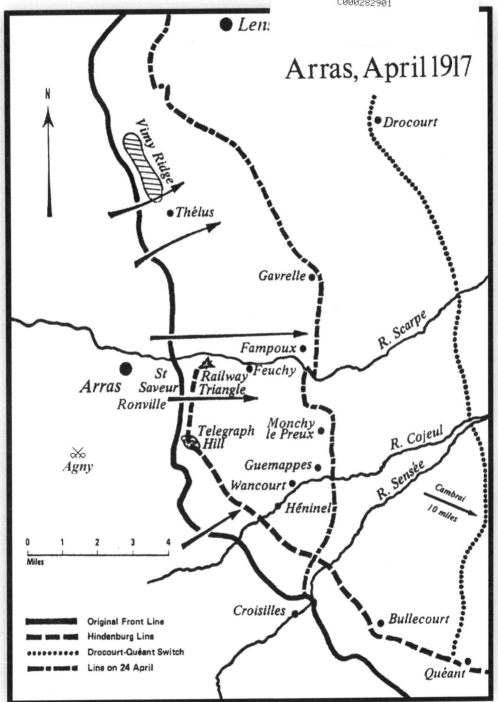

Arras, April 1917

N

Lens

Drocourt

Vimy Ridge

Thélus

Gavrelle

R. Scarpe

Fampoux

Feuchy

Arras

St Saveur

Railway Triangle

Ronville

Telegraph Hill

Monchy le Preux

R. Cojeul

Agny

Guemappes

R. Sensée

Wancourt

Héninel

Cambrai
10 miles

Croisilles

Bullecourt

Quéant

0 1 2 3 4
Miles

▬▬▬▬ Original Front Line
▬ ▬ ▬ Hindenburg Line
••••••••• Drocourt-Quéant Switch
▬ ▬ ▬ Line on 24 April

EDWARD THOMAS

EDWARD THOMAS

From Adlestrop to Arras:
A Biography

Jean Moorcroft Wilson

BLOOMSBURY
LONDON • NEW DELHI • NEW YORK • SYDNEY

Bloomsbury Continuum
An imprint of Bloomsbury Publishing Plc

50 Bedford Square   1385 Broadway
London   New York
WC1B 3DP   NY 10018
UK   USA

www.bloomsbury.com

**Bloomsbury, Continuum and the Diana logo are trademarks of
Bloomsbury Publishing Plc**

First published 2015

British Library Cataloguing-in-Publication Data
A catalogue record for this book is available from the British Library.

Library of Congress Cataloguing-in-Publication data has been applied for.

ISBN: HB: 978-1-4081-8713-5
ePDF: 978-1-4081-8714-2
ePub: 978-1-4081-8715-9

2 4 6 8 10 9 7 5 3 1

Typeset by Integra Software Services Pvt. Ltd.
Printed and bound in Great Britain by CPI Group (UK) Ltd, Croydon CR0 4YY

To find out more about our authors and books visit www.bloomsbury.com.
Here you will find extracts, author interviews, details of forthcoming events and
the option to sign up for our newsletters.

For Cecil Woolf
&
in memory of
Sir Martin Gilbert (1936–2015)

THE EDWARD THOMAS COUNTRY

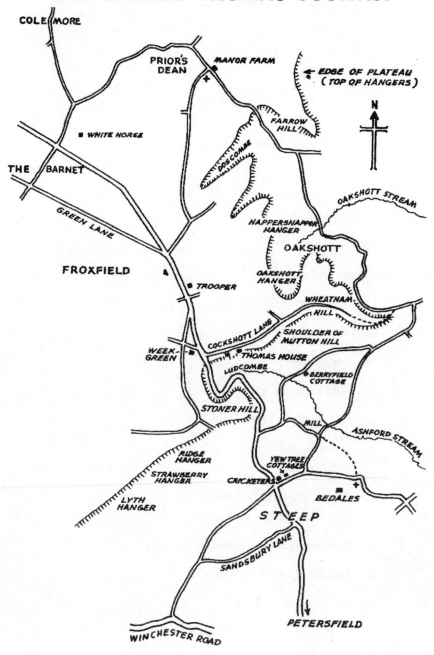

CONTENTS

LIST OF ILLUSTRATIONS

First Plate Section

1. The Thomas family c. 1894

2. 61 Shelgate Road, London, SW11

3. Mary Elizabeth Thomas, 1896

4. Edward Thomas, 1898

5. Helen Berenice Noble and Edward Thomas

6. Edward Thomas, 1898

7. Helen Noble, 1898

8. The Lincoln College Torpids Crew, 1899

9. Edward Thomas in his rooms at Lincoln College, Oxford, 1899

10. Edward Thomas at Oxford, 1899

11. Helen Thomas and Merfyn, 1900

12. Edward Thomas and Merfyn at Ammanford, 1900

13. Thomas family, with Edward, Merfyn and grandmother, 1902/3

14. Helen Thomas with Merfyn, c.1902

15. Rose Acre Cottage, with Edward and Merfyn Thomas

Second plate section

Edward Thomas's Father's Ancestry

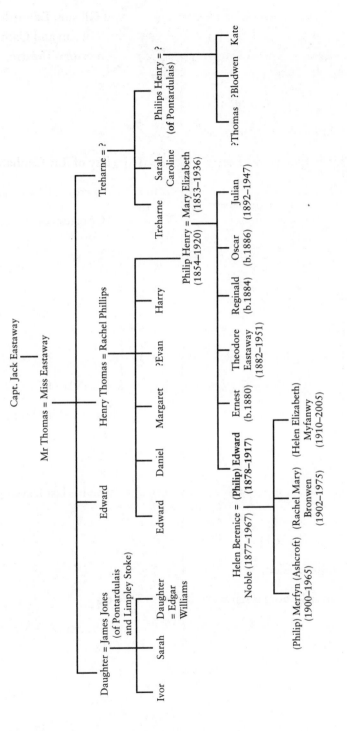

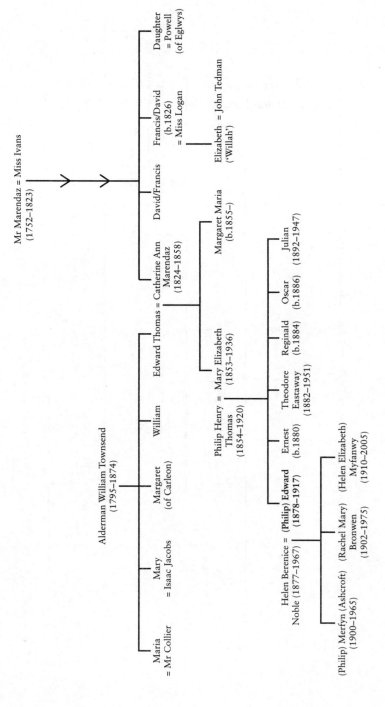

Edward Thomas's Mother's Ancestry

'Sir, the biographical part of literature is what I love most. Give us as many anecdotes as you can.'

Dr Johnson

Line Drawing of Edward Thomas by his brother Ernest Henry Thomas, 1905, National Portrait Gallery, London.

INTRODUCTION

A stopped watch, a half-filled clay pipe and a pocket-diary with curiously creased pages were among the personal effects of Edward Thomas sent home to his distraught wife after his death at the Battle of Arras on 9 April 1917. From such sad memorials she drew what comfort she could, coming to believe that her husband's body had remained unblemished and that the shell which killed him had done so simply by drawing the breath from his body. The true details of Thomas's death have remained obscured, generations of biographers repeating Helen Thomas's highly subjective version. I am now able to give the actual, very different facts here for the first time.

Thomas did not live to see the first edition of his poems, which were not published as a collection until after his death, but they have never since been out of print. For almost a century his work has attracted strong advocates and disciples, including some of the best-known names in modern poetry – Thomas Hardy, W. H. Auden, Dylan Thomas, Philip Larkin, Ted Hughes and Seamus Heaney among them. (Hughes famously called him 'the father of us all'.) He features on the First World War memorial plaque in Westminster Abbey, yet his status among the privileged few to appear there is still uncertain. His name is perhaps not currently as widely known as that of Rupert Brooke, Wilfred Owen, Siegfried Sassoon or even Isaac Rosenberg.

Yet with the exception of Rosenberg and his fellow-Modernist David Jones, Thomas's 'distinctively modern sensibility' (to use F. R. Leavis's phrase),[1] is probably the one

1

most in tune with our twenty-first-century outlook. As his great contemporary admirer Andrew Motion has pointed out, Thomas occupies a 'crucial place in the development of twentieth-century poetry',[2] forming something of a bridge or hinge between Georgian poets like Gordon Bottomley and Lascelles Abercrombie and fully fledged Modernists such as Ezra Pound and T. S. Eliot, whom he anticipates. After a lifetime study of Thomas's work and its context Edna Longley sees him as 'situated on the cusp of history and on the brink of modern selfhood',[3] one of the half-dozen poets who 'remade English poetry' in the early twentieth century.[4]

A characteristic poem by Thomas, in contrast to the apparently more 'composed' work of the Georgians, gives the sense of a jotting down of random impressions and feelings, expressed in quiet, reflective speech. His exploration of such topics as memory, identity, disintegration, directionlessness and loss anticipate many of the themes of modern poetry. In addition, his verse is, as Longley also argues, 'psychoanalytical before psychoanalytical criticism', his 'ecological vision' a pioneer of 'ecocriticism' and his environmentalism prophetic of our own concerns.[5] A poem like 'Old Man', for instance, which opens with a meditation on the herb of that name otherwise known as 'lad's love', unfolds through the simple action of a child 'pluck[ing] a feather from the door-side bush / Whenever she goes in or out of the house' and the narrator wondering how much she will recall of the scene in later life. It is a deceptively artless start which enables the poet to arrive without apparent contrivance, yet with a sense of inevitability, at his regretful conclusion:

> As for myself,
> Where first I met the bitter scent is lost.
> I, too, often shrivel the grey shreds,
> Sniff them and think and sniff again and try
> Once more to think what it is I am remembering,
> Always in vain. I cannot like the scent,
> Yet I would rather give up others more sweet,
> With no meaning, than this bitter one.
>
> I have mislaid the key. I sniff the spray
> And think of nothing; I see and I hear nothing;
> Yet seem, too, to be listening, lying in wait

For what I should, yet never can, remember:
> No garden appears, no path, no hoar-green bush
> Of Lad's-love, or Old Man, no child beside,
> Neither father nor mother, nor any playmate;
> Only an avenue, dark, nameless, without end.[6]

The elusiveness here, as Motion suggests, 'is so scrupulously reflected in the disarmingly low-keyed tone of voice'[7] that it is not difficult to see why Thomas has suffered some neglect. Yet the poem could have been written yesterday, so contemporary are its content, technique and what Philip Larkin has called Thomas's 'almost infinitely-qualified states of mind'.[8]

Thomas's verse was, in fact, written between 1914 and 1917 and his most famous English contemporaries were all war poets. Here, too, he occupies a significant central position. Neither as jingoistic as Brooke, Julian Grenfell, or Sassoon before he experienced front-line conditions, nor as critical of the conflict as the later Sassoon or Owen, Thomas's more measured approach most nearly resembles another relatively neglected war poet, Charles Hamilton Sorley. In both cases, and despite a considerable age difference, their attitude towards the war is remarkably mature and perceptive from the start. They also share a strong sense of the past and profound love of the countryside. In Thomas's case this eco-historical sense leads him, in poems like 'The Gallows' and 'The Combe', for instance, to correlate the war with human violence to other species, a concept which again resonates with modern readers:

> The Combe was ever dark, ancient and dark.
> …But far more ancient and dark
> The Combe looks since they killed the badger there,
> Dug him out and gave him to the hounds,
> That most ancient Briton of English beasts.[9]

There are those who would deny that Thomas is a war poet at all, including such respected critics of the genre as Bernard Bergonzi and John H. Johnston. Some prefer to include him in the 'Georgian' camp, or to label him a 'Pastoral', 'Nature' or a 'Mystic' poet.[10] Even here there is no consensus. The belief that war poetry, to qualify as such, must deal only with actual fighting appears simplistic in view of Thomas's powerful achievements in this area. Though none of his poems were written in France, all (save a few undergraduate dabblings) were composed after the outbreak of war, which tinges many and directly inspires not a few of them. The war is always hovering as a sinister, metaphorical background to the English countryside. An ostensibly pastoral poem like 'Haymaking', for instance, is no less a reflection of what Thomas himself called the 'dark chaotic character'[11] of war than 'This is no petty case of right or wrong' or 'In Memoriam (Easter 1915)' which refers more openly to the war:

> The flowers left thick at nightfall in the wood
> This Eastertide call into mind the men,
> Now far from home, who, with their sweethearts, should
> Have gathered them and will do never again.[12]

For as Larkin wrote in a review of Wilfred Owen's *Collected Poems*: 'A "war poet" is not one who chooses to commemorate or celebrate a war, but one who reacts against having a war thrust upon him.'[13] Robert Frost, who played a crucial role in Thomas's turn from prose to poetry in late 1914, wrote to Edward Garnett after Thomas's death: 'His poetry is so very brave – so unconsciously brave. He didn't think of it for a moment as war poetry, though that is what it is. It ought to be called [echoing Thomas's 'Now all roads lead to France'] Roads to France.'[14] Despite being included in most Great War anthologies, however, there is truth in Longley's claim that Thomas 'eludes or disturbs the category "war poet"' as he does those of 'Georgian', 'Pastoral', 'Nature' or 'Mystic'.[15] ('I ain't a mystic,' Thomas himself wrote to Bottomley.[16]) It may be that this problem in placing Thomas is another factor which has militated against his wider acceptance. An age of ever-growing interdisciplinary studies may now be more receptive to his versatility and wide range.

His life alone makes for absorbing reading: his marriage to Helen, the daughter of his first literary mentor, James Ashcroft Noble, while still at Oxford; his dependence on laudanum; his rejection of a safe Civil Service career and determination to make a living by writing; his friendships with many of the well-known magazine editors and writers of the Edwardian and early Georgian period – Edward Garnett, Rupert Brooke, Gordon Bottomley, Joseph Conrad, Lascelles Abercrombie, Hilaire Belloc, Wilfrid Gibson, Walter de la Mare and many others; his thoughts of suicide; his infatuation with a schoolgirl over a decade younger than himself and later a beautiful, but married woman; his meeting with Robert Frost in 1913 and subsequent shift from prose to poetry, even more unusual than Sassoon's move in the other direction; his relationship with Eleanor Farjeon, who entered into a curious three-sided relationship with him and his wife; his decision to enlist in the army at the age of 37; and his death in France on 9 April 1917, the first day of the Battle of Arras. It is the stuff myths are made of and posterity has been quick to oblige. While making his name better known, however, this has threatened to obscure his worth as a writer.

The first and most enduring of these myths is that when Helen Noble's pregnancy obliged Thomas to marry before even finishing his degree, he was then forced to support his wife and family by accepting any work available and that all his subsequent prose is 'hackwork'. One admirer of his poetry, for instance, referred as recently as 2008 to Thomas 'churning out' prose.[17] Yet Thomas's critical biography of Richard Jefferies is a classic of the genre and still a standard work on the subject, his topographical and travel books, like *The South Country*, *The Heart of England* or *In Pursuit of Spring* anticipate by many years the experimental work of writers such as W. G. Sebald and his meditative essays and impressionistic fiction are still well worth rereading. In addition, his many reviews and articles frequently break new ground. (He was the first to recognize the genius of Walter de la Mare, W. H. Davies and Robert Frost, for example.) The beauty, subtlety and insight of his best prose are unsurpassed and in a significant number of cases have links with and a direct bearing on the poetry which followed. 'Rain', for instance, can stand on its own as a disturbing poem about solitude and death:

> Rain, midnight rain, nothing but the wild rain
> On this bleak hut, and solitude, and me
> Remembering again that I shall die
> And neither hear the rain nor give it thanks
> For washing me cleaner than I have been
> Since I was born into this solitude.
> Blessed are the dead that the rain rains upon:
> But here I pray that none whom once I loved
> Is dying tonight or lying still awake
> Solitary, listening to the rain,

Either in pain or thus in sympathy
Helpless among the living and the dead,
Like a cold water among broken reeds,
Myriads of broken reeds all still and stiff,
Like me who have no love which this wild rain
Has not dissolved except the love of death,
If love it be towards what is perfect and
Cannot, the tempest tells me, disappoint.[18]

Read in the context of Thomas's life, which reveals that 'Rain' was written in army barracks in early 1916, the significance of the poem becomes clearer – 'Myriads of broken reeds all still and stiff', for example, directing the reader's imagination towards corpse-ridden battlefields in France. But looking at it in conjunction with his prose work *The Icknield Way* brings out an even greater depth to the poem.[19]

Another, related myth is that Thomas was grindingly poor, whereas his earnings between 1906 and 1912 were about the equivalent of a university professor's. Admittedly Thomas's income was not as secure as an academic's and he probably had to work harder for it, but he did not live in penury; he could still afford to employ the household help denied to the really poverty-stricken. While this particular myth is less damaging to Thomas's reputation as a writer, it nevertheless helps to perpetuate the rather distorted picture of a Grub Street hack painted by some biographers and critics.

Other aspects of the legend, such as the claim that Thomas was a true 'Celt' (whatever that may be), or that he found 'serenity and fulfilment' in the army,[20] are equally in need of re-examination, especially in light of the copious new material which has emerged since the last authoritative, full biography by R. George Thomas was published in 1985.

Perhaps the most serious distortion of the Thomas story concerns his character and here a new biography is urgently needed. The impression given by a significant number of those who have written on him is that he was almost permanently depressed. While it is true that he suffered from severe depression at times and had several nervous breakdowns, however, there is another side to him which needs to be brought out if he is to be fully understood. Otherwise his attraction for his contemporaries and his ability to form close friendships remains puzzling. Eleanor Farjeon, who fell deeply in love with him, warned one biographer: 'Remember that when his moods weren't on him like a sickness, when his nerves weren't harassed by overwork and anxiety…he was among other things the best talker, the best thinker, the most humorous…His power of friendship was as great as his need of it.'[21] She also warned that his was a 'complicated nature – the Cretan labyrinth was not more tortuous – and though the thread is often knotted and ravelled, it is always true in fibre, twisted with nothing that is second-rate.'

The humour may have been sardonic at times but it was rarely in doubt. His clergyman friend, Jesse Berridge, noted that 'his sense of the ridiculous often approached hysteria to my sober view and it was very catching'. Complaining to Bottomley in 1907 of being too busy with trivial work, Thomas concluded, for example: 'Never mind; I am now, being just 29, insured against death, accident and disease – and shall get £500 if I lose both eyes or even both legs (but I am not sure about the legs).'[22] As Richard Emeny notes, the standard picture of Thomas as 'faun-like…a man so exquisitely sensitive that one could imagine him…modelling for the Death of Chatterton' is seriously misleading; he was 'in fact a very tough customer indeed – physically and mentally'.[23]

The iconic studio photograph of Thomas which accentuates his handsome, refined face, brooding eyes, sensitive mouth and delicate yet powerful hands must bear some of the blame for this interpretation. Was it seeing this photograph that inspired Norman Douglas's claim, for instance, that there was 'something of the Byzantine angel; ethereal, refined, aloof' about him and that what he lacked was 'a little touch of bestiality'?[24]

Helen Thomas's two posthumous books on her husband, *As It Was* and *World Without End*, must also take some of the responsibility for the Thomas legend. Beautifully written and almost unbearably sad, they may nevertheless be as misleading as the photograph. In fairness to Helen, she never claimed that they were strictly autobiographical, using the fictional names Jenny and David for her main protagonists, as though to distance the material from her own married life. (Only in recent editions have they been renamed Helen and Edward.) She was prompted to write partly as therapy for her distraught condition following her husband's death, and it is dangerous to take her books literally, as many critics have done. Though parallels with the Thomases' life are many, recent evidence has shown that at least one of the central episodes – the idyllic honeymoon in 'Dad' Uzzell's Wiltshire cottage – is not strictly true. Yet a 1978 reissue of Thomas's *Richard Jefferies* claims that the picture of Uzzell's original cottage on the dustjacket is where 'Helen and Edward Thomas spent their honeymoon'.[25] This in itself is not necessarily serious but it does show that at least some of what Helen wrote is not to be taken as the literal truth. If, as I suspect, it was created from wish-fulfilment, then it suggests that her account is far from objective, for understandable reasons. It certainly warns the reader against interpreting the story literally, whether it concerns other events or the Edward-figure, 'David'. The fact that generations of scholars have done so, often without corroborative evidence from a more reliable source, underlines the need for an up-to-date assessment.

Even those who suspected the accuracy of Helen's account as autobiography felt understandably reluctant to question it while she and her children were alive. This was particularly true if they had received the family's help and co-operation, as most biographers did, including Professor Thomas.

Now, over a quarter of a century after the publication of his *Edward Thomas*, a franker treatment of certain areas of his life is possible. The handling of his relationship with Helen, for example, suffered notably from such constraints. While it has always been clear that Helen remained deeply in love with him all her life, it has not always been possible to explore the full range of his feelings for her without risking offence. As the recent publication of an undergraduate poem from his letter to a close friend, Harry Hooton, in 1898 suggests, the true picture is more complex than the official version and implies that he was already questioning their relationship at this early stage.[26] Five years later, after the birth of two of their three children, he confided to his diary: 'No-one knows how difficult I find it to live with Helen, though I admire her, like her, perhaps love her.'[27] And in 1904 he wrote to Helen herself: 'If I could only love you and show my love as much as you deserve how happy would you (and I) be!'[28] A year later he told another close friend: 'What I really ought to do is to live alone. But I can't find the courage to do the many things necessary for taking that step. It is really kind H[elen] and the dear children who make life almost impossible.'[29] This was not a passing phase: a decade later in 1915 he wrote to Frost concerning the possibility of joining him in America: 'There is no one to keep me here [in England] except my mother.'[30] Yet his final letters to Helen from France are signed 'All and always yours'.

It is not prurience which calls for a franker examination of Edward and Helen's relationship. Without a fuller understanding of Thomas's complex character, it is impossible to appreciate his work completely. Given the considerable amount of new material which has come to light since 1985, the record needs to be brought up to date and, in a number of cases, adjusted.

Since there is no complete edition of Thomas's letters, diaries, notebooks and prose writings, it has been necessary to go to original sources wherever possible. This has included spending a month at the Harry Ransom Center, University of Texas at Austin, studying not only the full collection of Thomas's letters to Garnett, but also the countless letters to Garnett about Thomas after his death, letters from Thomas to Clifford Bax and other friends and following up references to Thomas in Bax's personal diary. Material at Bryn Mawr in the Claud Lovat Fraser Collection has also yielded significant details about Thomas's personality, as well as his relationship with Lovat Fraser's close friend, Ralph Hodgson. Thomas's letters to a fellow travel-writer, Norman Douglas, at Yale have helped illuminate Thomas's important links with the *English Review*, as well as with Douglas himself. Walter de la Mare's letters to Rowland Watson deposited in the Berg Collection of the New York Public Library earlier this century, though written after Thomas's death mainly about raising money for a memorial to him, have provided new information. Even material already known has rewarded revisiting; Thomas's 80 Field Notebooks in the Berg Collection, for example, have thrown new light on areas of Thomas's personal life either previously unknown, or obscure. The earlier ones, as well as the later, have proved particularly helpful in understanding his poetry and placing it in context. Recent published material has also aided an understanding of Thomas; Robert MacFarlane's *The Old Ways* (2012), in particular, has offered fresh insights into the importance of walking to Thomas and different ways of approaching his travel books.

New material has continued to emerge. As recently as 2006, when I had already started writing my biography, a scholar at the University of Virginia discovered an unpublished poem by Frost, 'War Thoughts at Home', which it seemed to me was written in response to news of Thomas's death. Not one of Frost's best, it is nevertheless of real interest, suggesting as it does that the influence between the two poets was by no means one way. Frost's influence on Thomas has been well documented but this recently found poem indicates that Thomas also affected Frost. The scene appears to be an isolated house in the woods very like the one Helen and the children moved to at High Beech after Thomas enlisted. Birds play a prominent role in the poem, as they do in Thomas's poems but less so in Frost's. Glyn Maxwell claims that the first stanza, with its 'alertness to the processes of sight and thought, defies imitation,'[31] but its careful observation, low-keyed yet highly charged language, unobtrusive metaphor and easy movement are not unlike Thomas's. And its concluding lines bring to mind Thomas's own war poems, which so often fix on everyday objects – fallen leaves, broken reeds, rain, for instance – with symbolic overtones:

> She draws down the winter shade
> And it glows with an early lamp
> On that old side of the house
> The uneven sheds stretch back
> Shed behind shed in train
> Like cars [i.e. carriages] that long have lain
> Dead on a side track.[32]

At the very least, 'War Thoughts at Home' confirms the two men's shared approach to poetry. It is not surprising, therefore, that the words which come closest to conveying Thomas's essence as a writer come from his own review of Frost's *North of Boston*. Describing this book as 'the most revolutionary' of modern times but 'one of the quietest and least aggressive', Thomas sums up Frost's poetry in words which apply equally to his own: 'It speaks and it is poetry.'[33]

1

BEGINNINGS (1878–1880)

E dward Thomas's sensibility strikes most readers as so modern that it comes as something of a shock to realize that he was born a Victorian, into an era of horse-drawn omnibuses, four-wheeled carriages, gas lighting, gin-palaces, crinolines and live-in servants for all but the poorest of families. There were as many as six to eight postal deliveries a day in London, but the telephone was virtually unheard of. In 1877, the year before Thomas's birth, the Russo-Turkish War broke out and the University of London voted to admit women to degrees in medicine. In politics the Tories, under Disraeli, were in power, the Whigs (or Liberals), under Gladstone, in opposition, a situation which would cause Edward Thomas's father, an ardent Liberal, to fight even harder for his party. Tennyson still reigned as Poet Laureate.

Origins fascinate most people, especially their own. They were of more than usual interest to Edward Thomas, who studied the past professionally, as a history scholar at Oxford, and, imaginatively, as the teller of *Norse Tales*, *Celtic Stories* and other works. He would draw up his own family tree at the age of 29. But his engagement with his past began much earlier, aged 5, with a visit to his parents' native home of Wales. It was here he conceived a 'passion for Wales' which never left him. Inspired partly by his own ancestors and partly by the country's colourful history his passion culminated, he recalled, in his singing of Thomas Moore's 'Minstrel Boy' and his 'harp':

> I knew only of *Welsh* harps [my italics]. I supposed the minstrel boy with his wild harp slung behind him was Welsh [i.e. rather than Irish as Moore intended] and as I sang the song I melted and trembled with a kind of gloomy pleasure in being about to die for Wales, Arthur's and Llewelyn's Wales, the 'land of song'. While I shivered with exhaltation repeating his words:
>> Though each man else betrays thee
>> One sword at least thy rights shall guard,
>> One harp at least shall praise thee,
>
> It might have been my harp and my sword.[1]

Welsh scenery, too, inspired Edward as a child. Rivers like the Ebbw and the Usk, he remembered, 'cut across my childhood with silver bars, and clouded it with their apple-flowers and their mountain-ash trees and ma[d]e it musical with the curlew's despair and the sound of the blackbird singing in Eden still'.[2] Looking at a map of Britain at the age of 30 he could still write, with a proud roll-call of his family names and haunts: 'the West calls, out of Wiltshire and out of Cornwall and Devon beyond, out of Monmouth and Glamorgan and Gower and Carmarthen, with a voice of dead Townsends, Eastaways, Thomases, Phillipses, Treharnes, Marendaz, sea men and mountain men'.[3] His pride in his heritage emerges clearly: 'Each man of us is as ancient and complicated, as lofty-spired and as deep-vaulted as cathedrals and castles of old.'[4]

Thomas's own London birth on 3 March 1878, at 10 Upper Lansdowne Road, Lambeth, seemed to him an 'accidentally Cockney nativity'.[5] But it was one that shaped his life as surely as his Welsh ancestry; it is misleading to view him solely in terms of Wales, for he grew to love England, particularly its southern counties, just as keenly. Researching for *The South Country* made him realize how important it had become to him by 1908: 'this country, though I am mainly Welsh, [is] a kind of home…These are the "home" counties. A man can hide away in them. The people are not hospitable, but the land is.'[6] He would celebrate and try to capture 'Englishness' both in prose works like *The Heart of England* (1906), *The Icknield Way* (1913) and *In Pursuit of Spring* (1914) and in poems such as 'Adelstrop', 'The Manor Farm' and 'Haymaking'. One of his most ambitious verses, 'Lob', written while he was compiling *This England: An Anthology from Her Writers* (1915), shows how precious 'Englishness' had become to him by the time war broke out in 1914 and how well he would convey it. After reading 'Lob', Robert Frost wrote to him: 'I never saw anything like you for English.'[7] And Walter de la Mare, on hearing of Thomas's death in the First World War, would claim that 'a mirror of England' had been 'shattered'.[8]

Thomas saw no contradiction in his dual allegiance. He seems to have shared the attitude of Mr Stodham in his semi-autobiographical novel, *The Happy-Go-Lucky Morgans* (1913), who asks: 'Do you love the wilderness? Do you love Wales? If you do, you love what I understand by "England". The more you love and know England the more deeply you can love the wilderness and Wales.'[9]

This love of England as well as Wales may have stemmed from his mother, with whom he identified more closely than with his father. For Mary Elizabeth Thomas had been born in Headingley, Yorkshire, and was partly English as well as Welsh. It is significant that when her son sketched in his family tree in 1907 he began, not only with his mother's family, but with the English branch of it – the Townsends of Yorkshire origin. She and her family 'proudly preserved' the memory of her grandfather, Alderman William Townsend (1795–1877), and his descendants.[10] One of Edward's earliest memories was of visiting two daughters of Alderman Townsend with his mother on that first visit to Wales in 1883, his mother's aunt Mary (Mrs Isaac Jacobs) in Swansea and her aunt Margaret at Caerleon, both carefully recorded in his autobiography and on his family tree.

He did *not* visit, however, the two great-aunts who brought up his mother and her sister after their mother died in 1858, when Mary Elizabeth was 4; it had been an unhappy experience for the girls, who had christened their aunt's home, Hill House in Newport, 'Hell House'. The great-aunts' names are omitted from Edward's family tree. His maternal grandfather (the girls' father), however, is prominent, with a note in his grandson's handwriting that, 'though an English name', Edward Thomas Townsend, if not born in Wales, had 'long lived at Neath and Port Talbot'. He had 'trained as a doctor', but (in a prophetic reminder of Thomas's own life) had 'married very early and had to do what he could'. He took up a more lucrative job as an accountant and died, like his wife, when his eldest daughter (Edward's mother) was only 4, her sister Margaret even younger.

It was a sad but romantic story made even more appealing to the highly imaginative young Edward Thomas by the fact that his maternal grandmother's father had been a 'Marendaz', Marendaz's own father (Thomas noted) 'reputed a "German"', but presumably Spanish or Portuguese.[11] There is little in Thomas's description of his mother to suggest Mediterranean blood, however, either in looks or temperament. Her features were delicate and clear-cut, her hair a light golden-brown, her eyes blue; her temperament seems to have displayed none of the flamboyance associated with Spanish or Portuguese genes. Edward, who adored her, referred to her 'uncertainty…her melancholy, unconfident way'.[12] 'She is diffident and sad and not clever,'[13] he would tell a close friend as an adult. Except in the last feature her eldest son resembled her. Even as a child he identified with her shy, introverted nature, and in other ways, too. His mother's 'straight nose and chin,' he tells us, made a profile that 'for years formed my standard'.[14] His earliest memories were of her gentle presence and of her singing, a remembered bliss to him. His first notion of femaleness was the memory of her 'not quite dressed, in white bodice and petticoat, her arms and shoulders rounded and creamy smooth'.[15]

Similarly, her role as a devoted mother and housewife, whose life revolved around her husband and six sons, seems to have become a model of what he would expect his own wife to be when he married. Her continual pregnancies throughout his childhood may well help explain his own reluctance to have children later on. At all points of crisis in his life thoughts of his mother would recur, whether he was contemplating suicide, considering leaving the country, or facing the possibility of death in France, when he would remember to make copies of his poems for her. As an adult his mother sometimes appears to take precedence over his wife. He believed himself to be her favourite son.

One of Mrs Thomas's most important roles in Edward's childhood was that of intermediary between him and his father, Philip Henry Thomas, an 'eloquent, confident, black-haired, brown-eyed' Welshman. The words are Edward's, who saw his father as 'all that my mother was not'.[16] It is tempting to accept this neat dichotomy and argue that Edward, so like his mother in many ways, was also completely unlike his father. Edward wrote a poem to his father in 1916, so devastating that it remained unpublished until 1949, when it confirmed this as the popular view. It is certainly one which the poem itself encourages:

> I may come near loving you
> When you are dead
> And there is nothing to do
> And much to be said.
>
> To repent that day will be
> Impossible*
> For you and vain for me
> The truth to tell.
>
> I shall be sorry for
> Your impotence:
> You can do and undo no more
> When you go hence,
>
> Cannot even forgive
> The funeral.
> But not so long as you live
> Can I love you at all.
> *In the first draft this line read 'Far out of your reach'.

While it is worth noting that Edward addressed but did not send this poem to his father in his lifetime, there is no denying that it is a shocking statement and one which cannot be explained simply in terms of an Oedipus complex, whatever the charge of 'impotence' in stanza three suggests. There is no doubt that he appears to have been less proud altogether of his paternal ancestors, placing them second in his family tree in 1907 and devoting less space to them. As with his mother's branch, he began with their most prominent *English* forebear, Captain Jack Eastaway, a sailor from Devon who settled in Glamorgan and one of whose daughters married a Thomas. Nevertheless, his father's family was mainly Welsh, also less middle class overall than his mother's – small farmers and railway workers. When Edward paid visits to his paternal grandmother, Rachel (née Phillips) Thomas, who had moved with her husband, Henry, to be near the Great Western Railway works at Swindon, he remembered her Welsh friends remarking 'how well my father was doing, my grandfather who had long been dead having only been a [railway] fitter'.[17] He would adopt his father's family name of 'Eastaway' as a pseudonym less from pride in it than for its sound. Only one of the five explanatory notes on his family tree is devoted to his father's branch. In addition (whether his own choice or not), though his first given name is 'Philip' after his father and his paternal grandmother's maiden name, he was known by his second name, 'Edward' (nicknamed 'Edwy'), echoing his mother's father's name, Edward Thomas Townsend.

This preference, if it was one, must not be exaggerated. After that first visit to his mother's family at the age of 5, Edward was to enjoy many holidays with his father's relatives, in particular with his grandmother, Rachel Thomas, at Swindon and his father's cousin, T. Treharne Thomas and his family at Pontardulais, in South Wales. Yet there is no denying that Edward had a difficult relationship with his father, which the marked difference between them helps to explain. Beside the obvious physical contrast between the short, stocky, dark Welshman and his tall, slim, fair son, there were more important ones of temperament. Whereas Edward and his mother were introverts, given to melancholy and brooding, Philip Henry Thomas was a classic extrovert, certain of what he wanted from life and confident of achieving it. He failed completely to understand his eldest son's uncertainty and lack of self-confidence. Rowland Watson, while collecting memories of Edward Thomas after his death, came across an anecdote about Philip Henry recalled by one of Edward's friends: 'Once, when staying with Edward, he said, "I have never in my life done or said anything I am ashamed of." The son looked down at him and said, "May God help you." '[18] Edward himself wrote of his father's scorn when he gave up a school race in the one thing he excelled at, walking, *not* because he was losing or was exhausted, but because he 'hated being pursued' and could not stand the possibility of being beaten: 'My father blamed me for cowardice, and for years after used to say to me at intervals: "Ah well, it's no use, I suppose. It's just that mile race over again." "Half-mile," said I.'[19]

Philip Henry never gave up his determination to better himself. This strength of character, combined with a powerful intellect, enabled him to rise from a humble background to become a teacher, learn three foreign languages and to pass the Home Civil Service Entrance Exam at Executive level with distinction. His plans for his equally clever, more privileged son, however, met with great resistance. A notable achiever himself, he was honestly puzzled by Edward's lack of worldly ambition. His son's sense of futility and failure may have been partly his father's unintentional doing.

One aspect of Philip Henry's extrovert nature, and another pronounced difference from his son, was his love of an audience. While Edward would be unable to consider a teaching career seriously, because of crippling shyness, Mr Thomas held forth with relish. His remarkable gift for public speaking was developed at the old Battersea Town Hall, known as the Battersea 'Parliament', which included such notable public figures as Stanley (later Lord) Buckmaster, John Burns and Horatio Bottomley. He also lectured on various subjects in many parts of the country and spoke every Sunday at Battersea Town Hall for the Ethical Society, becoming well known in Positivist circles, eventually occupying the pulpit at the Church of Humanity in Holborn.

For father and son differed in their interests as well as temperaments. Mr Thomas's job at the Board of Trade debarred him from taking office with any political party during Edward's childhood, but at his retirement in 1914 he would stand as Liberal Parliamentary candidate for South Battersea, whereas Edward rarely involved himself in politics throughout his life. A brief flirtation with politics at school was clearly motivated by an attempt to please his passionately committed father. Writing to tell his father, who was away on holiday, of his impressive exam results in French and grammar, he continues, 'there is still unmarked an essay we had to write either on "Bicycling" or the "General Election". Of course I did the "General Election of 1892 was a great political crisis, – a struggle between privilege and reform".'[20] Nor did he respond to the Positivism which had replaced his father's more conventional Anglican and Methodist upbringing, and led him to become a Unitarian. Edward's boredom at any kind of religious service – and these were generally Unitarian as a child – fills many pages of his autobiography and his resentment at his father for making him attend them is strongly expressed. He believed that 'the radical and free-thinking influence of home' had caused him to 'neglect' in his writing 'the feeling that belonged to my own nature and my own times of life'.[21] From a young age he turned to nature to satisfy his religious needs, another interest not shared by his father.

However, father and son did have some things in common and there is evidence to suggest that Edward was quite close to his father as a child. In the same letter to him reporting on the 1892 election, for instance, he tells his father about the pigeons he collected, implying a shared interest, and ends with the hope that he will be home in time to attend Edward's Sports Day. Both father and son were intellectually more than able. And even though Edward made a good deal less effort to 'improve' himself than his father, he found school work no real challenge, in general, and frequently came top in exams. Like his father, he took easily to languages and would eventually read Latin, Greek and French fluently. They shared a love of words, the father reading to his son from an early age and publishing a book of his own, *A Religion of This World*. They both also loved music, in particular folk-song. Both were good with their hands, Edward in later life making some of his own furniture.

Ironically, it may have been one of their most marked similarities, their independence, which made relations between them so difficult at times. Perhaps, as Rowland Watson suggests, each in his own way was 'self-centred, and neither had capacity to bridge the gulf'.[22] Though Philip Henry Thomas's stern moral outlook and expectations of a Victorian pattern of behaviour became increasingly unacceptable to his eldest son, Edward would show himself to share some of these values once he had children of his own.

Edward's youngest brother, Julian, also subjected to his father's inflexible standards, nevertheless believed that Edward was unfair to their father when he wrote: 'nothing I ever heard at home attracted me to literature or the arts'.[23] Julian argued that:

> To my father he owed more than he would ever admit, in especial the art of reading aloud, and through this the appreciation of poetry. One pleasant memory at least I have of the painful Sunday afternoons that he describes – my father's reading aloud from *Hiawatha*, which began when he realized the failure of 'improving' literature to arouse any interest whatsoever in any of us. Only one more musical voice have I heard, and that was Edward's own...He read in an almost unaccented monotone, slowly, clearly, so that not one word, not one shade of meaning was lost. Many years later he read aloud his first poem to me: and then, all too soon, that voice was stilled.[24]

Beside reading and singing to Edward his father also helped him with his school-work; it was his interest, combined with 'the pleasure of being top', which made Edward 'do such homework as [he] did'.[25] Philip Henry also tried to broaden his son's education by sending him in his early teens to evening classes on botany, paying for special lessons in Latin and Greek and taking him to public lectures. 'At Kelmscott house I heard Grant Allen recommending State endowment of literary genius,' Edward recalled: 'I saw William Morris and was pleased and awed.'[26]

Though all six sons rebelled against his strict standards, Philip Henry Thomas genuinely wanted to instil worthy principles in them, reading them poems like Leigh Hunt's 'Abou Ben Adhem', for instance, to 'inspire a love of virtue'.[27] But he was not as harsh in this as Edward implied. When his eldest son, caught out in a wrongdoing, showed genuine remorse, even he was forced to admit how kind and forgiving his father could be.

Above all, Mr Thomas encouraged Edward when he started to write as a teenager, even helping him to refine his style. A later mentor, James Ashcroft Noble, responding to Edward's early paper on Richard Jefferies, wrote: 'I have not examined it carefully, sentence by sentence – indeed that has already been done by your good father.'[28] Whatever Mr Thomas's shortcomings, there is no doubt that he wanted the best for his sons. In Edward's case this would begin early and radically change the educational expectations that someone of his social standing may have had.

2

'All Being, Doing and Suffering' (1880–1888)

Edward Thomas's description of his childhood gives little hint of what was to come. It reads like the experience of many other lower-middle-class boys of the period, rather than the formative years of someone who would emerge as one of the most subtle and sensitive writers of the twentieth century. The emphasis falls largely on outer not inner happenings. 'I don't know what I was,' he writes later to a close friend of this period. 'I only know what I did and, later on, sometimes what I thought.'[1]

Up to the age of about 4 'a sweet darkness enfold[ed] his life with a faint blessing'.[2] One of his few memories from this period was 'the voice of one singing as [he] sat or lay in her arms', the songs (he afterwards worked out) of his mother, then of her younger sister Margaret.[3] Music was already a significant element in Thomas's life, though it was never to play a central role. When he started to plan his autobiography in 1913, 'Music' was the first item he noted in a list of only seven topics he wanted to cover.[4]

Unlike the tortured being he would become, one of his other memories of his infancy was of being 'at peace with life', wherever he was. Less surprisingly for someone who grew passionately close to nature, his sharpest sense of happiness at this time was 'out of doors...ly[ing] in the tall grass and buttercups of a narrow field at the edge of London'.[5] (This was almost certainly in his birthplace, Lambeth, still then on the fringes of London and the country.)

Many clearer memories followed after the age of 4. The setting was now Battersea. When Edward was nearly 2 and another child due, his hard-working and ambitious father had managed to move his family in 1880 from their South Lambeth lodgings to a house of their own at 2 Tremorvah Villas, 49 Wakehurst Road, where they were to remain until Edward was 9.[6] The house itself was a modest, pale-brick semi-detached on two floors, situated in a rash of new terraces that had erupted along the edge of south London as the railway reached the area. Running parallel with Battersea Rise, Wakehurst Road was in two halves, climbing up opposite sides of a slight valley, along the bottom of which ran the main shopping centre, Northcote Road. The local school lay at the end of the street.

Wakehurst Road was, therefore, convenient in a number of ways, but its greatest advantage for Edward as a child was its proximity to Wandsworth Common, only minutes away. This allowed him and the younger brothers, who followed at two-year intervals during his nine years in the house, easy access to an area of relatively untamed nature. Even before they could walk the youngest children would have been taken there for an airing.

When it was too wet or too dark to be out of doors, 49 Wakehurst Road, despite its modest size, provided its own 'playground', in the form of a long passage which ran from the front to the back door. Here, when Edward had a brother old enough to run, they 'raced up and down the passage,' he recalled, 'to be pounced upon by the servant out of a doorway and swallowed up in her arms with laughter'.[7]

It is hard to square this scene of carefree childish exuberance and adult affection with some of Thomas's later descriptions of his family, in his autobiography, as 'quiet' and 'stiff'.[8] They were, he suggests, the opposite of 'cheerful', with little 'ease and jollity'.[9] There were 'few visitors', and 'friends seldom came to the house'. His memories of Christmas are particularly bleak, the main impressions being 'disappointment, chapel, a heavy dinner and crackers, some squabbling, comparison of our presents, tea…supper'.[10] Yet his unflinching honesty, one of the virtues of his book, compels him to wonder, retrospectively, whether the fault lay partly in himself:

> I think I had always an eager haste to unveil the mystery, always a flattering look of wonder which always sank dead like an extinguished torch into disgust with the imperfect thing. If it had only been something better or different. It mattered not how many or good were my presents:

they fell below an indefinite imagined standard. If they were simply below last year's it was worse.[11]

The reflections of the 35-year-old Thomas looking back, this is one of the few indications of the restless, dissatisfied man he would become. The remainder of his account is full of the typical pleasures of childhood: of playing hide-and-seek, of ringing neighbours' bells and running away, of asking for sweets in the shop with invented names, of breaking the greenhouse glass in a large, deserted garden nearby, of smoking illicit cigarettes from rolled brown paper. It was, as he told John Freeman, 'all being, doing' – and 'suffering' when his parents realized he had been smoking.

Some of these activities were undoubtedly carried out with his younger brothers in what, despite Thomas's criticisms, must have been a lively household. Five, later six, growing boys could hardly have been less than a handful, the noise-level high. Edward was followed by Ernest, then Theodore, Reginald, Oscar and Julian, and, though he denied any close relationship with them later, all five of his younger brothers remembered childhood pursuits with him. Mrs Thomas was rarely without a servant to help, as well as a washerwoman who came every Monday from Lambeth and fascinated Edward with the mid-morning bread, cheese and beer she was given in their teetotal household. Though the 'general domestics' (as they were called) rarely stayed more than a year or two, he recalled most of these women, especially the younger ones, with evident affection – Eliza, Emily, Jane, Martha, Alice, Clara and so on. He was already appreciative of their femininity in that predominantly male household, their patience and kindness, their 'sweet looks or presence'.[12] His father, brothers and schoolmasters are treated far less tenderly.

The only constant female presence in his family life, however, was his mother and, to a lesser extent, her sister, Margaret, when she came at regular intervals to help with the births of his five brothers. More lively and outgoing than his mother, she came to represent for him early on another appeal of the feminine, one which would complicate his life and change its direction as he grew up. For it was not just 'the grace, smoothness and gentleness' of his aunt Margaret's voice which gave him pleasure: she also afforded him his 'first conscious liking for the female body…at the sight of her sitting less than half dressed in a chair, her head bent and one foot on to which she was pulling the stocking lifted from the floor'.[13]

Margaret Townsend was the relative closest to Edward throughout his life. She had educated herself beyond her sister's level to the standard required of a governess, an education which included wide reading in literature. She watched admiringly as Edward began to write and was proud to agree with a gentleman in her railway carriage who happened to be reading one of her nephew's early nature essays and claimed that 'he out-Jefferies Jefferies'.[14] When she became a companion-secretary to a wealthy American lady who stayed in Oxford, she visited him several times there. After she left England in 1904 or 1905 to settle permanently on the west coast of America and became involved in Theosophical circles, they continued to communicate by letter for the rest of his life. His letters to her are full of details of his writing and of literature generally. Hers to him have not survived, but were evidently concerned partly with her search for religious truths. Though Edward did not always agree with her, her approach to life, so different from his pragmatic father's, may (as R. George Thomas suggests) have given 'approval to [his] sudden spurt of interest' in later childhood 'to the affective literature of Richard Jefferies and, even more, to the reading of poetry for its own sake'.[15]

More than a decade after Thomas left home he was to write a book called *The Feminine Influence on the Poets* (1910). He may have been thinking partly of his own early childhood, which was shaped by women. Apart from his mother and his aunt, the first school he attended, for instance, had a female head and he remembered only female teachers there. Since he entered the infants department in mid-1883 (under his baby nickname, 'Edwy') and was there until he moved up to junior school in April 1886, where the boys were separated from the girls, the first eight years of his life were dominated by women.

Belleville Road School was situated a few hundred yards from the Thomases' house, between Wakehurst and the parallel Belleville Road from which it took its name. A relatively small, two-storey Victorian building, which still functions as a school, it was one of the first of what were known as 'Board Schools'. Following the 1870 Education Act, these were set up to provide universal education at elementary level. During Edward's time a small fee was still payable and one of his most vivid memories of Belleville Road School, apart from the smell of carbolic soap and the caretaker ringing the bell for lessons, was of depositing his 'weekly fourpence' on the teacher's desk.

Board Schools were funded by the local council rates, still only compulsory until the age of 10 during Edward's five years at Belleville Road School, and its curriculum was fairly basic. It would not change greatly over the the next 20 years and, like another less socially privileged poet killed in the First World War, Isaac Rosenberg, Edward was expected to master little more than the three Rs – Reading, Writing and (A)rithmetic – with a great deal of rote learning in history and geography; multiplication tables were chanted aloud, historical dates, rivers and bays of England learnt by heart. Edward, who actually enjoyed learning the names of, for instance, the tributaries of the Thames, nevertheless thought of Belleville Road later as a 'clockwork' school.[16] Sometimes he found 'addition, subtraction, multiplication and parsing...tediously easy'.[17]

No languages other than English were taught and no serious attempt at a musical education was made. Yet one of the things Edward remembered with most enjoyment was certain hymns, a verse of which was dutifully sung before and after each lesson. He also, like Rosenberg, enjoyed drawing from an early age and, though little attempt was made to teach art either, he took particular pleasure in maps, as he would throughout his life. He loved sketching in Great Britain, then 'inking in the coast lines with red, and making mountain ranges with thin parallel strokes arranged in herringbone fashion'.[18] (Predictably he 'never tired' of the western coasts.) His greatest criticism of his education at this stage was that he was taught to read before he was taught to write, which he argued resulted in him 'writing like a book, not like a human being'.[19]

'The best of life,' for Edward, however, 'was passed out of the house and out of school.'[20] He remembered far more of what he did 'before and after than in school',[21] of games enjoyed in the playground and the surrounding streets. Since his friends were mainly boys from his own and neighbouring roads, the games often continued long after lessons ended. He always, in any case, had at least one younger brother with him by the age of seven. Unlike his account of lessons, his list of games played is extensive and, in some cases, quite detailed – rounders, (spinning) tops, marbles, hoops, hide-and-seek, leapfrog. An early love of names shows itself in his inclusion of more esoterically called pursuits like 'Egg-cup', 'Cherry-Stones', 'Buck along' and 'Fly the garter'. When a friend in adult life, Norman Douglas, compiled his book on *London Street Games* (1916), he stressed the point that he wanted 'to demonstrate the inventiveness of children, not to write a professional treatise', the reason he gives for 'piling up the games into a breathless catalogue' as Thomas does.[22] Thomas, who was in close contact with Douglas by the time he started writing his autobiography in December 1913, may have been influenced by Douglas, whose first instalment of *London Street Games* appeared in the *English Review* in November 1913.[23] If the Board School curriculum made minimal demands on its brightest pupils in its classrooms, Edward's list of games suggests that they were not lacking in 'inventiveness' outside it.

Best of all, however, were the activities pursued on Wandsworth Common, completely away from both school and home. One hundred and seventy-five acres of coarse grass, shrubs and trees, it was the nearest these Battersea Board schoolboys got to nature, and a stimulating escape from their suburban streets. Even the railway line which cut the Common in half on its way north-east to Clapham Junction could not detract from its appeal. If anything the deep bushy cutting with its possibility of foxes, was an added attraction. The Common remained, in Thomas's own words about another of London's open spaces (Hampstead Heath), 'this fragment of the wild', where the 'uneven wildness due to nature and excavation make up for its small extent'.[24] Edward and his friends could spend a whole day on Wandsworth Common without thinking it small. An uneven piece of uncultivated, gravelly land, it had several ponds where the boys – girls are not mentioned – could paddle. Another diversion was to catch frogs there and Edward, who reveals a fascination with violence and cruelty at several points in his memoir, admits his 'half-shrinking, half-gloating curiosity' at their brutal dissection by older boys.[25]

Thomas's life-long love of angling was also born on Wandsworth Common, where he fished for sticklebacks and gudgeon in the long pond on the far side of the railway, with a worm tied on a cotton line, or impaled on a bent pin. The first book that 'touched [him] deeply' before the age of ten was Isaak Walton's *The Compleat Angler* which gave him 'a brief entry into an indefinite alluring world of men rising early in the morning and catching many fish, and talking to milkmaids who had sung songs with beautiful voices, and using strange baits'.[26] Fishing would have for Thomas the 'serenifying' effect that horse-riding had on Siegfried Sassoon. Apparently on one occasion, while visiting Joseph Conrad and his family later in life, he sat happily fishing for hours with Conrad's son, Borys, though neither had a hook attached to their lines and the pond was guiltless of fish. The fact that what he called Walton's 'different, embalmed enchanted life' appealed so soon to Thomas suggests an innate romanticism, which had been nurtured in early childhood by traditional fairy-tales and, later, by the poems and novels of Sir Walter Scott and tales of King Arthur and his Knights of the Round Table.[27] Accounts of more recent adventures in wild places, such as Robinson Crusoe, or of actual journeys by explorers like Samuel Baker, also appealed to him. The 9-year-old boy, who imagines travels for the Watercress Man in *The Heart of England* (1906) – 'sleeping the boy knew not where, perhaps not at all, but going on and on, certainly not to church, but perhaps to places with mountains, icebergs, houses in the branches of trees, great waters, camels, monkeys, crocodiles, parrots, ivory, cannibals, curved swords' – gives some idea of the effect these books already had on his imagination, however philistine he claimed to be at that age.[28]

Edward was read to from an early age, often by his father. When he and his two younger brothers caught scarlet fever, for instance, Philip Henry Thomas would read them *The Cuckoo Clock* and the opening of *Great Expectations*, which affected his eldest son deeply and would influence his description of his own childhood later on.

These readings were mainly prose, but even when the books were 'improving' ones, as they often were in this Victorian household of strict moral standards, Edward found them enormously enjoyable. His favourite book, read to him before he could read for himself, filled such a large space in his early memories that it became two separate books for him retrospectively – *Fairy Know-a-bit* and *A Nutshell of Knowledge*. (The correct title is *Fairy Know-a-bit, or a Nutshell of Knowledge* by 'A.L[ady].O[f].E[ngland]', the pseudonym of Charlotte Maria Tucker, published in 1866). The loss of this book in later childhood left Edward longing for the 'Key of Knowledge' he thought it contained. Even as an adult he would feel he had 'mislaid the key' when he tried to understand the past.[29]

Thomas is at pains to point out, however, that his books did 'not hamper my games, nor alter them in any way, except to enhance them imaginatively'.[30] He was 'still well content to remain, except during these readings, a citizen's son of London in the eighties of the nineteenth century, but a citizen with a sometimes fantastically light grasp of facts'.[31] He played as hard as ever and took up another activity which also became a lifelong passion, walking. At a time when children of his class were allowed a great deal more freedom to roam the streets than today, he regularly made the three-mile trip to Wimbledon Common by various routes and found the streets he passed through full of interest: 'a cage of pigeons or rabbits or guinea-pigs...or an old man with some trait of surliness or quaintness...or a chestnut-tree where we had to stop to throw up at the "conkers", or a shop where we had once bought a specially good halfpenny cake'.[32] Names, again, fascinated him, 'Allfarthing Lane' being a particular favourite. Later he would extend the territory to include Richmond, where the Park gave an even better idea of the countryside which lay beyond the London suburbs.

Edward was about 10 when he first experienced the real countryside for himself. His visits to his paternal grandmother in Swindon would open up not only the Downs, plains and forests of Wiltshire, which lay at its door, but also a way of life very different from that of the London suburbs, partly through the influence of a local writer, Richard Jefferies. These holidays, independent of home save for the company of a younger brother, would also allow Edward to roam even more freely than in London and to meet characters who seemed to spring from the countryside itself – poachers, tramps, gamekeepers, gypsies and the like. If there was any equivalent for him of Wordsworth's 'fair seed-time', it was in Wiltshire. His account of his own awakening to nature (though in prose not verse) resembles Wordsworth's in the strong, mystical, Romantic vein it reveals: to him Wiltshire was 'paradisal', 'a blessed place'.[33] He came to believe that 'half [his] soul was there'.[34]

Edward remained grateful to his grandmother for making these visits possible. He loved the journey through the West Country to Swindon, the approach past stone- (not brick-)built houses to her little ivy-covered cottage at 19 Cambria Place in the railway village of New Swindon.[35] The row of low houses which seemed to Edward's childish eyes 'like bull-dogs small, but strongly built',[36] faced a large park, with the countryside only a short walk away along the canal running directly behind the chapel at the back of number 19. The area, which had been settled mainly by railway workers from Wales, was known as the 'Welsh Colony',[37] and Rachel Thomas's kitchen could have come straight out of a Welsh village. 'No room was ever as cosy as my grandmother's,' Edward remembered:

> Its open range was always bright. There was a pair of bellows frequently in use. A brass turnspit hung from under the mantelpiece. The radiant steel trivet was excellent in itself but often bore a load of girdle cakes or buttered toast or more substantial things. An old brown earthenware teapot stood eternally upon the hob. Tea-caddies, brass candlesticks, clay pipes and vases full of spills, stood on the mantelpiece.[38]

His grandmother baked prodigiously, 'pies with pastry a full inch thick', various fruit tarts, but 'above all', she made 'doughy cakes, of dough, all spice and many raisins', which Edward thought 'as much better than other cakes as Swindon was much better than other towns, and always as much better than other so called doughy cakes'.[39] She cooked, shopped, cleaned, did almost everything, though her unmarried daughter, Margaret, would sometimes take over the baking of the doughy cakes, delighting her nephew by de-stoning the raisins with her teeth when she thought no one was looking. His portrait of 'Aunt Rachel' in *The Happy-Go-Lucky Morgans* (1913) would be a composite portrait of a woman of his aunt's generation, but based largely on his grandmother, who represented for him what was already becoming an outdated model of the domestic feminine role.

Yet for all Edward's appreciation of Rachel Thomas, who was in her mid-sixties when he started spending long holidays with her, he did not instinctively love her, as he did his mother. While recognizing that she was 'marvellously kind and necessary', he never felt close to her. Whether it was a clash of temperaments, too similar temperaments, his own inability to love easily (which would later cause problems in his marriage), or simply an extension of his attitude towards his father, whenever there was any quarrel, he admitted feeling 'contempt mingled with my hate of her inheritance from semi-rural Wales of George the Fourth's time'.[40] She seemed to him 'bigoted, worldly, crafty, narrow-minded and ungenerous'.[41] He found her religiosity particularly oppressive, not hearing her singing hymns to herself (in Welsh), but the way she dressed him in his uncomfortable

Sunday best, herself in black, and dragged him to church. The service struck him as no more inspiring than his father's Unitarian rituals, 'dreary discomfort' in which, as in London services, 'the hymns were green isles'.[42] Afterwards he would be taken to see her friends who, when they wanted to hide something from him, would speak Welsh, a language he never learnt. Their cliquishness was one aspect of their Welshness he did not appreciate; he made no allowances for the possibility that his grandmother might still feel in exile from her native Tredegar.

Edward felt more affectionate and more positive towards his uncle Harry, Rachel's youngest son. Twenty-three or -four when his nephew got to know him and a fitter at the Swindon railway works, he seemed far more easy-going and spontaneous than his civil servant brother, Edward's father, and the nearest Edward had got by the age of 10 to a countryman. 'Uncle Harry – a study of careless joyousness in a rigid house,' Thomas would note in 1907 – 'also the mingling of Devon, Spain and Wales'.[43] On his day off, Sunday, after a late breakfast, he would take his nephews to his local club for a drink, followed by a ramble out of town along the canal. More like someone their own age than a grown man in his behaviour, he would introduce them to rat-hunting with dogs and stones, or play games like ducks and drakes with them and teach them country skills such as peeling off the bark of willows. After another visit to his club for a second ale or pipe of shag, he would get them back home for his mother's one o'clock meal of roast lamb, green peas and mint sauce, with rhubarb and custard to follow. While Harry enjoyed her home-cooking, however, they bickered constantly over his relaxed attitude towards the gardening and his other household responsibilities. He would leave home for a new life in South Africa in 1891 when Edward was only 12 or 13.

Harry Eastaway Thomas was too impatient to make a good fisherman, but his replacement on later similar country rambles, David Uzzell, was an expert in all country matters and one of the most formative influences of the young Thomas's life. It was while fishing with the local boys in the late 1880s that Edward first met 'Dad', as he called him 'in the Wiltshire style'.[44] Born at Kemble, Cirencester, in about 1845, 'Dad' grew up a wild, strong, lawless youth, serving first in the militia, then taking odd jobs mowing and harvesting, later becoming an 'errand man' in Swindon. As his great strength diminished, however, he began to repent of his youthful excesses and by the time Edward met him was a teetotaller and caretaker at the Salvation Army Barracks at New Swindon. He and his wife lived there with one of his three sons, who worked in the same railway factory as Harry Thomas. But 'Dad' remained an essentially tough character, thinking nothing of digging out a corn from Edward's foot, for instance, with his sharp little pocket-knife without apology. Edward, whose interest in girls started at an early age and grew rapidly, was particularly appreciative of Dad's 'fond[ness] of talking of love w[ith] hearty lustfulness and some curiosity, but no mean ribaldry', his conclusion usually being a remark Edward was to repeat often in his later writings, 'Well, well what a thing it is.'[45] 'Dad''s refusal, or inability, to conform to the Victorian middle-class need to hide anything to do with sex or the human body from children – as though adults were 'doing without sex', as Thomas put it – made 'Dad''s extraordinary freedom 'both amusing and alluring', as well as liberating to the boy.[46] Edward's initial impression of 'a wicked old man' quickly gave way to a belief that 'all men were like him', a conviction reinforced by the activities of various couples he witnessed emerging from the undergrowth by the side of the canal, but that 'most of them were inferior in honesty' to 'Dad'.[47] Thomas's later efforts to be direct about his own sexual impulses were undoubtedly influenced by his conversations with 'Dad'.

Initially, however, it had been Uzzell's physical robustness and country knowledge which attracted Edward, who instantly became a disciple of this 'finely made fellow', with his ramrod-straight back, 'his clear steel blue eyes' and his unlined 'bull strong face, sunburnt like his sinewy neck'.[48] He knew all about birds and their nests, encouraging Edward's own budding interest in them, and in collecting their eggs. He could imitate bird-notes 'to the life', 'the hollow note of the bullfinch…the chuckle of a jackdaw or the chiding of a sparrow-hawk at its prey…a young rook's cry whilst gobbling a worm'.[49] It was his expertise that helped Edward to learn the names of all the wild flowers. Uzzell was also a skilled herbalist, preserving the leaves and roots of many plants, which he used to cure a wide variety of complaints, including (he told Edward frankly) unwanted pregnancies.

Some of 'Dad''s youthful rebelliousness survived in his bitterness towards the Church and the State and his insistence that there was a separate law for the rich and the poor. This may, in turn, have encouraged Edward's own growing disaffection with religion and his sympathy with a certain type of working-class man. The relationship between himself and 'Dad' was to be among the most enduring of Thomas's life. When, later on, he wanted to evoke an ideal of 'Englishness' which would relate to England's history, folklore, literature and the countryside itself, 'Dad' would serve partly as his model, lying behind his creation of the robust Chaucerian figure of 'Lob' in the poem of that name:

> At hawthorn-time in Wiltshire travelling
> In search of something chance would never bring,
> An old man's face, by life and weather cut
> And coloured, – rough, brown, sweet as any nut, –
> A land face, sea-blue-eyed, – hung in my mind
> When I had left him many a mile behind.

The narrator's 'search of something chance would never bring' was begun in Wiltshire, his county of adoption, where his relationship with 'Dad' Uzzell and, to a lesser extent, Harry Thomas showed him an approach to life that was far more instinctive and spontaneous than his parents', relating more closely to the earth. If he had a tendency to idealize such men, together with the gypsies, tramps and labourers he also met in the country, it was perhaps because he longed to be like them. From an early age he felt cursed by a self-consciousness he believed the chief cause of his later problems and depression. With 'Dad', and men like him, he could share vicariously in a less cerebral way of life. The figure of 'Dad' and what he represented for Thomas appears not just in 'Lob', but in various figures through all the writing to follow.[50]

3

'THE FOOLISH YEARS' (1889–1893)[1]

Edward Thomas's growing self-consciousness was exacerbated at the end of 1888 by his father's decision to send him to a private school. With characteristic pragmatism, Philip Henry Thomas had calculated that, if Edward was to gain a coveted scholarship to Battersea Grammar School, and thus a respectable but free education, it would be worth investing in a more ambitious programme than the Belleville Road Board School could provide. Edward was duly enrolled at a local private prep. school, St John's Hill House. It was a particularly strong contrast to the Board School he had attended in Swindon for part of the summer term of 1888, whose pupils both his grandmother and her daughter thought 'too low' for him. Though he denied sharing their feelings, he undoubtedly did consider himself superior to the Board School pupils he had encountered up to the age of 10, confessing his sense of superiority, for instance, in announcing to them 'that my father [is] an "Officer" in the Civil Service'.[2]

He is unlikely to have felt socially superior at St John's Hill House School, where the 50 or 60 boys were of a distinctly higher social class, as he thinks it worthwhile noting, 'the sons of tradesmen, professional men, moderately well to do clerks and men of small independent means'.[3] About half the pupils boarded and used their privileges to dominate the day boys. While the geography and history lessons offered continuity to Edward, the mathematics grew a great deal harder and handwriting needed more attention. Two subjects entirely new to him were Latin and physiology, which evidently fascinated Edward and his schoolfellows, who listened 'as if the body were a newly discovered machine and we were angels'.[4] Paperchases were the only organized communal sports activity and it was during one of these runs that Edward discovered a piece of country which seemed to him 'exactly like the real country at Swindon': 'here were private but not inaccessible copses, hedges with oaks in them, and wandering paths, rough lanes, scant cottages'.[5] It was at Merton, only six or seven miles from Battersea, that he kept his recently discovered love of the countryside alive. He enjoyed one run in particular, despite being left behind by the rest of the school, when he met an older boy in the same position and ate bread and cheese with him at a pub in Merton, an event he described in 'A Sportsman's Tale'. The boy was Arthur York Hardy, who would become the closest friend of his teenage years.

At St John's Hill House, however, it was neither sport nor lessons that preoccupied the boys, but pets. From the boarders' silkworms, the senior boys' white rats to the pigeons, hares, rabbits and guinea pigs kept by the rest, they filled Edward's thoughts and emptied his pockets, as he bought, sold or exchanged pets with the other boys. His love of birds, encouraged by 'Dad' in Wiltshire, led him to choose pigeons and he would later fill several pages of his autobiographical novel, *The Happy-Go-Lucky Morgans*, describing them. Pigeons also led, indirectly, to his only apprenticeship in carpentry as he made coops for them in the workshops of a fellow-pupil's father, where he was taught to use a saw, hammer, screwdriver and brace.

As Thomas thought it significant to point out, his companions 'were now boys exclusively'.[6] Without sisters of his own and only rare visits to his female Welsh cousins, the possibility of getting to know girls was limited to his friends, none of whom had sisters of his age. His next school, which he transferred to after the headmaster moved St John's Hill House to the country, was also confined to boys. This made girls, when he did meet them, mysterious and different, and led to a certain amount of idealization of them, which sisters of his own might have quickly dispelled. In 1887, before leaving his Board School, he had become 'very fond' of a girl in his neigh-bourhood, Mabel Looms, 'lifted her in his arms to prove his superiority' over his rival for Mabel, Charlie Thornley. A great fan of Scott's heroic poems and Rhoderick Dhu at the time, he liked Mabel to see him with a toy sword at his side.[7] He even wrote letters to her, a fairly precocious activity in the context.

Edward's second private school, which he does not name, was clearly intended to continue his preparation for the Grammar School scholarship. It was about two miles away in Battersea, too far to return home for lunch and the main significance of this for Edward, now 11, was eight or nine hours a day at a stretch in what he remembered as 'greenless streets'.[8] While he continued to enjoy the usual playground games, like leapfrog, he looked forward to playing cricket and football organized by the boys on nearby Clapham Common, with its trees and open spaces.

The curriculum was similar to St John's Hill House, with the addition of French which Edward evidently liked, reading French books later on in the original. Another additional subject was chemistry, which he disliked. Evening lectures on sound, light and heat, which his father insisted he attend, also failed to appeal. Despite being several years behind most of the other boys in all subjects, he was seldom lower than fourth in class, more often than not first.[9] He had a quick, retentive brain and almost everything came easily to him. He felt little interest in the subjects themselves. Even poetry, represented by Byron's 'The Prisoner of Chillon', left him cold; he was, he emphasizes, in 'a period of prose which the place encouraged',[10] the beginning of what he called 'the foolish years' from 11 to 15.[11]

By sending Edward to private schools his father was taking him further away from his son's adult ideal of the 'natural' life of country living, carried out within a stable if limited environment. Removing him from the 'local' school not only took him away from the area physically, but also from the friends he had made there. It distanced him socially from his earliest environment and even from the two brothers nearest to him in age, Ernest and Theodore ('Dorie'), who remained at the local Board School. 'Not even yet,' Thomas wrote in 1913, 'can I recall anything distinctly of my brothers beyond the fact of an inconstant feud with the eldest of them.'[12] Though he at no point names any of his brothers in his autobiography, we know that this was Ernest, who was very like his father in physical appearance, darker, shorter and more athletic in build than Edward. It is possible that Edward identified him in other ways with his father, which may explain why they disagreed so much. It may also account for his extraordinary writing out of Ernest from his childhood. Ernest was only two years younger, was his constant companion on his long holidays at Swindon, where they fished, went bird-nesting and trespassed together, as was Theodore, another two years younger again. Both subsequently had vivid memories of the time they spent with Edward, including not only the fishing, trespassing and bird-nesting in Wiltshire but also long walks with him in London as boys, and several visits to him after his marriage. Yet all Thomas records in any detail was his repeated quarrelling with Ernest, whom he does not name. (Things would improve later.) He had better relations with Theodore, who would become a distinguished engineer and with whom he would stay for a month or two in 1908, neutral ones with Oscar and Reginald ('Reggie') and warmer ones with his youngest brother, Julian.

Once Edward started at his second private school in 1889 he saw even less of his brothers or the rest of his family. He was, in any case, living in his own world, an exciting one of boys' adventure stories, devouring books by Mayne Reid, who had replaced his earlier passion for James Fenimore Cooper and G. A. Henty. His reading at this time gives no hint of what was to come, except in its extent: he loved 'blood and thunder' books, especially, stories with titles like *The Headless Horseman*, *The Scalp Hunters* or *The Secret of Adam's Peak*.

Edward dismissed the pupils at this second private school as 'a coarse rough lot, worse than the Board-School boys', a remark which suggests that he was still highly conscious of the social implications of his father's decision.[13] His attitude may have been influenced by his aunt Margaret Townsend's shock when he went to tea with a boy whose father owned a public house, albeit a very large one. With what seems like inverted snobbery he declared: 'I preferred the sons of Swindon mechanics and labourers to the sons of Battersea tradesmen and clerks.'[14]

When Thomas describes his successful move to Battersea Grammar School as a Free Scholar aged about 12, the first thing he notes is the superior class of the boys there. He thinks it worth pointing out that, while resembling those at private school, at least superficially he found them 'more refined...their speech was better; their code of honour more strict; and there was an *esprit de corps* amongst them', terms which might be used to describe pupils at a public school.[15] Instead of increasing his confidence, however, this contact with the greater 'refinement' seems to have made him less, not more secure socially and even more self-conscious. When his aunt Margaret invited her three eldest nephews to spend a holiday with her in 1892 at Burnham, in Somerset, where she was looking after children whose parents were in India, his feelings of social inadequacy came to the fore. The eldest boy, who had just left the public school his younger brothers still attended and was destined for the Royal Military College, Sandhurst, caused Edward to feel 'anxious not to show my more awkward manner' and made him 'conscious of being shy, timid and sneaking'.[16]

The education itself at Battersea Grammar School he found almost as undemanding as at his two previous schools, and he continued to come top in English, history and geography, and near the top in most other subjects. He worked just hard enough to retain his scholarship and to satisfy his father's expectations of him, finding his schoolbooks dull on the whole. His father's efforts to stimulate an interest in a variety of subjects continued to fail almost completely; Edward preferred to learn his botany, for instance, from a countryman like 'Dad' Uzzell, rather than from books or lectures. He tolerated the special lessons in Latin verse and Greek grammar his father arranged only because to do otherwise would have brought 'worse nuisances'.[17] He responded poorly to lectures which later on would have interested him. Grant Allen recommending State endowment of literary genius, for example, was something that would concern him personally in adult life. Even his father's enthusiasm for literature failed to extend his eldest son's interests beyond the adventure stories or natural history his schoolfellows were reading.

The one area where Philip Henry Thomas did succeed in involving Edward for a time was politics. An active member of the local Liberal Party, he succeeded in convincing his son that 'Mr Gladstone was a glorious, great and good man' and that all Conservatives were 'an inferior race, partly because they were wicked, partly because they were stupid'.[18] Edward accompanied him on Sundays to political meetings at Washington Music Hall (now the Battersea Palace) at 32 York Road, Battersea, to listen to John Burns, Keir Hardie and the Socialists and once saw the Irish Republican Michael Davitt there, fresh out of prison, 'dark, straight and austere with his armless sleeve dangling'.[19] He canvassed for the Liberals in the General

Election of 1892 and followed its progress keenly, as his remarks to his father show.

Edward's interest in politics was short-lived, however, and would not survive in any organized sense in adulthood, when he insisted that he could not 'grasp' politics.[20] If he had any political convictions at all, they tended to be of the 'Dad' Uzzell variety, more of a protest against the lot of the agricultural labourer than a coherent system of beliefs. At any rate his rare period of accord with his father over politics did not last and they were soon at loggerheads again, especially over Philip Henry's insistence on his attendance of the morning service at his Unitarian chapel and a full report on the sermon at Sunday lunch.

Edward's final rejection of his father's world coincided with his awakening to poetry at the age of 15. He had found no poetry in the Shakespeare plays he had been forced to read at school, regarding blank verse as a form of prose,[21] though he did glimpse 'certain human heights and depths' in plays like *Henry V* and *Richard II*. But gradually his parents' large collection of poets, which included most of the classics – Chaucer, Spenser, Keats, Byron, Shelley, Tennyson and Browning – began to interest him. Starting with the rote learning of parts of 'In Memoriam', he began to linger over poems like Tennyson's 'The May Queen' and Gray's 'Elegy Written in a Country Churchyard'. Ernest Thomas remembered that in about 1893 or 1894, while they were still sharing a bedroom, 'every night after we had got to bed, he would keep me awake by repeating from memory yards of poetry, particularly Keats and Shelley, which he had been reading that evening'.[22] Ernest was more interested in the visual arts and would eventually go to art school (producing his own pencil portrait of his older brother). Edward's nightly recitations caused 'arguments and quarrels which lasted for several years'.[23]

But the best of life for Edward was still spent out of doors, where he started to read his favourite poetry to his best friend at Battersea Grammar School, Arthur Hardy. Their budding relationship at St John's Hill House (Arthur becomes 'John' in *The Childhood of Edward Thomas*), when they had got lost together on a paperchase, had been cut short by Edward's move to another school. But Arthur, two years older than Edward, had preceded him to Battersea Grammar, where they quickly became inseparable. The only lasting friendship of Edward's schooldays, it was based on shared tastes but contrasting temperaments and backgrounds. 'We were two entirely different natures,' Thomas wrote in 'A Sportsman's Tale', his thinly disguised account of Arthur (now called 'Harold' while the narrator himself becomes 'John'): 'he was a cricketer, a sportsman, a dancer, and could jump over spiked railings as high as his shoulder'.[24] Though Arthur 'looked rather stupid' at school, and with people generally, Edward admired his confidence 'in the fields which seemed to him a mark of grace'.[25] He was also conscious of Arthur's greater social confidence; his speech seemed 'more refined', his manner 'freer and more generous', his house 'larger' and Thomas remembered feeling 'some shame' of his own 'slightly inferior social position'.[26] A handsome, fair boy with large regular features, Arthur's appearance also appealed to Edward, who was susceptible to beauty in either sex from an early age.

Their shared interests centred round typical schoolboy pursuits of the time – moth- and butterfly-collecting, fishing and bird-nesting – but their greatest passion was for nature itself. One of their first excursions at Battersea Grammar was back to the spot they had discovered together on that failed paperchase, Merton. Their appreciation of this 'piece of pure country', and other nearby open spaces, went through a number of phases in their four years' rambling together. First, the 'wild unconscious play', when they hardly distinguished between the open fields and the neighbourhood of towns, except to prefer the fields.[27] Next came the 'hunting stage' when they 'deliberately played at savages', followed by a phase of collecting birds' eggs, flowers and insects, and of stuffing birds and animals.[28] Finally, they arrived at the 'poetical stage' when nature became a setting (as it had for the young Wordsworth) for something less physical but no less exhilarating as Edward read his latest poetic discoveries to Arthur – Theocritus, Spenser, Marvell, Gray, Blake, Wordsworth, Shelley, Coleridge and Keats. Sometimes he would listen to his less intellectual friend, with his 'handsome heavy face reciting [Shelley's] "The Revolt of Islam" with a grave, puzzled expression under his rapture'.[29] He would devote a whole chapter of *The Happy-Go-Lucky Morgans* to the relationship between a similarly close pair of friends, Philip and Arthur.

Arthur would give up reading poetry and revert to a more physical life, joining the South African police in 1902, but the friendship would survive, leading Thomas to dedicate *Light and Twilight* (1911) 'To

A[rthur] Y[ork] H[ardy] 1891–1911' after Hardy returned to England in 1910 and they had taken a ten-day holiday together in Wales. 'Our friendship,' Hardy told James Guthrie after Thomas's death, 'was so much a "spiritual" one that we could always take up the thread again pretty much where it had been dropped. I know no-one who can begin to take his place in my thoughts.'[30]

In the early 1890s Edward's autumns, winters, springs and early summers were spent in London with Arthur his constant companion, but his summers were still passed mainly in Wiltshire with 'Dad' Uzzell. Another Wiltshire influence which had encouraged his interest in poetry was the writer Richard Jefferies, who had grown up near Swindon at Coate and had described the surrounding countryside in loving detail. One of the first books of Jefferies's Edward discovered, probably among his father's well-stocked library, was *The Amateur Poacher* (1879). What he admired in the Wiltshireman's books was partly the contrast with his own existence as lived in London: 'the free open-air life, the spice of illegality and daring, roguish characters – the opportunities so far exceeding my own, the gun, the great pond, the country life, the apparently endless leisure.'[31] It was a world he could inhabit by simply opening *The Amateur Poacher*, which became an important part of his own way into writing. Under Jefferies's influence, as well as the more practical need to write a school essay about his holidays, he, too, began noting natural details on his outings – birds, plants, trees, clouds, seasons. When eventually some of these observations appeared in his own first book, *The Woodland Life* (1897), it seems fitting that it should open with the final words of Jefferies's *The Amateur Poacher*: 'Let us get out of the indoor narrow modern days, whose twelve hours somehow have become shortened, into the sunlight and the pure wind. A something that the ancients thought divine can be found and felt there still.' His father would reject the Christianity of his youth for, first Unitarianism, then Positivism, but Thomas would depart further still from conventional religion, finding his own meaning largely in nature (though he refused to call it a religion). 'Almost as soon as I could babble,' he told an admirer (in a paraphrase from the play he first read at this time, *Henry V*), 'I babbled of green fields.'[32]

Thomas's discovery of poetry, also at this period, gave him (in his own words on Morgan Rhys in *Beautiful Wales* (1905)): 'a second world in which he henceforward moved with a rapture which I do not always observe in the religious'.[33] In religious matters, Thomas wrote in what sounds like a statement of his own views, '[Morgan] remains so pure a sceptic that he has never yet learned that there is anything about which to be sceptical'. Thomas himself believed that this 'so-called matter-of-factness in combination with a rich imaginativeness is perhaps a Welsh characteristic'.[34]

The combination of nature, poetry and the writings of Jefferies had, by the end of 1893, almost given birth to Thomas the writer. It needed one more factor added to the equation, and yet another change of school, to complete the process.

4

St Paul's and Helen Noble: Alone Together (1894–1897)

By sending Edward to one of London's two great public schools, St Paul's, at the age of 15, his father was severing yet another link with his son's Board School beginnings. It was a move which even cut him off from the more socially acceptable Battersea Grammar School. On going to public school, Thomas recalled, he had 'without thinking of it dropped all connection' with Battersea Grammar.[1] He never once returned, his only surviving link being Arthur Hardy, who remained his close friend during four terms at St Paul's from January 1894 to Easter 1895, though not a pupil there himself.

Edward's own explanation for his apparent coldness towards his former schoolmates other than Arthur was shyness: he dreaded 'the mere coming face to face with anyone who was not an intimate'.[2] This fear would often be interpreted in later life as aloofness. At St Paul's it almost certainly prevented him from making new friends easily and left him feeling intensely isolated. His description of his protagonist, Philip's, suffering in his unpublished novel *Fiction*, sounds very similar to his own suffering on arrival at St Paul's:

> A feeling that I was horribly conspicuous made me wish to hide myself. For the people were no longer a negatively friendly element which the individual slid in and out of…Perhaps

I discovered something they had in common, but what I saw chiefly was that they were different from me. I was alone, and I found myself saying over my name to myself to intensify my individuality, to bring about a conviction that though alone I was strong. Thenceforward I was always wanting to take the joys of solitude and of society in their extreme forms, and was alternately miserable from lack of company or the presence of uncongenial company.[3]

Edward's failure to win a scholarship to St Paul's, as his father had hoped, was not a good beginning for someone hampered by shyness. He had always previously been able to shine academically when he chose. Now, for the first time in his life, he found himself struggling hard near the bottom of the class. St Paul's History Eighth had been formed the previous year to cater for boys wanting to read history at either Oxford or Cambridge. Edward was among the youngest in it, by as much as two years at the start. He was also a long way behind in Latin, Greek and science, weak in Maths and French, and little better in history and divinity. (He came seventh out of eight boys in the form overall after six months and bottom in classics and French.) Only in English and drawing did he do well initially. Yet he carried out his work steadily and his form-master, R. F. Cholmeley's, real concern was about Edward's apparent lack of 'interest in life generally'.[4] After the form's two scholars left for Oxford in the summer of 1894 the age gap narrowed and Edward's work began to improve. By Christmas 1894 his Latin, French and mathematics were progressing, and his English and Drawing were deemed 'good', and his history 'very good'.[5] From seventh he had risen to second out of eight boys and Cholmeley thought him 'quite the ablest in the form, considering his age', though he still wished 'he were a more sociable person'.[6]

The problem was clearly not academic. The real challenge for Edward was social. The whole school, with the confidence of its ancient traditions and social cachet behind it, 'impressed and alarmed' him, from its imposing headmaster, Mr Walker, downwards. He felt 'humbled', even by boys of his own age, many of whom 'wore men's clothes, carried their books in bags like clerks', and seemed to him 'grimly earnest... thinking of only work and success'.[7] Others intimidated him by their air of wealth and 'more refined voices' than he was used to.[8] Even their clothes seemed infinitely superior to his own 'ready-made' ones.[9] He saw himself as unimportant, isolated, out of place, and only not despised because 'utterly unnoticed'.[10] He felt completely 'alone', a word which recurs many times in his record of this period. He was 'alone' on his train journey to and from the school, still then situated in Hammersmith Road, near Hammersmith Roundabout, he took his lunch 'alone' at midday, he watched (but does not record playing) rugby 'alone', or walked by the River Thames 'alone' in his free time, 'sometimes in such wretchedness', he claimed, that he 'wanted to drown [him]self'.[11]

It was the start of the bouts of depression which would afflict Thomas throughout his life, brought on, it seems, by a sense of inadequacy or inferiority. Yet both his schoolmaster's and fellow-pupils' remarks about him at this time suggest that he had no firm grounds for his feelings. Lucian Oldershaw, a friend of G. K. Chesterton (who had recently left St Paul's) and one of the History Eighth's two scholars, described his meeting with the adolescent Edward as memorable. They had both been invited to dinner by another classmate, R. E. Vernède, later a poet and novelist who would also be killed in the First World War. The three of them had 'talked books' all evening and when Oldershaw and Thomas left together, they continued to do so:

> We walked for hours about the streets of Notting Hill and talked and talked [Oldershaw wrote]. What we talked about (it was mainly the classical poetry of the eighteenth century!) did not seem to matter much. I felt we were communing with something deeper than words. I felt something of the same awe and excitement I had experienced four years before when tramping round Warwick Gardens with Chesterton... When we parted at midnight, physically tired but spiritually exalted, I found myself quoting what I could recall of Keats's sonnet, a new planet had swum into my ken.[12]

Oldershaw's reaction to Thomas and other facts which emerge from Edward's detailed daily account of his life from January to March 1895, his last term at St Paul's,[13] suggest that he exaggerated his isolation in retrospect, though the feeling itself may have been real enough. Instead of the single debate which he describes in *The Childhood* (1938) as a humiliating experience, his diary records that he participated in a number, at least two of which he was chosen to open.[14] He was elected to the committee of the 'St Paul's School History Form Debating Society', later noting that its

Vice-President, R. Smalley, was 'up for a scholarship at Lincoln, Oxford'.[15] His self-contained manner may have discouraged other friendly overtures apart from Vernède's. E. C. Bentley, one of the form's two scholars on Edward's arrival, remembered him as 'exceptionally reserved and quiet'.[16] The reserve was almost certainly an attempt to hide his lack of confidence and growing self-consciousness, but Thomas himself appeared to think it stemmed from something more sinister. His alter ego in *Fiction*, Philip, at the same age believed that 'there was something at the back of my mind, not quite hidden from myself or my schoolfellows, - a weight, a darkness, - which was against intimacy'.[17] As with the 16-year-old Edward, this dark 'something' had 'taken away all [his] irresponsibility'.[18]

Whether Mr Thomas's decision to remove Edward from St Paul's was a reaction to this change in his eldest son is impossible to say. It may have stemmed from more practical, financial considerations. It was certainly not because there was any doubt of Edward's academic ability. The headmaster himself, Mr Walker, had told Mr Thomas that he 'had no doubt' that 'he would get a scholarship' if he stayed on.[19] Still set on a career in the Civil Service for his son, however, Mr Thomas stuck to his decision. Edward, on the other hand, as a direct result of attending St Paul's, now wanted to go to Oxford, or, at least, 'to do something in connection with learning or literature'.[20] His father, Mr Thomas, with more forbearance than his son credited him with, agreed to enquire about an apprenticeship for him at the *North Wiltshire Herald*, the paper where Richard Jefferies had worked. He did so on 13 March but when the reply came a week later stipulating a five-years' apprenticeship, was 'not willing' to allow it.[21]

Edward was already a fledgling journalist, however, having started to write magazine articles with the encouragement of the minister of their Unitarian chapel, W. G. Tarrant.[22] The minister, whose own publications would include a book of verse as well as the history of Unitarianism and a selection of his sermons and lectures, had detected promise in the youth and would be responsible for his first publication in a children's magazine, *Young Days*: ' Wrote article for *Young Days* called "Birds in March",' Edward noted on 14 January 1895.[23] He also recorded proudly on 23 January 1895: 'Editor of *Young Days* pleased with my article – wants one for April!' Only a day later he is 'thinking seriously about writing a book: "Rural Walks" '.[24]

Though doubtful about the title, he had especially decided to include a chapter, 'Peewit Fields', in it, his interest in birds already strong. ('I like birds more than books,' he had written on the flyleaf of a St Paul's algebra book in poor Latin.) Ideas for both the essays and the book had grown out of his admiration for Jefferies's detailed accounts of the Wiltshire countryside, which Edward had tried to emulate in his school essays. The sights, sounds, smells, even the touch of the plants, birds, landscapes and skyscapes he had noted on his visits to his grandmother, were recreated.

Jefferies himself had been greatly influenced by Gilbert White's *Selborne*, the natural history of a small corner of Hampshire, and Edward's next step was to order White's *Selborne* with an introduction by Jefferies. He also joined the Selborne Society and started to read their magazine, *Nature Notes*, which would review at least two of his books in its pages.[25] By 9 February 1895 he was beginning a third article, 'Birds in May'.

The Rev. Tarrant was also indirectly responsible for the publication of Edward's first book, when he introduced him this same year to a new member of his congregation, James Ashcroft Noble. Noble, a convinced Liberal and Unitarian, was a northerner by birth and largely self-educated. Nevertheless, he had become a successful man of letters by the time Thomas met him, a reviewer for the *Spectator*, *Academy* and *Daily Chronicle*, as well as editor of the literary supplement of the *Manchester Examiner*. He had published a number of books, which included poetry, a collection of his reviews and essays and a study of the sonnet in England.[26] Perhaps because of his own early struggles in Liverpool, he was always ready to help unknown young writers, such as the nineties poets Richard Le Gallienne and William Watson, and Gordon Bottomley, who would himself become something of a mentor to Thomas.

Noble's move to Wandsworth in 1893 had been his second attempt to establish himself in London, partly to be nearer the centre of literary activity but also for health reasons. Only 50 when Thomas finally met him in person in the autumn of 1895, he would be dead less than a year later of tubercular laryngitis, his rapid deterioration poignantly documented in his letters to the 17-year-old Edward between October 1895 and February 1896. He would be too ill to read his young disciple's last letter to him of early April 1896, thanking him effusively for his 'surpassing kindness and insight', for 'bringing light where there was uncertainty'.[27]

At their first visit, which took place some time after Edward returned in August 1895 from a summer spent mainly in Swindon, Noble was still hard at work in his study overlooking a little garden at the back of 15 The Grove, Wandsworth, where he sat at his knee-hole writing desk constantly smoking cigarettes and sipping weak whisky and water.[28] Tarrant had already sent him a sample of Edward's work, which Noble greatly admired – his three daughters had privately christened him 'The Genius' – and, despite the youth's pronounced shyness, they started to discuss it. The death of Noble's first son, Philip, and a falling out with William Watson after he jilted Noble's best friend's daughter, had left him in need of a protégé. As Noble told Edward early on, he reminded him of his 'boy Philip', who had died young, and not just because of their shared first name.[29] Since he had 'no Philip left to me', he wrote, 'he would have to be proud of' Edward until his younger son, Lancelot was 'old enough to do something to be proud of'.[30]

Noble quickly began to treat Edward like a son, though he was careful not to undermine his father's authority with him. (When Edward expressed resentment at what he considered Mr Thomas's harsh treatment of him, Noble was anxious to defend the father's decisions, especially his insistence that Edward should continue to study for the Civil Service exams.) He was enough of a Victorian, despite his nineties credentials, to agree with Mr Thomas that Edward was too young to read Rousseau's sexually explicit *Confessions*. He eventually asked if he could call Edward 'Phil', 'because you know I think of you as my own boy'.[31] Though this experiment was quickly abandoned in favour of 'Edwy', his fatherly role continued as the established writer guided the aspiring one a step nearer to a literary career. He gently offered improvements to his essays, anticipating what a number of Edward's later editors would suggest, that Thomas should 'throw in a little more topography or outline so as to give the interest of individuality to each picture'; 'a place-name,' Noble believed, 'would do something to localise the scene'.[32] He did not hesitate to dismiss Edward's attempts at verse as 'a pleasant little twitter'.[33]

Noble also introduced him to the work of new writers – the sixteenth-century antiquary John Leland, whom Edward enjoyed, Walt Whitman, whom he did not – and set up invaluable contacts for him with many friends in the literary world, most profitably with Mr Fletcher, editor of the *New Age* (of which Noble was part-owner), and Mr Perris, sub-editor of the *Speaker*.

By 6 November 1895 Edward had had his essay 'Wild Fruits' published in the *New Age*, a far more prestigious magazine than *Young Days*. George Cotterell of the *Yorkshire Herald*, alerted by Noble, wrote a glowing letter praising his 'youthful Jefferies', whom he declared 'a prodigy'.[34] E. T. Cook of the *Westminster Gazette*, C. J. Longman of *Longman's Magazine* and Richard Holt Hutton of the *Spectator* are among other possible contacts mentioned. Noble also mooted the possibility of 'a little book of his essays' as early as November 1895 and it was at his suggestion that Edward decided to add his nature diary for a year to it. Again it was Noble who put him in touch with his own publisher, William Blackwood, about the project leading to the publication of *The Woodland Life* a year later.

The relationship was far more than a literary one, however. Noble was the first, after 'Dad' Uzzell, of a number of father figures for Thomas. His letters would be among the few spared by Thomas when he systematically burnt his papers before leaving for France in January 1917. Their tastes in literature did not always coincide; Edward would continue to prefer Shelley and Keats to Wordsworth and Tennyson, and he showed no sign of agreeing with Noble that Elizabeth Barrett Browning was a more suitable poet for potential 'sweethearts' to read than Shelley and Keats (as Noble's daughter would learn). But they were both passionate about literature, both idealists of a kind, both deeply serious without being prudish. Noble did not hesitate to try to help Edward work out his attitude towards women and sex. (There appears to be some censorship of their correspondence here, possibly by Helen Thomas (née Noble)!) Noble was intensely sympathetic towards the conflicts of a youth emerging into manhood and encouraged Edward to confide in him in a way he had evidently not been able to talk to his own father. Noble's sending of a passage from Conan Doyle's *The Stark Munro Letters* shows great sympathy for what he suspected Edward was experiencing – in Conan Doyle's words:

> The shrinking, horrible shyness, alternating with occasional absurd fits of audacity...the longing for close relationship, the agonies over imaginary slights, the extraordinary sexual doubts, the deadly fears caused by non-existent diseases, the vague emotion produced by all women, and the half-frightened thrill by particular ones, the aggressiveness caused by fear of being afraid, the sudden blackness, the profound self-distrust ...[35]

In addition Edward's introduction to Noble helped fill the gap left in his life by his father's sudden withdrawal of him from St Paul's and, with it, his hope of getting to Oxford. At last Edward could seriously consider himself a writer. In fact his three-day walk from London to Wiltshire from 15 to 17 April, around the time Tarrant put him in touch with Noble, may have been taken partly to gain more copy.[36] It was certainly the start of a pattern which would result in a number of topographical books based on long walks or cycle rides – *Beautiful Wales* (1905), *The Heart of England* (1906), *The South Country* (1909), *The Isle of Wight* (1911), *The Icknield Way* (1913) and *In Pursuit of Spring* (1914).

Noble had an equally significant effect in a quite different area. For it was during Edward's visit to the Noble household in autumn 1895 that he got to know Noble's middle daughter, Helen Berenice Noble, then just 18. Helen, who wore wire-rimmed glasses and was not outstandingly pretty, considered herself 'plain'. She also suffered from a sense of intellectual inferiority, created mainly (she believed) by the superior academic achievements of her older sister, Irene, and her younger one, Mary, to such an extent that she had begged to be allowed to leave school at 16.[37] She was already convinced that she would never find anyone to love her and give her the children she longed for. So that she did not initially hope for more than friendship from her father's latest protégé. Her account of her first meeting with Edward in her largely autobiographical novel, *As It Was* (1926), however, suggests a more than intellectual attraction to him:

> My father introduced us and our eyes met – the boy's solemn grey eyes rather overshadowed by drooping lids with long lashes. He did not smile, but looked very steadily at me and I at him as he took my hand with a very hard and long grip…though I thought him shy and awkward and silent I liked him and wanted to see him again.[38]

Her description of Edward at this time is the first of many to show how striking he was:

> [Edward] was tall – just six feet – and slim, with a broad chest and shoulders, which he carried well – loose-limbed and athletic. He had a beautifully shaped head with a fine brow, and thick fair hair, worn rather long, curved a little over his forehead and ears. His nose was

long and straight, his mouth very sensitive, with the upper lip slightly overhanging the lower. The chin was strong. The eyes were grey and dreamy and meditative, but fearless and steady, as if trying to pierce to truth itself…His hands were large and powerful.[39]

Helen makes it clear in *As It Was* that, despite her own lack of confidence, it was she who took the initiative, opening the door to Edward, seeing him off at the end of his visits, even, eventually, insisting on a goodbye kiss. Her father, influenced by the nineties' movement's belief in the 'New Woman', allowed his daughters more freedom than was usual for the time; even their clothes were freer, the corset and crinoline a thing of the past for them. By January 1896, when her father had returned from a vain attempt to improve his health at Ramsgate, he is encouraging Edward to take Helen on one of his long walks, unchaperoned. Even before the first of these, however, Helen has 'a plan' for 'the Genius' and herself, which she frankly confesses to her best friend, Janet Aldis:

> I think it will succeed although it will take ages, for he is fearfully shy, and I am likewise affected. He wants a girl friend and I want a boy friend, and I like him (or at least what I know of him) and I think he likes me, I *think* it would be good for both of us if we could be friends. I wonder if we shall.[40]

Noble's letters to Edward leave no doubt as to his approval. It is as though the dying man, who was especially close to his middle daughter, wanted to leave her in the right hands. It was his intervention which brought about the first long walk to Richmond on 9 January. A year later Edward would send Helen a handwritten anthology of some of his favourite poems to mark the anniversary of what had clearly been a highly emotional occasion; the very terseness of his diary entry covering the original event supports this. When they repeat the walk to Richmond on 7 February 1896, his diary entry suggests that the day has flown past and that everything has become even more intense than usual in her presence: 'It is night before we know it – the sunset – twilight lost in listening to the thrush and wren in the tree-shadowed lane.' (They are late reaching home.) The inclusion of Browning's 'A Lover's Quarrel' in the same notebook, following half a torn-out page, hints that they are already on a romantic footing. ('Love, if you knew the light / That your soul casts in my sight').[41]

Before Edward left for another long stay in Swindon in mid-February he had dared to call Helen 'Sweet', she recorded, and during his six weeks' absence they corresponded faithfully. Arthur Hardy was sent as a substitute for his friend to 6 Patten Road, Wandsworth, where the Noble family had moved during James Ashcroft Noble's visit to Ramsgate.[42]

This budding romance was harshly interrupted by James Ashcroft Noble's death on 3 April 1896, though it may also have helped to seal it, by offering each of them a surrogate for the dead man. But Mrs Noble, who had approved of the relationship while her husband was alive, now began to discourage it. She had already forbidden Helen to visit Edward's collection of books and birds' nests alone and also to write to each other, though they had ignored the embargo on letters. Helen believed that her mother was 'jealous' of 'this quiet, reserved, clever boy' with whom she had 'no point of contact'. But Mrs Noble may simply have feared that Helen's impetuous, passionate nature might overcome the young couple's repeated resolve to keep the relationship 'pure'. They were idealistic but also highly sensuous beings; as Edward's nature essays had already shown, he responded intensely to the senses, particularly those of sight, sound, touch and smell. His passion for poetry, much of it by Shelley at this time and shared with Helen, was not calculated to cool the blood of two adolescents embarking on their first real relationship with the opposite sex. Thomas himself admitted that he was 'perpetually drunk with sunsets and Shelley' at this period, a far from ideal diet for restraint.[43]

For restraint was needed as they grew more intimate, despite Helen's repeated assurances of their 'purity' to her mother. Edward became increasingly tormented by his unsatisfied urgings, encouraged inadvertently by the 'sweet' submissiveness and willing participation of the young woman he now called his 'Anemone maid'.[44] One very real threat to his restraint was Helen's naïve belief that 'freedom' is the only way to greater purity.[45] Another of her ideals, which would test her to her limits later on and which would in practice allow Edward more 'freedom' than herself, was that they should tolerate affections outside their relationship, albeit platonic ones.

When Mrs Noble finally succeeded in separating them and Helen was sent as a nursemaid to family acquaintances, the Webbs, in Margate in mid-1896, Edward's physical frustration became almost unbearable, his only outlet his letters to Helen, which he filled with his own passionate feelings towards her. As he tried to live up to their shared ideal of complete truthfulness between them, his style (as he points out in 'How I Began') started to develop: 'Now it was that I had a chance of discarding or of adapting to my own purpose the fine words and infinite variety of construction which I had formerly admired and imitated in fairly cold blood.'[46] Though the letters have not survived, Helen's replies make it clear that his frankness included references to his fight against erections, nocturnal emissions and masturbation, which cold baths could not entirely subdue. Their letters became a substitute for sex to some extent, with Helen supplying Edward with innocently inflammatory details about the female body and physiology, gleaned from her more worldly-wise friend, Janet, and a book secreted from her father's study. Later they would solemnly visit museums together to study the human form as depicted in some detail by Greek sculptors. Helen, who was prouder of her firm young body than her face, would eventually take her clothes off for Edward, spontaneously, little realizing the added strain this imposed.[47]

They were very young and very earnest. Edward began to use weights to tone up his body, Helen to develop hers with swimming, both believing, with the still fashionable philosopher Jean-Baptiste Lamarck, that such physical improvements and appropriate mental preparations would guarantee superior offspring. Their love, they thought, would better the world. Though neither of them believed in the marriage ceremony – they had devoured Shelley's 'Epipsychidion' together – by January 1897, less than a year after Noble's death, they were wholly committed to each other. 'I suppose we are what is called engaged,' Helen wrote to Janet that month:

We at first wanted to know each other, then knowing became friends, and every day as our knowledge increased, greater liking, deeper sympathy, and so on to love and feeling our love, knowing it to be true, pure and everlasting; then the desire for the perfect life of unity, and then of giving the world the benefit of our love by a little child. And so for that time we live now, both of us, and we are perfectly happy, and the waiting is not weary, but good and happy for us both.[48]

Edward was not yet 19 when Helen made this announcement of their unofficial 'engagement' to her friend. There is no record of his parents' reaction to the couple's evident commitment to each other. However, it is unlikely that his father, a highly effective, practical man ambitious for his clever son's advancement, would have thought it sensible. In fact it may help to explain his uncharacteristic change of mind over Edward's desire to go to Oxford, which he made known only a month after Helen's January announcement of their 'engagement'. While this volte-face may have also been in response to outstanding results in the Civil Service exams, as R. George Thomas suggests (citing Philip Parrish's achievement in *Fiction* to support this), Mr Thomas might equally well have wanted to separate Edward from Helen for three years while he matured. One of his conditions for agreeing to Oxford was that Edward and Helen should not write to each other after he left for university. Mrs Noble entirely agreed with the embargo. She believed that Helen and Edward were 'too young to love truly' and determined to prevent the match.[49]

The question must now be asked whether they did both 'truly' love? There was never any doubt in Helen's case. As she wrote after Edward's death: 'I lived only as I gave and gave and gave to him and never gave enough never satisfied my desire to love.'[50] At the start Edward had no hesitation in telling Helen that he, too, 'love[d] without limit or doubt, you only, your body and spirit and memory'.[51] There is evidence to suggest, however, that in time her love would come to oppress him. Just over a year later, in another attempt at verse, he starts with a reference to 'April's oversweet / Anemone and marigold' and ends 'We cannot always love.'[52] The poem was sent to a male friend but not to Helen.

Even at the height of his passion for Helen, Edward expresses serious doubt about his ability to love 'truly':

> I wonder does this letter appear no more than the product of my brain? [he writes to her on 21 June 1897] In truth, I do seem to live more upon my brain now. It needs your presence to make me dare to feel passion. Yet…I am nonetheless [more] moved towards you, little one, than when I wrote such wild letters, apparently full of imaginative passion, but in which disease and Shelley entered largely. I can never satisfy my passion, nor approach its satisfying, except actually in your arms, little one. I am aloof, and cold, and embarrassed at other times; and partly, then, because of its incompleteness and the restraint even upon its incompleteness.

He would remind her with brutal honesty twenty years later: 'You know that my usual belief is that I don't and can't love and haven't done for something near 20 years…you know how unlike I am to you, and you know that you love, so how can I?'[53]

As Thomas himself emphasized, they were very different people: she whose homeliness of appearance was matched by a homeliness of taste; he inordinately susceptible to physical beauty in either men or women. Helen's impetuousness contrasted sharply with Edward's nature, which was (in his own words) 'so clear and critical'.[54] Helen herself described him as 'complex, subtle and sensitive', herself as 'primitive'.[55] She was a simpler, less uncertain person than Edward, whose insecurities were already marked by the time she met him.

There are two distinct schools of thought over their relationship, which divide, broadly speaking, into those who believe their differences were complementary and those who consider them incompatible and that Helen held Thomas back, that he became (in George Meredith's metaphor) a 'rapid falcon in a snare condemned to do the flitting of the bat'.[56]

The first view is articulated most convincingly by Helen herself, who writes lyrically about their life together with all its ups and downs, in her two novels, *As It Was* and *World Without End*. After his death, she told one of his close friends, Edward Garnett, that her 'real' life had been 'inclosed' in the years she knew and loved him:

> Nothing before that matters [she continued] and nothing after that. We grew up together, and though all those years were not all happy, we were necessary to each other, he with his sensitiveness and his self consciousness always recoiling upon himself and wounding him desperately; his pride and Celtic suspiciousness and readiness to hurt himself with the [tiniest/ toughest?] weapon…all that and more intricacies of temperament make happiness, an even habit of happiness quite impossible. But when happiness came it lifted the soul…high as before it had been plunged down to the ultimate depths. The one thing he depended on always and knew would not fail him tho' I daresay it had been – it often was – the cause of some terrible agony for him and so for me, for me and so for him, was our love, or shall I say my love, for that anyway I do know …[57]

Unconditional love, however desirable it might seem, is not always easy to receive and Thomas would later express grave doubts about his early choice of life partner. The second viewpoint is that he was too young to decide wisely at the age of 18 and that it arrested his emotional development at the adolescent stage. First love is generally an overwhelming experience but it is often part of a learning process and not necessarily suitable for a lifetime's wear. It was probably particularly difficult for someone as highly sexed as Thomas evidently was to distinguish his physical need of Helen from the rest of his feelings towards her. It was also reassuring for someone so recently bruised by his sense of inferiority at St Paul's to receive such unqualified admiration, however irritating it might become to him in time.

In 1897, however, Edward suffered no such doubt and their main problem was sufficient patience to survive the period of separation imposed on them by Mrs Noble. She continued to find work for Helen which took her away from home – a stint as governess to the son of a Russian and Austrian couple,[58] as 'mother's help' to an excitable Frenchwoman and her son at Rugby, governess to the Ward children in Bedford, followed by a period with the Andrews family at Sandgate in the second half of 1898. Though Mrs Noble periodically forbade them to correspond, Edward's passionate letters to Helen continued and were eventually read by Mrs Andrews, who promptly gave Helen a week's notice. These letters have not survived but, judging by Mrs Andrews's reaction, they expressed Edward's physical frustration and erotic imaginings in some detail.

By this time Edward had been at Oxford a year. But if his father's hope had been to lessen his son's attachment to Helen by sending him there, it failed. Nevertheless Thomas's world was opening and in a way that would eventually exclude Helen from certain areas of it altogether.

5

A Glimpse of Paradise
(October 1897–September 1898)

> There was for a short time, amidst but not of the University,
> a student whom I cannot but count as [Chaucer's] 'clerk
> of Oxenford'. He came from no school, but straight from a
> counting-house. All his life he had been a deep, unguided
> delver in the past.
>
> – Edward Thomas, *Oxford*, 1903

When Thomas came to write his book *Oxford* in 1903, three years after leaving the University, he drew heavily on his own time there, with one notable exception; he says little of the life of the non-collegiate student ('tosher'). Yet the first third of his entire stay in the city of 'dreaming spires' was spent as an unattached scholar, and that not the least intense part of it. At the time, however, it seemed to him that he was living merely 'in parenthesis', while he worked towards his true goal.

Thomas arrived in Oxford in October 1897 in time to establish himself in lodgings at 113 Cowley Road, to the east of the city centre, and to sit the mandatory Matriculation examination. 'Matric' was more normally taken at school, but his premature departure from St Paul's meant that he had both to prepare himself for it and enter it independently. But as St Paul's had shown, he could work hard and effectively when necessary and on 16 October he was able to inform his new correspondent Harry Hooton, the future husband of Helen's best friend, Janet Aldis, 'I matriculated today before the Vice-Chancellor of the University, and, in consequence, I am left a little freer of time and heart.'[1] He had 'feared failure' in what turned out to be an easy exam for him, so had 'worked to the exclusion of all'.[2]

It was the first of many hurdles Thomas faced in his determination to be part of that privileged world he had first glimpsed at St Paul's. In order to manage on the limited financial support his father was able to offer, he also needed to win a scholarship; his selection of Balliol, Merton and Lincoln was both ambitious and realistic. Then, in addition to scholarship work, he had to study for 'Responsions' (known as 'Smalls' or 'Little-Go'), another entrance requirement which involved attending an additional three hours of set lectures daily, plus further work at Latin and mathematics. Any notion of Thomas as a dreamy aesthete living only in his imagination must fade in the face of his resolute handling of such challenges.

Thomas was helped at a practical level by an institution set up to offer male students in his position a university education without the cost of college membership, St Catherine's Club, later Society and eventually St Catherine's College. (The female equivalent would eventually form St Anne's.) Membership enabled him to prepare for 'Little-Go', the next exam facing him: 'Lectures of a useless kind for Responsions occupy three hours for six days a week,' he complained to Hooton four days after matriculating.[3] He was also studying hard and independently for the Balliol History Scholarship in November.

Yet Thomas was still finding time for his own writing. Encouraged by some kind responses to his first book, *The Woodland Life*, when it was published by William Blackwood in the spring of 1897, he continued to submit work to the *Speaker*, where many of the book's essays had first appeared.[4] By 1897 these juvenile efforts, written mostly when he was 17 and all before he was 19, would seem to him 'poor enough'.[5] He was determined to move on from a manner he described as 'largely founded on [Richard] Jefferies's *The Amateur Poacher*, [Charles] Kingsley's *Prose Idylls*, and Mr Francis A. Knight's weekly contributions to the *Daily News*, but doubtless with tones supplied also by Shelley and Keats, and later on by Ruskin, De Quincey, Pater and Sir Thomas Browne'.[6]

Thomas was still bent on making writing his career, the £80 a year or so paid by the *Speaker* for his later essays an added incentive. But the writing itself would be quite different from *The Woodland Life*, he vowed, in both style and content. As evidence of this he pointed Hooton towards what he called his 'prose fancies' being published regularly by the *Speaker* in 1897. These centred round a mythical character called Basil 'after a little cousin of that name...a puppet I introduce to represent myself [he told Hooton], who has a most tragic meeting with the spirit of nature...and falls "slain in life by the frost of a great melancholy"; and so on; all very sublime but a little uninteresting to everyone but myself'.[7] 'Some things I write in prose I feel ought to be in verse to have effect,' he added, 'but I am too old to begin such an arduous art'.[8] The setting is very like the area of Wales he had visited as a child and revisited the summer before starting at Oxford.

A number of Thomas's long series on the same subject of 'Basil of the Woods' were, as he had hoped, 'impose[d] on *The Speaker*' over the next few years. It was an impressive achievement for a youth of 19 studying for his scholarship exams and a far cry from the debut in an obscure children's magazine. Nevertheless, the 'great melancholy' Thomas attributed to his 'puppet' Basil, was real enough and not helped by his attempts to move on from the Romantic poets to more modern, less upbeat writers such as Hardy, Meredith, Pater and Flaubert (in French). He had spent the summer of 1897 reading Rousseau's *Confessions*, also in the original.

'Then there is Swinburne,' Thomas wrote to Hooton shortly after his arrival at an Oxford where some undergraduates were roaming the streets at night chanting his intoxicating rhythms out loud.[9] But Thomas's enthusiasm for Swinburne's 'laudable hexameters' did not survive his discovery that Swinburne, who had called Shelley 'the greatest lyric poet' a decade before, by 1897 thought him 'empty and worthless'.[10] Long before his own attempts to bring poetry nearer to natural speech rhythms, he was already rejecting Swinburne's verse as artificial and too divorced from life. In the words of his later book on Swinburne, commissioned shortly after the poet's death in 1909, he would explain more fully why he had failed to appreciate him: 'Other poets tend towards a grace and glory of words as of human speech perfected and made divine, Swinburne towards a musical jargon that includes human snatches, but is not and never could be speech.'[11]

It was one of the many devastating criticisms in Thomas's highly perceptive, scrupulously fair analysis of Swinburne, which infuriated his admirers when it was published in 1912, and may account for the fact that the book was remaindered shortly afterwards.

Thomas's choice of writers like Hardy, Meredith and Rousseau, in preference, was hardly 'feel-good' literature, however, for someone who felt intensely isolated, as at St Paul's. He was not literally without friends: there is mention of another student, Leonard Wharton, and he renewed contact in his first month with at least two boys he had met at St Paul's, Lucian Oldershaw and Ian MacAlister. His isolation was more a state of mind, a reflection of his sense of himself as an outsider.

By the beginning of December, when he had taken and failed the Balliol scholarship and was concentrating on Responsions, he was still attending three lectures daily, allowing himself only one short walk per day and spending his evenings reading 'Smalls' work, or some book of English prose or poetry, or Catullus. 'But whether in or out, I am always alone,' he wrote to MacAlister.[12] When anybody did visit him, he suspected that they came 'out of charity'.[13] Another barrier to friendship, as MacAlister himself would find and Thomas admit, was that this 'solitariness' was 'partly choice', since he was 'never so content as when alone'.[14] He felt 'a painful awkwardness and reserve' in company,[15] and was already using the word 'diseased' to describe what he had diagnosed as his central problem: self-consciousness.[16]

Yet Thomas did find real pleasure in congenial society, and Ian MacAlister, who would go on to become Secretary of the Royal Institute of British Architects and be knighted for his services, was to become one of his closest friends and staunchest supporters. MacAlister's description of the start of their friendship in Oldershaw's rooms sounds very like Oldershaw's account of his own excitement in Thomas's company at St Paul's:

> I was shy. He was even shyer and he hardly spoke at all. But when I left to go back to College he went with me and we talked till we reached the gate. Then we turned and I walked back with him to his lodgings [i.e. in the Cowley Road]. Then he turned and came back with me to Merton. That long talk was really the beginning. He was for a time unhappy and out of his element in Oxford and I felt that his intimate outpouring to

me was something of a comfort to him. The fact that we were both shy lads was indeed a help.[17]

While MacAlister, who had stayed on in the History Eighth of St Paul's, knew more in his narrowly specialized subjects, he believed that Thomas was 'far above him intellectually' and would have no problem winning a scholarship to Merton, Thomas's next goal, as well as 'Mac's own college'.[18] Thomas was not convinced: partly through 'over-reading... partly by letting my fancy have its own way,' he told Mac, 'I have succeeded in making myself quite unable to hold my own in any situation that needs reflection, reason, argument. So far I fail and fail.'[19] Another failure to pass Responsions this December did not help.

The self-doubt, alternating with confidence in his abilities – he believed he 'deserved a scholarship'[20] – increased Thomas's sense of isolation at Oxford in his first year, despite friendly advances from Oldershaw, MacAlister and Leonard Wharton, another Old Pauline. But Mac persisted and, after a 'very restrained start', they would eventually achieved the 'genuine intimacy' Thomas hoped for'.[21] He found MacAlister 'admirable' from the start, 'a moral character, especially by contrast with me; generous and unselfish; with fine judgement and sanity'.[22]

MacAlister had another quality Thomas appreciated and would always welcome in a friend, a willingness to accompany him on long walks. Thomas had started reading Matthew Arnold before arriving in Oxford and was almost certainly familiar with Arnold's lyric celebrations of the surrounding countryside, 'The Scholar Gypsy' and 'Thyrsis'. Over the next three years he would explore the area exhaustively, often in Mac's company, round Fyfield to the west, Wheatley to the east, Boars Hill in the south and Wood Eaton to the north. He writes glowingly in *Oxford* of one walk in particular (it could stand for many):

> that goes the round from Folly Bridge, through South Hinksey to the 'Fox' at Boar's Hill (where the scent of hawthorn comes in through the window with the sound of the rain and the nightingale); and then away, skirting Wootton and Cumnor, past the 'Bear' (with its cool flagged rooms looking on a field of gold, and Cumnor Church tower among elms); and back over the Hurst, where [the undergraduate] turns, under the seven firs and solitary elm to ponder the long, alluring view towards Stanton Harcourt and Bablock Hythe.[23]

Thomas's fondness for country pubs, born no doubt out of gratitude for the rest and refreshment they offered, emerges clearly in this passage. He would continue to enjoy them on the many subsequent journeys round the British countryside, in particular for their wide social mix, their welcome, their anonymity and their sense of history.

Thomas's failure to win a scholarship to Mac's college, Merton, in January did nothing to spoil their friendship and by March 1898 Mac was introducing him to another friend, reputed 'perhaps to be the wittiest talker of his time', Hamilton Fyfe.[24] Thomas, who had never passed through the public school phase of hero-worshipping other boys and being attracted to them physically, now seemed to fall in love with almost every attractive young man he met. He had already declared his 'love' for Harry Hooton in long, humorous letters, and by March 1898 feared that his 'shadow worship' of Fyfe 'should make a princess of him, if I spoke'.[25] As his letters to Hooton show, he also feared rebuff yet his self-consciousness, which would render him such a sensitive recorder of feelings, especially in poetry, made him suspect that 'perhaps it is not the coldness or indifference of others which alone keeps one without a friend, but possibly the defects...of myself'.[26] Despite such self-doubt Fyfe would become a friend and walking companion at Oxford.

Friends were not the only distraction in his second term; writing to Helen almost daily now occupied more of his time. Curiously, he appears to have written to her only twice during the autumn of 1897, though not because both sets of parents had forbidden it (which they had) or because he needed to work long hours (which he did). As he explained to her on 14 November 1877 with the devastating honesty that would mark their whole relationship: 'I wrote Mr Hooton a long letter yesterday and Friday, in fact so long I feel you might be justly angry. But you know why it was long, and yours short: – all is uncertain, and unknown between me and him: – we have no uncertainties. Therefore you are content sweet Helen?'[27]

He was sufficiently self-aware, however, to write at the end of his marathon efforts to Harry: 'Perhaps Helen would sigh if she saw the long letter to you.' The fact that he felt he had to make an effort to 'keep' Harry but not Helen might justifiably have made her question his priorities.

Was Edward starting to take Helen a little too much for granted? His letters, when they begin again in earnest, are full of terms which suggest a sense of condescension, a slightly patronizing tone – 'my own sweet little one Helen, my anemone maid, sweet heart,' he addresses her on one occasion, combining three of his favourite terms for her at this time.

Helen's acceptance of him was, however, unconditional, her 'joy' and 'content' in their relationship unaffected by the demands he made on her.[28] She was still working as a mother's help away from home and saving every penny towards their own future together and even his occasional reprimands about her carelessness with money and frequent demands that she send him some of it could not shake her devotion. When he started writing poems, later in 1898, one of them would contain his ominous reference to finding himself 'Weary of April's over-sweet – Anemone and marigold.'[29]

Distractions like these from the unremitting study of his first term achieved (as Thomas had suspected it might) a fresher approach to the Lincoln scholarship, which he sat and won in March. Norman Brett-James, elected to an Exhibition in the same exam, recognized at once the 'maturity of Thomas's literary powers' which had gained him the top scholarship; he greatly admired the 'brilliant intuition' and imaginative grasp which led Thomas *not* to choose between the two subjects set for the exam that year, 'Vox Populi, Vox Dei' ('The Voice of the People is the Voice of God') and 'Might is Right', but to combine both into one answer.[30] Brett-James never doubted that Thomas 'very obviously deserved' the first place he was awarded and was inclined to attribute it partly to the fact that at 20 Thomas was slightly older than his rivals.[31] But it was more than just a matter of age, at his most confident and relaxed, with his sense of isolation and self-doubt in abeyance, Thomas's subtlety and invention was far above the average as he would later show. In 1898 he rejoiced in being 'top of the whole set' in the Lincoln exam, boasting to 'Dad' Uzzell: 'I do look grand in my long black gown.'[32]

The pleasure of winning a scholarship was marred by the need to pass Responsions before he could take it up. He had failed the exam for the second time in March, so was greatly relieved to pass it at his third attempt on 14 June 1898. Though he was still referring to the 'entire solitude of [his] life' in May, he was beginning to join in University activities and continued to make friends. He had been horrified at the possibility of falling at this last hurdle.

The most carefree year of his adult life lay just ahead of him. Buoyed by a rare sense of inclusion and success, he looked forward to seeing 'Dad' Uzzell during his stay with his grandmother at Swindon in mid-July, instructing his old friend, 'mind you put yourself in fighting trim against my visit'.[33] One of the 'fine times' he envisaged with the ex-poacher was to 'go out all night' as they once had on a walk to Burderop Park just south of Swindon, when they had 'heard the night-jar' and seen 'the sun rise'.[34]

The Swindon trip was also a duty-visit to his grandmother and, once over, Thomas was free to leave for Wales at the end of July. It had become 'sacred ground' for him[35] and in his new buoyant mood he was hoping to add – 'maybe only a gleam' – to its ancient literature which he venerated, the *Mabinogion* in particular: 'anything old is romantic to me,' he told MacAlister. It was a very different young man who presented himself at his father's cousin's house in Pontardulais, ten miles north-west of Swansea, from the 'lad…[with] awkward manners, silent gaucherie, unsuitable dress, and down-covered chin' Philip Treharne Thomas recalled from the previous year.[36]

Edward's descriptions of his six-week stay, first at his father's cousin's, then at Ammanford, five miles north-east of Pontardulais, paint a picture of a young man escaping into an almost prelapsarian world, very different from the one he inhabited in London and Oxford. 'The good Welsh people have changed me into the animal I always potentially was,' he writes to Hooton on 17 August, 'I eat and sleep, and my most serious work was yesterday – binding the sheaves of wheat in a strong sun; I really did work hard, and at the end had tea sitting round a cock of wheat with the reapers and binders.'[37]

The Pontardulais house was full of third cousins, sons who worked in the local tin-mines or factory, black-haired, black-eyed daughters who wore rich silk clothes which delighted Thomas's senses. Yet he gave no names in his letters to Helen, Hooton or MacAlister, creating the effect of an Arcadian dream, peopled by simple rural folk (despite their industrial background), who flattered him in every conceivable way. So that it comes as a slight shock to learn that three of his brothers accompanied him to Wales this summer: Reggie staying with him at Pontardulais, Ernest and Oscar lodging with other relatives in Cwmavon.

Edward's escape into an Arcadia of non-intellectual joys could only ever be partial, though he was always ready to praise the virtues of hard physical labour and he made it clear to his relatives that he also needed to carry on writing. His aunt, Welsh-speaking, motherly and anxious to please, put him into the hallowed front-parlour, 'a room so absurdly encumbered with cheap decorations', according to him, that he could not work there and insisted on using the kitchen, the centre of activity, always busy, often crowded and noisy.[38] Frequent meals were served there as the various sons and daughters came off their shifts in the local tin-mine or factory. Edward seemed positively to welcome these constant distractions; though later he was to complain bitterly when his own family tried to carry on their everyday life around him.

It is hardly surprising that his literary output was more modest than usual; it is remarkable that he managed to write at all in such noisy surroundings. Yet he started on another of his 'birth-doomed transcripts from Malory – enlargements – or what you will about Elaine' and her relationship with Lancelot which 'fascinated' him.[39] In addition he almost certainly completed his paper for the *Speaker*, 'Wayside Pleasures', here, which reflects his growing interest in wild flowers at Pontardulais, where he was adding to his knowledge of at least the names. Unsophisticated rural delights, he implies in his letters home, are what he needs.

Thomas would continue to stress his preference for the simple and functional over the elaborate and sophisticated throughout his life. But his enthusiasm for gypsies, tramps, poachers and agricultural labourers in general can seem at times something of an affectation in view of his own evident need for the more refined joys of intellectual discourse. It is clear, for instance, that even during his idyllic stay in Wales, he was grateful for the stimulus offered by a young Welsh poet, John Jenkins, known to all by his Bardic name, Gwili. He had first met Gwili – 'the only man of any reading and intellect in the area' in his opinion – the previous year. While keeping up with his reading, he relished the chance to exchange ideas with a practising poet and Welsh-speaker. Gwili, less than six years older than Edward, was already winning prizes for his poetry and in 1901 would gain the crown at the National Eisteddfod, as well as respect as a Baptist preacher of advanced views. A perennial student, he had studied at both Bangor and Cardiff universities and would later go on to Jesus College, Oxford, inspired perhaps by his talks with the young Oxford student in 1998.

Though he had not yet managed to complete a degree, he was teaching at the Gwynfryn Academy at Ammanford, an idealistic institution, for mainly adult males, run by another Welsh bard, Watcyn Wyn. Born in Hendy, Pontardulais, Gwili had first met Edward there on a return visit to his birthplace. Edward's own visit to Ammanford in 1898 would consolidate their friendship.

The two men were sufficiently alike yet also different to suit each other well. Edward, so fastidious and spare both in appearance and with words, found Gwili 'in many ways a coarse barbarian outwardly', overdependent on his womenfolk to look after him.[40] There would be times when he wished Gwili were 'keener, more enthusiastic, more angular, more argumentative'.[41] A 'jovial' man, Gwili spoke rapidly and continuously and laughed so much that Edward could understand only half of what he said.[42] He was also full of the same 'lenience, tolerance and concessive gentleness' as the Treharne Thomases towards Edward, something he feared as breeding 'conceit' in him.[43] Lacking such qualities himself, he did not hesitate to pronounce Gwili's stories and journalism, for instance, 'mean in thought…second-rate *in English*, at least'.[44] Yet he also recognized in the preacher-poet 'a real fineness of spirit' which overcame such differences.[45] Their shared passion for poetry involved them in long discussions on the Welsh metric system, which Gwili was able to explain. Unsuccessful himself in the stricter verse metres, Gwili worked in the freer ones, which would win him the Eisteddfod Bardic crown, a preference which may also have influenced Edward's own experimental approach to poetic metre 15 years later. Gwili certainly increased Edward's knowledge of Welsh literature, translating much of it for his own non-Welsh-speaking friend. Together they made plans for him to translate Thomas's July *Speaker* article 'Summer' as his modest contribution to Wales's literature.

Gwili was also the countryman Edward longed to be and took him on long walks in the neighbourhood of Ammanford: to Carreg Cennen, the ruins of a medieval fort which towered in the distance near Llandeilo, to Golden Grove, also near Llandeilo, the ancestral seat of the Vaughans and another rich source of legend; to Llyn Llech Owain (the lake of Owain's stone), the source of the River Gwendraeth near Gorslas and another fertile site of legend. All these places and more would be remembered fondly by Gwili in his elegy to 'Edward Eastaway'.

Edward, in his own tribute to Gwili, would point to further shared interests. Like himself, Gwili was a keen swimmer, despite having damaged his eyesight in his native river (the Gwili), yellowed by vitriol from the local factory. In describing how much the Gwili meant to his friend despite nearly blinding him, Thomas revealed other shared passions, including a love of rural South Wales, especially its coastal regions, and fishing: the passage from 'Digressions on Fish and Fishing', in Thomas's *Horae Solitariae* (1902) was based on Gwili and the 'revered angler' in it instantly identified as her father by his daughter, Nest Bradney.

By the end of his summer in Wales Edward could say with conviction that 'except in the case of Gwili, the people were to me only a sweet atmosphere in which I could most perfectly enjoy the legends and songs of Wales'.[46] He had been particularly moved by the songs, which Gwili's sister sang to him, clearly with amorous intent. Edward's reassurance to Helen that it was 'in fact ... partly you that I saw when I held her'[47] could not have reassured her, serving only to underline his responsiveness to the sister as well as to the music.

The sensuous life Edward had led in Wales made it all the harder for him to restrain himself physically with Helen after his return, especially given her uninhibited response to him. Helen was now working as a mother's help for the Andrews family in Chiswick and after his return Mrs Andrews allowed Edward to visit Helen in her room unchaperoned. Returning to London on 7 September, he had had nearly a fortnight to contemplate their reunion on the nineteenth. It was evidently a passionate one, since after anxiously asking if she is 'quite well' in his letter to her the next day, he continues:

> I think you cannot help pondering on our meeting last night. And quite rightly. You poor little one were the victim of a pure overwhelming desire, and I of a smaller desire by no means pure; and I feel much more abject than if that desire had been satisfied. I was trying to think in the correct way about right and wrong as I travelled home last night. Of course all kinds of schemes came – we would read stiffly together etc. Somehow I feel as if it were purer – certainly it would be honester – 'to do the thing we fear'. But nothing of course would induce me to make a miserable thing out of you and a fool of myself. Could we not find out some means? You understand.[48]

Helen did 'understand', but was no bolder than Edward about investigating contraception and the problem was shelved. But Edward's few quiet weeks with his family in late September and early October, filled with reading and writing, walks with Arthur Hardy and visits to the Nobles, were abruptly ended by Mrs Andrews's sudden dismissal of Helen for what she called her 'illicit connexion' with Edward.[49] Alerted perhaps by Helen's behaviour, she had secretly begun reading Edward's passionate letters to her young employee. Helen, secure in her unqualified devotion to Edward, did not feel guilty, but she served out her last week with the Andrews miserably, worried about the reaction of her mother. Edward was both humiliated and furious. After an 'insolent' reply to his letter of complaint to Mrs Andrews, by 19 October he was contemplating legal action.

6

Paradise Gained (1898–1899)

What a thing it is to be an undergraduate of the University of Oxford! Next to being a great poet or a financier, there is nothing so absolute open to a man. For several years he is the nursling of a great tradition in a fair city: and the memory of it is above his chief joy. His follies are hallowed, his successes exalted, by the dispensation of the place. Surely the very air whispers of wisdom and the beautiful... That time is the one luxury he never regrets. It is a second childhood, as blithe and untroubled as the first, and with this advantage over the first that it is not only good, but he knows that it is good. What games! What walks! What affections! are his. Time passes, we say, although it is we – like children that see the square fields receding from their swift train – that pass.

                               – Edward Thomas, *Oxford*, 1903

Mrs Andrews's abrupt dismissal of Helen had threatened to cloud Edward's long-awaited arrival at Lincoln College on 14 October 1898, even leading him to thoughts of suicide. But Helen's apparent serenity and Lincoln itself triumphed. From the time he caught his 'first delightful glimpse of the grey, main quadrangle...so quiet and deserted, filled with the gaudy crimson of flying creeper leaves', through dinner in the small but perfect medieval dining-hall, to the moment he sat down in his own room at the end of the evening, everything delighted him.[1] Five days later, in a letter to Hooton, he is still revelling in that 'first glimpse of the little College…the grey aged walls of the main quadrangle'; it is, he believes, a 'good omen'.[2]

According to a family friend, Thomas had been obliged to take more luxurious rooms than he would otherwise have chosen,[3] possibly ones situated over former student John Wesley's rooms in the oldest of the quadrangles, the original fifteenth-century site of the college. There is no indication, however, of Thomas regretting this first set of rooms, which he describes as being 'of pleasant aspect, large, and comfortable, tho very bare so far: St Catherine (Raphael) looks very lonely on one wall, Tintern Abbey [a favourite since childhood] and a nodding bunch of wheat on the other'.[4] He would quickly line his walls with what his fellow-scholar, Brett-James, remembered as a 'charming collection of books of all periods and most varieties, first editions of poets and essayists, books by Izaak Walton, Cobbett, Jefferies and [W. H.] Hudson'.[5]

Lincoln is one of the smaller Oxford colleges. Lytton Strachey's tutor would suggest it to Strachey's father as a 'suitable alternative to Balliol' when, like Thomas, Strachey failed to get into the more prestigious, larger college a year after Thomas in 1899.[6] Consisting of about 65 undergraduates, most of whom had not passed through what Strachey's tutor called 'the great public schools', he believed Lincoln's 'more modest and intimate climate' would be more suited to 'a boy like Lytton, silent, maladroit and of a literary turn'.[7] Tucked away in The Turl between Broad Street and The High, and sandwiched between Exeter College and All Saints Church, it was both private and convenient.

The contrast with Thomas's 1897 arrival at Oxford as a non-collegiate scholar could hardly have been greater; where once he had been, literally, an outsider, walking in daily from his lonely 'digs' in Cowley Road, he was now inside at the centre, with a sense of belonging, which he reinforced with a number of new acquaintances.

On his first day at Lincoln, for instance, Thomas had made friends with his next-door neighbour, Lionel Cornish, one of the few identifiable models he was to use in *Oxford*. He had already met Cornish at the Lincoln scholarship exam in the summer and had described him then to Helen as 'too brilliant, beautiful, successful' to care for him: 'what can an athlete such as he,' he asks, 'with good looks, fine health, perfect temper, moderate abilities, and outdoor habits' find in common with himself?[8] In a rare show of spontaneity, he called Cornish 'a delightful being', who had 'charmed' Thomas and everyone else by his few words before the viva voce examination at Lincoln.[9] The similarities with the 'clean, brave, and modest freshman' of section eight of 'Undergraduates of the Present and Past' in *Oxford* are unmistakable, particularly Cornish's seemingly effortless athletic achievements. (Outstanding at running and the long jump, Cornish would win many honours in the Amateur Athletic Association championships and represent Great Britain in the 1908 Olympic Games.) Thomas also found him physically attractive, as he did not hesitate to tell Helen with his usual frankness: 'Just a little thin, otherwise lovelier far than Apollo.'[10] It would be the first of a number of infatuations with young male under-graduates at Lincoln, which continued into his second year.

Cornish, an instantly popular figure, may have encouraged the less outgoing Thomas to make other friends at Lincoln, or at least to participate in college activities where he might meet like-minded people. They both joined the Literary Society, the Davenant, for instance, where Thomas would become close to other members, H. E. Mann and Martin Freeman. Mann, who was the President of the Davenant in autumn 1898 and gave the first paper on 'Henrik Ibsen', was impressed by Thomas's knowledge of books and his papers to the Society; he remembered one in particular on 'Natural Magic' in literature. Thomas delivered at least one other paper, 'The Relation of Prose to Poetry in the Nineteenth Century', described by Norman Brett-James as 'very illuminating', 'on the birth of the Nineteenth Century, the wave of Revolution, the break-up of Europe and the threatened destruction of society, and the genesis of a new literature, as exemplified in the poems of Coleridge and Wordsworth'[11] – which 'showed a wealth of reading and a grasp of principles calculated to challenge all or most of those who heard him'.[12] Though Mann was two years ahead of Thomas at Lincoln, they would go down at the same time and see each other occasionally in London. An even closer friend in later life was Martin Freeman, who shared Thomas's growing interest in folk-songs as well as literature. Thomas respected Freeman's sound literary judgement and appreciated his willingness to join him on 25-mile walks. They would remain friends for life. The more leisured, wealthier Freeman would rent a cottage in 1905 to which Thomas could escape from family distractions and write; in 1907 he would contribute an essay on 'English Country Songs' to Thomas's *Book of the Open Air* and in 1910 Thomas would dedicate his *Feminine Influence on the Poets* to his friend.

Cornish, who excelled at rowing as well as his many other athletic activities, was probably also responsible for introducing Thomas to the sport. Another undoubtedly autobiographical passage in *Oxford* concerns a freshman who finds himself persuaded to become an unlikely member of the college rowing team. Like the youth in his book, Thomas evidently showed 'some good points at the river', being 'painstaking and neat'.[13] By 28 November, just over a month after his arrival, Thomas is rowing in the 'fours' for Lincoln, is awarded his 'colours', and selected as 'bow' for the college Torpid Eight in February 1899. He takes to wearing the brightly coloured blazer which accompanies these honours. His new friends now include more athletic types, J. O'Brien, H. V. Collins and H. B. Davies. He is proud of the physical prowess constant rowing practice has brought him and boasts of 'winning a wager with 8 pound dumb bells', which proves his increased strength.[14]

In such hearty company Thomas also starts drinking, sometimes heavily, though he knows his teetotal father would disapprove. He has already begun to smoke excessively, preferably a clay pipe, which becomes something of an affectation with him. He also indulges in 'low talk', he tells Hooton, his excuse being the need to 'forget' the unpleasantness of Helen's dismissal. Describing himself as 'quite rowdy', he appears proud of the fact that it was he who 'officiated with the scissors at the cutting of an odious lovelock from the brow of a certain freshman' and to revel in his 'bad' reputation.[15] People think him 'filthier', he believes, than his 'shy talk' merits.[16] Robert Frost, in whom Thomas would confide frankly, remembered him boasting that he was distinguished at Lincoln 'for the ribald folk songs he could entertain with – not to say smutty'.[17] The sudden rise in popularity of the undergraduate in *Oxford* who has read Rabelais almost certainly reflects a corresponding rise in Thomas's popularity at Lincoln at this time. The melancholy, near-solitude of his first non-collegiate year is now replaced with a 'light-hearted[ness]' for which he feels it necessary to apologize to Hooton by mid-November.

By Christmas 1898 Thomas is experimenting with opium, in the form of laudanum; taken ostensibly to deal with a bad chill, it is clear from his reference to De Quincey's *Confessions of an Opium Eater* at the time that he is also interested in the 'delicious terror' he experiences under its influence. He would continue to take it at times of stress for the next seven years. No longer the restrained, even repressed young man terrified of losing control he was when Hooton first met him, he now seems proud to be able to tell Hooton:

> ...I can listen to 'Circus Girl' music, I can topple into bed *off* the verge of drunkenness more than once: swear: use slang creditably: howl choruses – even the foul choruses of the Varsity...: also I can be heartily sick and well rid of it all, and able to talk the most modest common-places of affection or business at home.[18]

Thomas's piece for the December 1898 *Speaker* reflects his experience at Lincoln more sympathetically when he describes a young student who, like himself, enjoys the sound of bells ringing out at night as he sits in his 'pensive citadel' among the rooftops. As Thomas was to note in the opening passage of his surviving Lincoln diary, 'The sound of bells ha[d] something peculiarly concordant with [his[spirit', an aesthetic need which was temporarily suppressed on arrival at Lincoln.[19] By Christmas 1898 his attitude is still, in his own words, 'devil may care indifference', which he continues to blame on his 'early despair' over the Mrs Andrews affair.[20] To the onlooker, it sounds more like the typical reaction of a young man from a fairly sheltered, puritanical background first encountering the outside world for himself.

Thomas's time at Lincoln College was not an entirely negative experience, however. It was during the course of what he clearly regarded as dissipation that he met another two men who became friends for life. The meeting took place through the first of these, John Hartmann Morgan, who introduced Thomas to the second, Edmund Sidney Pollock Haynes, in his rooms at Balliol in December 1898. (It is not clear exactly how Thomas met Morgan, who was Welsh. It was possibly through his Welsh relatives, or another Welsh connection, John Williams, the retired headmaster of a school at Swansea, Waun Wen, whom Thomas would visit on a number of occasions later.) Morgan, two years older than Thomas and already a graduate of the University College of South Wales, had a brilliant career ahead of him. He would go on to become a professor of Constitutional Law at the University of London, a brigadier in the British Army and an MP. As worldly as Thomas was not, he would try to help him in his various crises; Thomas would welcome his advice but rarely follow it.

Haynes, a fellow-student at Balliol, was also destined for a brilliant career. It was not just Haynes's privileged background which ensured his success, though he could look forward to a comfortable position in his father's law office after Oxford. He had been a King's Scholar at Eton, would write 20 books before his death in 1949 and make a name for himself as a champion of Divorce Law Reform. Though outwardly even less like the reticent Thomas than Morgan, he had more in common with him in the areas that counted. For instance, they planned to write a novel together, *Olivia Paterson*, which, though never completed, gives some insight into their university life.[21] They enjoyed each other's conversation greatly. 'His talk was in those days much of books,' Haynes remembered. 'He seemed to know Aubrey's lives almost by heart and he could invent passages of seventeenth-century prose the authenticity of which was never questioned'.[22] Thomas, in turn, wrote admiringly of Haynes's 'fine conversation about Latin and Teutonic literature' in his field notebook for 1899.[23] For as they talked they often walked long distances together round the Oxfordshire countryside, usually, Haynes recalled, to Shotover, Cumnor and Bagley Wood.[24] Many Sundays were passed in this way. (Thomas's dedication of his book about another great walker, *George Borrow*, to Haynes in 1912 was perhaps in acknowledgement of this.) Alternatively they explored the rivers Isis and Cherwell, 'bathing, sculling, talking and eating as the mood came'.[25] They were particularly appreciative of each other's sense of humour, which Haynes regretted not seeing emphasized in Helen's later account of Edward, but then theirs was a different relationship.

Only five months older than Thomas, Haynes nevertheless adopted a protective attitude towards him from the start. Time and again he would come to his friend's rescue, sometimes with practical advice, which Thomas usually ignored, more often with money. Generous, kind and stimulating, Haynes would remain a loyal friend throughout Thomas's life. They would review each other's books positively, though according to Haynes they both preferred each other's conversation, visited each other and took at least one holiday together.

At Oxford Thomas was suspicious of what he called the 'brilliant, vicious society at Balliol' and considered Haynes 'utterly immoral'.[26] It would be Haynes, however, who worried about Thomas's increasing dependence on opium and tried to wean him off it. As Thomas recognized from the start, Haynes had 'many fine feelings and purposes'.[27]

By the time Thomas began to take opium in December 1898, his work was beginning to suffer from his changed life-style. There had been no obvious effect on it during his first term at Lincoln, when he worked hard to please his tutor, Owen M. Edwards. Thomas felt fortunate in having a Welshman to supervise him and he would dedicate his next book, a collection of essays, *Horae Solitariae*, to his professor. Edwards's interests extended far beyond his specialist area of seventeenth-century political thought and he evidently encouraged Thomas to indulge his own wide interests, especially in literature.

Besides representing his home town, Merioneth, as a Liberal MP during Thomas's time at Lincoln, Edwards would also become Chief Inspector for Education in Wales. His greatest passion, however, was for the revival of Welsh as a literary language, one which coincided with Thomas's own admiration for Welsh poetry and song. By August 1898, under Gwili's influence no doubt, Thomas had come to believe that a poet, 'especially a lyric poet ha[d] an infinitely greater chance [in Wales] than in England, a greater chance of perfection in his art and in his fame'.[28] Not for the first time he mourned the fact that he had 'come to London' to be born.[29] Lacking the necessary knowledge of Welsh, however, he thought that even in English he 'might do something by writing of Wales'. It was Edwards who would enable him first to fulfil that hope by inviting his student to write an introduction to the work of the Welsh poet John Dyer for his Welsh Library Series in 1903.

While preparing it, Thomas would confess to a friend: 'Long ago I found [Dyer] a pleasant oasis in the midst of the eighteenth century and its coffee-houses and its rhymes as like one another as Windsor chairs or policemen. But he is little else & it was not easy to avoid showing that I thought so in my introduction.'[30] It would be another two years before Thomas wrote his own book on the subject, *Beautiful Wales* (1905).

Meantime, Thomas used his second review of Edwards's own book on *Wales* (1901) to thank his tutor indirectly; beside puffing younger poets, Gwili (whom he would also thank in his introduction to Dyer's poems) and 'older poets like Watcyn Wyn and Mr Edwards himself', he praised Edwards for being 'at once sternly accurate and poetically true'.[31]

Edwards, described by one fellow-countryman as 'the best-loved Welshman of his time'[32] was also a conscientious teacher, reputed to spend 'a disproportionate amount of time on his tutorial work at Oxford'. He encouraged Thomas to enter early for the college exam ('Schools') in December 1898, in which Thomas was successful, and for the Lothian Essay Prize, in which he was not.[33] Thomas also sat the Law Preliminary exam. According to MacAlister, one main reason Thomas admired Edwards was because his personality and methods 'had nothing donnish about them'.[34]

Thomas would remain grateful to Edwards for his guidance, though he would later refer to him as 'the venerable but unfriendly Edwards'.[35] He had need of it, for Modern History had a demanding syllabus, requiring him to pass exams in the Continuous History of England, the General History of a period selected by the student from a choice of topics and a Special Portion of History, or Special Historical Subject, using original authorities. Candidates had also to demonstrate a knowledge of both Constitutional Law and Political and Descriptive Geography. A Subject, or Period of Literature, to be submitted for approval, was an optional addition. The recommended textbooks for such a course were made even more daunting by the fact that the books could be written 'in any language', though the two main ones apart from English were French and German. (Thomas may have justified his continued reading in French and German Literature – Flaubert, Gautier, Goethe, among others – on these grounds.)

Lucy Newlyn, in her illuminating edition of Thomas's *Oxford*, quoting *The History of the University of Oxford* that 'Modern History set out to prepare graduates to fill influential positions at home and abroad',[36] queries just 'how suitable it was for Edward Thomas'.[37] The answer must depend to some extent on his choice of topics. Evidence suggests that he chose to specialize in his tutor's own area of expertise, the seventeenth century, and to submit the optional paper on literature, from the same period, Haynes testifying to his friend's complete familiarity with the diarist John Aubrey and other seventeenth-century writers. Thomas himself quotes most liberally from Milton, Cowley, Donne, Marvell and other seventeenth-century writers throughout *Oxford* and in the chapters he wrote for *Olivia Paterson*; his alter ego, Langton, chooses to give his extension lectures on two historical figures from the seventeenth century, the Earl of Clarendon and Viscount Falkland.

For all his influence, Owen Edwards does not appear to feature in Thomas's 'Dons Ancient and Modern' chapter' in *Oxford*, most of which, he told Gordon Bottomley, was 'imaginary'.[38] Only one of the dons was 'taken from life,' he adds, 'the one like William Morris'. The original was F. York Powell, a distant cousin of Thomas's as he afterwards discovered. Perhaps this was his reason for making the flamboyant Regius Professor of History and ancient folklorist an exception by describing him in *Oxford*. Thomas is almost certainly the imaginary student who finds the don 'the most unpedantic man in the world', and that 'to walk with him, in all weathers, to Wood Eaton, Sunningwell, Fyfield, Northmoor [was] to go with a walking and genial embodiment of the north west wind and a dash of orchard scent'.[39] R. George Thomas suggests that Thomas's interest in Old Icelandic poetry and saga, first sparked by William Morris, was fed by his personal attachment to York Powell. It would later lead him to publish a book on *Norse Tales*. The only student in his own admission who is *not* 'imaginary' attends lectures 'outside his course', an allusion perhaps to Thomas's own fascination with York Powell.[40]

York Powell's lectures were not the only distraction by Thomas's second term at Lincoln. Extensive daily rowing practice for the February Torpids ('toggers'), often followed by a so-called 'drunk' in the evening with his recently made friends, was one of these. The earliest dated entry in his surviving notes on his life in the college, is a description of a 'Lincoln Smoking Concert' in March 1899 and catches the flavour of such occasions well:

> Scene: the Hall Band on the dais. Benches all round, chairs in the body.
> Music and songs: then Spanish Castanet dance played by band.
> Interval for wine: everyone returns halfscrewed.
> Music seemed to grow wilder. Candles fell from brackets. Fumes of tobacco and wine. People begin to shout accompaniment, then to throw down candles. Finally the hall was cleared of chairs, and all

joined hands and danced madly – the band playing fiercely. No light except by the band, the rest in darkness. How the dance ended I don't know.[41]

Another distraction from work was his relationship with Helen, which had entered a new phase. Possibly as a result of the more physical life he was leading in the rowing team, perhaps influenced by the less idealized attitude towards sex he encountered among some of his new companions, Edward now began to find the limits he and Helen had imposed on their love-making even harder to bear and, with Helen's help at Christmas, had finally acquired contraceptives. Her new job was with a friend of Janet and Harry Hooton, Beatrice Logan, who lived in some style in St Peter's Square, Hammersmith. Beatrice's bohemian views made it possible for Edward to stay overnight with Helen a temptation too far. Under the influence of Mrs Logan's artistic, free-thinking young friends, who included the poet Charles Dalmon and the actor Franklin Dyall, Helen was a willing participant in their full love-making. Helen had, with her father's encouragement, always thought of herself as an emancipated young woman and, under Beatrice's guidance, she happily embraced 'free love'.

While Edward would become friends with at least two members of the Logan circle – Dalmon and Dyall – and listened carefully to their discussions on beauty and art, morality and the 'new woman', he was 'unimpressed', according to Helen, and sat among them like a 'judging Sphinx'.[42] But he was no doubt also influenced by their views. His fears of an unwanted pregnancy now dealt with, as he thought, he indulged his physical needs joyfully. By February 1899 he is writing Helen 'hopelessly voluptuous' letters, longing for her 'throbbing bosom' and 'tingling limbs' and 'dreaming of [her] breasts, [her] hair, [her] eyes in the silent darkness of night'. He was following his own instructions to Helen to 'think always of the Spring days and nights we shall soon enjoy' to the exclusion of more mundane matters like college assignments.

Yet another distraction and influence was Thomas's growing interest in the Aesthetic Movement. In *Oxford* he makes a love of words the reason one of his sample undergraduates turns to it: 'Wherever the word has been cherished for its own sake, in all "decadent" literature, he makes his mind at home.'[43] Thomas's earlier reading of Walter Pater is now supplemented by a study of Oscar Wilde, John Addington Symonds and others. Pater's influence would be short-lived and afterwards 'scrupulously exorcised' (as Cooke so nicely puts it)[44] by Thomas in his 1913 study, *Walter Pater*, written as he worked his way towards 'wring[ing] all the necks of [his] rhetoric – the geese'.[45] As his own prose became simpler and closer to speech rhythms, Pater's writing seemed to him to display 'an exquisite unnaturalness'.[46] From referring to Pater's 'nearly perfect style' in 1898, less than a decade later he would be telling Gordon Bottomley that he got 'more and more dissatisfied with Pater', whose works seemed 'fatally external to him'.[47] Pater's belief that the artist, especially the poet, should strive to withdraw his thoughts from ' "the mere machinery of life" to the spectacle of men and their grandeur', would strike Thomas, as he started to contemplate writing his own poetry, as nothing more than a 'kind of higher philately or connoisseurship'.[48]

While still at Oxford, however, Thomas remained under the spell of Pater and his fellow-aesthetes and, unfortunately, also 'begins to write' like these, 'in a style which, along with his ornate penmanship, would occupy a lifetime, and result in one *brochure* or half a dozen Sonnets'.[49] Even his dress was affected and became, Helen recalled, the 'elegantly negligent' style of 'the young aesthete of the day', in strong contrast to the good but well-worn tweeds he wore in later life.[50] Though he was not, nor ever would be, ready to 'gather rosebuds' with abandon, by early 1899 he was less ready to reject the pleasures of the moment for the strict moral standards inculcated in him by his upbringing.

Whatever the causes of Thomas's changed behaviour, it began to affect his work and by the end of February 1899 he was behind with his essays. The College Boat Race in Eights Week in late February went badly, Lincoln's boat suffering the shame of being 'bumped' five times and coming in next to last. Though the college did not deprive the team of its colours, as Thomas had feared, he felt humiliated. Released from the tyranny of the long daily rowing practices, however, he now tried to remedy the 'sad falling off' in his work his tutor had noted.[51] By working late each night he caught up on his overdue essays and was able to complete one of only two papers published in the *Speaker* this year, together with a piece for the *JCR*, a short-lived university magazine. He also managed to see something of his aunt, Margaret Townsend, visiting Oxford as companion to a wealthy

American woman, and to resume more regular long country walks with friends, most often Haynes and MacAlister, until the latter's absence with typhoid fever this summer.

By the end of Thomas's second term at Lincoln, it seemed as though he was finding some kind of equilibrium in his new life, despite celebrating his twenty-first birthday on 3 March with an excess of wine and subsequent hangover. But he was knocked off balance completely in early May 1899 by some unexpected and, to him, highly unwelcome news.

7

Paradise Lost (1899–1900)

The news of Helen's pregnancy in early May 1899, at the beginning of Thomas's third term at Lincoln College, was to have far-reaching consequences. His year of more light-hearted enjoyment came to an abrupt end, as he faced his responsibilities and the probable consequences.

His father, when the news eventually reached him, would argue that the culprits were 'alcoholic drink', 'libidinous' French novels and 'smoking to excess', in that order.[1] No doubt he would have added opium to the list, if he had known of it, together with Helen's move to Beatrice Logan's more relaxed establishment. Edward himself accepted that 'perhaps the licentious life of Oxford with which – with wine and wild talk, grave and gay – I have entered with all the zest that was to be expected from one who has spent so many years in solitude – that this life may have heated my blood somewhat unnaturally'.[2] Written four days before the marriage he felt obliged to undertake, there is an apologetic, far from joyful tone to this account Thomas offered Hooton.

Helen, on the other hand, suffered no doubts nor regrets, though she saw no need for marriage. Her version of events in *As It Was* makes it clear that she was delighted to discover that she was having Edward's child: 'a calm, deep, secret joy' had entered her spirit, it was 'as it could not help but be', and she felt 'content and happy with a sense of fulfilment'.[3] Nearly 22 and far more mature than Edward, she had longed for children and welcomed the pregnancy. Since she was the one physically responsible for contraception, it is not impossible that, consciously or not, she had allowed it to occur. It certainly seems as though she might have been expecting it, since she told Edward the news less than a month after the date of conception, which they agreed had been 6 April.

Edward's attitude was so much less straightforward, that Helen had to ask him directly if he 'too, felt any joy at the thought of a child'.[4] He assured her that he had 'felt it considerably' but only a week before the baby's birth he admitted to Haynes that he had 'no sentiments of attachment to the being to come'.[5] He also wondered whether it was 'decent' to rejoice in the conception of their child.[6] For however vigorously he appeared to reject his father's values, he was probably influenced by them. 'Remember it is not a nice business at all; there's nothing heroic about it,' he writes to Helen: 'we cannot expect the end of it to be anything but cheap and nasty patchwork'.[7] His first instruction to her had been that his parents 'must not know'.[8]

There seems to be an element of shame here. But Edward, knowing his father would disapprove, also faced the prospect of having his parental contribution to Oxford withdrawn. He had become uncharacteristically extravagant at Lincoln, indulging in fine china and expensive books and pictures, as well as elaborate clothes, to satisfy his growing admiration for the Aesthetic Movement. Even with strict economy, however, he knew he could not manage on Lincoln's £60 bursary and the £80 he could expect to earn, at most, from his freelance writing. (His father had stipulated that part of his earnings must be contributed to his family's household expenses.) Just as he felt he was coming into his own at Lincoln, there seemed a distinct possibility that his time there must end abruptly. Having rejected his father's advice to train for a secure job in the Civil Service, he was unqualified for anything likely to earn him an income on which he could comfortably support a family.

Thomas's main concerns by May 1899 were, therefore, practical, centring largely round money. Ironically, just prior to the child's conception, he had published a paper praising 'Indolence',[9] with copious references to Keats, gypsies and Watts-Dunton's novel *Aylwin* (1898), which features gypsies and tells the story of Henry Aylwin's love for a Welsh girl, Winifred.

(Thomas had spent a memorable evening with two gypsies a few months previously in the rooms of a fellow-student, Trench.) It now looked probable that his own chance to enjoy indolence was coming to an end. A later friend, who knew him well, would argue that Thomas needed 'leisure and energy of spirit to find himself', but that this premature responsibility deprived him of both.[10] While Edward had no doubt that he and Helen must marry, despite their idealistic opposition to the institution, at barely 21 he was not ready for it. He would refer later to marriage 'continually encrusting the soul'.[11]

Haynes for one, while as sympathetic as Morgan to Thomas's plight, believed it would be better for Helen to have an abortion than that Edward should risk his prospects with a premature marriage. Nevertheless, when Edward insisted on going ahead with it, Haynes lent him £10 immediately and promised to get him tutoring work during the long vacation. Even before the birth of the baby, Edward asked him to be its godfather: 'You have already done more for the infant than most godfathers do in a lifetime!'[12]

Journalism brought in another two or three pounds in mid-1899, though Thomas's paper on Malory was rejected by *Literature*. Helen also hoped to be able to access the legacy left her by her father, but she anticipated problems with her mother, who was reluctant to part with it. The couple's financial position looked bad.

The clandestine ceremony took place at Fulham Register Office on 20 June 1899, attended by Beatrice Logan and her future husband, Mr Potbury, who 'witnessed' the wedding, together with Janet Aldis, now married to Harry Hooton. Helen had felt 'surprise and disappointment' when Beatrice, despite her emancipated talk, and Janet had both urged marriage.[13] Edward then returned to Oxford and Helen to St Peter's Square, Hammersmith, which Beatrice was leaving in July. Since they believed they could keep the marriage secret, Edward was obliged to follow his father's plan, to send him to Swindon, where his grandmother was dying, then back to Wales for the summer. The Hootons offered their house in Gipsy Hill as a temporary refuge for Helen after her job with Mrs Logan came to an end and she planned to rent rooms in Carshalton, Surrey, for the birth itself.

Edward found it 'a pain and a terror' to continue to hide his marriage from his parents, however, despite fearing his father's reaction, and by July was anxious to let him know of it.[14] Hooton was deputed to inform both families of the news once Edward was safely in Wales and on 12 August Mr Thomas's terse response arrived: 'Mr Hooton has made some revelations. What are the facts?' 'So here I am,' Thomas wrote to Haynes from Ammanford:

> ...in a pretty state, with no letter since Tuesday from Helen, and not a notion of my father's attitude; tho from what I can judge the above laconism is worse than a tirade. There's not a human being here I can talk to; or, if I did, they would reply in the neo-Baptist vein. All my mock-heroic position is upset. I was looking forward to my garret in Carshalton, with more or less lyrical work, interspersed with pot-boiling...and now it looks as if my father is going to play the long-suffering saint. The present obvious solution is laudanum [i.e. opium]. Of the future I cannot make anything. One thing is certain. I can't live at home.[15]

Once again, Edward is not being fair to his father. While Mr Thomas was unable to resist lecturing his son on the evil of his ways at Lincoln, he behaved better than expected. Punctilious about money, he was worried about the £60 bursary Edward had already received from Lincoln. However Edward chose to portray him, he was proud of his eldest son's ability and could see the value of him completing his degree, still hoping he might use it to enter the Civil Service at a high level afterwards. He agreed, therefore, to continue his allowance for another year. He and his wife also showed sympathy towards Helen. Mrs Thomas visited her immediately and offered her a home with them at Shelgate Road while she waited for the birth. Though Helen would have much preferred to remain independent in rooms in Carshalton and Edward found the thought of going home 'distasteful', they accepted the offer, Helen mainly for Edward's sake, Edward because he reasoned that, if his father refused to let him leave home to earn a living, 'Why should he not be the victim of his own decision.'[16] As it turned out, Helen got on well with 'the little mater', as she called Mrs Thomas affectionately. Her kindness, together with her experience of six births of her own, was reassuring, especially since Helen's own mother refused to speak to her. It had been agreed, finally, that Helen would draw her legacy in monthly payments and pay her own household expenses to Mrs Thomas.

Once Edward knew that his future at Lincoln was assured, he began to relax again, telling Helen rather tactlessly how much he was enjoying his 'rich' holiday in Wales without her. ('Day by day,' he recorded in his notebook at the end of August, 'grows my passion for Wales.'[17]) He did not feel 'a bit reformed by this exposure', he informed her, vowing 'I *will* enjoy that last year at Oxford: Damn the respectable.'[18] Meantime, he instructs her to listen to good music, study worthy pictures and sends her a list of suggested reading, to provide an 'improving' environment for their unborn baby. His letters are by turns dictatorial and loving.

By 12 October, back at Lincoln, Thomas proceeds to carry out his vow to enjoy his final year. While keeping Helen to a tight budget, he continues to indulge himself in clothes, books and wine. Just over a month later, only two months before his child is due, he admits to being 'strangely fascinated' by a freshman, Brook, with his 'abundant black hair... narrow white face, almost vulpine, noticeable long red lips and white teeth, sparkling and frank grey eyes'.[19] His passion for Brook, who is frightened by Thomas's reputation ('my character, my "atheism", my drinking'), is very similar 'to what [he] had experienced in love of a woman', though he 'emphatically' denies that there is any 'sexual excitement' in it.[20] Nevertheless, his infatuation interferes with his work. Even the birth of Philip Merfyn Ashcroft Thomas at Shelgate Road in the early morning of 15 January 1900, when Helen 'took the ordeal like an athlete' and he survived 'fortified by laudanum', did 'not have any great effect' on his behaviour, he claimed.[21] While Helen spent the next six months writing him loving letters detailing every aspect of their new baby's development, Edward continued to fall in love with young men. Brook had been followed by 'young Parsons'[22] and in February he became infatuated with another Lincoln freshman, W. E. ('Lucy') Elsey, in whose company he attended the Magdalen Friday service.

A 'great part of [his] enjoyment' at this choral service was caused 'by the presence of Elsey,' he wrote, but it was more than that – 'the fresh youthful faces of the choir: and their angel voices ascending amid that severely ornate stone and multitudinous candles, and the solemn organ... with stops that in opening seemed to let me hear the music of heaven through open doors'.[23] For Thomas worshipped 'Beauty' (his capital letter) in almost any form and needed it badly. One of his greatest fears about his unborn baby, for instance, had not been for its health but its appearance: 'My only wish is that the child may be comely to look upon.'[24] Once Merfyn had passed muster, Thomas turned his attention to Elsey. Besides accompanying him to Magdalen, Elsey also visited him at his lodgings, where Thomas and his friends drank Marsala, absinthe and whisky to excess, though Elsey left early.

Thomas continued to drink heavily at times, despite (possibly because of) his new responsibilities. His excuse to himself was a sadness verging on depression, which he tried to 'drown in wine', a depression which only lifted occasionally in the company of others: 'Stand alone I cannot,' he wrote in February 1900: 'Tender and simple love is necessary to me; in spite of my foulness I can give it – but receive it I never do.'[25] It is already apparent that he did not find Helen, however devoted, enough.

It is difficult to associate the Thomas who fell in love with young men and drank heavily with the writer who would observe life so acutely and delicately later on. His behaviour was no doubt partly the reaction of an immature youth rebelling against premature responsibilities. But he also had a need for beauty which Helen could not satisfy. However much it hurt her at times, it was an essential ingredient of his character. Haynes described him as 'always hyperaesthetic as regards impressions, and the beauty of Oxford sank deeply into him'.[26] Agonizing later about his restlessness and inability to love, in his poem 'Beauty', where his feelings of isolation and coldness are emphasized through the imagery of an un-sunlit river, he nevertheless tries to explain this need and its power to heal:

> …But, though I am like a river
> At fall of evening while it seems that never
> Has the sun lighted it or warmed it, while
> Cross breezes cut the surface to a file,
> This heart, some fraction of me, happily
> Floats through the window even now to a tree
> Down in the misting, dim-lit, quiet vale,
> Not like a pewit that returns to wail
> For something it has lost, but like a dove
> That slants unswerving to its home and love.
> There I find my rest, and through the dusk air
> Flies what yet lives in me. Beauty is there.
>
> (*Annotated Collected Poems of Edward Thomas*, p. 58)

This poem, which would be written in January 1915, was inspired directly by a passage from his field notebooks describing an experience on 8 April 1910, when he sat at his table with his son and his second child, Bronwen. 'Tired, angry[,] ill at ease' (words he repeats exactly in the opening lines of the later poem) he catches a glimpse of 'beauty in [the] dim-lit quiet vale w[ith] its...trees, its white gables, and its gentle curvy Downs just visible' and recognizes that the loveliness of the landscape causes 'some little thing' in him 'to fl[y] to it' and 'be happy', though another side of him continues 'sad and sick and weary'.[27] Already in 1900, he was dependent on beauty for survival. By May 1900 he felt ready to die 'for the sight of a beautiful face, the touch of a beautiful hand, the sound of beautiful voices'.

With finals looming, in his last term Thomas had moved into rooms at 17 Worcester Place with P. J. Maine, who shared his interest in folklore. Ironically, since the move had been made in an effort to escape his too-sociable life in college, Maine turned out to be very gregarious and they usually had friends to share at least one of their two main meals daily. Though Thomas had finally passed the mandatory Divinity exam at his third re-sit in March, he still had a lot to catch up on. Yet in April he was lunching with Hilaire Belloc to learn all about a new weekly Belloc was launching, the *Pilot*.[28] It would be the start of a lifelong friendship with Belloc, whom Thomas already thought 'prodigious'.[29] Though he believed him 'too unstable and fantastic to be anything more than a literary man',[30] he was full of admiration for his performances at the Oxford Union debates, describing (though not naming him) in *Oxford* as 'a stiff, small, heroic figure, with a mouth that might sway armies, a voice as sweet as Helicon'[31] and quoting his 'ardent' poetry there.[32]

Thomas's excuse for lunching with Belloc when he ought to have been revising, he explained to a fellow-student and -writer at Lincoln, H. B. Davies, was that he felt so exhausted he could not work and so accepted all offers of hospitality. Another of these was an invitation to dine with a friend of Haynes's, the barrister William Clarke Hall, an ex-Balliol man who lived at Thames Ditton with his recently married wife, Edna (née Waugh). Haynes had described her to Edward as his 'Beatrice' and Edward, too, had found her 'exquisite' when he met her briefly at Balliol the previous summer, thinking her, if anything, *too* attractive.³³ In April 1900 he tells Davies that she is ' "too white" as Browning says; her eyes are too large and beautiful'.³⁴ Edna seemed to him almost 'too beautiful to live'. So long as *he* lives, tells Davies, he will 'make pilgrimages to her annually': 'She is the Aesculapius of my spirit' and 'has oil and wine for the phlebotomy of time'.³⁵ Her talents as an artist – she had won a place at the Slade aged only 14 – added to her attractions. It is clear from the letter Helen wrote to Edna after Edward's death that, with his usual, at times brutal, frankness, he had not concealed his admiration from his wife, who knew his need for a beauty she did not possess: 'why wasn't I beautiful for Edward?' she asks Edna. 'I did so long to [give him?] beauty not to take it from him, not to take but give, to have hair and eyes and mouth and that something else that helped him.'³⁶ It is Edward's 'old adoration' of Edna, she claims, that makes her treat Edna as her 'confessor': she felt herself, by comparison, such a 'common or garden woman'.³⁷

There is no hint of sexual excitement in Thomas's description of Edna to Davies, yet his physical needs are very strong indeed by 1900. His letters to Helen describe in some detail the disturbance this causes him in her absence, his fevered imaginings of their next love-making. In telling her of his disappointment at having to miss the two nights they had hoped to spend together in late 1899, he had written, prophetically as it turned out, 'For the flesh is very weak, and my desires are simply overpowering at times and I could almost pick up a woman of the streets if it were safe in a pedantic City like [Oxford].'³⁸ By the summer of 1900 his fathering of a child (which has leaked out) has given him something of a reputation at Lincoln, which may have encouraged him to behave more recklessly than usual.

For whatever reason, towards the end of May, in the middle of his finals, he fell ill with what the doctor diagnosed as gonorrhoea, almost certainly caught from a prostitute on 19 May as he celebrated the Relief of Mafeking with his friends. Only a year before he had written self-righteously to Hooton: 'I suppose prostitutes were made because men had inordinate desires; now men have desires because there are prostitutes.' He refused to be tolerant about prostitutes, he declared, 'even [if] I am called prudish in revenge'.³⁹ His diary makes no mention of a prostitute, nor does his description of the celebrations to Helen (understandably), though it does convey the frenzied atmosphere, when the whole of Oxford, it seems, took to the streets. Huge bonfires were lit by the students and, according to Thomas, 'all the women, married or otherwise, allowed themselves to be promiscuously kissed by the University; in fact most men employed themselves in recording as many kisses as possible'.[40] Whether Helen recognized 'kissing' as a euphemism at the time or not, Edward was soon forced to tell her of his illness and its probable cause.

Helen's restraint in the circumstances was remarkable, if her surviving letters can be trusted to give the full picture. Only once, and that possibly before he had told her of his illness, does she reprove him even slightly, when he appears to have forgotten the importance of the holiday they had planned to take together after finals, writing peevishly, 'it would be insanity to go arcadizing with bankruptcy and the gutter ahead':[41]

> You do not realise all the strain physical and mental that I have had during the last year [Helen replied]. You leave me for a life perfectly congenial to one side of your nature, but for me there is no recompense, nothing to make up for you, nothing on which I can throw myself mentally and so forget my solitariness. That is only one, though the greatest, of those things which have made it so difficult for me to feel as well, and as cheerful as I used to feel....
>
> ...You see, Edwy, your somewhat hard and cold way of saying things hurt me rather. I try my very best and succeed in writing to you as cheerful as may be, that I may not increase your despondency, but rather raise your spirits, but I am not utterly careless indeed.[42]

Edward immediately apologizes. It is possible that if Helen had stood up to him more often, their relationship would have been more successful. He himself believed that he needed someone who was 'strong not too tender'.[43]

By early June Thomas was very unwell, suffering from high temperatures and extreme physical weakness. The doctor he visited prescribed protargal, a silver proteinate used to treat gonorrhoea before the advent of antibiotics. He also advised strict dieting, no alcohol and complete rest. Thomas found the whole experience humiliating and felt rather sorry for himself, especially after his friends had gone down: 'I am without any tender or even joyous hand and voice. That for one who has been, or tried to be, free-handed and sympathetic with so many, who has almost cried out for pity and endearment, is heart-breaking,'[44] Though not exactly a hypochondriac, he was unused to illness and felt sorry for himself when it struck.

In retrospect Thomas would give gonorrhoea as an explanation for his failure to gain the First that had been predicted. It is true that having to sit ten three-hour papers over six days would be demanding at the best of times. Looking back over the letters which preceded his illness, however, it seems likely that it was not just gonorrhoea which had prevented him getting a First. He had been distracted by college life and by anxiety over Merfyn's arrival. 'My malady is fearfully complex,' he had written to Helen only a month after the baby's birth, 'it is regrets, anxiety, disappointments, weakness, laudanum, wine, love of beauty and lack of beauty, books, men and women – a thousand things combined.'[45] His depression and anxiety had been exacerbated by Helen's fears that she may, through carelessness, have become pregnant again in 1900. (Edward had clearly ignored Haynes's highly practical suggestion a few months earlier: 'the avoidance of another such catastrophe' by using a contraceptive himself, an idea he found distasteful.[46]) Other distractions were the papers he had to produce, added to his university work, to supplement his father's modest allowance – five for the *Speaker* from October 1897 to July 1898, three for the *Speaker* between 1899 and July 1900, together with one for *Literature* and one for the *Atlantic Monthly* during the same period.

By 10 May Thomas had 'given up hope of anything above a fourth'[47] and by 25 May six days after the Mafeking celebration but before the full physical results have hit him, he confessed to having been 'wickedly idle' for the last year.[48] He predicts 'a Third at most and possibly a plough fail.'[49] However hard he now worked (and he did), he believed there was not enough time to make up for his past laxness. His subsequent illness partway through his exams only exacerbated the situation.

Reading Thomas's letters to MacAlister from London, when he was still recovering from what his parents were led to believe was overwork, it is clear that Thomas subsequently convinced himself that had he not contracted gonorrhoea, he would have got a better degree:

> It's leaked out that my early papers were 'very good' but fell off just when I was first attended by the doctor, – on which I sent in a certificate and there was talk of giving me the class earned by my best papers, which meant a long viva such as I could not endure.[50]

Even by mid-July Thomas still felt unfit for the shorter viva he faced a few days later. In the event he achieved a second-class degree – 'a bitter disappointment to his father', according to Helen.[51] While better than Edward feared, it was not good enough for him to continue at Oxford, or to try for a Fellowship, which had been one option. A later friend, Norman Douglas, would argue that Thomas was 'intended by nature for the life of bachelordom in collegiate surroundings'.[52] Edna Longley, on the other hand, maintains that, with his suspicion of academia, it was probably a good thing he was not offered the choice of continuing at Oxford.[53]

If, as seems likely from Thomas's letter to Bottomley about *Oxford*, he is the undergraduate in section two of chapter four, it is clear that he regarded his second-class degree as a failure, since he tells Bottomley that that particular student leaves 'without success'. There were other extenuating circumstances. The first member of his family to attend Oxford, his strict and sheltered upbringing had not prepared him for its many temptations, nor for its brilliant social life. Immature and lacking in social confidence, he had been overwhelmed by the sense of ease, intellectual as well as social, he had encountered, especially on his visits to Haynes and Morgan at Balliol. But the question still arises as to whether Thomas had been wise in going to Oxford at all. Had he got his predicted First, it might have given him the confidence he lacked, as St Paul's School had shown. He had no practical need of a degree for the occupation he was determined on as a writer and it had meant a certain amount of sacrifice on his own and his family's part to send him there.

R. George Thomas argues that Oxford provided 'a gentle transition from two years of freedom after St Paul's' and the 'severer demands' of 'family and social life',[54] and that it was the only sustained period when he had to try to come to terms with the expectations of a society that held strong attitudes incompatible with his private world. He also suggests that Thomas 'brought away from Oxford a greater readiness to understand the interests and pursuits of the audience he was to address'.[55] William Cooke claims, less abstractly, that 'it gave him his first real intellectual and social companionship', 'a period of leisure he would never know again',[56] and an opportunity to indulge his love of literature. As John Moore puts it, 'he had found men who talked his language and thought his thoughts'.[57] The books he read then, Moore points out, lasted him throughout his life, as did the friends he made.

Thomas himself implies, through his alter ego in *Oxford*, that, besides all these things, he had fulfilled more intangible aims:

> He wants to be a scholar, and fears to be a pedant, he wants to learn a wise and graceful habit with his fellow-men, and fears to be what he hears called a gentleman. He wants to test his enthusiasm and prejudice, and fears to be a Philistine. He wants to taste pleasures delicately, and fears to be a [*bon*] *viveur* or an aesthete.[58]

Thomas is undoubtedly describing himself when this unnamed student who, like himself, gains a second-class degree 'by means of legible handwriting, clear style, and amusing irrelevance' goes down 'careless of success, ready to do anything so long as he can escape comfortable and conventional persons, and quite unable to be conspicuous'.[59] Yet he has also 'been to the garden of the Hesperides and brought back apples that he alone can make appear to be golden in his rare moments of health'.[60]

8

GRUB STREET (SEPTEMBER 1900–SEPTEMBER 1901)

Edward Thomas left Oxford addicted to books and opium. He had no money and serious debts.[1]

At the height of his troubles with his father, in August 1899, over his premature marriage, he had written to Haynes: 'One thing is certain: I can't live at home.'[2] Yet a year later it seemed his only option. His modest earnings from the *Speaker* had dried up and not been replaced by further commissions from *Literature* and the *Atlantic Monthly*. Though still determined to make his living by writing, he was not earning nearly enough from it by autumn 1900 to support Helen and Merfyn. Meantime, Mr Thomas senior had continued to play what his eldest son rather ungratefully described as 'the long-suffering saint' and allowed him to return to the family home in Shelgate Road.

Mr Thomas had paid all Edward's medical bills as well as financing a holiday in Wales for Helen and Merfyn when a planned voyage to Spain or the Canary Isles with Morgan had fallen through, but relations between father and son continued to deteriorate. So that when Edward again rejected his father's suggestion of a safe job in the Civil Service in October 1900, Mr Thomas thought 'it would be best for [him] to go out into the world', that is, to find (and pay for) his own accommodation.[3] His decision, Edward told MacAlister, who was writing to him regularly from Oxford, 'has made me buckle to in a way surprising to myself'.[4]

He had already approached his Oxford tutor, Owen Edwards, about the possibility of a schoolmastership in Wales; on 6 October he wrote more urgently asking for 'any suggestions whatever'.[5] Edwards had nothing to offer, so two days after writing to him Thomas set off on the first of his many visits to Fleet Street in search of journalistic work. He approached at least seven editors and, though he purported to find it an 'amusing' as well as 'tiring' undertaking, he was depressed by the largely unenthusiastic response he received. *Literature*, he told Mac, gave him 'one wretched book to review', the *Daily News* came to 'no decision', the *Star* 'was (of course) rude', the *Academy* 'stupid', the *Literary World* 'made no promises', the *World* was 'undecided' and the *New Century* 'penniless'.[6] (Later he would try John Buchan, who had, like Thomas, just left Oxford, and become acting editor of the *Spectator*. Though Buchan seemed 'favourably disposed' towards him, nothing came of that either.[7] Only Henry Nevinson of the *Daily Chronicle* was positive, promising to put Thomas down to review poetry, essays and other elevated literature.

While Thomas described Nevinson only briefly as 'genial' after his first meeting, Nevinson's account of the occasion is much fuller, underlining the young Oxford graduate's problems in asking for work:

> One evening after my first return from the Boer War, a person of unknown name was announced, as many such there were, and, cursing aloud or silently, I awaited his entrance. Can a man stride with a proud and melancholy shyness? If so, he strode in that manner. He was tall, absurdly thin, and a face of attractive distinction and ultra-refinement was sicklied over with nervous melancholy and the ill condition of bad food or hunger. Almost too shy to speak, he sat down proudly and asked if I could give him work. I enquired what work he could do, and he said 'None.' At once recognising my former self in him, I asked whether he would like some reviewing on any subject, and on what. He replied that he knew nothing of any subject, and was quite sure he could not write, but certainly he did want work of some sort. I asked if he would not care to try a short review of a scholarly book I was just throwing away; for if he could not do it, that would make little difference to me or to anyone else. I urged him repeatedly, and at last, with extreme reluctance, he consented, and nervously took his leave, just mentioning that his name was Edward Thomas, lately

from Lincoln College, Oxford...Of course, he at once became one of my very best reviewers, and soon one of my dearest friends. Shy and reserved of feeling he always remained, too self-distrustful till nearly the end.[8]

Nevinson's first reaction had been to say to himself 'Yet another poet', but other editors may, as Hooton suggested, have 'resented his quiet manner', mistaking it for 'the aloofness of a proud young aristocrat', rather than the shyness it partly was; though Hooton conceded that it was also 'in part a disdain of the sort of man to whom he had to appeal'.[9] It was not an attitude calculated to get him work. Nevinson was the exception at the start and would never fail to find work for Thomas while he remained literary editor of the *Daily Chronicle*, sometimes asking for three reviews in just over a week. From 23 November 1900, when Thomas produced his first (scathing) review of the popular poet Harold Begbie's *The Handy Man*, together with six other collections of poetry, until Nevinson left to resume his war-reporting abroad in December 1903, he published at least 150 pieces by Thomas, judging him 'one of my three best reviewers, the other two being Lionel Johnson and William Archer'.[10] He also introduced Thomas to, among others, the publisher J. M. Dent.

Though Thomas lacked Nevinson's radical, crusading spirit and political commitment and could not always praise the many books he produced, he 'liked and admired' the man.[11] Despite their twenty-two years' age difference, they became good friends, Thomas being invited to Nevinson's London home, and Nevinson being invited to spend weekends with the Thomases on his frequent returns from foreign trouble-spots. His claim to know Edward 'very intimately' is supported by his various descriptions of him and Thomas's dedication of *The Heart of England* to Nevinson in 1906.[12]

Though Thomas was grateful to Nevinson for reviewing, he complained bitterly about the work itself which, he would tell a young disciple in 1908, he found 'fearful...drudgery', continuing: 'But no other course was open to me when I left Oxford. I took a poor degree and had no money. You are right when you said...I did not take to reviewing for choice.'[13] Reviewing, he believed, 'encrusted the Soul'.[14] Varying his metaphor, he complained elsewhere that another huge parcel of books had come for him 'to gulp and vomit and return to the vomit'.[15]

By the time reviewing work had dried up in 1914, Thomas had written over 1,900 reviews containing more than a million words. He had had sometimes to read 15 books for a single review, and this amounted on average to one review every three days for 14 years.[16] He was a conscientious reviewer and the work took up most of his energy; at times he was forced to work from nine o'clock in the morning to one o'clock at night to meet his deadlines.[17] One time-consuming factor was his scholarly insistence on always checking his facts. Another strain was the determination to be completely honest, even about books written by friends. Not everyone appreciated his candour as much as Walter de la Mare, who wrote of his honesty that 'the true cause' of poetry was 'better served by an uncompromising "Trespassers will be prosecuted" than by an amiable "All are welcome"'.[18] The Bishop of Derry may not have felt the same when, in his first review for the *Daily Chronicle*, Thomas hailed the bishop's poems with the biblical words: 'There is nothing new under the sun.'[19] The poet Sturge Moore, who would write admiringly of Thomas after his death, nevertheless referred to 'the opinionated savage youngster' that Thomas had been before he 'saddened and mellowed' in later years'.[20] Ezra Pound, who did not appreciate Thomas's reassessment of his initially enthusiastic response to his *Personae*, reacted very badly indeed to his candour.

Thomas's conviction that reviewing was 'derived writing', 'the coining everything into hasty words',[21] plus the long hours involved, led to his greatest complaint, that it drained him of the time and energy for his own, more imaginative writing, the essays and prose-poems he favoured at this time. He was already describing himself as a 'prose-poet' by November 1900.[22] Though he dreamt about 'original writing', he would tell a friend in 1905, he rarely managed 'to get out pen and paper for it'.[23]

Reviewing was undeniably 'drudgery' in one sense. But whether it was a wholly negative experience for Thomas is not so easy to decide. When Nevinson gave Thomas his first books to review in late 1900, it not only saved him from an ignominious return to his family, but it would start him on a course which would supply his 'bread and butter' money for over a decade. Even at the start he earned £52 in less than a year, enough to pay at least half of his rent. It would eventually bring in a modest but sufficient income for Thomas and his family, while allowing him a certain amount of independence. On the few occasions he tried working in an office, or a job with set hours, he hated it and he turned down at least one teaching post at this time. His wide and ever-increasing knowledge of literature would quickly establish him as a leading authority, particularly on modern poetry. As his reputation became established, he was often allowed the books he wanted to review, or to suggest others not on offer. Thomas Seccombe, a scholar and man of letters and himself extremely well read, claimed that Thomas's 'knowledge of poetry soon took me out of my depth' and testified that to the younger men of that time Thomas became both the wise King Rhadamanthus and the monstrous watchdog Cerberus: 'He was the man with the keys to the Paradise of English Poetry.[24] Walter de la Mare, when he referred to 'the generous help and encouragement many living poets owe[d] to Thomas', included himself in their ranks.[25]

Thomas was rarely wrong about a poet's worth, though his praise of writers like Charles Doughty and Sturge Moore has not convinced posterity. However time-consuming the work, it seems to have given him a security other than financial that he badly needed. The need to work hard daily to produce the reviews he did may have helped ward off a depression which settled on him frequently when alone and without work. The length of review allowed to him, as R. George Thomas points out, 'suited his own temperamental desire to write continuously for about 1,200 to 1,500 words'.[26] And the wide variety of books offered him allowed him to use his knowledge of French, German, Latin and Greek, as well as of nature and poetry, to good effect. De la Mare, for one (Thomas suspected), preferred his reviews to his prose books on 'landscapes and people'[27] and James Milne, who would replace Nevinson at the *Daily Chronicle* in late 1903, believed that 'possibly some of [Thomas's] best work was his criticism'.[28] Only when Thomas started on what he dismissed as 'hack-writing of books', and was threatened with the loss of reviewing did he concede that 'low' as reviewing was, it was 'only for today and [could] be shaken off', whereas his continuous writing of commissioned prose books was 'more damaging to freedom and reputation'.[29] The most serious aspect of both these freelance activities was that it sentenced Thomas to nearly a lifetime of anxiety and uncertainty, forever dependent on editors, forever waiting for the postman's knock. Already anxious and uncertain enough by the age of 22, it would leave him even more vulnerable to depression. His fits of melancholy certainly grew more pronounced once he started on his freelance career.

Though Thomas would periodically contemplate other work, he would continue to live mainly by reviewing for the next decade and more. (He would turn down the offer of a schoolmastership at £120 a year, because it left no time or energy for his own work.) Reviewing was a profession which allowed him, however hurriedly, to write books of travel and biography and, even more importantly to him, poetic essays on his own choice of subject. On 16 November 1900, for instance, only a fortnight after moving to his own accommodation, he is telling Mac that he 'laughed for joy over a page describing [his] neighbours and surroundings', even though Helen said it was 'all pure fiction'.[30] The piece referred to was 'Recollections of November', which would appear in his second book, *Horae Solitariae*; in 1902, the 'surroundings' Earlsfield, at that time a newly developed, working-class suburb of Wandsworth, and the accommodation the top three rooms of a house at 117 Atheldene Road.

Thomas thought his 'November' piece 'the best thing' he had done 'for some years' and was depressed that 'no magazine, or journal, or newspaper in England' would print it.[31] (the *Atlantic Monthly* did, eventually, a year later.) Apart from its literary merits the essay gives an interesting glimpse of Thomas's initially positive response to what he tells Mac is a 'very comfortable flat', which 'without any expense' he is having distempered 'in French grey, a colour I greatly love'.[32] Though 'Recollections of November' acknowledges that his street is 'brand-new', 'suburban', even 'mean', lacking both sunlight and vitality, its very dreariness stimulates him to imaginative heights, where the neighbouring navvy trudging to work daily becomes 'a superb labourer who, if he were of stone, and not of gnarled brown flesh, might stand in a temple of fame' as the heroic Roman dictator 'Cincinnatus'.[33] Likewise, some insignificant poplar trees, half-denuded of their leaves and struggling to survive, are imagined as being 'in love with their own decay, like old and widowed ladies that have lived on into these flat unprofitable times'.[34] Poverty, Thomas now maintains, 'is really the Tenth Muse'.[35]

Disillusionment quickly set in. Drafting a letter to Haynes's friend, the exquisite Edna Clarke Hall, only a fortnight after the move to Atheldene Road, to thank her for her gift of roses, he refers disparagingly to 'this misty hollow, this dismal street, this tiny flat' as 'an ugly experience'.[36] He begs for her to come 'to see ME' (Helen is inserted as an afterthought), arguing that her beauty would enrich this 'labyrinth of red brick'. His bitterness extends even to the profession he had so recently been longing for: 'I now live – if living it may be called – by my writing, "literature" we call it in Fleet Street (derived from "litter", as we say "a litter of pigs" or "he made an awful litter"). It's a painful business'.[37]

Thomas's letters to Mac from his 'dismal muddy street' grow even gloomier. He describes the icy rooms, his meagre meals, his ill-health, his lack of money, his Oxford creditors who are threatening court action, and his squalid, noisy, sinister neighbours in the flat below. By 1 January 1901, he is telling Mac that any letter he might write to him 'would only be a long-drawn mental equivalent of suicide'.[38] By 8 February, when Helen and Merfyn have been away a week at Ramsgate, he admits that 'three or four times' he has 'come to [his] wit's end' and thought of the revolver he has evidently acquired for just such an occasion.[39] While his wife and son's departure has been undertaken to 'lighten the burden', they had been his only comfort and their absence has made him 'nearly sick with horror' in the 'empty, absolutely empty house'. This was one of the first of a number of suicide threats and symptomatic of a serious problem in Edward's marriage. Given frequently to 'intense [nervous] irritability', he could not live comfortably with Helen, yet could not live without her.[40]

Whereas in 'Recollections of November' Edward had managed to find some romance in the London streets, in his next essay, 'February in England', in keeping with his mood everything in the city seems grey: 'Grey roofs, grey ships; indeed, only one immobile ruddy sail of a barge, drifting up, coloured the Quakerish raiment of the day. By dipping my pen into the grey Thames ripple I am fain to make grey the reader's mind grey as it did mine.'[41] This piece, which opens lyrically in the country and closes equally poetically with a description of rural Wales, uses contrast to point up the drabness and deathliness the narrator sees in London – 'Death in life', he quotes from 'The Ancient Mariner'. It is a contrast which undoubtedly reflects Thomas's own thoughts as he compares the loveliness of Oxford and its surrounding countryside with the suburbs of Wandsworth. 'It is not the same air you breathe', he tells Mac, still at the University.[42]

As at Oxford, Thomas turned to opium to deal with his depression, though in doing so he may have made it worse. His diary entries show him taking opium daily and on the rare occasions he resists it, taking a double dose the next day – meantime noting on 21 December 1900, 'Read [de Quincey's] "Opium Eater" for 1000th time.'[43] While regarding it as a way of dealing with almost everything, from toothache to tiredness, he does sometimes wonder if it might actually be part of his problem. Yet he still takes it, he declares by mid-January 1901, to 'keep me alive'.[44] It gives him 'vivid' and 'horrible' nightmares, his 'waking' nights 'full of dreams' and his sleeping 'full of the actual'.[45] At times he uses the drug to help him work, trying 'to set [his] fancy working in a definite line under P[ersian] O[pium]', at others quite unable to work for longer than a few hours because of it.[46] The physical effects are alarming: a 'large piece of P.O.' makes his body 'itch almost all over', his 'sense of hearing becomes horribly keen', but at the same time he experiences 'wild sensations of silence' with a feeling that 'some fearful crash was coming'.[47] Haynes, with whom he lunches regularly, is deeply concerned.

A more practical reaction to his depression is to plan a move. He longs for 'a glimpse of the country', he tells Mac on 1 January 1901, or at least an escape from the drab surroundings of Atheldene Road. In the first week of February he asks Mac if he can lend him money to finance the second of his many early moves, five in four years. Each time he hopes to make a fresh start, that things will be different and better in new surroundings.

The move, to 7 Nightingale Parade, Nightingale Lane, Balham, was, in fact, an improvement in a number of ways. (He uses it to try, unsuccessfully, to give up opium.) His parents, still at Shelgate Road, were nearer and they visited often, continuing their kindnesses: Mrs Thomas rarely arrived without a beefsteak or a cake for them and Mr Thomas was still ready to put Edward in touch with possible employers when he decided periodically to try for a full-time job. (As Edward grudgingly conceded: 'By dint of great breadth of view on Father's part' and 'a great patience on mine, my relations w[ith] this gentleman are slowly ripening into a genial if distant acquaintanceship'.[48]) The neighbourhood itself Thomas finds 'better…quieter and healthier', situated as it is halfway between Wandsworth and Clapham commons.[49] He has found four rooms for ten shillings cheaper than usual because they are over a laundry receiving office, though it is quiet. There is also the option of a fifth room for only an extra shilling, which will resolve one of the problems, his need for a separate study.[50]

Although there had not been nightingales in 'Nightingale Lane', at least since Thomas was a boy, when the name was 'a fine music for [his] boyish ears', it was still a pleasant road of large houses with leafy gardens and lawns.[51] The flat itself was 'a great improvement, much warmer and safer in every way'.[52] There was a problem getting rid of an old lady who occupied two of the rooms and refused to move, but he was hopeful of a new beginning. He took up carpentering more seriously and made a sofa for Helen. He also started to socialize more.

One of his first visits, outside of his close Oxford circle, was to friends of Helen's older, unmarried sister, Irene, Duncan and Peggy Williams. Peggy, an artist, would marry Jacob Epstein after her divorce from her civil servant husband, Duncan, but there was already something of a bohemian flavour to their gatherings at Clovelly Mansions, Gray's Inn Road, in January 1901. And while Edward enjoyed meeting Duncan, 'a compact little Welshman with a fine voice', according to a later friend, Arthur Ransome,[53] and was pleased to see the 'dear little poet Dalmon' (who also lived in Gray's Inn with Franklin Dyall), he was still suspicious of the world they moved in: 'I hate these professionally Bohemian people who adore the great Sodomites', he wrote in his diary.[54] But Duncan would become a good friend, who would help Thomas, through his knowledge of folk-songs, when Thomas came to write his *Pocket Book of Poems and Songs for the Open Air* (1907) and spend several weekends with him and Helen after they moved to the country.

An even better friend made on these visits to Gray's Inn Road in 1901 was Jesse Berridge, whose wife, like Peggy Williams, was an artist. Berridge's first impression of the newcomer to their 'voluble and amusing circle' was of someone 'rather remote, kindly, giving the impression of reserves of knowledge, or of perhaps a suppressed anxiety'.[55] Berridge, though four years older than Thomas, was evidently a little in awe of him. The premature death of Berridge's father had prevented him from going to university, which may help to explain his attitude. But they had many other things in common: both had married young to the sorrow of their more conventional parents; both had been forced to keep their marriage secret for a time – Berridge from the bank where he worked; both were living in rented rooms in one of the recently built London suburbs – Berridge in Southfields; both had a wife and young son to support on a low income; and both were trying to write, though in Berridge's case, not for a living. Both loved the classics and Thomas tells Berridge of 'a Greek play' he has been writing but just burnt in June 1901.[56] They even looked slightly similar, slim but strongly built, fair and good-looking.

Even more importantly for Thomas, Berridge shared his love of walking. From the start, when Thomas suggested an excursion to his favourite country spot, Merton, they would take many long walks, later bicycle rides together. It was Berridge, unbeknown to Thomas's readers, who was partly the original of 'the Other Man' in the long cycling tour which formed the basis of *In Pursuit of Spring* (1914). ('You mustn't give away the fact that the Other Man is rather a lie,' Thomas would instruct Berridge on 3 May 1914.)

There were differences, however, as each of them pointed out. When telling Robert Frost in 1915 that Berridge 'might have been the original of Torrance' in his one novel, *The Happy-Go-Lucky Morgans*, Thomas added 'but Berridge is much better – the saintliest, honestest, best-natured man imaginable, doesn't like everybody but thinks ill of nobody.'[57] (Berridge was a devout Christian, unlike Thomas, and would go on to become a clergyman.) For his part Berridge expressed his sense of their differences in his explanation for their *not* collaborating on a novel together: Thomas's 'honesty and recognition of the imperatives in his own experience and outlook, would not coalesce with my rather pretentious idealism.'[58] Despite these and other differences they remained friends for life. In 1912 Thomas would dedicate *Norse Tales* to Berridge and his family and one of his last meetings in England before leaving for France would be with Berridge.

The friendship between the two was well established by May 1901. But even having a good friend near at hand and evenings in congenial company could not make Thomas happy for long. Work prospects did not noticeably improve, though he struggled to establish new contacts; the old lady occupying rooms in his flat proved stubborn; and he started to talk ominously of 'nerves' to Mac. He was ill in March and felt neglected by his Oxford friends, apart from Mac and Haynes. His only refuge by March was 'dreams' of Oxford, which seemed to him more than ever an 'enchanted' place.[59] He spent his evenings reading Arnold's poetic evocation of it in 'Thyrsis' and 'The Scholar Gypsy'. By April he was 'getting on his own nerves' and felt 'absolutely run down', despite a holiday at Westgate in Kent with Haynes, who was still worried about his opium consumption.[60] A long-deferred visit to Oxford in June only made him more depressed. And when he did find the time to do his own writing, he judged his essays 'as unsaleable as ever'.[61]

Once again the answer seemed to him to lie in a move, this time to the country. Both he and Helen believed, in common with many town-dwellers at the start of the twentieth century, that a child should grow up (in Helen's words) 'in the freedom and beauty of the English countryside'.[62] Edward had read – and would later quote – Jefferies's advice: 'If you wish your children to think deep things – to know the holiest emotions – take them to the woods and hills, and give them the freedom of the meadows'.[63]

Two weeks' holiday at the 'delightful, little, uninteresting village of Horsmonden' in mid-Kent with Helen and Merfyn in July, when he planned to be 'healthy and stupid' and 'do nothing but fish all day long', provided a spur and by August Thomas was taking several trips to Kent in search of a cottage.[64] By 13 September 1901, he was 'very tired of London'.[65]

He was also suicidal again and made an attempt to kill himself on 8 August, his depression brought on perhaps by helping his parents to move out of his childhood home, Shelgate Road, with its memories of more carefree times:

> 11.30 p.m....I took over 1oz of old laudanum, meaning to take 1½oz but failing from nausea – Tonight perhaps [would] have succeeded in dying if Helen had not found me and given emetics.
> 1.00 a.m. The chief symptom was a throbbing of temples and incapacity to concentrate attention on a book for more than 3 minutes, though I was not sleepy ....
> 2.00 a.m. My motive for accepting emetics was a sense of caddishness for leaving Helen to depend on someone else. Sickness ¾ hour after emetics. I did not want to die though I disliked living, for in the more dangerous moment[s] I had no revelation of anything in death that was interesting, nor expected Death would unveil anything except worms.[66]

Helen, not surprisingly, was 'very melancholy' herself, as well as (Edward noted) uncharacteristically 'sluttish'. Something radical had to be done and they finally resolved to move out of London.

9

Rose Acre Cottage (October 1901–July 1903)

E dward failed to find the romantic cottage he and Helen had
in mind for a price they could afford. But he did eventually
discover an affordable house in Kent, a mile from the attractive
village of Bearsted, two miles from Maidstone and only ten
minutes' walk from the railway station. On 12 September 1901 he
reported to Mac he had almost completed on an agreement to rent
'a pretty house and gardens at Bearsted'. With Helen he was much
franker, returning from his bicycle ride into Kent to view it and
announcing that he had found them a house for only £32 a year, he
warned her not to expect 'any sort of beauty in it'.[1]

Though Helen could not believe that a house with such a
promising name as 'Rose Acre' could be anything but lovely, she
was bitterly disappointed by her first sight of it:

> It was a square box built of bright red brick, with slate roof
> and four uninteresting windows and a cheap stained-glass
> door in the middle. It stood nakedly on the top of a little
> hill in a railed-off piece of rough ground, untidy and bare
> and uncultivated, full of couch-grass and the ranker kinds of
> weeds. Inside there was a narrow passage with a room on each
> side papered with hideous red paper. Nothing could have been
> more unlike what I had imagined.[2]

Thomas himself was soon referring to Rose Acre as 'an ugly little
house'.[3] 'All other houses I look back on and see spiritual,' he

observed in his field notebook nine years later. 'This alone is unsubduable.'[4] Part of the problem was that he and Helen had fed largely on Romantic literature and expected a country cottage, especially one called 'Rose Acre', to resemble something from Wordsworth, Keats or Tennyson, preferably to be thatched and certainly to have roses in evidence. Objectively speaking and by twenty-first-century standards their cottage (which no longer exists) was a reasonably attractive if modest country dwelling and a distinct improvement on Nightingale Parade. For the first time the Thomases had a whole, detached house of their own. They also had a good-sized garden, even if it was riddled with weeds.

With respect to the garden at least, Edward was positive, beginning at once to tame it, the first of his many efforts to create the garden of his choice. Despite his disparaging remarks – 'the garden is ground to be dug (and to grow chiefly couch [grass])'[5] – it is clear from his offer to help Jesse Berridge with his own garden a few months later, that he enjoys gardening, or at least finds it an anaesthetic against melancholy: '…"*il faut cultiver notre jardin*". I find in gardening the properties of Lethe and Styx.'[6] Despite the physical strain involved in breaking up Rose Acre's heavy, uncultivated soil, he would find the garden 'a good friend' and gardening the 'best physic for [his] depression.'[7] Hard, regular work outdoors 'did [him] good against [his] will.'[8]

One aspect of gardening which particularly appealed to him was being self-supporting in fruit and vegetables. (Helen would become largely responsible for the flowers.) The first thing he did, as a surviving plan for one of the gardens shows, was to map out where his apple, pear, plum, cherry and nut trees, as well as soft fruit cages, would go; vegetables followed, methodically. His field notebooks contain long lists of plants and seeds sown each February and March. His pleasure in these annual rituals comes through in his poem, 'Sowing', which highlights another aspect of gardening he loved, the close contact with nature, from birds to stars, even the rain. It allowed him to enjoy all his senses, which combine in the last stanza of the poem to experience the rain, which he *hears*, as the *touch* of 'a kiss' or 'a tear' (a simile he will use again in 'Like the touch of rain'):

It was a perfect day
For sowing; just
As sweet and dry was the ground
As tobacco-dust.

I tasted deep the hour
Between the far
Owl's chuckling first soft cry
And the first star.

A long stretched hour it was;
Nothing undone
Remained; the early seeds
All safely sown.

And now, hark at the rain,
Windless and light,
Half a kiss, half a tear,
Saying good-night.[9]

Like most serious gardeners, Thomas was grateful for donations, frequently soliciting them from friends. He would thank Gordon Bottomley, for instance, for numerous presents of cuttings of the herbs bergamot, rosemary and 'lad's love', or 'old man', the last inspiring one of his finest poems. Another is sparked off by his love of garden smells:

Digging

Today I think
Only with scents, – scents dead leaves yield,
And bracken, and wild carrot seed,
And the square mustard field;

Odours that rise
When the spade wounds the root of tree,
Rose, currant, raspberry, or goutweed,
Rhubarb or celery;

The smoke's smell, too,
Flowing from where a bonfire burns
The dead, the waste, the dangerous,
And all to sweetness turns.

It is enough
To smell, to crumble the dark earth,
While the robin sings over again
Sad songs of Autumn mirth.[10]

A poem like 'Digging' suggests, as Edna Longley argues, that 'reciprocity with "the dark earth" integrates mind and body...in a lingering present day epiphany'.[11] It was a sense of integration that Thomas otherwise seldom experienced: he rarely felt (as he did in 'Sowing') that 'Nothing undone / Remained' after a day's writing.

Another weapon against depression was visits from friends, whom the Thomases could now accommodate at Rose Acre. Harry and Janet Hooton were among the first to be invited for a weekend, when Edward promises Harry 'to take a long walk and get hungry and drink beer', though his own preference would be to 'hang in the corner of a field, any field here, and hang till I am cured, like bacon'.[12] It is difficult to reconcile Thomas's apparent gloom with his friends' fond memories of visits. Duncan Williams, for instance, another early visitor, found it:

> a pleasant experience at any time to visit him in his country cottage, to spend the day in fishing or sauntering, and the evening in talk, to fetch the supper beer in a jug from the inn up the lane, to introduce or to learn of some newly discovered old song of the English or the Welsh folk, and sometimes to set off with him after dark for an all-night tramp. His keen powers of observation gave him an intimate knowledge of animal and plant life, his ear would frequently catch the cry of a bird when he and his companions alike were apparently immersed in conversation.[13]

Jesse Berridge, wife and son are also urged to visit, together with MacAlister, Haynes, Morgan and Nevinson, among others, most of whom do. In April 1902 his oldest friend, Arthur Hardy, comes to say goodbye before he leaves to join the South African police.

New neighbours were another distraction. The vicar, the Rev. John Scarth, in his last year of the 60 years' incumbency, talked to Thomas of Oxford and, less predictably, of his interest in ghosts. He seemed undismayed by his young neighbour's agnosticism and would later get him work with the Psychical Research Society. The Thomases' immediate neighbours, a retired wine merchant, Mr Crossman, and his wife, also invited them to dinner and the men afterwards indulged their fascination with maps, allowing Thomas to trace out on his neighbour's old maps forgotten footpaths, which he would afterwards explore. Located a few miles from the Pilgrims' Way, Bearsted encouraged his interest in ancient, historic routes.

Thomas's work was possibly his most effective way of fighting depression, however much he complained about it. He started at once an essay on a local professional gardener, whom he identifies only as 'Brown' in his 'Bearsted Notes',[14] almost certainly the original for 'Hengest: A Kentish Study'. This was one of the last pieces to be added to the book of essays he was hoping to publish, *Horae Solitariae*. Reviewing also kept him busy on the whole. Though he complained to Hooton of being 'dependent on the caprices of two uninterested Editors' (that is, of the *Daily Chronicle* and the *Week's Survey*, which had started sending him books in 1901), his income gradually increased.

There was never, nor could be, enough money to allay Thomas's anxiety, however. Before the end of his first month at Rose Acre he had sent out over 20 articles, in the hope of earning more, but 12 had come back, and he fully expected the other 8 to do so.[15] But he found consolation in smoking clay pipes and playing with Merfyn, whom he appreciated more as the child's vocabulary increased. His greatest pleasure lay in the surrounding countryside, which he found just as 'exquisite' as he had before his move there; it perhaps 'soothe[d] [him] too much and encourage[d] a mild despair' which he believed his 'favourite vice'.[16] Though there were carefree days out with Helen and Merfyn, his son eating blackberries, Edward stealing young trees to plant in his garden, his overriding mood was one of 'melancholy', which he was beginning to think 'largely...physical'.[17] Helen wrote that many days were 'saddened' for the family by his 'anxiety'. Unlike her husband, she believed that his melancholy 'had its roots in no material circumstances but came to cloud his spirits and our life, unbidden and uncontrollable'.[18] She was convinced it was inherited from his mother. Edward's detailed account of his 'despair' only three months after he had diagnosed it as 'largely physical' in October 1901, certainly suggests that it was more mental than physical, 'a sort of nervousness, a continuous palpitation and a sense of something approaching that never comes'.[19] A reference to guns at the end of this account adds a sinister note to this confession: 'I don't mean a sense of approaching good or bad luck, but merely a sense of something coming, as if [I] had heard a report and waited for the other barrel.'[20]

Edward's dread of something ominous approaching was given concrete form shortly after this letter to Mac of 9 February 1902, when Helen told him that, despite their precautions, she was pregnant again. Even she, who longed for more children, feared the effect it might have on Edward and agreed to try for an abortion. In a period when abortion was illegal in most circumstances, she consulted the more worldly Beatrice Logan (now Mrs Potbury) and her sister Irene, but neither could, or would, help, Irene reminding them of the expense it would involve. This had, for once, not occurred to Edward, who responded: 'It is of course utterly unimportant when compared with the doubled responsibility on two feeble minds and the anxiety before the responsibility begins.'[21] By 14 March he seemed resigned to the arrival of 'the little misfortune', which he describes cynically as 'some mark of our activities'.[22] Helen made one more attempt to terminate the pregnancy in London, but that too failed. What should have been a joyful event for her had become a nightmare. In her desolation she turned to Janet Hooton, still her closest friend:

> I know I shall love [the baby] when it lies in my arms, perhaps all the more because I know it will have only me to depend on for love: but now I cannot have any happy thoughts of it. I think of it only with tears in my eyes and a fierce pain in my heart, an intolerable aching which wears me out body and soul. It is terrible to me more than to most people perhaps for down crash come my purest ideals. I feel accursed because of this sweet thing lying near my heart. You ask why I do not want it? Because we are very poor; because it means more anxiety for Edward and more work for him. Home will become unendurable to him. Even now poverty, anxiety, physical weakness, disappointments and discouragements are making him bitter, hard and impatient, quick to violent anger, and subject to long fits of depression
>
> …He is selling some of his dearest books to pay for baby clothes and doctor, etc. and as he packs them up I know how he is rebelling at fate, how hard life seems to him, how he regrets it all. But on me who love him more than my life the burden falls doubly. I can no longer be…the one he looks to for all his joy, for all the sweetest things of life. He cannot love, Janet, he cannot respond to my love. How can he when all is so dark, and I, I have deprived him of it all, the joys of life and love and success.[23]

Helen and Edward would blame themselves for each other's misfortune throughout their married life, Helen for her husband's need to take on uncongenial work to support a family and Edward for condemning his wife to the life of poverty and hardship and denying her the many children she longed for. But Edward's reaction to the pregnancy almost certainly stemmed from more than money worries. While it is true that they were not well off, they were not on the poverty line. His reaction is more likely to have stemmed from the further tie a second child represented to marriage and a family, one more obstacle to the peaceful pursuit of his own work he had envisaged.

Fortunately Thomas's attention was soon distracted by the need to read proofs of his second book, *Horae Solitariae*. After repeated efforts to find work at all the popular magazines of the day had failed,[24] he had sent out proposals for a book of his own essays and what he called 'prose fancies' or 'prose-poems', to several publishers. (His request to one of the best-known agents of the day, James Pinker, to represent him had been rejected.) It was only after Haynes, with his usual generosity and concern for Thomas, had offered to pay some of the cost of production that they were accepted for publication by Gerald Duckworth. Partly to thank him, no doubt, Thomas had opened his collection with an epigraph taken from a poem Haynes had entered (unsuccessfully) for the Newdigate Prize at Oxford, 'Arcadia': 'Dreams have their truths for dreamers.'

These are words with which Thomas could identify closely and many of the pieces in *Horae Solitariae* attempt to describe his own dreams, or 'reveries' (his word). The collection is dedicated to another Oxford figure, Owen Edwards, and at least four of the sixteen pieces were written there, or inspired by the place – 'Two Scholars', 'Caryatids', 'On the Evenlode' and 'Horae Solitariae' – and show how widely his reading had been there; Lord Chesterfield jostles with Lamb, Victor Hugo with Thoreau. The dreams reflected in the early writings are of the joys of nature, of leisure, of the classics, of female beauty, of rural hospitality. The later pieces, written mainly in London – 'Recollections of November', 'February in England', 'A Gentle Craftsman', 'Digressions on Fish and Fishing' – express dreams of escape, especially to Wales. The two pieces written in Kent, 'Hengest' and 'Isoud of the White Hands', celebrate his discovery in that county of the joys of gardening and of following country lanes and footpaths, 'footprints perhaps of the immortals'. Common to them all is a sense of the poetry of existence. Though this manifests itself too flowerily at times for modern tastes, especially in the Oxford essays, where the influence of Pater and the Decadents is strongest, there are passages which anticipate the best of the later prose and poetry. The farmer's daughter in 'On the Evenlode', for instance, is the first of Thomas's beautiful but mysterious women, whose 'whole expression was one of holy wistfulness, but changed ceaselessly and even contradicted itself, like a picture seen again in other days: it was full of the sorrow there is in laughter, the joy in tears'.[25] She is encountered again in 'Isoud of the White Hands', where a 'pale glorious face' is seen fading into the dusk and, as Jan Marsh argues, becomes an image of the countryside's perfection. Despite the beauty and joy surrounding such a vision, she notes, this face is usually tinged with sadness: 'Dryad or angel, she represents that lost and inaccessible happiness which Thomas hoped to recapture in the "unique geniality" of the Kentish landscape.'[26] She would feature significantly in Thomas's poetry.

Thomas claimed that the 'worst things' in *Horae Solitariae* came 'first',[27] suggesting that he believed his writing had improved since Oxford. Nevertheless he read through his book 'with pleasure' when it was published in June 1902, though he made an exception for 'Epitaphs', put in only at the request of a friend.[28] When *Horae Solitariae* and *Rose Acre Papers* (1904) were reprinted in 1910 only three pieces came from *Horae Solitariae*, none of them from the Oxford days.

The reviewers were kind to Thomas for the most part, only gently criticizing what Thomas himself would later call *Horae Solitariae*'s 'airs and graces' and Haynes would describe as 'editions de luxe' stuff.[29] *The Times*, for example, praised his 'gift of a happy, if somewhat elaborate discourse.'[30] Most to his taste, because most understanding of his aims presumably, was the *Athenaeum*'s praise, which contradicts any suggestion that Thomas was unappreciated in his lifetime; this lengthy piece concludes with the words: 'This is one of the books which keeps alive in unfriendly days a tradition of scholarship and philosophic living to which we trust the world will return.'[31]

Thomas's own final verdict on *Horae Solitariae* would be mixed: 'sentence by sentence it is good, essay by essay it is bad',[32] but its publication was an unmixed blessing. He was now represented in public not by his juvenile *Woodland Life*, but by a more mature work which had received wider recognition. This gave him the confidence to carry on with his creative work at a time of great self-doubt. It also offered him his first contact with a man who would nurture that side of his writing and later become a close friend, Edward Garnett.

Yet Thomas was 'not cheered by all of this'.[33] His preferred work was still largely rejected, for reasons which Garnett, a shrewd, often inspired reader for several well-known publishing houses, identified in words which also explain his own admiration for it: Thomas's 'imaginative reveries,' he argued, were 'too pure in tone, too delicately haunting in their poetic appeal, to be apprehended by one in five hundred of the reading public'.[34] Even when his writing was published, it enjoyed, at best, modest sales and his attempts to write 'pot-boilers' always failed.

What depressed Thomas more than rejection of his work or even lack of money by mid-1902, however, was his inability to go on writing: 'I haven't enough strength to sit in a chair,' he tells Mac, 'I can't even read for more than five minutes…Can you wonder that I sometimes take opium?'[35]

By the end of June when work is still slack and he is tired of the struggle to pay the rent on Rose Acre, Thomas starts to look for a cheaper house. Even another holiday at Horsmonden, spent mainly fishing, 'standing up to his ankles in a black bog watching a usually motionless float', could not shift his settled depression this summer.[36] While England was in festive mood, celebrating the coronation of King Edward VII on 22 June, Thomas himself sat in Rose Acre feeling like 'a fowl on an addled egg'.[37] (He had noted the death of Queen Victoria on 22 January 1901 just as morosely in the diary he started writing again at Atheldene Road: 'The queen died. I hadn't a penny left to buy a stamp.') August and September he found 'sad months',[38] the birth of his second child looming.

One small consolation, which would increase greatly with time, was the start of a friendship with Gordon Bottomley. Four years older than Thomas, Bottomley was also like him virtually unknown in 1902, when he had published only two slim volumes of poetry and a verse play, but would later establish himself as part of the northern arts scene and one of the Georgian poets loosely gathered around Edward Marsh, who brought out a series of *Georgian Poetry* anthologies from 1912 to 1922. (Bottomley would be represented in all but the last of the five volumes.) He would also establish himself as one of a group of poets, which included Yeats, who would attempt to revive the verse play; *King Lear's Wife* being his best-known work in the genre. His main poetic influences were the later Victorian poets, the Pre-Raphaelites and William Morris.

Bottomley recalled Thomas's first letter to him as being from Oxford, 'an amusing letter in which he said he addressed me with the same confidence as that with which an idiot addressed a letter to God and posted it in a red pillar-box'.[39] (A sense of humour was evident on both sides from the start.) The date of Thomas's initial letter was, in fact, 30 September 1902, when Bottomley's first play, *The Crier by Night*, may have aroused his interest. His review of this, which came out two months later, underlines their distinct difference in literary taste, yet also expresses admiration for 'a natural magic' in the verse.[40]

Bottomley was already in regular correspondence with Helen, whose father, James Ashcroft Noble, he had greatly admired, especially his *The Sonnet in England* (1893). When Bottomley sent some of his own work to Noble, the latter had sent it on to another protégé, Edward Thomas. After Noble's death in 1896, Bottomley began to include Helen in his letters to the family and, after her marriage, Edward, too.

Bottomley, like Noble, suffered from a tubercular complaint, in his case one which affected his lungs, and by 1902 he had been living a mainly invalid existence for ten years. Though born a Yorkshireman, by 1902 he had passed many years in the romantic limestone country of the north-west, between Windermere and the sea-coast of Low Furness and North Lonsdale, detained there by his ill-health. The two poets would not meet until 1903, on one of Bottomley's rare visits to London. After that Thomas would gladly make the long train journey to the Lake District to visit Bottomley whenever possible.

The two men were different in a number of ways apart from literary style. Bottomley, despite his ill-health, gave an impression of physical robustness, 'a large, kind, shrewd, observant, brown bear of a man with a strong beard', according to Edith Sitwell.[41] Whereas Bottomley thought that Thomas 'resembled Haydon's life-mask of Keats in feature and expression', though quite unlike that tubercular young poet in other ways, being 'tall, straight, manly – always lean and sinewy, moving with a long, tireless countryman's stride'.[42] While Bottomley was forced to rest, often to lie in bed most of the day, Thomas (he recalled) 'walked greatly... in the north... mainly over and among the hills and fells which surround[ed] the foot of Windermere'.[43] Whereas Bottomley would not marry until 1905, at the age of 31, Thomas's own early marriage was registered by Bottomley as a 'premature assumption of the responsibilities of life' which 'tended to make him an employé of publishers and editors, a writer of books to order'.[44] (Bottomley would consider Helen's portrait of her husband, in *As It Was* and *World Without End*, as 'two below-stairs novelettes'. According to one of his later visitors, Stanley Snaith: 'his references to these confections came as near to rancour as his native benignity would allow'.[45]) Most significantly of all, Bottomley and Thomas had different literary aims, as well as styles, at the start, though these would lessen with time, as each influenced the other. Bottomley was primarily a poet and verse-dramatist, Thomas a prose-writer whose favourite form when they met was the essay, in which, he argued, 'there was scope... for everything a man could need to say'.[46] Thomas, while anxious from the start to promote Bottomley's publications, did not hesitate to criticize his style. In response to one of Bottomley's early publications, *White Nights*, for example, he told his friend, with his usual frankness, that he found something to like but in the diction 'a good deal to regret'.[47] Bottomley's was a 'jewelled and blossomy vocabulary', according to Thomas, a diction influenced heavily by Dante Gabriel Rossetti and the 'Decadents', whom Thomas himself was beginning to reject by 1902.[48] Bottomley quickly came to believe that Thomas should be writing poetry, not just the 'prose-poems' he identified in his early work. He would be one of the first to be shown Thomas's poetry when it began to 'run' and, though it was very different from his own, was gradually influenced by Robert Frost's theory behind it, 'that THE SOUND OF POETRY is PART OF ITS MEANING'.[49]

Despite these differences the friendship was, as Snaith argues, 'a marriage of true minds'.[50] They shared a deep love of literature, including the classics, which transcended any differences on the subject. Thomas's letters are full of new writers he has discovered, or requests for literary information from a man who is even more widely read than himself, despite a limited formal education.

Bottomley was also very musical, encouraging Thomas's own interest in folk-songs. Bottomley's background was partly Scottish and their shared sense of a Celtic heritage was one more tie between them. Once Thomas started visiting Bottomley in 1904 yet another similarity would emerge, their interest in the life of ordinary country people.[51]

R. George Thomas calls Bottomley Thomas's 'ideal reader'[52] and there were undoubtedly benefits to him from the relationship. Apart from practical matters like proofreading, or supplying music for songs, Bottomley became one of Thomas's few trusted confidants. He appeared to understand him better than Thomas understood himself at times. He could talk to Bottomley of almost anything, including his opium-taking, his depression, even his infatuation with an 18-year-old girl. While he called Bottomley 'Comforter', Bottomley called him 'Edward the Confessor'.

One area Thomas did not normally discuss in any detail in his letters to Bottomley was his family life, possibly because he thought Helen would do so. But in his third letter to Bottomley, of 31 October, having already sent a postcard to announce the birth of his second child on 29 October, he tells Bottomley: 'Helen and the girl are very well, and Helen at least is cheerful, but I am still excited and can hardly read – work pours in more often than it used to, and of a difficult kind sometimes. So the only peaceful talk I can joy [sic] now is reading letters and going over the Christian names of women.'[53] His letter to Jesse Berridge, whose own wife had just given birth to their second child in September, is more explicit:

> …item, a daughter [who] arrived at 10.45 last night leaving Helen out of breath but cheerful. Don't congratulate: perhaps in 1920 you may. 'It' is an ugly, healthy thing, with a lot of black hair and blue eyes. Helen is very well today…what shall we [call] it? There are no ugly names I find. I incline to Mary, Rachel, Maudlin, or – Megalostrate![54]

'Maudlin' and 'Megalostrate' were fortunately resisted and Bronwen ('Branwen' is a leading character in the *Mabinogion*) was added to 'Rachel' and 'Mary', keeping alive the tradition of Welsh names started with Merfyn.

Thomas would rapidly lose the detachment suggested by his letter to Jesse about his daughter. Unlike his relationship with Merfyn, from whom he had been separated for several months after his birth, he bonded rapidly with Bronwen, who quickly became his favourite. Though he had grown to appreciate Merfyn more once he and Helen started to live together, as time went by their relationship became more difficult. Both were too reserved for easy communication. Thomas would admit to Bottomley that he was 'not always patient of [Merfyn's] petulance and inverte-brateness...he is very much like me'.[55] Merfyn's own feeling was that he 'did not understand [his father] nor he me': he claimed to have 'happy memories' of their life together, 'of his gentle kindness, of his knowledge and appreciation of the countryside and the simple things in life'.[56] Yet a coldness would persist between the two until just before Thomas's death. Part of the problem may have lain in Thomas's hope, when Merfyn was still a baby, that he would be able to 'control and guide the thing I loved'; as he told Mac: 'Briefly, I suppose, I wanted to make [Merfyn] what I should have liked to be myself but couldn't.'[57] He became a conscientious but not warmly loving father to his son, perhaps unconsciously mimicking his own father's relation to him. A close friend of the family, Eleanor Farjeon, observing Thomas with his son on numerous occasions, would ask: 'Don't you think you are unnecessarily hard on Merfyn?' – to which he would reply, 'Perhaps I am – but it gives him something to kick against', a rather chilling response.[58]

With Bronwen there was never any question of her father resisting her, partly because she dealt with him so skilfully. Temperamentally quite different from either Edward or Merfyn, she was a joyful extrovert from birth. Eleanor Farjeon, who understood Edward more than most, described Bronwen as someone 'who adored her father and was adored by him' and who 'seemed to know by instinct that the way to help irritability is not to be hurt by it'.[59] Her nature was 'very gay', Eleanor recalled: 'to a sharp accent from her father she answered airily – "Very well, very well, my dear sir!" and did what he wanted smilingly'.[60] Though she differed from her father in significant ways – she did not enjoy long walks, for instance – she shared other important interests with him, in particular his love of wild flowers. Edward fondly recorded her reaction as a young child to the loss of a wild rose she had picked but broken while she walked home: 'It's gone. It's broke! It's gone, its gone, gone, gone.'[61] Bronwen's childish word would provide the germ for one of Edward's most poignant poems of loss, many years later, 'Gone, gone again'. Above all he appreciated his daughter's sheer joy in life, so often denied to him. When Bronwen was only 4 he would note in a folder marked 'Projects':

Bronwen's vivacity in talking, laughing, running, merely looking at you w[ith] wide eyes, or throwing her head right back so as to thicken her white neck in abandonment of laughing – her life is like a flame burning straight [as? among?] dry wood so that one wonders how it can last – the joy of the flame tearing through obstacles, careless, unconscious, determined, vivacious – She flames along as she runs, her laugh is a flame, her eye is a flame and we must [look?] at it.[62]

The story he did write about Bronwen, 'The Flower-Gatherer', which imagines the death by drowning of a young girl, shows how much he valued but feared to lose his flame-like elder daughter. She complemented him in a way neither his son nor his wife could.

Though 'work poured in', as Thomas told Bottomley, two days after Bronwen's birth it could not prevent his 'quarterly alarms' about rent. This second child, who added to Helen's joy, initially seems only to have increased his anxiety. Even the news that, with the death of the poet Lionel Johnson, he would become chief reviewer for the *Daily Chronicle*, could not lift him from his settled depression. His choice of reading at this time is revealing – his old favourite, Robert Burton's *Anatomy of Melancholy*, Boethius's *Consolations of Philosophy*, Apuleius's *Metamorphosis* and Thomas à Kempis's *Imitation of Christ*.

His melancholy was increased by the departure of MacAlister, still one of his closest friends, for a job in Canada, as a military attaché to a Canadian general. By 25 December 1902, after a day spent with Helen and the children, he told Mac that he 'often wanted to go away and walk and walk for a week anywhere so long as it is by an uncertain road'.[63] His melancholy, he maintains, quoting Browning, 'grows old along with [him]'. He despairs, not only because his reviewing leaves him little time for his own work, but that he has no time simply 'to be non-literary and free to think or better still not to think at all…to let the wind and the sun do my thinking for me, filling my brain'.[64] This Christmas letter closes with thoughts of death, to the time when he will be 'a part of a great calm under nettles and yews and grass'.

It was not, therefore, just the need to earn money that made Thomas leave for a stay in London on 11 February 1903. It was also an equally strong need to get away from his family, a break from his irritability Helen seems to have welcomed on this occasion. This need for separation, mainly on Edward's but sometimes on Helen's part, would recur frequently until he left for the army in 1915. A 16-mile walk along the Pilgrims' Way shortly after Bronwen's birth had evidently not been enough to satisfy Edward's urge to get away. Nor had a brief visit to London for research on the edition of the poet John Dyer he was preparing for Owen Edwards's Welsh Library Series.

Yet it is equally true that once away from the noise and distraction of family life, Thomas would begin to feel unbearably lonely. He complained bitterly of his isolation in Kent, away from his friends, but felt even more isolated in London in February 1903, despite being in frequent contact with his parents, brothers and friends. However, he had resolved to stay a month.

It was a fate from which Nevinson rescued him, with characteristic generosity. The publishers A. & C. Black had asked Nevinson to write 50,000 words on Oxford, to accompany a series of pictures by a well-known artist of the day, John Fulleylove, but he was too busy with other commitments and suggested that Thomas might like to do it instead. The fee would be £100, a large amount of money by Thomas's standards. Though it was not a job he fancied, he accepted Nevinson's offer gratefully and was highly relieved when the publishers agreed to the change, their only proviso being that Thomas must provide 60,000 rather than 50,000 words for the same fee, to be delivered by the end of July 1903.

Thomas wrote at once to Helen, whom he knew would be delighted by the news. His own reaction was more mixed: while grateful to be relieved of immediate money worries, he disliked the tight deadline and the journeyman aspect of the writing, suspecting that the text would be subservient to the illustrations. But at least he could now legitimately return home. So, after a short (and remarkably sober) visit to Oxford, ostensibly to research his book, he was back in Bearsted, with £20 in his pocket from the advance. He could now carry out his intention of leaving 'the ugly little house', Rose Acre, and settling in a more romantic cottage on the village green. For the fourth time in less than three years, he hoped that a change of house might work magic on his melancholy.

10

'The Valley of the Shadow'[1]: Ivy Cottage, Bearsted Green (July 1903–May 1904)

'We are to move to a pretty, old house on the village green, with a pair of lime trees on the two strips of lawn in front. It is covered with ivy and has shuttered windows, and a dormer in the roof,' Thomas wrote to Bottomley on 17 April 1903 in a letter which conveys a renewed sense of hopefulness. His letter to MacAlister, two months later, after the family migrated to Ivy Cottage, Bearsted Green, is even more positive: 'We like it immensely,' he enthuses uncharacteristically of the small, tiled, half-timbered cottage which faced the 'wide, shaded and quaint' village green.[2] It was the house he and Helen had dreamt of when they first planned to move to the country. Each time they came down from the bleak, windy heights of Rose Acre, they had coveted Ivy Cottage. It had eventually become available in mid-June 1903, just as Thomas was paid the remainder of his advance on *Oxford* and was able to afford the rent.

Town-born and bred, Thomas loved the rusticity of village life, from the farmyard noise of fowls, ducks and pigs at the back of Ivy Cottage to that of his neighbour, the village wheelwright, 'whose hammer [was] quite a peaceful melodist'.[3] For the first time since their arrival in Kent, both he and Helen felt (as an old labourer's wife told them) that they were 'in the middle of everything'.[4]

Helen, who did not suffer from Edward's shyness, loved the social side of village life, of getting to know Mrs Adams, Mrs Ivens and Mrs Farewell, for example, and gossiping with the landlord of the local pub. Edward enjoyed his carpentry lessons from their wheelwright neighbour, which concluded more often than not with a visit to the same pub and more gossip.

Helen shared Edward's hope that a change of house might improve their difficult family life and for a time it seemed as if the move to Bearsted Green might do just that. 'At first,' she wrote, 'we were so busy and so happy settling down in our new house – and this time one which we both loved – that [I hoped that] the cloud that I dreaded so much would dissolve, and that we should be free of it for ever.'[5]

Edward was, in any case, simply relieved to have finished writing *Oxford* to a tight deadline and to begin with he was happy in his relative freedom. But his efforts to get to know the villagers were not entirely successful; he found the majority of his neighbours somewhat wary of him. The simple country workmen he tried to contact were (unlike their vicar who had retired and moved away, as had the retired wine-merchant, Mr Crossman) either suspicious of newcomers, or frightened of someone much more educated than themselves – 'quite kindly,' he noted, 'but a little mystified.'[6] He is unlikely to have been able to talk to them about *Oxford*, currently going through the press.

Work on the book had, nevertheless, been a distraction and, according to Helen, 'helped ward off the dreadful attacks of melancholy.'[7] Publication itself, set for autumn, held the promise of recognition and more congenial commissions. Thomas had had to write it at great speed and was not proud of the finished product, liking only 'one or two' pages in it.[8] 'It is neither good hackwork nor good Edward Thomas,' he told Mac, whom he had included in the planning almost from the start.[9] The initial outline, sent to Mac on 16 March 1903, suggests how little time there had been to conceive of anything but the simplest scheme, with a chapter on each of the topics he wanted to cover:

I	History of a typical college (dateless & partly fanciful)
II	Dons – a series of types
III	Undergraduates– a series of types
IV	College Servants – [a series of types]

The only significant additions made to these topics would be an introductory chapter 'On Entering Oxford' and 'In a College Garden'. The
result, like most of the travel books to follow, would be a curious mixture,
part history book, part autobiography (despite Thomas's denials), part
guidebook especially to the countryside round Oxford, mapped out in a
series of walks, and, above all, a eulogy to the city which remained Thomas's
'great good place' throughout his life.

John Moore argues that it was a 'thousand pities' that the publishers
demanded the book so quickly, 'for *Oxford* was a book which Edward
wanted to write'[10] – 'I should have liked to take years over it,' he told
MacAlister.[11] But the need to work swiftly sometimes brought out the
best in Thomas. While he may be right to imply that *Oxford* was not
the best he could do, it is nevertheless a charming, and inadvertently
revealing book which loves its subject, the walks especially well done. His
insights into undergraduate life at Oxford at the end of the nineteenth
century also reward reading.

The writing of *Oxford* had kept Thomas busy not just with the
writing but also with several trips for research to both Oxford and
London. During two or three of the London visits in May and early
June he had enjoyed meeting Bottomley, who was taking advantage of
an unusual respite from his lung troubles to spend a month there. So this
meant that besides his usual research in the Reading Room of the British
Museum, Thomas had the pleasure of getting to know Bottomley in
person. Bottomley still remembered, over 40 years later, Thomas's 'mellow
voice with an attractive huskiness' as he called out in Bottomley's hotel
apartment to introduce himself.[12]

Just as *Oxford* had helped ward off melancholy in the first half of 1903,
however, the effort needed to meet the deadline may have brought it on in
the second half of the year, Helen believed:

> The Oxford book was a tremendous strain, and that added to anxieties
> about money and so on, have altogether shattered his nerves. He can

now write no more than he is obliged to do, and that with difficulty. His mind once so rich in thought and idea has become incapable of either and he sits whole days doing absolutely nothing.[13]

The change had not been immediate. In July and August Thomas had still been able to take walks along the Pilgrims' Way, almost certainly with future books and essays in mind. But *Oxford* had left him 'dried up' and he felt he would 'never do good, slow, leisurely work again'.[14] But he had managed to carry out his reviewing for the *Daily Chronicle*, producing at least 35 reviews for the paper between mid-June and the end of December. 'I have a resigned doggedness in doing what I must to live,' he told Mac.[15] Gardening, too, he managed, finding it even more helpful in his increasingly despairing state.

By the beginning of September, at Helen's insistence, Edward consulted a London physician, Dr Segundo, who diagnosed 'intercostal neuralgia', a rare pain condition in which the patient feels pain around the ribs, and prescribed arsenic, strychnine, cod-liver oil and 'plasmon' cocoa, together with a 'good' diet containing plenty of meat, plus regular habits, freedom from worry and a more active social life. Very little of this was calculated to help Thomas. To be fair to Dr Segundo, psychiatry was still in its infancy and the discoveries of pioneers such as Jung and Freud in Vienna had not yet reached England. Virginia Woolf, who experienced a number of nervous breakdowns, would find like Thomas that treatment in England at the beginning of the twentieth century consisted mainly of encouraging the patient to put on weight.

One helpful part of Dr Segundo's treatment, at least for Helen and the children, was to send Thomas away for a holiday to Swindon. However frank Helen sometimes was in her account of their relationship, she rarely spoke honestly of the suffering imposed on Edward's family by his breakdowns, perhaps out of shame. She omits to mention crockery thrown at the wall in a rage, or the cloth pulled furiously from beneath the tea-time meal, for example, incidents reported later by close friends. But in her second letter to Mac, still in Canada, in 1903 she admitted: 'Edwy's condition seemed to get worse, and I felt that if immediate action was not taken I should collapse too...you see in the terrible state of nervous and irritability things occurred here which could not be helped in a household with two young children...It was a terrible time for the least annoyance

...a thing out of place, the children's chatter – affected him as a fearful calamity.'[16] Yet perversely, 'the only people [Edward] liked to see were the two children' who not surprisingly, he told Mac, 'were not fond of seeing my silly, haggard face'.[17] Worst of all for the home-loving Helen was her husband's apparent dislike of home during such attacks.

His three weeks' holiday in Swindon helped Thomas a little. Though still 'irritated and bored by everything and everybody', in avoiding work as much as possible and spending whole days out of doors walking and fishing he did 'pretty well'.[18] With more congenial company than his aunt and grandmother, he believed he would do even better. The only people he spoke to were a tramp and a labourer, which made his father accuse him furiously of 'condescension'.[19] Yet his old problem remained: 'I can't write. I feel as I did before I came here, quite barren and stale.'[20]

Helen, meantime, was taking a ten-day holiday in the Lake District with friends, leaving Merfyn and Bronwen with her mother-in-law. Shortly after she arrived back in Bearsted, Edward himself returned, unable to 'endure being away from home any longer'.[21] Once there, all the old symptoms returned: 'Restlessness is becoming a disease with me,' he wrote to Mac,

> I hardly know why. I am always finding fault and cannot sit down for half
> an hour without remembering that the servant has forgotten to do some
> small thing, and off I go to do it, spoiling my work and temper. I really
> feel that I shall never again be able to write my best.[22]

It was at this point Helen asked Mac for help. If he could lend her the money due to her from the remainder of her legacy (£60) the following January, and was willing to invite Edward to visit him in Canada, both she and the doctor believed that the sea air on the crossing, a complete change of scene and time with one of his oldest friends would help. MacAlister agreed at once, but Edward refused to go, 'afraid' of such a long sea-journey and radical change, as well as of spending so much money, whoever provided it. (MacAlister, in the end, had insisted on *giving* Helen the money for the fare.) Helen's urgent pleas almost changed Edward's mind, but he found the perfect excuse to stay: 'the "Chronicle" is to be re-organised at the end of the year,' he tells Mac, '...and I must be on the spot when the new editor is installed'.[23]

In fact, when the change of editors at the *Daily Chronicle* took place, Thomas was not 'on the spot' to urge his claims, but staying in Warminster with another Oxford friend, Morgan, who was working there. His condition had worsened again in late November and, after another few days in Swindon fishing with his artist brother, Ernest, he had gone on to share lodgings with Morgan on Salisbury Plain. His time was spent mainly in writing reviews and talking to Morgan: 'So much talking I never did before and I am led to believe that it is good for me.'[24] Morgan himself was apparently in a similar condition and they 'talked furiously...We get on very well and have many long talks, both critical and autobiographical and I feel myself stimulated, and I am conscious of more purely intellectual powers that I generally am,' Edward wrote to Helen not very tactfully....'He makes me think afresh...we are seldom dull and never bored.'[25] Dutifully sticking to his regime of expensive remedies, including the cod-liver oil and 'plasmon' cocoa, he pleased his doctor by putting on almost a stone in weight, as instructed. But he was still unable to write anything of his own.

This inability to return to his more normal creative work seems to have been both the main cause and the main result of his depression. No one who tries to understand Thomas can ignore his recurring bouts of melancholy. While Helen continued to believe that they were a result of a 'morbid...and introspective temperament,'[26] Edward himself attributed it to a much wider range of possible causes, though he also suspected that they lay more in the mind than in the body. After a particularly bad spell in which he had 'hoped for death', he told Mac:

> I am not physically weak. I sleep very well and long. I can walk 25 miles in a day or fish for 12 hours and then walk 10 miles without much discomfort. On the other hand, I am sometimes terribly fatigued by half a mile or by 2 hours writing, and I sit down and wish I could sleep for ever: sometimes I sit for hours and can do nothing but submit to the play of the imps that bring into my mind the most mad and trifling and undesired thoughts...[27]

At the same time Helen observed that 'the least physical unwellness ma[de] Edward at once depressed and irritable' and Thomas believed that his 'great enemy' was 'physical exhaustion'.[28]

When looking for possible causes, Thomas's first thought was to wonder if his 'indiscretions and intemperance in alcohol, opium and tobacco, ha[d] at last taken effect'.[29] However, while accepting that they had been 'serious', he could say with perfect honesty that since moving to Bearsted Green in June 1903, he had 'lived moderately in every way', apart from possibly working or walking too much at times. He still took opium when finding it particularly difficult to write and it may, eventually, have acted as a depressant, but he had too many responsibilities and not enough money to indulge in alcohol, tobacco or opium excessively.

Thomas's second thought was to wonder if 'continued journalism [had] at last destroyed my always slender capacity for writing what I liked'.[30] Yet when his review work started to dry up in 1911, he would tell Bottomley that his depression at that point was linked to 'the necessity of producing many books instead of a few and much reviewing'.[31] Work, even reviewing, was 'the only thing', he claimed that helped him fight his 'usual devils'.[32] He never held his journeyman work entirely responsible for his depression.

One of his greatest fears by 1903 was that he was losing his 'religious attitude' towards nature.[33] Though he found this almost too painful to admit, he believed it helped to explain his depression this year, since it made his own writing even more difficult. While 'one little note used to recall much of the glory of former days out of doors,' he tells Mac, 'now it is barren and that means a great deal, because I cannot bring myself to write about anything else'.[34] This inability to enter into nature completely left him with a sense of desolation he would try to pin down in 'The Glory', when he began to write poetry eleven years later:

> The glory invites me, yet it leaves me scorning
> All I can ever do, all I can be,
> Beside the lovely of motion, shape, and hue,
> The happiness I fancy fit to dwell
> In beauty's presence...[35]

Yet even in the mapping out of his despair, Thomas reveals his intimate knowledge of nature – 'the pale dust pitted with small dark drops', for example – as he describes his attempts to grasp the essence of what he sees:

> ...Shall I now this day
> Begin to seek as far as heaven, as hell,

Wisdom or strength to match this beauty, start
And tread the pale dust pitted with small dark drops,
In hope to find whatever it is I seek,
Hearkening to short-lived happy-seeming things
That we know naught of, in the hazel copse?

The duality of his thoughts and feelings, his sense of having only a joint tenancy of them, which would express itself most memorably in 'The Other', is hinted at here in a poem which veers between joy and despair, verbalized in a series of paradoxes and questions reflecting this uncertain state:

Or must I be content with discontent
As larks and swallows are perhaps with wings?
And shall I ask at the day's end once more
What beauty is, and what I can have meant
By happiness? And shall I let all go,
Glad, weary, or both? Or shall I perhaps know
That I was happy oft and oft before,
A while forgetting how I am fast pent,
How dreary-swift, with naught to travel to,
In Time? I cannot bite the day to the core.

The final image here of biting into an apple gives physical expression to the deep, simple satisfaction which eludes the narrator. Without stating it, Thomas has conveyed his most persistent problem, the inability simply to be, as nature herself appears to do, instead of 'sickled o'er with the pale cast of thought'.[36] Poetry itself may offer the only possibility of resolving the problem, the narrator's equivalent of the freedom of the birds' wings.

Another possible reason Thomas gave Mac for his depression – 'the dirtiness and confusion of my house' – was the most serious problem of all, not because Helen's housewifely abilities really mattered, nor just because it highlighted a temperamental difference between them which could never be resolved, but because Edward perceived it as a problem and reacted violently: 'Practically not an hour of my day passes without some irritation caused by this:...some tell me this irritation is an effect of my state of health of mind. Perhaps so. I believe it is the cause and apparently it is ineradicable.'[37]

Almost as an afterthought Thomas adds to his list of possible triggers for depression, 'lack of company, lack of money'. Not only is Helen not sufficient 'company', he implies, but he also holds her responsible, through 'small extravagances' and 'great mismanagement', for the lack of money. Both charges are unfair. He would have worried about money whatever his circumstances: it was one way in which his constant anxiety revealed itself. (Bottomley remembered Thomas telling him that his greatest fear was of bankruptcy.) As for company, even in congenial male company, Thomas felt alone: 'with me,' he claimed, 'social intercourse is only an intense form of solitude'.[38] As William Cooke points out, 'he seems to have had enormous difficulty in experiencing himself "together with" others...and "at one" with himself. Instead he could experience himself only in despairing aloneness, which accentuated his introspection to the point of acute self-torment.' 'He was isolated without being self-sufficient and without being able to muster any normal sense of human solidarity.'[39]

Despite all this Thomas was convinced that his salvation depended on a person, but that person could not be Helen, was unlikely to be any woman. Though it would probably be an exaggeration to say, as Haynes did, that his 'melancholy instantly disappeared' with close male friends,[40] he was sometimes able to forget his problems in their company. His brother Julian claimed the same and objected strongly to John Moore's life of Edward of 1939, 'which makes him out to be a sort of imbecile kept just within the borders of sanity by the too loving tenderness of his wife'.[41] Helen's 'too loving tenderness' was in fact part of the problem, according to Edward, who wrote in his diary in autumn 1903: 'If I walk 25 miles and have fishing or forcible stimulating company at the end of it, I am almost happy. If I walk ½ mile or less and come here [i.e. Bearsted] and find Helen sympathetic I am fatigued and almost dying, calling for death.'[42] A more astringent, or more detached, response to her husband's outbursts might have helped curb them. It is significant that his irritability seems not to have manifested itself with his male friends. Helen herself realized that her all-forgiving tolerance was not always good for Edward, and 'used to wish and pray to be different': 'if only I could be angry at his unkindness instead of hurt, I thought it might be better for him. If only I could take no notice, instead of pretending not to do so. How I longed to be able to alter my nature.'[43] Helen also believed, however, that though Edward had told her frankly that he could not 'love' her, he needed her for his survival. In 'saner times,' she told Mac, she realized that 'his troubles are of his own making almost entirely.'[44]

Thomas would finally accept that neither he nor the doctors he consulted in turn could find the root cause of his depression: 'Or rather I think *I* [my italics] do,' he told Bottomley, 'but it is so many things.'[45] Nowadays we might be tempted to label him as 'bipolar', yet he suffered none of the manic phases of that illness. Perhaps, in the end, it was simply, as he himself described it, his 'writer's melancholy which he must have':[46] 'For work that depends always and entirely upon a man's own invention and impulse always lets the artist down into deep waters of misery now and then.'[47] It certainly compelled him to 'seek as far as heaven, as hell' and gave him insights denied to less tortured people.[48]

One practical result of Thomas's depression, throughout his marriage, was guilt at the effect this had on the family. As a consequence he was often absent from home; his three-week stay with Morgan in December 1903 would set the pattern. With equal predictability, he would return home calmer, as he did on 22 December 1903. He had missed his family and was glad to be back with them, but inevitably the mood did not last. By the end of the month, after only a week at home, he was off again. The reason he gave on this occasion, as on so many later ones, was the need to find more work. Yet his quick visit to London on his way home from Warminster, when he had finally met the *Daily Chronicle*'s new literary editor, James Milne, as he took over from Nevinson, had established that, far from suffering from Nevinson's departure as he had feared, Thomas had benefited. For, however dismissive he was of Milne as an 'illiterate and clannish Scot',[49] Milne regarded him as his best reviewer and urged him to sign his pieces. Thomas quickly found the extra work he claimed to need, at the *World* as well as the *Daily Chronicle*, and was even asked to write another 'colour' book by the publishers of *Oxford*, A. & C. Black – on Holland – which he turned down.

It is quite clear that Thomas's reason for going to stay with Helen's sister and brother-in-law, Irene and Hugh McArthur, in Chancery Lane, for the whole of January 1904, was as much from restlessness as a need to consolidate his position at the *Daily Chronicle*. He was also able to enjoy the male company he missed so much in the country. Besides spending time with established friends, like Berridge and Duncan Williams, he made at least one new one, Arthur Ransome. Thomas met Ransome through an old school friend, Tom Clayton, a 'cheerful and serene and puzzling man,' according to Thomas,[50] who was in the habit of visiting the St George's vegetarian restaurant, at 37 St Martin's Lane in London, where two floors up, in the smoking-room, Clayton played chess with his brother. He may indeed have introduced Thomas to the St George's, which was to become an important focus of his life during the next decade, the location of an informal literary salon Thomas established once his visits to London settled into a regular pattern. London at the turn of the twentieth century was full of such meeting-places, some more formal than others. Thomas already knew the Pharos Club in Henrietta Street, nicknamed the 'cock-and-hen club' because it allowed women members, and the Yorick Club nearby in Bedford Street.

Arthur Ransome, fresh from the provinces, remembered vividly his first meeting at St George's with Edward Thomas, 'a man with a fine-cut, sad face, looking very much unlike a townsman.'[51] They left the smoking-room together, Ransome accompanying Thomas to a nearby booksellers, Thorp's, where he regularly sold the books he had just reviewed, then along the Strand and Fleet Street to the *Daily Chronicle*, for more books to review. He also met Thomas later at Duncan Williams's 'at homes' in Gray's Inn Road, where he felt he was 'tolerated' for Thomas's sake. When he took Thomas home to meet his family in Balham, however, they took one look at his rough country tweeds, considered 'most unsuitable for wear in London' and christened him 'Teddy Tommy'. Ransome's widowed mother, still hoping for a solid career in business for her son, included Thomas among the 'dangerous Bohemian' friends she feared were encouraging his literary ambitions.

Ransome, six years younger than Thomas, admired him and his writings greatly. To begin with Thomas responded positively, inviting him to keep him company at Bearsted Green in March 1904 when, according to Ransome:

> ...he and I and his dog Rags used to walk ourselves tired, eat bread and cheese and onions in a country inn and come home to smoke long clay pipes which we lit with spills twisted from the leaves of the books of would-be poets he had reviewed and knew to be unsaleable even to

our most omnivorous benefactor Mr Thorp. Thomas had a home-made bookshelf by his fireside and kept it stocked with verse meet for the burning.[52]

Shortly after the visit, Thomas would tell Bottomley, who knew Ransome well from his childhood holidays in the Lake District, that he had found Ransome 'very pleasant company' and thought him 'a remarkable boy'.[53] More importantly their long talks together had inspired Thomas to start writing again, his first essay for fifteen months. Ransome also found a publisher for a collection of four of Thomas's essays, 'bad, old published stuff,' according to the author, two of them ('An Autumn House' and 'Rain') dating back to Oxford days and written with what one of the book's few reviewers called 'a gold nib upon vellum'.[54] Thomas's collection, *Rose Acre Papers* (1904), would be second in a series started by an Ulverston printer (and friend of Ransome's) at the Lanthorn Press, following Ransome's *The Souls of the Streets* (1904). Thomas would dedicate his book to Bottomley, whom he considered indirectly responsible for publication through his admiration for one of the essays, 'Cleopatra (the Tragedy of a Poor Poet's Cat)'. Though not proud of *Rose Acre Papers*, he was even more dismissive of Ransome's book as 'prose in sugar'.[55] Its main interest for Thomas was the portrait of 'a man who knew himself', called Merlin: 'The keenness of his intellect has been sharpened on himself... He pierces in half an hour to the heart of a book, and sees what the author had arrived at, how far he had failed and why... He sees so clearly the pettiness of others that he cannot believe in the greatness of himself.'[56] 'Many independent people see me in "The Man who Knew Himself"', Thomas commented wryly to Bottomley.[57]

Thomas had returned home to Bearsted in February because Helen had fallen ill. The doctor had blamed insanitary drains in their quaint old cottage, which was also extremely cold and damp in winter. When the 17-month-old Bronwen caught pneumonia in March and nearly died, the Thomases decided to move again. Even without the series of family illnesses – Edward suffered from one of his worst fits of depression after an infected throat – they would probably have come to the same decision, with its promise of another new start. Once the drains at Ivy Cottage were fixed, as they were, there seemed no other reason for the move.

They had initially planned to move into 'red-brick country', no more than 18 miles from London, but finally decided on another house in the country. Meantime, almost certainly with the encouragement of Helen, he accepted an invitation to visit Bottomley and his family at Well Knowe House, just outside Cartmel. His week's stay in mid-April would set the pattern for the visits to follow, even after Bottomley had married in 1905 and left his parents' house. Part of Thomas's time would be spent writing, part taking solitary walks, since Bottomley was largely confined to his house, and a great deal of it talking with Bottomley 'in happy intimacy'.[58] Apart from keeping up with his regular reviewing work on this first visit, Thomas worked on a story he had started in one of his gloomiest moods in Kent, 'The Skeleton', which he discussed with Bottomley. Conceived initially as 'two pictures: first a beautiful, many-sided youth in Spring, and next his skeleton in Autumn, and I, or the teller of the story have murdered him', it suggests that Thomas held himself responsible for the death of his own youthful promise and hope. (As Thomas wrote in his field notebook this same month, 'like many a young man who loves life too passionately, he was sometimes in love with death'.[59]) With Bottomley's help it would eventually be published in the *Venture*, run by a friend of his, John Baillie. When Thomas dismissed his story and complained 'there is no form that suits me', Bottomley suggested he try the prose-poem, possibly the first to do so.[60]

Evenings at Well Knowe House were mostly spent listening to Bottomley play the spinet, or sing old folk-songs such as 'Somer Is Icumen In', with Thomas contributing some of his own favourites. His visit, he told Bottomley shortly after his return to Kent, had left him 'calmly glad' and 'decidedly better', an effect Bottomley would continue to have on him: 'Well Knowe is going into my memory, along with Oxford and the Pilgrim's Road and the Surrey and Wales and Wiltshire I knew as a child.'[61]

Predictably the calm was short-lived and by 12 May 1904 Thomas was 'busy, tired and neuralgic' and 'had still not found another house'.[62] A few days later the local paper advertised exactly what he and Helen wanted and they rented it immediately. Less than a week later they had moved in.

11

ELSES FARM (MAY 1904–OCTOBER 1906)

The new house was a large square farmhouse standing away
from the road in the midst of its own fields. Oast house, cow
sheds, stables, hayricks and a huge barn were grouped about it
on two sides. On the other side was a large garden and orchard,
and in the front was a little garden opening into a field in which
stood great oak trees, and in whose coppice-like hedges sang
innumerable nightingales.

– Helen Thomas, *World Without End*

Helen's description of Elses Farm conveys the pleasure both she
and Edward took in it throughout their stay. It was one of
the few of his numerous rented houses that Thomas liked without
reservation from the beginning to the end. He described himself
as 'deeply contented' there at times, an unusual admission from
him.[1] The fact that he was also as depressed, periodically, as in all
his other houses only shows how vain were the many moves he and
Helen made in the hope of improving his state of mind.

Yet there is no doubting the enjoyment that he, as well as the
whole family, derived from Elses Farm, to which they moved in
late May 1904. It was conveniently placed in the Weald of Kent,
near Sevenoaks and four miles equidistant from Tonbridge and
Penshurst. Helen particularly appreciated the house itself, its large
rooms, long, flagged passages leading to dairies and storerooms

and its 'immense' kitchen and scullery, with huge brick oven and two large coppers, one for brewing beer, the other for washing clothes.[2] She loved learning how to bake bread in the brick oven from the innkeeper's wife, Mrs Turner, who also helped in the house. She even enjoyed the heavy housework and gardening involved, 'anything which gave my strong body exercise and which satisfied my spirit with its human necessity'.[3] She was also delighted by the way Merfyn, at 4½, and Bronwen, at 19 months, responded, growing especially fond of the 50 or so cows in the meadow in front of the house and learning to know them by name.

Edward's equally positive response made itself felt in his work. After nearly three years' exploring rural Kent on foot he was familiar with the cycle of work on the land, but at Elses Farm gained a closer knowledge of it. Since the house was situated in the middle of a working farm, he was surrounded by its seasonal activities, from ploughing and sowing or planting, to the harvesting in early autumn of both hops and hay, at which he, Helen and the children sometimes helped. And though his poetry was not written until a decade later, the knowledge he absorbed at Elses Farm would feed into it, as well as into his prose. The close observation of 'February Afternoon', for instance, where 'Black rooks with white gulls following the plough / So that the first are last until a caw / Commands that last are first again'; the 'team's head-brass' of the horses pulling the plough in the poem of that name; even the description of 'Tall nettles' which inhabit neglected corners of farmyards was almost certainly informed by his first intimate contact with farming. 'Swedes', too, harks back to this period: the striking imagery of 'the white and gold and purple of curled fronds / Unsunned' when the swedes are uncovered, as being:

> ...more tender-gorgeous
>
> At the wood-corner where Winter moans and drips
> Then when, in the Valley of the Tombs of Kings,
> A boy crawls down into a Pharaoh's tomb
> And, first of Christian men, beholds the mummy,
> God and monkey, chariot and throne and vase,
> Blue pottery, alabaster and gold.[4]

was first conceived in *The Heart of England*, written at Elses Farm. And his personal involvement in the rituals of haymaking, little changed in rural

Kent at the turn of the century from ancient times, enabled him to write the evocative closing lines to 'Haymaking':

> ...All was old,
>
> This morning time, with a great age untold,
> Older than Clare and Cobbett, Morland and Crome,
> Than, at the field's far edge, the farmer's home,
> A white house crouched at the foot of a great tree.
> Under the heavens that know not what years be
> The men, the beasts, the trees, the implements
> Uttered even what they will be in times far hence –
> All of us gone out of reach of change –
> Immortal in a picture of an old grange.[5]

Hop-picking at the beginning of September was another important ritual which the Thomas family joined in, as Edward Garnett witnessed. Garnett, the publisher's reader responsible for Duckworth's publication of *Horae Solitariae*, had got to know Thomas personally by the time he moved to Elses Farm. A mutual friend had taken Thomas down to Garnett's country house, The Cearne, near Limpsfield, and, on his return visit to Thomas at Elses Farm, Garnett had coincided with the hop-harvest. The scene lingered in his memory 'as an idyll of gracious youth': 'The charm of Thomas in the freshness of his strength, of his beautiful eyes and hair which shone in the sunlight, brown bleached to fair gold, appeared at its best in the open air, recalling the people of the "Mabinogion", or some hero myth, such as that of the Argonauts.'[6]

It was not a compliment Thomas could return. By 1904, at the age of 38, Garnett had lost the strikingly romantic looks of his youth and put on weight, appearing to Walter de la Mare only a few years later as 'a ponderous, wild-looking figure, very tall, with grey, jowled cheeks and thick-lensed glasses: a frog-like face, or – as some writers thought, watching his alarming approach at a literary party, every possible button undone – more like an outrageous great grizzly'.[7] Fortunately, Thomas was undeterred by what another writer, Henry Green, called Garnett's 'pale-faced, menacing' appearance, and Garnett became a good friend and staunch ally.

As a publisher's reader not just for Duckworth, but also Cape, Dent and Fisher Unwin, Garnett was a particularly useful contact for Thomas as the younger man struggled to establish himself in the London literary world. His recommendations would secure the publication of several collections of the work Thomas most wanted recognized, his imaginative pieces. Like Bottomley, Garnett realized from the start that Thomas was basically a poet and encouraged him in that direction. He believed that Thomas's self-consciousness was 'akin to [his] sensitiveness and both due to [his] youthfulness'.[8] Garnett was also responsible for Duckworth commissioning two of Thomas's best travel books, *The Heart of England* (1906) and *The South Country* (1909). When Garnett set up his own literary lunches at the Mont Blanc (and later the Villa Villa) in late 1905, early 1906, Thomas would be among the first invited to join writers like Conrad, Belloc, Galsworthy, Hudson and Ford, and useful literary editors such as Thomas Seccombe, Rolfe Scott-James and (later) Norman Douglas of the *English Review*. Ten years older than Thomas and a leading figure in the literary world – he had encouraged, in some cases discovered, D. H. Lawrence, W. H. Hudson, Liam Flaherty and Conrad, among others – Garnett's support of Thomas was of crucial importance to him in 1904 and the following decade.

Garnett's kindness offset what W. H. Davies remembered as a 'most destructive mental punch', which he attributed to his Irish origins and 'natural wit'. Davies remembered one occasion in particular when Garnett's words 'g[ave] pain, which he was very quick to rectify':

> ... It was when some one asked Edward Thomas for his address. At that time Edward Thomas, being ill-paid for his work, had accepted several commissions to write books on different subjects, and these books were being announced by the different publishers. So when Garnett heard the question of Edward Thomas's address, he, thinking of all those books, answered quickly: 'Every publisher in London has it.' Thomas, who was overworked and in bad health, began to defend himself by asking how could he help it, was he not forced, etc. When Garnett heard this, and saw the effect of his words, it was not long before he smoothed things over, saying – 'Yes, yes, Thomas, we know that it can't be helped!'[9]

Sadly, for such a shrewd judge of literary merit and as he himself recognized, Garnett had his limitations as a writer. An accomplished editor, of the letters of Conrad, Hudson, Galsworthy and Thomas to himself, for instance, he never quite succeeded in the more original work attempted, either in the prose-poems of his first book, *An Imaged World* (1894), or with his biographies of *Hogarth* (1911), *Tolstoy* (1911), *Turgenev* (1917), or with plays like *The Breaking Point* (1907) or *The Feud* (1909). His failure was all the more pronounced beside the success of his wife, Constance Garnett, whose translations of the Russian classics dominated the field, or the genius of those he so carefully nurtured. Thomas, who believed like many others, that Garnett's powers lay in his ability to recognize and help genius (though he did not include himself in that category), was greatly admiring of him, dedicating of *The South Country* to him in 1909.

Garnett's first stay with the Thomases in 1904 came towards the end of a long line of visitors to Elses Farm that summer. Besides visits from both sides of the family, the Hootons also came for weekends. The most frequent guests, however, were Edward's friends – Haynes, H. B. Davies, Maine and MacAlister, who returned from Ottawa this summer. Nevinson, Ransome and Duncan Williams also spent weekends there. Such relentless hospitality is remarkable in someone who constantly worried about money: food alone for the visitors must have added significantly to the household expenses. It is also curious in someone who was always working towards one deadline or another; meeting the visitors at the station, taking long walks with them and entertaining them for several days, sometimes even on weekdays, must have eaten into valuable writing time. And Thomas still claimed that, however many people surrounded him, he was always alone. Perhaps the visitors served as a buffer between himself and Helen, whose relationship proved to be no better at Elses Farm than in previous houses. He had hoped, as usual, for a respite from their problems, but, just as he thought they were settling down, their servant fell ill at the end of August and he was 'off to irritation and housework again'.[10]

The servant's illness may have brought things to crisis, but it was not the root cause, as Thomas admitted to Bottomley when, four weeks later, he left home for London again, this time to take a room in a lodging-house Ransome had discovered in Chelsea:

> I found that my work – even my bad reviewing – was suffering more & more from a silly but unavoidable nervous interest in the children's movement in and out of the house, and equally silly but unavoidable interference in little household things, and a continual

wearing irritation. This affected my temper and I thought it wise to try
the effect of a change.[11]

This particular change did little to improve his mood, but it did bring him
into closer contact with Ransome, who remembered his three-weeks' stay
at 1 Gunter Grove with both affection and amusement. Like others of his
friends he could testify that Thomas was 'not always melancholy', breaking
out into Welsh songs, while their landlord, a postman, slept peacefully
below, and causing the startled man 'into tumbling out of bed'.[12] One of
Ransome's friends was equally entertained when she caught a glimpse
from the top of a horse-drawn omnibus of Thomas and Ransome 'walking
gravely along in the gutter, one behind the other, carrying between [them]
a green-varnished deal writing-desk' on which Ransome planned to write
his 'masterpiece'.[13]

When Thomas, who was in any case worried by the extra 15 shillings
a week he had to earn to pay for his room, decided suddenly to leave only
three weeks' after arriving, Ransome was sad. (He was also irritated by a
subsequent suggestion that Thomas's room had been squalid.[14]) He was
extremely sorry to lose Thomas's company. Unfortunately, closer proximity
with Ransome had the opposite effect on Thomas. He remained grateful for
the publication of *Rose Acre Papers* that Ransome had engineered, which
made its appearance, together with Ransome's *The Souls of the Streets*,
during his Chelsea stay. But his attitude towards Ransome's writing and
the man himself, only slightly critical at the start, was hardening, possibly
partly from jealousy of the younger man's facility and rapid progress in the
literary world. His nickname for Ransome became 'the Electrician' because,
like the advertisement for a lavatory pan disinfectant, he was 'healthy but
limited'.[15] His own lack of confidence in his writing, he believed, might be
rectified by some of Ransome's certainty. Looking back in 1908 he would
realize: 'I cherished him because he was the nearest approach to a blithe
youth I happened to know and it is natural I should be angry with him for
rather speedy disillusionment.'[16]

It was not disillusionment with Ransome or his room, however,
which caused Thomas to leave Chelsea in September 1904, nor did he
return straight to his family as Ransome supposed, remembering his abject
words, 'I ran away from home every day, but always came back for tea.'[17]
Thomas's daily soliciting of work from editors and publishers during his

London stay had resulted in a commission to write the text for another 'colour' book for A. & C. Black on Wales. Though he had turned down Methuen's offer of a similar book on Holland and a commission to produce a biography of either Marcus Aurelius or Swift – 'few authors have a nobler record of performances left undone'[18] – he could not resist a book on Wales, despite a punishing deadline: 'The fools of course have waited till the last moment,' he told Bottomley, 'and I expect to have less than three months for the whole.'[19] The very appeal of the subject made it all the more regrettable that it would, of necessity, be a rushed job.

Only three days after Black's commission was agreed Thomas was off again, this time with Helen for a stay with his father's relative, Mrs Phillips, at 'Oaklands' in Ammanford. The decision to include Helen may have been in an effort to improve their deteriorating relationship this autumn; if so, it does not appear to have worked: not only does Helen, unusually, omit it from her account of 1904, but less than two months after it Thomas is telling Hooton that he dares not invite him to 'such a house of misery…Everything is as bad as it could be – Debts. Disagreement. Dirt.'[20] The situation had become so bad that he had 'taken to opium again,' he confessed, which gave him 'an indifferent hour at least tho' it is always disappointing'.[21] Only with the regular use of opium would he be able to finish his book on Wales. By the end of the year after a miserable Christmas in which flu was added to first Edward, then Helen's sufferings, he was warning Hooton *not* to talk to Helen 'about herself and me. Chance has hurried things on and at present we are worse than ever: both of us unable to make anything tolerable out of our new relations.'[22]

These 'new relations' were presumably agreed on during Edward and Helen's stay at Ammanford. He makes no mention of them to Mac, nor does he mention the presence of Merfyn with them, instead reporting: 'We spend all the daylight out of doors, make a few notes, read a little and go very tired to bed.'[23] When she leaves after a week, the tone of his letters changes noticeably. Though his plan, to walk and train into North Wales, is frustrated after three days (and 60 miles) by badly blistered feet, his enthusiasm is unmistakable. To Mac, who has been unable to accompany him as Thomas had hoped, he writes: 'My walk in the mountains of Carmarthen and Cardigan was splendid. It rained all the time as I walked through the wildest and yet most hospitable country I can imagine. The people and the land were adorable.'[24] They were, he tells Jesse Berridge, now training to be a clergyman, 'immortal days.'[25]

On his return to Elses Farm, in an effort to make working conditions there more bearable for his almost permanently irritable state, and to save money by working at home, he moved his study upstairs to a quieter but less attractive north-facing room. Installing his books of modern poetry on a shelf over the fireplace, he 'nervously' tried 'to make use of all [his] books and reading,'[26] hoping Mac would be able to lend him Thomas Pennant's *Tour in Wales* or *Welsh Minstrelsy*. 'Loaded' as he was with books and notes, he anticipated further trips to London for research.

In the event most of Thomas's research at the British Museum Library – 50 closely written pages of notes – was abandoned: 'I have decided to omit all history,' he told Bottomley.[27] Although he purported to have no plan and to be unable to write, by 22 December 1904 *Beautiful Wales* was half-finished. His conscientiousness about deadlines and the need to send in each chapter as it was completed made him more ashamed than usual of the finished product. Yet the book rises well above the level of the guidebook and commentary A. & C. Black commissioned. By ignoring what was expected in such a series – that is, a text subservient to Robert Fowler's illustrations, a practical guide through the whole country and an introduction to its most famous sites – he makes room for his own vision of Wales, anticipating innovations in the travel book over the next century. In a gently satiric introduction he pokes fun at 'the lovers of the Celts', whom he views as 'a class of "decadents"…and of aesthetes.'[28] 'The great disadvantage of Wales,' he mocks, 'seems to be that it is not England.'[29] Having thus disposed of the so-called Welsh 'experts', he goes on at once to give an unashamedly personal account of the country's attractions for *him*. And, despite his grumbles about the constraints theoretically imposed on him by his commission, this allows him to express himself in a way not very different from that of his essays. He recalls some of the old Welsh legends from the *Mabinogion*, such as Sir Gawaine and Sir Uwaine and their adventures with three mysterious 'damosels', or the myth of Llyn Llech Owain, related to him by Gwili. He is best when he describes his own reaction to features such as 'the little unnecessary pool that waited alongside a quiet road and near a grim, black village', which produced 'neither a legend nor a brook', but which makes him think 'that after all, the pool means the beauty of a pure negation, the sweetness of utter and resolved despair, the greatness of Death itself'.[30] Far from preventing him from pursuing his own work, *Beautiful Wales* (as he interprets his commission) allows him to give voice to the many dreams, visions and memories with which he lives.

The need to meet a deadline was, for the most part, a positive thing. 'Task work is good for me,' he wrote to Bottomley on 27 February 1905, two days before his deadline. 'I am a thing of habit, and the regular work of these last three months has been far easier than the irregular which has not been half of it in bulk.' Another way Thomas dealt with his deadline, and which also allowed him to write what interested him, and to use his copious notes made in his three-day tramp, was to make the second half of his book a calendar of Wales for every month of the year, with landscapes for each. He had already used this simple structural device in *The Woodland Life* and in *Beautiful Wales*, as in that first book, he makes it an excuse for a series of prose-poems. (Later still a similar attention to the seasons and their different landscapes would provide him with the subject for numerous poems.) Thomas called these passages 'marvellously irrelevant as a rule', but they are very like the kind of writing he enjoys. Proof of how similar these passages are to the writing he aims at, as well as how 'irrelevant' some are to the book, is the fact that he inserts essays written previously for himself – on London suburbs, for instance – into his supposed guide to Wales. Many, however, are clearly based on Wales, the opening of his section on 'April', for example:

> For half a day there was now a world of snow, a myriad flakes falling, a myriad rising, and nothing more save the sound of rivers; and now a world of green undulating hills that smiled in the lap of the grey mountains, over which moved large clouds, sometimes tumultuous and grey, sometimes white and slow, but always fringed with fire. When the snow came, the mountains dissolved and were not. When the mountains were born again out of the snow, the snow seemed but to have polished the grass, and put a sharper sweetness in the song of the thrush and the call of the curlew, and left the thinnest of cirrus clouds upon the bare field, where it clung only to the weeds.[31]

It was the 'gentle, austere beauty' of passages like this which convinced Bottomley that *Beautiful Wales* contained some of Thomas's best prose.[32] He was of great help throughout, supplying books and pictures Thomas believed might inspire him, turning the Welsh schoolmaster-bard, Watcyn Wyn's translation of his native songs into verse for English readers and allowing Thomas to include his own poem, 'Apple-Bluth', in his section on April, as well as reading proofs as they came in.

Despite Bottomley's encouragement, Thomas continued to be almost wholly negative about *Beautiful Wales*. 'What will you say of my 25,000 words of landscape?' he asks Bottomley as he completes the book, 'nearly all of it without humanity except what it may owe to a lanky shadow of myself – I stretch over big landscapes just as my shadow does at dawn...!'[33] In a momentary reversal of roles, Bottomley was for once more negative than Thomas about his landscapes. Thomas's response to this is revealing: 'I regret you don't like the landscapes. For landscapes are what I seem to be made for...'[34] To Mac he would write, after seeing 'a dozen reviews of "Wales"' that were 'all favourable but mystified. Nobody has accepted the challenge of my method and appraised its results. All they say is "how nice, and how odd, and why doesn't he mention places?"'[35]

Beautiful Wales is not all landscape, however. Thomas included seven or eight characters besides himself. These, too, he dismissed as irrelevant. Yet his fourth chapter, sketching in 'Two Ministers, a Bard, a Schoolmaster, an Innkeeper, and Others', not only manages to capture some convincing Welsh 'types', but is also highly entertaining, particularly in its portrayal of two ministers. Mr Jones, for example, 'has a book-shelf containing nothing but sermons and theology, which he had read'. And Mr Rowlands, who 'is six feet and two inches in height, seventeen stone in weight, and has a voice in proportion' and who, 'when he stands up, one supposes that he can never sit down' and vice versa. Bottomley regretted the almost complete absence of Welsh women from the text, to which Thomas replied: 'I didn't forget the women: I was afraid of them'.[36] Bottomley was also sorry that he had omitted some verses of 'The Maids of Carmarthen' from his text. Yet one of Thomas's own concerns was that, in an effort to fit his own word-count, he had padded his book with overlong quotations from Shelley and Borrow. He had been conscious of George Borrow, whose books, including *Wild Wales* he had read at Oxford, throughout the writing of *Beautiful Wales*, later writing a sympathetic biography of him for Chapman & Hall, drawn to him partly by his Celtic connections. 'Borrow was a big truculent outdoor wizard,' Thomas wrote, 'who comes to our doors with a marvellous company of Gypsies and fellows whose like we shall never see again and could not invent'.[37]

R. George Thomas, himself a Welshman, sees *Beautiful Wales* as 'a neglected goldmine for any Welshman who wishes to understand his own heritage', but regrets Edward Thomas's failure to formulate bigger ideas about Welsh history and contemporary Welsh culture and society.[38] Thomas's decision to omit all history, however, suggests that it was never his aim to explore Welsh politics in a way that his father, for example, might have done. Instead he attempts to convey, often in mystical terms, what Wales might mean to any sensitive reader of landscapes.

Completed to time, by 1 March 1905, just two days before Thomas's twenty-seventh birthday, *Beautiful Wales* was his fifth book in eight years, a considerable achievement despite his sense of failure, and would set the pattern for many of the books to follow. By June he was also busier than ever as a reviewer, with the *Academy*, *Speaker* and *Outlook*, as well as the *Daily Chronicle* and the *World*, giving him more work. He reviewed ten books alone for the *Academy* in June and July. He was particularly proud of the fact that, until the *Academy* was taken over by Harmsworth and had its literary space reduced, he and Martin Freeman had been asked by its literary editor, Harold Child, to help shape the magazine's literary policy, over *Academy* dinners which he professed to dislike: 'Freeman and I are…getting a lot of impressionism amongst the heavy stuff,' he boasted to Bottomley.[39]

Some of Thomas's extra work resulted from his own more frequent visits to editors and publishers in London, other commissions came through Garnett. An equally important factor by mid-1905, however, was his acquisition of a literary agent, Charles Francis ('Frank') Cazenove. The introduction may have come from Ransome, whose main source of work by 1905 was the *Week's Survey*. This was situated in Henrietta Street, also home to several literary agencies, including a small firm founded by George Perris, whose partner was Cazenove. Ransome's 'first friend' among these agents was Cazenove, who started working for Perris in 1902 and as Thomas's agent in 1904, with the commission for *Beautiful Wales*. It is likely that Ransome had mentioned Cazenove to Thomas, as he had to John Masefield,[40] though Thomas already knew Perris through Noble. It was the start of a relationship which would continue, with one short break, from 1904 to 1914, terminated sadly, by Cazenove's death from cancer in early 1915.[41] It was Cazenove, therefore, who handled the various book commissions which followed quickly as the result, no doubt, of his efforts – *The Book of the Open Air* (1907), *The Pocket Book of Poems and Songs for the Open Air* (1907) and an introduction to Borrow's *The Bible in Spain* (1906).

The youngest member of Perris and Cazenove's firm, Thomas Burke, who would himself become a successful writer, recalled Cazenove as 'that now almost extinct thing – a *literary* agent', a man 'capable of judging and appreciating new literature, and understanding the mind of the literary artist'.[42] He did for 'pure literature', Burke claimed, what Garnett did in a much wider field and was, from the start, a firm believer in Thomas's writing, 'working for years at a return which scarcely covered his postage costs in their correspondence'.[43]

Thomas was not just a frequent correspondent, but a regular visitor to the agency's offices in Covent Garden, where his arrival seemed to Burke 'like the entry of some rare Presence. His appearance was austere and intellectual…He was beautiful to hear. I often thought that if Christ were to take form in the modern world he would have something of the appearance of Edward Thomas.'[44] Thomas may have looked Christ-like, but his demands on his agent were certainly not. Cazenove needed all the qualities Burke attributed to him to deal with Thomas tactfully. He was never a 'popular' writer and his work was not easy to place. He could also be difficult about contracts, as his letter to Cazenove about Dent's commission for *The Heart of England* shows. When Dent lowered his initial offer slightly, Thomas told Cazenove firmly: 'I cannot allow Dent to dock the sum promised [i.e. from 100 guineas to £100, a reduction of £5]. So I will drop the game if he does not give way.'[45] When Thomas did just that, turning down the commission despite the need for the money, it took all Cazenove's tact to resolve the situation.

With Cazenove's input Thomas became even busier, and more harassed. Helen, meantime, had taken practical steps to deal with his inability to work at home yet his need to be near his family. She had appealed to MacAlister, again, about the possibility of finding a room for him to work in, away from the noise of two young children but near enough to walk to daily. Mac had appealed to their wealthy Oxford friend, Martin Freeman, and by 16 April 1905, Edward was working in 'a little cottage half a mile over the fields' from Elses Farm, rented by Freeman but used only occasionally by him for weekends.[46]

Stidulph's Cottage, Egg Pie Lane, would help ward off Thomas's irritability for a time. By May he 'went there to business for six hours regularly' every day, he told Bottomley, the discipline of the routine providing comfort.[47] So, too, would the constant stream of visitors to Elses Farm again this summer. But despite the company and the increased demand for his work, he felt 'more miserable than ever'.[48] Once again he turned to opium. His inability to write 'prose-poems' to order for the *Daily Chronicle* was the cause but, more seriously, he blamed the lack of 'somebody strong and tender' to look after him. He felt he was getting 'worse and worse…and no week, – hardly a day, – passes without my thinking that I must soon cease to try to work and live'.[49] He felt lucky to have 'the oblivious minutes at sunset or midnight,' he told Bottomley:

> for at all other times, whether I am reading or writing or talking or trying to sleep, I am plagued by such little thoughts as how much I shall earn this week or what train I shall catch tomorrow or whether I shall have my letters by the next post, and such big thoughts as whether anything is worth while, whether I shall ever again have hope or joy or enthusiasm or love, whether I could for any length of time be quite sensible in taking food, sleep, drink etc.[50]

His most shocking confession comes last, that he lacked a 'motive': 'You see – I must have a motive and to be honest, my responsibilities to Helen and Merfyn and the dear and joyful Bronwen is not a motive.'[51] So desperate was he, that he felt that 'true and thorough insanity' would be a relief. He longed for 'some one to help'.[52]

Bottomley's reply has not survived, but it is clear he did his best to help. Thomas was well aware that he needed to be less self-conscious, as Bottomley must have suggested, but felt unable to change himself. At the same time he assured Bottomley that he need not fear Thomas's suicide, because he was 'too distracted and undetermined ever to do more that be perplexed in the extreme and in vain'.[53] He believed he ought to live alone, but had not the courage to do so, he told Jesse, who was also trying to help him: 'It is really the kind H[elen] and the dear children who make life almost *impossible*.'[54] Everything seemed to be 'dissolving'.[55]

He made various efforts to help himself. His visits to London, which by 1905 had become regular weekly or fortnightly ones, usually on Tuesdays and/or Wednesdays, were not just to find work, but also to meet friends and escape from his family. His Wednesday afternoon 'teas' at St George's were now a fixture and the means of making new acquaintances as well as meeting old ones. Haynes, Freeman and MacAlister and more recent friends like Nevinson, Dalmon, Berridge, Ransome and Garnett would come regularly to the smoking-room on the second floor when they were in town. Thomas himself would become known as 'the Iambic', less in reference to his eminence as a critic of poetry than to his rhythmical weekly or fortnightly appearances in London.

Thomas also attempted to fight off depression with long walks, though this was less successful. His plan to follow the Pilgrims' Way to Canterbury with Martin Freeman, for instance, ended after only 25 miles because of badly blistered feet again, though he enjoyed one night sleeping under corn sheaves in a field before having to limp home. R. George Thomas believes that Thomas's frequent trouble with his feet was a sign of incipient diabetes, as did Thomas himself, but it may have had more to do with the fact that he wore football boots for walking, because they were much cheaper than conventional hiking boots. A more serious reason for not walking than blisters, however, was his conviction by mid-August that: 'Exercise is fatal. During long hard work I am splendid, but the moment I stop I am at my worst and the effect may last a week.'[56]

Another remedy for depression was his own work and, encouraged by Garnett on one of his visits in mid-September, Thomas was also trying to write more imaginative pieces, which he now called 'Illusions' or, more jokingly, 'Ejaculations in Prose'.

All these attempted remedies seem only to have increased Thomas's self-consciousness. But one thing which may have helped towards the end of 1905 was his meeting with the poet W. H. Davies and his efforts to help someone who seemed to be in a worse situation than himself. He had already enjoyed playing patron to Mac and, to a lesser extent, Jesse, by giving them helpful contacts in the literary world. He had also shown himself ready to help younger, or less successful writers like Thomas Burke, who as a 'bungling beginner' had found his honest response to the poems he showed him more helpful though just as kind as other established authors he approached.

Thomas had been brought into contact with Davies through reviewing work. Though he constantly complained about it, one advantage, as he had acknowledged in *Beautiful Wales*, was the excitement of reading the work of a 'fresh modern poet, straight from the press before anyone has praised it, and to know it is good'.[57] Though in the case of Davies he was not quite the first – St John Adcock in the *Daily News* and Arthur Symons in *Outlook* had both already praised him highly – he could be proud of the fact that he was among the first to recognize Davies and, in the words of the poet's biographer, 'the man who was to do more for him than anyone else'.[58]

The poems in question, *The Soul's Destroyer*, had come to Thomas to review by an unusual route. Davies, who had published his collection at his own expense, had sent copies out to well-known authors, asking if they wished to buy one. George Bernard Shaw, attracted to the poems' 'freedom from literary vulgarity which was like a draught of clear water in the desert', had paid for another eight copies to be sent to 'such critics and verse fanciers as he knew of, wondering if they would recognise a poet when they met one'.[59] Thomas, together with Garnett and Israel Zangwill, was among those who both received a copy and recognized a poet. Intrigued by this unknown versifier who gave his address as a doss-house in the East End of London and influenced by his own fascination with tramps, beggars and gypsies, Thomas took the (for him) unprecedented step of visiting Davies at his lodgings in Marshalsea Road *before* writing his review for the *Daily Chronicle*. His first impressions, on 11 October 1905, go some way to explaining the curious relationship between the two which followed:

> A small narrow-headed black-haired Monmouthshire man, with the childish slightly uncomfortable smile (with the mouth) of Welsh people, and still a Welsh accent. One leg; the other lost on railway in U.S.A. He is of Maindee n[ear] Newport (where Mother lived) and was a picture frame maker, but had and has eight shillings a week left by his sea-captain grandf[athe]r, and left Wales ten years ago, spent five years in U.S.A. and Canada doing odd work – fruit farm, and railway, and then five years in London.[60]

Davies's South Wales' connections naturally interested Thomas. So, too, did the unworldliness of this man seven years his senior: 'He has quite the shy manner of a Welshman who has just come to London,' Thomas added to his notes the next day, 'and looks and speaks as if quite unspoiled by experience or by the glory of a review by Arthur Symons.' Davies's determination to be free of worldly responsibilities at whatever cost and his complete dedication to poetry were equally appealing to Thomas. Most of all, he admired the lyric simplicity of Davies's best poems in an age when it was not in fashion in verse. Bottomley, who was not concerned with what was fashionable, agreed with Thomas, writing to him 'we are surely still amid a good age for English poetry when such a virginal, pristine, bloomy, lisping, limpid, innocent talent as his can exist'.[61]

Thomas's review, ten days after his visit to Davies, did a great deal to secure Davies's reputation, especially coming from a man known to have exacting standards and a great literary sensibility:

> Mr William Davies...has been active and passionate. He has been poor and careless and hungry and in pain. 'I count us', he says, in his 'Lodging-House Fire', which is as simple as a cave man's drawing on bone, and yet of an atmosphere dense with sorrow:
>
> > I count us, thirty men,
> > > Huddled from winter's blow,
> > Helpless to move away
> > > From that fire's glow.
>
> ...His greatness rests upon a wide humanity, a fresh and unbiased observation, and a noble use of the English tongue...In subtlety he abounds.[62]

The review was illustrated with many other quotations and sales of *The Soul's Destroyer* increased dramatically.

Davies felt that Thomas's review was better than his work deserved, but he took the money it generated gratefully and returned to Wales, where Thomas visited him on his own, brief visit to John Williams at Swansea in late November 1905. It was in Wales that Davies started to write *The Autobiography of a Super-Tramp*. When the first draft – and his money – were finished he returned to England to a situation ideally suited for him to benefit from the advice of two men well acquainted with the publishing world, Thomas and the even more experienced Garnett. For Thomas, identifying only too easily with Davies's financial difficulties, had offered to share Stidulph's Cottage with him; he would continue to work there daily but Davies could both work and live there. The cottage was a tiny, two-roomed building, with a kitchen-living-room on the ground floor and a bedroom on the first. Thomas had to pass through Davies's room to his own and always found him 'solemnly happy' at his work.[63] Furnished only in the most primitive fashion by the Thomases, the cottage nevertheless represented freedom for Davies, who proudly displayed on the kitchen mantelpiece the small library he was accumulating, again due to Thomas's kindness. 'If you have any spare copies of even the most elementary poetry,' Thomas wrote to Bottomley on 24 July 1906 (as he tried to persuade his landlady to allow him to stay on at Stidulph's Cottage and Davies to live there), 'I should be glad to transmit them.' Bottomley duly sent Browning, who joined Wordsworth, Shelley, Sturge Moore, Byron and Cowper on the mantelpiece. Davies was to stay at the cottage for more than three years, his rent paid for mostly by Thomas, even after he had been given notice to quit Elses Farm by the end of September 1906 and despite his constant anxiety about money. Richard Stonesifer argues that 'the freedom and quiet peace' of the Weald had a positive effect on Davies's poetry, enabling him to express his true lyric powers, free at last from the 'shadows of the past'.[64]

Thomas was equally generous and thoughtful towards Davies in other ways, some of them highly entertaining. The story of his replacement of Davies's broken wooden leg, though it has been told before, is worth repeating for the insight it gives into both writers. A few months after Davies's arrival at Stidulph's Cottage his prosthetic leg, which had seen some hard tramping in all weathers, collapsed beyond repair. Since Davies himself had no money, Thomas set about raising funds from friends to replace it. Meantime, he took steps for a makeshift one which would at least keep Davies mobile and, sensitive to Davies's fear of any of the villagers learning of it, took it to a local wheelwright to make under the guise of a 'Curiosity Cricket Bat'.[65]

Thomas also made sure that Davies felt welcome at Elses Farm, where he became a great favourite with the children, who christened him 'Sweet William'. He usually ate his evening meal with the family and then, over beer and tobacco in front of the fire, would read his current draft of his *Autobiography* to them. Thomas, like Garnett (who had also been shown the manuscript), believed that the work badly needed revising and rewriting, for Davies had almost completely passed over his tramping experiences in America and England in favour of more lurid adventures in low places. Even had he found a publisher willing to publish it at the time, it would, in Garnett's and Thomas's opinion, have attracted the wrong kind of interest. Davies did not take kindly to suggested alterations, but did what they asked. When *The Autobiography of a Super-Tramp* appeared, with a preface by Bernard Shaw, who had also chosen the title, it was a great success, earning Davies some money at last. He showed his appreciation for Thomas's help by insisting on taking over payment of the rent at Stidulph's Cottage. His surviving letters to Thomas also express his gratitude, as well as his continued dependence on him for advice and approval.[66] Thomas, he was to write in *Later Days*, was his 'first and oldest literary friend'.[67] He also dedicated *New Poems* to Thomas in 1907.

Thomas would continue to help Davies all he could. Besides reviewing each of his publications, some more positively than others, though always sympathetically, he introduced him to Garnett's Mont Blanc Tuesday lunches and his own Wednesday teas, where Davies met a wide range of useful literary contacts, like Nevinson, Hudson and Ashley Gibson. He also introduced him to Cazenove, whom he believed would do more for Davies than his current agent, Pinker. Though, as Thomas drily put it to Bottomley, he felt that he and Davies were 'not born for one another', he grew very fond of Davies and was sad to think of having to leave him in September 1906 when his lease on Elses Farm expired. Davies himself was devastated, regarding it as a personal tragedy.

12

BERRYFIELD COTTAGE: 'WHEN FIRST I CAME HERE I HAD HOPE' (DECEMBER 1906–FEBRUARY 1907)

> When first I came here I had hope,
> Hope for I knew not what. Fast beat
> My heart at sight of the tall slope
> Of grass and yews, as if my feet
>
> Only by scaling its steps of chalk
> Would see something no other hill
> Ever disclosed...[1]

Thomas's move from Kent to the Petersfield area of Hampshire in November 1906 took him west and nearer to his own particular 'heart of England'. His book of that title, *The Heart of England*, was written in Kent and published in October 1906, the month before he moved into Berryfield Cottage at Ashford, and Hampshire did not feature significantly in it. Situated as it was, however, between the two other counties he had grown to love and know intimately, Kent and Wiltshire, Hampshire would quickly become central to his vision of England and Englishness. It would feature prominently in his next topographical book, *The South Country*.

Thomas's last months at Elses Farm had been particularly busy. Added to his usual reviewing for the *Daily Chronicle*, he had contributed regularly to the *Bookman* and the *Academy*, occasionally for the re-formed *Speaker* magazine, and had several longer articles published. He also collaborated with Frank Podmore, a prolific writer on psychical research as well as a founder of the Fabian Society, on a series of articles on Apparitions, Thought Transference and related topics for the *Grand Magazine*: 'He exudes information and I string it into ropes and coils of pearls,' Thomas explained to Bottomley.[2] This foray into the psychical world did not surprise his younger brother, Julian, who remembered Edward as always having been interested in such matters. Some of his stories do suggest that his mind was open to another world beyond the material, agnostic though he was. His review of Arthur Symons's *Spiritual Adventures* the same month that he was collaborating with Podmore points to more than a professional assignment. In addition, he was working hard on four commissions, the most challenging of them a book he wanted to write in theory, but in the event found very difficult, *The Heart of England*.[3]

Walter de la Mare believed that *The Heart of England* 'came freely and from the heart'.[4] Though that was true only of parts of it – Thomas had great difficulty in reaching the agreed word-count of 65,000 – there are many passages which reflect the author's pleasure in describing the countryside he loved, its landscapes, its rituals, its seasons, its characters, its ancient folk customs, its traditional songs, its old inns and, in some detail, its trees, flowers and birds:

> The brook rises in a clear, grey, trembling basin at the foot of a chalk hill, among flowers of lotus and thyme and eyebright and rest-harrow. Here the stone curlew drinks, and above is the gently rounded escarpment, ancient, and yet still young compared with the dusky spring which has something gnomish and earthy about it, though it takes the sun. It drops in thin, bright links over the chalk, and then for a time loses its way in playing with cresses and marsh marigolds, spreading out so finely that hardly will the ladybird drown that falls therein – falling at length in a cascade from one dead leaf to another down a hedge bank. Below, it nourishes the first forget-me-nots, by a gateway where it slips across the lane, and is dew-fed by the vetches and clovers that swaddle the posts of the gate. ('The Brook'[5])

The ideal form for this wealth of material, however, eluded Thomas. His search for what he would call (in relation to *The South Country*) 'a good framework' would remain a problem for him in his full-length books about the countryside until *In Pursuit of Spring* (1914), when he hit upon the 'simple plot' he wished someone had given him earlier: 'Not a lot of ramifications, recognition scenes, etc., but just a progressive narrative that can help me to get out, first my knowledge of the Suburbs, then, for contrast, the country.'[6] When Dent, perfectly reasonably, asked for a synopsis of *The Heart of England*, he found it virtually impossible to oblige.

Judging from the finished work, in the absence of a clear plan Thomas used his book like a capacious carpet-bag, into which he packed detailed observations of nature from his field notebooks, stories he had contemplated, brief character-studies, half-finished essays and his ideas on a variety of subjects, including suicide, happiness and music. Like his early models Browne and Burton, he was cavalier about genres. He tacks a long passage on his love of music, especially folk-song, on to what starts out as a visit to an old country inn. He also includes not just the words but also the music for a number of the songs named. The result is a collection of the 'small things' he preferred to write, loosely strung together.

There are times in *The Heart of England* when Thomas's tendency towards poetry surfaces. 'The Metamorphosis', for instance, which Bottomley admired, is a chapter of one page only, simply but lyrically, describing 'a proud ash shedding its leaves after a night of frost.'[7] Likewise Thomas's praise of the ship, the chariot and the plough, in his second chapter, 'Faunus', besides anticipating his later poem 'As the team's headbrass', is a prose-poem in itself:

> How nobly the ploughman and the plough and three horses, two chestnuts and a white leader, glide over the broad swelling field in the early morning! Under the dewy, dark-green wood-side they wheel, pause and go out into the strong light again, and they seem one and glorious, as if the all-breeding earth had just sent them up out of her womb – mighty, splendid and something grim, with darkness and primitive forces clinging about them, and the night in the horses' manes.
>
> The ship, the chariot, the plough, these three are, I suppose, the most sovereign beautiful things which man has made in his time, and such that were his race to pass away from the earth, would bring him most worship among his successors.[8]

Another favourite of Bottomley was 'Earth Children', a more extended piece which shows Thomas's ability to portray country characters, or rather 'types', though there are elements of 'Dad' Uzzell and his wife in this account of an ancient couple in their declining years. Another successful section based on two main characters is 'The Fox-Hunt' which helped convince Garnett that Thomas was really a poet and even Thomas thought it 'pretty good'.[9]

There are, in fact, germs of future poems scattered throughout *The Heart of England*. The moment in chapter I ('Leaving Town'), for example, when 'all the birds sang stormily'[10] anticipates 'Adlestrop', when 'all the birds / Of Oxfordshire and Gloucestershire' sing in unison. And in chapter XXXV, a fanciful dream of the congregation of a country church going to heaven, Thomas describes the gamekeeper and the squire in terms which prefigure not just Thomas's own, well-known encounter with a gamekeeper in 1914, but also his poems 'An Old Song 1' and 'The Gallows':

> The gamekeeper stood, with smoking gun barrels, and a cloud of jay's feathers still in the air and among the May foliage about him. Pride, stupidity, servility clouded his face as in his days of nature, and above him in the oaks innumerable jays laughed because beauty, like folly, was immortal there.
>
> The squire, more faint, and whether to his joy or not I could not discern, was standing under a bough on which hung white owls, wood owls, falcons, crows, magpies, cats, hedgehogs, stoats, weasels, some bloody, some with gaping stomachs, some dismembered or crushed, some fleshless, some heaving like boiling fat, and on them and him the sun shone hot.[11]

Bottomley's praise of the poetry in the heart of England was offset by criticism of what he saw as a piling up of landscapes again, as in *Beautiful Wales*. Thomas himself was even more critical, dismissing his book (with reference to two of his favourite nature-writers) as 'Borrow and Jefferies sans testicles and guts'.[12] As he told Nevinson, to whom the book is dedicated, he believed it contained 'a good deal of my worst [work]', though he also felt it contained his 'best works' to date.[13] He was particularly apologetic about three pieces written in 1902 or earlier ('Village', 'Frieze at the 4 Elms' and 'August'), which he had inserted in a panic when the publisher Dent informed him that he was 5,000 words short of the agreed length. Another curious insertion in a book about England is a final chapter on Wales, 'The Castle of Carbonek', ostensibly a mythical castle from Arthurian legend but in reality firmly based on Penard Castle near Swansea. By keeping his topographical books deliberately vague – 'he localises virtually nothing, and he individualises as seldom', Thomas Seccombe would point out in his *Times Literary Supplement* review[14] – Thomas was able to use old or extraneous material until his publisher insisted on place-names. Until then, he would continue to reinterpret the 'travel' book according to his own needs and was proud of it: in longing for 'some really good man [to] praise my "ship, chariot and plough", my "Earth Children", " Metamorphosis" etc.,' he tells Bottomley, 'I feel that perhaps they are really good and am almost sure they are new'.[15] He was greatly disappointed when the *World* and the *Standard* merely commented 'what a cheery knowing companion he was for a day in the country' and the *Academy* that he was 'affected'.[16] Though there were more positive reviews, he vowed that it would be his last 'colour' book, in which his words were less important, he felt, than the pictures and which were normally expensive to buy.

Fortunately, the reviews appeared in earnest the month Thomas moved his family to Berryfield Cottage in November 1906, when there was plenty to distract him. His writing had prevented him from paying all but a brief visit to approve the house in advance and the search for it had been left to Helen. It had been she who insisted that they must find a good school for Merfyn, who was about to turn 7 and growing beyond what she could teach him; as Edward's work and impatience with his son increased he had become less and less involved in his education. After some research and reading of J. H. Badley's writing, Helen decided on Bedales, the co-educational school Badley had set up in 1893 in the village of Steep, near Petersfield. On a visit to the school, she also found a house she liked and knew they could afford. Situated only a mile from Steep at Ashford, it was in one of Hampshire's most beautiful woodland areas, nicknamed 'Little Switzerland' by its admirers for its dramatic scenery. After two months of homelessness, staying with family, and friends, the Thomases moved into their grey stone and flint[17] former farmhouse at the foot the Shoulder of Mutton Hill.

Edward's pleasure in the house and its surroundings never faltered: 'This house and the country about it make the most beautiful place we ever lived in,' he wrote to Bottomley a few days after their move there: 'we are now become people of whom passers by stop to think: how fortunate they are within those walls. I have thought the same as I came to the house and forgot it was my own.'[18] Normally cautious and always anxious about money, he would even make an attempt to buy Berryfield Cottage when there was a threat of losing it later on. It would be scene of some of his happiest, as well as unhappiest years, and some of the busiest.

Helen's reaction was equally as enthusiastic. Whereas at Elses Farm she had concentrated on its vast farmhouse kitchen, at Berryfield she was more conscious of the outside: the large, old-fashioned garden which stretched in front of the house running parallel to the lane; the yew tree by the gate which sheltered a gold-crested wren; the lane itself so deep and dark that the entrance to it from the main road looked like the entrance to a tunnel. The rough field of wild flowers which bordered one side of the property and led to Stoner Hill; the stream which flowed past the house on the other side through a wild water-meadow full of forget-me-nots, meadow-sweet, mare's tails and loosestrife; the foxes and owls inhabiting the surrounding woods, whose eerie cries at night added to the mysterious and romantic appeal of the place.

Edward started exploring the countryside around immediately, delighted by their proximity to Gilbert White's Selborne, William Cobbett's birthplace at Farnham and the historic city of Winchester. He was less keen on getting to know Bedales and left this to Helen, who was determined to learn all she could about the school and its staff. She already admired all she thought it stood for, its 'co-education...its love of the open air, its unscholastic freedom of discipline, its freedom from monied snobbishness and its social life, simple, free and happy'.[19] Despite the last named quality, she found it difficult to break through the staff's 'cultured reserve', but would eventually win them round through a combination of perseverance and friendliness. Their approval was shown by an invitation to teach part-time in the preparatory school attended by Merfyn, a group of about 30 boys and girls aged between 7 and 12 or 13, under the headmastership of Russell Scott.

Helen would come to believe that she had been 'taken in' by the Bedales' staff and would write less sympathetically of them in retrospect.

While she remained convinced that they were 'kind, serious, intellectual people' with a belief in worthy causes, temperance, votes for women, hygiene and liberalism – and she enjoyed the social life they offered her – she would begin to tire of their well-ordered lives, so unlike her own:

> None of them were rich, but none were poor... they all – so it seemed to me – had led and would always lead the same quiet comfortable lives, rational, well balanced. Their politics inclined to Socialism and they were on more than usual friendly terms with the villagers... they were moderate in all things; they read the best books and the *Manchester Guardian*, and loved the best music, and had replicas of the best pictures on their walls. Their homes were in faultless taste outside and in. Their simple oak furniture was made by skilled craftsmen, and their curtains were hand-woven. Their meals were lavish and good, inclining to brown bread and vegetarianism and, of course, non-alcoholic.[20]

Helen's relations with Bedales' staff were, however, close for a number of years, whereas their distance from the tortured passionate inner life of Thomas was too great to bridge. Relations between them, with a few exceptions, remained cool. Though he would frequently abstain from tobacco, alcohol and meat, he never believed that there was virtue in such a choice and could have no real sympathy with those who did. According to Helen, he was regarded by the majority of Bedales' staff as a 'solitary wandering creature who worked irregularly, who drank and smoked in village inns, who had no political beliefs or social theories, and was not impressed by the school or its ideals'.[21] 'I don't like Bedales folk,' Thomas would tell Bottomley after eight years experience of them. 'All I like [are] the hills ...'[22]

Thomas would describe the countryside around Berryfield Cottage in some detail in *The South Country*. But before doing so he had four other jobs to complete, two of which had been commissioned before he left Elses Farm. In January 1906 he had agreed to edit *The Book of the Open Air* for Hodder & Stoughton, to appear first in twelve monthly parts, then in two bound volumes. His letter to one of his contributors, W. W. Wright, in July 1906, gives some idea of the work's aim and scope, that is 'to give a precise but picturesque impression of nature in England by means of a series of essays on birds, mammals, trees, etc.'[23] W. H. Hudson, W. Warde Fowler and Edward Clodd, he tells Wright, are among the contributors. As his further letters to Wright show, Thomas was a conscientious editor and the undertaking enormously time-consuming, as he responded to a long list of naturalists of various persuasions and their contributions, if these eventually materialized. Whether like Hudson and Douglas Dewer, they were well known or unknown, like Miss Emily Sharpe, who wrote him an article on butterflies and moths, he responded equally carefully to their efforts.

Thomas also suggested articles on less obvious 'Open Air' topics, such as 'Nature in English Poetry', which he asked Bottomley to write, and another on English country songs, which Martin Freeman undertook. He himself contributed articles, presumably on topics of his own choice, on Gilbert White and Richard Jefferies as well as another nature diary along the lines of *The Woodland Life* and *Beautiful Wales*. He also provided introductions for both volumes, when they were published in book form in 1907 and 1908 respectively. The endless letters involved in editing 'this foolish book', he told Hudson at the end of March 1907, had become 'most wearisome and unsatisfying' and was 'mak[ing] everything else so'.[24]

There was one positive aspect to the undertaking, however: a much closer relationship with Hudson himself. The two had already met at Garnett's literary lunches but got to know each other better through *The Book of the Open Air*. The 46 letters which have survived from Thomas to Hudson, stretching over a period of ten years from August 1906, give a clear idea of what drew the two men together. Their discussions range from 'kite country' in Wales, Hilaire Belloc's early verses, the beauty of the landscape round Berryfield Cottage, shared literary friends, Hudson's health, and that of his much older wife, peacocks' cries and Thomas's current work. 'I love the man,' Thomas told Bottomley less than two years after the letters start, 'though I don't mistake that particular piece on "Furze" for great literature when I say it gives me extraordinary pleasure. The tenderness and wildness of it – the mention of those hard big hands of his – the modesty, ease and serenity of it...But of course it is nothing like his finest work except in its candour.'[25] With the exception of William Morris, there was no other writer whom he sometimes would have liked to have been. William Morris's

Message of the March Wind, though nothing like Hudson, reminded him of Hudson as 'a noble piece of humanity'.[26]

When Thomas died not long after his last letter to Hudson on Christmas Day 1916, the normally reticent Hudson wept at the news, expressing his own feelings for Thomas more briefly, but just as poignantly to Helen: 'I loved him as my own son'.[27] From the start Hudson had felt an 'esteem', 'affection' and 'admiration' for Thomas which mirrored Thomas's own.[28] Though separated widely by age and experience – Hudson was nearly 40 years older than Thomas and had grown up in Argentina – they shared many interests and attitudes. Both were dedicated naturalists with a special interest in birds; Thomas treasured Hudson's gift of his *Adventures among Birds* as 'about the best bird book there is'.[29] Both were also, to quote Thomas on Hudson again, 'the substantial miracle of a naturalist *and* an imaginative artist in one and in harmony [my italics]'.[30] Hudson shared Thomas's dislike of 'the way in which scientific people and their followers are satisfied with *data* in appalling English'.[31]

They were even similar in appearance, their leanness and air of distinction suggesting ascetic tendencies and a marked individuality. Douglas Goldring, who sat next to Hudson at one of Garnett's Mont Blanc lunches and was struck by his 'tall, thin, careworn' appearance, was delighted by Ford Madox Ford's comment that 'Huddy' (as he was known to friends) 'moved like an [American] Indian', adding his own observation that 'he was almost as swift and noiseless as a bird'.[32] Thomas was critical of William Rothenstein's portrait of Hudson in 1907 because, rather than suggesting 'an eagle in a palace court', it suggested 'an eagle at the zoo and content to be there'.[33] De la Mare's chosen metaphor for Hudson was a falcon with a falcon's piercing eyes which looked 'strangely out of place in London'.[34]

Hudson was among the first to claim that Thomas was 'essentially a poet', convinced that 'in his nature books and fiction he leaves all there's best and greatest in him unexpressed'.[35] Hudson understood more clearly than most the negative effect that Thomas's piling-up of commissions had on his writing and also on his mental equilibrium. De la Mare recalled that the two men were extremely close over many years, as close as such reticent men could be. They were close enough for Hudson to invite Thomas to join the select group of his friends who met weekly at his house at 40 St Luke's

Road, Bayswater. He would advise Thomas over his nature books, write a testimonial for a lectureship Thomas thought he wanted and support an application to the Royal Literary Fund for him in 1914. Thomas, in turn, reviewed all Hudson's books enthusiastically and dedicated his biography of Richard Jefferies to him in 1909.

Hudson himself referred to 'the bond uniting us', chief reason for which, he believed, was that 'we were both mystics in some degree'.[36] Though Thomas denied this, at least in his own case, he has left a passage in his field notebooks about a visit to Hudson which hints at a shared sense of another world outside the material one:

> Sat with Hudson talking slowly but easily and the lamp not lit – talking of poetry and of South Americans and outside it is still and hazy and children are playing w[ith] subdued voices w[hich] clearly proclaim the Spring and tho' I hear no birds it is [as if] I'd heard the first blackbird and a robin and a distant thrush at [the] edge of infinite countryside. Hudson does not like the children playing outside but I do as it creeps in during the pauses in the firelit big gloomy solitary room.[37]

They might differ over children – Hudson was childless – and, more importantly, over poetry, but the bond uniting them would survive his criticism of the verses Thomas sent him, even beyond the grave: 'Not many people in this world feel the loss of a friend so acutely for so many years,' de la Mare would write of Hudson's feeling for Thomas, long after Hudson's own death (aged 81) in 1922.[38]

Thomas would send the first of many requests for Hudson's advice about the commission which followed *The Book of the Open Air* – *The Pocket Book of Poems and Songs for the Open Air* (1907) – as well as asking leave to quote a sentence from him as a motto for it.[39] Once the first volume of *The Book of the Open Air* was published in 1907, he was able to concentrate on this task, which he enjoyed far more, an anthology of some of his favourite poems and songs. Grant Richards had asked him, via Cazenove, to compile this on the strength of Thomas's *Daily Chronicle* review of *Traveller's Joy*, edited by W. G. Waters, on 28 June 1906.

It was Thomas's love of the open air, but even more so the mystical side hinted at with Hudson, which helped cement a second important relationship he made in 1906, with Walter de la Mare. His description of one such shared mystical moment in his field notebooks shows how close the two men became. The occasion was a visit in 1909 to de la Mare, who had rented a cottage for a month that summer to be near Thomas:

> 9pm Parting with de la Mare at Goose Green by shadowy thickets in a few mouths of roses in this gloom – far off the dark wavy outline of our hill ag[ain]st a pale sky streaked with grey ruins of a calm delicate sunset...– a distant train sounding like a mere echo – no voice, no [song?] – the air getting misty, the grass wet, scent of honeysuckle – My feeling of deep confidence & ease as if nothing c[oul]d. touch me as if I were floating over the beautiful land off to the dark bush-like poplars, the hills, the church, Metures, Gemma and Vega, as if I now knew there was something in me wh[ich]. no future c[oul]d. touch, whether I am soon to die...or to know a death, these things may hurt but I go on till I am indistinguishable from the dark land & the sky wh[ich] is so soft & glorious & comforting high overhead, its glory entering me & giving me strange joy both alone & as I talk to de la Mare ab[ou]t why it wd. be so great to be able to write down the feeling of this gloomy thicket by Goose Green & us & the sky. How hollow seems earth as if the abode of ghosts have fled away & [deserted?] a feeling of infinity & eternity.[40]

If proof were needed of the importance of this experience for Thomas, it is made even more explicit in his story 'The Stile', published two years later in *Light and Twilight* (1911). The repetition of key phrases ('deep confidence and ease' (which becomes 'deep ease and confidence') and 'soon to die', striking metaphors ('a few mouths of roses' becomes 'white roses like mouths') and shared references to the scent of honeysuckle, the dark outline of the hills and the stars, leave no doubt as to 'The Stile''s genesis and also emphasize how heavily Thomas still relied on his notebooks by 1911, despite Bottomley's advice. 'The Stile' also tries to make more explicit the shared mystical moment pointed out in the field notebook:

> I found myself running, without weariness or heaviness of the limbs through the soaked overhanging grass. I knew that I was more than the something which had been looking out all that day upon the visible earth and thinking and speaking and tasting friendship. Somewhere – close at hand in that rosy thicket or far off beyond the ribs of sunset – I was gathered up with an immortal company, where I and poet and lover and

flower and cloud and star were equals, as all the little leaves were equal ruffling before the gusts, or sleeping and carved out of the silentness. And in that company I learned that I am something which no fortune can touch, whether I be soon to die or long years away. Things will happen which will trample and pierce, but I shall go on, something that is here and there like the wind, something unconquerable, something not to be separated from the dark earth and the light sky, a strong citizen of infinity and eternity. The confidence and ease had become a deep joy; I knew that I could not do without the Infinite, nor the Infinite without me.[41]

Thomas, who believed himself to be 'very much on an everyday ordinary level except when in a mood of exultation normally connected with nature and solitude', felt that by comparison with de la Mare he was very ordinary indeed – 'essentially like other men in the train'.[42] (Siegfried Sassoon felt the same.) It was a view that de la Mare rejected; he saw Thomas as someone who not only glimpsed another world, but who helped inspire a sense of mystery in others. 'Sotto Voce', one of three poems de la Mare wrote about Thomas, conveys a similar sense of magic to 'The Stile', of something beneath the tangible surface.

Thomas had first contacted de la Mare in the summer of 1906 for permission to include one or two poems by him in Thomas's *Pocket Book* anthology. He had reviewed de la Mare's *Songs of Childhood* in 1902, unaware that its author 'Walter Ramal' was a pseudonym for the poet he now approached.[43] 'I regret that I saw nothing in it except the nonsense pieces,' he told Bottomley in July 1906, 'while I now see that it is poetry.'[44] But he 'thanked God' that he had at least quoted the whole of one poem from it, 'Lovelocks'.[45] He was relieved to find that he had reviewed de la Mare's novel for adults, *Henry Brocken*, more positively in 1904.[46]

De la Mare's relative obscurity in 1906 may have been one reason Thomas wanted him in his anthology, as Judy Kendall suggests;[47] he was anxious not merely to repeat familiar poems by well-known poets in it. His request for 'one or two' poems from de la Mare becomes three – 'The Child in the Story Awakes', 'Keep Innocency' (Thomas's personal favourite) and 'Bunches of Grapes' – as he rapidly responds to de la Mare's 'subtle honesty' and his admiration for Thomas's reviewing.[48] The stiff 'Dear Sir' of his first three letters quickly softens to 'My dear sir' in the fourth and finally (via

'Dear de la Mare') to 'My dear de la Mare' in just over six months. De la Mare is invited to visit Berryfield Cottage almost immediately, though the two do not meet physically until March 1907 – at the 'Mecca' in the City of London, a restaurant near de la Mare's place of work.

Accompanying this increase in personal warmth would be Thomas's growing appreciation of de la Mare's work. His review of de la Mare's *Poems* (1906) less than three months after writing to him,[49] is the first of his many attempts to help a writer who, though five years his senior, was far less well known and in an even more difficult position than himself. De la Mare's daytime job as an accountant for an Anglo-American oil company, to earn money to support his wife and four children, made Thomas more appreciative of his own relative freedom to write, as well as more sympathetic towards him. He would continue to review de la Mare regularly and positively until that area of his work dried up and could boast in 1915 that he had 'probably reviewed [de la Mare] more than anyone else'.[50] He also introduced the older writer to editors and publishers he thought might give him work, Nevinson and Elkin Mathews, for instance, and, in 1911, the literary editor of the *Saturday Westminster Gazette*, Naomi Royde-Smith, a meeting which would affect de la Mare's life profoundly. Thomas would take him to Garnett's Tuesday lunches, invite him to his close circle of friends at the St George's restaurant and propose him as a member for an even more exclusive literary club, inaugurated in 1907 in honour of Henry Fielding, the Square Club.[51] Most importantly Thomas would help de la Mare with his writing, which de la Mare sent him in proof. Much of Thomas's advice about poetry would anticipate his own practices in verse later on.

De la Mare's release from a desk job in 1908, with the granting of a Civil List Pension which Thomas had helped win, would mark a turning point in their relationship, coming just as Thomas himself was about to start on a desk job of his own. As de la Mare quickly established himself as a 'name' in the literary world, he was able to offer assistance to Thomas. He had from the start helped Thomas with suggestions on his prose books but once he began work as a reviewer for *The Times Literary Supplement* as well as the *Westminster Gazette* and became a reader for Heinemann's, his influence counted for as much, if not more, than Thomas's and he was happy to use it on his behalf. In 1909, for instance, he shared his good fortune in being given life membership of the London Library with Thomas by taking books out for Thomas (though not strictly speaking legal). He was later to use his connection with *Georgian Poetry* after Thomas's death to urge Thomas's inclusion, offering to stand down himself if need be. His efforts to get Thomas a Civil List Pension on two occasions mirror Thomas's own earlier efforts to get de la Mare one.

It could not have been easy for a man as proud and insecure as Thomas to accept this reversal of roles lightly and there are signs that it irritated him on occasions. In his letters to Bottomley and Helen in October and November 1912, for instance, he complains that de la Mare is 'a too busy man now – never quite unpuckering in our scanty meetings', so busy with his success that he leaves 'all the efforts' to organize their meetings to Thomas, 'while he does nothing'.[52] And when de la Mare is awarded an extra £100 for his Civil List Pension in 1915, Thomas clearly finds it galling: 'he was making £400 at least,' he tells Frost, admitting frankly 'I was annoyed especially as I am told I have no chance myself as being too young and not as well known as others who will be applying', ending rather more comically: 'If he didn't give me such opulent dinners when I went there I should mind less.'[53]

These were understandable outbursts at a time when Thomas was feeling more than usually depressed and desperate and did not destroy what was one of the closest friendships of Thomas's final decade. De la Mare would be one of the few people to whom he sent his poetry under his own name in 1915 and one of even fewer friends he told of his infatuation with a schoolgirl in 1908. He also felt close enough to de la Mare by 1911 to confess freely his suicidal thoughts. Theresa Whistler believed that Thomas and the poet Mary Coleridge were the two great friendships of de la Mare's life and wrote that the mention of their names 'brought a tone into his voice that no others ever did... They were the pole-stars in his sky, and no other friendships, however intimate or long, affected him so centrally.'[54]

De la Mare had been one of the first poets Thomas approached when he started work on his *Pocket Book of Poems and Songs for the Open Air.* With his usual independence he interpreted his brief freely as a licence to produce the kind of anthology he would 'like to possess', one which would above all avoid '*Golden Treasury* obviousness'.[55] There would be an emphasis on folk-songs, to a large number of which he would (with Bottomley's help) give melodies.

Thomas had already shown in *The Heart of England* how important music was to him – 'Music, the rebel, the martyr, the victor – music, the romantic cry of matter striving to become spirit.'[56] He was now to demonstrate his further claim that 'of all music, the old ballads and folk songs and their airs are richest in the plain immortal symbols…in themselves epitomes of whole generations, of a whole countryside'.[57] The songs would be mainly English but would include some Latin, French and Welsh examples. They would range from medieval lyrics and well-known pastoral airs to the English folk verses recently collected by Sabine Baring-Gould and Cecil Sharp. Some less well-known sea-shanties would be contributed by his friends Tom Clayton and Jesse Berridge, whose father had been a sea captain. The book would be dedicated to Helen, who treasured his ritual of singing these songs to his children at bedtime, and who would pick out some of the tunes he wanted to include on the piano for him.

Another taste Thomas would indulge in his anthology would be for epitaphs copied from gravestones in old country churchyards and noted down carefully in his field notebooks. His guiding principle was to include 'such things as I like to think about when sitting down or walking in the country'.[58]

There would be poetry by standard authors – Chaucer, Shakespeare, Spenser, Herrick, Blake, Wordsworth, Coleridge, Shelley, Keats, Byron, Milton, Marvell, Browning, Swinburne, Tennyson – but wherever possible Thomas would choose their less familiar work. Contemporary poets, where included, tended to be friends, like Bottomley, Dalmon and Davies, as well as de la Mare. Bottomley, whose knowledge of poetry equalled Thomas's and whose knowledge of music surpassed his, continued to suggest material for inclusion as far as the proofs, which he then helped correct. Thomas was proud of his songs – 'glorious…the best short collection in the world', but he wished he 'thought as well of the poems'.[59] He suspected that in his effort to avoid the obvious and the familiar, that his poetry was 'not all good and not all popular enough'.[60] He certainly did not expect to make as much money out of his book as E. V. Lucas had out of what Thomas called rather dismissively his 'genial Open Road anthology'.[61] But *The Pocket Book of Poems and Songs for the Open Air* remained in print until 1950 and he had gained great satisfaction from editing it. It also strengthened a musical strain which would influence his own poetry when he came to write it.

Even working on a book which pleased, or at least interested and stimulated him was not enough to banish Thomas's depression for long. By late December 1906, with *The Pocket Book of Poems and Songs of the Open Air* finished and only the tidying up of the hardback edition of *The Book of the Open Air* outstanding, his 'devil' was on him again, he told Bottomley:

> the present is of the old sort; even a little worse, since I have had but one visit from a friend since I came here, have had so much work that only twice have I been able to walk all day, and for some reason have attained a degree of self-consciousness beyond the dreams (which makes me spend hours, when I ought to be reading, or enjoying the interlacing flight of three kestrels, in thinking out my motives for this or that act or word in the past until I long for sleep).[62]

Rational as the first part of this explanation sounds, it is no real explanation for his mood. He could be equally depressed by the prospect of less work than too much and by 1912 would claim that 'work' was 'the only thing' that would cure him.[63] And his complaint about having seen only one friend at Berryfield Cottage ignores the fact that he had been there only a month when he made it. He also fails to take into account the fact that he had recently started two of the most important friendships of his life and was daily expecting a visit from Bottomley's friend and collaborator, the artist-craftsman, James Guthrie.

Thomas had seen some of Guthrie's work in Bottomley's *Midsummer Eve*, which he had reviewed for the *Daily Chronicle*,[64] but had never met the man in person. Now shortly after his move to Hampshire Bottomley alerted both men to the fact that they were virtually neighbours, knowing that the seven miles between Berryfield Cottage and Guthrie's house at South Harting, south-east of Petersfield, would present no problem to either. By 16 February 1907 Thomas reported to Bottomley that he had finally met Guthrie the previous day:

> I had done three long days reading and writing and the morning being lofty and blue, I walked to South Harting…and met him and his wife

and three children and found myself infinitely more at ease than I usually am with strangers. We seemed to hit it off in a lazy way quite comfortably and he walked back with me in the evening as far as Petersfield which was midway. I saw lots of his work and I like his landscapes more and more ...[65]

Guthrie, born in Glasgow in 1874 but brought to London as a child, was an artist, printer, poet and craftsman who had established his own private press at the Pear Tree Cottage, Ingrave, Essex in 1899, before moving to Kent as Thomas did (Shorne in Guthrie's case), then to West Sussex, near to its border with Hampshire. His final move would be to what he called, in recognition of one of his chief mentors, 'Blake country', Flansham, on the Sussex coast. His son Robin's description of his father after his death in 1952 suggests similarities between Guthrie and Thomas, despite their different disciplines: 'His uncompromising attitude to art and to living itself was truly remarkable...It was a life of perpetual struggle and disappointment kept vitalized by invention and love of doing things.'[66]

In other respects, Guthrie and Thomas differed significantly. Though worse off than Thomas in some ways, with a sick wife, three small children and very little money, Guthrie remained cheerful throughout and even tried to cheer Thomas out of recurrent depressions. And where Thomas was often silent but always articulate, Guthrie was 'inarticulate but not silent', Thomas would come to feel. He found Guthrie's many 'pretty little schemes' frankly 'fantastic' and was unable to relate to them.[67] Even where they shared something, like their love of nature, their approach was quite different; Guthrie recalled: 'Upon our early walks, we used to compare our different ways of looking at nature; the one literary (translating things seen into words) and the other artistic (looking for form and colour). I teased him about trying to fit Keats into what he saw, and he me for finding a sentiment where I ought to consider shapes.'[68] Guthrie believed that they learnt something from each other and Thomas's introduction to *Guthrie's Second Book of Drawings* (1908) confirms that he had at least been shown how to look at pictures.

One of the interests of Thomas's friendship with Guthrie, which lasted until his death, is the side of himself he revealed to the older man. While conceding that 'nobody who knew Thomas would pretend that he was evenly patient, wise or forbearing', Guthrie remembered him for his active sense of friendship and his quiet way of talking. Like many good talkers he was at his best with a single chosen companion; for the presence of a third party tends to distract and disturb, to introduce a foreign element of criticism or banter, in which the spirit of the best conversation evaporates. This was especially true where Thomas was concerned, and it accounts for the ironic reserve which some noticed in him when in a mixed company. His attitude then was that of an observer, unwilling to venture an opinion where there were already too many. Shy as he was, he did not suffer fools gladly, nor permit any personal liberty against himself.[69]

Guthrie also emphasized the musical side to Thomas, who joined in their family singsongs on his visits to Flansham, often singing one of his own favourites, such as 'The Wraggle Taggle Gypsies, O!' The middle Guthrie son, Robin, remembered what 'a tireless and passionate swimmer' he was, ' "bathing to excess" with [the three boys], playing with them near the shore, then suddenly leaving them to swim far out to sea till his head was a speck in the distance'.[70] He also remembered him as a 'rather unusual "visitor" who turned up at odd times, generally after we were in bed…leaning on the end rail dispensing sweets'.[71] When the three boys put on little plays, 'he would invade the stage or sit back petting [them] with fragments of biscuit'.[72] Clearly Thomas was more relaxed than usual with the family. Guthrie, according to Eleanor Farjeon who knew them both well, became 'one of [Thomas's] staunchest friends'.[73]

Guthrie was one of the few people who saw a positive side to what others dismissed as hack work. 'It was not all – hard going,' Guthrie maintained, 'and sometimes he found a subject in which he took a lively interest.'[74] Thomas was to light on such a subject and produce one of his most successful prose books only two months after his first meeting with Guthrie in February 1907, *Richard Jefferies: His Life and Work*.

13

HOPE AND LOSS OF HOPE
(JANUARY 1907–DECEMBER 1909)

I f Edward and Helen were still hoping that a new house meant
a new start, they were quickly disillusioned. After helping them
move into Berryfield Cottage, Helen's mother had died suddenly
in early January 1907. Although Helen had not been close to Mrs
Noble, especially after her marriage, she needed an emotional
support Edward was unable to give.

His first few months at Berryfield had been crowded ones.
The move itself was followed by an intense period of preparation
of the garden for his ritual sowing of vegetables in February and
March. Fruit trees and bushes would be planted and added to over
a relatively long period, but seeds could not wait if the Thomases
were to have vegetables throughout the year. His writing also kept
him busy, with reviewing still coming in regularly. *The Pocket Book
of Poems and Songs for the Open Air* was completed for publication
in early 1907 and followed by an extensive revision of the first
impression, which was full of misprints. Despite this activity, by
April he had suffered 'two bad spells of languor and melancholy'.[1]
Cutting his smoking from eight pipes to two per day had not
helped. He longed for 'a little money to turn round for a year,' he
told Bottomley, 'to make sure whether there is anything I should
want to do if I had not to do reviewing'.[2]

Yet the same May letter makes it clear that the problem did not lie in the need to review sometimes as many as four times a week for the *Daily Chronicle, Bookman* or *Morning Post*; even when this taskwork was finished for the day, the malaise remained:

> I can't read for pleasure. I tried gardening: it annoyed me…It is no use walking, for I do nothing but feed my eyes when I walk, and it has at last occurred to me that is not enough – a man in the country must be a naturalist, an historian, an agriculturalist, or a philosopher, and I am none of them. I have no 'interests' at all, and I know that beauty can bore and infuriate one who is seldom passionate.[3]

Thomas's more animated discussion of ideas for books which might 'help [him] out of reviewing',[4] suggests that his only hope of a cure might still lie in writing, but on a subject he enjoyed rather than endured. His first thought was of something similar to *The Heart of England*, 'dally[ing] with *The South Country* to include a bit of history – perhaps the history of England from the point of view of one parish or great house', an idea he would shelve for another year.[5] Another possibility was a collection of pieces on English poets, an opportunity to write about his favourites, a scheme which would be realized in *A Literary Pilgrim in England* (1917). What he really wanted to write was about his 'chiefly pathetic memories of the Suburbs – their grave charming Queen Anne [house]s, now tumbling down at the feet of the villa-builder', his own special memories of their 'little bits of waste ground' and 'their quite new houses so difficult to like and yet to be liked'.[6] He suspected that less than a hundred people would want such a book and no publisher would commission it. But he would write about the suburbs in other guises, as a way to the country in his travel books, in his essays and in fictional form in his one novel, *The Happy-Go-Lucky Morgans*.

Thomas would eventually settle on another legacy from childhood, the naturalist Richard Jefferies and his native county of Wiltshire. His admiration for Jefferies had come through in the titles of his two most recent books, both of which echo Jefferies's *The Open Air* (1885). His adolescent essay on Jefferies lay far behind him, but he knew that Garnett had written at least one more recent article on him and looked to him for advice and any new information about the naturalist. Hutchinson's reader (and de la Mare's brother-in-law), Roger Ingpen, expressed interest in a life and criticism of Jefferies of not more than 80,000 words for an advance of £100. It would take until July 1907 to agree a contract, by which time Thomas had already started work. Rarely had he felt so enthusiastic about a subject and he insisted on a reasonable time in which to write it.

A few days in May with a friend made at the Mont Blanc in March, Stephen Reynolds, who lived in Devizes, had refreshed his love of Wiltshire. And his fortnight with Gordon and Emily Bottomley at Cartmel in June appears to have dispelled his fear of producing merely 'a bad life of a good man'.[7] Garnett was equally helpful and encouraging. He was able to introduce Thomas to Jefferies's widow, as Thomas had hoped, as well as suggesting other lines of enquiry. By the end of June Thomas had arranged to meet Mrs Jefferies at Chiddingfold in Surrey, only 22 miles from Steep. By early July, the contract fully signed, he set to work in earnest.

School holidays arrived shortly afterwards, however, and Helen took the children away, leaving Edward to fend for himself and Martin Freeman, who came to keep him from the solitude he dreaded: 'So what with cooking, washing up, talking and…daily work', he had little time for his book.[8] But by mid-August he was installed at Broome Farm, near Swindon, preparing to 'plough through Parish Registers, explore Jefferies country, talk to anyone who had known him' and perhaps even fish 'for one or two whole days'.[9]

The three weeks in Wiltshire passed quickly. Despite several dead-ends, he gathered some useful information and made a few good contacts. But he feared that he would have to use Jefferies's books as his chief source and quote more than he liked doing, a fault which mars the finished work. A further problem was that, with his usual anxiety about money, he had agreed at the same time to write a life of George Borrow for Methuen, who had been impressed by his introduction to Borrow's *The Bible in Spain* the previous year. Helen describes the fortnight she spent with Edward in Wiltshire as 'one of the happiest times of my life'.[10] But Edward's letter in September to Bottomley shortly after his return home indicates that he had not shared her joy in their rare time alone together, complaining of being 'not well, worried, hard at work, discontented with myself and everyone I see…and troubled by a lot of sleeplessness'.[11] It is clear from what follows, both in the letter and in his life, that he believes only an extreme emotion could rouse him from his lethargy: 'Why have I no energies like other men? I long for some hatred or indignation or even sharp despair.'[12] His glimpse of a possible salvation a few months later in the 'love' he had believed it 'impossible' to feel would vanish almost as soon as it appeared, but it would give him a moment of intense joy such as he had rarely experienced before.

One symptom of Thomas's depression which Helen found particularly difficult to bear was his constant irritation with the family and frequent trips to escape home. A fortnight's visit to London in early November, staying with his parents and the Hootons, was followed by another visit to Stephen Reynolds at Devizes in early December, both in the name of research. No sooner back home, he was preparing to go away again to somewhere quiet and distraction-free for the actual writing of Jefferies's life. According to Helen, it was a nerve-specialist friend who had suggested it; if so, it was almost certainly at Edward's prompting.

Fortunately Janet Hooton was able to help. She and Harry rented a cottage at Minsmere, near Dunwich in Suffolk, next to her parents, the Aldises, and their close friends and relatives the Webbs, for whom Helen had worked in 1896. It was the smallest unit in a little coastguard station of black cottages standing far from all other houses on the edge of a sandy cliff. Four of the eight cottages were leased to William Trego Webb, his wife and eight children, three to the Aldis family and the last to the Hootons, who used it as a retreat from their home at Anerley in south London. A room at the seaward end of the building was used as a communal recreation space. The Hootons not only lent Edward their little cottage but also arranged for someone to look after him there.

Edward planned to leave for Suffolk just after Christmas, a festivity he enjoyed for once 'because Bronwen excelled herself in joy and expressions of joy and even Merfyn was never peevish'.[13] Setting out on 27 December, he stopped in London to consult a leading nerve-specialist, Dr Thomas Savill, who diagnosed his problem as 'neurasthenia'. Savill's definition of this was 'a gradual increase in nervousness and unusual fatigue at the end of [a] day's work', occurring most commonly in those aged between 25 and 40 and those who lead indoor sedentary lives.[14]

Thomas makes light of this consultation when reporting it to Bottomley, claiming that the doctor 'messed [him] about, commanded abstinence from alcohol and sugar and almost abstinence from tobacco, and gave [him] a wonderfully compounded medicine (bismuth, bromide) and small green tablets',[15] but he immediately began to feel better. (Bromide was used commonly as a sedative at the time, bismuth to treat dyspepsia.) He also found Dr Savill's severe diet, which appealed to his strong ascetic tendencies, reassuring. As Thomas himself suggested, however, his marked improvement in health and spirits at Minsmere was just as likely to have been a result of the sea air and the lively company of the Aldis family with their three grown-up daughters next door. Another reason for his sense of well-being during his first month in Suffolk was that his work was going better than usual, his careful preparation and the congeniality of the subject allowing him to write more freely and enjoyably than for a long time.

But the most likely reason for Thomas's unusually positive mood in January 1908 was his powerful attraction to a daughter of the Webb family, 'a girl of seventeen [she was actually 18] with two long plaits of dark brown hair and the richest grey eyes, very wild and shy'.[16] 'It is a good many years since I felt such a strong unreasoning liking for anyone,' he confessed to Harry Hooton, who knew the girl in question, Hope Webb, well. He said he was attracted to her by 'her perfect wild youthfulness and remoteness',[17] but there seems also to have been an element of 'forbidden fruit' in the relationship. The fact that Hope had been a child in Helen's care – an irony probably not lost on Helen – and that she reminded him in some ways of his own daughter, Bronwen, lends almost incestuous overtones to the affair. His poem 'Celandine', written nearly a decade afterwards, undoubtedly about Hope – 'Her nature and name / were like those flowers' – celebrates a flame-like quality, a brightness of eye which he found in both Bronwen and Hope; it also links the first finder of celandines to an entry in his field diary for March 1909 noting that 'Bronwen found the first Celandine':[18]

Celandine

Thinking of her had saddened me at first,
Until I saw the sun on the celandines lie
Redoubled, and she stood up like a flame,
A living thing, not what before I nursed,

The shadow I was growing to love almost,
The phantom, not the creature with bright eye
That I had thought never to see, once lost.

She found the celandines of February
Always before us all. Her nature and name
Were like those flowers, and now immediately
For a short swift eternity back she came,
Beautiful, happy, simply as when she wore
Her brightest bloom among the winter hues
Of all the world; and I was happy too,
Seeing the blossoms and the maiden who
Had seen them with me Februarys before,
Bending to them as in and out she trod
And laughed, with locks sweeping the mossy sod.

But this was a dream: the flowers were not true,
Until I stooped to pluck from the grass there
One of five petals and I smelt its juice
Which made me sigh, remembering she was no more,
Gone like a never perfectly recalled air.[19]

Edward, who continued to be entirely frank with Helen, told her that Hope, her favourite as a child, was now beautiful, timid and unsophisticated, that she had walked with him on the beach, spoken of the books she was reading and of her love for the open air, the sea and the flat marshes of Suffolk: 'He said she was like a wild, timid sea-bird, and that only very gradually had he overcome her shyness.'[20] In a repetition of his adolescent relationship with Helen, he lent Hope books and introduced her to his favourite poets. He makes the link between Hope and his improvement in health and spirits clear when he tells Walter de la Mare of the effect her departure for school has had on him, also of the connection he makes between Hope and this overwhelming experience of love:

And the place has become chiefly superficies [surface] ever since. She is…a particularly lovely age to me because when I was that age I knew only two of my coevals, one I married and the other is in South Africa, and in the presence of this new one I had the sharpest pains and pleasures of retrospection, longing and…[21]

Thomas's attraction to Hope seen in this context implies, as Edna Longley argues, that 'an aspect of his sexuality [had] remain[ed] arrested at, and hence fixated on, the adolescent moment – also, that premature domesticity caused the arrest',[22] a theory borne out by Thomas's next two sentences to de la Mare: 'I am now making absurd attempts to return to that period by means of letters [to Hope]. You see I have a young head on my decrepit shoulders.'[23] The physical chasteness forced on him by the circumstances, but the licence allowed to his imagination in her absence, fitted in well with his creation of, perhaps even preference for, idealized women: 'You are right when you propose an unassailable vision of her,' he writes to Bottomley after Hope has left Minsmere.[24] He was to celebrate her not only in his next two books, *The South Country* (1909) and *Rest and Unrest* (1910), but in his poetry many years later.

Though his correspondence with Hope allowed him to fantasize about her for the remainder of his stay at Minsmere, the relish went out of his life. While his notebook becomes more lyrical than ever, it becomes more despairing: 'It is a rotten world where everything is fleeting yet the soul desires permanence even for its brief unprofitable emotions such as my love for —' he writes on 20 February.[25] Though work on his Jefferies book proceeded reasonably well, his view of the landscape changed significantly after Hope left the area. From having found nearby Dunwich 'beautiful…a heaving moor of heather and close gorse up and down and ending in a sandy cliff about 80 feet perpendicular, and the black, peat strewn fine sand below', once the presence which had irradiated it had gone, he was telling Bottomley that he did not 'like the country on the whole, only two or three miles of moor, Sandy cliff, flat marsh and sea'.[26] 'And even that,' he added frankly, 'is a remembered dream now that the child I told you of has become a phantom face and a kind but moderate letter-writer' – words written only days before Helen was arriving to spend his last weekend at Minsmere with him.

Despite Hope's disappointing letters, however, Thomas was both devastated and humiliated when on his last night at Minsmere he was told by her father, a retired Anglo-Indian and man of letters, William Trego Webb, to stop writing to her. 'After saying goodbye Webb said "I hear you have been having a little correspondence with Hope…She is very busy and has to write letters to us, her brother, her sisters – I think it had better cease." '[27]

Only four days previously, Thomas had 'dimly foreseen a guttering candle, a flicker, a smell and an awakening to find the fire as well as the light gone out, the house gone cold and dark and still and the one thing possible a shivering undressing and so to bed and the usual dull torment before I dare to rise and begin another day'.[28] Now, to make it much worse, he felt himself cast in the role of a child-seducer.

Throughout the whole affair no one seems to have taken Hope's possible involvement in it seriously except Helen who, after reading Hope's letter to her 'Auntie' (as she called Helen), suspected that she was falling in love with Edward. But even Helen, like the rest of the people involved, seems to have regarded Hope as a child, though at 18 she was the same age as Helen when she met Edward and older than Edward when he became involved with Helen. She was, in fact, a young woman about to leave home for university. It may or may not be significant that Hope never married; perhaps she was unable to find anyone to compete with the attraction of a handsome, older man, a writer like her own father.

Edward's letters to Helen from this period can throw no light here, since they have not survived, almost certainly because they were too painful for Helen to reread as it dawned on her that Edward, who had told her that he 'could not love', was in love with her former protégée. Suffering torments of jealousy, she wrote him long, injured letters, followed immediately by loving, conciliatory ones:

And Hope's written again to you, and you to her I suppose. I wonder (I do really so please tell me, I'm quite serious) what you want her to develop into, or what you want 'it' to develop into. You are fond of her, but you can't make her fond of you without making it difficult for her. Is it to be the friendship of a middle-aged man, a man of letters etc. etc. and of a simple schoolgirl, the sort of idyllic affair your biographers will dote on – a passionless, innocent, intimate, uncleish, loverish affair that makes one wish in reading the biography that 'I' had been the girl. Is it to be of that sort? Or is she meant to slip unconsciously into something more, with sentiment in it, and heart openings, and in fact a love affair, or what? It puzzles me. I mean your attitude to her, what you want, what's it all about?

Helen's public version of events, written much later, underplays the strength of Edward's passion for Hope, implying simply that the Suffolk stay had done him good and that he returned home looking 'splendidly well and…in the best spirits'.[29] Thomas's first biographer, R. P. Eckert, accepted Helen's version of events, concluding that when he returned home 'his love for his wife had not lessened; if anything, it seemed greater than before'.[30] Helen's own choice of biographer, John Moore, is even more upbeat. Describing Edward's infatuation with Hope as 'a brief pleasant folly', he repeats Helen's comforting rationalization that Edward's anger at Mr Webb's edict meant that 'he was surely well again: bad temper was more healthy than despair'.[31] Having emptied his pockets of the pebbles he had collected with Hope, Moore continues, 'he suddenly found that he could laugh at himself and that the episode was over'.[32] R. George Thomas, on the other hand, argues that 'the consequence of the nine weeks at Minsmere was the emergence of a more flexible, less idealistic, but essentially loving relationship between Helen and Edward which provided Helen with a more identifiable role to fill in the home, at Bedales, and in the neighbourhood'.[33]

If, by this, R. George Thomas means that Helen could no longer believe in an 'ideal' love between them, then perhaps so. Helen had certainly 'gone through a crisis' in her life, she told Janet: 'and I *think* I'm wiser and know I'm sadder. In trying to look into things, I believe it's my ideal that has been smashed; it was so high and shining and fair, but it was not useful – so it fell'.[34]

Edward was in an even worse state, confessing to de la Mare less than a fortnight after his return that his 'mind ha[d] been in Hell these many days' and that he found living 'only just possible'.[35] Two days later Helen noted that since returning from Minsmere Edward had been 'terribly nervy, depressed, desperate, as bad as ever' and that 'all [her] hopes ha[d] fallen into many fragments'.[36] By the end of March Edward felt as though he were 'crawl[ing] along the very edge of life, wondering why [he] didn't get over the edge'.[37] 'The change from the strong east winds off the sea, the regular uninterrupted life at Minsmere, to this milder place full of "little" responsibilities, the garden bedraggled after a sudden winter,' he explained to Bottomley, 'meant something.'

By October comes Thomas's reference to marriage 'continually encrusting the soul'[38] and a month later on 29 November he wrote in his diary, 'tried to shoot myself'. At the same time he was attending a Dr Bramwell for his second treatment. He had already visited Dr Savill five times between March and 2 October, when he decided that Savill was 'perfunctory' and switched to Dr Bramwell. But three days after his second visit he decided that he 'disliked' him, too, and cancelled his next appointment. He felt as despairing as at any time since Oxford.

Part of Thomas's depression stemmed from his decision to accept a post as an Assistant Secretary with the Royal Commission on Ancient Monuments in Wales and Monmouthshire, which his father had engineered. On paper he had seemed ideally suited to the job. It held out the promise of field trips around Wales, some interesting research and only an occasional day spent in the London office. Theoretically the evenings and whole days would be free for his own writing. The reality turned out to be very different. He was expected to be in his office – a dark office in Great George Street, Westminster – every day from ten till six, which meant cramming his own work into the evening and late nights. Since a daily commute from Petersfield to London was impracticable, he had to spend the week in town with family or friends, a situation he disliked. The promised trips to Wales turned out to be one trip to Swansea, a town he found 'horrible' as well as 'sublime'.[39] When the true nature of the job became apparent, his only reason for not resigning till Christmas was to placate his father. MacAlister's appointment as Secretary of the Royal Institute of British Architects had possibly encouraged Thomas to take an office job, but de la Mare's release from his clerkship in an oil company at approximately the same time may help to explain his decision to leave the Commission as soon as decently possible.

The deciding factor was the impossibility of carrying on with his own work. By August 1908, when he accepted the post, Thomas had already agreed to write *The South Country* he had earlier proposed for Dent, as well as to edit and introduce *The Plays and Poems of Christopher Marlowe* for Dent's Everyman Library. He was still intending to produce a life of George Borrow and determined to carry on with his reviewing work, which he did not want to lose. Most pressing of all was his need to complete his biography of Richard Jefferies. He had sent in the main text to Hutchinson in July but had still to compile a bibliography, provide an index and correct proofs, an onerous job even with Bottomley's help. Having spent more time and effort over this book than on any previous work, he was anxious to do it full justice.

Whether Thomas succeeded or not is debatable, despite Q. D. Leavis's well-known praise of *Richard Jefferies* as 'a classic in critical biography, to stand with Lockhart's *Scott* and Mrs Gaskell's *Bronte*'.[40] Tastes in biography have changed since 1909, when *Richard Jefferies* was published, and modern readers would probably agree with Thomas's fear that he had included a disproportionate amount of quotation from Jefferies's work: 'I have had to quote so much in order to make my special claims for him quite clear and I shall be buried under the load of his good things and produce only an untidy anthology.'[41]

Yet there are 'good things' from Thomas as well as Jefferies in his biography. His admiration for Jefferies's work, never in doubt, enables his readers to appreciate the Wiltshireman's gifts, above all his 'power of using words' (and in doing so, Thomas's own):

> Nothing is more mysterious than this power, along with the kindred powers of artist and musician. It is the supreme proof, above beauty, physical strength, intelligence, that a man or woman lives. Lighter than gossamer, words can entangle and hold fast all that is loveliest, and strongest, and fleetest, and most enduring, in heaven and earth.[42]

Thomas's assessment of Jefferies's many fiction and non-fiction books, including his classic children's book, *Bevis* (1882) and an early attempt at science fiction, *After London* (1885), is stimulating and perceptive, particularly his own account of his favourites, *The Amateur Poacher* (1879), *Round About a Great Estate* (1880), *Dewy Morn* (1884) and *Amaryllis at the Fair* (1887). Perhaps best of all is Thomas's piece on Jefferies's autobiography, *The Story of My Heart* (1883), in which it becomes clear how closely he identifies, consciously or not, with his subject. He understands from first-hand experience Jefferies's profound love of the country, especially Wiltshire, his time spent in the suburbs of south London, which he both hated and loved, his difficult personality, his curious, rather sardonic sense of humour, his prose-writing always straining at the edge of poetry and his problems as 'a poorish, isolated writing man' – though Thomas himself was no longer 'poorish' or 'isolated' by 1908.[43] He could empathize with Jefferies's fits of depression, his pursuit by 'the Terror'. And he was drawn to Jefferies's mystical streak to the extent of asking Jesse Berridge for books on mysticism, which Berridge felt was 'much more than an effort towards

ABOVE: The Thomas family
1894. (Left to right) Philip
Henry Thomas, Julian, Ernest,
Edward, Reginald, Oscar,
Theodore, Mary Elizabeth
Thomas.

RIGHT: 61 Shelgate
Road, London, SW11,
(right-hand house).

RIGHT: Mary Elizabeth
Thomas, 1896.

FAR RIGHT: Edward
Thomas, 1898.

Helen Berenice Noble and Edward Thomas,
aged approximately eighteen.

Edward Thomas, 1898.   Helen Noble, 1898.

ABOVE: The Lincoln College
Torpids Crew, Lent term, 1899.
Edward Thomas second from left,
back row.

ABOVE: Edward Thomas in his
rooms at Lincoln College, Oxford,
Michaelmas term, 1899.

RIGHT: Edward Thomas
at Oxford, 1899.

ABOVE: Thomas family, with Edward,
Merfyn and grandmother, 1902/3.

RIGHT: Helen Thomas
with Merfyn, c.1902.

ᴛᴏᴘ: Rose Acre Cottage, with
Edward and Merfyn Thomas.

ᴀʙᴏᴠᴇ ʀɪɢʜᴛ: Ivy Cottage,
Bearsted.

ᴀʙᴏᴠᴇ: Elses Farm, The Weald,
Kent.

ʀɪɢʜᴛ: Edward Thomas, 1905.

ABOVE LEFT: Henry
Nevinson.

ABOVE: Edward Garnett.

LEFT: W.H. Hudson.

BELOW LEFT: W.H. Davies.

BELOW: Walter de la Mare.

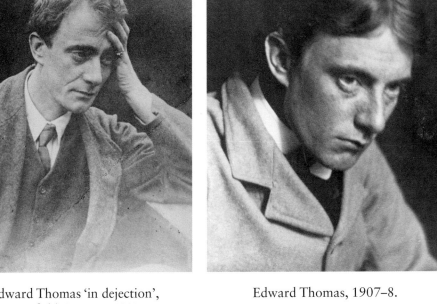

Edward Thomas 'in dejection',
Berryfield Cottage, 1907.

Edward Thomas, 1907–8.

Helen with Bronwen and Merfyn, a studio photograph
taken at Petersfield, New Year, 1907.

LEFT: Berryfield Cottage, Steep.

BELOW: Wick Green, above Steep.

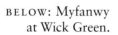

BELOW: Myfanwy at Wick Green.

BELOW RIGHT: 2 Yew Tree Cottages, Steep.

literary understanding of Jefferies and Maeterlinck'.[44] The mention of Maeterlinck shows how interested Thomas became for a period in the Belgian playwright, though by the time he came to write his study of him for Methuen in 1911, he was already suspicious of his esoteric tendencies and by completion felt 'intense disgust for the later work'.[45] While he retained his admiration for Maeterlinck's earlier work, especially *The Life of the Bee*, his final judgement was that he was 'nothing but wind'.[46] (Ironically, Maeterlinck himself liked Thomas's book on him.)

Thomas's view of Jefferies, on the other hand, remained constant, his enjoyment of Jefferies's love of 'the free open-air life, the spice of illegality and daring roguish characters' unchanged.[47] (What he could not know is that he would also die at the same early age as Jefferies, 39.) When, in his opening chapter, Thomas launches into a detailed description of Jefferies's native Wiltshire, it is a charming account written from first-hand knowledge and love of the county. Meantime, Jefferies virtually disappears from the scene, slips out of focus. As Bottomley had noted of *The Heart of England*, an overemphasis on landscape can swamp other things, in this case Jefferies's character and development. On the other hand, the positive effect of Thomas's identification with Jefferies emerges in his understanding of his choices and reactions as a boy and young man, worshipping and writing about nature.

Thomas's own assessment of his biography as he finished his first draft was fair, possibly erring on the harsh side: 'The book is not, cannot be organic. It may have a lot of small lights, but no light on the whole man. Trying to mingle biography, criticism and mere exposition of his matter, I have made confusion.'[48] The critics were kind but Thomas was not satisfied. He hoped to get 'nearer to a real book form' in his next work, *The South Country* (1909).[49]

Thomas makes the topographical nature of *The South Country* clear in his opening paragraph. After telling his readers that his title comes from Hilaire Belloc's poem of that name, he explains what he understands by 'the south country' and, in doing so, conveys his love and first-hand knowledge of his subject as he had in *Richard Jefferies*:

> it includes…the counties of Kent, Sussex, Surrey, Hampshire, Berkshire, Wiltshire, Dorset and part of Somerset. East and west across it go ranges of chalk hills, their sides smoothly hollowed by Nature and the

marl-burner, or sharply scored by old roads. On their lower slopes they carry the chief woods of the south country, their coombes are often fully fledged with trees, and sometimes their high places are crowned with beech or fir; but they are most admirably themselves when they are bare of all but grass and a few bushes of gorse and juniper and some yew, and their ridges make flowing but infinitely variable clear lines against the sky…This then is my South Country. It covers the South Downs, the Icknield Way and the Pilgrims' Way, and the crossroads between them and the Thames and the sea, a land of hops, fruit, corn, high pasture, meadow, woodland, heath and shore.[50]

Robert MacFarlane sees *The South Country* as more than a straightforward travel book, claiming something 'hypermodern about the book's collage-like feel, its shifts and bucks' which distinguishes it sharply from other Edwardian nature travelogues; and compares the experience of reading it to a 'Google-Earth flyover of the chalk counties: zooming in here, settling there, lifting off, scrolling on'.[51] Thomas, he argues, 'pioneered the walk as art-act, as artefact' decades before Guy Debord and his Situationists devised the idea of the *dérive* or 'randomly motivated walk' in the 1950s.[52]

Helen Thomas, less controversially, sees *The South Country* as 'one of the happiest' of Edward's prose works and one of his best sustained pieces of prose-writing.[53] But her explanation for this – that it was written at a period of 'comparative ease and tranquillity' – is less convincing.[54] He had rarely felt less 'tranquil' than he did between May and October 1908 when *The South Country* was drafted. Nevertheless the writing of it did offer him some relief, allowing him to revisit the Suffolk coast and Hope Webb imaginatively and in an acceptable form. For, despite his careful delineation of an area south of the Thames and Severn and east of Exmoor, he also includes East Anglia ('only for the sake of contrast,' he hastens to tell his reader), in particular what is recognizably Minsmere, a section included ostensibly to convey the end of winter in Suffolk.[55]

Hope herself is almost certainly described in the same section, though the account purports to be that of a 4-year-old rather than 18-year-old girl:

She is beautiful and straight as the July corn, as the ash tree standing alone by the stream. She is fearless as fire, bold and restless as wind, clear-hearted, simple, bright and gay as mountain water; in all her actions a daughter of the sun, the wind and the earth. She has loving looks for all. From her fair broad naked foot to her gleaming hair she is, to many, the dearest thing that lives.[56]

The hint of sexual attraction in that glimpse of 'naked foot' appears again in the character of a 17-year-old girl described later in the book by a man who is, in effect, the first real incarnation of 'the Other', long before Thomas's poem of that name is written. The man, not named, is 'tall', 'dressed in grey', 'hardly over thirty', works in a sunless office in winter, loves 'rain best of all', 'belongs to the suburbs', believes himself to be a 'superfluous man' and quotes Sir Thomas Browne at length, resembling his creator closely in all these and other ways. So that when this man tells his story of his attempt to escape to the country and his love for a 17-year-old girl who lives in Suffolk, it is impossible not to identify her with Hope again: 'She was tall and straight with long brown hair in two heavy plaits, a shining, rounded brow, dark-lashed grey eyes, and a smile of inexpressible sweetness in which I once or twice surprised her, pleased with the happiness and beauty of her thoughts and of Nature.'[57] Like Thomas, the teller of the story ('A Return to Nature') knows his Shakespeare, quoting *Cymbeline* to express his desolation when he has 'lost' her, or thinks he has:

> …Not comforted to live
> But that there is this jewel in the world
> Which I may see again –

The whole episode centring round the Hope figure is one of the most interesting parts of *The South Country*, pointing forward to his use of an alter ego, 'the Other', and revealing his growing attraction to the possibilities of fiction rather than travel-writing to express himself, an impulse which will lead to his next literary effort, *Rest and Unrest*, where Hope again is almost certainly present as the idealized figure of a young woman in 'The Fountain'.

The South Country, dedicated to Garnett, who had been a great help in writing *Richard Jefferies*, contains other insights into Thomas's life beside the impact of Hope Webb on him. He had made several trips round Surrey, Sussex and Kent in preparation and used his intimate knowledge of Hampshire and Wiltshire as well. But he also 'dragged in' (his phrase) Cornwall, not part of the South Country as he defined it, mainly because he had visited it for the first time just before starting to write. His five-day trip with one of his few Bedales friends, Geoffrey Lupton, had impressed him greatly and he was reluctant to waste the copious notes he had, as usual, taken.

Six years younger than Thomas, Lupton was a big man with a magnificent physique; with his blond hair, bright blue eyes and red beard, he reminded Helen of a 'Viking or a young demi-god'.[58] He was also a man of few words and those few often 'brusque', she remembered. Though in many ways very different from Thomas, he was the ideal walking companion and they covered at least 16 miles a day, getting up at 5 a.m. and going to bed at 9 p.m., as they walked down the Cornish coast from Tintagel to St Ives and round Land's End to Penzance. But while Thomas's field notebook gives precise names – St Endelion, Port Isaac, Tintagel, Camelford, Polzeath etc. – his section on Cornwall in *The South Country* is noticeably free of them, despite his promise to Dent to be more specific. It is as though he is trying to get to the essence of the places he visits and scorns such externals. In its wildness, ruggedness and wealth of local legends Cornwall reminded him at times of Wales and he would revisit it the following summer with Haynes.

Besides using his notes on Cornwall to fill his word-count, Thomas also recycled pieces already published in magazines and elsewhere. One piece, not recycled but a remnant of his idea of writing a whole book on the subject, is his chapter on 'History and the Parish', which reveals what Edna Longley defines as 'his post-Darwinian approach to "the mystery of the past"; his ecological vision',[59] again ahead of his time:

> Someday [Thomas writes] there will be a history of England written from the point of view of one parish, or town, or great house. Not until there is such a history will all our accumulation of information be justified. It will begin with a geological picture, something large, clear, architectural, not a mess of insignificant names... The peculiar combination of soil and woodland and water determines the direction and position and importance of the ancient trackways; it will determine also the position and size of the human settlements.[60]

History of the kind Thomas had studied at Oxford is rarely present in *The South Country*, though there is a description of one of the hunger marches through London which started in 1905, showing that, despite his claim to be apolitical, he was concerned at the extreme inequalities in society by that date.

Dent, however, had wanted something different, with real place-names and a solid-looking framework. Instead Thomas presented him with his own interpretation of the travel book as a vehicle for his thoughts and impressions on a wide variety of subjects, sprinkled with quotations from his favourite poets: 'My mind is lyrical or if you like jerky and spasmodic,' he wrote to Bottomley by way of explanation.[61] Phrases from the book would anticipate his poetry.

When the sales of *The South Country* proved disappointing, Dent's fears were realized and he would not ask Thomas for another so-called travel book, leading Thomas to believe that it was 'the last of its tribe.'[62] Bottomley, for one, rejoiced: 'Landscape was never valuable to you,' he tells Thomas shrewdly, 'except as a transition to more personal things.'[63] Yet if he agreed with Thomas that *The South Country* was in some respects his 'worst' book, he also argued that it was his 'best' so far, with its 'personal element', its 'character-sketches' and its supreme 'historic sense.'[64] Perhaps, as Robert MacFarlane suggests, the best way to think of this book is 'as a dream-map', that is 'an act of imaginative cartography, a chart of longing and loss projected onto actual terrain.'[65]

Thomas's work on *The South Country* had been hampered by his need to proof-read *Richard Jefferies* and work for the Royal Commission, but he managed to complete it, more or less by October 1908. His sense of release when his father reluctantly agreed to his leaving the Royal Commission at Christmas that year expressed itself partly in his decision to write something entirely for himself, with no thought of payment. He had already told de la Mare that he wanted to do no commissioned work for a time, 'just to see if anything occurs to me. So far I have never had an opportunity of writing a book I wanted – I mean really wanted to whether I had time and payment or not.'[66] An unusual scarcity of review work in the first three months of 1909 provided a rare opportunity to experiment with this idea and in January Thomas wrote again to tell de la Mare that he was 'without work and…writing stories without events, queer dull, sombre, languid things which nobody will ever print or see.'[67]

It was almost certainly his feelings for Hope which led to this burst of creativity unparalleled since his undergraduate days. He had suffered for ten months and tried to commit suicide in November 1908 over her; nevertheless she had given him a sense of rejuvenation. And on the anniversary of his arrival at Minsmere he was finally able to sublimate his feelings in a series of essays, sketches and stories, some inspired directly by his stay there. From the beginning of 1909, he told his two greatest supporters and advisers, Bottomley and Garnett, he had experienced 'an extraordinary energy in writing' and by the middle of February had 'done nothing else'.[68] He suspected that his efforts would be 'too unpleasant, or too fanciful, or too quiet' to appeal to the newspapers or magazines and they would certainly lack the obvious popular appeal of writers like G. K. Chesterton or Arthur Ransome. But he would, in fact, sell a significant number of them to the papers before publication in book form. Though the impulse finally petered out in March 1909, partly, Thomas believed, through the undermining effects of a long, hard winter, he was convinced that the result was 'better work or in a better direction than all but the best of the old'.[69]

These short prose pieces have been regarded by many critics as practising ground for the poems to come and seen as dealing at greater length with themes which would be treated more succinctly in his poetry. 'The Fountain', for instance, an account of the feelings aroused by a beautiful girl, may seem prolix when compared with his poem 'Beauty', which condenses all the complexity of Thomas's need for and reaction to beauty. Garnett, who was instrumental in publishing many of these prose pieces in *Rest and Unrest* and *Light and Twilight* claimed that they are the work of a poet 'in essence and in outlook': 'Many score of his prose pages [in those two books and *The South Country*]...are filled with passages of haunting loveliness, the impressions of a creative, brooding mind and eye sensitive to infinite shades of beauty in the life of the English countryside'.[70] Garnett cites 'Olwyn', 'The Flower-Gatherer', 'A Group of Statuary', 'Mothers and Sons', 'July', 'The Maiden's Wood' and 'Snow and Sand' in evidence.

To regard these prose pieces as failed poems, however, is to underestimate Thomas's achievement. Writing in 1909, at a time when the short story was redefining itself in England and trying to break free of its nineteenth-century conventions – the need for a story, plot and characters, of a beginning, middle and end – Thomas anticipates many of the features of the Modernist short stories of Katherine Mansfield, D. H. Lawrence, Virginia Woolf, James Joyce and others. These are pieces in which, as the poet John Freeman points out, 'reverie and imagination, together have woven a situation, a story, an air of sadness or beauty, of longing or ineffectuality – short character studies, passionate prose lyrics, sketches of nervous states edging upon morbidity'.[71]

Thomas's diary for 1909 shows that he was reading Turgenev regularly during the composition of his sketches, almost certainly under the influence of Garnett, whose wife, Constance, had translated a collection of the Russian's short stories in 1897 as *A Huntsman's Sketches* (Thomas's own story, 'A Sportsman's Tale', though not published during his lifetime, echoes Turgenev's title story, sometimes translated as 'A Sportsman's Sketch'). Thomas was also reading Tolstoy, Conrad, Poe, all writers who value mood and atmosphere over story and plot. With the benefit of hindsight, it is clear that Thomas was ahead of the Modernist short story writers in making these foreign writers his models rather than, say, Dickens or Conan Doyle.

One interest of the stories today lies in the autobiographical content of these prose pieces. Apart from the recreation of Hope Webb in 'The Fountain' and 'The Attempt', which gives a detailed account of Thomas's attempt to shoot himself in November 1908, almost every one of the 23 sketches of *Rest and Unrest* and *Light and Twilight* (1911) reveals some fresh aspect of his life or feelings. His morbidity, for instance, is well to the fore in the story 'Milking', in which a farmer milking the last cow of the day broods on the death indoors of his deformed, seventh child, or 'The Flower-Gatherer', in which a lovely child wanders to her death in the river, or 'Hawthornden', in which the man who was 'always home to tea' dies attempting to get back home to eat his wife's sweet cakes, a particularly virulent example of Thomas's self-disgust. Other stories, like 'Home', 'Olwen' and 'The Castle of Lostermellyn', express Thomas's love of Wales. (He had been rereading the *Mabinogion* and would take Merfyn on a ten-day visit to Wales in April 1909.) Stories like 'Sunday Afternoon', which explores the relationship between Mr and Mrs Wilkins and their grand-daughter, Cathie, puzzling on first reading, turn out to be based on an actual incident, in this case a scene at Minsmere between Janet Hooton's parents, the Aldises, and their grand-daughter Jane, who had become very fond of Thomas. His field notebook account of her 'convulsions of crying' because he had left the communal living-room are reflected faithfully in his story as is the harshness of her grandmother's 'clear, hard' voice as 'soulless as a piston' and his own comforting of the child 'throbbing with the corners of her lips twisting the world with sorrow', her breath coming up to him 'with perfect sweetness all the time, sweet as new bread, mown grass, or gorse after the summer rain'.[72] While such delicate observations in both his notebooks and stories do indeed anticipate the poetry to come, it should not be allowed to diminish Thomas's achievements as a prose-writer.

As Thomas had suspected from the start, this new work was even less profitable than the old. He was not surprised, therefore, when it proved quite impossible to persuade a publisher to accept it as part of a guinea guidebook. Fortunately, Garnett was able to persuade Duckworth to publish them in *Rest and Unrest* (1910) and *Light and Twilight* (1911), dedicated respectively to Ian MacAlister, whose wedding in January 1909 coincided with Thomas's first efforts (his excuse for not attending the ceremony), and Arthur Hardy, who had returned to England from South Africa. By the time the first of these, *Rest and Unrest*, was published in February 1910, Thomas was making yet another new start in a house built specially for him.

14

'Your Hurried and Harried Prose Man': Wick Green (December 1909–December 1910)

'With respect to your present troubles and anxieties, would it not be wise, seeing that authorship causes you so much trouble and anxiety, to give it up altogether?'

'Were you an author yourself,' replied my host, 'you would not talk in this manner; once an author, ever an author – besides, what could I do? return to my state of vegetation? No, much as I endure, I do not wish that.'

– *George Borrow*, 1912, p. 206

The move to a new house at Froxfield, 700 feet up on a beech-covered hill above Ashford Hanger, was a long time coming. Perhaps if 'Wick Green' had taken less time in the planning and building, Thomas would have had fewer expectations of it. The idea had been suggested by Lupton who, after an apprenticeship to his family's engineering firm in Leeds, had trained as an Arts and Crafts architect under Ernest Gimson and returned to the area of Bedales where he had been a pupil. He had bought a piece of land at the top of Shoulder of Mutton Hanger in the same sale of the Ashdown Estate which had seen the Thomases' lease of Berryfield Cottage threatened, and had built himself a house and workshop there. Though the Thomases were, in the event, allowed to stay on at Berryfield and even made an attempt to buy it, they had already had to contemplate moving. So they were grateful for Lupton's offer to build them a house next to his own in Cockshott Lane, fitted out in William Morris style, and to rent it to them at whatever price they could afford. His proposal had been made in May 1908 and he and Thomas had explored the idea further during their five-day trip to Cornwall the following month.

Lupton's proposed house for Edward and Helen was, after the completion of his own, his first independent commission and he took a great deal of trouble over it. When the house was finally ready for them in the autumn of 1909 it would be the result of many consultations between the three of them. One of Edward's requirements had been a study detached from the house and Lupton obliged with a small thatched building a hundred yards from it at the edge of the hanger, part of which served as an apiary. Ernest Rhys, who visited him there, recalled that 'the bees seemed a natural part of [Thomas's] equipment on a hot day and you could smell the honey'.[1]

With the plans for the house agreed by August 1908, Lupton had started laying foundations in the early spring of 1909. His insistence on making as much as possible himself, manufacturing his own bricks and nails and cutting, planing and shaping locally sourced beams, meant relatively slow progress, but by late April 1909, on Thomas's return from Wales with Merfyn, Thomas's study at least was almost completed.

Another unforeseen benefit of Thomas's relationship with Lupton was an introduction to Jacques Raverat, who had been at Bedales with 'Lumpit' (as Lupton was nicknamed) and visited him regularly at this time. Raverat had gone up to Cambridge in 1906 to read Maths and had met, among others, his future wife, Gwen Darwin, and the poet Rupert Brooke there. A mysterious illness (later diagnosed as multiple sclerosis) would force him to leave Cambridge and to settle in the South of France, but when he first met Thomas he was still part of the Cambridge group, the 'Neo-Pagans' which included Brooke. On 7 December 1909 Raverat would invite Thomas to dinner with Brooke in London, a prelude to another meeting between Brooke and Thomas later in the month.

It was Raverat, too, who had introduced Thomas to the medic attempting to cure his then undiagnosed illness, Dr Bramwell. By January 1909 Thomas reported of Dr J. M. Bramwell that he had 'made some extraordinary cures by suggestion (without hypnotism) – almost daily'.[2]

Even after he could no longer afford further treatment Bramwell had managed to 'convince' Thomas that he suffered 'not from my stomach but from myself. He hopes to cure me of the elaborate self-consciousness which he says is at the root of everything wrong in me.'[3] Bramwell even persuaded Thomas not to worry about what he ate. By 13 February Thomas was referring to his 'improved health and self-control (due to my new doctor)': 'I work, I walk and I sleep and I hardly ever make people miserable.'[4]

Another important meeting was with Joseph Conrad at Aldington in November. He had been introduced to the Polish writer by Garnett two years previously when Conrad made one of his rare appearances at the Mont Blanc lunches, but this was his first significant contact with him. Despite Conrad's friendliness, Thomas was 'uneasy' with him, he told Bottomley later, finding himself saying things he 'neither meant nor wished it to be supposed [he] meant', overawed partly perhaps by his appearance:

> He looks something like Sir Richard Burton...black hair and moustache and beard and a jutting-out face, and pale thin lips extraordinarily mobile among the black hair, flashing eyes and astonishing eyebrows, and a way of throwing his head right back to laugh which he often does at things which tickle him.[5]

Thomas had admired Conrad's work since Garnett had introduced him to it in 1905, *Youth* in particular, which he had been reading before embarking on his short prose pieces. The relationship never became close, but he would propose writing a book on Conrad to Martin Secker in 1912 and dedicate his *Walter Pater* to him in 1913. He would also visit him, in preference to his family, on one of his last weekends in England in 1916.

Thomas had been taken to see Conrad in November 1909 by a more regular attender of Garnett's lunches, Perceval Gibbon, 'a pallid, dark-haired Welshman with a great command of the technique of the magazine short story', of particular interest to Thomas just before he attempted his own.[6] According to Douglas Goldring, whose short-lived magazine, *The Tramp*, would publish three pieces by Thomas in 1910, it was Gibbon's Welshness, as well as his skill at short-story writing, which recommended him to Thomas.[7] He was not apparently put off by what Goldring called Gibbon's 'equally great addiction to hard liquor'.[8]

Goldring and Gibbon were both part of a group of writers gathered round Ford Madox Hueffer (he would change his German name to 'Ford' during the First World War), as he launched his *English Review* in 1908 over a fishmonger and poulterer's at 84 Holland Park Avenue. Ford, like Gibbon, was a regular at the Mont Blanc, one of the many useful contacts offered to Thomas by these lunches, and by June 1909 Thomas was reviewing for him. His positive notice of Ezra Pound's *Personae* for the *English Review* that month caused consternation among the less open-minded members of the Square Club, according to Edgar Jepson.[9]

Another name and address new to Thomas's diary for 1909 is that of Ashley Gibson, considered by Thomas a nice but not highly gifted man. Gibson gives, nevertheless, an entertaining account of Thomas's visits to London. It is thanks to Gibson that we know of his nickname, 'the Iambic', because of his rhythmical appearances at St George's restaurant. A freelance journalist himself, Gibson often saw Thomas in Fleet Street, where (he recalled in his *Postscript to Adventure*) Thomas:

> looked what he was, a hind let loose. Tall lean figures in shaggy tweeds are nothing by-ordinar in that thoroughfare. But none other has or had quite that way of carrying himself. He walked with a sort of lope, half springy and half lackadaisical. And noting – as how could they fail to – the face under the favourite hat of fisherman's frieze, from youth to prime a face austerely beautiful, vivid in the intensity of its tan, candour of its blue eyes, and bleach of Saxon hair, sensitive passers-by almost gasped. I have seen lots of ordinary people, responsive to this stranger's quite extraordinary physical distinction, turn round in the street and watch him out of sight, an introspective Pan whose arm pressed to its side not the syrinx but, odd anomaly, a couple of review books.

Gibson was able, in this same Fleet Street, to find Thomas work with the *Literary World*. But his main interest is as a friend and admirer of Ransome, whose move to the Steep area after his wedding in March 1909 may explain Gibson's appearance in Thomas's diary that year. Despite the fact that Edward and Helen had been witnesses at the wedding, only six months later Edward was telling Harry Hooton: 'We see little of the Ransomes. She is not attractive and he is her slave.'[10] Jealousy may have entered into it. Ransome's success continued and he and his wife, Ivy, 'gad[ded] about a lot – motor rides, flights to the North, to Paris, to

Boulogne' and there is a certain wistfulness in Thomas's final comment: 'They have no children.'[11]

Thomas's main socializing was, in any case, in London not Steep. The image he projected of an isolated, depressed man is almost comically contradicted by his diary, and not just for 1909. He might complain to Bottomley that he 'hate[d] London; no exercise, no air, and continual belly-ache and head ache and discomfort all over'.[12] He might also believe that 'it is not good for me to see people as I listen to so much that I don't understand – politics, art and so on – and pretend to take an interest and say...foolish things' and that 'people despise me'.[13] But it did not stop him visiting the capital regularly and seeing far more people than his work required. Besides the Mont Blanc lunches on Tuesdays and sometimes the Villa Villa on Wednesdays, where business was in any case combined with socializing, or his attendance on Fleet Street editors, he also still met regularly with friends like Mac, Haynes, Hooton, Freeman and many others during his usual two-day visits. Lunches, teas and dinners were all booked up despite the protests of isolation. His monthly attendance at the Square Club alone, which involved the membership fee, the cost of the dinner in a central London restaurant and an overnight stay, suggests that he enjoyed socializing more than he admitted. He even sat to the portrait artist (John) Kelt Edwards, who also painted Owen Edwards and his father's friend, David Lloyd George. There were at least two sittings but the portrait, if ever completed, has not survived.

By the end of 1909, as the prospect of moving into Lupton's new house became more real, Thomas enjoyed an unusually long spell of feeling better, a combination of Dr Bramwell's treatment, his own study away from the family, the possibility of having his more creative work published, the prospect of a new start and two months of satisfying if back-breaking work, creating a garden out of Lupton's stony, clayey site. It was in this mood that he finally agreed to Helen's desire for another child, the price she may have extracted for his infatuation with Hope Webb. By the time the move to Wick Green took place on 16 December 1909, she was in bed feeling 'unwell', almost certainly pregnant.[14]

Theoretically Wick Green, built according to Edward and Helen's specifications, was everything they had ever wanted in a house. A long, low building

facing south, it had windows on all sides except the north, looking out over
what Edward initially judged 'a mighty view', towards Chanctonbury Ring
and the ridge of the South Downs seven miles away.[15] Helen found a good
maid and was able to give time to the large garden with Edward, who was
still busily creating his vegetable patch and planting fruit trees. Her 'special
bit' of garden was the built-up terrace running along the whole length of the
south wall below the ground-floor windows. The only level part of the plot,
she soon had it 'gay with flowers, and dropping over the edge great clusters
of aubretia and white and yellow alyssum'.[16] Here Lupton, at her request,
had built into the wall of the house an alcove where, as she became more
heavily pregnant, she could sit and sew looking out over the magnificent
view. The house itself had more room for friends to stay and was surrounded
by fields and woods full of badgers and foxes, inviting exploration. 'Yet
somehow,' Helen wrote, 'we could not love the house':

> The heavy oak was raw and new, and seemed to resent its servitude in
> beam and door and with loud cracks would try to wrench itself free.
> There was nothing in their exposed position to protect us from the wind,
> which roared and shrieked in the wide chimneys, nor have I ever heard
> such furious rain as dashed vindictively against our windows…Often
> a thick mist enveloped us, and the house seemed to be standing on the
> edge of the world, with an infinity of white rolling vapour below us.[17]

Edward's reaction began less than a month after they moved in. Whereas
their lofty position had made him feel at the start 'as if all earth were my
pedestal',[18] less than three weeks later he was writing in his field notebook
for 6 January 1910, 'third day of thick grey mist w[ith] beaded yew tree
dripping and scarce any wind – as a rule you can only see 100 y[ar]ds ahead'.
He was already feeling cut off from life, as if each of his days were 'like
Sunday – curtained, waiting'. By 26 January he was 'tired and depressed'
again and began adding a new note daily to his diary – on the weather, with
'wind' and 'mist' prevailing. His obsession with the weather would continue
as long as he lived at Wick Green: 'We think of nothing else practically,' he
wrote to Bottomley a year after moving in: 'The wind and rain knocks at
all our windows all day and night.'[19] Knowing Bottomley's interest in Norse
legends, which had resulted in 1907 in a collection of poems dedicated to
Thomas, *The Riding to Lithend*, he compared Wick Green in the rain to the

underworld of Scandinavian mythology, 'the Nifleheim that men ultimately emerged from': 'it is like living before the creation'.[20] When Thomas came to write his own version of *Norse Tales* (1912), he would include his own experience in that of King Gangler, who steps out of his hilltop house to find that 'the night's storm had washed away all the rest, and there he was shipwrecked in a sea of clouds and mist, rocking and swirling about round about ....This sea must have been like Nifleheim.'[21] One friend felt that Wick Green might have come straight out of William Morris's Norse-based saga, *News from Nowhere*.

Years later Thomas could still recall the sensations created in him by exposure to the weather at Wick Green. His first completed poem, 'Up in the Wind', reflects this. So, too, even more extremely, does 'Wind and Mist', which centres round a conversation between the narrator and an imaginary passer-by who echoes Thomas's initial enthusiasm for the house and with whom the narrator agrees: he has seen 'that house / Through mist look lovely as a castle in Spain, / And airier'. Yet, having lived in it, and known 'every nook of it', he confesses to 'hating it':

> ...Doubtless the house was not to blame,
> But the eye watching from those windows saw,
> Many a day, day after day, mist – mist
> Like chaos surging back – and felt itself
> Alone in all the world, marooned alone.
> We lived in clouds, on a cliff's edge almost
> (You see), and if clouds went, the visible earth
> Lay too far beneath and like a cloud.
> I did not know it was the earth I loved
> Until I tried to live there in the clouds.[22]

Thomas's fears, of being alone, of being cut off from the earth he loved, are reinforced by the relentless wind and mist at that height, even in summer, especially the wind. Like a twentieth-century Ancient Mariner, he needs to tell the passer-by of its effect on him.

> You would not understand about the wind.
> It is my subject, and compared with me
> Those who have always lived on the firm ground
> Are quite unreal in this matter of the wind.

> There were whole days and nights when the wind and I
> Between us shared the world, and the wind ruled
> And I obeyed it and forgot the mist.
> My past and the past of the world were in the wind.[23]

In Thomas's retrospective view of Wick Green in another 1915 poem, 'The New House', the wind began to moan on his very first night there, foretelling in his mind the period of increasing depression and eventual breakdown which would follow:

> Old at once was the house,
> And I was old;
> My ears were teased with the dread
> Of what was foretold,
>
> Nights of storm, days of mist, without end;
> Sad days when the sun
> Shone in vain: old griefs, and griefs
> Not yet begun.
>
> All was foretold me; naught
> Could I foresee;
> But I learnt how the wind would sound
> After these things should be.[24]

'The New House' is one of Thomas's bleakest poems, a re-enactment of the narrator's sense of dread, symbolized for him by 1915 by the wind. But the wind itself, like the rain, would also become a force for good, a source of inspiration in later poems (like 'Aspens' and 'The Wind's Song') and it is more than likely that Thomas was displacing his sense of hopelessness and entrapment in 1910 from its true source to a more neutral external cause.

Thomas was undoubtedly disturbed by the thought of another child: Myfanwy's birth in August 1910 would lead to one of his severest breakdowns. Even before her arrival he had started to worry about money again, despite continuing to earn enough from his reviews and articles to support his family comfortably. The move to a larger house in itself was enough to revive all his neuroses about finances. And his response, which was to take on yet more work, only added to his anxieties. Between 1910 and the beginning of 1913, 13 books would appear under his name. Few, if any, self-respecting writers could contemplate such an undertaking without a sense of anxiety and dread. Even discounting his two collections of prose pieces, *Rest and Unrest* and *Light and Twilight*, written mainly in 1909, *The Tenth Muse* (1911), which is a reprint of the eighth chapter of *The Feminine Influence on the Poets* (1910), and *The Rose Acre Papers* (1910), a reissue of his *Horae Solitariae* (1902) with two additional essays from *The Rose Acre Papers* (1904), there still remained nine new books he was committed to completing in just three years. In addition he would agree to write introductions to Isaac Taylor's *Words and Places in Illustration of History, Ethnology and Geography* (1911), William Cobbett's *Rural Rides* (1912) and to edit a *Pocket George Borrow* (1912). He also started researching and writing *The Icknield Way* (1913) during this period. For the first time in his career the term 'hackwork' is possibly justified for some of these books, professionally carried out but without the full commitment he had felt towards previous works. His need to concentrate and work, often from early morning to late at night, had never been greater.

Thomas's response to all these pressures was to escape to his study. Though sharing a similarly dizzying view towards the Downs through its long end window, and even more exposed to the weather, it became a refuge for him, a place even more of his own than Stidulph's Cottage had been. In his impatience to escape family distractions he had moved in even before the windows had been glazed. But there was a fireplace when he needed it and he made himself a large table and bookshelves tailored to his needs. In the flowerbed by the door he planted his favourite herbs – thyme, old man, tansy, rosemary, lavender – some of them given to him by Bottomley and propagated by cuttings each time the family moved. (Helen, in turn, would take cuttings from them after his death to plant on his grave in France.)

Some of the resulting books are his least successful, starting with *Windsor Castle* for Blackie's Beautiful England series. He considered this a 'dirty' job, taken on in January 1910 for completion the following month.[25] Written on the strength of rapid research in the British Museum Reading Room and a brief visit to Windsor, where his Republican sympathies were offended by the need to actually go into the castle, it is an unsatisfactory book, full of historical 'facts' but giving no sense of Windsor Castle itself. It is clear from an entry in his field notebook during his visit there, that his interest in history by 1910 was almost solely literary: 'Chief period is

18th Century of Collins' Persian Eclogues and Pope's Windsor Forest. See colours of the banners etc in St George'[s].'[26]

Thomas's other travel book of this period, *The Isle of Wight* (like *Windsor Castle* the text to Ernest Haslehurst's illustrations in Blackie's *Beautiful England* series) is less perfunctory but well below his best. In it his approach to history becomes even more literary, opening with references to Coleridge, Keats and Conrad and including often extended passages on Fielding, Drayton, Ruskin, Tennyson, Whitman as well as the three writers he is proposing for other commissioned books in 1910, Lafcadio Hearn, Borrow and Swinburne. Welsh literature also makes an unexpected appearance. Judging from the more conventional, brief account of the island's history tacked on at the end, Thomas's publishers were not happy with the way that he had, as with *Beautiful Wales*, *The Heart of England* and *The South Country*, interpreted his commission according to his own interests. They would certainly not have approved of the tone in which Thomas after a lightning two-day visit to the island, writes about it:

> The Isle of Wight contains the most-advertised of beauties, so that it might be supposed difficult to see the beauty for the praise. It is under the further disadvantageous advantage of being very easily approached and traversed. A man could see everything that he is expected to see in a Bath chair or in dancing slippers; it is all as easy as lighting a bought cigarette. The only inconveniences are the bad and expensive railways, and other people.[27]

That 'Bath chair' does the island no favours. Once again Thomas, consciously or not, is subverting the form of the travel book for his own ends. It would hardly attract visitors to the island to read in his later passages of 'landladies in thousands and visitors in tens of thousands' and of the 'tyranny' of hill top monuments, or 'follies'.[28]

Another feature of the travel book Thomas fails to deliver is an account of famous beauty spots. There is some landscape, sensitively described, but of an obscure spot that has caught his imagination. Overall he appears to regard the Isle of Wight as an extension of mainland Hampshire, as indeed it once was. There are a number of references to features of the area round Steep, such as 'Butser Hill' and the 'little white inn' near his home.[29]

A further irregular feature of this intended guidebook is Thomas's inclination to invent stories rather than stick to facts. The sight of an unlit farmhouse across a field, for instance, sets his imagination alight with the tale of a young man returning 'with few honours and few hopes' from university to his ailing father and cousin Margaret, an intriguing unfinished story which has an autobiographical ring to it. But it seems singularly out of place in the guidebook Blackie had requested. Yet Thomas was puzzled and annoyed when the publishers turned down his suggestion for another book for their series.

By the time *The Isle of Wight* was published on 5 December 1911, Thomas had completed three other commissions, all linked quite consciously by him to his 'willing[ness] to accept anything' to pay for the 'increased expenditure' of the move to Wick Green and prospect of a new baby.[30] The first of these, *The Feminine Influence on the Poets*, was written with even less pleasure and more haste than usual. From the title onwards – not Thomas's choice – he found *The Feminine Influence* 'a wretched, wretched book'.[31] His original suggestion, to write 'on the influence of women on English poets', proved too general, so he decided to concentrate on the attitude of poets to individual women and 'the idea of women and so on'.[32] Even his modified plan involved extensive research, far more than the three months he had set aside. His preparation had included a study of the poems and letters of poets as varied as Keats, Landor, Wordsworth and Donne, but, nearly two months into the project and still 'without plans', he was debating whether to include the Provençal and Italian poets as well.[33] Asked for his advice, Bottomley had replied wittily, ' "Women and Poets" is quite a large subject, my dear Edward; especially women.'[34] He was quite scornful of 'weariful old Provençal artificiality…the whole simply caused by living in too warm a climate; also of Petrarch and even of Dante'. Thomas takes his advice, but his range is still extremely wide, from Beowulf to Yeats and Sturge Moore, further evidence of the many years he had spent reading and reviewing British poetry.

Thomas further complicated his work by asking poet-friends like Bottomley and Berridge for an account of how any one of their love poems came to be written, material he included in his book but anonymously. He particularly liked Bottomley's claim that 'all poems are love poems', replying that it was 'exactly what [he] had hit upon [him]self in one of [his] cloudy cogitations'.[35]

Despite all the problems anticipated by Thomas and his doubts about the finished work, *The Feminine Influence on the Poets* allows him to discuss his favourite poets and also to criticize the few he fails to admire, like Herrick, and periods he dislikes, notably the eighteenth century. The first chapter on women's position through the ages and the attraction of old ballads rises well above dry research. His difficulties with Helen, for instance, become less puzzling in the light of his remark that 'women are still a race apart. They are foreigners, their world is another world, ever at hand, ever unavoidable, ever mysterious; and through this world is man's nearest path to the strangeness of things.' Even more revealing is his statement that God's gifts to women were 'deceitfulness, weeping and spinning' and that they brought 'confusion' to man. Likewise a passage on Donne's difficulties with a family to support but very little money, offers further insights into Thomas's state of mind in 1910.[36]

Thomas had rushed to complete *The Feminine Influence* before the new baby's expected arrival in mid-August. Apart from a note made the night before – 'Helen in gr[eat] pain' – he greeted his third child's birth early on Tuesday, 16 August, with no apparent emotion in his diary entry: '12.30am for doctor / 4.50 baby born / Gardening / to W[est] Harting to de la Mare / To bed 10.' His field notebook suggests stronger, though still suppressed, feelings.[37] His description of the birth in 'Wind and Mist' five years later, as he points to the room in which it occurred at Wick Green, conveys no joy at the event and some apprehension:

> …In that room at the gable a child
> Was born while the wind chilled a summer dawn:
> Never looked grey mind on a greyer one
> Than when the child's cry broke above the groans.[38]

The greyness without suggests a greyness within as Thomas, though relieved that Helen's difficult labour was safely over, contemplated his extra responsibilities. While glad it was a girl, he already had a daughter he adored, the one member of his family who seems not to have been a source of irritation by 1910; it would take him longer to establish a close relationship with his third child, Helen Elizabeth Myfanwy. Partly because of prevailing attitudes, he was not closely involved with her birth and left only two days after it for London and to pay a second, longer visit to Conrad, then to Belloc, Garnett and Ralph Hodgson. After another few days at home, he was off again for a fortnight in Wales. The first ten days were spent at Tregaron with Arthur Hardy, feeling increasingly alienated by their diverging tastes as adults: while Arthur wanted to fish all and every day, he chose to walk. A further few days were passed visiting John Williams in Swansea and Gwili at Ammanford.

Both Merfyn and Bronwen had been sent away for a month to avoid having them at home for the delivery and it may be that Helen encouraged Edward to visit Wales after the birth because it made it easier for her to recover under the nurse's care. (Her childless sister and brother-in-law, the McArthurs, paid the nursing bills.) It could also have been a response to Edward's evident depression over the arrival of another child.

His first real opportunity to get to know his new daughter was on his return from Wales in mid-September, when Myfanwy was already a month old. But he did eventually start to bond with 'Baby', or 'Baba', as she was called, singing Welsh songs to her as he gave her her nightly bath by the fire. Though she lacked Bronwen's striking prettiness, he grew to be proud of Myfanwy in a different way, writing to his aunt Margaret (Townsend) when she was four, that 'Baby seems to be much cleverer than either [Merfyn or Bronwen] and more independent, but I suppose the youngest often seems so[39].' There would be real affection in the poem he wrote to his youngest child before leaving for France, and she would appear, directly or indirectly, in four of his other poems.

In 1910, however, Myfanwy appears to have represented a threat, one more strain on Thomas's already overtaxed nerves. Looked at objectively, it had been a good year, with a move to a bigger, more luxurious house and at least four new friendships to celebrate. The first of these, with the bowler-hatted, pipe-smoking poet Ralph Hodgson, a singular figure in London's literary world always accompanied by one of a series of bull-terriers, started with a letter from 'Hoddy' on 21 January 1910, to which Thomas replied by return. Lunch followed five days later in London, the beginning of regular meetings at one of the vegetarian restaurants Hodgson haunted, more often than not the Eustace Miles in William IV Street. Hodgson also became a regular at Thomas's St George's teas. When Hodgson looked back nostalgically from his home in America thirty-five years later to 'some of the old spots I have loved so much', one of the only three places he named would be St George's – 'if it still exists…the coffee house in St Martin's Lane where we used to meet…(W. H. Davies, Edward Thomas and others)'.[40]

By the time the friendship started Thomas had reviewed one of Hodgson's poetry collections, *The Last Blackbird and Other Lines* (1907)[41] and would go on to review others, all positively. But it was not first and foremost Hodgson's verse he admired. By 25 November 1910 he was seeing a good deal of Hodgson and telling Bottomley 'you would like him, such a vigorous and simple nature, careless, generous'. The artist Claud Lovat Fraser, who collaborated with Hodgson on illustrated sheets of verse for the Poetry Bookshop, remembered him insisting: 'I am not a literary man, and I don't take joy of their company. It is misery to me to know that every word I say is being weighed up and measured…There is no jolly humanity about them. No give me the honest honourable Philistine in preference to them and the bull-terrier breeder above them both.'[42] The side of Thomas that admired gypsies, pedlars and working-class men would have responded to that. He would also have appreciated de la Mare's claim that Hodgson was 'independent as the North Pole'.[43] As mainly bookish men, both Thomas and de la Mare were fascinated by what Theresa Whistler calls Hodgson's 'flavour, character, gusto, unexpectedness…all…sun-shot through with idealism and a passion for beauty'.[44] A similar mix of characteristics had drawn Thomas to W. H. Davies, made even richer in Hodgson by a less limited intellectuality. As Whistler points out, there was 'nothing naïve about Hodgson's potent, ranging mind'[45] and there were long discussions between Thomas and Hodgson about poetry, as well as the dogs and birds they both loved so much. Like Thomas, Hodgson's approach to art was nature-loving and suspicious of anything too Modernist, though he was nearer to the Georgians in sympathy and practice.

Thomas visited Hodgson's home in Bookham, Surrey, at least twice in 1910 and Hodgson quickly became a regular visitor to Wick Green, spending many weekends, or longer, there.

> We all loved him [Helen remembered]. He looked – in those days – like one of the prize-fighters he loved to talk about. He was the most indolent man I have ever met. He used to sit in our living room, with his feet on the mantelpiece, smoking his pipe of shag which he kept in an enormous indiarubber pouch…When his money ran out he would

draw a picture for a magazine [he was a talented black-and-white artist as well as poet], but otherwise talk and playing with the children, who adored him, was his only activity.[46]

Hodgson only occasionally chose to walk with Thomas and his Irish terrier, Rags, but did stir himself sufficiently to give the Thomas children a bull-terrier bitch, Dinah, to guard them on the long, lonely trips down to Bedales. Sadly, Dinah, always sweet and gentle with the family, hated anyone who came to the house. When tradesmen, and even the postman, refused to risk being bitten, Helen reluctantly returned Dinah to Hodgson 'who was furious with us,' she remembered, 'for this concession to neighbourliness.'[47] He was an odd mixture, she remembered, given to 'unaccountable moods which almost seemed insane', as Thomas would discover in 1914 after the outbreak of war, when Hodgson's quarrel with him would be one possible factor in his decision to enlist.

Thomas's relationship with another poet, Harold Monro, also begun in 1910, would likewise end on a sour note. They had first made contact in 1909 through a mutual friend, James Guthrie, on one of Monro's trips to England from his home in Italy. A year younger than Thomas and of Scottish, rather than Welsh, parentage, Monro had enough in common with Thomas for him to invite Monro to come and see them when next in England. After studying at Cambridge and ending his first, unwise marriage, Monro had started the Samurai Press in 1906 and his whole life, like Thomas's, would be devoted to literature. His poetry, like Thomas's prose, had not brought him much recognition by the time they did eventually meet for lunch at Wick Green on 21 July 1910 during another of Monro's visits to England. When he returned for good a year later, after consulting Thomas about journalistic work for his younger partner in a homosexual relationship, Arundel del Re, Thomas would be 'glad'.[48] He would invite him to Wick Green for a weekend and urge him to find a house near him in Hampshire. When Monro finally bought a cottage, though not in Hampshire, he invited Thomas to stay with him there and when Thomas was on the verge of a breakdown in 1911, he would offer to lend him his house in Italy. He entered Thomas's life at a point when both felt despairing about their health and their future in general and they would find some comfort in each other for a time.

Thomas showed his appreciation partly by supplying unpaid reviews for Monro's *Poetry and Drama* magazine, a continuation of the *Poetry Review* Monro had started to edit for the Poetry Society in late 1911.[49] (Thomas would eventually agree to accept payment, but only for full-length articles.) He would also write an encouraging review of Monro's *The Chronicle of a Pilgrimage* (1909) despite initial doubts about it.[50] And his support of Monro's other publication, *Georgian Poetry*, would help to launch it successfully. Appearing six days after Monro's boldest experiment, the Poetry Bookshop, which opened officially on 8 January 1913 with a launch Thomas attended, his review of *Georgian Poetry 1911–1912* is restrained but positive. After listing the main contributors, many of whom were friends – some like Bottomley, Davies, de la Mare and Monro himself, close friends – Thomas concludes by isolating three 'Georgians' and recommending the volume to the readers of the *Daily Chronicle*:

> ...It shows much beauty, strength and mystery and some magic – much aspiration, less defiance, no revolt – and it brings out with great cleverness many sides of the modern love of the simple and primitive, as seen in children, peasants, savages, early men, animals, and Nature in general.[51]

It is a skilful outlining of what 'Georgian' poetry has come to mean, apart from its straightforward link to the reign of George V in which it was mainly written. Dominic Hibberd has argued that there can be 'no satisfactory definition of Georgianism', but then goes on to isolate certain characteristics: 'plain language, clear detail, realism, a strong feeling for the countryside and a belief...that the new poetry really was new, a radical departure from the grand rhetoric of the Victorians'.[52] It is not a definition which takes into account the magical world of de la Mare, or the visionary work of Bottomley, however. The least unsatisfactory definition is perhaps a negative one, that is, what Georgian poetry is *not*: it is not Modernist or Futurist, or highly experimental in general; however vague its boundaries, it does not include poets such as Ezra Pound, T. S. Eliot or Isaac Rosenberg (though Rosenberg would make a brief appearance in the 1916–1917 volume), all writing outstanding work during the Georgian period.

Georgian Poetry became an overnight success and there were to be five volumes of it in all. It had arisen partly out of Edward Marsh's close friendship with Rupert Brooke, whom he had met in 1905 on one of his many return visits to Cambridge. When Brooke's first slim volume of poems came out in 1911, Francis Meynell had suggested that Marsh review it for his friend Harold Monro's *Poetry Review*, and the team which was to produce *Georgian Poetry* was born. It needed only a chance remark by Brooke to bring the anthology into being. Monro agreed to be the publisher and Marsh was to find the poets, make and arrange the selection and distribute payment. The first number went into 13 editions.

Brooke's input would be mainly as contributor. By the time Thomas reviewed the first volume in January 1913, he had got to know Brooke fairly well. After his introduction to Brooke by Raverat and his dinner with him and Raverat in December 1909, he had tried to help Brooke in his pursuit of a Bedales pupil, Noel Olivier, mindful perhaps of his own infatuation with a schoolgirl less than two years earlier. Brooke had been forbidden to see Noel by her older sister, and was hoping Thomas would engineer a meeting by inviting them both to tea in the summer of 1910. There is no indication that the tea took place and Brooke stayed, not with the Thomases, but in a caravan in Lupton's gardens. He did, however, have a long walk with Thomas on that occasion.

Out of gratitude for his sympathy, or just because they got on well, Brooke invited Thomas to spend a weekend with him at the Orchard in October 1910. 'I have never been in Cambridge,' Thomas, an Oxford graduate, replied, 'and if you don't think it's too late in life for a first visit' – a reference to his nine years' seniority to Brooke – 'I shall very gladly come after an invitation such as yours.'[53] Apart from some dismay at the argumentative brilliance of Brooke's young friends, Thomas enjoyed his weekend and shortly afterwards invited Brooke to Steep again, to stay with him while Helen was away. They worked at their respective writing in the day and cooked for themselves, but in the evening sat talking. Thomas, who had not yet written serious verse of his own, also listened while Brooke read him his latest poems, many of them based on similar preoccupations to his own, as Jan Marsh has pointed out: 'a love of the countryside, dreams of idealised women and a longing at times to escape into oblivion';[54] also 'an irreverent attitude towards society and its institutions, and both were confirmed atheists'. It is hardly surprising, therefore, that when Brooke's first volume of *Poems* was published at the end of 1911, Thomas would review it in largely sympathetic terms:

> He is full of revolt, contempt, self-contempt and yet arrogance too. He reveals chiefly what he desires to be and to be thought…Copies should be bought by everyone over forty who has never been under forty. It will be a revelation. Also if they live a little longer they may see Mr Rupert Brooke a poet. He will not be a little one.[55]

Brooke had already included Thomas on a select list of friends to whom he wanted copies of his *Poems* sent. He would also persuade Edward Marsh, despite a puzzling coolness between the two older men, to invite Thomas to one of his breakfasts at Gray's Inn in February 1913. The occasion would be a failure and the experiment was not repeated. (Marsh 'put it down to dyspepsia', according to Brooke's biographer.[56]) But Brooke and Thomas would remain good friends, though it did not prevent Thomas voting for Wilfrid Gibson when Monro asked him to be one of a panel which chose the best poem of the year for *Poetry and Drama*. (Brooke's 'Grantchester' nevertheless was awarded the prize.) Only pressure of time would prevent Brooke from spending another weekend with Thomas before leaving for his trip to America, Canada and the South Seas in May 1913. He begged Thomas, however, to meet him in London, so that he could 'leave the Muses of England in your keeping – I do that anyway. Feed the brutes.'[57]

Thomas's last glimpse of Brooke would be at Gibson's house at Ledington, Gloucestershire, in June 1914, to discuss yet another verse publication, *New Numbers*. Hodgson, Monro and Brooke would all work closely together at the Poetry Bookshop and on *Georgian Poetry*, all are now considered Georgians, though Monro's poetry is often less conservative than the term implies. Thomas was still friends with all three of them when he first contemplated verse in 1914, yet when his own poetry began to flow at the end of the year it would be quite different from any of theirs.

15

THE BAX–BAYNES EFFECT (1911–1912)

I have been too squeamish, partly by nature and still more by
deliberately trying to get a position by the pose of seeming to
have one and to be able to refuse this and that. I have refused
several offers this year which I would not refuse now, because
I thought it was a mistake to cheapen myself and also I still
have enough ambition (so to call it) left to find utterly uncongenial work very humiliating. Still the bed is mainly of my own
making. I wish I could lie on it without making so much noise.
          – Thomas to MacAlister, 2 December 1911

Thomas had complained so often about both his book-
reviewing and the lack of it that, when it did start to dry up
in 1911, his friends may not initially have believed him. But there
was, in fact, a dramatic decrease between the end of 1910, when he
had at least 140 reviews and prose pieces accepted for publication
and 1911, when the number had almost halved; by 1912 it had
halved again. Apart from his reluctance to press for work, one
explanation may have been a change of editor at the *Morning Post*,
to Howell Arthur Gwynne, who asked Thomas for only one review
in 1911 and none in 1912.

Another cause was Thomas's preoccupation with commissioned work which he continued frantically to solicit through
Cazenove. No sooner had he completed *The Feminine Influence on*

the Poets in August 1910 than he agreed to write his book on Maeterlinck and another on *The Icknield Way*. By February 1911 he had started work on a study of Lafcadio Hearn and a fourth book, *Celtic Stories*, which he finished in April, with *The Isle of Wight* hastily cobbled together in between. In October 1911 he completed his rewriting of *Norse Tales* and began work in earnest on his life of George Borrow. No sooner had he finished a rough draft than he started work on 2 January 1912 on a critical study of Walter Pater and, while that was still in a rough draft, began researching his *Algernon Charles Swinburne*. July and August were devoted to a small book on *The Country*. When that, too, was finished, he noted in his diary, 'To London to look for work.' One result of this visit would be a meeting with Holbrook Jackson and work for *T. P.'s Weekly*. But that lay in the future and, apart from a series of promotional articles for the London Underground (arranged for him by his brother Theodore), he had no more commissioned work this year, possibly because of his sacking of his agent Cazenove in September 1912. (Cazenove would be reinstated by June 1913.) Faced with the prospect of a little leisure, however, Thomas immediately started work on his only novel, *The Happy-Go-Lucky Morgans*. He was a driven man.

Thomas's was a problem any serious but not best-selling writer faced by 1912. The age of patronage was more or less over, but the Welfare State and state subsidy of the arts had not yet come into being. There was no child benefit, social security or National Health System.[1] When Myfanwy became ill in 1912 with a mysterious complaint and Helen had to stay with her in hospital for a week, extra money had to be found to pay for it. Then there were Edward's frequent consultations with psychiatrists, his train fares and other living expenses when, as frequently happened, he was away from home for extended periods.

The Thomases were as self-sufficient as they could be, Edward growing their own fruit and vegetables and Helen making all their meals, bread and cakes. When Edward periodically gave up meat, as he did at the beginning of 1911 on yet another doctor's orders, the whole family would become vegetarian and money would be saved. Rents were cheaper in the country and some of their moves had been dictated by the need to pay less rent. But some expenses were unavoidable, notably the children's school fees, which were only partly covered by Helen's teaching at Bedales. Both parents were determined, nevertheless, to give Merfyn, Bronwen and Myfanwy what they believed to be the best education possible. (Edward is constantly asking friends for advice on 'good' but cheap schools during this period.)

Thomas was not alone in his dilemma of how to make enough money to live, yet allow time for his own writing. He was surrounded by friends in a similar position. Some, like de la Mare and W. H. Davies, had the problem solved for them by other people, who persuaded the government to give them a state pension. In Davies's case it was Thomas who was one of the prime movers, the other being Garnett. Together they were responsible for securing Davies the sum of £50 a year – a modest but sufficient sum for his needs – sending out a petition to friends and colleagues in the literary world which pointed out that:

> ... though Mr Davies's work has brought him fame and unquestioned rank in literary circles, the circulation of fine poetry is notoriously restricted, and the sales of Mr Davies's books, including *The Autobiography of a Super-Tramp*, has not yet yielded him a sum, yearly, exceeding the wages of a day labourer. While Mr Davies has no journalistic or other readily marketable gifts by which to increase his earnings, he is still in the prime of his creative productiveness, and may be expected to enrich further our imaginative literature.[2]

Ironically, when Thomas himself tried to get an annual pension for himself in 1914, he was turned down, though he would be awarded a one-off grant from the Royal Literary Fund.

Another solution to the writer's dilemma, and the most common one, was to find a job which brought in a regular income, preferably in the literary world. Many of Thomas's friends chose this course. Garnett, for example, was a reader for several publishing houses, Scott-James edited the *New Weekly*, Monro ran *Poetry and Drama* and Seccombe worked for *The Times*. Norman Douglas, a travel writer and novelist, was visiting London in search of such work when Thomas first met him at a Mont Blanc lunch in March 1911. He would be fortunate enough to be offered the assistant editorship of the *English Review* when John Mavrogordato left to cover the war in the Balkans for the *Westminster Gazette* in 1912.

Thomas and Douglas would become good friends once Douglas settled in England in 1912. A shrewd judge of character, Douglas has left what Bottomley thought one of the best analyses of Thomas's elusive personality, stating 'I have not found the Edward Thomas whom I knew for twenty years... anything like so completely or convincingly depicted as in the three or four vivid pages given to him in Norman Douglas's...*Looking Back*, a masterpiece of insight and evocation in which I recognize reality.'[3] Douglas's striking opening claim in that account – that 'there was something of the Byzantine angel about [Thomas], ethereal, refined, aloof'[4] – could *not* be made of Douglas himself, who was something of an earthy *bon viveur*. It is the contrast between the two men that Douglas emphasizes, particularly towards the end of the piece:

> What Thomas lacked was a little touch of bestiality, a little *je-m'en-fous-t-ism*. He was too scrupulous. Often, sitting at the Horse Shoe [pub] or some such place – often I told him that it was no use trying to be a gentleman if you are a professional writer. You are not dealing with gentlemen, why place yourself at a disadvantage? They'll flay you alive, if they can. Whereupon he would smile wistfully, and say that another pint of Burton [ale] would be my ruin.[5]

The contrast here is stark and makes the friendship which developed between the two all the more surprising. Douglas was aware of this and addresses it directly in the second sentence of his piece: 'Thomas was so austere in the matter of food and drink, so conscientious, so incurably monogamous, that differing from each other, we agreed perfectly.'[6]

Just how different Douglas and Thomas were emerges clearly in a contemporary description of Douglas in his capacity as assistant editor of the *English Review*, the setting where Thomas, as contributor, would have met him most often. By 1910 the *Review* had passed from Ford's editorship to that of Austin Harrison, who would run it until 1923. As well as sponsoring unknown writers, whom it often helped to establish – Ezra Pound, Wyndham Lewis, D. H. Lawrence, for example – it also published well-known figures like Henry James, Thomas Hardy, Arnold Bennett, John Galsworthy and W. B. Yeats. It was finally absorbed into *the National Review* in 1937.

The description is by Thomas Burke who, after describing Thomas's 'austere and intellectual appearance', moves on to Douglas, not only bringing out his differences from Thomas, but at the same time suggesting some similarities:

Douglas at that time had silver hair, the plump, ruddy face that indicates good living, the mouth of a wit and the brow of a scholar... [He] was always good, whether he was writing or talking, or just twinkling, and his comments on men whom the intellectual Press was treating as gods were frequent and free. He was so far in advance of the intellectuals and still [i.e. *c.* 1932] is...Douglas has the most fully-charged and fully-active brain of any writer I have met, not excepting Aleister Crowley. His scholarship alone is extraordinary, and when to that is added his control of style and his Voltairian wit, he seems to have more gifts than any one man should have. His books are rather literary treasures than everyday books; they belong on the shelves where one keeps the odd flavours Erasmus, Sterne, Butler, Huysmans; and there, I think, they will always have a place.[7]

Garnett, who saw the potential for a closer relationship between Thomas and Douglas despite their differences, proposed a joint weekend for them at The Cearne, writing to Douglas on 2 February 1912: 'Edward Thomas writes postponing his visit and proposing to come here, for the weekend, this day fortnight (Feb. 17th). I hope that will suit you also?'[8] Since Thomas's letters to Douglas (now at Yale University) start shortly afterwards, it seems that Garnett's efforts succeeded, though the visit to his house would not take place till later in the year.

Only seven letters from Thomas to Douglas have survived, dating from March 1912 to February 1913, but there were almost certainly others, since already by 6 December 1912 Thomas is inviting Douglas to stay with him for Christmas, not something he did lightly, and inscribed a copy of his *Algernon Charles Swinburne* to him the same year. It is perhaps a less serious loss than first appears as both Thomas and Douglas reserved their main energy for face-to-face discussion; their letters are usually brief and factual. Neither could afford much time for letters since they had both to earn their bread-and-butter doing the frankly humdrum, time-consuming reviewing which kept them (just about) solvent. Douglas described Thomas's need to write three, four, even more books a year when they met as 'a dog's life', claiming that he 'would rather be blacking boots'.[9] But Douglas himself reviewed books in every issue of the *English Review* from January 1912 until he left in March or April 1916, which sometimes involved reading nine books for a single review. Since Thomas's own review work had dwindled by

1912 he saw the *English Review* as an important opportunity and wrote to Douglas on several occasions asking for work. It is clear from his letters that he was sometimes, unwittingly, in competition with Douglas for the same book: 'Dear Douglas / Thank you for your letter and for offering me the contents of your pockets when you discover me picking them. However I hope I shan't hit upon another book that is already yours...'[10] The humour of both Thomas and Douglas emerges in such passages, as it does in that amusing story told by Douglas in *Looking Back*, which underlines how problematic money was for both of them:

> A point we had in common was that we were both badly off. It was therefore agreed that we should no longer write ridiculous articles, but open in some country village a small shop, one of those delightfully composite places where you could buy stationery and tobacco and chocolates and anything else; if we still cared to see friends, they would no doubt be able to run down for week-ends. Thomas said, 'If you'll find the capital I'll find the shop.' This is precisely what I failed to find, and the project was abandoned.[11]

Something else Thomas and Douglas had in common was that neither, strictly speaking, was English. Douglas's father was an aristocratic Scot who enjoyed the title of the Laird of Tilquhillie but lived mainly in Austria, in the Vorarlberg, where he ran a cotton factory. His mother was an Austrian. Douglas calls Thomas 'a Welshman (of an unusual variety)' and highlights another ironic similarity between them, that is 'that Thomas was more English than many an Englishman', as Douglas himself was.[12]

And in that long tradition of English writers such as Wordsworth and Coleridge, Thomas and Douglas were both great walkers as well as keen botanists, qualities which inform the travel books they both specialized in with infectious enthusiasm combined with impressive erudition. Thomas's response to Douglas's *Fountains in the Sand*, which he reviewed in the *Daily Chronicle* in December 1912, indicates how closely he shared Douglas's aims in travel-writing. Though they chose to write about very different landscapes – Douglas did *not* share Thomas's admiration for Richard Jefferies – their approach to travel-writing overall was quite similar and fairly unorthodox for the time, both tending to humanize the scene with people and incidents. Thomas felt unable to accept Douglas's invitation to accompany him to Calabria and to his house in Capri in 1912 but it is intriguing to think what he would have made of Calabria, far wilder then than now, and even more interesting to speculate what might have happened if Thomas had visited Italy with Douglas. Might Douglas have succeeded in 'Mediterreanizing' the rather repressed, very 'English' Thomas a little?

Douglas called Thomas 'incurably monogamous', but Thomas's infatuation with a schoolgirl in 1908 suggests that his sexual tastes were not completely different from Douglas's, himself attracted to schoolboys. Neither seems to have found equal sexual satisfaction in mature women and preferred male company, with few exceptions. They were both, basically, a 'man's man', most relaxed and most truly themselves in male company. Douglas went so far as to suggest 'publicly' (Bottomley claimed) 'that Thomas was intended by nature for the life of a bachelor don in collegiate surroundings'.[13]

What united Douglas and Thomas above all, however, was a hatred of cant and hypocrisy, a distrust of conventional morals. Mark Holloway has written of Douglas's

> core of absolute sincerity of regard for love and independence, for place and person and landscape, for fact and truth. This quality in Douglas could be called reverence: it was serious and devoted, though never ponderous, and it called forth, incidentally, a private morality, a sense of obligation, a code of behaviour that were as undeviating as any prescribed by conventional ethics.[14]

Thomas's own very similar attitude comes out clearly in the page he most admired in *Fountains in the Sand*. It is the point at which Douglas pours out his scorn against our so-called 'civilized' Western standards by comparison with the Arabs of North Africa, dismissed by many Westerners as 'poor primitives'.

It is tempting to imagine what might have happened if Douglas had been able to give Thomas even more work than he managed to find for him in the months after war was declared on 4 August 1914 but before Thomas enlisted in July 1915. For one main reason Thomas would eventually join the army was the ever-present need to earn money. When the war came, literary work was even scarcer, with Thomas's few commissions after August

1914 coming mainly from the *English Review* – presumably from Douglas. If such work had continued, Thomas might not have felt obliged to enlist and lived on into old age.

Another writer Thomas got to know better in 1911, Clifford Bax, represented a much smaller group of literary figures who had no need to earn money to support themselves and their writing. Bax, eight years younger than Thomas and not yet 24 when they first met, had been brought up with private tutors and surrounded by artists, musicians and writers at his parents' large, hospitable house, Ivy Bank, in Hampstead. He moved in a leisured, cultured circle largely unfamiliar to Thomas. After studying art at the Slade and Heatherley's, Bax had taken the equivalent of the Grand Tour, travelling abroad from 1904 to 1906, learning languages and gaining experience. In Dublin he had met the mystic artist and poet George Russell ('AE'), who quickened his growing interest in psychical research and spiritualism. Together they planned a magazine aimed at uniting the arts and philosophy, *Orpheus*, which would run from 1907 to 1913. One of Bax's attempts to help Thomas would be to commission and publish three pieces by him in what Thomas called his 'occultish quarterly'.[15]

Bax's first meeting with Thomas, in June 1910, had been almost certainly organized by Eleanor Podmore, wife of Frank Podmore, with whom Thomas had collaborated on articles for the Society of Psychical Research in 1906.[16] (Mrs Podmore was also the sister of the psychiatrist Dr Bramwell, who was treating Thomas for neurasthenia.) Bax had published only one book by this point, a paraphrase of *Twenty Chinese Poems* (1910); a second, *Poems Dramatic and Lyrical*, would follow in 1911. But a letter to Bottomley from Bax's lovely Elizabethan manor house in Wiltshire, Broughton Gifford, makes it clear that, while Thomas appreciated his host's hospitality, he does not feel the same about his poetry. Describing him as 'a local magnate, cricketer, theosophist and amusing talker who knows poetry because he likes it', Thomas adds, 'he will probably never write any'.[17] Even after Clifford started to make a name for himself with his first play, *The Poetasters of Ispahan*, in 1912, Thomas seems to have remained unimpressed, expressing more enthusiasm for his older brother, Arnold Bax, both as an 'excellent pianist and composer' and the author of verse and stories under the pseudonym Dermot O'Byrne, which Thomas 'enjoyed...very much'.[18]

A generous and hospitable man, Clifford would invite Thomas to stay with him on a number of occasions, both in Wiltshire and London, and would help him through one of the most difficult periods of his life. He would also recommend him to one of his publishers, Batsford, who commissioned *The Country* (1913) in 1912. (Thomas would abandon a second book commissioned by them, *Ecstasy*, in September 1913.[19]) Thomas would review at least one of Bax's books despite his reservations about his work.[20]

There was no real warmth between Thomas and Bax, however, who were probably just too different in temperament and tastes. When a mutual friend, Eleanor Farjeon, told Bax in April 1917 that Thomas had been killed at Arras, Bax wrote frankly in his diary on 15 April 1917: 'I am almost glad that I did not like him more. We never quite harmonised. Well I was happy at the Manor House. I saw a good deal of him. Daphne [Bax's first wife] liked him and he sometimes stayed six weeks or two months with us.'[21] By the time of Thomas's death, Bax would believe that Thomas was 'disappearing from [his] life' in any case.[22] But in 1911 and 1912 he was concerned for Thomas's welfare as it became clear that he was in an increasingly precarious mental state.

Despite all Helen's and the doctor's efforts, Thomas had started 1911 in a 'depressed and violent state'.[23] Exhaustion followed throughout February and March and by mid-April he took the unprecedented step of leaving for London late in the day 'to escape the children or allow them to escape me'.[24] The ominous eight blank pages in his diary which follow suggests that he remained in a highly perturbed state. The rest of 1911 was spent mainly away from home, walking with Merfyn in the West Country and visiting Swindon in May, then on the Icknield Way from Thetford to Odsey in June, in Wales in September, as well as making frequent trips to London. Nothing seemed to help and Helen eventually wrote to Haynes, as she had once written to MacAlister about his desperate frame of mind, receiving a generous cheque of £100 by return. This allowed Thomas to spend another six weeks in Wales, mainly at Laugharne, where he completed a rough draft of his study of Borrow. 'I am sorry to hear that Thomas has broken down again,' W. H. Hudson wrote to Garnett in November. 'Why will he work so incessantly and furiously?'[25] Yet it was work which helped to stabilize

Thomas in his current crisis: 'If I could have work *and remain alone to do it*,' he wrote to de la Mare, 'I think I could shut my mouth.'[26]

Even so Thomas started 1912 feeling as tired and depressed as ever; it was at this point that Bax intervened, inviting him to stay at Broughton Gifford in the spring, with a doctor he believed could help him, and whom Thomas had recently met, Helton Godwin Baynes. Brought into contact with the Baxes initially by the friendship of his father, Helton Baynes, with Clifford's father, Alfred, Godwin became a close friend of the family and Ellen Bax persuaded her husband to pay for Godwin to be able to leave the Baynes's timber business and take a degree at Cambridge. Visiting the Bax family in London, Godwin quickly became part of a group of young artists, writers and musicians who gathered round Arnold and Clifford at their house on Haverstock Hill, christening themselves the 'Hampstead Heathens', in emulation of Keats's group of friends. Known as 'Godwin' at this time (he would later adopt the name Peter), Baynes dominated the group, according to Clifford, 'by virtue of his gigantic physique, omniverous mind, universal goodwill, and overwhelming vitality':

> His appetite for joy was insatiable. Twenty-four hours gave not enough scope for his high spirits…He swam vast lakes, climbed perilous mountains, rowed in the Cambridge boat, trolled forth songs by the hour, heckled anti-Socialists on the Heath, passed examinations painlessly, read half the new books that came out, lectured on Walt Whitman, and even listened with interest to my exposition of Oriental mysticism.[27]

Though Clifford himself was not entirely overwhelmed by Godwin's flamboyant personality, the majority of people were, with Edward Thomas no exception at the start. As the artist in Clifford noted, Baynes 'drove the colour out of most men', who quickly became 'no more than his admiring adjuncts…like fishes flowing by hundreds into the whale, or courtiers of old time, who were happy for days if the King had vouchsafed them a kindly word'.[28] Eleanor Farjeon, who knew the group through her brothers and joined in many of their activities, makes an even more convincing case for the hero-worship which surrounded Godwin, helping to explain his initial impact on the normally sceptical Thomas:

> This giant rowing-blue from Cambridge (six-foot-four in his socks), with a heart and brain to match his physical prowess, was the most popular

man I have ever known. When he was talking to you he compelled you to feel that you were more interesting to him than any other person in the room, and I still think that at the given moment this was almost true. He was the sun-god of a dozen circles besides ours, and we found our firmament enlarged from other spheres with Thornycrofts and Radfords, Oliviers, Stracheys, and Meynells. College and medical friends, Fabian, literary, and musical friends, revolved in his orbit; the party began to glow when Godwin appeared. Maitland Radford, a young man of keen wit and shrewd judgement, assayed his values with a detachment not possible to most of us, and for 'Tiny' Baynes's empire invented the name 'Godwinia'.[29]

Everyone, it seems, wanted a piece of Baynes. Edward Garnett's son, David, for instance, who met him through family friends in Hampstead, claimed to have been responsible for introducing Thomas to him. While John Moore, who relied on Helen Thomas for much of his information, says it was Haynes who did so. Another possible candidate is the Thomas's neighbour at Steep, Dr Harry Roberts, who knew Baynes through his work among the poor in the East End of London; Thomas records having them both to dinner at Wick Green after the exchange of a few letters with Baynes, on 25 February 1912.

What is certain is that by 11 April Thomas was at Broughton Gifford being 'treated' by Baynes, the visit arranged by the ever-helpful Bax. Though Baynes had qualified as a physician at St Bartholomew's Hospital in London, by early 1912 he was already interested in Freud and psychology; he would later become a student of Jung in Vienna. When Thomas first consulted him professionally in April 1912, Baynes was about to leave for Paris to study hypnotism at La Salpêtrière, a hospital for mentally disturbed women. Thomas would describe Baynes's treatment of him as 'semi-hypnotic', in which the doctor suggested 'harmony and calm' to his patient. Together with discussions often lasting from breakfast to lunch, about subjects ranging from free-will and ideal republics to Arnold Bennett and the subjects of two of Thomas's current commissions, Swinburne and Pater, walks and cycle rides, the 'freedom and ease' of Broughton Gifford made Thomas feel extraordinarily cheerful'.[30] Baynes, he told Bottomley, was 'working magic with my disordered intellects'.[31] He left Broughton Gifford on 20 April describing his stay as 'the longest period of ease and cheerfulness' he could ever remember.[32]

Matthew Hollis believes that Baynes's method of treating Thomas 'opened the way for a more self-examined life', which led to the autobiographical writings and poetry that followed. However, Thomas's problem was not lack of self-examination, but an excess of it and Baynes might have done better to urge him to examine himself less, not more.[33] Constant self-analysis was one of the main problems. There is no precise account of how Baynes treated Thomas, at a time when he had had no formal training in psychoanalysis. Baynes himself dismissed it as 'try[ing] amateurishly to cure his Neurasthenia by suggestion' and later, after a vivid dream of Thomas, in 1920 'reproached' himself for 'taking a fee for my childish efforts'.[34] He believed the source of Thomas's neurosis to be 'the clutch of the erotic complex'. The most likely explanation for his initial success with Thomas is the sheer force of his personality. Frances Cornford, another poet on whom Baynes would have an overwhelming effect, spoke of 'an animal energy which emanated from him...his presence in a crowded room could make itself felt the moment he entered, like a mighty gust of wind'.[35] Thomas would become very dependent on Godwin in 1912 and 1913, visiting him (after Baynes's typically swashbuckling trip abroad to help in the Balkan War of late 1912 to 1913) at his house and surgery at 30 Victoria Park Square, Bethnal Green, where he ran a GP's practice as part of Harry Roberts's large East End combine.

Baynes's daughter, Diana, claims that her father would help Thomas to gain some insight into his recurring depression and that, when he stopped seeing Baynes, it would be partly through a suspicion that his 'dark times' might also be the source of his creative writing. But Thomas's decision would also stem from a sense of disillusionment with the too popular doctor: 'Godwin can't help me,' he told Eleanor Farjeon. 'When he first came to see me he made me feel that I was the most important person in the world to him. As I came to know his world I found he gave the same impression to everybody – and I don't like being one of a crowd.'[36]

At the start, however, Baynes had been of great help to Thomas. It was almost certainly he who persuaded Thomas to accept Bax's invitation to spend an uncharacteristically indulgent week at Broughton Gifford playing cricket with the group of young Hampstead friends in August 1912. Meeting Thomas at Winchester on 3 August, two days before the Cricket Week started (possibly to make sure he did not change his mind),

Baynes accompanied him on a walk to Devizes, by way of Salisbury, Wilton, Wishford, Tilshead and West Lavington. The first night was spent at a cheap temperance hotel, but only after 'alcohol elsewhere'.[37] They also boarded a non-stopping train as it slowed down at Dunbridge Station, to the 'annoyance of the guard'.[38] Clearly Thomas was in a more relaxed mood in Baynes's company.

The following ten days were among the most carefree of Thomas's adult life. Surrounded by men most of whom were a decade younger than himself, he reverted to his Oxford persona, rising later than usual, bathing daily in the River Avon, cycling or taking the horse-wagonette to the daily cricket matches at Melksham, Box, Trowbridge and Calne, as well as playing at Broughton Gifford itself. An indifferent cricketer, he was allowed to keep the score only in their first match – he enjoyed score-keeping, he said, because the score sheet reminded him of a sonnet[39] – but was persuaded to play in at least two matches, at Trowbridge and Calne. As the *Wiltshire Times* reported, he was lowest on the batting order at number 11, got two 'ducks' (that is, no runs at all), did not bowl and took no catches. Nor is he likely to have excelled at the chess and tennis tournaments also organized during the week, but probably did well at the paper games played after dinner in the music room, where he enjoyed Arnold Bax's piano-playing, 'like silver gnomes'.[40] He also heard Baynes singing folk-songs from Cecil Sharp's collection, Elizabethan lays and eighteenth-century drinking songs, in his warm baritone there and talked late into the night with his fellow-cricketers. He had got to know most of them quickly, he reported to Helen, after the first day's match at Devizes, finding Maitland Radford one of 'the nicest and cleverest' initially.[41] 'All but two', he found 'easy to get on with and make a good party'.[42] Clifford Bax remembered him talking often to his close childhood friend, Lynn Hartley, who, like Thomas, would be killed in the First World War. The two men Thomas wanted to meet again by the end of the week were the painter, later writer, Stacy Aumonier, and the playwright Herbert ('Bertie') Farjeon, who would introduce Edward to one of the closest friends of his last years, his sister, Eleanor. If Clifford Bax's account is true, this 1912 Cricket Week, like the one which preceded and followed it, was idyllic, a bucolic interlude in an ideal setting far from the contemporary issues of the day – the militant Suffragette agitations, the suspicions of a white slave trade, the railway strikes and the rumours of the imminence of war with Germany already circulating.

The effect on Thomas would not be permanent but it seems to have lasted until the end of the year. Though he turned down the suggestion of a camping trip in Wales with Baynes and friends on 22 August, only three days after his return from Broughton Gifford he set off on a bicycle tour with Merfyn, stopping first to visit Vivian Locke Ellis. He had known Ellis, a minor poet who had just opened an antique shop, since late 1910, when they began to meet at Garnett's lunches and St George's. But it was not until Ellis married a 'nice young rich wife',[43] and bought a rambling seventeenth-century house at Selsfield, near East Grinstead, that Thomas started to stay with him. He was particularly fond of the Ellises' extensive garden with its 'deep dark ghyll where they quarried the sandstone hundreds of years ago, now full of hazel and oak'.[44] He would spend over two months with them from 1913 to 1914 writing in a stone outbuilding in that same garden.

Thomas's opinion of Ellis's poetry varied; though never very high, he was to include two of Ellis's poems in his anthology of flower-poems. De la Mare (introduced to Ellis by Thomas) admired his verse sufficiently to include it in one of his best-known poetry anthologies, *Come Hither* (1923). And it was to de la Mare, staying at Cowden not far from Selsfield, that Thomas and Merfyn cycled next. After some roach-fishing and a great deal of talk with the de la Mares' other weekend guest, Hodgson, the Thomases were off again, for a visit to Davies, at Sevenoaks, followed by the Hootons at Coulsdon.

It was a typical trip for Thomas, who frequently took to the road to visit friends when restless. So, too, was his next journey, alone to Wales, ostensibly to research an article on Swansea for the *English Review* (almost certainly engineered by a sympathetic Norman Douglas). He was becoming anxious about money again:

> Evidently I can't get a living by writing [he tells Bottomley on 1 September 1912], unless I content myself with far less than I have got used to…Well and I don't know what to think of apart from writing. I occasionally allow my mind to wander towards some such thing as canvassing for advertisements and similar occupations for superfluous people, but not quite seriously yet.

Once again he considered other jobs, 'some kind of secretaryship (through Belloc)' or a librarianship in a South Wales college.[45] Meantime, he was grateful to have any work at all, especially if it involved a trip to Wales, and spent three whole days in early September researching his article in Swansea, before travelling on to see Gwili and his relatives at Ammanford and Pontardulais.

One sign of the liberating effect Bax, Baynes and their friends may have had on Thomas was his decision after returning from Wales to write a novel. Started on 22 October 1912 and written rapidly in just over two months, *The Happy-Go-Lucky Morgans* would allow him not only to give fuller rein to his imagination but also, through its autobiographical nature, to revisit the past in the way Baynes had encouraged him to do. Even without Baynes's intervention, there were a number of factors to explain what may seem like a puzzling change of direction. Years before when he was longing to write something quite different, Cazenove 'could only suggest fiction'.[46] Though Thomas felt unable to contemplate it at the time, he did suggest a little book on the suburbs, making a link between a novel and them which would be realized five years later in *The Happy-Go-Lucky Morgans*, set firmly in his childhood haunts in south London. When Cazenove again suggested fiction in 1912, he was readier to listen, telling de la Mare that he 'might write one autobiographical novel'.[47] By November 1912 he was hard at work on it.

In asking de la Mare's help in placing the completed novel, Thomas would admit to uncertainty about its title: 'If you think it right I will call it *A True Story of Balham*. In any case I thought of a foreword saying that all the characters *are* from life.'[48] Nine days after starting it on 22 October 1912, he had described it to Bottomley as 'a loose affair held together if at all by an oldish suburban home, half memory, half fancy, and a Welsh family (mostly memory) inhabiting it and collecting a number of men and boys including some I knew when I was from ten to fifteen'. The scheme allowed him to use 'all memory up to the age of 20' and he 'indulged [himself] freely'.[49] The family concerned are identified by most Thomas scholars as the Joneses of Thomas's autobiography, *The Childhood of Edward Thomas* (1938), who lived near the Thomases in Shelgate Road in a big, old house similar to the Abercorran House of the novel. But Edward's youngest brother, Julian, who shared seven years of his life in that same suburb, claimed that the house belonged to the Morris family, closely related to a Welsh poet, Lewis Morris, 'The Wilderness' of the novel, not in real life attached to the Morrises' house, was part of an old mansion, Battersea Rise House, nearby, a triangular three-acre field, with a pond covered with waterlilies and full of carp.[50] One of a number of titles Thomas considered for his novel was 'The Morrises of Battersea Rise'.[51] Other titles attempted to capture the spirit of freedom and ease he envied so much in his Welsh neighbours, referring to it as 'Happy-go-lucky days' or 'This life is most jolly of Balham story'.[52] Yet others emphasize the family's Welshness, having called their house after the original name for Laugharne (Abercorran), where he had been staying less than a year before, he toys with variations on this, such as 'Ann of Abercorran', 'The Morgans of Abercorran', or simply 'Abercorran'.[53]

Thomas made no pretence that his so-called 'fiction' was not thinly disguised autobiography. He even considered writing a preface for it, he told Garnett, 'stating that all the characters but one are from life and offering no prizes for identification'.[54] What he does not also tell Garnett, possibly because he himself had not realized it, was that all the characters are not only 'from life', but in many cases aspects of Thomas himself, as Hudson realized. Hudson's explanation – that 'a poet trying to write prose fiction often does this' – would anticipate by several years Thomas's turn to verse.[55] While Thomas is the pseudonymous narrator of the story, Arthur (the Christian name of his childhood friend, Hardy) Froxfield (from the place Thomas was living in 1912), he is also partly Mr Torrance, who was born in 'the house under the hill', like Edward's mother, and has published 33 books in 13 years, exactly like Edward, partly Philip Morgan in his growing love of nature and Shelley and partly the gypsy, Aurelius, a 'superfluous' man, the adjective Edward had used of himself to Bottomley a month before starting to write his novel. At the same time 'Philip', given Edward's first name, is also the narrator's companion on his walks into the country and sharer of his love of poetry, pointing to both Arthur Hardy and Helen as models, just as Mr Torrance has elements of the Unitarian minister who had first encouraged Edward's talents, Mr Tarrant. Both Mr Stodham and Aurelius, he admitted, resembled his poet-friend, Charles Dalmon.

All these characters, to a greater or lesser extent, reflect Thomas's feelings of being either dispensable, like Philip who dies at the end, or superfluous. Lucy Newlyn and others have seen Thomas as a 'marginal' man, biographically, temperamentally and economically, a theory which his analysis of the 'superfluous' man wholly supports. His own sense of outsidership, of belonging nowhere, emerges clearly in Arthur Froxfield's comment on Aurelius: 'The superfluous are those who cannot find society within which they are in some sort of harmony.'[56] If *The Happy-Go-Lucky Morgans* is full of the melancholy of the Celtic twilight, as one reviewer noted, it is because it allows Thomas to express his feelings more freely than in previous books: at 34 his predominant sense was despair at ever finding his true direction in life. The disposal of Philip at the end of the novel may be a recognition that his youthful aspirations had all died, leaving him more melancholy than ever.[57]

Thomas himself hoped that *The Happy-Go-Lucky Morgans* was 'something more than a connected series of essays', but its story-line of a boy's short-lived relationship with a family so much freer and more irregular than his own is slight and created mainly to explore his own dreams of freedom, both physical and imaginative.[58] Only after he had finished it did he realize what Garnett was quick to point out, that it is similar in a number of ways to Richard Jefferies's *Amaryllis at the Fair*, a novel based on Jefferies's own family at Coate, as they imperceptibly approach disaster. There is little narrative development in either book, both writers preferring to organize their material round short scenes and, in Thomas's case, a series of short stories.

The Happy-Go-Lucky Morgans lack of a strong story-line might not have mattered a decade later when Modernist writers like Woolf, Mansfield and Proust were helping to shift the focus from outer to inner happenings. In early 1913, however, when Thomas hoped that first J. B. Pinker (de la Mare's agent), then Garnett might place it, it was not easy. Though Garnett finally persuaded Duckworth to publish it, when it appeared in October 1913, it was received politely but without warmth. The absence of a 'coherent narrative' and 'the presence of much that is sheer fairy tale, though excellent of its kind' were Charles William Broadribb's reason for considering in his *Times Literary Supplement* review of 20 November 1913 that, 'on the whole… Thomas's novel made for rather patchy reading'.

An even more convincing sign of Broughton Gifford's liberating effect was Thomas's decision to visit Europe for the first time. Having previously turned down Monro's offer of his house at Locarno, Douglas's invitation to go with him to Calabria and Capri and Bax's to Sienna, Thomas suddenly agreed to accept the offer of a week's stay in Paris with Harry Hooton's friend, Jones, who was leaving for France the next day. The English representative of a French bank, Jones and his wife had an apartment in Passy, in the fashionable 16th arrondissement, at 32 rue des Vignes ('Passy,' Edward informed Helen on arrival, 'is a sort of St John's Wood [of London].'[59]) Harry, always anxious to help his wife's oldest friend cope with Edward's moods and depressions, volunteered the fare and his overcoat for the occasion and before he had time to change his mind Edward found himself leaving Britain for the first time in his life.

Passing the Weald and Elses Farm on the train to Folkestone, he arrived at the coast in a violent wind which diverted his boat, so that Calais, not Boulogne as scheduled, was his first view of France. Though he spent seven days walking the streets of Paris, he wrote only a quarter of a page of impressionistic jottings in his field notebooks, which suggests that there had been a dreamlike quality to the experience – 'rustic – wharfs – boulevards – latrines – bookstalls – steamer stages – Notre Dame – dark – new light of blue veiled purple – red etc'.[60] His diary entries are even briefer than usual, noting only the obvious tourist sights, which he inspected contrary to his customary refusal to visit such places even when the publishers of his travel books requested it – the Luxembourg Museum, Notre Dame, the Louvre, the Bastille, St Cloud and Sèvres, as well as the *quais* along the Seine. There are none of the usual references to work, books read for reviews and articles, with the writing of the same, to business letters received and answered.

Nor is there Edward's habitual record of his love-making (marked with an 'x'), since Helen, though invited by the hospitable Joneses, had not been allowed to join her husband. 'Mrs Jones asked,' he wrote to Helen, 'and I would have telegraphed. Only I can't bear the children being entirely dependent on Maud' (i.e. the Thomases' current 'help').[61] He settled with surprising ease into a life of leisure without her, walking in the morning, reading in the afternoon or visiting the opera with Mrs Jones, and dining late with Mr Jones when he returned exhausted from the bank. He was proud of his increasing fluency in spoken French, having previously only read it.

'I hadn't a dull moment, nor an unpleasant one,' he wrote to Janet Hooton on arrival home. 'No time for haunts of sin outside myself. Then the three hours railway to Boulogne in light mist was all delicious.'[62] It is a very different Edward from the gloomy, touchy man Helen and his children so often experienced. He had read only William Hazlitt's *Libor Amoris* while in Paris, attempted only one review and not once thought of the novel he had been so furiously engaged on in England.

The year 1913 has been fastened on as the start of Thomas's move towards poetry. But the process began earlier, in 1912, when his closer contact with Bax and Baynes and their friends allowed him to relive his undergraduate days with a group of gifted men only a little older than he had been at Oxford. In a sense it completed what had been an abruptly truncated rite of passage, his trip to Paris a few months later serving as a modest version of the travels experienced by his more carefree Oxford friends and helping to free his imagination for poetry.

16

Pursued by the Other in Pursuit of Spring
(January–September 1913)

Thomas completed *The Happy-Go-Lucky Morgans* on 30 December 1912 and, despite fearing lack of commissions, was immediately at work on other projects. By 8 January 1913 at the opening of Harold Monro's Poetry Bookshop, at 35 Devonshire Street on the fringes of Bloomsbury, for example, he was already reviewing books for Monro's *Poetry and Drama*. His review of the Poetry Bookshop's first publishing venture, *Georgian Poetry 1911–1912* would appear a week later. Despite what Thomas conceded was a 'chilly' review,[1] less than a month after that Monro invited Thomas to join Henry Newbolt, Ernest Rhys, Victor Plarr, Edward Marsh, T. E. Hulme and himself on a panel of judges to choose the best poem published in the *Poetry Review* under Monro's editorship.

Thomas had agreed to attend the Poetry Bookshop's opening on condition that Monro would protect him against his poets (or 'hostile bards', as Thomas put it to de la Mare)[2] and it is clear from his dealings with Monro that he did not identify wholly with the Georgian aims, as his poetry would demonstrate. But there had been one person at that event whom Thomas might profitably have met, had he not been so anxious to avoid contact with poets – Robert Frost.

He was, in any case, already hard at work researching another book, *In Pursuit of Spring*, an account of a journey by bicycle from London to Somerset. His proposed route covered 130 miles, which he researched in stages. He was already familiar with the way to and from London through its southern suburbs, a trip he had made a number of times by bike from Hampshire in an effort to save money on the train fare. He had also walked the next section of the route with Baynes, from Winchester through Salisbury and Trowbridge to the Somerset border for Bax's Cricket Week. It was this section he chose to repeat in February 1913 on his bicycle, carrying on after it into Somerset to Glastonbury.

Thomas's reason for starting his ride in Wiltshire was yet another invitation from Bax to visit Broughton Gifford, this time to meet someone who would become one of his closest friends over the next four years, Eleanor Farjeon. After meeting and liking her brother, Bertie, at Bax's in August 1912, he had seen Bertie and Godwin Baynes several times in the autumn of 1912. He had been introduced to Baynes's fiancée, Rosalind Thornycroft, and suggested that she join them for their next tea, together with Bertie's 31-year-old sister, Eleanor. It was on this occasion, in the Cottage Tea-rooms in the Strand, that Eleanor was introduced to Edward. Her 'first impressions were of his tall easy figure, his tawny colour, the grave pleasant tones of his voice, and a swift sidelong glance from his keen eyes when Bertie introduced' them.[3] 'To look and listen to Edward was enough,' Eleanor felt; 'he had a higher degree of beauty, of person, voice, and mind' than she had ever known.[4] Unfortunately for Eleanor, who fell instantly in love with Edward, the same could not be said of her. A short, plump, homely woman in glasses, she suffered even more by comparison with Rosalind Thornycroft, renowned for two qualities Edward valued highly, especially in women, beauty and grace.

The tea must have taken place shortly before Godwin left to help in the Balkan War on 13 November 1912 and Eleanor had longed to see Edward again. But it was not until she confided her feelings to Bax that another meeting was arranged between them in February 1913 at Broughton Gifford. (Eleanor's New Year's card to Edward had been politely acknowledged but with no suggestion of another tea.) When, after taking her for a long walk through muddy Wiltshire fields, Edward advised her to 'tread as if you were walking in a dream', she had no problem following his advice, since she was, in a sense, in a dream in his company. Later, in a series of sonnets devoted to Edward, she takes up the image again to describe the uplifting power of her love for him:

> ...Only when love across the heavy fields
> Divinely treads to labour with the clods,
> He breaks the goad that life is glad to yield,
> And lifts the yokes that bowed us to the clods...[5]

It was clear to Eleanor from the start that Edward did not feel a reciprocal sexual attraction to her and she would be horrified to discover later on that her mother had feared that they were having an affair. But Edward *was* drawn to her as a fellow-writer, whose knowledge and love of literature almost matched his own, as did her intelligence and wit. Eleanor would have no problem, for instance, in working out his clue to Helen as to his whereabouts in France in 1917: 'What do you think of Armed Men in Tears as the title of my next book?' While this puzzled Helen, Eleanor instantly guessed that he was near Armentières.[6] Though Eleanor was only at the beginning of a long writing career that would include stories, plays, poems and revues for both adults and children, he would quickly come to rely on her for literary advice. At Broughton Gifford in February 1913, for example, he read her and Bax the beginnings of a collection of odd little fables he was inventing, fragments of mock folklore based on homely proverbs, Eleanor recalled. Almost certainly under de la Mare's influence, he was planning to write a series of stories for children to illustrate the birth of proverbs. The title for this, *Four-and-Twenty Blackbirds*, may also have been inspired by de la Mare – his *Peacock Pie* – with Thomas unable to resist the link between his 24 stories and the blackbirds baked in a pie. It was an idea he had been working on in his field notebooks, jotting down in January 1913, for instance, 'Bird in the Hand / Birds of a Feather / Ill wind / All my eye / East West Homes best'.[7] And in *The Happy-Go-Lucky Morgans* he had described how Arthur and Philip go trespassing, 'with great hopes of four and twenty blackbirds or so'.[8] Encourged by Eleanor and Clifford's praise he would persevere with his collection, despite problems placing it, and when *Four-and-Twenty Blackbirds* was eventually published by Duckworth in 1915 would dedicate it to 'Eleanor Farjeon and Clifford Bax'.

It was the first of many occasions on which Edward would use Eleanor as a sounding-board. He could rely on her honesty, he believed, to tell him the truth. (Her criticism of his relationship with Merfyn would show she was no coward.) Equally importantly to him, he could also be as honest with her as he was with Helen. Indeed, his response to what Eleanor later called her 'long fanciful story', *The Soul of Kol Nikon* (1914), written 'very much under the influence of the Celtic Twilight',[9] was not what an aspiring writer would want to hear from one of London's leading critics, but she took it bravely and well.

When Eleanor finally dared to 'touch on his psychological problems', he was equally unflinching, telling her at length of 'his own coward evil', that is 'self-consciousness carried as far beyond selfishness as selfishness is beyond self-denial...and now amounting to a disease': 'I suppose every man thinks that Hamlet was written for him, but I *know* he was written for me.'[10] Their honesty with each other, Eleanor believed, allowed her to indulge in what Edward called her 'passionate quarrelsomeness' and allowed him to have 'warm and kind feelings' for her, 'when he wasn't too unhappy to do so'.[11] He valued her 'power to be part of the home life of you all,' she told Myfanwy, 'taking his moods as they came, as you all had to'.[12] While she was with them, she believed, 'he never had to be not-himself. So it was possible, without added constraint on him, for me to see him suffering and making Helen suffer.'[13]

A less crucial but important aspect of their relationship was Eleanor's practical help in typing out his manuscripts for him, an incidental benefit being the suggestions or queries made as she did so. Edward accepted her offer with great relief but some guilt, conscious from the start of her powerful feelings for him, though no word was ever said of 'how deeply and completely I loved him,' Eleanor wrote long after his death.[14] What precisely Edward felt for her she never knew, but it would be a comfort to her after his death to believe that he had 'sometimes depend[ed] on [her] love as one of the fixed things in his life which he had no need to question or to torment himself about'.[15]

The friendship between Edward and Eleanor developed rapidly, with meetings when he was in London, either for tea at the Cottage Tea-rooms, a fruit-lunch at Shearns, or a visit to Eleanor's family home in Fellows Road. By March 1913 he was offering her and Bertie the loan of Wick Green for the Easter weekend, friends included, since Helen and the children would be at the seaside in Norfolk and he would be 'walking somewhere'.[16] (In fact, he was cycling once more through Wiltshire and Somerset still in *Pursuit of Spring*.) Once he and Helen had finally given notice to Lupton in January, it may be that they cared less about other people invading Wick Green. They may, on the other hand, have begun to feel prouder of their house built so magnificently on the top of Stoner Hanger. It certainly enchanted the Farjeons and their Hampstead friends, the Corders, the Baxes, the Antoniettis, Myra Hess, Godwin and the Thornycroft sisters, Joan and Rosalind. Edward's response to Eleanor's grateful letter of thanks was to invite her to meet his wife.

It is impossible to tell from Helen's glowing account of Eleanor's first visit to Steep how exactly she had felt when Edward wrote to say he wanted to invite his new female friend to visit. His infatuation with Hope Webb lay only five years behind them. Her response to Eleanor, a 'short, and warm and touchingly humble' letter, hoping that Eleanor 'would not be disappointed in her' and emphasizing that she 'wasn't intellectual but "very primitive"',[17] suggests that, consciously or not, she was anxious to disarm Eleanor in advance.

This first visit to Steep had been delayed initially by Edward's pressure of work. More research on *In Pursuit of Spring*, concluded in late March with a bicycle ride to the Quantocks with Jesse Berridge, was followed by a few days spent at Dillybrook Farm, near Bath, with de la Mare. On this occasion, too, they shared a semi-mystical moment as the thrushes burst into song at twilight, an experience Thomas would later describe in his poem 'March' and de la Mare in his 'Dust to Dust'.[18] April was spent writing the book itself in London and May in his typing its 75,000 words (amateurishly) at Wick Green, 4,000 words a day. He was also preparing *The Icknield Way* for the press. By the time he was freer of work, in June, Eleanor herself was busy elsewhere.

In Pursuit of Spring was completed at approximately the same time as his two other books on the English countryside were published. *The Country* was an essay-length piece for the Batsford Fellowship series in which Thomas lays out his views on the difference between town- and country-living, at a time when there was a distinct 'back-to-the-land' movement. *The Icknield Way*, published by Constable in August 1913, is a more substantial account of a journey along one of England's most ancient roads, undertaken by Thomas in stages over the course of a year, but given as a single ten-day journey in the book. Unlike most of his previous travel books, both *The Icknield Way* and *In Pursuit of Spring* have a clearly defined outline. *The Icknield Way* is shaped simply round a journey with a purpose, an idea Belloc had helped popularize with his *Old Road* (1904) and which R. Hippisley Cox, T. E. Peake and others had continued. (Belloc's *Old Road* and *The Stane Street* were part of the same series published by Constable.) Thomas freely admitted their influence, and was in touch with both Belloc and Hippisley Cox, choosing for his journey the old road that runs from Norfolk through Cambridgeshire, Bedfordshire, Hertfordshire, Buckinghamshire, Berkshire and Wiltshire into Dorset. It was his publisher's wish rather than his own inclination that made him give a specific route full of concrete details; he continued to prefer a less rigid form which allowed more rein to his imagination. 'I am writing my Icknield Way,' he told Bottomley in July 1911, 'and am at the worst of the mere archaeology.'[19] He was also less interested than Belloc in topographical detail, which he uses more as a springboard for passages already tending towards the vividness and concentration of poetry; his description of a path through Marmansgrave Wood, for example, anticipating a poem like 'Tall Nettles':

> It was a broad and hedgeless track, often riddled by rabbit burrows which were masked by nettles. At its best it was a rough, tussocky sheaf of cartways. Everywhere sand and flints, parallelograms of fir trees, nettles, and more nettles and the smell of nettles. Rarely it passed a square, now, or several years ago, given to corn. I like nettles, especially with elder trees in blossom above them, as at Lackford Road Heath, half-way along.[20]

One of the clearest examples of Thomas's move towards poetry is the description of rain which concludes the next to last chapter, foreshadowing his poem on the same subject by at least five years. It is 'mutter[ed]' by a ghostly character who prefigures the Other Man in *Pursuit of Spring*:

> Now there is neither life nor death, but only the rain. Sleep as all things, past, present, and future, lie still and sleep, except the rain, the heavy, black rain falling straight through the air that was once a sea of life. That

was a dream only. The truth is that the rain falls for ever and I am melting into it. Black and monotonously sounding is the midnight and solitude of the rain. In a little while or in an age – for it is all one – I shall know the full truth of the words I used to love, I knew not why, in my days of nature, in the days before the rain: 'Blessed are the dead that the rain rains on.'[21]

Such passages show Thomas at his best, unconstrained by the need to give specific details or accounts of tourist sites. He was, however, genuinely interested in the old roads. His dedication to Harry Hooton, which refers to walking with him on the Pilgrims' Way 'many a time', becomes lyrical as he remembers it 'always among beach and yew and Canterbury bells, and always over the silver of whitebeam leaves'.[22] His response to ancient pathways would reveal itself most memorably when he turned to poetry proper:

> ...Roads go on
> While we forget, and are
> Forgotten like a star
> That shoots and is gone.
>
> On this earth 'tis sure
> We men have not made
> Anything that doth fade
> So soon, so long endure.[23]

Thomas was particularly struck by the 'pathos of old roads worn deep and then deserted and only surviving in parts – for centuries they seemed so necessary – men set out on them at dark and now they are no more than a place in which men have lived and died content'.[24] But it is Thomas's naturalist's eye and poet's ear which distinguish him most sharply, his interest in the smaller details – the life of insects, birds and plant-life – in a tradition which goes back to Gilbert White at the end of the eighteenth century, through Jefferies and Hudson. They were all, as Hudson put it, 'travellers in little things'.[25]

Despite this, *The Icknield Way* is nearer to the guidebook Constable requested than Thomas's previous travel books. Each chapter, after the introductory ones 'On Roads and Footpaths' and 'History, Myth, Tradition, Conjecture and Invention', takes the reader through one of the ten days' walks. It is enlivened by personal details, of shabby clothes and sore feet; humorous asides – the narrator 'recommend[s]' any form of transport, 'elephant, camel, horse, mule, donkey, motor-car, waggon, or cart, anything but a covered cab or a pair of hobnailed shoes' rather than 'feet'; poetic insights, the road described as 'a symbol of mortal things with their beginnings and ends always in immortal darkness', though he confesses to finding the flat roads of Cambridgeshire 'without mystery'.[26] More than any other poet since Wordsworth, Thomas's walking led to lyrical writing.

Cycling, too, as *In Pursuit of Spring* shows, inspires Thomas to poetry, though still technically in prose. He had taken to cycling relatively late and initially 'hate[d]' it, regarding it more as a necessity than a choice.[27] But by early 1913, faced with a journey of 130 miles and time pressing, he begins to see merit in wheels, writing to Helen after cycling to Wiltshire: 'I confess I do like cycling because I get moving air, views, and exercise without being reminded of the poorness of my body. Driving might be something like it but not quite because one really is doing something and the attitude is not entirely unheroic.'[28] His brother Julian, who had walked many miles with him along the Icknield Way, was again asked to accompany him for the first part of the journey for *In Pursuit of Spring*, through the south London suburbs to Salisbury Plain; he was probably relieved that it was by bike since he remembered setting out each morning on the Icknield Way at five or six o'clock and walking 30 or 40 miles until their muscles ached and their feet were blistered and sore.

There were some drawbacks to cycling, especially when it was 'cold and softly raining':

> In cycling chiefly ample views are to be seen, [but] the mist conceals them. You travel too quickly to notice many small things; you see nothing save the troops of elms on the verge of invisibility. But walking I saw every small thing one by one; not only the handsome gateway chestnut just fully dressed, and the pale green larch plantation where another chiff-chaff was singing, and the tall elm tipped by a linnet pausing and musing a few notes, but every primrose and celandine and dandelion on the banks, every silvered leaf of honeysuckle up in the hedge, every patch of brightest moss, every luminous drop on a thorn tip.[29]

As such passages show, despite his misgivings cycling does not prevent Thomas breaking into the prose-poems Robert Frost would note in this book. And it is the less conventionally beautiful aspects of nature which appeal to him – the dandelions and nettles as well as the primroses, celandines and honeysuckle:

> But these things also are Spring's –
> On banks by the road side the grass
> Long-dead that is greyer now
> Than all the Winter it was;
>
> The shell of a little snail bleached
> In the grass; chip of flint, and mite
> Of chalk; and the small bird's dung
> In splashes of purest white...[30]

On the whole, however, cycling is presented as a positive, at times semi-mystical experience in which Thomas feels himself 'a great deal nearer to being a disembodied spirit than I often can be'.[31] Untroubled by the tiredness he increasingly experienced when walking and undisturbed by 'people or thoughts', he 'fed through the senses directly, but very temperately, through the eyes chiefly, and was happier than is explicable or seems reasonable', in what he believed to be the 'pleasure of [his] disembodied spirit'.[32]

These occasional trance-like states during his cycle ride for *In Pursuit of Spring* may help to explain the first explicit reference to 'the Other Man', who appeared sporadically throughout, almost like an hallucination. Early in the journey the narrator sees the Other Man buy a chaffinch in a bird-shop, before releasing it 'with an awkward air' shortly afterwards. He sights the Other Man frequently on the road to Morden, loses him at Ewell, only to meet him again on Epsom Downs. The Other Man reappears at Salisbury, where they discuss one of Thomas's favourite topics, clay pipes, next at Bemerton, where the narrator defends one of its former vicars, the mystic poet George Herbert, whom the Other Man then mocks. When he next materializes on the road from Trowbridge to Shepton Mallet, he shows an interest in and knowledge of birds equal to Thomas's and, like Thomas, turns out to be a writer of travel books:

> 'I wrote one all about this valley of the Frome... But no one knows it was the Frome I meant. You look surprised. Nevertheless, I got fifty pounds

for it.' 'That is a lot of money for such a book!' 'So my publisher thought.'
'And you are lucky to get money for doing what you like.' 'What I like!'
he muttered, pushing his bicycle back uphill, past the goats by the ruin,
and up the steps between walls that were lovely with humid moneywort,
and saxifrage like filigree, and ivy-leaved toadflax. Apparently the effort
loosened his tongue. He rambled on and on about himself, his past, his
writing, his digestion; his main point being that he did not like writing.[33]

The Other also shares Thomas's faddish taste in health-foods and his
wariness of strangers. His final appearance is at Kilve, in Somerset, to check,
like Thomas, if it really had 'no weather-cock' as Wordsworth's 'Anecdote
for Fathers' claimed. In all these scenes he allows Thomas to express views
and tastes so similar to the author's own that it is impossible not to see
him as an aspect of the author's own self. (He avoids 'difficulty in telling
truths', as Thomas saw it.[34]) The Other Man is also, as P. J. Kavanagh points
out, a 'device for throwing derision at himself'.[35] Long before it became a
familiar strategy, Kavanagh argues, Thomas is 'publicly debating in front of
his reader his doubts about whether he can write [his book] at all'.[36]

After starting treatment with Baynes in 1912, Thomas could not have
been unaware of the possible link between the 'double' in literature and
Freud's 'id' or Jung's 'shadow', the side hidden from public view, also the
seat of creativity. In Jungian psychology a crucial stage in what Jung calls
the 'individuation' process is to face this 'shadow', or 'other' side, and to
integrate it with the conscious, public persona, since for some it may be that
'the dark side of his being, his sinister shadow... represents the true spirit
of life as against the arid scholar'.[37] Unlike Freud, Jung sees the 'double' or
'shadow' simply as a complementary opposite, which needs to be recon-
ciled. Only when one side of the personality is repressed and subordinated
does damage occur.

Thomas's decision to feature the Other Man as an actual character in
his work is prefigured in his field notebook for the period: 'Other Man –
wraith – when seen at Salisbury I was not sure he had existed before'.[38] This
was the culmination of a series of allusions in previous works of clearly
recognizable alter egos: the melancholy city-worker of *The South Country*
who flees London every summer, a variety of characters in *The Happy-Go-
Lucky Morgans* and the narrator's 'ghostly double'. 'The Pilgrim', too, in
the short story of that name, is another candidate put forward by Andrew

Motion: 'a poet of a kind who made a living out of prose'.[39] And as Stan Smith points out, much of the opening of *The Country*, which Thomas was preparing for the press in 1913 as he followed his itinerary for *In Pursuit of Spring*, 'is taken up with a monologue by that country-born city-dwelling clerk' – the opposite of the city-born country-dwelling Thomas – 'a fictive alter ego who allows the author both to utter and to distance himself from the opinions expressed'.[40] Thomas's letters and diaries also reveal a sense of a dual, even multiple personality. As early as 1906 he had told Bottomley that he felt 'destined to reflect many characters and to be none' and had written in his field notebook three years later that he had 'no opponent but self'.[41] By 1911, his 'worst year', he told MacAlister that his head was 'almost always wrong', with 'a sort of conspiracy going on in it' which left him 'only a joint tenancy and a perpetual sense of the other tenant' and what he might do.[42]

Thomas was familiar with the figure of the Other in literature. Even before the *Doppelgänger* of German Romanticism popularized the concept, Sir Thomas Browne had written in one of Thomas's favourite books, *Religio Medici* (1642): 'There is another man within me, that's angry with me.' Having read Poe 'over and over again' by 1908, Thomas would have known Poe's 'William Wilson' (1839), the story of a 'double' who pursues the protagonist.[43] He would also have been familiar with Stevenson's *Dr Jekyll and Mr Hyde* (1886) and Wilde's *The Picture of Dorian Gray* (1891). And he had almost certainly read Conrad's *The Secret Sharer* (1910).

Like most of these writers, Thomas was less concerned with the Gothic elements often attaching to the double, or other, than the psychological truths they might help to embody. In his own case, the introduction of the 'Other Man' into *In Pursuit of Spring* suggests that he might at last be dealing with a long-repressed side of himself. Shortly after the book was completed, for instance, he had finally faced the unpalatable fact that he could no longer live with Helen. Their early marriage had cut off sides of himself he was now ready to explore. By doing so, in Jung's terms he was attempting to integrate his two selves. The period of immense creativity which followed not long after could be seen (again in Jungian terms) as the manifestation of this.

His turn to poetry is certainly the most tangible evidence of a change in Thomas. One of his earliest verse efforts would be a poem called 'The

Other', in which the narrator is mistaken for a man who closely resembles him as with *In Pursuit of Spring*. Despite his 'fear', the narrator actively pursues the Other in the poem through a quest-like landscape, leaving behind him both the 'dark wood' from which he has emerged and 'the inn in the sun'.[44] In the second of the eleven stanzas he 'travelled fast, in hopes I should / Outrun that other'. He pursues him, he tells the reader, 'To prove the likeness, and, if true, / To watch until myself I knew'. And self-knowledge does appear to follow after a long, hard journey, when suddenly at twilight among desolate scenery he 'stood serene, / And with a solemn quiet mirth, / An old inhabitant of earth'. In this unaccustomed mood of serenity, comparable to Wordsworth's 'spots of time', Woolf's 'moments of being' or Joyce's 'epiphanies', the narrator is able to accept that what he once called 'melancholy', because it was not 'happiness', might be a positive experience – 'Moments of everlastingness'.[45] When his confrontation with the Other eventually takes place, the narrator cannot explain his motives in pursuing him and 'slips away'. Nevertheless he has faced the Other and has become completely aware of him, even though there seems little likelihood of reconcilation between the two:

> And now I dare not follow afterwards
> Too close. I try to keep in sight,
> Dreading his frown and worse his laughter.
> I steal out of the wood to light;
> I see the swift shoot from the rafter
> By the inn door: ere I alight
> I wait and hear the starlings wheeze
> And nibble like ducks: I wait his flight.
> He goes: I follow: no release
> Until he ceases. Then I also shall cease.[46]

All his adult life Thomas had been taking journeys like this, through dark woods to bright comforting inns, observing minute natural details as he travelled; only now is their full significance beginning to be revealed to him in the pursuit and acceptance of the Other.

Facing the Other – if that is what Thomas was doing – did not make him any easier to live with, as Eleanor discovered when her visit to meet Helen finally took place in early August. This had been deferred yet again in July, when the Thomases moved late in the month from what Eleanor called their 'glorious position on the ridge' at Wick Green to Yew Tree Cottage, a semi-detached house that had just been completed, she remembered, on a 'raw plot of ground' near Bedales in Steep. Built by a wealthy Socialist aristocrat, it was one of six cottages intended for workmen. When the rents, though fairly moderate, discouraged the villagers from applying, Edward and Helen decided to take one. Edward's dislike of Wick Green, together with Yew Tree Cottage's much lower rent, its convenient position near Merfyn and Bronwen's school and its more easily manageable garden, finally convinced him to move to what seemed, after the grand scale of Wick Green, a tiny cottage. Helen, undeterred by the lack of an indoor bathroom, limited bedroom space and combined living-room and kitchen, saw this eighth move in 13 years, as she had so often before, as a chance for a fresh start. 'It's awfully cosy and pretty and I love doing all the work,' she wrote to Janet Hooton a fortnight after the move. (They had also given up their servant, to economize further):

> It is I who am making a home for Edward, the only time I've had it all in my own hands, and I believe it's going to be the happiest home we've ever had. I know I shall do my best, and my dear old boy is trying too. Yes! Isn't he handsome but he's more than that. I've never met a man who could come anywhere near him in looks or in character either. If only he had a little more native hope and joyousness, so that all this bitter discouragement and anxiety had not driven him to despair. But I don't give up hope, I feel he *must* come out all right. He's tried hard during these last two years to kill my love for him but it's just the same as it always was, it's my great treasure, the thing that keeps me going, that is my life, that and the children. In my heart I have memories so splendid that I am rich in happiness tho' I spend very many days of utter misery. Sometimes I think he does not love me any more, and my soul goes into a panic of terror, and then out of the darkness comes some wonderful gleam that gives me new hope, new life, new being and I start again. And now in this cottage it's all going to be easier.[47]

Despite Helen's enthusiasm and however resolutely she set about making Yew Tree Cottage home – bright curtains at the windows, scarlet geraniums on the windowsills – two months after the move Edward made his decision to leave Helen and his family, ostensibly for good. Helen refers in her letter to two years of intense strain, but judging from Edward's diary he had experienced it for much longer than that. Moving to smaller, more cramped living-quarters only exacerbated the situation for him. Though Lupton allowed him to keep on his study at Wick Green, where he worked daily, his irritability began to spiral out of control, even in the presence of Eleanor during her first visit on 9 August. Edward, who had spent a few more days with Bax and his friends at Broughton Gifford's annual Cricket Week, arrived back in Steep at the same time as Eleanor, who was walking with Helen from the station. 'He was not in a good mood,' she recalled, and to cover the slight embarrassment, she chatted about cricket, asking after the other members of the team, whom she knew well – the Bax brothers, Stacy Aumonier and her brother, Bertie. That evening at supper she saw the first sign of Edward's uncontrollable irritation with his family, sparked off (according to Eleanor) by 'some nothing Helen said or did, or hadn't done'.[48] On this occasion the storm passed without spoiling the evening, but Eleanor would witness many other times when it did not. As her visits became more intimate, she 'saw how he was the greatest sufferer when he could not help "inflicting five persons at once"'.[49] Only Bronwen, who did not react to such behaviour, seemed able to cope with it. Eleanor felt great sympathy for Helen, whom she had liked immediately, but felt unable to help.

Eleanor never experienced Edward's irritability personally, even during the whole week they spent together on the Norfolk Broads with Stacy and Gertrude Aumonier and Merfyn, who had been left in his father's care while Helen holidayed in Switzerland for three weeks with her sister, Irene. After meeting at South Walsham, they were towed to Ranworth Broad in their houseboat to start their leisurely cruise through Norfolk. While Stacy wandered off to paint at their daily moorings, Eleanor and Edward took walks, which showed her his natural way with country people and his keen eyesight. (Like Helen, she was short-sighted.) Only when Edward and Stacy occasionally fished together was she deprived of his company. It was a happy time, with no sign of the irritability which had so shocked her at Steep.

After another week of childcare for Edward, looking after Bronwen, as well as Merfyn, at Flansham, near the Guthries, however, all the old problems returned. Depositing Bronwen with Myfanwy at their aunt's house, Thomas stayed on in London, paying what was probably a last visit to Godwin at Bethnal Green, before he and Rosalind left for a country practice at Wisbech. Whether as a result of yet another session with the psychiatrist or not, two days later, on 7 September 1913, Thomas made the first tentative move towards his mature poetry.

Thomas had gone straight from the Bayneses to stay with Ellis and his wife at Selsfield. Already thinking seriously of leaving Helen, Selsfield House seemed a possible alternative. He liked the Ellises but was not too close to them for comfort. He also admired the surrounding Surrey countryside and thought the size of the house would allow for a reasonable amount of independence. His mood was particularly bleak by early September, his notebooks making it clear that his depression had been building up during the year. Entries from May to June, for example, include a quotation from Coleridge's 'Ode to Dejection' about his natural surroundings: 'I see but cannot feel how beautiful it is.'[50] And by 29 June he is asking himself: 'Is it worse in my curst state to see this beautiful hot windy weather and hate it and myself because I can't enjoy it – or to have foul weather and realise how it would tend to damp my spirits (but would it?) if I were not curst.'[51] His work, too, was going badly. With the completion of *In Pursuit of Spring* he had only *Four-and-Twenty Blackbirds* and his book on *Ecstasy* to work on, and his chief qualification for writing about ecstasy, he maintained, was his 'intimate and long-standing acquaintance with the opposite of ecstasy': he 'knew well the "grief without a pang" described with some flattery in Coleridge's "Dejection".'[52]

Thomas had also reached a crisis in his writing life; neither his novel nor his travel books nor his literary criticism satisfied his search for the right medium. His short stories, which he favoured, were more difficult to place. He would spend his time at Selsfield experimenting in a number of genres, among the fruits of which would be his autobiographical account, *The Childhood of Edward Thomas*, published long after his death.

All these factors came together on the night in question to produce a momentous reaction. It was in the early morning of 7 September 1913 that a sleepless Thomas wrote in his field notebook a quite different entry from the usual detailed notes of his natural surroundings, though these become woven into his account of the experience.

It is Sept. 7th of the year and of me. All night the 100 firs by the Ardingley rd. sound like a far forest or sea. Then at 4.30 the cocks crow, none near, and a robin begins to sing its pausing mute [?] open song & sounds quite monotonous and quite expressionless outside in the dark hushed garden. He continues and the light grows and the firs never cease and I try to sleep but can only try to compose verses on the occasion, beginning something like

> The 7th of September
> Of the year & of me [This line crossed through by ET]
> The sere & the ember
> Of the year and of me
> There will always be firs to moan
> And robins to sing at cold dawn.

Despite its brevity and incompleteness, anyone familiar with Thomas's poetry will immediately recognize the features which go into this fledgling attempt 'to compose verses on the occasion': the use of a common sensation or occurrence, such as the passing of the seasons, the reference to birds and trees, the choice of rhymed, or half-rhymed over unrhymed verse, and, most memorably, the sense of isolation and of something just beyond the poet's reach. Here he is, as F. R. Leavis would argue, writing 'on the edge of consciousness'.[53]

Many of the poems to follow would contain literary allusions; this first effort seems more dependent than most on them. Thomas, partly through his book reviews since his early twenties, was enormously well read and a lifelong admirer of Shakespeare. The echo of Macbeth's lament as he sits lonely and deserted, facing his end – 'My way of life is fallen into the sere, the yellow leaf' – is unmistakable, reinforcing Thomas's own sense of despair as he writes the lines. There is almost certainly a hint, too, of Byron's last poem, 'On This Day I Complete My Thirty-sixth Year'. Thomas himself was in his thirty-sixth year in September 1913, and would certainly have known the piece. Byron's second stanza opens with its own debt to *Macbeth*, 'My days are in the yellow leaf.' Behind both lie Shakespeare's sonnets on ageing, in particular Sonnet 73: 'In me thou see'st the glowing of such fire, / That on the ashes of his youth doth lie.'

It is tempting also to speculate if Macbeth's lines, or Byron's last poem, both uttered by a man resolved to face the possibility of death in battle, came back to Thomas a year later, as he faced his own decision about enlisting. But a more fruitful question, perhaps, is how this unpublished fragment affects our view of Frost's role in Thomas's development as a poet. While it does not devalue the importance of Frost's encouragement, it does suggest that Thomas would have gone on to write poetry without his intervention. It certainly refutes Thomas's own, self-consciously Shakespearian claim that Frost was the 'onlie begetter' of his verse. The friendship with Frost has understandably fascinated generations of readers and critics. We must be careful, however, not to give it undue prominence and so distort our view of Thomas's turn to poetry.

The most interesting speculation of all, however, thrown into relief by this notebook entry and its context, is that by 1913 Thomas was coming to terms with his depression and starting to deal with it through poetry. Faced with his inability to sleep, a familiar feature of depression, he 'can only try to compose verses on the occasion'. It is the beginning of a strategy which, in the last years of his life, as his verses began to 'run', was to lift him above a despair which by 1913 not even his greatest hope, Dr Godwin Baynes, had been able to cure. It was not joining the army (as some of his friends would suggest), which changed Edward Thomas. Rather, as this long-buried notebook entry hints, it was the decision to write poetry to combat despair.

17

'THE ONLY BROTHER I EVER HAD'
(6 OCTOBER 1913–MARCH 1914)

We were greater friends than almost any two ever were
practising the same art [...] He gave me standing as a poet –
he more than anyone else [...] I dragged him out from under
the heap of his own work in prose he was buried alive under.
                    – Robert Frost to Grace Walcott Hazard Conkling,
                                                28 June 1921

When Thomas met Robert Frost in the smoking-room of
St George's restaurant, St Martin's Lane, on 6 October
1913, it was the start of a literary friendship rivalled only by that of
Wordsworth and Coleridge, Rimbaud and Verlaine, or Owen and
Sassoon. For Frost and Thomas's interaction was to have equally
significant consequences in both personal and literary terms.

The meeting itself was a miracle of chance. It might so easily
have been a repeat of an earlier occasion – the launch of Harold
Monro's Poetry Bookshop on 8 January 1913 – when Frost and
Thomas had been in the same room, already knowing a number of
the same people, but had failed to meet. Similarly, if Thomas had
kept his appointment with Eleanor Farjeon on 6 October, he might
not have been introduced to Frost, either at all, or in time to gain
the benefit he did from that friendship. Or if he had committed

suicide the day before, as he had intended after one of his 'private hell[s] of depression', prevented only by de la Mare's persuasion – though he still had 'the saviour' [a gun?] in his pocket on 6 October.[1]

Instead, prompted perhaps by curiosity, or simply trust in the man who had arranged the meeting, Ralph Hodgson, he wrote to Eleanor on 5 October asking her to forgive him if he failed to turn up the following day: 'I have an appointment of uncertain time with an American just before and may not be able to come'.[2] When he and Eleanor did eventually meet, she remembered, he did not name the American.[3]

Yet Frost was to become, in Eleanor's words, 'the greatest friend' of Thomas's life[4] and their rapport at his first encounter was instant. For Frost it was as though they were (to quote his later poem on the subject, 'Iris by Night') 'elected friends'. So strong was his sense of affinity that he claimed Thomas as 'the only brother I ever had'.[5] Though Thomas was less forthcoming than the exuberant American, he would write his own poem about their intercourse, especially on the long walks they would take together the following summer:

The sun used to shine while we two walked
Slowly together, paused and started
Again, and sometimes mused, sometimes talked
As either pleased, and cheerfully parted

Each night. We never disagreed
Which gate to rest on. The to be
And the late past we gave small heed...[6]

Apart from some superficial similarities – of age (they were both in their thirties, Frost, at 39, the older by four years), of appearance (both were physically attractive, Thomas strikingly so) and of circumstances (both married young and had a dependent family) – there were other more fundamental likenesses, especially of temperament. Though each had a well-developed sense of humour and was very good company, especially at their ease among men, they suffered equally from periodic bouts of deep depression and, in Thomas's case at least, suicidal thoughts. Both were prone to what might nowadays be called psychosomatic illnesses, though these recurrent failures of health were very real to each of them. Whether this stemmed partly from their circumstances or vice versa is impossible to say, but here again the resemblances are conspicuous. Both entered early into rushed marriages, had children very young, failed to live up to academic expectations and struggled for over a decade to support their families, Frost as a schoolmaster and farmer, Thomas as a journalist and prose-writer of what he considered 'hack' work. By the time they met, neither felt they had succeeded in what they had set out to achieve, and both experienced a repeated sense of defeat, self-abasement and personal failure as a husband, father and writer. Yet both were sustained by a passionate love of the countryside – Thomas's intimate knowledge of trees, for instance, mirroring Frost's own – and both found consolation in literature. Their shared enthusiasm for the classics and their early love of the Romantic poets, as well as Hardy, Emerson and Thoreau, alone gave them many points of contact.

Despite all these similarities, it was their differences initially that led to the extraordinary development in their relationship which marks it out. When Frost was introduced to Thomas in the autumn of 1913, it was at Thomas's request. As one of London's best-known literary critics, respected particularly for his sensitive response to contemporary verse, Thomas had already reviewed Frost's first published book of poetry, *A Boy's Will* (1913). Ironically, given Frost's present-day fame and Thomas's relative obscurity, Frost himself was virtually unknown at the time, unlike Thomas, whose travel books, biographies and numerous reviews had won him wide recognition in literary circles. Though Frost's poems were starting to appear in American magazines before he left for Europe in September 1912, he had not been published in book-form until he reached England. But he was determined to make his name as a poet. Selling the small farm he owned in New England and supported by a recently increased annuity of $800 from his grandfather's estate, he had come to a country where he believed his chance of recognition would be greater, the choice between England and Canada having been decided apparently by the toss of a coin. There is little doubt that in being one of the first respected critics to recognize Frost's genius, Thomas helped start the American on the road to success.

Yet Frost, who had unhesitatingly cultivated some of the best-known players on London's literary scene in 1913 – Ezra Pound, Harold Monro, Wilfrid Gibson, Ralph Hodgson, Lascelles Abercrombie, among others – seems to have made no such effort to woo Thomas. Their friendship appears to have grown spontaneously from a genuine liking and admiration for each other and for each other's work. After a second meeting, on 22 December 1913, at which Frost had promised to introduce Thomas to the Imagist poet F. S. Flint, Thomas would invite Frost to spend a night at his parents' home in Balham to avoid a late journey back to his rented house in Beaconsfield. And by the end of January 1914 Thomas had evidently confessed to Frost his growing unhappiness with his wife, from whom he was temporarily separated, and his desire to leave her for good: would his 'dear Frost', he wrote, look for cheap lodgings for him near the Frosts in Beaconsfield? Even after Thomas's decision to return to Helen and his family in February 1914, he would still be planning to see Frost in London, or to cycle over from Steep to Beaconsfield, a good day's ride, ending one such letter: 'I wish you were nearer so that we could see one another easily and our children.'[7] Their talk, when they managed to meet, was that of kindred spirits.

So that when Thomas went on to write yet more reviews of Frost's second English publication, *North of Boston* (1914), he would not consciously be doing Frost a favour, though that was the result his reviews would have. He was simply recognizing in the American's technique the effects he himself admired in poetry, had aimed at in his lyrical prose and would eventually realize in his own verse.

Describing *North of Boston* as 'the most revolutionary' book of modern times but 'one of the quietest and least aggressive', Thomas had written in the *Daily Chronicle* on 22 July 1914:

> These poems are revolutionary because they lack the exaggeration of rhetoric, and even at first sight appear to lack the poetic intensity of which rhetoric is an imitation. Their language is free from the poetical words and forms that are the chief material of secondary poets. The metre avoids not only the old-fashioned pomp and sweetness, but the later fashion also of discord and fuss. In fact, the medium is common speech... They depend not at all on objects commonly admitted to be beautiful; neither have they merely a homely beauty, but are often grand, sometimes magical. Many, if not most, of the separate lines and separate sentences are plain and, in themselves, nothing. But they are bound together and made elements of beauty by a calm eagerness of emotion.

Reading this and Thomas's previous reviews Frost must have realised that he had finally met someone who recognized the value of what he called his 'sound of sense' theory. It was an area which he and Thomas would explore exhaustively in August 1914, the month they spent together in Gloucestershire.

When Thomas left Yew Tree Cottage to lodge with Vivian Locke Ellis and his wife at Selsfield House, East Grinstead, at the end of October 1913, shortly after meeting Frost, the American was one of the few people to be told that he was intending to leave his wife for good.[8] The ostensible reason he gave, as he had so many times in the past, for his extended absences from the family home, was the need for peace and space in which to write. Heinemann appeared to have accepted his book of proverbs, *Four-and-Twenty Blackbirds*, and he was, as always, anxious to earn money with a new one.

After completing work on a short book about Keats, he quickly turned to his own life. *The Childhood of Edward Thomas* was possibly inspired and certainly helped by his rereading of the opening of *Great Expectations* in 1913, with its vivid recreation of childhood, and his review of Walter de la Mare's *A Child's Day* (1912).[9] This autobiography, unpublished in his lifetime, takes him up to the age of 16, significantly the period just before he met Helen, whom he may, consciously or not, have been trying to 'write out' of his life. Though he dismissed the book as 'mainly an occupation' and 'a tame literal matter of fact absolutely unrhetorical autobiography',[10] he evidently enjoyed the much looser writing it allowed after the constraints of his commissioned works: 'I am reconstructing my past from the age of 4–16, without using any documents or any other person's recollections', he informed the poet John Freeman on 11 December 1913. 'It will depict simply what I *know*, hardly at all about what I *think*, of myself, without explanations, or interpretations, or inventions.'[11] He planned to 'put down almost every trifle because if it turn[ed] out well nothing w[ould] be trifling'.[12] By letting one incident 'flow out of another', he realized he risked 'chaos', 'a child's garden of prose altogether run wild', or simply 'a disjointed series of short passages', a fault of all his previous books, he believed.[13]

It is a way of writing that anticipates the poetry which would follow a year later in a number of ways, as Edna Longley points out: 'close focus, little comment, no unitary "self", sound and image taking the lead'.[14] So close is the connection between the prose of his autobiography and his poetry that whole phrases from *The Childhood of Edward Thomas* are repeated in the poems. As Thomas reaches back into his past at the beginning of his life-story, for instance, he recalls: 'more simply and completely than any spent indoors at that time one day above others. I lay in the tall grass and buttercups of a narrow field at the edge of London and saw the sky and nothing but the sky.'[15] Just over a year later, on 10 January 1915, he would open one of his early poems, 'A Lofty Sky', thus:

> Today I want the sky,
> The tops of the high hills,
> Above the last man's house,
> His hedges, and his cows,
> Where, if I will, I look
> Down even on sheep and rook
> And of all things that move
> See buzzards only above: –
> Past all trees, past furze
> And thorn, where naught deters
> The desire of the eye
> For sky, nothing but sky.[16]

It is as though both the prose and poetry are tapping into the same imaginative source. For almost the first time the writer was allowing his creative powers to take precedence over his more self-conscious faculties.

Thomas worked quickly and as happily as he ever could at *The Childhood* in his writing-room at Selsfield House, a stone outbuilding in the garden, recording his affection for it three years later in 'The Long Small Room' according to his daughter, Myfanwy:

> The long small room that showed willows in the west
> Narrowed up to the end the fireplace filled,
> Although not wide. I liked it. No one guessed
> What need or accident made them so build.
>
> Only the moon, the mouse and the sparrow peeped
> In from the ivy round the casement thick.
> Of all they saw and heard there they shall keep
> The tale for the old ivy and older brick.

When I look back I am like the moon, sparrow and mouse
That witnessed what they could never understand
Or alter or prevent in the dark house.
One thing remains the same – this my right hand

Crawling crab-like over the clean white page,
Resting awhile each morning on the pillow,
Then once more starting to crawl on towards age.
The hundred last leaves stream upon the willow.[17]

Framed by the willow, and despite its association with 'weeping', the poem starts buoyantly with the narrator's affection for this small, awkwardly shaped writing-room. But a sense of mystery and melancholy is introduced in the middle two stanzas with 'the moon', 'the casement thick', 'the old ivy and older brick' and 'the dark house', which is deepened by the moon's, sparrow's, mouse's and narrator's inability to 'understand', or more ominously, 'alter or prevent in the dark house'. Written in November 1916, only two months before going out to fight in France, about a room occupied while the future of his marriage is in danger, this is almost certainly an allusion to the poet's own insecurity about his future, an interpretation which the elegiac note of the last stanza reinforces. The narrator's hand 'crawling' painfully 'crab-like' over the page is seen as a process taking him inexorably 'towards age', if not death in France. The image of decay and dissolution is strengthened in the last line by the shedding of leaves in autumn, the point at which Thomas originally started his poem. It is a conclusion he fears has a sort of 'Japanesy suddenness of ending'.[18] Only three months earlier he had written of the autumn of the year 'and of me', 'the sere and the ember'.

Nevertheless Thomas's mental state gradually improved at Selsfield House. Apart from a brief trip home at the end of November, a visit from W. H. Davies in early December and a long walk to see Bottomley, who was spending a second winter at the poet R. C. Trevelyan's house 20 miles away on Leith Hill,[19] there were few interruptions to his routine until his second meeting with Frost in London on 22 December.[20] Helen and the children arrived at Selsfield House the next day to spend Christmas with him, but their stay was no more successful than Thomas's own brief return home in November, when he had found things 'worse than they were'.[21]

When Myfanwy fell ill there and Helen stayed on to nurse her, Edward escaped to London early in the New Year of 1914, with Merfyn and Bronwen. He was as undecided as before. Nothing had changed.

It was, therefore, as a distraction rather than in a festive mood that he agreed to attend Monro's monthly dinner for his poets at Pecorini's restaurant in Frith Street, Soho, on 6 January 1914.[22] Hodgson's friend and collaborator, the artist Claud Lovat Fraser, who also attended, has left an entertaining account of the mood of 'some twenty-odd poets of various degrees', a 'quaint crew' which included J. C. Squire, T. E. Hulme and an unknown man who said 'I presume we're all celebrities here.'[23] Lovat's description reinforces the impression that Thomas was rarely as melancholy with his friends as with his family, despite the general gloom of the gathering: 'A mournful dismal affair [Fraser records] – R[alph] H[odgson] however made our end of the table uproarious – Monro, de la Mare, Thomas and self were quite cheerful but even then things were chilly, despite [Hodgson's] earnest entreaties to Thomas to recite "The Boy Stood on the burning decadent".'[24] When the host, Monro, left unceremoniously with Hodgson to play billiards, the dinner gradually broke up, but Hulme invited Thomas, Fraser and de la Mare (with whom Thomas had arrived) to a party across the road at 67 Frith Street, where he lived with his friend, Mrs Ethel Kibblewhite and her two children.[25] Lovat Fraser's reaction to what followed was almost certainly shared by Thomas:

> All the lights were dimmed and obscured. It had an eerie 'Edgar Allan Poe'-ish air – Upstairs in a large subdued room were many vague people. The whole impression was one of nightmare – I was introduced to Epstein, a beastly-looking fellow, God help me! And there were many bone-less (not my word, but apt) beings like unhealthy exhalations from [Aubrey] Beardsley's mind – one was a particular little horror with sunken eyes and a brown toupée. A man! a little thing past all vice – 'A toupéed spook', as de la Mare called him.[26]

Lovat Fraser felt he was 'under the influence of a horrible dream' and found 'an awful unreality in those many people chattering stories of "devil-worship" or whatever the themes were.'[27] Eventually he, Thomas and de la Mare 'broke loose' from the party and left, depositing de la Mare at Victoria Station on their way home, Thomas to join Bronwen at his parents' home.

Thomas returned shortly afterwards to Selsfield House, where he remained until the Locke Ellises left for Italy in mid-January and he had to find alternative lodgings. Since he had not yet decided to return to his family, but disliked being on his own, he was grateful for Clifford Bax's offer of accommodation in his London flat at 11 Luxemburg Gardens, Brook Green, in Hammersmith. 'No brook. The green all white and the white dirty,' Thomas would write to de la Mare, once installed there, but was appreciative all the same.[28] Bax had recently left his own wife, Daphne, to live with the actress Olga Antonietti, a decision of which Thomas approved. Writing to Eleanor Farjeon he reasons: 'I know that Daphne would be no better and Clifford the worse for making any attempt to abide by the letter of their marriage, especially as there is money enough to keep them separately.'[29] (Thomas's own lack of money to maintain two households was undoubtedly a factor in his own indecision about leaving *his* wife.) Less than a month later, beside sending his 'love and blessing' to Bax in his difficult situation, he was telling Eleanor that he liked Bax's mistress, Olga, 'decidedly'.[30] And by mid-January 1914 he was installed with Clifford and Olga in Hammersmith. He seemed no nearer to returning to Helen than in the previous October.

It was at this point that Frost intervened, according to his granddaughter.[31] Thomas had been in touch with him throughout the separation from Helen, at a time when he urgently needed advice, and his decision to return home was almost certainly influenced by Frost. Thomas was definitely depending on him for literary advice at this period. He was grateful, for instance, for Frost's approval of his autobiography and quite ready to abandon the continuation of it, covering his life after 16, at Frost's suggestion. Thomas's title for the second volume, *Fiction*, suggests the problems he found in describing his experiences *after* he met Helen, particularly since it was started on 24 February 1914, just after he finally returned to his family at Steep. If, as he intended, the second volume was to be an account of his life after *The Childhood*, he must have felt there were problems in this undertaking once he started on it. Perhaps he realized that in describing his relationship with Helen he would hurt her. At any rate he completely changed his original plan and turned his protagonist into a small boy orphaned at an early age, again reminiscent of Dickens's creations in *Great Expectations* and *David Copperfield*. As R. George

Thomas has suggested, it is 'almost as if [Edward] Thomas was trying to create, in his fiction, an alternative pattern his life might have followed'.[32] If so, he failed to convince either Frost or his imagination and his work on *Fiction*, unlike *The Childhood*, went very slowly indeed for a normally fluent writer. Two pages a day was all he could manage and finally, after Frost's negative reaction, he gave up this second attempt at a novel in April 1914. His other main task in February, as he lingered on with Bax in Luxemburg Gardens, was a book of literary pilgrimages. He had agreed to write this in the absence of any other reasonably well-paid project, but disliked it, if anything, more than work on *Fiction*, and referred to it disparagingly throughout the writing of it as 'the vile 'Omes and 'Aunts'.[33] (*Homes and Haunts of English Writers* was the working title of what would eventually be published as *A Literary Pilgrim in England*.[34])

Thomas had started work on *A Literary Pilgrim* in the autumn of 1913, but was still drudging away at it daily by the spring of 1914. He had finally returned home on 17 February and was 'glad to be back and to watch the plain and downs' from his study window, he told Eleanor in one of his many letters to her of this period.[35] She herself, though she makes no reference in print to the Thomases' separation, expresses herself delighted to see them reunited; it was probably a great relief to her to hear from Edward on 22 February that the family were 'all well and liking each other'. She felt honoured to be invited to his thirty-sixth birthday on 3 March 1914, even daring to kiss him as well as Helen goodnight before she went to bed. Her role was quickly becoming that of confidante to both parties. She was also by this time a willing, unpaid secretary to Edward, whose autobiography she had just started typing. Though she 'loved him with all [her] heart', she knew that to tell him so would oblige him to end their friendship.[36]

It was an unusual triangle in which these three adults found themselves. Frost, who had become very close to Thomas by 1914 and who would witness this three-sided relationship at first hand, maintained that Helen hoped to 'conquer' Eleanor, a potential rival, 'with magnanimity'.[37] After reading some draft chapters of Helen's autobiographical *World Without End*, Frost's conviction of her manipulativeness would emerge very clearly. In one chapter, he told a friend with barely concealed irony, Helen has Edward invite to the house a girl he has met and come home full of admiration of [i.e. Eleanor]. She gives herself away by calling this girl 'this paragon of women'. But she finds the minute she sees her (how homely she is) that she can conquer her with magnanimity or conquer her jealousy of her with magnanimity. All women are sisters that the same man loves, she tries to make herself think.[38]

Frost is particularly sickened by an incident Helen describes in detail, when the three of them are in the woods listening to a nightingale:

E[dward] says to the two of them We are knowing but the nightingale knows all. Then he kisses his wife and to keep the score even his wife makes him kiss the other woman [i.e. Eleanor]. She pretends to think that is large and lovely but I happen to know it was a dose she was giving him and rubbing in. These things are hard to do sincerely. And unridiculously.[39]

Though Frost would recognize Helen's first book, *As It Was*, as 'a good piece of work in a way', he wondered 'if she wasn't in danger of making E.T. look ridiculous in the Innocence she credited him with. Mightn't men laugh a manly laugh? E.T. was distinguished at his college at Oxford for the ribald folk songs he could entertain with – not to say smutty.'[40] He may, of course, have been jealous of Helen's relationship with Edward, just as she appears to have been of Frost's with him. Nevertheless, it is interesting to hear the views of one of Thomas's closest male friends at this period. Other male friends would feel the same.

Eleanor herself felt nothing but love for Helen, by her own account, and years later she would be horrified to hear this three-sided friendship described as a *ménage à trois*, with its implication of a sexual liaison. Meantime, in early 1914 it carried on as it had begun, with Thomas's every need attended to by one or other of the two women. When he needed to get away from his family again in early May, Eleanor was there with an invitation to spend a week with her, her brother and a friend in a cottage lent to her at Kingham, in the Cotswolds. His slightly grudging acceptance – yes, if he could bring his work – did not stop her from enjoying a whole week of his company virtually by herself. And in August 1914, when the entire Thomas family would arrange to spend nearly a month's holiday together, for the first time ever, Eleanor was invited to spend part of it near them. Eleanor herself maintained that it was 'to meet the Frosts',[41] but it is hard not to suspect that she was being used as something of a buffer between Helen and Edward, who was finding prolonged close proximity to his family increasingly difficult to bear.

Thomas's main distraction this year, however, would be not Eleanor, but Frost. His women friends, few in number, could rarely compete with the men in his life and Frost attracted him more than most. No sooner had he paid the Frosts a visit during their final days in Beaconsfield in late March 1914 than he would be arranging to visit them at their new home in Gloucestershire. And by the end of April, he would have spent a week near Frost's rented cottage at Ledington. Barely back home in May, he would be arranging, with uncharacteristic eagerness and determination, yet another visit for June, this time during his and Helen's supposedly 'time alone together' break. And not content with Frost's visit to him at Steep in July, he would be arranging a further visit to him, this time a whole month in August. Less than two months after that he would return again, alone, for another two stays. Frost drew him like a magnet and these visits, the August and October ones especially, were to have an influence on his life in at least two important areas.

18

'While We Two Walked Slowly Together': Thomas and Frost in Gloucestershire (April–July 1914)

> But Ledington, my dear Robert, in April, in June, in August.
> – Thomas to Frost, 16 March 1916

> [Thomas] more than anyone else was accessory to what I had done and was doing. We were together to the exclusion of every other person and interest all through 1914–1914 was our year. I never had, I never shall have another such year of friendship.
> – Frost to Amy Lowell, 22 October 1917

No one who traces Thomas's movements in the year following his introduction to Frost in October 1913, and the letters between them, can doubt Frost's role in galvanizing Thomas into writing the poetry which he had experimented with the month before he met him. There were other factors which influenced his dramatic change of direction, the eventual outbreak of war, for example, and other friends, such as Nevinson, Bottomley, de la Mare and Eleanor Farjeon, had already suggested the possibility. But it was Frost who gave him the confidence to consider writing poetry in earnest, during their holidays together at Ledington in April, June, August, October and November.

Ledington was the hamlet to which Robert and Elinor Frost moved themselves and their four children from Beaconsfield in April 1914. Homesick for rural New England, they wanted to experience an English spring in less urban surroundings and two of the friends Frost had made among London's literary establishment helped them to realize their dream. Lascelles Abercrombie and Wilfrid Gibson, both prominent members of the Georgian poets by 1914, shared the Georgians' desire to live in the country in a simple way – even if it meant only at weekends. (Unkind critics dubbed them the 'Weekend Cottagers'.) First Abercrombie, then Gibson had discovered one of the loveliest corners of England and were quick to encourage Frost to join them there.

Approximately two miles south of the quaint Herefordshire town of Ledbury, Ledington lay just over the border into Gloucestershire, and not far from the county line with Worcestershire. Situated between Dymock and Redmarley D'Abitot, it was characterized for Thomas by 'the red marl, the green grass and the Leadon, a beautiful stream here among the woods'.[1] For Frost, used to the wider, more open spaces of America, it was the scale and crowded scenery which first struck him: 'The fields are so small and the trees so numerous along the hedges,' he wrote to an American friend a month after his arrival, 'that, as my friend Thomas says in the loveliest book on spring in England [*In Pursuit of Spring*], you might think from a little distance that the country was solid woods.'[2] Elinor, a shadowy figure who nevertheless experienced life deeply, was even more lyrical about the area:

> I wish I could make you feel what a lovely country this is [she wrote to her sister less than three months after moving to Ledington]. When we first came, the meadows were covered with yellow daffodils and the cuckoo had just begun to sing…The pastures here are so rich that they are just as green as the mowing and wheat fields, and they are separated by dark green hedges and bordered by huge elms. Great flocks of sheep and herds of cows are everywhere.[3]

It was the daffodils, once grown there commercially for their dye, which had given another poet connected to the area, John Masefield, the title of one of his best-known works, *The Daffodil Fields* (1913), and the first stanza of his lyrical celebration of these 'west lands', 'The West Wind':

It's a warm wind, the west wind, full of birds' cries;
I never hear the west wind but tears are in my eyes.
For it comes from the west lands, the old brown hills
And April's in the west wind, and daffodils.

Abercrombie would note the 'yellow shine of daffodils' in several poems describing his Gloucestershire home, The Gallows (named after a poacher who had been hanged there).[4] So, too, would Gibson. But it was Thomas, with his love and knowledge of birdsong – as well, incidentally, of Masefield's poetry – who would come nearest to Masefield's more comprehensive appreciation of the area, in an essay inspired partly by his 1914 visits to Frost, 'This England'. Both the title and argument of this piece[5] make it clear that this small patch of countryside, over all the other beautiful parts he had explored so extensively during his 36 years, came to symbolize for Thomas all that was loveliest and worth fighting for when war was declared. His first impression shows how instantly it had appealed to him:

> In April here I had heard, among apple trees in flower, not the first cuckoo, but the first abundance of day-long-calling cuckoos; here, the first nightingale's song, though too far-off and intermittently, twitched away by gusty nights winds; here I found the earliest mayblossom which by May Day, while I still lingered, began to dapple the hedges thickly, and no rainfall, yet the land was sweet.[6]

The greater part of Thomas's time on this first and all four subsequent visits, would be spent with Frost. Though he arrived on 22 April with the responsibility of his two older children, Merfyn, now 14, and Bronwen, nearly 12, this quickly vanished as they rapidly made friends with the Frost children, Leslie (a girl), Carol (a boy), Irma and Marjorie, who were roughly their own age. Thomas's week with Merfyn and Bronwen in Laugharne where he had spent six weeks in 1911, had been undertaken from a sense of duty, but the children had 'enjoyed themselves', he reassured Eleanor Farjeon, who remained anxious about his relations with Merfyn.[7] Thomas was still working daily on *A Literary Pilgrim*, as well as his *Fiction*, which was 'crawl[ing] tediously,' he told Eleanor, 'towards the chief episode'.[8] So the stay in Wales had not been much of a holiday for him, especially since he had caught a cold and felt 'wretched'.[9]

At Ledington, however, with Merfyn and Bronwen happily occupied with the Frost children and their father there to tempt him, he spent the subsequent week mainly walking and talking. (The combination became so familiar to anyone who knew Frost that his family referred to his activity simply as 'walks-talking'.) Thomas, looking back on this first visit to Ledington, where he and the children had lodged with Mr and Mrs Chandler at Oldfields (later Old Fields), described his daily routine with evident nostalgia: 'Once or twice or three times a day,' he remembered, he used to cross the three meadows, pass through the gate and over the two stiles that separated him from Frost's house, Little Iddens, and arrive at 'the little house of whitened bricks and black timbers', with its 'vegetable garden in front with a weeping ash and a bay tree, a walnut in a yard of cobbles and grass behind, a yew on the roadside, an orchard on the other'.[10] An attractive mix of ancient beams, whitewashed exterior and leaded windowpanes, Little Iddens was, nevertheless, extremely primitive by most standards even in 1914, with its tiny kitchen, narrow staircase, low ceilings, old-fashioned stove, outside lavatory and lack of running water. But the rent was cheap and the unworldly Frost family lived mainly out of doors during what seemed to them the lovely spring and summer of 1914.

Thomas's poem about his time with Frost at Ledington, 'The Sun Used to Shine', emphasizes the outdoor nature of their daily routine. So does his prose recollection in 'This England', which anticipates much of the poem's content: 'How easy it was to spend a morning or afternoon in walking over to [Little Iddens],' he wrote, 'and then strolling with my friend, nearly regardless of footpaths, in a long loop, so as to end either at his house or my lodging.'[11] In both essay and poem he attempts to convey the pleasure of those walks, often undertaken (as he preferred) without a map, through 'orchard and grass, gently up and down, seldom steep for more than a few yards'.[12] Their walks varied in length, from a stroll down the lane to see Gibson at Greenway, longer rambles across the Beauchamp Estate to visit Abercrombie at Ryton, to May Hill, six miles away, or to the British Camp at Malvern. Both Frost and Thomas enjoyed long walks, though Edward's days of 25-mile hikes were behind him. The striking pair became a familiar sight that summer, Edward tall, loose-limbed and almost shockingly beautiful (according to Catherine Abercrombie), Robert, 'a thickset man, not as tall as Edward, with a shock of grey hair,' Helen recalled, 'his face

tanned and weather-beaten and his features powerful'.[13] Like Edward, his
eyes were 'blue and clear' but shaded, she noted, by 'bushy grey eyebrows'.

It was the talk accompanying these walks, however, that most interested Thomas, as his essay makes clear, 'If talk dwindled in the traversing of
a big field, the pause at the gate or stile braced it again. Often we prolonged
the pause, whether we actually sat or not, and we talked – of flowers,
childhood, Shakespeare, women, England…'[14]

Above all, like their literary predecessors, Wordsworth and Coleridge
on their long tramps through the Lake District and Somerset, Thomas and
Frost talked of poetry. And like Wordsworth, to whom Thomas would
compare Frost in two of his reviews of *North of Boston* published this
summer, Frost would expand his revolutionary theory of language. Often
referred to as 'the sound of sense', it is perhaps better described as 'the sound
of a sentence'. After listening to Frost expounding his theory that, 'Just so
many sentence sounds belong to man as just so many vocal runs belong to
one kind of bird',[15] by the end of 1914 Thomas would be contemplating
writing a book on 'what [Frost's] new definition of the sentence mean[t] for
literary criticism'.[16] Like Wordsworth Frost was fighting against 'writ[ing]
in a special language that has gradually separated from spoken language'.[17]
'The poet's pleasure,' he believed, 'must always be to make his own words as
he goes and never to depend for effect on words already made even if they
be his own.'[18] This struggle to remain (in Thomas's words) 'free from the
poetical words and forms that are the chief material of secondary poets'[19]
and focus primarily on the sound of words, which would in any case (Frost
argued) convey their sense, led Frost to a Wordsworthian respect for 'the
language really used by men'.[20]

Frost's theory would be memorably demonstrated for Eleanor Farjeon
when she visited the Ledington community in August that year. Strolling
along a country lane with him and Edward, she remembered Robert 'talking
of what he called the "cadence" in the human voice, when accompanied by
the speech that came natural to it'.[21] As they walked they saw in the distance
a man standing on top of a cart, forking up corn or manure from below:

> Frost stopped and shouted a question across the fields – it might have
> been, 'What are you doing there, this fine afternoon?' but whatever the
> words the man could not have heard them. He too shouted some answer
> that rang through the air, and it was impossible for us to distinguish

what he said. But the cadence of the answer was as clear as that of the question. Robert turned to Edward. 'That's what I mean,' he said.[22]

Eleanor never doubted that this was 'one of the revealing moments to Edward, a moment in which his own cadence was made clearer to himself, so that those who ever heard the movement of his beautiful reflective voice can hear it now in the simplest utterance of a small unforgettable,

Yes, I remember Adlestrop – '[23]

Long before 'Adlestrop' or any other of his poems were composed, Thomas had already written to Bottomley that Frost's 'getting back to pure speech rhythms is going to do good'.[24] The date of this letter, 29 May 1914, suggests that not only had Frost spent their first extended period together expounding his favourite theory but that he had begun to strengthen Thomas's own inclinations in poetry long before he started to write it in earnest. It seems ironic, however, that Thomas should have expected Bottomley to share his excitement over Frost's ideas. For as William Pritchard has pointed out, Frost's theory of language would distinguish his practice not only from that of his Victorian and post-Victorian forebears in England and America, 'but also from the radical aesthetic Pound was insisting upon in his Imagist pronouncements, and even – for all his friendly affiliations with them – from the Georgians: Wilfrid Gibson, Lascelles Abercrombie, W. H. Davies' – and, I would suggest, Bottomley.[25]

Pritchard may be right to argue, as he does, that 'Frost's theory would serve as a standard by which Thomas could measure his own experimental work', but its influence must not be exaggerated. For as Thomas himself was to point out to Frost shortly after the April visit, it was in a sense only a timely expression of a position he had also been working towards:

> You really should start doing a book on speech and literature, or you will find me mistaking your ideas for mine and doing it myself. You can't prevent me from making use of them: I do so daily and want to begin over again with them and wring all the necks of my rhetoric – the geese. However, my [book on] 'Pater' would show you I had got on to the scent already.[26]

In fact, Thomas had been 'on the scent' even earlier than 1913 (the year his *Pater* was published) as his books on *Maeterlinck* (1911) and *Swinburne* (1912) show. And, to be fair, Frost never viewed the situation as that of one writer influencing another. He saw it, rather, as a process of mutual discovery, which he, Frost, happened to have expressed and put into practice first. 'What we had in common we had from before we were born,' he wrote to a friend after Thomas's death. 'Make as much of that as you will but don't tell anyone we gave each other anything but a boost.'[27] He saw himself and Thomas as 'Siamese twins in a literary sense, with a spiritual bond holding us together.'[28]

It was during this April visit, too, that Frost told Thomas that he was a poet. Thomas, he would later explain to Harold Roy Brennan, had 'lost patience' with the minor poetry he had to review, 'and it took me to tell him what his trouble was.'[29] Thomas was suffering, Frost argued:

> ...from a life of subordination to his inferiors. Right at that moment he was writing as good poetry as anybody alive but in prose form where it didn't declare itself and gain him recognition. I referred to paragraphs here and there in such a book as The Pursuit of Spring and pointed them out. Let him write them in verse form in exactly the same cadence and we would see...[30]

Fourteen years before meeting Frost, Thomas had already argued that the main difference between nineteenth- and twentieth-century literatures stemmed from 'the apparent destruction of the boundaries between poetry and prose', a development he traced back to Wordsworth's claim that 'there neither is, nor can be any *essential* difference between the language of prose and metrical composition.'[31] Seven years later in a review of Baudelaire's *Poems in Prose*, translated by Arthur Symons, Thomas was actively recommending the form,[32] as well as experimenting with it himself. So that this immediate response to Frost's suggestion comes as little surprise.

Less than three weeks after this first visit to Gloucestershire Thomas was able to report to Frost: 'I go on writing something every day. Sometimes brief unstrained impressions of things lately seen, like a drover with six newly shorn sheep in a line across a cool woody road on market morning...'[33] That this was another tentative step towards poetry is clear from a second passage in the same letter: 'I wonder whether you can imagine me taking to verse. If you can I might get over the feeling that it is impossible...' When his first formal poem, 'Up in the Wind', emerged it would be closely related to one of his own prose pieces. It would also bear some similarity to the dramatic verse narratives of Frost he was studying in *North of Boston* this year. (After reading 'Home Burial' and 'The Housekeeper', Pound would tell Frost that he was really trying to write short stories.[34]) But Thomas's worry that his poetry might be too heavily influenced by Frost – 'Is this North of Bostonism?' he asked Frost of his prose-poems on 19 May 1914 – would prove groundless. Once under way his verse would reflect his own 'cadence', or voice, as Frost believed it should.

Thomas would associate his start in poetry with the area where he had first seriously considered writing it during his walks and talks with Frost. His attempt to explain his aims and attitude towards it, 'Words', would be written on May Hill, just over a year after he had first visited it with Frost. The manuscript of 'Words' was headed ' "Hucclecote" – on the road from Gloster [*sic*] to Coventry' and was written 26–28 June 1915, following a visit to a friend made through Frost, J. W. ('Jack') Haines at Hucclecote. Haines remembered that while he 'botanised' on the slopes of May Hill, Thomas 'sat on the hill…composing the beautiful poem "Words", which he brought down completed for us at breakfast the next morning'.[35] A complete broad dome from a distance, May Hill offered an even more dramatic view from its summit, which Thomas described in 'This England', 'command[ing]' views of 'the Severn and the Cotswolds on the one hand, and on the other the Wye, the Forest of Dean, the island hills of North Monmouthshire, dark and massive, the remote Black Mountains pale and cloud-like, far beyond them in Wales'.[36]

'Words' opens with a plea to the Muse, one in which the poet's own sense of unworthiness emerges in his comparison of himself to faulty, or mundane, things ('a crack in the wall', 'a drain') rather than to the more elevated imagery of larks and wind-harps of his Romantic predecessors:

> Out of us all
> That make rhymes,
> Will you choose
> Sometimes –
> As the winds use
> A crack in the wall
> Or a drain,
> Their joy or their pain
> To whistle through –

Choose me,
You English words?[37]

The narrator then goes on more confidently to remind us of his life-long apprenticeship to words in imagery which underlines his determination to be simple and direct, yet highly evocative and true to his heritage:

I know you:
You are light as dreams,
Tough as oak,
Precious as gold,
As poppies and corn,
Or an old cloak:
Sweet as our birds
To the ear,
As the burnet rose[38]
In the heat
Of Midsummer: ...

The paradox of 'worn new' thirteen lines later enables Thomas to convey the essence of his poetic theory and practice with the directness and simplicity he desires:

But though older far
Than oldest yew, –
As our hills are, old, –
Worn new
Again and again:
Young as our streams
After rain
And as dear
As the earth which you prove
That we love ...

The description of words in terms of the English landscape here perfectly mirrors Thomas's own revelation about poetry the previous year as he walked the hill he now alludes to, with Frost: but further topographical references – to Herefordshire, Wiltshire and Kent, as well as Wales, imply that his 'words' will be his own, deriving from his unique ancestral mix and subsequent experience:

> Make me content
> With some sweetness
> From Wales
> Whose nightingales
> Have no wings, –
> From Wiltshire and Kent
> And Herefordshire,
> And the villages there, –
> From the names, and the things
> No less.

The paradox of 'nightingales without wings', referring to the fact that the nightingale's habitat is said to stop short of Wales, encourages the reader to interpret the birds symbolically, as poets, in this context. Similarly Thomas will use the paradox 'fixed and free' in his last stanza to draw attention to the apparently contradictory nature of the poet's craft, a contradiction mirrored in the opposite actions of 'dancing' and 'standing' still:

> Let me sometimes dance
> With you,
> Or climb
> Or stand perchance
> In ecstasy,
> Fixed and free
> In a rhyme,
> As poets do.

Thomas linking of 'rhyme' with poetry in the last three lines may signal his determination to distinguish his work from Frost's, especially the mainly blank verse of *North of Boston*, though it could also be an attempt to distance himself from the 'free verse' of Modernists like Pound. In essence, however, Thomas's poetic theory in 'Words' reflects Frost's much-voiced own.

The traffic was not entirely one-way, however. There are signs that Frost, in turn, was influenced by Thomas this year with regard to poetry. He had begun his stay at Ledington regarding Gibson as an impressive poet and his greatest literary friend in England. But even before Gibson's fairly critical review of *North of Boston* in the *Bookman* of August 1914, or his failure (as Frost saw it) to support Frost in a feud with a local gamekeeper in November, there are signs of disenchantment, for which Thomas is the most likely source.

Thomas had already met Gibson, who was the same age as himself, by the time he stayed near him and his newly married wife, Geraldine, in Gloucestershire. Gibson had not arrived in London from his native Northumberland until 1912, but as a founding member with Marsh, Monro and Brooke, of *Georgian Poetry*, he quickly became an established part of the literary scene. Thomas had also reviewed Gibson's work quite often, from at least 1902 onwards.[39]

From a romantic, quasi-medieval start with poems like *The Golden Helm* (1902), in which Thomas had detected 'a strong flavour of saccharine',[40] Gibson had turned by 1910 to poetry on humbler subjects, becoming known, like Masefield, as 'the People's Poet'.[41] Thomas welcomed the change.[42] A fair, if at times severe critic, he described Gibson's *Akra the Slave* (1911), for example, as 'the most interesting thing' of his to date.[43] He was ready, likewise, to acknowledge Gibson's achievements in *Fires*, Book I (1912). But he still had serious reservations about both the man and his work; when invited to Monro's Poetry Bookshop launch on 8 January 1913, for instance, he specifically named Gibson as one of the poets Monro must promise *not* to 'assault' him with if he accepted.[44] Yet as Thomas himself pointed out to Bottomley in May 1914, he did 'like [Gibson's] later work', albeit 'temperately'.[45] But his earlier, more caustic remarks had been noted, it seems, and relations between the two men were never more than polite.

Frost, still very close to Gibson in early 1914, seems to have been unaware of these tensions and continued his regular strolls of about a mile to the Gibsons' thatched cottage, the Old Nailshop at Greenway, during Thomas's stay. Thomas's admission to Bottomley shortly afterwards – 'Gibson and I are too conscious of what we used to think of one another' – suggests that the visits were not entirely a success.[46] And on a number of occasions they would be turned away at the door by Geraldine Gibson, who would inform them that 'her husband was in the throes of a long poem and must not be disturbed'.[47] Frost's and Thomas's 'fairly contemptuous ridicule' at what seemed to them Gibson's self-importance may have been tinged, as Helen suggests, with 'a little honest jealousy', since Gibson had by 1914 become a successful poet, especially in America.[48]

Even without an element of jealousy, however, Gibson's behaviour was not calculated to win Thomas over and it is no surprise to read in his letter to Frost about a second planned visit to Ledington, this time with Helen, in June: 'By the way, I rather think it won't be necessary to go down to Greenway [i.e. to see Gibson]. I should like my wife to meet Abercrombie, but there is not time for both and perhaps one without the other would be unseemly.'[49] After the August visit Thomas would tell Bottomley that he saw 'too little of Abercrombie, too much of Gibson'.[50] Helen went even further, characterizing Gibson as 'very small and mean'.[51]

Yet most people found Wilfrid Wilson Gibson – or 'Wibson' as Rupert Brooke affectionately called him – a kind and friendly man. D. H. Lawrence, for instance, not an easy person to please, had told Marsh in 1913 that he thought Gibson 'one of the dearest and most lovable characters' he knew,[52] and Thomas's failure to get on with Gibson is puzzling. Though his criticism of Gibson's work would become harsher afterwards, in April 1914 he was still largely positive about it. Two of his most recent reviews, in fact, singled out Gibson for praise.[53] And in any case as an experienced critic he was quite capable of separating the writer from his or her work and liking the former while not admiring the latter.

Abercrombie is a case in point. 'I do not know his equal for keenness and warmth,' Thomas would tell Bottomley in April 1914, yet by that time he would have serious reservations about Abercrombie's work.[54] Perhaps he felt less threatened by the slightly younger poet, who was also not quite so close to Frost in early 1914 as Gibson and, therefore, gave no cause for jealousy. Thomas particularly disliked self-importance in a writer and, if Helen is to be believed, Gibson suffered from a strong sense of it. Whereas Frost's anecdote about W. H. Davies, who would stay with the Gibsons this summer, indicates that Abercrombie was more modest though scarcely less successful. As Davies was rushed the three miles through narrow lanes on his wooden leg from the Gibsons' house to the Abercrombies' at Ryton, he was told that Abercrombie was 'the greatest poet in England': 'But that's what Davies thinks he is himself,' Frost added. 'And that is what Gibson, or Gibson's wife thinks Gibson is. (Gibson and Davies both make more out of their poetry than Abercrombie…)'[55]

Thomas 'liked' Abercrombie personally when he met him for the first time in April 1914.[56] His opinion of Abercrombie's work, however, had developed in the opposite direction to his views on Gibson's. It had started with admiration: '[Abercrombie] is good, there is no doubt,' he wrote in 1908 to Bottomley, who already knew Abercrombie as a fellow-poet on the northern arts scene.[57] The book which invited this praise was Abercrombie's first collection, *Interludes and Poems* (1908), which had also drawn him to the attention of Brooke, hence to Marsh and other Georgian poets. Thomas went so far as to describe Abercrombie in 1909 as 'one of the youngest and most interesting of poets now alive'.[58] By 1911, however, when Abercrombie, having married and settled in the Dymock area, had self-published his second book, *Mary and the Bramble*, Thomas was not quite so enthusiastic. While he found the versification in this story about the girlhood of the 'Mary Virgin', 'vigorous', he felt that the attempt had 'few charms except an evident delight in naiveté'.[59] He had fewer reservations about Abercrombie's verse play 'The Sale of St Thomas' (published in *Georgian Poetry 1911–1912*) and was kind about his second poetry collection, *Emblems of Love* (1912) and a second play, *The Dramatic Sense: Deborah* (1913); *Speculative Dialogues* (1913), too, is praised 'for "those heady virtues" which poetry commends'.[60] But the praise is heavily qualified. ('I admire it, as Keats admired the attitudes of men fighting in the street...'[61]) And by the time Abercrombie shows him proofs of *The Massacre of Innocents* in the summer of 1914 he does not 'think much of it'.[62]

Abercrombie himself had shown 'heavy derision' for Thomas's *Swinburne* (1912),[63] but it is unlikely that Thomas was retaliating. He was simply – and perhaps naively – hoping to help Abercrombie towards better work, freed from some of the preciousness, as he saw it, of Georgian practice. Abercrombie himself seems to have borne no grudge; he would be one of the first to help publish Thomas's poetry. According to Abercrombie's nephew, his wife, Catherine, was 'incredibly protective'[64] of her husband, and became (in Thomas's words) a 'little hostile' towards him. So that despite Thomas's anxiety 'always...to like' Abercrombie, the friendship never developed, though Catherine continued to think Thomas 'the most beautiful person [she] had ever seen'.[65]

By the time Thomas visited Abercrombie and Gibson in April 1914, they had finally published the first part of the little magazine they had planned, together with Brooke and another poet-playwright,

John Drinkwater – *New Numbers*. Thomas had had little or no contact with Drinkwater, in contrast to the other founders, but he would review his work on at least five occasions in 1914.[66] Given the lukewarm reception of Drinkwater's poetry by this stage, Thomas was surprisingly lenient, 'facility' being his most serious charge against it. In fact, when he congratulated Gibson, Abercrombie, Brooke and Drinkwater on the 'first instalment of their joint venture' (*New Numbers*) he praised Drinkwater's four short pieces as 'reveal[ing] the purity and aspiration of his spirit, the lucidity and formality of his style at their best'.[67] But in his second review of *New Numbers* for the *Daily Chronicle*, where he is given less space, he fails to mention Drinkwater's work at all and his attitude would harden over time. So that by the fourth issue of *New Numbers*, in February 1915, he would be labelling Drinkwater 'hopeless', though not publicly.[68]

This fourth part of *New Numbers*, despite including Brooke's immensely popular '1914' sonnet sequence for the first time, would, for a number of reasons, be the last. Viewed variously at its launch as an offshoot of Marsh's *Georgian Poetry*, or a rival to Monro's *Poetry and Drama*, its end would go largely unnoticed in a country at war. But it was in its first youth when Thomas arrived for his April 1914 visit, with Part II about to be published. By the time he returned there in June 1914, Part III was in active preparation and his visit would coincide with that of the fourth poet involved, Brooke, seeming to Thomas 'browner and older and better-looking after his tour' of Canada, America and the South Seas.[69]

Thomas, who had described Brooke's contribution to *New Numbers*, Part I, as 'brilliant',[70] also enjoyed his company and would overcome his reluctance to see Gibson for the chance of talking to Brooke again. Despite the brevity of his stay with Helen, he would spend part of it with Brooke at Gibson's cottage. Brooke arrived at the Old Nailshop on 24 June and stayed overnight and Edward and Helen travelled up by train – through Adlestrop – the same day and met him there that same evening. The meeting of so many important poets of the period was memorable to at least one of them, Gibson, who wrote nostalgically of it 11 years later in 'The Golden Room':

> Do you remember that still summer evening
> When, in the cosy cream-washed living-room
> Of the Old Nailshop, we all talked and laughed –

Our neighbours from The Gallows, Catherine
And Lascelles Abercrombie; Rupert Brooke;
Elinor and Robert Frost, living a while
At Little Iddens, who'd brought over with them
Helen and Edward Thomas? In the lamplight
We talked and laughed; but, for the most part, listened
While Robert Frost kept on and on and on,
In his slow New England fashion, for our delight,
Holding us with shrewd turns and racy quips,
And the rare twinkle of his grave blue eyes?

We sat there in the lamplight, while the day
Died from rose-latticed casements, and the plovers
Called over the low meadows, till the owls
Answered them from the elms, we sat and talked –
Now, a quick flash from Abercrombie; now,
A murmured dry half-heard aside from Thomas;
Now, a clear laughing word from Brooke; and then
Again Frost's rich and ripe philosophy
That had the body and tang of good draught-cider,
And poured as clear a stream.[71]

Thomas's visit, brief as it was, had only been made possible by 'burning [his] candle at three ends', according to him, so plagued was he with work.[72] Most of May and three-quarters of June had been spent in Steep working on the last stages of *Fiction* before abandoning it, on a last push to complete *A Literary Pilgrim* for Methuen and on some book reviews, including two of *North of Boston*. He also continued to experiment with prose-poems. His three-day visit in mid-June to Gordon and Emily Bottomley, who had recently moved house within the Lake District, resulted in an actual poem about the new house, though Thomas would not write it down until over two years later:

The Sheiling

It stands alone
Up in a land of stone
All worn like ancient stairs,
A land of rocks and trees
Nourished on wind and stone...[73]

Even the stay with the Bottomleys had had to be combined with work on reviews and an article on 'Midsummer' for *T.P.'s Weekly*, though he also enjoyed visiting a house built by Mrs Gaskell's daughter 'about the time that nice lady died'.[74] He had still not completed *A Literary Pilgrim* and a commission to edit an anthology, *The Flowers I Love*,[75] by the time he and Helen set off for Ledington on 24 June.

The fact that Thomas had worked so hard to make this second visit possible, when he had already arranged to spend the whole of August at Ledington, shows how impatient he was to continue his dialogue with Frost. And Elinor Frost's description of Edward after his first visit as 'quite the most admirable and lovable man we have ever known',[76] together with Frost's repeated urging to return soon, suggests that the appreciation was mutual.

Helen Thomas observed after finally seeing her husband and Frost together that June, it was 'at once obvious that they were very congenial to each other'.[77] She herself 'never became close to Robert as Edward was,' she admitted, and may even have been jealous of the unusual closeness between the two men. But since her own happiness depended largely on how fulfilled her husband felt, she could only welcome Frost's effect on him. She was presumably reflecting Edward's opinion as well as her own when she wrote of Robert 'encourag[ing] Edward…to think of himself as a potential poet, and thus…to give Edward his deepest intellectual satisfaction and pleasure'.[78]

Relations between Helen and Frost would deteriorate after Edward's death, especially once Frost had read Helen's largely autobiographical novels, *As It Was*, and (parts of) *World Without End*. He objected particularly to Helen telling the reader how Thomas 'carr[ied] her off to bed on his last leave of absence before going to the front'.[79] On their first meeting in June 1914, however, relations were friendly enough for Helen to join in with Edward's invitation to Robert to spend a weekend with them at Steep in July.[80] Since the joint August holiday was less than six weeks away, it is another sign of how much Edward longed to be with Frost at this time. 'His wanting me,' he told Eleanor Farjeon, 'is some encouragement.'[81]

Thomas spent the rest of July, as he had May and June, trying to fulfil his commitments, particularly the dreaded 'Omes and 'Aunts' book (*A Literary Pilgrim*), which had dragged on longer than any of his previous commissions. He also concentrated seriously on putting together the flower anthology, in which he was hoping to include verses by Frost, as well as other poet-friends. (He wanted to include Frost's 'A Tuft of Flowers', or 'A Late Walk', or 'Mowing', but warned Frost to 'remember I have got to include, so to speak, Shakespeare and Jesus Christ'.[82])

Another idea for a new commission reflects his growing commitment to poetry this summer, a proposal to Monro for 'a sort of introduction' to between 'twelve and twenty living poets'.[83] He was also planning to revise the short book on Keats he had written at Selsfield House. But the greatest encouragement towards poetry lay in Frost and by 3 August 1914 he was eager to leave for Ledington again.

19

THE SUN USED TO SHINE
(AUGUST–SEPTEMBER 1914)

> Now it was August, and again no rain fell for many days, the
> harvest was a good one, and after standing long in the sun it
> was gathered in and put in ricks in the sun, to the contentment
> of men and rooks. All day the rooks in the wheat-fields
> were cawing a deep sweet caw, in alternating choirs or all
> together, almost like sheep bleating, contentedly, on until late
> evening. The sun shone, always warm, from skies sometimes
> cloudless, sometimes inscribed with a fine white scatter miles
> high, sometimes displaying the full pomp of white moving
> mountains, sometimes almost entirely shrouded in dull
> sulphurous threats, but vain ones.
>
> – 'This England', *Nation*, 7 November 1914

When Thomas set off with his son, Merfyn, on 3 August
1914 to cycle to Ledington, war had not yet been declared.
It seemed, at the start, a typical August Bank Holiday Monday with
everyone out enjoying the sun. But when they broke their journey
at Swindon, to see Edward's old friend Jesse Berridge and to show
Merfyn Coate reservoir, the evening papers were full of war's
imminence. Factory hooters would sound throughout Swindon
when, on 4 August, England officially entered a conflict which
already involved not only Serbia, Austria, Hungary, Germany,

France and Belgium, but also countries as distant as Russia. This was on a scale and of a kind never before experienced by the English, whose last major engagement had been fought far away in South Africa by a small army of mainly professional soldiers. The need to enlist much larger numbers of volunteers and to muster every available soldier, reservist and territorial was urgent and created havoc with all the usual systems of transport and communication, as Helen Thomas discovered when she set off for Ledington herself on 4 August by rail. Burdened not just with her two young daughters and their dog Rags, but also a Russian pupil from Bedales, Peter Mrosovski, who had been refused permission to leave the country, she 'never forgot' the journey which ensued, 'the disorganized train service, the crowds at the stations, reservists being seen off by friends, trains full of men going to join the ranks, and complete chaos everywhere'.[1]

It was not until the early hours of the following day that she and the children arrived at Ledington, having had to make the last part of the journey in a taxi she could ill afford. After a drive of 15 miles through the Malvern Hills under a large harvest moon and trouble with the local policeman over her obviously foreign charge, it came as a great relief to see Edward waiting for them at the gate of their lodgings, Oldfields.

There are curiously few references to the war by Thomas during this period, though he did admit to Eleanor Farjeon on 2 August that while 'busy getting ready' to leave on holiday, the family had been 'talking rubbish about War'.[2] Yet by this date the immediate causes of the war had been building up for more than a month and the underlying ones went back at least half a century. While the average citizen might not reasonably be expected to understand what had brought Europe to this explosive point – the Slavs' desire for self-government, or Germany's territorial ambitions, for instance – Thomas, as an Oxford history scholar, might have been expected to show more involvement. Even at Oxford, however, he had seemed more interested in literature than history and the recent dramatic incidents which had finally detonated the First World War appear to have been of less concern to him than another chance to discuss poetry with Frost during the American's brief visit to Steep on 17 July. In one of his few allusions to the political situation in the same 2 August letter to Eleanor, for example, he refers to it only as a possible incentive to turn to verse in his mid-thirties: 'I am a little at a loose end after sending off [*A Literary Pilgrim*] yesterday.

Who will want the thing now. I may as well write poetry. Did anyone ever begin at 36 in the shade?'³

While the assassination of the Austrian Archduke by a Serb patriot on 28 June 1914 signalled trouble for the politically aware throughout Europe, Thomas had been spending the day peacefully with Helen and their ex-Bedales friends, the Hodsons, in Coventry, on their way home from visiting Frost, and looking forward to another visit to the Russian Ballet two days later. When Germany declared her readiness to support Austria in a war against Serbia on 5 July, Thomas had been thinking of suitable poems for the flower anthology he had promised to edit for T. C. & E. C. Jacks.⁴ After Austria's ultimatum to Serbia on 23 July, followed by Russia's promise to support Serbia, then, a day later, France's promise to support Russia, he was still planning innocent, peacetime activities, such as a visit to the Goodwood Races the following Wednesday. Even Germany's explicit declaration of war against Russia on 1 August, and against France on 3 August, provoked no obvious response from Thomas, who was busy sending off his completed *A Literary Pilgrim* and preparing for his holiday in Gloucestershire. Germany's invasion of neutral Belgium, which finally prompted Britain's declaration of war against her, goes likewise unremarked by him.

Part of the explanation for this apparent indifference may be geographical. Had Thomas been in London on 4 August 1914, it would have been virtually impossible for him not to become more affected. But at Ledington, deep in the countryside, there were as yet few signs that England was at war. Apart from the local policeman's reaction to the Russian boy in her charge, the effects were largely indirect, sometimes quite comical. Edward told Eleanor Farjeon, for instance, that 'Frost's immediate reaction to the war was the feeling that he must provide for the duration,'⁵ which meant, Helen Thomas remembered, the walls of Frost's rather bare living-room being 'stacked up with ramparts of shredded wheat packets, tins of rather cheap sugary biscuits and boxes of highly scented soap'.⁶

There are other less amusing manifestations, though none had serious consequences. The locals, sanguine on the whole about the outcome, were nevertheless wary of 'anything or anyone unaccountable,' according to Eleanor: 'the chink of light between the curtains, the unfamiliar accent of a stranger'.⁷ To begin with, Edward reported, 'Frost's New Hampshire intonation had been suspect, and some of the natives had thrown stones at his windows, deciding he must be a Hun'.[8] After receiving several anonymous letters the local policeman had finally interviewed Robert, who was furious. In a reversal of their later reaction to Frost's brush with an officious gamekeeper, Edward was merely amused and the holiday atmosphere returned.

The only tangible way in which the war made itself felt in the first half of the month was that it delayed Eleanor Farjeon's arrival. The Thomases had suggested that she should spend part of August with them to meet the Frosts, but her brother Harry had been holidaying in France and was still stranded there. She could not leave her mother to worry about him on her own, she felt, so a later date for her arrival was fixed.

Otherwise the Thomases and Frosts spent an indulgent time: 'talk and strolling and odd games of cricket' filled most days, according to Edward.[9] He and Robert, Helen recalled, 'were always together and when not exploring the country, they sat in the shade of a tree smoking and talking endlessly of literature and poetry in particular'.[10] On the rare occasions when it rained everyone assembled in the Frosts' cottage. Since it possessed only two chairs, the four adults and eight children all sat on the floor, talking or singing the folk-songs Edward loved so much. While Germany swept rapidly through Belgium into France in the opening days of the war, they might be sitting in Little Iddens trying to remember the words of 'Mr John Blunt', or 'Au Jardin de Mon Père'.[11]

As the Battle of the Frontiers in Alsace and Lorraine approached on 14 August, life still seems to have continued uneventfully for the little Gloucestershire community. The children occupied themselves and each other in preparing another issue of the Frost family magazine, *The Bouquet*, to which Edward as well as Robert would contribute.[12] Since a number of issues (produced in a single copy and circulated round the two families) were lost, there is no knowing whether August had its own number. If it did, it may have contained Edward's poem 'The Lyre', which his daughters remembered him contributing to *The Bouquet*. While this is a modest achievement, clearly written with children in mind, it is worth quoting here as a possibly early attempt to follow Robert's advice to start writing poetry:

This is the constellation of the Lyre:
    Its music cannot ever tire,
For it is silent no man need fear it:
Unless he wants to, he will not hear it.

If this is indeed Thomas's first semi-public poem it is interesting to see how elevated the imagery of the poet, as a lyre, is in contrast to the later metaphor comparing the poet to a 'drain' or 'crack in the wall'.

Frost had ample opportunity to guide Thomas towards poetry this month since, despite the latter's virtuous work intentions, the greater part of their time was spent talking. It seldom rained, so this meant that they passed it mainly out of doors, Thomas told Hudson, 'on short excursions, seldom further than Whiteleaved Oak at our end of the Malverns'.[13] By August, he noted, the orchards had begun to produce their crops of 'small brown perry pears, as thick as haws' and 'chiefly cider apples, innumerable, rosy and uneatable'. But, as he also remembered, 'once or twice [he and Frost] did pick up a wasp's remnant, with slightly greasy skin of palest yellow, that tasted delicious'. Such passages from 'This England' suggest that for Thomas his time with Frost in Gloucestershire had a touch of the Garden of Eden and its apples about it. There is only a hint, in his poem on the same subject, 'The Sun Used to Shine', that 'rumours of the war remote' might bring the idyll to an end. Almost everything else has an Arcadian feel to it. The farmhouse, in which he lodged, for instance, was surrounded by 'large orchards in which were grown the choicest of dessert plums', the outside 'hung with delicious fruit' which the Thomases were allowed to pick – 'greengages and large golden or purple juicy plums'.[14]

It was not all as idyllic as it sounded, however. One problem, only hinted at in Helen's account of their stay, was her lack of rapport with Elinor Frost. While her husband's intimacy with Robert Frost might have been expected to bring her closer to Elinor, she retained 'only a vague memory' of her as 'a rather nebulous personality' with 'none of the physical strength or activity of her husband'.[15] It is clear from Eleanor Farjeon's description that the two women had little in common: 'Elinor Frost, fragile and weariable, was not the naturally joyful housewife that Helen was, the home-maker who bustled from job to job on a breath of laughter.'[16] There was certainly some disapproval in Helen's attitude towards Elinor, though she did not voice it beyond commenting on her haphazard housekeeping. She was particularly struck by Elinor's preparations for the midday meal, which appeared to consist solely of taking 'a bucket of potatoes into the field and sitting in the grass to peel them – without water'.[17]

More seriously, Helen and Edward were, in his own, understated words, 'doing rather moderately' at Ledington.[18] By the middle of the month, he felt 'very irritable indeed', he confessed to Eleanor. Despite his attempts to explain this in terms of Merfyn and the Russian boy being 'bored', or Myfanwy having had 'a very bad fall', it seems more likely that it was the last reason he listed – 'the quarters [being] too close' – which was the main cause of the problem.[19] The first long holiday he had taken with his family, he was unable to escape regularly to London for the night or on longer research trips for a travel book. He could not even get away to Wales for a week with Frost, as planned. For by mid-August the war was beginning to make itself felt even in dozy Ledington. Mr Chandler, the Thomases' 44-year-old landlord and a soldier of 21 years' service, had been 'sent for to Hereford' on the morning of 14 August.[20] This meant that Edward and Robert might be needed to take on some of his farm-work. Even if not, there were other problems attached to their proposed Welsh trip. For as Edward explained to an understanding Eleanor, still having problems arranging her own holiday with them, 'travelling has new inconveniences and things cost even more than ever here, so I don't know what they'll be at inns'.[21] Of one thing only was he certain at this point, that he had no intention of 'serving [his] country'.[22] According to Frost, Gibson hated the war, Abercrombie hated the Germans and Frost himself hated the Germans but not the war, and none of them had yet felt obliged to enlist.

Instead Thomas contemplated 'turning plain reporter and giving *unvarnished* [my italics] reports of country conversations about the war'.[23] Two things prevented him, however; Frost's active discouragement, which is rather puzzling in view of the American's approval of the war; and a suspicion that 'varnish' was precisely what the public wanted. 'Do you read Harold Begbie, for example?' he asked Eleanor.[24] Begbie was a journalist, a popular writer on religious and social issues whom Thomas may have met in the offices of the *Daily Chronicle*. Even a short extract from Begbie's poem published this month in the *Daily Chronicle* makes it clear what Thomas meant by 'varnish':

Fall In

... Why do they call, sonny, why do they call

> For men who are brave and strong?
> Is it naught to you if your country fall,
>   And Right is smashed by Wrong?
> Is it football still and the picture show,
>   The pub and the betting odds,
> When your brothers stand to the tyrant's blow
>   And Britain's call is God's?[25]

'What a low fiend Begbie is,' Thomas wrote to John Freeman, almost certainly in response to this poem.[26] If Begbie's was the first example of war poetry he encountered, it is not surprising that he seems consciously to have avoided the genre when he started to write poetry himself not long afterwards. And Begbie's jingoistic appeal to Englishmen in the name of God was by no means an isolated example of the kind of verse produced at the outbreak of war.[27]

Such outpourings may even have delayed Thomas's start in verse altogether; he is anxious to point out to Bottomley, for instance, that by 25 August he is '*not* [my italics] writing poems like all those London bards'.[28] In a letter to Monro of 14 September, offering an article on war poems for *Poetry and Drama*, he admits to having found them 'particularly wretched on the whole, except those done quite deliberately like Begbie's and they are even more hateful'.[29] Why, he asks Monro five days later, was it 'so often bad'?[30] But since he believes, as his subsequent article on 'War Poetry' in December 1914 would show, that the public 'want something raw and solid, or vague and lofty and sentimental', he argues that 'they must have Mr Begbie to express their thoughts, or "Tipperary" to drown them'.[31] It was Begbie and his fellow-journalists, like Edward's own father, who would provoke him into writing the nearest he ever came to a direct war poem, setting out his own more measured approach to the conflict:

> This is no case of petty right or wrong
> That politicians or philosophers
> Can judge. I hate not Germans, nor grow hot
> With love of Englishmen, to please newspapers.
> Beside my hate for one fat patriot
> My hatred of the Kaiser is love true: –
> A kind of god he is, banging a gong.
> But I have not to choose between the two,
> Or between justice and injustice ...

In the second half of this poem, Thomas reflects on his own reaction to the crisis, rational or otherwise:

> … Dinned
>
> With war and argument I read no more
> Than in the storm smoking along the wind
> Athwart the wood. Two witches' cauldrons roar.
> From one the weather shall rise clear and gay;
> Out of the other an England beautiful
> And like her mother that died yesterday.
> Little I know or care if, being dull,
> I shall miss something that historians
> Can rake out of the ashes when perchance
> The phoenix broods serene above their ken.
> But with the best and meanest Englishmen
> I am one in crying, God save England, lest
> We lose what never slaves and cattle blessed.
> The ages made her that made us from the dust:
> She is all we know and live by, and we trust
> She is good and must endure, loving her so:
> And as we love ourselves we hate her foe.[32]

John Pikoulis has accused Thomas of being 'more than a little sentimental in this poem,'[33] but if he is it is a rare lapse on his part. In any event, 'This is No Case', as Bernard Bergonzi points out, shows an awareness far removed from such straightforwardly patriotic poems as Julian Grenfell's 'Into Battle' or Rupert Brooke's '1914' sonnet sequence. It is an awareness relating to the countryside Thomas knew so well and hinges on the distinction (in William Cooke's words) 'between subtle (private) patriotism and deliberate (public) patriotism,'[34] a distinction Thomas makes in his article 'War Poetry'. Far from being 'sentimental' or rhetorical, he appears to be questioning himself with his usual rigour on possible reasons for enlisting. And what more convincing argument could there be in his case than his long-standing love of English landscapes ('the storm smoking along the wind / Athwart the wood') and her literature ('God save England,' he echoes from one of Shakespeare's most patriotic plays, *Henry V*, though he also conjures up the witches' cauldron from *Macbeth*, which suggests the evil of war)?[35]

'This is No Case' would not be written down until 14 months after the outbreak of war, but it rehearses many of Thomas's arguments with himself on the subject. While it could be argued that it was the war itself which provided the final impetus towards poetry, he had more immediate concerns about its likely effect in mid-August 1914. Despite feeling 'more secluded here from realities than ever,' he told John Freeman, even after Mr Chandler's call-up,[36] Mrs Chandler had been obliged to raise the supposedly fixed terms for board at Oldfields. But Thomas was getting no new work to fund the increase and could see no likelihood of any, as a flurry of letters between himself and his literary agent shows. His proposal of a book of the prose sketches Frost had suggested ('call it "Thick and Clear" ' Thomas joked with Cazenove) failed to appeal.[37] But Cazenove did like his idea for 'a series of country rides…to relate solely to the war's influence'[38] and within a week was able to report some interest in it: Austin Harrison, who had published Thomas's 'Swansea Village' article in his *English Review* in June this year, was ready to discuss the idea. Thomas then travelled to London on 28 August to debate terms, returning on 29 August. Eckert, who interviewed Frost for his account of this period, reported that Edward's relations with Helen were so bad at this point that she insisted on the American going with her to Ledbury station to meet him.[39] Despite Thomas's success – Harrison had agreed to pay £25 for 5,000 words, plus travel expenses – when he heard his wife's enthusiasm over what to him was a literary trifle, he 'straightened up,' according to Frost, 'even taller than he was [and] stiffened, irritated in spite of himself'.[40] The three of them walked back to Ledington 'strung out in a row along the road, Thomas and his wife trying to avoid each other'.[41]

Frost never deviated from this view, telling Eleanor on his last visit to England in 1957 that, in Gloucestershire that summer, he 'saw how [Helen's] enthusiasm and optimism irritated [Edward]'.[42] When Eleanor finally joined the group at Ledington on 20 August 1914, Frost believed that Helen had 'pretended to tease [Edward] about [Eleanor], and pushed [Eleanor] on to him as though familiarity would make him tired of [Eleanor]'.[43] Eleanor denied this story by 1957, but was forced to accept that she and Robert, who both 'loved Edward beyond all, fe[lt] differ-ently about Helen'.[44] (Eleanor wrote in this same piece, ' "we both loved

[Edward] more deeply than any man we have known", I said, and [Robert] nodded'.) While conceding that Robert knew Edward better than she did – 'for a man talks to a man' – she argued that she knew Helen better than Robert did – 'for a woman talks to a woman'.[45] She was also forced to consider Robert's theory that 'love can be hate too':

> ...And it was not Helen's fault [Eleanor continued] that Edward was an abnormally sensitively-irritable man; when he was so she may have been unwise in dealing with it but he would have been so in any other home circumstances, with other people who could not heal or help him. For this is the nature of neurotic irritability, and people who fail with it may fail by trying to do something, when nothing can be done.[46]

Eleanor told Robert that in their four years of friendship Edward 'was never once irritable' with her; 'but then all intimacy was kept unexpressed,' she added, acknowledging that 'if I had been his wife I would have had to take the brunt of his moods and done worse with them than Helen. And hate might have been the other side of love for me too.'[47]

This is an admirably fair summary of the situation from someone who loved Edward and Helen deeply. However, it overlooks the possibility that, while it may not have been either partner's 'fault', the marriage was an unfortunate mismatch of temperaments. As Frost saw it, Helen's 'emotion was too lush for [Edward] and irritated him' beyond his usual irritability, driving him on one occasion at least to throw a teapot at the wall.[48] If Edward's poem, 'No one so much as you' is really about Helen not his mother, as seems likely, his own perception of their differences makes the gap between them seem quite unbridgeable, since the narrator describes himself and Helen respectively in the closing lines as 'a pine in solitude / Cradling a dove'. Frost may not have been far wrong when he argued that one of Thomas's motives for enlisting had been to get away from Helen.[49]

Though Eleanor objected strongly to a radio programme in the 1950s describing her relationship with Edward and Helen as a *ménage à trois*, it is clear that she served a useful function in the Thomases' marriage, particularly in the summer of 1914. She was not just of practical help, bringing Edward some of Coleridge's works, so that he could make up a shortfall of some 10,000 words in his *A Literary Pilgrim* manuscript by adding Coleridge to his list of writers. Her sympathy towards and understanding of both Helen's and Edward's problems enabled her to calm what had evidently become a tense situation and to change the dynamics slightly. 'Everyone was glad to have you,' Edward told her shortly after the holiday had ended, tacitly acknowledging the problems they had faced in his following sentence: 'I felt as if I were rather the grub in the apple.'[50]

Despite these tensions Eleanor herself enjoyed her fortnight in Gloucestershire greatly. Her lodgings with Mr and Mrs Farmer, an elderly country couple she imagined to have stepped out of a novel by Thomas Hardy and George Eliot respectively, delighted her. She grew very fond of her quarters at their 'plain and solid house', Glyn Iddens, just up the lane from the Frosts and the Thomases. She also grew accustomed to the large jug of powerful cider they served with her meals in place of water, a habit which stood her in good stead when her hostess insisted on giving the local 'covey of poets' a 'supper'.[51]

This meal, on a 'gargantuan scale' like everything else at Glyn Iddens, ended with two memorably comic moments. The first occurred when Mr Farmer, eyeing the 'enormous Stilton in an advanced state of [maggoty] ripeness' at the end of the huge meal, told Eleanor gleefully: 'I likes it…when they looks out o' their little winders and wags their tails, but I don't like it when they squeals between my teeth.'[52] The second shows Edward in a rare moment of relaxation in mixed company, as they finished their meal with the cheese:

> I rose [Eleanor remembered], and Helen rose, and Elinor Frost. Mr Farmer rose. The Poets attempted to rise, relapsed on to their seats, and regarded each other with comical consternation. They were perfectly sober, though exceedingly gay; but the gallons of strong cider, against which I had been inoculated, had gone to their legs, and not one of them could stand without support.[53]

Eleanor liked to boast afterwards of the night when she 'drank all the poets in Gloucestershire under the table'.[54]

Mrs Farmer's 'supper' for the Poets must have taken place some time between Eleanor's arrival on 20 August and Edward's departure at the beginning of September to research his *English Review* article. His agent's stern reminder that 'nothing must be said' in it 'which will stop recruiting', was probably unnecessary, since Thomas himself was already starting to identify more with the Allies' cause than at the war's outbreak. According to Eleanor, he was even 'considering enlisting', though she appears to attribute this to things being 'very bad in every way – worse than I have ever known them' between the Thomases.[55] The British Expeditionary Force had fought its first two serious engagements of the war, the Battle of Mons on 23 August and Le Cateau on 26 August, and news of its retreat on both occasions would have reached Thomas, even at Ledington, by 27 August. As *The Times* warned on 26 August, the fighting had 'so far gone ill' for the British, who were retreating, exhausted, from the Germans eastward of the Meuse. Thomas's reaction to the news, as he walked with Frost under a 'stout orange' harvest moon, shows him confronting his own indecision about enlistment, possibly for the first time:

> …At one stroke, I thought, like many other people, what things that same new moon sees eastward about the Meuse in France. Of those who could see it there, not blinded by smoke, pain or excitement, how many saw it and heeded? I was deluged, in a second stroke, by another thought, or something that overpowered thought. All I can tell is, it seemed to me that either I had never loved England, or that I had loved it foolishly, aesthetically, like a slave, not having realized that it wasn't mine unless I were willing and prepared to die rather than to leave it as Belgian women and old men and children had left their country. Something I had omitted. Something, I felt, had to be done before I could look composedly at English landscapes, at the elms and poplars about the houses, at the purple-headed wood-betony with two pairs of dark leaves on a stiff stem, who stood sentinel among the grasses or bracken by hedge-side or wood-edge. What he stood sentinel for I did not know, any more than what I had got to do.[56]

The sentinel-like betony would appear again in the poem he also wrote about this moment of revelation under the harvest moon, 'The Sun Used to Shine', together with the other flower he had noted on his walks with Frost that August, the so-called 'autumn crocus' (colchicum), which he imagines elsewhere as having risen out of 'a subterranean world…into which the multitudes of the earth…seemed to have gone down to tranquillity'.[57]

... We turned from men or poetry

To rumours of the war remote
Only till both stood disinclined
For aught but the yellow flavorous coat
Of an apple wasps had undermined;

Or a sentry of dark betonies,
The stateliest of small flowers on earth,
At the forest verge; or crocuses
Pale purple as if they had their birth

In sunless Hades fields... [58]

Both flowers become faint symbols of the battlefields he was beginning to envisage, the betonies standing guard, like sentinels, over the troops, the crocuses 'Pale purple as if they had their birth / In sunless Hades fields'. The latter reference is almost certainly a reversal of the Persephone myth, as Edna Longley points out, in which the goddess returns from Hades' underworld each spring, Thomas's crocuses prompting the ironic thought that the soldiers who die in Autumn 1914 will *not*, unlike Persephone and the crocuses, return inevitably to life. The moon, too, becomes symbolic, indicating the shared humanity of the narrator with the soldiers, as the poet struggles to travel imaginatively to the front, ultimately in vain:

... The war

Came back to mind with the moonrise
Which soldiers in the east afar
Beheld then. Nevertheless, our eyes

Could as well imagine the Crusades
Or Caesar's battles. Everything
To faintness like those rumours fades –
Like the brook's water glittering

Under the moonlight – like those walks
Now – like us two that took them, and
The fallen apples, all the talks
And silences – like memory's sand

When the tide covers it late or soon,
And other men through other flowers
In those fields under the same moon
Go talking and have easy hours.[59]

Written in May 1916 almost a year after Thomas himself became a soldier, 'The Sun Used to Shine' may also be an anticipation of his death less than a year after that. The sudden shift in the last two stanzas from the past to a very different present, and a future in which 'other men through other flowers' will walk and talk, appears to equate the narrator with the 'fallen apples' or 'memory's sand / When the tide covers it'. The simple, easy movement of the rhyming four-line stanzas, where one line frequently runs on to the next, even across verse breaks, mirrors the two men's calm, unhurried stroll and conversation, their pauses both in walking and talking and, at least for the narrator, a quiet resignation at the end of their musings about the war in what appears to be superficially their Eden.

Thomas left on his fortnight's research for 'Tipperary' (as his first article for the *English Review* was to be called) shortly after this moonlight revelation and what he encountered during his trip almost certainly reinforced his sense that he ought to 'do' something for his country.

20

THE ROAD TAKEN (SEPTEMBER–NOVEMBER 1914)

> ...There is now no man living with whom I can be completely myself – Frost nearest of all, but I think not quite, because I am a little anxious to please him.
>
> – Edward Thomas to Helen Thomas, 11 October 1914

On 30 August 1914, when Thomas was about to set off on his research trip for 'Tipperary', he wrote to de la Mare: 'If the war goes on I believe I shall find myself a sort of Englishman.' His letter opened with a reference to Rupert Brooke having joined the army, a fact repeated in letters to several other friends this autumn,[1] and rivalry with Brooke may have added another incentive for him to enlist. He would certainly appear critical of Monro for *not* having joined up by November and would be correspondingly admiring of T. E. Hulme for doing so: 'the only one of that sacred band', he wrote to Frost, adding ironically that 'the rest stayed at home for their country's good'.[2]

Though Thomas himself would continue to hesitate, the pressure on all fit men to enlist was increased by a series of further Allied defeats in the autumn of 1914. The Germans' victory over the Russians at the Battle of Tannenberg at the end of August had given a decisive start to the war on the Eastern Front and British morale had been further lowered by more heavy losses of British and French troops at the Battle of the Marne (6–10

September) and the first Battle of Ypres (19 October–22 November). In Britain most people were beginning to realize that the war would *not* be 'over by Christmas'. In reality, the opposing western armies had dug themselves in along a line stretching from the Belgian coast to Switzerland, a line that was rarely to move more than ten miles either way during the next four years. Nevertheless, war fervour continued, Britain's overall mood still accurately reflected in Brooke's '1914' sonnet sequence. Thomas's contribution at this stage would be confined to writing about this mood as he found it at first-hand.

His itinerary for his research trip – through Coventry, Birmingham, Sheffield, Manchester, Bradford, Leeds, Hartlepool, Sunderland and Newcastle-upon-Tyne – was clearly planned to help him establish how the 'man in the street' was reacting to the war. A great deal of his time would be spent 'in pubs talking to workmen and eavesdropping'[3] and the result – an unusually early example of 'vox pop' or mass observation – is an invaluable record of popular feeling about the war at its start. He learnt many interesting facts, about recruitment and employment in particular, some quite unexpected. It probably came as no surprise to learn that there was lack of work in trades like jewellery-making in Birmingham, for example, but less predictable to discover that coalminers in Newcastle, for instance, had suffered from unemployment because their colliery had supplied coal to Germany before the war. (Many of the unemployed workers had enlisted and some ultra-patriotic employers, apparently, were deliberately dismissing younger unmarried men 'in order to drive them to enlist'.[4]) Other trades appeared to flourish. Boot-makers in Leicester, for instance, were so busy making boots for the British and French armies, he discovered, that they had to turn down a substantial order to supply the Greek army with them. And the harness-makers of Walsall were overwhelmed with work, supplying horses at the front, as were the explosives factories of Elswick. But only the publicans really profited, Thomas argued, since in general everyone had to work harder for less pay.

It was not just the pubs which were busy. Thomas saw that the streets, parks and other public places were 'thronged...bands played in the streets – at Newcastle bagpipes – to quicken recruiting'. Football matches were a favourite recruiting place. And though the war was not discussed publicly – you were branded a Socialist if you did so – he seems to have had little difficulty in getting people to talk to him openly about other related topics. A Coventry man, for instance, argued that the working classes were doing their duty, but not the middle class – he called it the 'second class' – 'these young fellows who are neither man nor girl, and think about their socks all day'. Opinions on the enemy varied surprisingly, from those who maintained that 'the Germans are a rotten lot' to those who admired 'German strategy and organisation'. One youth in Manchester even ventured to suggest 'they must be a fine race of soldiers' and a Coventry man went so far as to argue that 'the German people were as good as ourselves'.

Yet this man like everyone else, Thomas found, 'was sure of victory' and no one could 'stomach the idea of English soldiers retiring and retiring', as they had recently been forced to do at Mons and Le Cateau. Patriotic feelings ran high and scores believed that it was 'the greatest war of all time'. There is little doubt that such widespread and heartfelt patriotism from ordinary men and women strengthened Thomas's own identification with England. A week into his trip he was writing to Jesse Berridge, 'The obvious thing is to join the Territorials.' Only the fact that he could not 'leave other people to keep [his] family,' he added, prevented him from doing so; he repeated, 'I am slowly growing into a conscious Englishman.'[5]

The war had thrown everything into confusion for Thomas as well as almost everyone else and he seems to have drawn consolation from the one certain employment he had, in writing about it. He particularly enjoyed reporting the many rumours and legends that circulated, some of them entertainingly absurd, such as the story that two million Russians had travelled down through England by night and were waiting for the Germans at Ostend.

'Tipperary' concludes with a passage which reflects Thomas's own position by the end of his trip on 10 September:

> Probably there are two kinds of patriot: one that can talk or write, and one that cannot; though I suspect that even the talkers and writers often come down in the end to 'I do not understand. I love.' It must happen more than once or twice that a man who can say why he ought to fight for his country fails to enlist. The very phrase: 'to fight for one's country', is a shade too poetical and conscious for any but non-combatants.

As Thomas repeated in several letters at this time, his own plans were 'uncertain'.[6] He had hoped to complete the writing up of his article in Carnforth, combining it with a visit to Gordon Bottomley and his wife. But Bottomley was suffering one of his frequent relapses and Thomas returned to the crowded little cottage at Steep to finish 'Tipperary', due at the *English Review* offices on 15 September. Two days before completing it, he was telling Eleanor that 'when it's done I shall find out what sort of soldier they still want at Petersfield'.[7] Yet only six days later he appeared still to be considering Frost's idea of living with him in America, writing to him (with reference to their last moonlight walk together):

> I doubt if I shall get any nearer soldiering than I did then, chiefly for fear of leaving many tangles behind and not being able to make any new ones for perhaps a long time. So I shall probably see you before the year's old. I might go to Wales and see you on the way back. But I must first see if there is any paid work to do.[8]

There were, in fact, to be two visits to Frost 'before the year's old'.

First, however, Thomas tried to deal with the more pressing problem of finding paid work. On the same day that he wrote to Frost, 19 September, he was asking Monro if he would be interested in his proposed article on 'War Poetry'. While waiting for a reply, he continued with a piece he was writing for the *Nation* describing the August holiday with Frost and his reaction to the outbreak of war, 'This England'. But apart from a few reviews and review articles for the *Bookman* and *Poetry and Drama*, there was little to reassure him financially and even less to distract him from his indecision about enlisting. Not since his undergraduate days had he had so much time to reflect on his own situation. He even considered going on with his autobiography.

One slight distraction was a plan for Frost to move his family within walking or easy cycling distance of the Thomases. But the cottage in question, owned by an aspiring poet, Mary Wilson Gardner, whom Frost had met at the opening of the Poetry Bookshop, was either not suitable, or not available, when the Frosts' lease of Little Iddens came to an end in mid-September. The Frosts moved instead into one of the Abercrombies' adjoining cottages at Ryton and Thomas's hopes of meeting Mrs Gardner's flaming red-haired artist daughter, Phyllis, were disappointed.[9] (Reputedly very attractive, Phyllis had been one of Brooke's several romantic entanglements.) It was a rare instance of Thomas showing his interest in beautiful women openly, one more indication perhaps of his growing discontent with Helen.

Another slight distraction was a cycle ride on 17 September to James Guthrie at Flansham, where he enjoyed a swim in the 'cold rough sea'.[10] But the visit was brief and the same problems faced him on his return. He was off again a week later to look for work in London, staying once again with the hospitable Bax and Olga.

Even more restless than usual, he next decided on a trip to Wales, citing the need to gather material for a second *English Review* article on popular attitudes towards the war. This time, he proposed to concentrate on 'what country [rather than town] people say about the war'.[11] But by the time he 'had done walking and riding and afflicting Helen with long journals,' he told Eleanor, he 'couldn't write in Wales'.[12] Instead he had visited his old friends, John Williams ('the Deacon') at Swansea and Gwili at Ammanford, enjoying long bicycle rides through the Black Mountains and the Brecons in between. It was not until he got to Gloucestershire, on his way home, that he started collecting material in earnest, one of his first nuggets being Eleanor's old landlady Mrs Farmer's observation to Frost's eldest daughter, Lesley, 'that the Kayser's hambition was to eat his Christmas dinner in London'.[13]

Though part of Thomas's motive in cycling to Wales had almost certainly been the hope of seeing Frost on his way home, the visit had been in doubt until the last moment. Frost had left for a fortnight's stay in Edinburgh at the beginning of October, but had caught flu and arrived back early in Gloucestershire, exhausted, on 9 October, to be met by an equally ill, worn-out wife and sick son. Elinor Frost had, nevertheless, managed to write confirming Thomas's visit. Clearly neither she nor Robert wanted to miss seeing him and Edward arrived at Ryton on 14 October just as Abercrombie left to join his wife and their new-born baby in Lincolnshire. With 'Robert not very well', their normal walks seemed threatened, until the appearance of Frost's recent acquaintance, J. W. ('Jack') Haines.[14]

A local solicitor and friend of Abercrombie, Haines shared Frost's passion for botany as well as poetry and the two had already taken long walks together. When Thomas arrived the three of them spent at least one afternoon together, Haines recalled, 'wandering about the little valley of the Leadon, then full of beautiful, unusual, autumn flowers, such as the primrose-leaved mullein, the small teasel, and the spreading bell-flower, all of which delighted [Thomas]'.[15] For the most part, however, they 'loaf[ed] and talk[ed]', the 'languid, still weather' lending itself to idleness.[16] As Haines remembered, there was 'much talk of Poets', mainly of Doughty, W. H. Davies and de la Mare. Thomas had been 'meditating' a poem about gypsies only a few days previously, after passing one of their caravans near Cockett as he cycled into Swansea, and could hardly have found more fertile grounds for such a project.[17]

Haines's first impression of Thomas was of 'a dreamy man of slow speech and deliberate opinions, infinitely interested in little things'.[18] He struck Haines as someone who 'had thought and talked over all the bigger things until he was tired of them'.[19] Thomas would stay with Haines at his home in Hucclecote, near Gloucester, on several occasions beside the one which inspired his poem 'Words'. His last visit would be only a week before leaving for France. They would also exchange letters.

Thomas enjoyed this stay at Ryton so much that he postponed his return, asking Helen to forgive him and telling her how much he was enjoying the 'great soft still days' in Gloucestershire.[20] He loved the Abercrombies' garden, with its old, bent apple tree and lavender, borage and evening primrose still flowering in it, and was almost certainly thinking of this autumnal idyll when he came to write 'October':

> ... The rich scene has grown fresh again and new
> As Spring and to the touch is not more cool
> Than it is warm to the gaze; and now I might
> As happy be as earth is beautiful,
> Were I some other or with earth could turn
> In alternation of violet and rose,
> Harebell and snowdrop, at their season due,
> And gorse that has no time not to be gay,
> But if this be not happiness, – who knows? ...[21]

Thomas's ride home through the West Country reminded him, like his trip to Wales, how much he loved his country and less than a fortnight later he was telling Frost that he had 'just made [himself] ill with thinking hard for an hour', up in his hill-top study, that he 'ought to enlist next week in town' (i.e. London).[22] His father's visit on 27 October and his inflammatory, jingoistic talk, rather than discouraging this thought, appears to have concentrated his son's mind on essentials. However, it is clear from 'This is no case of petty right or wrong', that he could not accept his father's black and white view of the situation.

When Thomas arrived in London at the beginning of November, rather than enlisting as he thought he 'ought', he spent a week seeing friends and discussing possible illustrations for *Four-and-Twenty Blackbirds* with Hodgson's artist-friend, Lovat Fraser. Still opting to write about the war rather than fight in it, no sooner had 'This England' been published in the *Nation* on 7 November, than he was 'in the thick of [writing] Tipperary ii' ('It's a Long, Long Way') for the *English Review*, as well as completing 'War Poetry' for Monro.

Once both articles were handed in by 13 November, his thoughts turned again to enlisting. He was also undoubtedly affected by Hodgson's charge of lack of patriotism when they met at their usual haunt, St George's. His own account of the matter, on 9 or 10 November, to friends – that 'Hodgson flung off today labelling me pro-German' – lacks detail.[23] But he was more specific about it to Helen, who later recalled: 'In the course of conversation somebody said: "Germans are afraid of cold steel", and Edward said "Everybody is afraid of cold steel". At that Ralph Hodgson shouted at Edward, "You damned pro-German" and stalked out of the restaurant.'[24]

Thomas may deliberately have omitted to tell Helen that, according to another witness, Hodgson also 'kicked over tables and chairs on his way out'.[25] Though Thomas remained convinced that he was right about the fear of 'cold steel', he was greatly saddened by the incident and, as he told their mutual friend Monro, 'almost enlisted afterwards in repentance'.[26] He could 'almost face bayonets to bring [Hodgson] round,' he confessed, 'but not quite'. But this taunt from an old friend hurt deeply. While Helen was able to attribute Hodgson's outburst to his 'unaccountable moods which sometimes seemed almost insane', Thomas tried to argue his case rationally with him: 'I think what you say is just enough,' Thomas conceded on 19 November 1914, 'and I hope it will not be long before we can meet.'[27] Hodgson, who had himself already enlisted despite his age

Clifford Bax.

BELOW: (Helton) Godwin Baynes, as a newly qualified doctor.

LEFT: Edward Thomas at Broughton Gifford.

RIGHT: Edward Thomas (third from right) at Calne, with the group staying at oughton Gifford or Cricket Week.

LEFT: Eleanor Farjeon, 1913.

BELOW: Robert Frost, 1913.

ABOVE: The Georgians (left to right) John Drinkwater, Wilfrid Gibson, Edward Marsh, Lascelles Abercrombie, Geraldine Gibson and Catherine Abercrombie, outside the Birmingham Repertory Theatre, May 1914.

BELOW: Adlestrc Station Platform, as it was.

LEFT: Old Fields, the Thomases' lodgings.

RIGHT: Little Iddens, the Frosts' lodgings.

LEFT: The Old Nailshop, the Gibsons' house.

RIGHT: Glyn Iddens, Eleanor Farjeon's lodgings.

LEFT, ABOVE AND BELOW LEFT: Edward Thomas, Steep, 1914.

BELOW: Helen Thomas, Steep, 1914.

Hut 35. Edward Thomas second from left, middle row.

Edward Thomas on leave
at Steep, 1916.

Ralph Hodgson in Royal
Artillery uniform, 1916/17.

Signatures on the reverse of the group photograph
of Hut 35, December 1915.

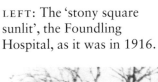
LEFT: The 'stony square sunlit', the Foundling Hospital, as it was in 1916.

RIGHT: Edward Thomas with Gordon Bottomley on his last leave, late 1916.

LEFT: Edna Clarke Hall.

BELOW: Codford Camp.

LEFT: Edward Thomas's grave at Agny, near Arras.

BELOW: Bronwen, Myfanwy and Merfyn Thomas, shortly after Merfyn enlisted in a Kentish regiment in early 1918.

and ill-health (he suffered greatly from haemorrhoids) and would serve in coastal defence, refused and Thomas concluded sadly: 'He and I are not meeting till the war is over. I am not patriotic enough for his exuberant taste.'[28] One of Thomas's first actions after he did finally enter a recruitment office would be to visit Hodgson's regular resort, the Poetry Bookshop, to ask Monro's secretary, Alida Klementaski, to 'tell Hodgson I've enlisted.'[29] It would take another six months for Hodgson to relent and 'send his love': 'so I am forgiven,' Thomas told Frost.[30]

Thomas went so far as to get a Parliamentary Recruiting Committee form by late November, but as his plans to visit Frost again that month make clear, he had still not made up his mind. He filled the interval between stays by writing two more of the prose-poems Frost had admired, possibly in order to have something to show him when they met. Both pieces form the basis for two of his earliest poems. The first, 'The White House' (later 'Horse') – based on Thomas's local inn, 'The White Horse', on the Froxfield plateau above Steep, which he had revisited in early November – is dated 16 November and provides the germ of his first completed poem, 'Up in the Wind' of 3 December 1914.[31] His second prose-poem, heralded by a reference to the herb known as 'old man' (or 'lad's love') and written on 17 November, similarly underpins his poem of that name dated 6 December 1914. 'I don't find the war shuts me up,' he would write to Hudson on 26 November: 'In fact it has given me time to please myself with some unprofitable writing.' He told his aunt Margaret Townsend on 23 November that having 'used [his] leisure to write things [he] had in mind', he had 'come to an end for the present' and was 'sitting up in his study on the hill with nothing whatever to do either to please others' or himself.[32] His fifth visit to Frost this year, he implied, was to fill in time, but his careful preparation of the two prose-poems, together with Frost's continued encouragement to change from prose to verse, makes it more likely that he was preparing to launch himself into poetry. When he arrived at Ryton on 25 November events themselves would help propel him towards what for him was an act of great daring, though the same events would make him wonder whether he might not be the coward Hodgson had labelled him. The need to prove himself may have contributed both to his decision to turn to poetry and, ultimately, to his enlistment.

Edward's letter to his aunt two days before leaving for Frost's suggests that he had been pondering the question of enlistment very hard indeed:

> ...I have been thinking a good deal from time to time, trying to decide whether to enlist or not. I don't want to: only I feel that it is the only thing to do if a man is able bodied and has nothing else to do. And who can do anything else much now? The war must probably last many months, more than a year, longer. The only satisfaction I get is in realizing that so many men in a civilized age are capable of this kind of extravagant courage and endurance.[33]

His letter ends with the news that his brothers Theodore ('Dory') and Oscar are both trying 'to get work in France', where they believe 'their knowledge of transport would be useful', information that may have also been responsible for reigniting the question in his own mind.

Thomas was still 'trying to decide whether to go into the army', according to Frost, when he reached Gloucestershire on 25 November.[34] Frost remembered them sitting 'in front of his big open fireplace' to ward off the cold and Thomas debating endlessly on the topic. 'Whenever Thomas had any kind of decision to make, however small, he'd talk out the alternatives until you'd wish he'd just make up his mind.'[35] It was Thomas's indecision, Frost claimed, that prompted his poem 'The Road Not Taken' (original title 'Two Roads'), partly as a gentle dig at his friend:

> Two roads diverged in a yellow wood,
> And sorry I could not travel both
> And be one traveller, long I stood
> And looked down one as far as I could
> To where it bent in the undergrowth;
>
> Then took the other, as just as fair,
> And having perhaps the better claim,
> Because it was grassy and wanted wear;
> Though as for that the passing there
> Had worn them really about the same ...

Thomas's response to a later draft, of June 1915, shows clearly that not only had he first seen 'Two Roads' *before* he started writing poetry himself (on 3 December 1914), but that he trespassed on occasions himself – with some relish, according to his brothers and to Haynes, who regularly trespassed with him during their Oxford rambles: it also helps explain Thomas's initial lack of enthusiasm for the poem.

> Honest man (Marlborough used to think he was honest), I have found 'Two Roads'. It is as I thought. *Not having then begun to write I did not know that is how it would be done.* It was just its neatness. I don't pretend not to have a regular road and footpath system *as well as doing some trespassing. On looking at it again* I complain only of a certain periphrastic looseness in 'the passing there had gone to them both about the same. [My italics][36]

Less than a fortnight after his late November visit to Frost, Thomas would write his own poem on a similar theme, 'The Signpost', which looks very like a response to Frost's 'Two Roads' and strengthens the likelihood that he first read a draft of it during that November visit:

> I read the sign. Which way shall I go?
> A voice says: You would not have doubted so
> At twenty.[37]

The last line – 'wondering where he shall journey, O where?' – may well reflect Thomas's indecision over enlisting, but it also applies literally to his practice while out walking. 'No matter which way he went he was always sorry he didn't go the other way,' Frost claimed.[38]

By the end of his November visit Thomas would have good reason to regret 'The Road Not Taken', since the path he and Frost did choose on one of their walks through Ryton's 'yellow woods' would lead to their well-known encounter with the local gamekeeper. Referred to simply as the 'gamekeeper incident', this has been described many times, most fully by Frost's grand-daughter, Lesley Lee Francis. And though she based much of her version on what Frost and the rest of the family told her, hers is also fairest in its assessment of what was, in essence, a clash of cultures. The difference in social attitudes between the majority of Americans and British was even more pronounced in 1914 than it is today and this seems to have been the root cause of the problem.

Abercrombie rented The Gallows, where the Frosts were staying, from Lord Beauchamp, who owned the surrounding estate. The nearby wooded game preserve was watched over by a fierce keeper named Bott, but there was a tacit agreement that Abercrombie and those of his friends perceived as 'gentry', such as the Gibsons, could walk, even picnic there. It may be that Frost and Thomas assumed that the same privilege extended to them, or Frost may not have known of the embargo in the first place. (Thomas almost certainly did, writing later in his adaptation of 'The Lincolnshire Poacher', 'An Old Song', 'I roamed where nobody had a right but keepers and squires and there / I sought for nests, wild flowers, oak sticks, and moles, both far and near'.[39]) So that when Bott, who carried a shotgun, ordered them peremptorily off the land, they were morally outraged – at least, Frost was – but technically guilty. The American, who failed to appreciate what seemed to him an arcane English class system, was particularly nettled at being called a 'damned cottager' by Bott, whereas Thomas, who had grown up under such a system, felt unable to question the gamekeeper's order.[40] According to Francis's account, he 'retreated', though whether 'in fright', as she claims, or from a realistic assessment of the situation, is not recorded. Myfanwy claimed that 'my father would certainly not have got into a fight with a country-man who was looking after the landowner's wood', sure that Thomas 'understood our ways, and Frost had a very quick temper in that when the village policeman did *his* duty by calling on the "alien" every so often, Frost said to him "if you come here again, I'll shoot you" '.[41] But Thomas did subsequently agree to accompany a furious Frost to the gamekeeper's house, where Bott's response to Frost's threat to 'beat him up' if he harassed him or his family again was to point his shotgun at Thomas. It is difficult to believe that 'what happened next' – that is, Thomas instinctively backing away from a twelve-bore shotgun held by a fiery-tempered gamekeeper – 'would be,' as Matthew Hollis claims, 'a defining moment in the friendship of Robert Frost and Edward Thomas, and would plague Thomas to his dying days'.[42] Whether or not the incident was witnessed by a 12-year-old boy, who made the unlikely claim decades later to be on his way *to pick hops in late November*, seems immaterial. Thomas's reaction was perfectly understandable, so, too, was his retrospective wish that he had stood up to Bott, who had no call to point his gun at anyone. As Francis suggests, 'the gamekeeper incident assumed emblematic proportions in his vacillation [about enlistment] but could not have affected the inevitability of the outcome, for which we find complex motivation'.[43] And there is no sign whatever that it affected his close friendship with Frost.

More complications followed. First Bott reported Frost to the local constable, who issued a summons against him for threatening bodily harm. Then Gibson, to whom Frost appealed in Abercrombie's absence, refused to intervene. (His own cottage was on the Beauchamp Estate.) Next Abercrombie, alerted by letter, consulted his solicitor-friend, Haines, with the intention of taking out a counter-summons against the keeper. Only after hearing Thomas's more moderate, more nuanced version of events, which placed the original incident in the woods, rather than on the road as Frost had claimed, did Abercrombie drop his litigious intentions, writing to Haines again, on 4 December:

> Many thanks for your most sensible letter. My sole reason for writing to you [i.e. on 1 December] was on account of the alleged insult on the road, which, if true, was clearly intolerable and to be put a stop to somehow or other. Thomas's description of it, however, scarcely bears out Frost's, and I now believe he [Frost] has rather exaggerated the incident in a way which he is a trifle inclined to: I mean he is particularly sensitive to anything remotely resembling insult or deliberate annoyance to himself. This is not the first time he has been aggrieved. – As to the wood incident, he had, of course, no right there. I have permission, but that does not imply permission to my friend. The strange thing was that the keeper, knowing where Frost was staying (so Frost says), should have been so unpleasant.[44]

Abercrombie believed that 'the secret of the whole thing' was that Frost did 'not know how to talk to such folks as keepers'; the American could be as condescending in his own way as he thought the English 'gentry' were, referring to people like Bott, for instance, as 'the peasant kind'.[45] A truce was reached only when Abercrombie asked his sister, Ursula, to use her considerable influence in the district, resulting in the charge against Frost being dropped and a personal letter of apology sent to him by Lord Beauchamp.

Though Thomas, like Frost, would joke about the event later – 'Thomas says it is the best testimonial I have had and I must get my publisher to use the gamekeeper in advertising me,' Frost wrote to Monro, in December 1914 – there is no doubt that the whole episode left Thomas feeling that he may have been a coward. If 'An Old Song' is drawing on his own experience, as it appears to, then there is both confession and regret in its fourth stanza:

> Since I've thrown away a chance to fight a gamekeeper;
> And I less often trespass, and what I see or hear
> Is mostly from the road or path by day...[46]

According to Frost, Thomas would tell him after his enlistment that he regarded it as a 'test of his courage, which he felt had failed him in the Gamekeeper episode' and that this was 'the real incentive of his joining up, to prove his courage, by going into danger.'[47]

But Frost's reported claim that it was Thomas's reaction to the gamekeeper incident which led eventually to his enlistment may or may not be true. A more certain and equally dramatic fact, somewhat overshadowed by Bott and his gun, is that it coincided with Thomas's turn seriously to writing poetry. It is possible that the need to prove himself, at least to Frost, after what he perceived as his failure may have provided the final stimulus in turning him into a poet.

21

'THE ONLY BEGETTER' (DECEMBER 1914)

But I am in it and no mistake. I have an idea I am full enough but that my bad habits and customs and duties of writing will make it rather easy to write [poetry] when I've no business to. At the same time I find myself engrossed and conscious of a possible perfection as I never was in prose. Also I am very impatient of my prose, and of reviews and of review books. And yet I have been uncommonly cheerful mostly. I have been rather pleased with some of the pieces of course, but it's not wholly that. Still I won't begin thanking you just yet, tho if you like I will put it down now that you are the only begetter right enough.

> – ET to RF, 15 December 1914

Despite Thomas's claim, Frost was not 'the only begetter' of the poetry which began to pour out of him in December 1914. Quite apart from his own attempt of 7 September 1913 and possibly his need to prove himself after his retreat from the gamekeeper, he was faced with a blank future. Once his 'War Poetry' and 'Anthologies and Reprints' review articles had been published in *Poetry and Drama* and 'It's a Long, Long Way' in the *English Review* at the beginning of December 1914, no more commissions seemed likely. A direct result of the war, this left Thomas in a financially precarious yet curiously liberating position. For the first time in 14 years he had few or no deadlines to meet and time for himself. 'There is little work that has to be done, so I do the other kind,' he explained to Bottomley, adding apologetically that he 'kept making excuses for not trying to join the army'.[1] That this was not from lack of patriotic feeling is clear from his article, 'It's a Long, Long Way', where he expresses his own deep love of his country: 'If England seems threatened you feel that in losing her you would lose yourself; she becomes plainly and decidedly "the dear realm of England"...'[2] While he hesitated to take a step which would mean leaving Helen and the children for a completely different life-style, however, he could still express his patriotism in his more familiar medium, words. It was a problem he had been debating for some time. Having read so much war poetry he found bad, yet believing in the power of verse, what more natural than that he should finally do what Frost had been encouraging him to try for months, and turn to poetry himself?

> I suppose writers generally have been people who tasted far more things [he writes to Helen] than they ever swallowed and digested. But Shelley bothered for a time about politics...and Tennyson started at any rate to join a body of volunteers to fight (I think) in Spain. And I dig in the garden. I suppose it is something I only feel how far too little it is to give my imagination of the lives of men reality.[3]

He was, in any case, 'starting to write shorter and shorter things', as he told Bax.[4] He had 'got past poetical prose,' he believed, and begun to feel that in poetry he could 'use [his] experience and what [he was] and what [he] kn[e]w with less hindrance than in prose, less gross notebook stuff and mere description and explanation'.[5] By 3 December he had completed his first poem.

There are few situations which test the friendships of writers more than success in the same field. ('Complimenti, you bitch,' Pound wrote to Eliot after reading the first draft of *The Waste Land*: 'I am wracked by the seven jealousies.'[6]) Since Frost was more jealous than most of his poetic powers, there is no greater proof of the strength of his affection and admiration for Thomas than the encouragement he continued to offer him once his poetry began to flow. However threatened he may have felt by Thomas's extraordinarily accomplished start in verse, he rejoiced in it and offered expert, detailed advice at every stage. Thomas, in turn and despite his extreme sensitivity to criticism, welcomed Frost's help and adopted many of his suggestions: 'Tell me all you dare about [my poems],'[7] he was instructing Frost by the middle of December 1914.

Thomas's first piece, 'Up in the Wind', was evidently sent to Frost shortly after its completion in December, but he had been working on it for at least a month, switching between poetry and prose as he did so. Relatively few writers make a successful transition from the one medium to the other and even fewer from prose to verse. Hardy is the outstanding example of the latter and was undoubtedly in Thomas's mind as he made his own move. But Thomas was possibly unique in one respect, and that was in basing his poems, at least to begin with, on a previous prose passage.

Yet as 'Up in the Wind' shows, his transformation of prose into poetry was no simple matter of dividing the prose into verse lines. As he had written to Bottomley in 1908: 'Poetry in verse is at one with the tides and the pulse; prose is chaos cut up into beds and borders and fountains and rustic work like a garden. A merely great intellect can produce great prose, but not poetry, not one line.'[8] In fact, in this particular case, he had started writing the poem a fortnight *before* the prose piece in his field notebook in a series of notes and phrases for it:

> I could wring the old girl's neck
> That put it here
> A public house! (Charcoal burner)
> But she's dead long ago
> by bringing up and quite outdoing
> The idea of London
> Two woods around and never a road in sight
> Trees roaring like a train without an end
> Only a motorist from far away
> Or marketers in carts once a fortnight
> Or a few fresh tramps ignorant
> of the house turning.[9]

He then continued in prose, writing his descriptive piece, 'The White House/Horse' on 16 November, as possibly needing to express his thoughts more expansively before attempting to concentrate and reorder them into poetry. Eleven days later he combined both, jotting down a prose note which would be used in his poetic version.[10]

The changes Thomas made between the prose version and the final draft of his poem reveal more clearly than any of his many writings *about* poetry that he knew from the start where it differed essentially from prose and what his own aims were. Whereas the prose version opens with a long description of the inn, the emphasis falling on the isolated natural setting, the poem starts more arrestingly *in medias res* with the violent outburst of the 'wild girl' who returned from London to work there. (He had noted his field notebook for 1911 (no. 47) a 'barmaid' in a Welsh inn with a 'Cockney voice'.)

> 'I could wring the old thing's neck that put it here!
> A public-house! It may be public for birds,
> Squirrels and such-like, ghosts of charcoal-burners
> And highwaymen.' The wild girl laughed. 'But I
> Hate it since I came back from Kennington.
> I gave up a good place.'

The 'story' Thomas contemplated telling in his prose version 'would *not*,' he writes, 'have included either the "old girl" or the landlord's indignant cockney daughter'. It would, instead, have tried to 'interpret the look that the house had as you came up to it'.[11] Yet precisely by concentrating on the 'old girl' and the 'landlord's indignant cockney daughter' in his poem, he conveys the isolation and wildness of the situation vividly as well as its contrast with urban living and a sense of the past:

> …Her Cockney accent
> Made her and the house seem wilder by calling up –
> Only to be subdued at once by wildness–
> The idea of London, there in that forest parlour,
> Low and small among the towering beeches
> ………………………
> But the land is wild, and there's a spirit of wildness
> Much older, crying when the stone-curlew yodels
> His sea and mountain cry …

Thomas's detailed prose notes, which he was starting to deplore, are not so much abandoned here as subjugated to a central drama and its themes, as the wild girl explains in the course of the poem, however indirectly, her choice of the country over the London suburb of Kennington, of the wild over the tame. As Jan Marsh notes, 'dramatically, the poem balances the ideas of the imagined past against the actual present, and of the town against the country'.[12]

Another theme developed in the verse but not in the prose version despite its greater length, is the disturbing effect of constant wind at a great height, an experience which had contributed to Thomas's own need to leave Wick Green by 1913. The symbolic overtones of the poem's title, 'Up in the Wind', become apparent as the landlord's daughter relates her reaction to the inn's missing signboard, which the narrator laments:

> But would you like to hear it swing all night
> And all day? All I ever had to thank
> The wind for was for blowing the sign down.
> Time after time it blew down and I could sleep.
> At last they fixed it, and it took a thief
> To move it, and we've never had another:
> It's lying at the bottom of the pond.
> But no one's moved the wood from off the hill
> There at the back, although it makes a noise
> When the wind blows, as if a train were running
> The other side, a train that never stops
> Or ends. And the linen crackles on the line
> Like a wood fire rising.

Such autobiographical details as Thomas's feelings about wind may be incidental; is it relevant to note, for instance, that he was born near Kennington where the girl has been in service? But there is no mistaking the importance the poet places on the girl's – and Thomas's own – preference for the country. The final scene, of the girl gazing out of doors at the calves drinking from a pond, is moved from the middle of the prose piece to round off the poem, as the narrator asks her 'What about Kennington?':

> She bent down to her scrubbing with 'Not me:
> Not back to Kennington ...
> I reckon I shall stay ...
> Look at those calves.'

Between the open door
And the trees two calves were wading in the pond,
Grazing the water here and there and thinking,
Sipping and thinking, both happily, neither long.
The water wrinkled, but they sipped and thought,
As careless of the wind as it of us.
'Look at those calves. Hark at the trees again.'

Thomas's belief that his early poems were 'like quintessences of the best parts of [his] prose books – not much sharper or more intense'[13] is disproved by his very first effort, which also contradicts his claim that his poetry has not 'been Frosty very much'. For 'Up in the Wind' shows the clear influence of Frost. A long, blank-verse 'conversation piece' in the manner of Frost's 'Home Burial', 'The Death of a Hired Hand' or 'A Servant to Servants', like them it is related largely through one or more of the protagonists, who live in a lonely place and in a difficult situation. Thomas worried about such an influence, according to W. H. Davies. Davies 'never forgave himself', his biographer writes, 'for his unintentional blunder in telling Thomas, who showed him three of his first poems without disclosing their authorship, that they certainly were the work of Robert Frost', since it was so evident that Thomas 'lacked faith in the individuality of his own work'.[14]

It was probably in an attempt to escape being 'Frosty very much' that Thomas largely avoided blank verse after 'Up in the Wind', – as he told Frost 'tho (or because) I like it best'.[15] When Eleanor questioned him about the difficulty of rhyme a month later, he was able to report: 'No, I don't believe rhyme is at all a *bad* trouble. I use it now more easily than not and always fancy I leave the rhymed pieces as easy as the rest...'[16] When he assured Frost that the rhymes 'dictated themselves decidedly', however, it is hard not to suspect that he was at some level trying to distinguish himself from his mentor. He would also concentrate mainly on shorter lyric poems. While his own explanation to Bottomley – 'I think for the length of a lyric' – may contain some truth, Edna Longley's suggestion, that he felt the need to create 'a kind of sibling differentiation', is also convincing.[17]

Even in this first complete poem, the influence of Frost must not be exaggerated. Thomas's language, while just as close to the speaking voice as Frost's, is quite distinct from the American's. As Vernon Scannell has pointed out, the 'easy colloquial movement and the unforced but striking imagery' of the girl's remarks on the wind, for example, are all Thomas's own. Just as the characters of the two men were different – Frost appearing so much more robust and optimistic than the melancholy, indecisive Thomas – so their verse is, for the most part, quite distinctive in feel.

Thomas's second poem, 'November', for instance, completed a day later than 'Up in the Wind' on 4 December 1914, though inspired partly by his November visit to Frost when it was probably begun, is far less 'Frosty' and more indicative of what is to come. Much shorter, at only 18 rhymed couplets, it also anticipates many other Thomas poems on the countryside and its seasons. Both in the title and opening couplet he names, as he is to do in other poems, a specific month, which he then describes in characteristically unromantic yet loving detail: there is 'mud' as well as 'clean... clear... sweet... cold' skies in his 'November'. It is evidently important to him from the start to tell us the worst – 'I should prefer the truth or nothing'[18] – as well as the best, in order that we should appreciate the best, a creed summed up in 'November's concluding lines:

> Another loves earth and November more dearly
> Because without them, he sees clearly,
> The sky would be nothing more to his eye
> Than he, in any case, is to the sky;
> He loves even the mud whose dyes
> Renounce all brightness to the skies.[19]

Contrast, the poet implies, is vital to a full appreciation of life. This emphasis on the duality of existence, with its constant awareness of 'otherness', shapes many of his poems into mini-dialectics, leading frequently (as in 'November') to the use of contrast, paradox, antithesis and oxymoron.

'November' is far from Thomas's best work, yet it is an impressive achievement for a virtual beginner, showing few signs of the novice. His fear that this 'unexpected ebullition' might be nothing more 'than a doting replica of youthful eagerness' was unfounded: it did, as he hoped, 'represent a culmination', as opposed to the early outpourings of even such great poets as Shelley and Keats.[20] Yet, as he told Bottomley in the same letter, these first poems did 'not get much correction on paper'.[21] There are relatively few changes between the two extant versions.[22] Even after conceding that Garnett might be right to detect a 'jog-trot' rhythm, some slight sententiousness and the influence of Shelley's 'The Sensitive Plant' at the end of 'November', he felt certain enough to leave it unchanged.[23]

Thomas's confidence in his own judgement is even more apparent in his third poem, 'March', completed on 5 December:

> Now I know that Spring will come again,
> Perhaps tomorrow; however late I've patience
> After this night following on such a day.[24]

Frost's influence can still be seen – 'Something they knew' (in line 28) echoes Frost's 'Something there is' in 'Mending Wall' – but faintly and in the more general sense of pointing Thomas to his own prose for inspiration for verse. 'March' also mirrors several passages from the book Frost selected as prose poetry, *In Pursuit of Spring*, which helps to explain Thomas's odd choice of March for a subject in December. The first chapter of *In Pursuit of Spring*, for instance, records 'volatile spring weather'[25] and includes a number of details repeated in the poem. And later in the book Thomas writes: 'All the thrushes of England sang at that hour, and against the background of myriads I heard two or three singing their frank, clear notes in a mad eagerness to have all done before dark; for already the blackbirds were chinking and shifting places along the hedgerows.'[26] Theresa Whistler locates the background to this passage as Dillybrook Farm, near Bath, where de la Mare visited Thomas in March 1913, and argues that the scene which inspired it also gave rise to de la Mare's poem beginning 'Heavenly Archer, bend thy bow' in *Motley*.[27]

In consulting *In Pursuit of Spring* for poetic inspiration, Thomas may also have been reminded of his section on Hardy in the same book. Citing the older poet's belief 'that "the longlegs, the moth and the dumble dore" know "earth-secrets" that he knows not,' Thomas maintains that in 'The Darkling Thrush' this creed is 'to be found in another stage, the birds' song in Winter impelling [Hardy] to think that "some blessed Hope" of which he was unaware, was known to it'.[28] Thomas reverses Hardy's message – in 'March' the narrator is aware, rather than 'unaware' of hope, reflected in his choice of spring rather than winter as a setting:

> What did the thrushes know? Rain, snow, sleet, hail,
> Had kept them quiet as the primroses.
> They had but an hour to sing. On boughs they sang,

On gates, on ground; they sang while they changed perches
And while they fought, if they remembered to fight:
So earnest were they to pack into that hour
Their unwilling hoard of song before the moon
Grew brighter than the clouds. Then 'twas no time
For singing merely. So they could keep off silence
And night, they cared not what they sang or screamed;
Whether 'twas hoarse or sweet or fierce or soft;
And to me all was sweet: they could do no wrong.
Something they knew – I also, while they sang
And after.[29]

Nevertheless, as this extract also shows, Hardy's and Thomas's thrush poems have significant points in common and the difference may be more apparent than real. In *World Without End*, where the Edward-figure ('David') calls Helen ('Jenny') and Eleanor Farjeon ('Margaret') out of doors to hear the nightingale sing, it is clear that he shares Hardy's belief in the 'earth-secrets' of birds: 'We are knowing,' 'David' tells them, 'but the nightingale has wisdom more than solemn old Jenny.'[30]

Other influences have been detected in 'March',[31] but essentially it is the first of Thomas's poems fully to anticipate what is to come. His first-hand knowledge of nature is revealed throughout: to adapt his own comment on Meredith, 'his [thrushes] are real [thrushes]'.[32] A command of natural detail, though characteristic of Thomas, is not, of course, unique to him, whereas the 'voice' and the point of view in 'March' are. The fluid movement of the speaker's mind from the opening ('Now I know that Spring will come again') to its reiteration in the final line ('that Spring returns'), in easy, largely collo-quial speech, marks most of Thomas's poems from this point on. Likewise, the pronounced awareness of the duality of life, of its contrasts, both in content – the 'Rain, snow, sleet, hail' and wind share the scene with the primroses and wildly singing birds – and technique – the use of paradox in 'cold burning', for instance. Characteristic also is the merging of the different senses in phrases such as 'quiet as the primroses' or 'a silence / Stained with all that hour's songs'. While Edna Longley may be right to link such instances of synaesthesia to Thomas's youthful experiments with opium, its persistence in his writing long after he had stopped taking it, suggests that it continued to reflect his own perception of natural phenomena. Typical, too, are the qualifications throughout the poem – 'perhaps to-morrow', 'almost warmth', 'however late', for example, reflecting Thomas's chronic uncertainty and indecisiveness. All these qualities help to distinguish his poetry, which entertains few preconceptions and, unlike the work of many of his Georgian contemporaries, finds beauty in unexpected conjunctions or places. It also emerges as the work of a poet who refuses to moralize.

Yet none of this fully explains the magic of Thomas's verse in 'March' and his best work generally. Thomas himself comes closer to it when he attempts to identify what he finds in the poetry he most admires:

> No remarkable melody; no golden words shot with meaning; a temperate use of images, and none far-fetched; no flattering on modern fashions in descriptions of nature for example; no apostrophe, no rhetoric, nothing 'Celtic'. It is the old miracle that cannot be defined: nothing more than a subtle entanglement of words, so that they rise out of their graves and sing.[33]

These words in praise of Ezra Pound are even more applicable to Thomas's next poem, 'Old Man', where he is at his most characteristic. His fourth poem to be completed in four days on 6 December, yet it shows no sign of strain and is one of his best, his own favourite among his early poems. Frost called it 'the flower of the lot'. It is a poem only Thomas could have written.

By the time he came to compose 'Old Man', he had written several times to Bottomley about the herb of that name, which he had brought back from Bottomley's Lake District home, Well Knowe.[34] He tells Bottomley in 1908, for instance, how another plant gift, bergamot, reminds him 'of sunny rain and the whiteness of Well Knowe whenever I see it'.[35] Two years later he was reporting that 'The Old Man … you gave me is now a beautiful great bush at my study door. The Bergamot is multiplied…'[36] He would take roots and cuttings when he moved to Yew Tree Cottage in 1913. Bottomley's gift of rosemary, symbol of remembrance, did not take, a significant loss in terms of the poem, in which the narrator can 'remember' nothing.

Apart from his piece on 'November', 'Old Man's Beard' is much closer to the poem which follows than the prose version of 'Up in the Wind' was; Thomas had also written in his field notebook on 11 November 1914, less than a month before completing his poem: '*Old Man* scent, I smell again and again not really liking it but venerating it because it holds the secret of something very long ago which I feel I may someday recall, but I have no idea what.'[37] His insistence here and in the finished poem on the failure of such a distinctive smell to recall the past is in direct contrast to the more common literary device of introducing something that suddenly brings back the past, Proust's madeleine being the best-known example of this.[38] This avoidance of the obvious in favour of more elusive sensations, arrived at only after difficulty, is one of the qualities which distinguish Thomas's poems at their best. His refusal, too, to be 'deft' in his verse in the way he is in prose, whatever its origin, gives him (as P. J. Kavanagh notes) affinities with the Modernists.[39] What Robert Wells calls the 'unfinish' of his verse is, as Wells argues, 'sufficiently new' in its way.[40] 'Old Man', for instance, might on a first reading strike the reader as being a jotting down of random impressions and feelings, expressed in quiet, reflective speech, but it is, at heart, an exploration of such universal topics as memory, identity, disintegration, directionlessness and loss.[41] Contrast, as in his first three poems, is an important feature in 'Old Man' and in the best of Thomas's work. The discrepancy between the apparent simplicity of method and the complexity of what is being said sets up a dynamic tension. In addition, the contrast in age between the child and the narrator allows the poet to introduce the idea of the passage of time, without strain. And the child's simple action of plucking the herb allows the narrator to introduce echoes of the Garden of Eden and the Tree of Knowledge which leads on quite naturally to a contemplation of different ways of 'knowing'.

'The Signpost' (see p. 291), completed on 7 December, is the last of this first group of poems to be dated. It may mark a temporary break, as Thomas's anxieties about finding paid work returned. He had written to Cazenove on 2 December, just prior to embarking on his poems, to suggest an anthology, book or article on 'what England means today'. Though the poems which followed in the next five days partially carried out this patriotic plan, he is still pursuing his idea of a book on England on 10 December, despite his agent's failure to respond.

Thomas's next dated poem, 'After Rain', does not emerge until 14 December, a week after 'The Signpost'. It is the first poem in a fresh working notebook, a sign of Thomas's intention of continuing in this new direction. It is also the first of his poems on one of his favourite themes in prose, rain. (see, pp. 5–6) As Coombes notes, an 'interesting "rain" anthology could be compiled from Thomas's writings'.[42] In keeping with his acute awareness of the duality of life, Thomas's rain can have both positive and negative connotations in his work. He sometimes finds rain 'a lively companion' on a walk[43] and in a period of fine weather confesses to 'enjoying the rain of the interval almost as much as the heat itself', especially in Oxford or a London garden,[44] a theme he had explored in his early essay 'Rain'.[45] Yet in another early piece, he notes as a possible 'subject' 'experiencing being alone in world murdered by everlasting rain…'[46] In *Beautiful Wales* (1905) he makes a clear link between suicidal thoughts and the 'pleasure' of rain, quoting Shakespeare's lines from *Cymbeline*.[47] 'After Rain' hints at some of these varied, often contradictory aspects rain holds for Thomas, especially in its paradoxical conclusion, where the raindrops are both 'dark' and 'bright'.

Like 'Up in the Wind' and 'Old Man', 'After Rain' has close parallels with a contemporary prose piece, in this case written the same day as the poem in Thomas's field notebook.[48] In the poem natural details of the prose passage – the yellow crab-apples in the leafless copse, the narrow purple band of dead leaves contrasting with the green grass, the shining raindrops – are given added impact by the personification of the two opposing elements, rain and sun, particularly in the phrase 'pale choked day'.[49]

Thomas himself felt sufficiently pleased with his poems at this point to risk showing them to someone other than Frost and Helen and on 15 December posted at least half a dozen of them to Monro.[50] His choice of Monro is both obvious and puzzling. On the one hand, they had been on friendly terms since 1909. They were still meeting fairly often, either at the Poetry Bookshop, the Mont Blanc or St George's restaurant and Thomas was regularly invited to Monro's 'dinners'. Monro was known to have a fairly open mind on contemporary poetry, publishing such avant-garde collections as *Des Imagistes* (which Thomas had reviewed), as well as the more traditional Georgian poets. Finally, Monro had just sent Thomas his own poems to look at, so what more natural than that Thomas should send Monro his in return?

On the other hand, Thomas's response to Monro's poems had been as frank as he always tried to be in his reviewing, a frankness which sometimes struck the recipient as harsh, even brutal. Monro had appeared to take it well – 'My letter was crude and yours is a tender response,' Thomas wrote with some relief on 15 December in the letter accompanying his own poems. Nevertheless there might have been some resentment on Monro's part. It was not the first time he had asked Thomas for his opinion on his work and on each occasion his friend had been less than positive. In addition, by mid-1913 their friendship may have cooled somewhat: 'I am on my way...not very willingly to Monro's with Hodgson', Thomas had written to Eleanor in July that year.[51] Hodgson's break with Thomas in November 1914, only a month before he sent his poems to Monro, could have been another reason not to expect too favourable a response from someone who was close to Hodgson. Then there was Monro's anger with someone he (erroneously) considered close to Thomas, Wilfrid Gibson.[52] Thomas may also have overestimated Monro's ability to respond to the experimental, or at least different, in poetry: it is rumoured that Monro had rejected Eliot's *The Love Song of J. Alfred Prufrock*, for instance, as 'absolutely insane/inane' in 1914.[53]

Despite all these factors, Thomas appears to have sent his poems off in a hopeful mood: 'If you think anything of them,' he told Monro, 'the writer, who wishes to be very strictly anonymous, would like to see a small book of these and others.'[54] In sending them to Monro, he stressed, he was 'deliver[ing him]self into [his] hands'. When, only four days later, Monro sent them back, apparently unread, his dejection was profound, though it failed to destroy his own faith in them: 'I am sorry,' he replied to Monro, 'because I feel utterly sure they are me. I expect obstacles and I get them.'[55] It was chiefly to save himself 'unnecessary pain', he explained, that he had requested 'no explanation', considering 'one blow...better'.[56]

Monro, who was to reject Thomas's poems again the following year, would try to make amends after Thomas's death. Though his offer to publish them came too late, he would organize a reading from Thomas's verse at the Poetry Bookshop in November 1917.[57] By 1920 he was ready to admit, in *Some Contemporary Poets*, that in rejecting Thomas, he might have overlooked 'the very poet whom the future will recognise as the true genius of our time'.[58]

More importantly, Thomas himself believed that in starting to write poetry he was making 'the nearest approach to self-expression I ever made'.[59]

22

This England (January–February 1915)

I can't imagine that as men are at present, and as I imagine they will long remain, a nation is of much use that is not capable of this violent folly, when the body and whatever of the mind can work with the body prevails and boasts itself. But I should like to avoid too much of this strain because it is not the strain of the men who are fighting or going to fight, but rather of morbid people in whom the balance or fusion of mind and body is impossible, and who admire frantically what is impossible to themselves.

– ET to Margaret Townsend, 23 November 1914

Thomas had still not made up his mind about enlistment by the beginning of 1915. Always aware of the 'road not taken', he continued to waver with Hamlet-like indecision suspecting that he had 'talked and thought too much about it' for action.[1] Eleanor personally hoped that he would accept Frost's suggestion of accompanying him to America when he returned in February 1915. Edward himself was still considering other options, such as teaching English for his ex-Bedales friend Hodson at Bablake School in Coventry, or a job in the historical section of the War Office.[2] Both positions would have been a perfectly respectable option for a man of 36 with a wife and three children to support.

Yet Thomas continued to feel guilty: 'There is no business to allege as a reason [for not enlisting],' he wrote to de la Mare, 'and I imagine that I am going to dig in the garden and save minor expenses, while considering whether I can in reason and decency enlist. I wish they would conscribe me and settle my hesitations.'³ Even Cazenove's surprised response to his ditherings – 'I should have thought your calls were elsewhere' – did not prevent him from feeling the need to make excuses: that he 'would sooner enlist in London with a friend', for instance.⁴ His preparations for another article for the *English Review* 'about what people (myself included) mean when they say England' made him think even harder on his duty to his country.⁵ What his country meant to him is perhaps best illustrated by Eleanor's account of his response when she asked him (after his enlistment) what he was fighting for: 'He stopped and picked up a pinch of earth. "Literally, for this", [he said]. He crumbled it between his finger and thumb and let it fall.'⁶

For the time being, however, the only response he could manage was to write a series of poems on what he loved about England, from her old inns and country songs to her changing seasons, her trees, flowers, herbs and birds. With the exception of 'The Other', and if we include Wales in poems about his country, all his verse up to the end of 1914 would continue this process – 'Birds' Nests', 'The Mountain Chapel', 'The Manor Farm', 'An Old Song (I and II)', 'The Combe' and 'The Hollow Wood'.

Yet the need for volunteers from Britain was more urgent than ever. Turkey's alliance with Germany at the end of 1914 was only one of a number of reasons which led to a deadlock in the opening months of 1915. And Russia's appeal to Britain in January 1915 for help against Turkey led to Britain's decision to send troops to Gallipoli, to relieve pressure on the Caucasus and reopen the supply route to Russia through the Dardanelles. More men were required, not only for this campaign, but also for the equally pressing need to defend the Suez Canal in early February against a Turkish attack. A further plan, to send British and Indian troops to invade Palestine, to protect oil supply lines there, stretched the Allied resources to the utmost.

Thomas's letters are remarkably free of war news during this turbulent period. A badly sprained ankle at the beginning of January left him housebound for three weeks, at a time when he had even less paid work than usual to occupy him. While this enforced inactivity gave him 'only too much time for thinking', about all sorts of things, including enlistment, it also prevented him from taking any physical action and allowed him to concentrate on what still seemed to him the 'unlikely employment' of writing poetry.[7] From 4 January 1915, two days after he damaged his ankle rushing down the steep path from the Shoulder of Mutton to lunch and was still in bed, until 23 January when he began walking again, he wrote 16 poems, including his best-known, 'Adlestrop'.

It is clear that the inspiration for at least half of these came from passages in his field notebooks, which (he told John Freeman) he was rereading during his enforced leisure.[8] While the first piece, 'The New Year', owes its central idea more to Wordsworth's leech-gatherer and other old men met in lonely places, 'The Source' (written second and originally entitled 'The Source of the Ouse at Selsfield') harks back to his field notebook 64 entry for 7 September 1913 at Selsfield House, when 'the 100 firs by Ardingley Road sound[ed] like a far forest or sea':

> Half the night, too, only the wild air speaks
> With wind and rain,
> Till forth the dumb source of the river breaks
> And drowns the rain and wind...[9]

Thomas's powerful urge to write poetry, which had broken through on the same night he had written his notebook entry, finds its parallel in the image of the river bursting its banks, suggesting that one is as much a force of nature as the other.

During this stay at East Grinstead in late 1913, Thomas had also noticed a 'charcoal burner by blue hut piping slowly a bright old country tune and making it melancholy and bird like in the hollow deep valley',[10] a scene which concludes his next poem 'The Penny Whistle'. The poem itself links his love of folk tunes, natural detail and country folk, in a series of strong contrasts, between the 'new moon' in the 'naked frosty blue' and the brooks and the sun, between the vividness of the kingfisher and primroses and the 'black' charcoal burners, between their blackness and the white gleam of their washing and the letter a girl is reading. Visual contrasts are matched by aural ones as the brook's 'roaring with black hollow voices / Betwixt rage and moan' gives way to the charcoal-burner boy 'Slowly and surely playing / On a whistle an olden nursery melody'.[11]

A poem like 'A Private' is particularly close to Thomas's notebook sources, and makes most readers glad that he ignored Bottomley's repeated advice to abandon them, since it is one of his most moving poems about the effect of war on rural England. Two notes made in 1911 or 1912 form its basis: 'Hardy drinker sleeping out in hoarfrosty n[igh]t says he stayed at "Mrs Greenland's Hawthorn Bush"', then (a few pages later, by way of explanation) 'and the mead[ow] is big and sloping w[ith] many fine hawthorns (score or more fifty perhaps) scattered about (Mrs Greenland's Hawthorn Bush)...'[12]

The first draft of 'A Private', written on 7 January before Thomas had decided to enlist, comes across as a simple elegy for a 'labouring man' who slept outside because he chose to, or because he had spent all his money on beer, or because he had no money and did not care. France is not mentioned and the labourer's 'bright coffin' sounds like a reasonably innocuous reference to a natural death. When he answers the curious, who ask 'where do you sleep?', it is with a jokey reference to 'Mrs Greenland's Hawthorn Bush' as though this were the name of an inn. But in the final draft, written after Thomas himself is in the army, he adds to this snapshot of one familiar aspect of English life – the country pub – an allusion to the deaths taking place in France, including that of the labourer. In doing so, he creates a striking and pointed contrast between the pre-war Wiltshire downs and the current corpse-strewn battlefields of France. The 'labouring man' is now, more specifically, a 'ploughman' and also, with an allusion to his army rank, as well as his dislike of busybodies, 'A Private':

A Private

This ploughman dead in battle slept out of doors
Many a frosty night, and merrily
Answered staid drinkers, good bedmen, and all bores:
'At Mrs Greenland's Hawthorn Bush,' said he,
'I slept.' None knew which bush. Above the town,
Beyond 'The Drover', a hundred spot the down
In Wiltshire. And where now at last he sleeps
More sound in France – that, too, he secret keeps.[13]

Thomas's use of the metaphor of 'sleep' as a euphemism for death, its suggestion of a gentle but temporary release from everyday cares to describe a death which we suspect was anything but gentle or peaceful in France, creates a series of ironic contrasts between England and France, between past and present, peace and war. The last lines '…now at last he sleeps / More sound' forces the reader to consider what exactly is meant by 'sleeping'. The whole poem reflects Thomas's growing sense of the impact of war on the England he loved and is a suitably elusive memorial to the missing. It is also, if we take into account his later revision of it, his first poem to refer to the war directly.

Sometimes the notebooks provide only a small detail, but it is usually a telling one. In 'Snow', for instance, written a day after 'A Private' almost certainly to please the 4-year-old Myfanwy who was keeping him company, the lovely phrase 'the silence of snow' is taken from a notebook of five years previously.[14] In others the borrowing is extensive, as in 'Tears', 'The Cuckoo' and 'Man and Dog'. Like 'A Private', 'Tears' is based on at least two separate entries and shows that Thomas was able in reading back over his notes to make new links between them. His field notebook for April 1909 (no. 32), recording a visit to the Tower of London with Merfyn, notes 'British Grenadiers…in band in sunlight in still air', giving details of 'Eton jackets and fair hair and rosy faces', which would become in the poem an even more appealing picture of innocence, freshness and health: 'Soldiers in line, young English countrymen, / Fair-haired and ruddy, in white tunics'.[15] Without being jingoistic Thomas conveys the sense of patriotism the sight stirs in him, perhaps with the lines he had quoted from Jefferies in his biography in mind: 'So subtle is the chord of life that sometimes to watch troops marching in rhythmic order, undulating along the column as the feet are lifted, brings tears into my eyes.'[16] This 'chord' is struck also for Thomas by the quite different sight, noted a number of times in his notebooks, of what becomes in the poem 'twenty hounds stream[ing] by [him], not yet combed out / But still all equals in their rage of gladness / Upon the scent'.[17] Yet, as Cooke points out, not only do the two memories reflect in each other but *on* each other. For despite their superficial splendour, both hounds and soldiers also suggest a less attractive reality, that they are both geared to kill.[18] At the same time Thomas admits to being moved by both sights, especially that of the soldiers in the Tower courtyard playing 'The British Grenadiers':

> The men, the music piercing that solitude
> And silence, told me truths I had not dreamed,
> And have forgotten since their beauty passed.

Sometimes a prose passage from the field notebooks is turned almost word for word into a poem, 'A Gentleman' being a case in point – a conversation overheard in a pub in 1912 between a 'stranger' and a 'Gypsy dame'.[19] One of the most successful conversions of notes to verse, which followed two days after 'Snow', is Thomas's poem, 'Adlestrop'. Looking back through his notebooks for the previous year, he had seized on an apparently minor incident: 'Train stopping…at Adlestrop vi [i.e. June] 1914.' It was an event he had described only briefly at the time, not distinguishing it from several similar halts during the journey he and Helen had taken on 24 June 1914 to visit the Frosts in Gloucestershire. His contemporary prose account, opening with a description of the 'tiers above tiers of white cloud' over Battersea Park as they set off from his parents' home, continues:

> …then at Oxford tiers of pure white with loose large masses above and gaps of dark clear blue above haymaking and elms
>
> Then we stopped at Adlestrop, through the willows could be heard a chain of blackbirds songs at 12.45 and one thrush and no man seen, only a hiss of engine letting off steam.
>
> Stopping outside Campden by banks of long grass willowherbs and meadowsweet, extraordinary silence between the two periods of travel – looking out on grey dry stones between metals and the shining metals and over it all the elms willowy and long grass – one man clears his throat – a greater than rustic silence. No house in view Stop only for a minute till signal is up.[20]

Thomas's reaction to his recovered memory of that summer day provides him with 'Adlestrop''s opening stanza, the one Eleanor Farjeon cited as a particularly clear instance of his 'own cadence, the movement of his beautiful reflective voice':

> Yes. I remember Adlestrop–
> The name, because one afternoon
> Of heat the express-train drew up there
> Unwontedly. It was late June.[21]

As John Carey notes, 'Thomas's voice is not only distinctive, it is elusive, like a persistent regretful note heard at the edge of hearing'; his cadences, he argues, 'are the sound of a mind communing with itself'.[22]

By placing the precise but uncommon word 'unwontedly' so prominently at the beginning of the fourth line, Thomas emphasizes the unusual nature of the stop, which in turn creates a slight sense of unease. Yet there is no mention in the field notebook account of this journey on the Great Western Railway from Paddington to Worcester of the halt at Adlestrop being unscheduled. Indeed, it is unlikely that the Thomases' train was the 'express' specified in the poem, or that it stopped 'unwontedly', since the one daily express on that route in 1914 left too late to arrive at the time noted in the account, 12.45 p.m. While such details do not matter in themselves, they do give a valuable insight into Thomas's poetic methods, suggesting that just as he did not hesitate to conflate details from separate moments in the journey into observations on Adlestrop alone, so he changed the scheduled halt at the station on a stopping train into an *un*expected one on an imaginary express deliberately. (His first version of the poem specifies merely that the train is a 'steam' train, altered only later to 'express'.)

By introducing that word 'unwontedly' the poet also transforms the everyday into a realm of uncertainty and unknownness, begging questions he does not answer. In Thomas's hands the ordinary acquires extraordinary if indefinite significance. And it is partly the refusal to pin down the significance of such small, everyday events in his poetry which allows his readers to participate more fully in his poems by linking them with his or her own memories of apparently insignificant moments which nevertheless in retrospect become significant moments of being. As Margaret Drabble has observed: 'This is England, seen so briefly, so accidentally, so lastingly, from a passing train: who has not seen it so, and do we not all at times wonder if this is the only way to see it?'[23] It is crucial to the success of 'Adlestrop' that readers are able to identify with this almost universal experience of a sudden unexplained halt at a lonely country station which remains in the memory for no easily definable reason. The tension between the detailed outer scene, so vividly recreated from the notebook entry, and the sense that this is more than simply a description of a deserted, rural station takes the poem into the realm of what John Bayley has characterized as Thomas's 'subdued intensity':[24]

The steam hissed. Someone cleared his throat.
No one left and no one came

On the bare platform. What I saw
Was Adlestrop – only the name

And willows, willow-herb, and grass,
And meadowsweet, and haycocks dry,
No whit less still and lonely fair
Than the high cloudlets in the sky.

And for that minute a blackbird sang
Close by, and round him, mistier,
Farther and farther, all the birds
Of Oxfordshire and Gloucestershire.

The essence of rural England is here, its villages, its flowers, its skies, its harvests, and all the peacefulness that we associate nostalgically with such remote places. And a sense of loss is conveyed and perfectly reflected in the faintly regretful, almost elegiac tone of the poem, a sadness comparable to that of Keats's 'Ode to a Grecian Urn', which describes a similar 'silence', 'slow time' and a 'little town…emptied of its folk'. Yet 'Adlestrop' ends on an affirmative note as first a lone blackbird, then 'all the birds' in the surrounding countryside of Oxfordshire and Gloucestershire burst into song. Thomas may have remembered nothing much in real life of Adlestrop, but by naming it, choosing it for his poem he has singled it out and given it a human meaning.

'Adlestrop' was written in Thomas's bedroom in a deckchair, after three days in bed. The following day, 9 January, Thomas was 'downstairs – hopping' and eventual recovery began to seem more of a reality. So, too, did his possible involvement in the war and allusions to it become even more noticeable in his poetry. In 'Tears', for instance, written on 8 January, the possible fate of the young soldiers is evidently in his mind. And in the field notebook entry which underpins 'Man and Dog' this probable fate is spelt out when the 'short stiffish oldish man' Thomas describes meeting in November 1914, tells him that he was 'thinking about soldiers in France – terrible affair in cold weather', and hoping that they were not 'lying in trenches in this winter weather'.[25] In the poem based on this entry, after giving a potted history of the man's life and a detailed account of the 'small brown bitch' who goes with him everywhere (despite the fact that she deters farmers from offering him a 'shakedown' for the night) concludes:

… 'Many a man sleeps worse tonight
Than I shall.' 'In the trenches.' 'Yes, that's right
But they'll be out of that – I hope they be–
This weather, marching after the enemy.'[26]

The third of a number of poems structured round a dialogue between the narrator/poet and a country-dweller, 'Man and Dog' is the first to anticipate one of Thomas's most subtle discussions of the war between a soldier-narrator and a ploughman in 'As the team's head-brass'.

There are also hints in these poems written during Thomas's convalescence of his sense of entering new territory as he ponders the possibility of a complete change of life-style, and with it a plunge into the unknown. In 'Over the Hills', written the day after 'Adlestrop', the narrator recalls 'the day I passed the horizon ridge / To a new country' and 'the path I had to find', together with 'the inn where all were kind, / All were strangers'.[27] In 'The Lofty Sky' he feels 'like a fish that lives / In weeds and mud' and (in an echo of Yeats's 'Innisfree') 'would arise and go far / To where the lilies are'.[28] The poem which most effectively conveys Thomas's feelings at a time of a potential change of great magnitude is 'The Bridge', which would be written after a further two months of hesitation. It seems clear that he intended it to be read symbolically as the moment he is arriving at his lonely decision to leave the known, his family, friends and writing, for the unknown of the army and France:

I have come a long way today:
On a strange bridge alone,
Remembering friends, old friends,
I rest, without smile or moan,
As they remember me without smile or moan.

All are behind, the kind
And the unkind too, no more
Tonight than a dream. The stream
Runs softly, yet drowns the Past,
The dark-lit stream has drowned the Future and the Past.

No traveller has rest more blest
Than this moment brief between
Two lives, when the Night's first lights

And shades hide what has never been,
Things goodlier, lovelier, dearer than will be or have been.[29]

Haynes cites 'The Bridge' as expressing 'exactly the mood of a man who has walked all day and gained the mental repose that comes in the evening... It may be remembered that [Thomas] never talked so well as when walking with his elastic, long stride.'[30] 'The Path', written a fortnight after 'The Bridge', would make similar use of the landscape in its last line to convey Thomas's unsettled state: '...till, sudden, [the path] ends where the wood ends.'[31]

It would be misleading to suggest that every poem of this pre-enlistment period alludes to war, though all are, of course, written in the shadow of that conflict. The verses written between 15 and 23 January, for instance, with the exception of 'Man and Dog', are concerned rather with aspects of nature, such as bird-song ('The Cuckoo', 'The Unknown Bird'), the beauty of the everyday ('Swedes'), a visit to a 'Mill-Pond', or with more abstract subjects, such as 'Beauty', 'Ambition', 'Health' or 'Glory'. Yet another variation on the dialogue Thomas was already beginning to favour in poetry, 'Ambition' shows the narrator exploring an aspect of himself he 'never knew' until a particularly invigorating day of early spring, when 'the jackdaws began to shout and float and soar.'[32]

One of the last poems to be written during this initial outpouring of poetry, had been one of the first to be 'meditate[d]', 'The Gypsy', inspired by the sight of a gypsy caravan in Wales the previous October. 'Their gramophone and cosy lighted tent so near wind and stars' made him think 'how feeble and aesthetic [his] admiration of the mountains was, when [he] knew nothing of life on them.'[33] The gypsies' vitality had struck him forcibly at Selsfield House in December 1913 when, in a particularly depressed state, the twilight had seemed to him 'nothing but gradations of inhuman... dark, as of an underworld' in which his 'soul fled over it experiencing the afterdeath – friendless, vacant, hopeless.'[34] As in the poem which followed a year later, it was 'the spark in the Gypsy boy's black eyes as he played and stamped his tune', which had helped rescue Thomas from complete despair on that occasion. He had been drawn from his teenage years to what he believed to be the gypsies' freer life, lived in closer contact with nature than he ever managed to achieve. His notebooks are full of references to them, gypsy girls in particular, whom he describes with a mixture of romanticism and realism: 'Gypsy girl...w[ith] child and looked thro' me and never noticed my admiration...walking w[ith] a mouth organ – shockingly ill-fitting dresscoat and hat – dark almond eyes pink dark side-turning face hung down and stooping slouch...'[35]

The completion of 'The Gypsy' on 22 January and 'Ambition' on the twenty-third marks the end of Thomas's imprisonment indoors; on 24 January he was outside 'garden[ing] a little' and on the twenty-seventh travelling to London with his mother who had been visiting.[36] He had not enjoyed 'being obliged to be indoors in [his] tiny house with no outlook practically, within sound of 4 children very often squabbling and [his] wife over-worked, and worst of all with [himself] always [there]'.[37]

One purpose of Thomas's London visit would be to enquire about joining the National Service League, a patriotic organization set up in 1902 which advocated National Service or conscription. It had suspended its campaign when war broke out, however, a fact of which Thomas was unaware; so, too, apparently, was John Freeman, who had recommended it in response to an enquiry from Thomas on 16 January about information on 'any occupation going at the front of a non-militant kind'. 'Brooding over it' at Steep had not convinced Thomas that he would 'make much more of a soldier than that', but just 'to get rid of the thoughts' he had had that he ought 'to do something': 'I hate crowds,' he concluded, 'I hate uncertainty. So naturally I hate the idea of being in the army in any capacity.'[38]

Thomas had also consulted MacAlister about 'military employment', more specifically the Army Service Corps, which he believed would be 'active at the front but [do] no fighting'.[39] He was partly worried by not being physically fit enough for a fighting unit – 'flat feet and perhaps other deficiencies' – but also convinced that there were jobs he would 'be more capable of than shouldering a gun'.[40] The idea of killing a man seems to have been as 'distasteful' to him at this stage as joining the army at all.[41] One of his London calls on his late January visit would be to the Duke of York's Regimental Headquarters, to enquire about joining one of the Cyclists' Battalions of the Territorials, mainly responsible for reconnaissance and communications.

Nothing concrete came of Thomas's first serious attempt to enlist and his visit ended in disappointment with the need to cancel his planned weekend with the Frosts in Gloucestershire. His ankle was still too weak for more travel and the Frosts themselves were busy with last-minute details of their return to America. They had offered to take the 15-year-old Merfyn to join his ex-preparatory school headmaster, Mr Scott, out there. 'He badly needed to get away from me and from school life,' Edward explained to Mac, 'and I can't say I have begun to feel any pang.'[42] With Bottomley he was even franker, writing on 13 February, the day of Merfyn's departure:

> I don't pretend to expect this or that of it but I believe the time had to come to let him see what people were who couldn't make him do things as I can or a schoolmaster can but who nevertheless will expect him to give as well as take. However...I don't know except that he could not be worse off, even if the Germans torpedo the *St Paul* (an American ship).

It is a curiously detached response from someone as sensitive as Thomas in other areas, supporting Eleanor's charge of poor relations with his son. It was probably with her criticism in mind that he wrote to her about Merfyn shortly before his departure: 'I shall be glad for him but sorry for myself because it means the end of any chance of being anything to the boy.'[43] He found, in the words of his poem 'Parting', composed the day Helen took Merfyn up to Liverpool for his passage to America, that:

> ...memory made

> Parting today a double pain:
> First because it was parting; next
> Because the ill it ended vexed
> And mocked me from the Past again...[44]

The title of another poem written the same day suggests that Thomas felt that Merfyn was 'First known when lost'.

The whole question of whether Merfyn would be able to go with the Frosts to America had been uncertain until the last moment and Thomas had still not known for sure when he made his London visit on 27 January. The one successful outcome from that trip, apart from seeing friends like Eleanor and John Freeman, had been a commission from Oxford University Press for an anthology of prose and verse to give, Thomas hoped, 'as various an impression as possible of English life, landscape, thought, ambition and glory'.[45] His 'Note' to *This England*, as he would call his anthology, suggests that one of his aims was to counteract the flood of jingoistic writing inspired by the war:

> This is an anthology from the work of English writers rather strictly so called. Building round a few most English poems like 'When icicles hang by the wall', – excluding professedly patriotic writing because it is generally bad and because indirect praise is sweeter and more profound, – never aiming at what a committee from Great Britain and Ireland might call complete, – I wished to make a book as full of English character and country as an egg is full of meat.[46]

His intention was to include 'anything that makes us feel England particularly,' he told Eleanor who, like many of his other friends, was asked to offer suggestions.[47]

His own first thoughts were of 'Hotspur's ridicule of Glendower (and of all Celts)' in Shakespeare's *Henry IV*, George Herbert's 'The British Church' and Keats's 'Ode to Autumn', his second of classic English writers, poets like Chaucer, Milton, Wordsworth, Coleridge and Hardy, the diarists Evelyn and Pepys and prose-writers such as Bunyan, Latimer, Walton, Fielding, Cobbett and Borrow. More contemporary favourites also crept in, Doughty, de la Mare, Hudson and Bottomley. His aim was 'to arrange it so that it w[ould] be as simple and rich as a plum pudding', an appropriately English metaphor.[48]

Thomas's wide knowledge of English literature, recently refreshed by his research for *A Literary Pilgrim in England*, made him ideally suited for the job. It allowed him to include not only his own favourites and friends, but also two of his own poems written during the compilation of the anthology, 'The Manor Farm' and 'Haymaking', his first book publication as a poet. Thomas Seccombe, who called *This England* "the best…ever done', claimed that it was 'really an artist's note-book…annotating the life-enthusiasm of a born prose-master, whose love of his country was as generous as it was instinctive'.[49]

'The Manor Farm', written two months after Thomas's proposal of *This England* to Cazenove in October 1914, not only includes the title of the anthology in its last line, but also encapsulates the elusive quality Thomas wants to convey of Englishness. After describing a typically English village scene of ancient farmhouse, church and yew tree sleeping 'in a Sunday silentness' on a February day, broken only by the sound of three cart-horses 'swishing their tails / Against a fly', the narrator concludes:

> The Winter's cheek flushed as if he had drained
> Spring, Summer and Autumn at a draught
> And smiled quietly. But 'twas not Winter –
> Rather a season of bliss unchangeable
> Awakened from farm and church where it had lain
> Safe under tile and thatch for ages since
> This England, Old already, was called Merry.[50]

Another quintessentially English scene, 'Haymaking', is the subject of the second of his poems slipped into this anthology under his pseudonym Edward Eastaway. It, too, aims to convey what Thomas values most about England, centred for him round rural life, its seasons, its birds, its flowers, its trees. The detail is, as always, closely observed and calls to mind a painting by one of his favourite English landscape painters, Gainsborough, Morland or Crome, an unremarkable scene of treasured familiarity:

> The smooth white empty road was lightly strewn
> With leaves – the holly's Autumn falls in June –
> And fir cones standing stiff up in the heat.
> The mill-foot water tumbled white and lit
> With tossing crystals, happier than any crowd
> Of children pouring out of school aloud.
> And in the little thickets where a sleeper
> For ever might lie lost, the nettle-creeper
> And garden warbler sang unceasingly;
> While over them shrill shrieked in his fierce glee
> The swift with wings and tail as sharp and narrow
> As if the bow had flown off with the arrow.[51]

Thomas had to wait until autumn 1915 to see these poems in a book (Guthrie would include 'House and Man' and 'Interval' in the magazine *Root and Branch* a few months earlier and Thomas had included 'Eluned' in *Beautiful Wales*, but under the guise of a translation). His decision to include them, he said, was to make up a shortfall in the word-count at the last minute, but may well have stemmed also from a conviction that no one else would publish them. After Monro had sent them back unread in December 1914, Eleanor, only the second person to be shown his verse apart from Helen and Frost, had offered to approach *Blackwood's Magazine*. William Blackwood, who had published Thomas's first book, *The Woodland Life*, but declined the second, had started accepting work by Eleanor for his magazine by early 1915 and she was on friendly terms with him. Edward's diffidence about his verse, yet his desire to see it made public, emerges clearly in his response to her on 20 February: 'Here are four poems…for you to palm off on Blackwood if you can. I shall be enormously pleased if you can.' Her own letter to Blackwood accompanying the poems she sent shows how immediately she had understood and admired Thomas's verse:

> I want to introduce you to – not my own but the work of Mr Edward Eastaway. He is not yet known as a poet, but I think he will and should be. He is a man who feels England to her roots, and the poems are so deeply English in character, and seem so like a quiet and dignified growth of her earth, that I believe this is the right moment for them to appear, and you will know whether Maga [*Blackwood's Magazine*] is the right place. Though two of them touch in their own vein on our soldiers, they cannot be called poems of the war, but I do think they are essentially poems of Britain, and could have sprung only from the soil we love and are fighting for.[52]

Unfortunately, Blackwood found the poems 'something of a puzzle', though 'exceedingly interesting', and returned them promptly. Thomas himself then started sending them out to periodicals – the *Nation*, *The Times*, the *Spectator*, the *English Review*, the *Saturday Westminster Gazette*, *Country Life* and others. Many of the literary editors of these magazines were friends and would probably have looked kindly on anything sent in his own name, but he persisted, either from pride or fear, in keeping his pseudonym. Every one of the poems sent out between March and June was returned, their considerable achievement unrecognized in an era which veered between the comfortable Georgianism of poets like Gibson and Abercrombie and the challenging Modernism of poets such as Pound, Flint and 'H[ilda] D[oolittle]'. Only Thomas's close friends, Guthrie and Bottomley, let in on their true authorship from the start, would believe in them sufficiently in Thomas's lifetime either to publish or advise publishing them.

23

MARLBOROUGH AND THE FIELDS OF FLANDERS
(MARCH–JULY 1915)

Despite the indifference or outright rejection Thomas met with and his own indifference about the fate of his poems in early 1915, he continued to write them, often daily, sometimes more than one a day. By the beginning of March, with *This England* almost completed and a void threatening, he told Bottomley that he had no clear idea of 'what [he] really want[ed] to do' next, yet at the same time confessed: 'But I have begun to write in verse and am impatient of anything else. I am trying to test the unsympathetic world first by using a pseudonym.'[1] Promising to show Bottomley 'someday' what he was attempting, he speculates: 'Perhaps it is only like doing the best parts of my prose in verse and leaving out the connecting futile parts. That would be something if it were self-contained and better than the best of my prose as I imagine it is.'[2]

Thomas's final sentence concerning his turn to poetry – 'but it doesn't simplify the problem of living' – is particularly interesting, suggesting that this was very much on his mind. And it would be enlistment which would, in one sense, 'simplify the problem of living' for Thomas. Yet at the same time it may have been the desire to write verse which delayed his decision to enlist initially, since he believed that there would be no time for it in the army.

There is little doubt that his commission for *This England* and another one shortly afterwards – what he called his 'scraps of work' – in the first six months of 1915 'prevent[ed him] from quite seriously facing' the question of enlistment, though he was still trying to find 'something like a niche' for himself 'to crawl into' in the army, 'excepting a trench'.[3] Meanwhile his verse continued, 'occasional' only in the sense that he seized on almost every 'occasion' to write it. Merfyn's departure for America – though not that of Robert Frost and his family, who spent a last weekend with the Thomases on 6 February – was only one of a number of events marked in poetry that month. A discussion with Bottomley about houses, for instance, and the sighting of a 'magpie in oak tip like a weathercock' (in his field notebook 80), together with a previous prose piece on a man called Norgett in *In Pursuit of Spring*, would provide the germ for 'House and Man', a poem about the invasion of the outside world into a normally sealed domestic interior. It was a division Thomas felt he had failed to maintain at Wick Green, which he likened in retrospect to 'one of those carpets that can be used either side and failed to keep out the weather'.[4] (His two other poems on a similar subject, 'The New House' and 'Wind and Mist', would follow on 19 March and 1 April respectively.) Unlike Frost's 'An Old Man's Winter Night', which it may have influenced, 'House and Man' is also, like 'Adlestrop', about the workings of memory, possibly also his own indecision:

> But why I call back man and house again
> Is that now on a beech-tree's tip I see
> As then I saw – I at the gate, and he
> In the house darkness, – a magpie veering about,
> A magpie like a weathercock in doubt.[5]

A similarly close observation of birds, detailed in his field notebook on 4 February during some routine gardening, or on his way up to his study – '[they] perch simply in hedge and talk and chatter and whistle with heads up, making a sort of spiky beard under beaks' – would inspire the fifth stanza in 'The Barn' a few weeks later:

> Starlings used to sit there with bubbling throats
> Making a spiky beard as they chattered
> And whistled and kissed, with heads in the air...[6]

Other 'occasions', like his thirty-seventh birthday ('March the Third') or the sowing of seeds in March ('Sowing'), provide subjects for verse. Like many other poems by Thomas at this time – 'But these things also', 'The Barn and the Down', 'Two Pewits', 'The Path', 'The Wasp Trap', 'A Tale' – neither 'March the Third' nor 'Sowing' depend for their effect on the dramatic or extraordinary, but on the little, apparently unremarkable, familiar aspects of everyday life, which Thomas's acutely developed senses enable the reader to experience as if for the first time. The sight and sound of 'Two Pewits' in the 'after-sunset sky'; 'The Path' with 'the wood that overhangs / And under-yawns it' and 'that looks / As if it led on to some legendary / Or fancied place'; 'The Wasp Trap' hanging from the dead apple-bough and looking 'lovelier' in the moonlight than any star; 'the fragments of blue plates' on the site of the ruined cottaged like a 'periwinkle crawl[ing] / With flowers in its hair into the wood' in 'A Tale', 'the barn / At the edge of the town, / So huge and dark that it seemed / It was the hill' in 'The Barn and the Down', are all sights we have seen but not seen fully until Thomas shows them to us.

In 'The Barn and the Down' Thomas also gives an everyday scene symbolic overtones, the decrepit, empty barn providing an analogy for himself and his own feelings of physical frailty and uselessness as he continues to vacillate about enlisting, a theme which would find its fullest expression in 'There was a time':

> But now that there is something I could use
> My youth and strength for, I deny the age,
> The care and weakness that I know – refuse
> To admit that I am unworthy of the wage
> Paid to a man who gives up eyes and breath
> For what would neither heed nor ask his death.[7]

Increasingly as Thomas regains his physical strength, his thoughts turn to what the soldiers are enduring in France. It is a bird again, the melancholy cry of an owl, that partly inspires the poem of that name, written on 24 February 1915 but based on many earlier experiences of arriving at the end of a long walk, tired, hungry and cold, to look forward to 'food, fire and rest':

> ...telling me plain what I escaped
> And others could not, that night, as in I went

And salted was my food and my repose,
Salted and sobered, too, by the bird's voice
Speaking for all who lay under the stars,
Soldiers and poor, unable to rejoice.[8]

'The Bridge', written two days later and already quoted, also appears to concern itself with the war, more specifically Thomas's need to decide on his own role in it.[9] 'In Memoriam (Easter 1915)', written two days after the event, on 6 April, shows how even the most beautiful of sights – 'the flowers left thick at nightfall in the woods' – remind him of 'the men, / Now far from home, who, with their sweethearts, should / Have gathered them and will do never again'.[10]

Yet once again Thomas deferred making a decision as he set to work on his last commissioned prose book. No sooner had he finished *This England* and the indexing of *A Literary Pilgrim in England* than J. P. Collins, with whom he had been negotiating since mid-February, commissioned him to write 75,000 words on *The Life of the Duke of Marlborough* for Chapman & Hall. The life of an outstanding military hero who had won so many military victories for England was an obvious choice for a publisher in 1915. 'The achievements of the first Duke of Marlborough acquire particular interest at the present time,' Chapman & Hall's dust-jacket would declare, 'when Britain is once more fighting on the fields of Flanders for the freedom of the world.' The Allies' attempts to penetrate the German trenches at Neuve Chapelle, Aubers and Festubert from March to May had been unsuccessful, as had the Second Battle of Ypres, which was fought in the same area Thomas was writing about, from 22 April to 25 May 1915, the same period when he was researching and writing about Marlborough's life. The further heavy losses there would only confirm that the stalemate continued on the Western Front, which increased the pressure on the British to enlist anyone fit enough to fight.

For the time being, however, Thomas devoted his energies to writing *Marlborough*, a task for which he was ideally suited, on paper. An experienced biographer by 1915, Thomas had also specialized at Oxford in the period concerned, the seventeenth century. Yet he described Chapman & Hall's commission as 'by far the worst job I ever undertook'; he had accepted it because it had seemed the 'only chance of earning anything', he told Bottomley.[11] The prospect 'stifled' him, though he knew that he was 'lucky' to have any work at all in the circumstances.[12] It was not the kind of book he would have chosen to write, but he had finally been forced to accept that his own choice of subjects and more imaginative approach was unlikely to earn him money, except occasionally in magazines.

Thomas dismissed his completed work on *Marlborough* as 'undigested – useless', admitting to Frost that he had 'virtually paraphrased from old books and [his] memory of others, and hardly any more, except some argument about conduct and character'.[13] He found his subject, the Duke, such an uninspiring figure that he had deliberately had to play down the Duchess, because she would have made the Duke seem an even 'dimmer' figure than he was.[14] There is no doubt whatsoever that he had worked hard on his commission, as the 75 readers' slips taken out from the library at the British Museum for books on Marlborough, many of them in French, show. *Marlborough* is both competent and readable.

More importantly, *Marlborough* is a rare record of Thomas's feelings about the current war as the English faced first the sinking of the *Lusitania* by German submarines on 7 May, then the start of Zeppelin raids on London at the end of the month, events which largely negated the hope created by Italy's entry into the war on the Allies' side during the same period. In his account of another great soldier who preceded Marlborough, the Welshman Sir Thomas Morgan (1604–79), for instance, Thomas notes that 'he and his men fought all over the sands and the dyked lands where the English lie now (1915)' and that 'what was once a battlefield was likely to be so again'.[15] More specifically he points out that: 'Continually in Marlborough's letters he names the places everybody knows today. He posts 1600 men to Armentières... La Bassée was a central point in the long defensive French lines which were named after it. Mons was besieged again and again.'[16]

However little mention there is of specific happenings of the war in Thomas's letters and diaries for 1915, it is clear from such passages that he followed events on the Western Front closely throughout that year. It is also plain from his account of Marlborough's battles that he had no illusions about the brutal realities of warfare:

> They fought in armour by lantern and candle in galleries thirty or forty feet underground at Tournay; they mined and countermined, and blew men into the air or were blown up, by hundreds at a time; they were

suffocated by smoke, buried alive by falling earth, drowned by inunda-
tions; meeting unexpectedly sometimes these moles fought by mistake
with friends. What with cannon, bombs, grenades, small shot, boiling
pitch, tar, oil, brimstone and scalding water, the English Grenadiers had
scarce six sound men in the company after the siege of Lille.[17]

Apart from the armour and 'boiling pitch, tar, oil, brimstone and scalding
water', this could be a description of the Western Front in 1915. Other
passages outlining the gulf between 'soldiers on active service and soldiers
at home' suggest that by the time Thomas wrote it he no longer believed
that he could quieten his conscience with a safe desk job in England.[18] His
sympathy is all for the serving soldiers who faced the incomprehension of
'those who never saw their hardships'.[19] He quotes the author of a previous
life of Marlborough saying that the English public 'ought...to see the
dead horses in the miserable marshes of a rainy season; they should smell
"the stink of mortality"'.[20] Few or none of the poems Thomas had read
for his article on 'War Poetry' had included such realistic details; even
by mid-1915 its focus was largely on the uplifting nature of war and the
honour of fighting for England. Though Thomas would choose not to
include such grim details in his own poetry, he was ahead of many of his
contemporaries in facing the reality of war.

   Marlborough took approximately three months to research and write
and, to begin with, Thomas feared that it would dry up his poetry; 'Will
You Come?' appears to be an appeal to his muse not to abandon him. If so,
it is an anticipation of what his prose book might do to his poetic instincts,
rather than a reality, since his verse continued to flow during late March
and most of April. Indeed, he wrote one of his most successful poems, 'Lob',
during the period he was expecting to sign the commission for *Marlborough*.

   In its attempt to convey Englishness, 'Lob' is the verse equivalent of
This England, which had set out to anthologize 'what England means to
people'.[21] Thomas had known the character of 'Lob' since the age of 8,
when he had encountered him in the story 'Lob Lie-by-the-fire' by the
popular Victorian children's writer Juliana Horatia Ewing, which opens:

Lob lie-by-the-fire – the Lubber-fiend as Milton calls him – is a rough
kind of Brownie or House Elf, supposed to haunt some north-country
homesteads, where he does the work of the farm labourers.[22]

Ewing, whose 'Brownie' would inspire the Baden-Powells with the name of their girl-pack, then quotes the relevant passage from Milton's *L'Allegro* referring to the 'lubber-fiend', which Thomas himself would reread as an adult. Another admirer of Ewing, Rudyard Kipling, created his own version of Lob in *Puck of Pook's Hill* (1906), which Thomas almost certainly knew. But the influences go far beyond Ewing, Milton and Kipling: Lob is a culmination of Thomas's relish and admiration for a series of old countrymen encountered in life, literature and legend. A recognizable portrait of 'Dad' Uzzell opens the poem, appropriately so, since it was he who had first introduced Edward to the Wiltshire countryside which becomes the setting for 'Lob'. From one of his earliest essays, 'The Wiltshire Mole Catcher', onwards Thomas had written of such earthy types. 'Old Jack Norman.../ Jaunty and old, crooked and tall' in 'May 23' is a successor to Jack Horseman, 'the tall old watercress-man' with his 'Indian complexion' in *The Happy-Go-Lucky Morgans*, based on a real-life tramp, Helen claimed, his roguishness part of his appeal. Other watercress-seller tramps in Thomas's work are called 'Jackalone' (*The South Country*) and Jack Runaway. The 'Jack' in 'Lob', one of a number of generic names in the poem, is called 'Button', an ancient family referred to in one of Thomas's favourite authors, John Aubrey, underlining the theme of historical continuity which dominates the poem. Many of his poetic models echo his anthology choices for *This England* and are embedded in folklore. Puck, otherwise known as Robin Goodfellow, appears in Shakespeare's *A Midsummer Night's Dream*, as well as in Kipling's *Puck of Pook's Hill*, where Puck is 'the oldest thing in England'. (Eleanor had recommended 'Lob' to Blackwood for its 'old-wives, puckish spirit' and, though he rejected it, he agreed that there was 'a Puckishness about the piece which is very attractive'.[23])

Further models for Lob include the folk figures 'Hob' (or 'hob-goblin') and 'Hodge' (a generic name for the English farm-labourer). Thomas's extensive knowledge of folklore, from the folk-songs researched for *The Pocket Book of Poems and Songs for the Open Air* (1907), Irish folklore for *Celtic Stories* (1911), Scandinavian mythology for *Norse Tales* (1912) and English proverbs for *Four-and-Twenty Blackbirds* (1915) added to his familiarity with the works of Yeats, William Morris and Charles Doughty's *The Dawn of Britain* also help supply a rich background to this celebration of what Alan Hawkins calls 'village England' at a time when it appeared to be under threat.[24]

Thomas's aim in 'Lob' is both mystical and patriotic in the widest sense, that is to convey an impression of the continuity of English rural life through history in the character of Lob:

> … The man was wild
> And wandered. His home was where he was free.
> Everybody has met one such man as he.
> Does he keep clear old paths that no-one uses
> But once a life-time when he loves or muses?
> He is English as this gate, these flowers, this mire.
> And when at eight years old Lob lie-by-the-fire
> Came in my books, this was the man I saw.
> He has been in England as long as dove and daw,
> Calling the wild cherry tree the merry tree,
> The rose campion Bridget-in-her-bravery;
> And in a tender mood, he as I guess,
> Christened one flower Love-in-idleness,
> And while he walked from Exeter to Leeds
> One April called all cuckoo-flowers Milkmaids.
> From him old herbal Gerard learnt, as a boy,
> To name wild clematis the Traveller's-joy.
> Our blackbirds sang no English till his ear
> Told him they called his Jan Toy 'Pretty dear'.[25]

Thomas's fascination with place-names, already revealed in 'Adlestrop' – 'the name…only the name' – places England's linguistic history at the centre of its identity in 'Lob'. It also anticipates what Thomas called his 'household poems', written to his family a year later, in which place-names are seen as a precious heritage. 'Lob' represents as much of an 'other' side to Thomas in its own way as does 'The Other'.

Seventeen more poems would follow 'Lob' during Thomas's intense period of research on *Marlborough*, providing him with something of a relief from it and from thoughts of war. The only poem to make a direct allusion to the conflict, apart from 'In Memorian (Easter 1915)', was the last to be written before he started on *Marlborough*. 'Fifty Faggots', written as one of his 'reliefs' from his commission, he tells Frost, is 'founded on carrying fifty bunts (short faggots of thin and thick brushwood mixed) and putting them against [his] hedge' for future firewood.[26] Written only six days after the sinking of the *Lusitania*, it reflects Thomas's uncertainty about the future, hesitating as he still was between enlisting or joining Frost in America. After thinking how the faggots will provide a home for 'robin or wren' but will inevitably disappear to provide winter warmth, he concludes:

> ...Before they are done
> The war will have ended, many other things
> Have ended, maybe, that I can no more
> Foresee or more control than robin and wren.[27]

(Over a year later Thomas would tell Frost that the faggots had, in fact, been used for summer cooking out of doors, thus 'spoil[ing his] verses on the subject as far as they were a prophecy'.[28])

There would be only one poem composed during the writing of *Marlborough* from 18 May to 12 June, 'The Sedge-Warblers' (on 23 May), a piece in which Thomas sets out his poetic credo. He had noted 20 years previously in his diary that 'sedge warblers and whitethroats seldom sing'.[29] In choosing to celebrate the sedge warbler's 'song' above the bird favoured by his Romantic predecessors, the lark, he is continuing to redefine what is 'song', or a fit subject for poetry, as well as what constitutes 'beauty' and its relation to truth, as Yeats did in 'A Coat':

> ...And sedge-warblers, clinging so light
> To willow twigs, sang longer than the lark,
> Quick, shrill, or grating, a song to match the heat
> Of the strong sun, nor less the water's cool,
> Gushing through narrows, swirling in the pool.
> Their song that lacks all words, all melody,
> All sweetness almost, was dearer then to me
> Than sweetest voice that sings in tune sweet words.
> This was the best of May – the small brown birds
> Wisely re-iterating endlessly
> What no man learnt yet, in or out of school.[30]

It would be over a month before Thomas wrote his next two poems, which followed the completion of *Marlborough* on 19 June and a four-day bicycle ride with Jesse Berridge through Wiltshire to get rid of the thought of his book. Appropriately, the second of these, 'Words', composed on 25 and 26

June during a stay with Haines, is a plea to the muse – 'Choose me, / You
English words'.

The first of the two poems written at Haines's house, however, suggests
that Thomas's thoughts were occupied by more than poetry, the writing of
Marlborough having deferred rather than resolved his dilemma. In trying
to decide between the army and America, one thing weighed heavily with
him:

> I can't help dreading people both in anticipation and when I am
> among them [he wrote to Garnett on 24 June 1915] and my only way
> of holding my own is the instinctive one of turning on what you call
> coldness & a superior manner. That is why I hesitated about America. I
> felt sure that unless I could make a friend or 2 I could do no good. Nor
> do I think that any amount of distress could turn me into a lecturer.

Garnett's immediate response evoked a further one from Thomas which
helps to explain his attraction to the American option, despite its many
practical difficulties:

> ...it is all due to self consciousness and fear. What you call superiority
> is only a self defence unconsciously adopted by the most faint-hearted
> humility – I believe. It goes on thickening into a callosity which only
> accident – being left to my own devices perhaps – can ever break
> through. I long for the accident but cannot myself arrange to produce
> it! However, perhaps landing in New York quite alone, and under
> some stress, may do the trick, and I almost feel inclined to go if only to
> see whether it will happen so.[31]

Set in this context, the poem Thomas includes with his letter to Garnett, 'I
built myself a house of glass', needs little further explanation, based as it is
on what Thomas saw as the main problem of his life.[32]

Thomas also wrote to remind Garnett during this same stay in
Gloucestershire of one practical problem which made him hesitate to leave
for America and which had made his life more than usually difficult during
the previous three years – money. He had first asked Garnett if he would
be willing to recommend him for a Civil List Pension after hearing that
de la Mare had had his annual pension raised. By 24 June 1915, he was
hoping Garnett would approach Hudson for his support. Garnett did not
think Thomas's chances of getting a pension likely and advised him 'to go

to America and change [his] nature and become warm and approachable and give lectures and like Americans.'[33] 'So the outlook is difficult,' Thomas concluded by 25 June, his mind still not made up, though to Eleanor it seemed that 'America had never looked so certain.'[34]

A more powerful reason than either his crippling shyness or lack of money for not going to America was a growing conviction that he could not leave England while the war continued without making a contribution. Brooke's death on 23 April on his way to Gallipoli, while reminding him of the risks involved, may also have strengthened this conviction. By June he had just finished the articles on him, for the *English Review* and the *Bellman*, which had involved rereading Brooke's '1914' sonnets; though he did not rate them as 'pure poetry', he had found them 'eloquent' and felt unable to ignore their message, 'not having enlisted or fought the [game] keeper,' he told Frost.[35] By mid-June he, like most English people, had to accept that the Allies had 'not got the Germans beaten yet', but comforted himself with the report that 'we are really through the Dardanelles and [that] the price of wheat is falling', an idea Frost instantly destroyed: 'As for the war, damn it! You are surely getting the worst of it. You are *not* through the Dardanelles and we know that you are not. Nothing will save you but Lloyd George and a good deal of him. You must quit slacking.'[36] (A 'slacker' in American slang could mean a draft-dodger by 1915.) If Frost really wanted Thomas to join him in America, it was the worst possible response, especially given the ambiguity of his last sentence. Thomas could have taken 'You must quit slacking' to apply personally to him. He had been able to cope with Frost's teasing of him about his indecision in 'The Road Not Taken', but after this letter of 26 June, just as he appeared to have decided on America, he changed his mind again.

A fortnight later, on 9 July, he would take the first decisive step towards enlistment, his final separation from Frost prefigured in a dream of the previous month about his friend, its visionary quality and language reminiscent of 'Kubla Khan':

A Dream

Over known fields with an old friend in a dream
I walked, but came sudden to a strange stream.
Its dark waters were bursting out most bright

From a great mountain's heart into the light.
They ran a short course under the sun, then back
Into a pit they plunged, once more as black
As at their birth; and I stood thinking there
How white, had the day shone on them, they were,
Heaving and coiling. So by the roar and hiss
And by the mighty motion of the abyss
I was bemused, that I forgot my friend
And neither saw nor sought him till the end,
When I awoke from waters unto men
Saying 'I shall be here some day again.'[37]

24

The Extreme Decision (July–November 1915)

A man enlists for some inexplicable reason which he may translate into simple, conventional terms. If he has thought a good deal about it, he has made a jump at some point, beyond the reach of his thought. The articulate and inarticulate are united in the ranks at this moment by the power to make that jump and come to the extreme decision.[1]

On 9 July 1915 Edward Thomas took his first decisive step towards joining the army. Starting the day by practising basic army drill with his military friend, MacAlister, in a quiet part of Hyde Park – 'so that he would not feel utterly foolish when he first stood up with recruits much younger than himself'[2] – he then accompanied Mac to the headquarters of the Artists' Rifles in Duke's Road, opposite Euston Station, to enquire about enlisting. It was a decision he had 'half' arrived at, he told his parents, while having tea, then lunch with them on the previous two days.[3] His mother's opposition to the American plan and his father's extreme patriotism may have influenced his decision, but since both their responses were entirely predictable, the very act of consulting them suggests that Edward was ready to be persuaded.

His next move after calling at the Artists' Rifles was to make his will with Haynes ('leaving all my property to my dear wife, Helen Berenice Thomas'), indicating that he had, in fact, made up his mind completely[4] and also that he expected to be sent to France. Despite his reassurance to his parents that if he got a commission 'it would not (on account of my age) be of service, at first at any rate, if at all, in the trenches', he was clearly set on France.[5] 'I really hope my turn will come,' he would write to his aunt less than six months later, 'and that I shall see what it really is and come out of it with my head and most of my limbs.'[6] To claim, as John Pikoulis does, that he was 'not so much drifting towards death as placing himself before it', however, is to overstate the case.[7]

Thomas's choice of the Artists' Rifles is not hard to understand. It had been formed as a volunteer light infantry unit in 1860, mainly for artists, but had also included from the start those involved in the arts generally. Its badge, the twin heads of Mars and Minerva, which Thomas would have seen depicted in terracotta above the door of the Regimental Headquarters in Duke's Road, represented the Roman gods of war and of the arts respectively. A popular unit for volunteers, its membership broadened over the next 40 years to include professions other than the arts, such as lawyers and doctors, and by 1900 had been increased to 12 companies. But it was still restricted mainly to middle-class recruits and appealed particularly to those from public schools and universities. Priding itself on being a tough and efficient unit, at the outbreak of war in 1914 it had dispatched a fighting force to France. It had also taken on a special wartime role as an Officers' Training Corps and sent a number of its members to be officers in other units of its division, the 7th, while retaining its own active fighting force, winning numerous battle honours in 1917 and 1918 to add to those already gained in the Boer War.

It was as officer training material that Thomas would join the regiment. His fellow-recruits would include artists of all kinds, from Maresco Pearce, W. P. Robins, John Wheatley and Paul Nash, who would all become friends, to the cartoonist Sidney Strube (of 'Strube's Little Man' fame) and illustrator Alfred Leete, creator of the famous picture of Lord Kitchener in his 'Your Country Needs You' poster. Wilfred Owen, too, was to walk into the Artists' Rifles headquarters three months after Thomas and would overlap with him in training at Hare Hall Camp, though there is no evidence that they knew each other personally.[8] Other poet-members would include two minor Georgians, W. J. Turner and Edward Shanks.

Thomas was evidently reassured by the still slightly exclusive nature of the Artists' Rifles, though regretting that the war was allowing in a lower social class of men and that the corps was 'now only nominally reserved for the "professional" classes'.[9] He had considered an alternative, the Sportsman's Battalion of the Royal Fusiliers, but 'there,' he told his parents with barely concealed distaste, 'I might find a rowdy set, no better company than the ordinary crowd, whereas the Artists would be largely professional men'.[10]

The helpful sergeant at Duke's Road had arranged a medical for Thomas for Wednesday 14 July and he spent three of the four intervening days at Steep, 'clearing things up preparatory', he told Frost,[11] the only friend apart from Mac and Haynes to be informed of his intentions, since he was still fearing rejection on health grounds: 'Last week I had screwed myself up to the point of believing I should come out to America and lecture if anyone wanted me to. But I have altered my mind. I am going to enlist on Wednesday if the doctor will pass me.'[12] Frost was both 'sorry' and 'glad' at the news, believing that Thomas was doing it 'for the self-same reason I shall hope to do it for if my time ever comes and I am brave enough, namely, because there seems nothing else for a man to do…Only the very bravest could come to the sacrifice in this way.'[13] Frost wrote more frankly to Abercrombie that he thought that enlisting had 'made some sort of a new man and a poet out of Edward Thomas'.[14]

Besides writing to Frost and working in the garden of Yew Tree Cottage, Thomas's three days at Steep involved spending more time with his daughters, especially Myfanwy, who inspired at least one of the four poems written during this period of relative leisure, 'The Brook'. The incident on which it is based may have occurred the same day that he wrote it, during a walk with Myfanwy and Arthur Ransome's daughter, Tabitha.[15] As the narrator sits by a brook 'watching a child / Chiefly that paddled', all the poet's senses except taste are alert to the surrounding scene – the 'mellow' sound of the blackbird, the 'sharp' one of the thrush, the 'voices of the stream', the 'grey flycatcher silent on a fence', the sight of 'the waters running frizzled over gravel', the feel of the 'heat of the sun' for the butterfly, and the 'hot stone he perched on', and the 'scent like a honeycomb / From mugwort dull'. The narrator feels as if he and the child 'had been there since / The horseman and the horse lying beneath / The fir-tree-covered barrow on the heath /…Galloped the downs last' and experiences a strong sense of loss, perhaps as he contemplates joining the ranks of nameless soldiers, until:

> …the child's voice raised the dead.
> 'No one's been here before' was what she said
> And what I felt, yet never should have found
> A word for, while I gathered sight and sound.[16]

The elegiac tone of a goodbye to loved, familiar things, seen as though for the first, possibly the last, time, is unmistakable in 'The Brook' and in all three of the other poems written during Thomas's wait to take his medical. 'Aspens' celebrates 'the inn, the smithy and the shop', so familiar at village crossroads in Thomas's day, and may have been stimulated by another walk through Steep during his stay; an everyday sight he had taken for granted until forced to contemplate leaving it. His emphasis is not on the cheerful sounds coming from the smithy and the inn, but on the barely audible 'whisper' of the aspen trees, which (like his own faint poetic voice) 'is not drowned' and 'calls their ghosts from their abode':

> Over all sorts of weather, men, and times,
> Aspens must shake their leaves and men may hear
> But need not listen, more than to my rhymes.

> Whatever wind blows, while they and I have leaves
> We cannot other than an aspen be
> That ceaselessly, unreasonably grieves,
> Or so men think who like a different tree.[17]

Frost, who had written his own poem on 'The Sound of Trees' the previous year, thought 'Aspens' Thomas's 'loveliest of all to date' and needed no explanation.[18] But Eleanor did, Thomas having to explain to her that 'I was the aspen. "We" meant the trees and I with my dejected shyness.'[19]

A third poem, almost certainly originating in another farewell walk through Steep to the disused mill, 'The Mill-Water', is also dominated by a sense of loss, in this case of the 'talk and noise of labour and of play'. Only 'water that toils no more' can be heard, which 'falling, mocks / The music of the mill-wheel's busy roar'. The last line – 'Where once men had a work-place and a home' – suggests that Thomas had already said goodbye mentally to his own 'home' of nearly nine years.[20]

Yet Thomas, who had been dissatisfied with at least two of the three houses he had lived in at Steep and was rarely happy at 'home' for more than brief intervals, is unlikely to have been regretting an actual house, a suspicion strengthened by his last pre-enlistment poem, 'For These'. Here he sets out his ideal 'home', a place not so much of bricks and mortar but of a state of mind, which the poem implies can only ever be an aspiration. Significantly, this 'house that shall love me as I love it' is described only in terms of what lies outside it – ash trees visited by 'linnets, greenfinches and goldfinches', a garden full of sunflowers, 'a spring, a brook's bend, or at least a pond', all set on an 'acre of land between the shore and the hills'.[21] Most of all the narrator asks that 'something may be sent / To be contented with', an acknowledgement perhaps of Thomas's almost permanent discontent and a hint that he is hoping that will change.

'For These' was completed the day Thomas passed his medical on 14 July, a routine affair in which he and six other men, all except one much younger than he, were stripped, weighed, measured and made to hop round the room on each foot. Helen, who had been led to believe that he was in London looking for work, was informed immediately by telegram. While she had known of 'the struggle going on in his spirit' and had tried to prepare herself for the situation, when the telegram came she felt 'suddenly faint and despairing. "No, no, no," was all I could say; "not that." '[22] Three of Thomas's closest friends, W. H. Davies, Martin Freeman and Garnett, who was about to go out with an ambulance corps to the Italian front, were also told of the outcome the same day, de la Mare and Eleanor next.

Thomas had suggested to Eleanor that they meet for lunch the following day, but she felt unable to do so and telegrammed him to come to her house instead. As he entered the room, he bent his head and 'for the only time in our four years of friendship we kissed spontaneously,' Eleanor remembered.[23] When he confirmed his news, Eleanor, well aware of the potential danger he was placing himself in, said, 'I don't know why, but I am glad', to which he replied, 'I am too...and I don't know why either.'[24] Before long, Eleanor added, she did know why: 'Self-torment' had gone out of him, and I was glad because of that.'[25] Her feelings were not so very different from Helen's.

Thomas was one of the last of the remembered war poets to enlist: only Rosenberg and Owen (both out of England until 1915) joined up later. Many of the poets – Graves, Brooke, Nichols, Sorley, among them – volunteered at the start, Sassoon so keen to enlist that he put his name down even before England officially entered the war. But, with the exception of Brooke and Hodgson, few of Thomas's friends joined up, partly on medical grounds, like Abercrombie, Bottomley and W. H. Davies, partly because of their age, like Hudson, de la Mare and Guthrie.

Another delay followed Thomas's medical, while he waited to be 'attested' in the Artists' Rifles the following Monday, 19 July. Still technically free, he was able to return to Steep to write to inform the rest of his friends of his decision. His letter to Bottomley reveals more clearly than most his state of mind and expectations at this point, ending as it does: 'in a few months I expect to go to France to finish my training. Here then ends reviewing and I suppose verses, for a time.'[26] It would be less than a week, however, before the next poems were written. The enforced period of waiting with nothing more urgent to do than write to inform various editors that he was no longer looking for work and Hodson that he would not be taking the teaching job offered in Coventry, besides more letters to friends, more arranging papers and singing to the children, allowed his mind to lie fallow and to produce three poems in quick succession.

The opportunity to write his poems down occurred because of a damaged ankle, as in January. Rather than undergoing basic training after he was attested and kitted out with uniform, he found himself lame once more. The tough army boots worn during six hours of physical drill in Regent's Park on his first day damaged a tendon in his right heel and he was given sick leave until the following Monday. 'Don't tell anybody I aren't [sic] a soldier yet tho I am in uniform,' he instructed Eleanor.[27]

'Digging', the first of the poems which resulted, is another example of Thomas's ability to turn the everyday into a moment of revelation – in this case his habit of burying his evil-smelling clay pipes in the garden, together with a much older one he had discovered while digging. His historical sense, stimulated by his work on *Marlborough*, proofs of which he was correcting this same week, inspires him to create a comparison between Marlborough's famous battles and the current war he has entered, a subject fit either for 'tears' or 'mirth', possibly both the last line suggests:

What matter makes my spade for tears or mirth,
Letting down two clay pipes into the earth?
The one I smoked, the other a soldier
Of Blenheim, Ramillies and Malplaquet
Perhaps. The dead man's immortality
Lies represented lightly with my own,
A yard or two nearer the living air
Than bones of ancients who, amazed to see
Almighty God erect the mastodon,
Once laughed, or wept, in this same light of day.[28]

The narrator's apparent detachment anticipates that of 'God' in 'February Afternoon', who 'sits aloft in the array / That we have wrought him, stone-deaf and stone-blind[29].'

Thomas's ambivalence and sense of the past is shown again in the poem which followed 'Digging', 'Two Houses', in which the house that stood where a pleasant 'smil[ing]' farmhouse now stands introduces a darker note and a reminder of the events in France, 'as if above graves / Still the turf heaves / Above its stones' and 'the hollow past / Half yields the dead that never / More than half hidden lie: / And out they creep and back again for ever'.[30] A similar conflict between dark and light, between the world of sleep and dreams and that of daytime reality, is central to 'Cock-Crow', where the narrator's response to the bird's clarion call mirrors Thomas's response to the call to arms.

It would be nearly three months before Thomas returned to poetry. Determined not to disgrace himself as a soldier, he reported back for 'Light Duty' on Monday 26 July. But a new phrase enters the vocabulary of a man who had until now rarely had a moment to spare, 'hanging about', and he spent the next week at Headquarters doing just that. He was given nothing more demanding to do than cleaning rifles in the armoury. Nevertheless, he was beginning to believe that he might one day be a real soldier. His tendon survived the week of intensive drilling which followed with the regiment's 2nd Battalion, the Artists' main training unit in London which prepared new recruits for army camp in Essex.

One drawback of being stationed in London was that Thomas, for reasons of economy, lodged with his parents and his father was 'so rampant in his cheery patriotism' that he found himself becoming 'pro German every evening.'[31] His own feelings of patriotism, which on occasions almost reduced him to tears as he marched along in unison with his fellow-soldiers, were of a less obvious kind and brought him into conflict with his father once again. Even at his most patriotic Thomas believed that army talk of Duty and Discipline was little more than 'a lot of ordinary brutal morality masquerading as something very un-German and gentlemanly'.[32]

Lodging with his parents also meant that he was not forced into full contact with the other men in his unit, but could escape at the end of each day's training to see friends: 'So far I can't talk much to the men I am with,' he confessed to Frost. 'They don't seek me more than I do them.'[33] With Eleanor he was even franker: 'I don't like the men.'[34] Since he was expecting a commission fairly quickly, which would mean a transfer to another regiment, he may not have thought it important to bond with his fellow-recruits.

Despite these problems he could report to Frost after three weeks' hard training that his experience had made a significant change in him. His body now 'insist[ed] on real leisure', which left him by evening fit only for a little talk with friends like Locke Ellis, Davies, Freeman or de la Mare. Instead of sitting down daily to his writing, he 'drill[ed], clean[ed] rifles, wash[ed] out lavatories' among other duties.[35] He could look forward to sentry duty outside Headquarters and was proud to report that he now stood 'very nearly as straight as a lamp post' and 'apparently g[o]t smaller every week in the waist' and had to have new holes punched in his belt.[36] By 21 August he liked the life: 'I don't mind beginning my day [at 6.30 a.m.] with polishing buttons and badges and the brass of the belt,' he told Frost. 'I quite like the physical drill which is very strenuous and includes running, jumping, leap-frog etc.'[37] He had by now progressed to company drills and route marches. He had also had two inoculations for typhoid fever, which left him feverish for several days. In September came guard duty, night operations on Hampstead Heath and a little mapping practice at Rickmansworth.

It was nearly ten weeks after his first visit to Duke's Road, instead of the usual three or four, before his unit was transferred to army camp. The move had been delayed because the camp, at High Beech, near Loughton in Essex, was still being built and not ready on time to receive a company of 250 men. Despite finding the daily routine less demanding after his prolonged basic training, Thomas still had no energy for writing. 'As for reviewing,' he told de la Mare, 'it is almost as well there is none left for me. I couldn't do it.'[38] He had been unable to finish even the one review he had outstanding when he joined up. His reading had become confined to the standard manual for aspiring officers, *Company Training*, and to Shakespeare's *Cymbeline*, an unusual but appropriate choice, since in it the ancient Britons defeat an invading Roman army. His greatest mental effort was to proofread his *Four-and-Twenty Blackbirds* and index *Marlborough*, both of which were due to be published in October.

Thomas does not now look forward to more than a week at a time, although it is evident from his letters that he is highly conscious of the war – of the torpedoing of the SS *Arabic* in the Atlantic on 19 August, counteracted by a Russian naval victory and the presence of the British fleet in the Baltic, for instance, or, a fortnight later, of the failure of the Dardanelles campaign, 'only prolonged,' he believed, 'because it is not easy to draw back,'[39] or the start in late September of the Battle of Loos, which those in France were rumoured to hope would end the war. But he and his fellow-soldiers never discussed the war 'for more than a moment or two.'[40]

Orders eventually came through for a transfer to High Beech and on 17 September Thomas took a train for the half-hour journey to Loughton, walking another half-hour stretch to the camp through Epping Forest, 'oaks, hornbeams, beeches, bracken, hollies and some heather.'[41] Between seven and eight miles long and one to two miles wide, the forest lay high on a ridge and contained many tiny ponds and long, wide glades. He was already aware of two of the area's most important literary connections, having recently written in *A Literary Pilgrim* of Tennyson's stay at Loughton while writing 'In Memoriam' and John Clare's time in an asylum there. He would later discover another, Arthur Morrison, author of *A Child of the Jago*, whom he would meet while at High Beech.

Thomas would continue to find the beauty of the area a much-needed 'compensation' for conditions at the camp itself.[42] Built, ironically, on the site of a former pleasure resort high in the middle of the forest, High Beech Camp consisted of corrugated iron huts for the soldiers to sleep in, set around a large corrugated iron room previously used as a dining-room for the poor children who were brought out to Epping Forest, under the Shaftesbury Retreat scheme, to enjoy a day in the country. Conditions at the camp in September 1915, according to Thomas, were 'cramped and not over clean'.[43] The food was 'ill-cooked and ill-served', he told Haines after ten days of it, and had to be 'eaten in haste in a dark dirty room that the rain comes into'.[44] But hard physical work had given him an appetite and he ate whatever was served, with no ill-effects and none of his usual complaints of indigestion, a fact which makes it highly unlikely that he was suffering from diabetes, as he had sometimes claimed. De la Mare's present of a cake was much appreciated, greatly improving the plain midday meal of bread and cheese or sausage issued to the soldiers when out on field-work.

The work itself was mostly out of doors and even more strenuous than the London training. Apart from the chance to see the countryside, Thomas enjoyed the physical challenge, pointless though it often seemed. While he could understand the logic behind making simulated trenches, he thought it 'foolish' to give men such 'unmilitary work' as digging drains, carting clay and (however good he had become at it) carpentering.[45] He disliked the 'bully' supervising the jobs as much as the 'fox-hunting major' on whom he had to depend for leave.[46]

The biggest change at High Beech, however, was in Thomas's relationship with his fellow-recruits. Whereas he had felt 'an undigested lump' in the battalion in London, once in the close quarters of an army camp he began to make friends, visiting Loughton and a nearby pub, The Owl, with them for instance, on a number of occasions. (His move between A and B companies enabled him to get to know more of the men.) Not surprisingly, he was still unable to concentrate on any serious mental activity, which he blamed partly on the dirty, noisy conditions in the only available room, the canteen, which became even worse as winter approached. Whereas he accepted de la Mare's repeated offers of a cake gratefully, he firmly refused his suggestion of a book by the philosopher Herbert Spencer: 'I can read nothing, not even a paper: only "Company Training". Nor write...I don't think about books or writing except on a sleepless night when I sometimes make a few lines *and a half* and don't bother to write them down.'[47]

It would take yet another injury – this time damage to his knee – to produce another poem, one possibly based on those 'few lines *and a half*' of his sleepless nights. A further stimulus may have been Bottomley's news that he had shown some of Thomas's poems to Abercrombie, who liked them 'a good deal' and was considering including some of them in the *Annual of New Poetry* he was editing with Bottomley and R. C. Trevelyan. The most likely germ for 'October', the poem which resulted from having to rest for two days, however, was an earlier bout of sleeplessness in London, rendered 'tolerable' only by 'making blank verses' out of a letter written to Frost on 3 September 1915, which ended: 'It seems as if in my world there was no Autumn though they are just picking hops in Kent. On Hampstead Heath...I watched the bees at the bramble flowers and green blackberries and they looked so unfamiliar and with a kind of ugliness.' (Thomas would later explain to Eleanor that 'the original version [of 'October'] was in blank verse, but quite different'.[48]) Few poets can write of autumn without Keats in mind and his influence in 'October' makes itself felt not only in numerous echoes of his work overall ('No stir of air was there / ... where the dead leaf fell, there did it rest'), but also in an elaborate pattern of rhyme, assonance and syntactical unit, as Edna Longley points out. But the exact observation of seasonal change is Thomas's own – 'the green elm' starting to shed its leaves, the 'mushrooms small milk-white', the wildflowers he knew so well, the light breeze which fails 'to shake the fallen birch leaves from the fern', the 'scold[ing] of the squirrels' – as is the conclusion, where the poet turns from the outer to the inner life which, in Leavis's words, 'the sensory impressions are notation for' in Thomas's work.[49] And Thomas's focus, unlike Keats's, is not on the coming of spring but on his own failure to experience 'happiness' in such surroundings. Like 'The Other' and 'Melancholy', however, 'October' acknowledges that what the narrator calls 'melancholy' may change with the passage of time and that:

> Some day I shall think this a happy day,
> And this mood by the name of melancholy
> Shall no more blackened and obscured be.[50]

Many of Thomas's friends shared Henry Nevinson's opinion that 'being under orders in the army which admitted of no hesitation' brought about a profound change in Thomas, that 'the demon of melancholy left him' and that 'the energy of his soul had found its line of excellence'.[51] Haynes, for instance, claimed that 'life in the Army cured his neurasthenia'.[52] Bottomley, too, noted that on his last visit to them he was 'a happy, tranquillising presence, with a steadfast, gentle outlook on new dangers and old troubles;

newly and finely tempered, no longer moody or distracted about the future'.[53] Bax and Herbert Farjeon both believed that Thomas was happy for the first time since they met him. (Eleanor, who knew Edward far better than her brother, never claimed this.) His earliest biographers followed this line: John Moore writes rather grandly that he had 'shaken hands with the past and shut his eyes to the future, so that he was troubled neither with regrets nor apprehensions'.[54]

It is true that Thomas appreciated the regularity of army life and the security of a regular, if meagre, income of one shilling a day. He also enjoyed being physically fit (however gaunt and strained he looks in his photographs with Bottomley towards the end); Nevinson said that he had gained 'incredibly in health and stature and confidence'.[55] Yet Paul Nash, who believed he had witnessed one of 'the happiest bits of his life' while they were in the Artists' Rifles together, nevertheless told Bottomley that Thomas 'always seems to have been oppressed by some load of sadness and pessimism'.[56] And the poems themselves, unfiltered by politeness or the expectations of others, reveal what his letters rarely do during his army service. In 'Home', for example, after describing an enjoyable walk across beautiful countryside with his friends before returning to army camp, Thomas, as poet, insists: 'Happy we had not been there, nor could be, / Though we had tasted sleep and food and fellowship / Together long'.[57] His concluding stanza leaves little doubt that however much he assured his family and friends of his happiness, he was constantly 'homesick' for his old way of life:

> If I should ever more admit
> Than the mere word I could not endure it
> For a day longer: this captivity
> Must somehow come to an end, else I should be
> Another man, as often now I seem,
> Or this life be only an evil dream.

His letters to his closest confidant, Frost, reveal a state of mind nearer to resignation than happiness about the change: 'Does one really get rid of things at all by steadily inhibiting them for a long time on end?' he asked Frost. 'Is peace going to awaken me as it will so many from a drugged sleep? Am I indulging in the pleasure of being someone else?'[58]

Thomas might write of homesickness but it was evidently not for his actual home, since he visited Steep rarely during his initial months of training. Leave was not generous but even when he got it, generally every fortnight, he spent it mainly in London, though the train journey on to Steep was an easy one. And when he did make the effort, turning up unexpectedly to help nurse Helen through flu, he 'went down plump to the old level,' he confessed to Frost: neither Helen nor he had changed, he discovered, the house was chaotic and Helen was 'almost as much scared and surprised as pleased' to see him.[59] His letter would have come as no surprise to someone who believed, as Frost did, that Thomas had enlisted partly to get away from Helen.

On 24 October 1915 Thomas's unit was transferred back to London. During his three weeks of drill, trench-digging, map-reading and lectures and a week of digging clay and shovelling clinkers in mostly fine, warm weather, Thomas had been 'very well', he told John Freeman, and had 'enjoyed a good part of many days and some kindly company', the cold, uncomfortable evenings his only problem.[60] His fifth week, just before vacating the camp for winter, had been spent in musketry training, bringing the prospect of France that much nearer.

Three further weeks in London followed, Thomas (now promoted a rank from private to lance-corporal) spending the time from half-past nine in the morning until five in the evening instructing the men in map-reading. This was a skill which came naturally to him after many years of walking the countryside and he had finally conquered his fear of public speaking, so he enjoyed the 'school-masterish life' he was leading, 'help[ing] the men during lectures, explaining, doing their problems for them &c, and sometimes taking them out on Hampstead Heath'.[61] It was his first experience of giving orders and he gradually learnt to be 'less confidential in tone'.[62] Since he believed in the importance of map-reading and the use of the compass in warfare, he considered accepting the post of instructor when it was offered to him. Two things deterred him: it would mean remaining safely in England and giving up, or postponing, a commission. While he could see that it would be 'more reasonable to remain at home doing necessary work', honesty compelled him to admit to Frost that he did not want people to 'think less of him as a corporal at home than a lieutenant abroad'.[63] The army had increased rather than diminished his class-consciousness, as his reaction to his 'fox-hunting major' also showed.

In his absence at High Beech his literary life had gone on without him. Guthrie had published two of his poems ('House and Man', 'Interval') in *Root and Branch* and four of his prose books had been published, a reprint of *Maurice Maeterlinck*, *Four-and-Twenty Blackbirds*, *Marlborough* and *This England*, most of them receiving friendly reviews. And on his return to London he had discussed plans with James Smith of Oxford University Press for an anthology of narrative verse to follow *This England*, outlining a possible selection for it. (Frost had stayed with Smith in Edinburgh in late September 1914.) 'But who cares?' he asked Frost. 'Books are published *now* because publishers know things can only get worse as time goes on.'[64] Whereas in camp he found he could 'get on with people [he] had nothing in common with and almost get fond of them', as soon as he was back in London and able to spend time with his friends, 'the bond was dissolved' he told Bottomley.[65] He spent at least one long weekend at Steep, catching up on the gardening, lighting a fire in his study to air his books and seeing the artist Muirhead Bone, now living in Steep, and the Farjeons' doctor friend Maitland Radford, who was staying with the Thomases' next-door neighbours, the Fordhams, again. It was a relatively undemanding existence for Thomas and his fellow-recruits and nobody – 'least of all I,' Thomas confessed – looked forward to the planned return to camp life.[66]

When orders came through to proceed by train on 15 November to Hare Hall Camp, Gidea Park, Romford, Thomas travelled out there with his brother Reggie (now also in the Artists' Rifles) with no great expectations. But Gidea Park, a new garden suburb built only four years earlier with its own station a few miles from Romford, turned out to be an attractive place. Though the camp itself did not live up to Gidea Park's slogan of 'Dreams Come True', Thomas was pleasantly surprised to find it 'excellent'.[67] It, too, had been well planned, by architects and engineers from the Artists' Rifles, and spread out along tree-lined paths. Forty long wooden huts, designed to hold 1,400 men, surrounded several larger huts which housed the canteen, hospital, lecture room and sergeants' mess, as well as a YMCA café and quiet reading-room where Thomas would write some of his poems and letters over the next nine months. Situated on the north side of Hare Hall Park, the camp was conveniently close to a few shops and pubs on the main Colchester road and less than half an hour's walk from Romford. Living conditions were clean and tidy and not quite so spartan as at High Beech; they slept in canvas beds. 'But we think we would rather be on the floor at High Beech,' Thomas wrote to Frost, after two months of almost constant rain on the flat, clayey ground which held all the wet.[68] Another disadvantage was having to share a hut again, this time with between 25 and 30 men.

Though Hare Hall Camp itself was set on the 'dullest flattest piece of land imaginable', Thomas found the countryside around it 'beautiful'.[69] He and his fellow map-instructors had been set to work immediately to explore it, 'with a view to taking classes out' he explained to Eleanor.[70] Very different from his favoured 'South Country', he would nevertheless grow to love it for its understated charms, remembering perhaps the description he had quoted from Pater in its defence, in a review written 14 years earlier of Reginald Beckett's *Romantic Essex*: 'One of the true home counties by right, partly of a certain earthy warmth in the yellow of the sand below their gorse-bushes, and of a certain grey-blue mist after rain, in the hollow of the hills there, welcome to English eyes, and never seen farther south.'[71]

Thomas's response to his new surroundings during the first three 'beautiful cold sunny days' when the earth was 'thick with snow' was to write his first poem in over a month, 'There's nothing like the sun.'[72] Echoes of both the Shakespeare sonnets he loved ('My mistress' eyes are nothing like the sun') and Keats's 'Ode to Autumn' (again) are unmistakable:

> There's nothing like the sun as the year dies,
> Kind as it can be, this world being made so,
> To stones and men and beasts and birds and flies,
> To all things that it touches except snow,
> Whether on mountain side or street of town.
> The south wall warms me: November has begun,
> Yet never shone the sun as fair as now
> While the sweet last-left damsons from the bough
> With spangles of the morning's storm drop down
> Because the starling shakes it, whistling what
> Once swallows sang.[73]

It is a poem which supports his claim to his aunt Margaret, after less than a week at Hare Hall, that he had 'never been happier or better in health', though the last four lines suggest that he was not unaware of the implications of his training and the possibility that, in the words of the poem, he might not 'live long enough':[74]

> No day of any month but I have said –
> Or, if I could live long enough, should say –
> 'There's nothing like the sun that shines today.'
> There's nothing like the sun till we are dead.

Two other poems followed within the next ten days. First came 'The Thrush', written while on duty as hut orderly and focused on one of his favourite themes, the instinctive wisdom of birds compared with the more complicated knowledge man acquires only through hard-won experience and effort. (It is a theme Ted Hughes would tackle many years later in a poem almost certainly influenced by Thomas's, 'Thrushes'.[75])

The second of the poems, 'Liberty', addresses a subject already touched on in 'The Thrush', an extreme self-consciousness, which joining the army has partially cured, the narrator implies, the 'wiser others' being his more carefree fellow-soldiers:

> ... If every hour
> Like this one passing that I have spent among
> The wiser others when I have forgot
> To wonder whether I was free or not,
> Were piled before me, and not lost behind,
> And I could take and carry them away
> I should be rich; or if I had the power
> To wipe out every one and not again
> Regret, I should be rich to be so poor.[76]

Yet the poem ends on a familiar note of the regret he had hoped to banish, that he was 'still half in love with', not Keats's 'easeful death', though that may be implied, but 'pain, / With what is imperfect, with both tears and mirth, / With things that have an end'.

Thomas still found reading virtually impossible. By the time he began 'real work' again in early December as a map-instructor – taking 10 or 12 men out for five days at a time and trying to teach them the elements of 'map-reading, field-sketching, the use of compass and protractor and making a map on the ground with and without the compass' – he was reading less than anyone in his hut, he told Frost.[77] But some of the men he found 'very interesting' and the days passed easily. 'We are really rather comfortable here,' he reported from Hut 35, who are photographed as a group looking reasonably harmonious.[78] Two of the men he had liked most from High Beech had joined the map-instructors and were in his hut, and six of his 'old squad' had come with him from London. It was, however, yet another new set of people for him to get used to and he did so with uncharacteristic speed. Marching home with his fellow-instructors and 30 to 60 men after a long day's work, he would encourage them to sing together '"Mr John Blunt" and one or two other songs of mine'.[79] Most of his generation of volunteers had, after six months, left to become officers and he felt like an 'old boy' at school as the new boys arrived. It now seemed to him 'unlikely' that he would be able to afford to take a commission, he told Bottomley, and he was beginning to resign himself to continuing as a lance-corporal and map-instructor.[80]

Since leave was now scarce – one twenty-four-hour pass every fortnight, if he was lucky – the camp became his world. In his free time, which was on Wednesday afternoons and weekends during his first three months, he started to explore the countryside, often taking long walks with friends. Among his most frequent companions were the artists Charles Maresco Pearce, who was four years older than Thomas and had been his sergeant in London, Arnold Mason, seven years younger, and the Welshman John Wheatley, who was 14 years younger and would draw at least two portraits of him at Hare Hall.[81] Other friends included a schoolteacher and a game-breeder. One of his outings with friends would form the basis for 'Home' and show how close but also how limited these 'friendships of circum-stance' (as Sorley called them) were:

> Between three counties far apart that lay
> We were divided and looked strangely each
> At the other, and we knew we were not friends
> But fellows in a union that ends
> With the necessity for it, as it ought.[82]

Nevertheless, he enjoyed his walks with these men, some of them providing the inspiration for a number of the many poems – 43 out of 144 – he wrote at Hare Hall Camp. Both 'The Green Roads' and 'The Dark Forest', for example, were based on a walk he took, whenever possible, to the fragment of a forest six miles from the camp, which he found 'the best of all this county'.[83] Though he feared that the forest was 'perhaps too obvious a metaphor', an unsuccessful attempt at Maeterlinckian symbolism, and couches both poems in terms of fairy tales and folk legends – 'white goose feathers', 'a castle keep' and 'someone who goes to the forest but has never come back' ('The Green Roads'), the 'mighty multitudes' which 'ride about' and 'dwell inside' ('The Dark Forest') – both successfully evoke the war for which he and his fellow-soldiers are being prepared.

Even the constant 'Rain' he experiences at Hare Hall Camp is turned into a poem, in which the 'myriads of broken reeds all still and stiff' are a reminder of France and its battlefields. (see pp. 5–6) After lying in a 'bleak hut' with the 'wild rain' pounding on the corrugated-iron roof, the narrator's thoughts are never far from war, 'remembering again that I shall die',[84] but also admitting to a 'love of death' towards the end of the poem, another possible incentive to his enlistment.[85]

In 'Roads', written two weeks after 'Rain' on 22 January 1916, thoughts of France are linked backwards to his love of a landscape feature as symbolically fraught as forests for Thomas, making it quite clear what he expects of his future:

> Now all roads lead to France
> And heavy is the tread
> Of the living; but the dead
> Returning lightly dance....

It is the dead, he implies, who 'keep [him] company / With their pattering':

> Crowding the solitude
> Of the loops over the downs,
> Hushing the roar of towns
> And their brief multitudes.[86]

Suddenly, in the middle of January 1916, there is a distinct change in the kind of poetry Thomas is writing, a change which almost certainly started with one of his first walks at Hare Hall, to the house of the beautiful artist he had first met at Oxford in 1900, Edna Clarke Hall.

25

'A HEART THAT WAS DARK'
(NOVEMBER 1915–AUGUST 1916)

Thomas's poetry in the first half of 1916 suggests that he became as infatuated with Edna Clarke Hall as he had been with Hope Webb. Suddenly he started to write lyric love poetry quite different from the sombre reflections on war which had preceded it. So much so that by March he felt it necessary to reassure Frost that he would be careful 'not to *indulge* in a spring run of lyrics'.[1] Starting with 'The clouds that are so light' on 16 January and ending with 'After you speak' on 3 June, when he was faced with the thought of leaving the area, they introduce a new romantic note into his verse. Not since his juvenile poems to Helen at Oxford had he addressed a second person in such unconstrained terms:

> And even so now, light one!
> Beautiful, swift and bright one!
> You let fall on a heart that was dark,
> Unillumined, a deeper mark.[2]

The reference to 'your beauty' later in this poem makes it clear that it was not addressed to Helen, as does its emergence in a period when Edward has told Helen categorically, '...my usual belief is that I don't and can't love and haven't done for something near twenty years'.[3] It is significant, too, that Helen, who knew her husband so well, should have assumed that this was love poetry to

353

someone else and that he should have felt the need to reassure her, 'I have no dream girls, dearest. Don't you imagine it.'[4] His uncharacteristic claims of happiness at Hare Hall may also be linked to his reintroduction to Edna.

Edna and her husband, William, had moved from Thames Ditton to Upminster not long after Thomas's last visit to them there with Haynes in 1901 and by 1916 they had two young sons. They now lived in a handsome sixteenth-century house, Great Tompkins (known as 'Great House'), on Upminster Common, only three and a half miles from Hare Hall Camp. Thomas, despite his vow in 1900 to make a regular pilgrimage to Edna's beauty, had not kept in touch, but had probably been encouraged to visit her in Essex by Haynes, or by Maresco Pearce, who knew Edna from the art world. He and Pearce called on her shortly after their arrival at Hare Hall but Edna was in London and they were invited back to lunch the next day. Edna, meantime, had dreamt of Thomas the night of his first call and had told him so the next day, according to one of her poems to him:

> I spoke yesterday of that strange
> Heralding on your return that came to me
> You spoke to me of clay –
> Thus sitting quiet, my son upon my knee
> At open hearth where orchard wood did burn
> We met again with words spoke casually
> Of pshycic [sic] hours and heavy clay by turn
> Your words gave weight to what I had to say
> And mine did lightly penetrate your clay.[5]

While Edna's attempt to load their reunion with psychic significance was met with a lecture on the clayey nature of the soil in that area, an honourable attempt by Edward perhaps to keep clear of romantic involvement, her pun on 'penetrating his clay' in the last line suggests that, in her case at least, he failed.

Other entries in Edna's journal show that Edward's visits excited her and that her feelings were more than platonic. Emotionally and physically starved in a marriage to an older man who spent much of his time away from home and was, in any case, more attracted to young girls than mature women – his Oxford contemporary and friend, Ernest Dowson, referred to him as 'properly a worshipper and devout follower of the most excellent cult of La Fillette'[6] – she was also frustrated in her career as a painter. Thomas represented a world largely denied to her by late 1915. He was also much nearer to her in age and physically attractive. She was particularly interested in his poetry, which inspired her to write verses of her own, a number of which express her feelings for him quite clearly:

> O genius of Edward Thomas
> You are dearly loved –
> Give me your flowers.[7]

'Even those *not* penned in your name,' she told him, in a letter addressed to him after his death, were inspired by him.[8] Edna was anxious to stress that it was not just his genius which attracted her; she loved his 'smile at the corner of those lips where pride with tenderness dwell [*sic*] – There is ease in the quiet manner and in the blue of those eyes like thoughts shy and perfect as a bird, – elusive as the unknown bird he tells of in the earthy woodlands.'[9] Her account of their final parting is particularly revealing, both of her own feelings and of his failure to respond to them overtly:

> These eyes looked upon him, and may not do so again
> These ears heard his voice, and may not do so again
> This hand has touched his, and may not do so again.
> Yet with eyes of my new knowledge would I look upon him – I would
> again mark the gentleness and resolution of the contours of that face
> that had so haunted my imagination as I saw it last in light of the setting
> sun – he standing before me silent and unaware.[10]

Such entries, written in Edna's journal, read like posthumous love letters to a man who had almost certainly restrained himself from responding. They suggest that he made no protestations of love and no attempt at intimate physical contact. His one surviving mention of Edna at this time to Gordon Bottomley, who would have known her name from his familiarity with the art world, is impersonal, merely a report that 'Edna Clarke Hall lives near and Pearce and I go in to lunch[11].'

Edward had, in fact, written to tell Helen of his visits to Edna's house, but most of his many letters to her from Hare Hall Camp have disappeared, possibly because, like those written during his infatuation with Hope Webb, Helen found them too painful to reread. It is only because Helen herself wrote to Edna after Edward's death that we know for sure that he had kept his pact to be entirely honest with Helen and had told her of his visits. How honest she was in her letter to Edna is debatable:

> How glad I was when Edward wrote and told me he'd met you again, it was lovely for him to have you to talk to in all the strange life he'd now eagerly undertaken. I know how those little times at your house refreshed him and I was grateful to anyone or anything that brought into this work of his[?] something warm and human and beautiful.[12]

Was Helen really 'glad' to know how much Edward was enjoying his 'little times' with Edna, whom Helen knew from the one occasion they had met in 1900 was as beautiful as Helen felt sure she herself was not? Her suspicion that 'The clouds that are so light', written less than two months after Edward resumed contact with Edna, was written to another woman was probably not quietened by Edward's airy dismissal of it: 'Fancy your thinking I might have someone in view in those verses.'[13] (He would use a similarly ambiguous formula ('Fancy...') a month later to respond to her fears that the harsh poem to his father, 'I may come near loving you', was about Helen herself.) When at least six more love poems followed between February and June 1916 she undoubtedly felt suspicious and threatened.

The only evidence of Edward's response to Edna, if it can be regarded as such, lies in the poems themselves. While 'Those things that poets said', ending with a direct denial of romantic involvement ('I, loving not, am different') may be read as a further attempt to reassure Helen, 'The Unknown', regarded by him as one of his best, is harder to explain away: it is an account of a beautiful woman who 'lures a poet, / Once proud or happy, soon / Far from his door'; the final words, 'She / May not exist'[14] were perhaps added to calm Helen's fears. 'Celandine', though more likely to be about his daughter Bronwen and Hope Webb, is certainly not about Helen. Nor is 'Like the touch of rain', with its arresting opening simile of the effect of the beloved's touch 'on a man's flesh and hair and eyes', sensuous details possibly relating to his walks with Edna in the grounds of Great House and unlikely to be written to a wife he had tried to leave as recently as 1914. The implied parting in this poem – 'Go now' – may relate to an actual parting from Edna, or to an imagined scenario, but not to Helen whom he could not leave.[15] A similar situation is conjured up in 'It rains', where the poet invokes a mood of both happiness and sadness characteristic of the yearning regret which fills these spring 1916 lyrics:

> …And I am nearly as happy as possible
> To search the wilderness in vain though well,
> To think of two walking, kissing there,
> Drenched, yet forgetting the kisses of the rain:
> Sad, too, to think that never, never again,
>
> Unless alone, so happy shall I walk
> In the rain. When I turn away, on its fine stalk
> Twilight has fined to naught, the parsley flower
> Figures, suspended still and ghostly white,
> The past hovering as it revisits the light.[16]

The figures talking in an orchard among the cow parsley in the rain clearly hold as powerful sensations for Thomas as equivalent memories did for Hardy in his extraordinary series of love poems to his dead wife.

Even a more general poem by Thomas, 'Some eyes condemn', may be about Edna, who was fascinated by his eyes: 'thinking of your eyes, dear,' Thomas concludes, 'I become / Dumb: for they flamed, and it was me they burned'. [17] Still on the subject of eyes, there seems little doubt that 'After you speak', the last of this group of poems, is addressed to a beloved, possibly 'transcendental', as Edna Longley suggests, possibly real, whose 'eyes' and 'cheeks and hair' convey 'Something more wise, / More dark, / And far different' from the words she speaks, which suggest 'lust' rather than 'love'.[18] The poet becomes a 'lark', 'A mote / Of singing dust', which must 'Soar in lone flight / So far, / Like a black star'. Always the poet's remoteness, his inability to love fully, is emphasized, even when the object of his affection is highly desirable, as here.

Edna had given up full-time work as an artist by late 1915, only occasionally showing her work in galleries, but she had continued to draw and paint in watercolours and one of her many sketches was of the road leading to her house. Thomas's response to this, if her report can be trusted, gives one of the few hints of his feelings for her apart from his poetry: 'he said that he had often prayed they [i.e. the soldiers] would never be asked to march down there, because of the mystery it held for him,' Edna recalled.[19] The note she saw him making after viewing her sketch may have been one source for the poem which follows 'The clouds that are so light' – 'Roads' – one of the 'goddesses' in the opening stanza being Edna herself:

> I love roads:
> The goddesses that dwell
> Far along invisible
> Are my favourite gods.[20]

Whatever Thomas's exact feelings towards Edna were, there is no doubt that he was unusually contented at Hare Hall Camp during the period of their reintroduction in late November and December 1915. The recent discovery of signatures to a well-known photograph of him taken with 'Hut 35' shows that he was among men he already regarded as friends from London and High Beech, H. K. Vernon, J. L. Benson and Arnold Mason among them. (Mason, like Wheatley, would sketch Thomas during their months together, a sketch now lost.) The same could not be said of Helen, for whom it was a time of suspicions, possibly jealousy. The fact that she could imagine that his poem to his father, written on 26 December 1915 after a particularly unpleasant encounter with him, might be addressed to her shows just how unsure she had become of Edward's feelings towards her. (Ironically, one of the worst aspects of the experience, when Edward felt that his father had treated him with so much contempt that he had been ashamed to be alive, was that it caused Edward himself to fear that 'I had probably made Helen feel exactly the same.'[21]) For Helen to believe that a poem which ended 'But not so long as you live / Can I love you at all' was written to her shows how bad relations between them had become.

When he went on to write the second of what would become a series of valedictory poems to his family, the verse equivalent of the will he had made in Haynes's office, he feared that Helen would again believe that the poem he claimed was to his mother – 'No one so much as you', with its bleak fifth stanza stating 'I but respond to you / And do not love' – was about Helen herself. It is a suspicion he tries to pre-empt with another offhand remark: 'You might as well have concluded the verses to Mother were for you.'[22] Yet nothing he wrote about his mother suggests that he had ever stopped loving her in the way the second half of this poem implies. He was particularly concerned about her by early 1916, when an operation for cataract resulted in the loss of sight in one eye, and extremely grateful to Eleanor for visiting her as she convalesced. While the opening four stanzas of the poem fit in with what we know of his loving relations with his mother, with her timid, introverted nature and his defence of her against criticism of any kind, however, the last six stanzas do not:

> …My eyes scarce dare meet you
> Lest they should prove
> I but respond to you
> And do not love.
>
> We look and understand,
> We cannot speak
> Except in trifles and
> Words the most weak.
>
> For I at most accept
> Your love, regretting
> That is all: I have kept
> Only a fretting
>
> That I could not return
> All that you gave
> And could not ever burn
> With the love you have,
>
> Till sometimes it did seem
> Better it were
> Never to see you more
> Than linger here
>
> With only gratitude
> Instead of love –
> A pine in solitude
> Cradling a dove.[23]

These final six verses, in a quite different key from the first four, are almost certainly a separate poem to Helen, who came next, chronologically, on the list of what he once referred to as his 'Household Poems'. Instead, his official poem to her, 'And you, Helen', came at the end, an attempt it would seem to write a publicly acceptable version of his feelings for her and what he wanted to give her – youth, beauty, good sight, 'lands, waters, flowers, wine, / As many children as your heart / Might wish for'. Most significantly, in a tacit acknowledgement of the failures in their relationship, he wants to 'give you back yourself... And myself too, if I could find / Where it lay hidden and it proved kind'.[24] Written after his three poems to his children – in which he lovingly 'gives' some of his favourite Essex place-names to Bronwen (Codham, Cockridden, Childerditch, Roses, Pyrgo and Lapwater) in return for her continuing to find the first flowers of spring for him, and some even more fancifully named Essex places to Merfyn, but nothing more than Steep to the 5-year-old Myfanwy, whose 'small hands I would not cumber / With so many acres' – his poem to Helen is noticeably more guarded, hinting at a sense of guilt over their relationship.

Edward was, in any case, seeing even less of Helen by the beginning of 1916. Christmas had gone reasonably well, Merfyn's return from America providing common ground for rejoicing, but when Thomas returned to camp on 30 December 1915, he found that his old hut (Hut 35) had been broken up, the men separated. There was also a stricter application of the rules, with the two-mile out-of-bounds limit now rigidly enforced and leave even rarer than before, meaning fewer weekends still with Helen. It also meant that lunches with Edna on Thomas's free Wednesday afternoons were ruled out: her house, though an easy distance for a good walker like Edward, was outside the two-mile limit. Maresco Pearce's transfer back to London on 11 March may have made it even more difficult for Thomas to visit her, with the love poems a possible outlet for his frustrated feelings.

Thomas's responsibilities also increased with his transfer to D Company and Hut 15. Though he shared the hut with four other map-instructors and 15 new recruits, as the most senior man there, he was in charge. He was obliged to make sure that everyone was ready for an hour of parade and drill, to call the roll, see that meals were collected, served and cleared up by one of the recruits, the hut kept clean and a fund organized for the purchase of occasional luxuries. It was not a role he enjoyed. As he told Frost, he 'dislike[d] inflicting discipline', and his promotion to full corporal was delayed when he falsely reported his friend Arnold Mason present on Sunday 9 January, trusting that he would arrive shortly afterwards: Mason returned at seven o'clock the next morning and both men got into trouble.[25] Thomas was particularly galled that his younger brother Reggie, still in the same camp, got his second stripe before him. When 500 volunteers for

France were called for immediately, he even considered offering himself. An outbreak of measles among the men, which threatened to stop his leaves altogether, made February equally dreary and a chill which lasted ten days did not help matters. Maresco Pearce's departure in early March deprived him of one of his closest friends in the camp and he began to feel restless.

Thomas's restlessness, he believed, came from 'not being able to write a bit', yet this is contradicted by the facts.[26] By the beginning of March he had completed 14 poems since arriving at Hare Hall Camp, had had two accepted for publication in a magazine Guthrie had worked for, *Form*, six chosen for publication in book form by Guthrie himself and a request for a substantial number of contributions to *An Annual of New Poetry*. Abercrombie's response to his work, which Bottomley showed him, 'pleased [him] more than it could have done with any other man's name at the end,' he told Abercrombie.[27] Though he insisted on preserving his pseudonym, Edward Eastaway, this public recognition of his ability as a poet at last renewed his confidence.

News of the war Thomas also believed to be 'pretty good' by mid-March. Yet the Battle of Verdun had already begun in February 1916 and would drag on until December and the long build-up to another of the war's bloodiest battles, the Somme, had also begun. Meanwhile Thomas was writing hopefully to Frost: 'There is a prophecy abroad that [the war] will be over by 17 July. Helen says why not her birthday, which is a few days earlier.'[28] In the event, though the Battle of Bazentin Ridge, which ended on 17 July, would be a great deal more successful than the catastrophic opening day of the Somme, it would mark the start of a period of costly attrition, as German resistance strengthened.

Other less illusory consolations included visits from friends. John Freeman, for instance, took the train out to Gidea Park on Sunday 16 January, and again later in the year, to walk and talk and eat with Thomas in the fields around the camp; de la Mare visited at the end of April, with yet another cake. Thomas was also able to see Jesse Berridge, who lived just five miles away at Brentwood. Helen came once, though Eleanor, urged to do so, did not. By 14 April, now a full corporal, his past sin forgiven and earning one shilling and fivepence a day, Thomas was able to tell another of his faithful correspondents, Haines, that it was 'not a bad life. I find a lot to enjoy in it'.[29] His affection for his fellow-soldiers had increased as he made a conscious effort to bond with them through the places they knew best – 'There isn't a man I don't share some part with,' he told Bottomley.[30] It was a novel way of putting his travels to good use. He also grew fond of his captain, though unable to resist a parody of his good-hearted but clichéd speech to his men as they left for officer training: 'Pay attention. Stand easy. I just want to say a few words to you men who are going to the [cadet] school. I wish you all success. I hope you won't get into any trouble at all. Take care to mind your Ps and Qs and do everything top-hole.' Then, when he saw a rabbit in the fields: 'Company attention! Oh, look at that rabbit.'

On 19 May, on the pretext of needing dental treatment, Thomas attended the performance of Bottomley's one-act play, *King Lear's Wife*, which was being performed in London together with Gibson's *Hoops* and Brooke's *Lusitania*. He was accompanied by another of Bottomley's protégés, also in the Artists' Rifles, the artist Paul Nash. Though none of the three plays impressed Thomas greatly and he was not recognized by people like Sturge Moore, Marsh or Trevelyan, he enjoyed the outing with Nash. Eleven years younger than Thomas and destined to become an official War Artist, Nash shared a number of things in common with him, including time at St Paul's School. According to Mrs Nash, her husband found Thomas 'stimulating and sincere'.[31] Nash himself wrote that Thomas 'was always humorous, interesting and entirely lovable'.[32] Thomas welcomed Nash as a change from his usual two friends, Wheatley and Mason: 'He is wonderful at finding birds' nests,' he told Frost.[33]

Thomas's only 'grumble' at Hare Hall by mid-1916 was that he had even less time to write: an increasing scarcity of leave meant fewer railway journeys, during which the majority of his poems had been written. So he was ready for a change when the opportunity offered itself in early June. After realizing that the expenses of a commission would 'swallow up all his pay',[34] and determined 'not to do anything that rob[bed] Helen of her separation allowance', he had continued in his 'safe job [as a map-instructor], only too safe, with only too good company'.[35] He felt guilty on all sides, convinced that he must earn as much as possible to support Helen, yet also that he should be ready to take more risks for his country, to suffer more. So that when news that he had been granted £300 from the Royal Literary Fund reached him on 10 June, he was both 'grateful and disappointed', according to Eleanor, who had helped secure it with the signature of the eminent lady of letters, Alice Meynell.[36] It was not the Civil List Pension he had hoped for – he was too young and fit for that, apparently – but it did offer him a way out of his dilemma. Not only could he afford to pay for an apprenticeship for Merfyn, organized by his brother Theo with London Transport, but he could now apply for the commission he wanted without damaging Helen's financial prospects. The disappointment at not getting the pension he had applied for with the help mainly of Garnett and de la Mare, was minor compared with the relief of being able to resolve these two outstanding concerns.

Even the news that he was being turned out of his study at Wick Green by Mrs Lupton, while her husband was away in France, was made less painful by the fact that more money would make it easier to move from Steep, as Helen had wished to do for some time. With her husband in the army, the resolutely pacifist – to her somewhat self-righteous – stance of the Bedales staff had begun to annoy her. She also wanted to be nearer to Merfyn when he started his apprenticeship at Walthamstow in September. With the help of her sister Irene, whose husband Hugh had died in March and left her with time on her hands, the Thomases would eventually settle on a cottage near Edward's first camp at High Beech, 2 St Paul's Nursery.

In anticipation of his grant, by 6 June Thomas had already started applying for a commission in the Royal Garrison Artillery (RGA), initially in the Anti-Aircraft Corps, a branch responsible for the anti-aircraft defence of Britain. But without military influence of some kind, he expected to have to wait some time: 'You don't know an artillery colonel who might help,' he asked de la Mare, perhaps only half-joking.[37] His earlier thoughts of applying for some kind of 'Welsh Army job' with the status of officer had come to nothing.[38] When Bottomley asked him: 'Why Artillery? You can find enough danger anywhere, if you are bent on that, without taking on still more with guns, which are the affair of experienced professional soldiers', he replied: 'To get a better pension for my wife.'[39] It is an ambiguous answer, suggesting either that pensions were higher in the Artillery (which they were not) or that Helen could expect to become a widow earlier and therefore get her pension sooner. Certainly Edward could expect to be promoted sooner, since the number of its members being killed in battle was even higher than in the Infantry.

Thomas had been thinking of the RGA even before enlisting in the Artists' Rifles, writing to Eleanor in June 1915 that: 'If anybody said "You go and join the Royal Garrison Artillery and they will give you a commission", I believe I should go next month.'[40] Two of his friends, Rolfe Scott-James and G. R. Blanco-White, were intending to apply there and Harold Monro had already joined, though Thomas did not know this until later. He realized that his maths fell far short of what was needed for 'the big guns' – 'I believe they are the biggest,' he told Bottomley with what sounds like pride – but was confident that he could rectify that.[41] There was no doubt in his mind that he had made the right decision: he had wanted a change and in the Siege Artillery, which he settled on in preference to the much safer Anti-Aircraft Corps, he believed he would get it. 'Nobody,' he told Bottomley on hearing of his acceptance, 'is quite as pleased as I am myself and shall be when I am gazetted.'[42]

Thomas anticipated an even busier time ahead and it seemed more important than ever to write as many poems as possible. (Poetry, he had once told Eleanor, was 'the nearest approach I ever made yet to self-expression.'[43]) After finishing his verses to his family and a few more love poems in April and May, he had returned to more characteristic subjects with 'Tall Nettles'. 'Anything, however small, may make a poem,' he had written five years earlier in *Maeterlinck*, demonstrating this repeatedly in poems like 'Adlestrop', 'Swedes', 'The Path' and 'But these things also'. Thomas had written 'I like nettles' in *The Icknield Way* and now set about explaining this. For, as Bax argued, it was an unconventional choice of subject matter for a poem even by 1916. But, as J. C. Squire explains, Thomas was a poet of a 'peculiar and interesting kind':

> Most landscape poetry deals with certain special kinds of times and places, dawn, twilight or sunset, mountains, bleak moorlands, ripe cornfields, seas very rough or very blue, summer more than winter, strong moonlight more than the diffused light of an ordinary overclouded day. – Edward Thomas was unusual in avoiding the usual. Not only did he not go to nature mostly for decoration or for a material setting for his moods, but he did not *select*, unconsciously or deliberately, his subjects. Except that he avoided large towns and the conventionally romantic, one may fairly say that he was liable to write a poem about anything one might see at any time of day in a walk across the South of England.[44]

The understated description in 'The Nettles' of a neglected corner of a farmyard, with 'the rusty harrow, the plough / Long worn out and the roller made of stone', in which the narrator captures our attention by liking most:

> As well as any bloom upon a flower
> I like the dust on the nettles, never lost
> Except to prove the sweetness of a shower[45]

becomes another of those apparently commonplace scenes or experiences, anywhere and everywhere, which nevertheless acquire significance in retrospect and sum up so much of what is meant by Englishness. It is expressed, as Cooke suggests, 'in an undertone, overheard rather than heard'.[46]

Other poems written on familiar sights, such as cherry trees shedding their blossoms in May (the month 'The Cherry Trees' was written), contrast the comforting recurrence of seasonal events with the stark facts of a war, now in its third year, which had already claimed thousands of lives. Based on a remark of Myfanwy's during a walk together, when she mistook the fallen blossoms for confetti – 'Someone's been married' – 'The Cherry Trees' suggests that thoughts of France were constantly in her father's mind:

> The cherry trees bend over and are shedding
> On the old road where all that passed are dead,
> Their petals, strewing the grass as for a wedding
> This early May morn when there is none to wed.[47]

With the conciseness of an Imagist poem or a Japanese haiku, Thomas conveys, without needing to spell out, a powerful sense of loss and waste. Like his first poem of this type, 'In Memoriam (Easter 1915)', 'The Cherry Trees' records what is *not* – the men who will never return to pick flowers for their sweethearts in the first poem are now replaced with the young men who will, therefore, never marry. His short critical study of *Lafcadio Hearn* (1912) had focused his attention on the influence of Japanese on English literature, which he was already aware of in the poetry of Yeats, Pound, the Imagist poets generally and two closer friends, Bottomley and Dalmon. As far back as 1907 he had reviewed Elizabeth Bisland's *The Life and Letters of Lafcadio Hearn*,[48] as well as the work of the Japanese poet Yone Noguchi, who wrote mainly in English but advised English and American poets to experiment with the Japanese haiku ('hokku') form. He had met Noguchi several times and was almost certainly influenced by him.

The haiku's definition of a thing by its absence, an indirect rather than direct approach, is characteristic of Thomas's poetry as a whole and also reflects the way in which nature conveys its significance to him. In 'I never saw that land before', for example, 'the valley…the river small / The cattle, the grass, the bare ash trees', and numerous other apparently unremarkable features of the landscape, 'hinted all' but 'nothing spoke'.[49] For it was the impossible he aimed at in his verse, to 'sing / What would not even whisper my soul'. And in order to do that, the narrator concludes, he would have to use indirect communication 'as the trees and birds did, / A language not to be betrayed':

> And what was hid should still be hid
> Excepting from those like me made
> Who answer when such whispers bid.

'Bright Clouds', for instance, written a month later on 5 June, makes no overt reference to the war but its 'tall reeds / Like criss-cross bayonets' bring it sharply to mind. And 'The Gallows', based on stories told to Myfanwy, though ostensibly about a gamekeeper who strings up the corpses of dead animals to deter other predators, also evokes thoughts of France.

Even Thomas's most direct approach to war, 'This is no case of petty right or wrong', takes the form of one half of a debate he was having with his father. In 'As the team's head-brass' this debate is widened to include another speaker. (When Thomas had written to Frost in March promising 'not to *indulge* in a spring run of lyrics', he had resolved to 'try again to make other people speak', thus preventing the poet from giving a single point of view.[50]) In Edward's account of the poem's composition in a letter to Helen, it is the lovers who feature most prominently. But both the letter and the poem reinforce the view that his decision to enlist was closely linked to his feeling for the English countryside:

> As the team's head-brass
>
> As the team's head-brass flashed out on the turn
> The lovers disappeared into the wood.
> I sat among the boughs of the fallen elm
> That strewed an angle of the fallow, and
> Watched the plough narrowing a yellow square

Of charlock. Every time the horses turned
Instead of treading me down, the ploughman leaned
Upon the handles to say or ask a word,
About the weather, next about the war.
Scraping the share he faced towards the wood,
And screwed along the furrow till the brass flashed
Once more.
      The blizzard felled the elm whose crest
I sat in, by a woodpecker's round hole,
The ploughman said. 'When will they take it away?'
'When the war's over.' So the talk began –
One minute and an interval of ten,
A minute more and the same interval.
'Have you been out?' 'No.' 'And don't want to, perhaps?'
'If I could only come back again, I should.
I could spare an arm. I shouldn't want to lose
A leg. If I should lose my head, why, so,
I should want nothing more... Have many gone
From here?' 'Yes.' 'Many lost?' 'Yes: a good few.
Only two teams work on the farm this year.
One of my mates is dead. The second day
In France they killed him. It was back in March,
The very night of the blizzard, too. Now if
He had stayed here we should have moved the tree.'
'And I should not have sat here. Everything
Would have been different. For it would have been
Another world.' 'Ay, and a better, though
If we could see all all might seem good.' Then
The lovers came out of the wood again:
The horses started and for the last time
I watched the clods crumble and topple over
After the ploughshare and the stumbling team.[51]

This is another poem about the war's intrusion into rural England, again centring like 'February Afternoon' around the commonplace country activity of ploughing. Though ploughing at first glance seems the opposite of war, it, too, is made to reflect it, mainly through the imagery in the poem – the 'fallen elm', 'treading me down', 'scraping the share', 'screwed along the furrow', 'the blizzard' that 'felled the elm', 'the clods crumbl[ing] and toppl[ing] over' and 'the stumbling team', all of which bring to mind the men in the trenches. Even the 'flash[ing]' of the team's head-brass is reminiscent of ammunition.

The way in which the war is again set within the recurring cycle of nature, including human nature – the ploughing in spring, the lovers' retreat into the wood – allows Thomas to set up a contrast with the deaths in France of the ploughman's friend and many others who will never return, as the seasons and the lovers will. But on a more subtle level, the storm which fells the elm (a poem on the fallen elm by John Clare may lie behind this reference, as well as an actual blizzard of a few months previously) could be interpreted as a representation of the ploughman's dead friend, and, therefore, also part of the natural cycle. In other words, as in 'February Afternoon', war may be as much a recurring feature in man's life as the seasons. As such, it appears to be in some respects a challenge to, or contradiction of, Hardy's 'In Time of "The Breaking of Nations"', which it nevertheless echoes. Thomas's poem, unlike Hardy's, gives us the narrator/soldier's thoughts and feelings on war – Thomas was actually in the army by this time, whereas Hardy was not – as well, through a skilful use of dialogue, as the ploughman's. We are allowed both points of view and, because it *is* a dialogue, no greater weight is given to either. The ploughman, however, is allowed the last word: 'If we could see all all might seem good.' But the debate is still open; we could, if so minded, regard this ironically, especially coming from a non-combatant.

Though written in a less regular verse form than usual, the structure is very clear, controlling the material firmly within the framework of the lovers going into the wood at the beginning and coming out at the end, the ploughman's circuit as he ploughs, breaking up the conversation and reflecting, perhaps, the speakers' disjointed thoughts. It is, as the form itself suggests and Edna Longley argues, a poem about gaps, discontinuities and absences.

'No one cares less than I', completed the day before 'As the team's head-brass' and another dialogue of a kind, shows a similar readiness to face thoughts of death. By the time it was written in May camp life was regulated by bugle calls and Thomas, thinking perhaps of the association Rupert Brooke had set up in his '1914' sonnets between bugles and death ('Blow out, you bugles, over the rich Dead') and death and glory ('If I should die, think only this of me / That there's some corner of a foreign field / That is for ever England'), turns this to ironic ends to declare his indifference (real or assumed) to death in battle. An emphatic negative opens the poem and sets the tone, as it had in 'No one so much as you':

> 'No one cares less than I,
> Nobody knows but God,
> Whether I am destined to lie
> Under a foreign clod,'
> Were the words I made to the bugle call in the morning.
>
> But laughing, storming, scorning,
> Only the bugles know
> What the bugles say in the morning
> And they do not care, when they blow
> The call that I heard and made words to early this morning.[52]

Once again, as in Hardy's universe or in 'February Afternoon', God sits apart from it all.

These thoughts of death were undoubtedly linked to Thomas's decision to join the Royal Garrison Artillery, but once he had made a formal application in June, he marks it in a more playful fashion with a pastiche of two of his favourite folk-songs, 'Early One Morning' and 'Rio Grande'. The first revision of 'Early one morning', as it becomes, implies that the narrator is leaving his sweetheart because of her father's disapproval, but the final poem is less specific, still focusing on departure from familiar scenes but with the narrator making similar preparations to those Thomas was contemplating, such as burning his letters. So that when, in stanza five, the speaker tells us 'A gate banged in a fence and banged in my head' and in stanza six 'I could not return from my liberty, / To my youth and my love and my misery', it is tempting to interpret the whole poem autobiographically, especially the final stanza:

> The past is the only dead thing that smells sweet,
> The only sweet thing that is not also fleet.
> I'm bound away for ever,
> Away somewhere, away for ever.[53]

The war is always there in the background. Pondering on something as neutral as a dialect word he had first heard in 1895, for instance ('Aftermath called Lattermath in Wiltshire and Gloucestershire,' he wrote in his second field notebook), the memory prompts him to ask in 'It was upon', 'What of the lattermath to this hoar Spring?' in 1916.

'It was upon' was the first of three poems written when Thomas went sick on 21 June. It was his third sick leave since enlistment and worries about his own physical and mental weakness were uppermost in his mind in the third poem he produced during this lull, 'There was a time'. Garnett, who had known Thomas during the time he claims in the poem that 'this poor frame was whole / And I had youth and never another care', the period when 'weakness was all [his] boast', found the poem 'tense with the gravity of a long-delayed confession',[54] which is particularly true of the lines: 'I sought yet hated pity till at length / I earned it. Oh, too heavy was the cost'.[55] Eleanor, who could not be expected to welcome the reference to Thomas's possible death, thought the poem 'sick', to which Thomas responded: 'I thought it was more than a shade heroic.'[56] It is also evidence of his conviction that joining the army had provided an answer of sorts: 'I find less to grumble at out loud than I did ten years ago,' he had written to Frost the previous month: 'I suppose I am more bent on making the best of what I have got instead of airing the fact that I deserve so much more.'[57]

Thomas's implied decision in 'There was a time', to sacrifice himself for his country if required, came at a crucial moment in the war on the Western Front. The Allies' protracted bombardment of the Germans on the Somme, which started the day he wrote his poem, 24 June, failed to achieve its aim and the battle which followed would continue to claim the lives of thousands of men until it ended on 18 November 1916. The great demand for officers and men to replace them created enormous anxiety in the camp, Thomas reported to Eleanor in mid-July, and, for the second time that year, he considered volunteering for France immediately. His actions and words had for some time seemed those of a man saying goodbye. He had cleared out his study, taken a three-day walk with Helen, visiting friends like the Hootons and the Lock Ellises during leave to mark his first year of service, and written three poems charged with a sense of death or the unknown, 'The Green Roads', 'The Gallows' and 'The Dark Forest'. He also secured another £1 a week's pay for Helen from the Civil Liability Commission.

When, after three weeks of hard work improving his maths, he was formally accepted by the RGA on 28 July his relief was evident. Despite Helen's claim that, by the end of a year in the army, 'he hated it all, the stupidity, the injustice, the red tape, and the conditions of camp life',[58] the thought of going to an Artillery School and being 'out in France or who knows where in a few months' made him feel 'much happier' again, he told Frost, 'after months of panic and uncertainty'.[59] The increased pressures at Hare Hall Camp had left no time for the walks he had previously enjoyed there and if posted to the London branch of the Artillery School as he hoped, he would be able to see old friends. In his optimistic mood he even believed, at the height of the Battle of the Somme, that 'things [were] going right now': 'we have endured long waiting,' he wrote to Frost. 'I think we can stand anything now, even success.'[60]

Thomas managed to write only one more poem during his last few days at Hare Hall Camp, and that probably because he found himself once more in the camp hospital after yet another vaccination. 'How at once' starts optimistically enough, with the narrator's expectation that the swifts he sees migrating every May will return the following year, but it ends on a sombre note:

With other things I but fear
That they will be over and done
Suddenly
And I only see
Them to know them gone.[61]

Though he insisted that his poem was simply about 'natural history',[62] he undoubtedly had a sense, if not of foreboding, of something coming to an end. 'It is a restless time,' he admitted to Bottomley on 14 August as he made a 'huge bonfire' of his letters, papers and books at Steep, ostensibly in preparation for the move to a new house: 'All anchors will be up soon.'[63] The following day he was discussing the possibility of an edition of his poetry with de la Mare's brother-in-law, Roger Ingpen, who ran a small publishing house, Selwyn & Blount. Thomas had known Ingpen from his Balham, pre-Oxford days and also from his dealings with him as the reader for Hutchinson who had negotiated the commissions for both *Richard Jefferies* and *Lafcadio Hearn*. He was a fellow-member, too, of the

Square Club. Though the book would be a modest collection of 64 pages, published under Thomas's pseudonym in a small edition of 525 copies, it would be an important landmark in the growth of his reputation.

With only a week left before joining the Artillery, Thomas's thoughts were almost wholly on France, however. 'I wish suddenly I was an Officer going out now,' he wrote to Eleanor in mid-August: 'I am most impatient.'[64]

26

The Long Goodbye
(August 1916–January 1917)

Gone, gone again,
May, June, July,
And August gone,
Again gone by,

Not memorable
Save that I saw them go,
As past the empty quays
The rivers flow.

And now again,
In the harvest rain,
The Blenheim oranges
Fall grubby from the trees,

As when I was young –
And when the lost one was here –
And when the war began
To turn young men to dung...

Started on 26 August 1916, the day after Cadet P. E. Thomas presented himself for duty at the Royal Garrison Artillery in London, 'Gone, gone again' conveys a strong sense of nostalgia, regret yet resignation.[1] Based on an incident described in a 1908 field notebook – the 5-year-old Bronwen's repeated lament when the stem of the wild rose she picked had snapped as she walked home: 'It's gone. It's broke. – It's gone, it's gone, gone, gone' – Thomas's poem adds to the grief of the child an adult acceptance of what cannot be mended or changed.[2] His unflinching realism as he takes his final step on the road to France, or wherever else he might be sent, is reflected in the bleakest of imagery of desolation and decay. The allusions to recurring seasonal events – 'harvest rain' and 'Blenheim oranges', an old-fashioned variety of apple likely to appeal to Thomas – imply that the young men being turned 'to dung' (and, presumably, fertilizer for future apples) by the war is another inevitable process in life. The apples may be 'grubby', not only because of the sooty London rain, which was particularly heavy in the second half of August 1916, but also because, like the doomed young men, they are vulnerable to decay from either enemies or grubs.

A powerful sense of loss is present from the first word of the first line, 'gone', which is also the last word of the last line of Thomas's previous poem 'How at once' – 'to know them gone'. This is reinforced by subsequent allusions to a lost childhood, lost 'young men' and 'the lost one', almost certainly a reference to Edna Clarke Hall from whom Edward had recently parted on leaving Romford. ('It rains', written while Thomas was still seeing Edna, celebrates two people 'walking, kissing' in an orchard in the rain.)

'Gone, gone again' ends as it begins on a note of resignation and emptiness. Thinking of the old London houses Thomas had loved so much as a child,

> Outmoded, dignified,
> Dark and untenanted,
> With grass growing instead
>
> Of the footsteps of life,
> The friendliness, the strife …

the narrator concludes:

> I am something like that:
> Not one pane to reflect the sun,
> For the schoolboys to throw at –
> They have broken every one.[3]

Despite Helen's only too evident need of him, Thomas had suffered for most of his adult life from a sense of uselessness or redundancy, culminating periodically in thoughts of suicide. Though actual references to suicide stopped once he joined the army, it is clear from another poem of this period hinging on the word 'gone' – 'What will they do when I am gone?' – that his sense of superfluousness, if anything, increased: 'It is plain / That they will do without me as the rain / Can do without the flowers and the grass / That profit by it and must perish without.'[4]

Thomas sent 'Gone, gone again' to Eleanor from Handel Street in Bloomsbury, the branch of the RGA school to which he was assigned after reporting initially to their St John's Wood depot. On the eastern edge of Bloomsbury, it was not far from Monro's Poetry Bookshop in Devonshire Street and even nearer to the house Virginia Woolf had moved to with her brother and some friends in 1911, before her marriage to Leonard Woolf. Their house in the north-eastern corner of Brunswick Square backed on to St George's cemetery at the far end of Handel Street from the RGA Drill Hall. It would be yet another reminder of mortality for Thomas, who would use the imagery of graves, or 'tombs', in a second poem written during his Handel Street period, 'That girl's clear eyes'.

The Royal Garrison Artillery had existed as a separate branch of the Royal Artillery since 1899, when it was made responsible for coastal defence, mountain, siege and heavy batteries. New barracks at Handel Street had been opened in 1913. Since 1914, when the army had possessed very little heavy artillery, the RGA had grown into a vital component of the British forces on the battlefield, armed with heavy, large calibre guns and howitzers that were positioned some way behind the front line and had immense destructive power. Rigorous training for such dangerous work was needed for cadet officers destined for the front.

Thomas's first fortnight of training at Handel Street was spent 'learning about guns and wearing spurs'.[5] (The RGA were technically mounted troops.) Though feeling 'poor and feeble' after another vaccination and an abscess on his hand, he did not find the work physically hard: 'I learn to aim at invisible targets,' he wrote to Frost, 'to know the parts of a gun, the gun drill etc, the telephone by which we shall communicate, the work of an observation officers who watches the result of his battery's fire etc.'[6] But there was a great deal to take in and he was in a large group with 'rather few instructors'; he also felt slower and less apt than his much younger fellow-recruits, many of whom were engineers, surveyors and schoolmasters in civilian life, with a much better grasp of the maths involved. Being billeted at his parents' house again meant that he did not make new friends. On the other hand he did have an old acquaintance, Rolfe Scott-James, with him and he could visit other friends in the evening. Best of all, officer-cadets, he told Frost, were treated rather better and had fewer duties and responsibilities, less demands on one another, than in camp:

> The result is I am rather impatient to go out and be shot at. That is all I want, to do something if I am discovered to be any use, but in any case to be made to run risks, to be put through it. I have been saying to myself lately that I don't really care a fig about what happens. But perhaps I do. – I am cut off. All the anchors are up.[7]

In a poem written the day after this letter, Thomas repeats his sense of being cut off, of a lack of communication with the outside world, whether in the form of an unidentified girl or his fellow-soldiers: metaphors of concealment, of being sealed up and of death reinforce this central message:

> That girl's clear eyes utterly concealed all
> Except that there was something to reveal.
> And what did mine say in the interval?
> No more: no less. They are but as a seal
> Not to be broken till after I am dead;
> And then vainly. Every one of us
> This morning at our tasks left nothing said,
> In spite of many words. We were sealed thus,
> Like tombs.[8]

The 'stony square sunlit' and 'airy plane [tree]', together with 'the dark cloisters' and marching lines of schoolchildren, in the second half of the poem refer to Brunswick Square, where some training took place, and the neighbouring Coram's Fields, a seven-acre site housing the Thomas Coram Foundling Hospital of 1739, still standing in 1916:[9]

> ...Nor until now could I admit
> That all I cared for was the pleasure and pain
> I tasted in the stony square sunlit,

Or the dark cloisters, or shade of airy plane,
While music blazed and children, line after line,
Marched past, hiding the 'Seventeen Thirty-Nine'.

Such moments of pleasure were few, however, and Thomas's restlessness increased. By 17 September he was telling Jesse that he was 'not enjoying this half and half cadet stage a bit'.[10] Fortunately he passed his first exam which, despite his fears, he found easy, and on 20 September he accompanied the rest of his unit to the RGA's main training centre at Trowbridge, the county town of Wiltshire, eight miles south-east of Bath, near the Somerset border. Sent there to learn about the handling of the heavy guns, be brought to a peak of physical fitness and be given further instruction on the duties and skills of an officer, he found the work 'very hard and long and the conditions uncomfortable,' he told Bottomley after five weeks.[11]

There were consolations. It was a great relief to be out of London and in one of his favourite counties. Though Trowbridge was much further west than his childhood haunts around Swindon, he knew the area well from his visits to Bax at Broughton Gifford and his stays at Dillybrook Farm, near Bath, where he had written *Swinburne*. Situated at the junction of the A361 to Frome and the A363 to Bradley, near Trowbridge town centre, the barracks were within walking distance of attractive countryside, including the Mendip Hills only three miles away: 'It isn't bad and the weather is lovely,' he wrote to Eleanor on Monday 25 September, a few days after his arrival: 'Moreover the Saturday and Sunday were almost free, so I walked both to Dillybrook and to Bradford [near Broughton Gifford] by the fields. We are in tents and so we see the night sky. The trumpet blows for everything and I like that too, though the trumpeter is not excellent'. Edward's letters to Eleanor are a great help in understanding his poetry, this letter in particular. His enjoyment of the fine weather, some long walks in the countryside he loved, his delight in the night sky and the sound of the trumpet help to account for the positive, joyous note of 'The Trumpet' (written just after his letter to Eleanor):

Rise up, rise up,
And, as the trumpet blowing
Chases the dreams of men,
As the dawn glowing

The stars that left unlit
The land and water,
Rise up and scatter
The dew that covers
The print of last night's lovers

Scatter it, scatter it![12]

Yet this poem has often been read as an ardent call to battle, despite what is known of Thomas's attitude towards war. The poet's final exhortation, 'To the old wars; / Arise, arise!' could as easily be seen as an acceptance of necessity rather than martial fervour, the need to defend a world that is 'lovelier / Than any mysteries'.

Thomas remained at Trowbridge for seven weeks of intensive training, promoted to lance-bombardier (the Artillery equivalent of lance-corporal, and known as 'bomb' or 'lance-jack') shortly after arrival, which increased his work. From 6 a.m. to 7.30 p.m., apart from meals, he was lectured to about levers, pulleys and other gun-related matters. His evenings were spent reading up on the subject of the day. He did not leave the barracks except at weekends because the rules demanded that men change from their working uniform into cadet uniform before going out, and he was unwilling to do so. 'It is school again,' he complained to Bottomley at the beginning of October, 'and I am far from the top of the class,'[13] The teaching seemed to him 'improvised and atrocious' and to pass the required exams the men had to teach themselves in certain subjects, like hydraulics. He minded less about the demand for a high level of physical fitness, welcoming a strenuous afternoon of exercise, running, walking and particularly swimming: 'We had a swim yesterday in the Frome,' he told John Freeman in late October.[14] During weekends spent in camp he organized and led long walks or runs in the surrounding countryside.

His main worry was not the strict training but the family move to High Beech, which had been postponed repeatedly: 'Helen runs away so comfortably from affairs,' he had explained to Frost.[15] He was no longer free to organize the entire move himself, but he did manage to get to Steep to help prepare for it the week before it took place on 8 and 9 October. It was yet another goodbye, this time to the area which had been home to him for over a decade, and he records the occasion in 'When first I came here I had hope'. Walking down *his* hill the narrator feels that 'Hope now.../Just hope has gone for ever', a possible allusion to Hope Webb.[16] He also spent the week's leave he was given after sitting his second exam at 2 St Paul's Nursery, High Beech, helping Helen to settle in.

Edward loved Epping Forest and High Beech held some pleasant memories for him. While he almost certainly agreed with Eleanor that the house itself was unsatisfactory – 'bad...dismal and poorly planned...too temporary to settle in' – he relished its position 'right alone in the forest among beech trees and fern and deer'.[17] With his thoughts increasingly on France, it hardly seemed to matter where they settled. But he did worry about Helen, who had become uncharacteristically depressed as his commission and departure grew more likely. After her full social life at Steep, he feared that High Beech would be lonely for her and that the frequent Zeppelin raids in the area would increase her sense of isolation.

Helen herself made no secret of her dislike of their new house. For the first time in their married life she did not believe that a new house promised a new start and her lacklustre approach to the change increased the problems, which had begun with a 'grotesque nightmare' of a move with 'drunken men and books hurled pell-mell into cases'.[18] The house seemed to her frankly 'horrible...ugly, cold and inconvenient – an impossible place to make either pretty or comfortable'.[19] Her dissatisfaction sprang as much from Edward's remoteness, physically and emotionally, as from the house itself: 'single-handed,' she emphasizes, 'it took me a long time to get things ship-shape, and even when all was done there was a makeshift feel about the place which could not be eradicated, and which I hated it for': she felt as if she were 'waiting for I know not what'. An 'unutterable fear, an icy chill' had taken possession of her heart.[20]

Edward returned to Trowbridge from High Beech on 23 October to find that he had passed his second exam. While he rejoiced, Helen's fears increased. For him becoming an officer meant 'going out to France'; for Helen, his mother and Eleanor, it meant the strong possibility of his death.[21] When, after another three weeks, he completed his Trowbridge course successfully and was sent for a week to RGA barracks at Wanstrow, Somerset, for further training and exams, he regarded it as progress, while the anxiety of the three women deepened. Gazetted 2nd Lt P. E. Thomas on 20 November, he started to shop for equipment for France immediately, and set off with a relatively light heart the same day on a visit to Gordon and Emily Bottomley in the Lake District.

The worst was yet to come: writing to Eleanor from his new barracks at Lydd in Kent, where he was completing the last section of his training, he told her on 7 December 'the news we dreaded, and he desired,' as she puts it: 'they asked for volunteers to go straight to batteries in France and I made sure of it by volunteering. Don't let Helen know.'[22] But he had already made his intentions clear to Helen in his letter of 6 December, almost callously so, and she had felt 'the icy chill [taking] a closer grip, and the sense of statically existing – not living – [growing] more intense'.[23]

One reason for the increased demand for officers in France by late 1916 was the inconclusive ending to the long drawn-out Battle of the Somme on 18 November; it had claimed more than a million casualties overall, adding to the high cost of the failed Gallipoli campaign, and leaving the British Army more in need of reinforcements than ever. Lloyd George, who replaced Asquith as Prime Minister the same day that Thomas announced he was volunteering for France, faced an immediate demand for vigorous action. Lloyd George believed the Allies had found it in General Joffre's plan for a large spring offensive at Arras. One of the RGA units destined for Arras was the 244 Siege Battery, to which Thomas would be assigned on 16 December, the day after he passed his final exam.

To all outward appearances Thomas was unconcerned by the dangers of 'going out'; indeed at times he seemed eager to face them. Yet a number of things contradict this. His three-day visit to say goodbye to the Bottomleys, for example (taken during a week's leave between his Wanstrow and Lydd postings), suggests that he was very aware that he might not return. While he 'enjoyed every hour of it' and Bottomley remembered it as a particularly happy visit, it had ended on a sombre note:[24]

> There was talk and music and he sang (he always sang when he came to us): beside his folk-songs he had acquired a riotous collection of army-songs, which he sang with a mischievous quietness that made the rowdy ones much funnier than they were meant to be. He went [on] one or two long walks with my wife; at other times he sat with me in my open garden-house. One afternoon we spent a long time indoors watching a

marvellous storm gather...he said reflectively 'You are lucky.' I replied 'What, with my health?' He was silent for an appreciable time, then said still more quietly 'Yes.'[25]

Emily Bottomley had a strong presentiment on that visit about Thomas: 'He is going to die',[26] and in photographs taken during the visit Thomas has an almost skeletal look while the invalid, Bottomley, looks robust and full of life.

Jessie Conrad would also sense that the visit Thomas paid to her and her husband a few weeks later from Lydd would be his final one: 'There was something in his quiet resignation to his fate, that fate which seemed to both Conrad and myself to be sealed in some strange fashion that impressed us all.'[27] Three of the men who sat in Conrad's study on 9 December 1916 would die before the war was over, but not one of them seemed to her then to have that 'tragic air of fate and finality, [as much] as' Thomas, 'whose very gentleness seemed the strongest protest against the senseless taking of life. One felt his uncomplaining acceptance of the inevitable.'[28]

The most convincing proof of Thomas's state of mind at this time occurs in the poetry he was still managing to write on his long, roundabout journeys home to Essex. 'Lights Out', for instance, a description of his thoughts at the last trumpet call of the day, seems even at first reading more than a straightforward account of falling asleep:

Lights Out

I have come to the borders of sleep,
The unfathomable deep
Forest where all must lose
Their way, however straight,
Or winding, soon or late;
They cannot choose.

Many a road and track
That, since the dawn's first crack,
Up to the forest brink,
Deceived the travellers
Suddenly now blurs,
And in they sink.

Thomas had feared that 'The Dark Forest' of four months previously might be a 'bad Maeterlinckian' symbol, but it can be, undoubtedly, a place of threat in Thomas's poetry, and beyond it; the dangers of 'los[ing] [one's] way' and 'sink[ing]' into quicksands are made obvious. Even 'silence' and 'sleep' are given ominous overtones in this context:

> Here love ends,
> Despair, ambition ends,
> All pleasure and all trouble,
> Although most sweet or bitter,
> Here ends in sleep that is sweeter
> Than tasks most noble.
>
> There is not any book
> Or face of dearest look
> That I would not turn from now
> To go into the unknown
> I must enter and leave alone,
> I know not how.
>
> The tall forest towers;
> Its cloudy foliage lowers
> Ahead, shelf above shelf;
> Its silence I hear and obey
> That I may lose my way
> And myself.[29]

The forest is 'unfathomable', the way 'winding' or tortuous, 'deceiv[ing]' the traveller and leading to the 'brink'. In addition the destination is unknown and the sleep may be Shakespeare's 'sleep of death', his 'undiscovered country from whose bourn / No traveller returns'. The narrator's compulsion to 'go into the unknown' in stanza four, and to forgo 'love', 'ambition' and 'all pleasure' supports this reading, especially since it will end 'despair', one of Thomas's greatest problems in adult life.

Helen, whose own writing, ironically, helped to advertise Thomas's suicidal tendencies, nevertheless worried greatly that 'Lights Out' might be read as a suicide note. 'Though [it] obviously has undertones of death,' Myfanwy wrote much later, 'Mother was absolutely certain that the poem is initially about going to sleep, that my father would never have used a euphemism for Death or anything else.'[30] While it would be simplistic to interpret 'Lights Out' as a straightforward suicide note, however, the narrator's obedience to the silence of the towering forest, 'That I may lose my way / And myself' invites the reader to consider that possibility.

Wanstrow, from 13 to 17 November, had been something of an interlude. Not far from Frome, it was situated in 'beautiful country that I know a little,' Thomas wrote to Eleanor from the big empty house in which he was billeted, 'with two basins for forty-two men.'[31] It had been a far less demanding routine, working the men from 9 a.m. to 4 p.m. only – 'and then as much as we like'. Thomas had chosen to walk two hours in the evening before rehearsing for a concert in which he and three others were singing 'Mr McKinley', an American ballad on the murder of President McKinley, which Eleanor had taught him courtesy of D. H. Lawrence.

Lydd Barracks, which followed after a fortnight's leave, was less indulgent, a more sombre reminder of what lay ahead. But Thomas could still enjoy exploring this area on the south Kentish coast, previously unknown to him. In the fine, clear weather of early December 1916 he relished the flat shingle, even the long rows of low huts 'enormously' and found Lydd itself, a few hundred yards away, 'beautiful – an old group round a very tall church tower and a line of elm trees, the only tall things in all the marsh at all near'.[32] The tin huts which gave the camp its nickname 'Tin Town' seemed to him not nearly as ugly as he had expected.

When firing practice began in earnest on the shingle beaches, reached by an extensive single-gauge railway line, he began to feel 'nearer the real thing' and not just because of the continual sound of the guns on the ranges.[33] A letter written to Helen a week after his arrival conveys the sense of expectation, unrest and apprehension in the camp. He had shared his train journey to the Conrads on 9 December with three men from another squad who had just been told to get ready for Salonika. They had been stopped at the station while going off for an ordinary weekend leave and taken back to camp to get their things together for the 'adventure': 'Some people believe that our squad is for France and not Salonika,' Edward told Helen. 'In some ways I should prefer Salonika except that I believe there will be a desperate big mess there. I am afraid there will be a mess everywhere.

I am afraid things are very bad indeed.'[34] After having passed his final exam, he wrote to Eleanor five days later, more starkly, 'I am waiting my destiny.'[35] His 'destiny' turned out to be 244 Siege Battery, to which he was assigned on 16 December, and he would have another six weeks to wait while his battery, only halfway through its training, completed its preparations for the front.

Thomas had hoped to be in France before Christmas. He preferred not to have a Christmas in England just before going out, he had told Frost: 'I want to go soon, to get over the first and worst step [of parting].'[36] He was finding it increasingly difficult to enjoy his leaves for that reason. But the prospect of a Christmas in England without leave annoyed him, and he was delighted when it came through unexpectedly on 18 December. Eleanor, in whom he confided more than in Helen at this stage, was the first to know and managed to organize a gift of £20 for Helen to celebrate their Christmas in style. Helen's own account of preparing 'a great turkey', decorating the house, getting a Christmas tree for Myfanwy, who had never had a real one, rushing into London to buy Edward 'the best Jaeger sleeping-bag and thick gauntlet gloves and a volume of Shakespeare's sonnets', as well as sweets for the family and 'luxuries [they] had never tasted before, and wine as well', is breathless with excitement.[37] Edward's is far more restrained, 'very glad to be home' the most he will allow himself.[38] His poem written on Christmas Eve, 'Out in the dark', gives a much clearer idea of his state of mind, his mixture of excitement and apprehension as he waits to 'go out'. The poem, he explained to Eleanor, was inspired, once more, by his youngest child 'who speaks, not I'.[39] 'Did Mother tell you I wrote a poem about the dark that evening when you did not want to go into the sitting room because it was dark?' he asked the 6-year-old Myfanwy, making clear the central concern of the poem:

> Out in the dark over the snow
> The fallow fawns invisible go
> With the fallow doe;
> And the winds blow
> Fast as the stars are slow.
>
> Stealthily the dark haunts round
> And, when a lamp goes, without sound
> At a swifter bound

Than the swiftest hound,
Arrives, and all else is drowned;...[40]

Thomas's unconscious echo of Edward Grey's well-known remark on the eve of the First World War – 'the lamps are going out all over Europe' – strengthens the link to that conflict at this stage, especially when the narrator confesses his 'fear' in the third stanza, the one Thomas liked best:

And star and I and wind and deer
Are in the dark together, – near,
Yet far, – and fear
Drums on my ear
In that sage company drear.

The poem ends with a reminder of the weakness and insignificance of the personal life – 'the universe of sight, / Love and delight' which Thomas was enjoying with his family – before the 'might of...night' he faced in 'going out' (one of his most frequent phrases at this point). Echoing as it does what Thomas himself had characterized as Hardy's 'most tyrannous obsession of the blindness of fate, the carelessness of Nature, and the insignificance of Man', it is possible, as has been suggested, that 'Out in the dark' influenced the older poet when he came to write 'The Fallow Deer at the Lonely House'.[41]

Yet back at Lydd, on the next step of the journey to France, Thomas says he feels 'no trouble or anxiety'.[42] He has gained confidence as an officer, is proud of his unit, which boasts a 9.2-inch howitzer, believes his Officer Commanding, Captain Fenner, to be excellent and has begun to make friends with his fellow-officers. Apart from John Thorburn, already known to him, there were four others, two 2nd Lieutenants, a full Lieutenant and the Captain, all of them younger than himself, the youngest (at 19) half his age, in charge of a company of 150 men.

On 1 January 1917 he starts writing the diary he had abandoned on going to High Beech in September 1915: 'Shooting with 15 pounders and then 6" howitzers. All week at Lydd, I being F[ire]/C[ontrol officer] or observer daily, with mapwork for next day at night.'[43] Both the diary-writing and the shooting practice are a sign of the gravity of the situation and his own role in it. This final preparation for mobilization brings with it, at the end of the week, mobilization leave, spent mainly saying yet more goodbyes to friends – Bertie Farjeon and his wife Joan, Harry Hooton and Thomas's Parisian host, Jones, W. H. Davies, Haynes, Berridge, Tom Clayton and many others. He records his parting from Eleanor, which took place at High Beech after her last night's stay with the family on 8 January, in two words: 'Eleanor left'. Her own feelings, outwardly controlled as they had always been, were expressed more intensely in three of the sonnets she wrote to him after his death. After anticipating his 'go[ing] the way / Which in these bloodshot years uncounted men have gone', she describes their final farewell, when he had walked her down to the bottom of the hill leading into Loughton, and her gratitude that he had not, as he thought he might, met her in London three days later on his way back to camp:

> I thank you that you would not, friend.
> Not thanks for sparing a pain I would have dared,
> But for the change of mind which at the end
> Acknowledged there was something to be spared.[44]

Edward's parting from his mother two days later would be cushioned by the presence of all five of his brothers and his father at a last family dinner. Their real goodbye came the next morning when he left for Lydd. He says nothing of his mother but tells Helen of his father's last remark as he left the house 'and said goodbye with the words "I wish you had more belief in your cause to support you"'.[45] But when Helen criticized Mr Thomas for this, Edward responded with some insight, 'Don't be too hard on father. He did relent and walked with me to the train. He is just like me in that way.'[46]

The most painful parting was from Helen, an occasion she described in harrowing detail, particularly their last night. Several of Edward's close friends, such as Frost and Haines, felt embarrassed to be let into such intimate detail when they read it later in *World Without End*, convinced that the intensely private Edward would have hated it. Yet Helen herself clearly needed to write about an experience she had found so terrible that she did not think one could live through such agony. Her letter to her closest friend, Janet, as she began to recover very slowly from her severe nervous breakdown after his death, reveals how completely dependent her life had been on his:

> Three years ago today Edward went away from me. The snow was deep
> on the ground and he soon disappeared in a thick fog, and we cooied to

each other until we could not hear any more. I was left alone knowing that I would never see him, never hear him[,] never hold him in my arms again...Our life together was a restless sea, tide in, tide out, calm and glorious[,] despair and ecstasy; never still, never easy, but always vivid and moving, wave upon wave, a wild deep glorious sea. Our life was terrible and glorious but always life.[47]

The weight of such dependency was hard to bear and the strongest feeling Edward expressed after their parting was one of worry about Helen. (To Helen he wrote ambiguously 'All is well from now on.'[48]) Writing to Frost the day after leaving High Beech on 11 January for the last time, he assures him: 'I am quite well and in good spirits except when I think of Helen. I doubt if she is very strong to bear what she has to bear.' There is pity here – the pity expressed in 'No one so much as you' – and possibly also guilt that he has imposed the situation on Helen. After all, given his age, his family responsibilities and the fact that he had been invited to continue as a map-instructor with the Artists' Rifles, a skill he considered vital at the front, he could have remained in England honourably. He could also have opted for the Home Coastal Defence branch of the RGA, like Hodgson or the playwright Granville Barker, who had recently been assigned to it (much to Thomas's scorn). His volunteering for France was carried out in the full knowledge of its dangers and of how much it would distress Helen. His insistence on doing so may have sprung, as Frost believed, either from a need to prove himself to Frost and to himself, or from a need to get away from Helen. It could also have signalled a welcoming of the possibility of death, or simply come from a sense of duty.

In this same letter to Frost of 12 January Thomas also mentions Ingpen's decision to publish a selection of his poems, finally agreed over the winter months. In passing through London on his way to Lydd, Thomas handed over his selection to his publisher, carefully excluding the 18 poems chosen for Constable's *An Annual of New Poetry*. He had arranged for proofs of Ingpen's book, which would not be ready until after his departure for France, to be read by two of his most trusted friends, Eleanor and John Freeman. His last letter to Ingpen a week later would beg him 'not to make use of' his situation as a soldier bound for France, however tempting, 'now or in the event of any kind of accident to me, to advertise the book.'[49] The book was to be dedicated not to Helen but 'To Robert Frost'.

One poem written too late for inclusion in *Poems* (Selwyn & Blount, 1917) was 'The Sorrow of True Love', composed the day after he had confided his worries about Helen to Frost. In this context it reads less like a recognition of a 'true love' enjoyed by himself and Helen than an admission of pity and anxiety about her. Helen made a fair copy of the first five lines, which she chose to interpret as an acknowledgement of their 'true' love but which could possibly apply to Hope Webb (see line 4) or Edna Clarke Hall:

> The sorrow of true love is a great sorrow
> And true love parting blackens a bright morrow.
> Yet almost they equal joys, since their despair
> Is but hope blinded by its tears, and clear
> Above the storm the heavens wait to be seen.[50]

It is perhaps significant that Helen did not copy the conclusion to this bleak poem, which points to a less positive interpretation of his feelings as those of 'remorse and pity':

> But greater sorrow from less love has been
> That can mistake lack of despair for hope
> And knows not tempest nor the perfect scope
> Of summer, but a frozen drizzle perpetual
> Of drops that from remorse and pity fall
> And cannot ever shine in the sun or thaw,
> Removed eternally from the sun's law.

The clogged language and that final 'frozen drizzle', which conveys an even greater sense of hopelessness and depression than the 'cold drizzle' Thomas noted in his diary the day he wrote this poem, may reflect his tortured feelings as he looked back on his relationship with Helen. Though Helen had not yet sent on to him her Christmas present of Shakespeare's sonnets for France, Edward knew them well and his echoes from a number of them, particularly 'When in disgrace with fortune and men's eyes, / I all alone beweep my outcast state', reinforce a sense of failure and hopelessness.

'The Sorrow of True Love' would be Thomas's last completed poem. ('I can't write now,' he had told Frost on New Year's Eve, 'and still less can I read. I have rhymed but I have burnt my rhymes and feel proud of it.'[51])

It was written during his last weekend at Lydd, where he had to stay on in the empty camp to hand over to the incoming unit. Most of the battery were already at their final embarkation camp at Codford, no. 15, where he joined them on 15 January. On arrival he wrote yet another farewell letter to Eleanor, confessing that he had not tried to see her while passing through London as half-promised. Eleanor was grateful to be spared the pain, but Helen is unlikely to have felt equally glad that he did not seize a last chance to see her when he was given an unexpected leave on 22 January. Instead he visited Haines and his wife in Gloucestershire.

The Haineses thought Thomas seemed more cheerful and better physically, that he was 'glad to be done with waiting and to be going out', though they, too, had the distinct impression 'that he was not coming back and that he knew it'.[52] Paradoxically he showed little trace of the melancholy Haines had previously witnessed in him and 'was talkative and gay beyond his wont', discussing some new books of verse Haines had in the house, by de la Mare, Gibson and Davies, and naming de la Mare's 'Keep Innocency' as his favourite poem.[53] He also talked of his life in the army, of the men, their marching songs, the officers and 'most of all the guns; he liked them all,' Haines recalled.[54] When he left the next day, it would be with Haines's spare copy of Frost's latest collection, *Mountain Interval*, one of the few books he read immediately and would take to France.

Thomas was already familiar with the countryside round Codford from Hudson's *The Shepherd's Calendar* and his own trips through the area, which he now explored further on several long walks. One of these was to de la Mare's friends, the Newbolts at Netherhampton, for Sunday lunch. 'Someday I hope we shall live on Salisbury Plain,' he wrote to Helen.[55] He also took the men on route marches through the surrounding countryside, proud that he had not lost them on the way. Though he had always been good with his hands and a successful gardener, he enjoyed proving how capable he could be when called upon. He boasted of learning to ride a motorcycle on 19 January, for instance – 'I shall be unrecognisable at the end...find myself reading Rider Haggard,' he joked with Garnett.[56] He might grumble about them, but he listed his duties with some pride to Eleanor: 'I not only have to manage the mess and the cook but have to keep the accounts and pay the bills.'[57] As his future O/C, Major Franklin Lushington would write in a novel based closely on the 244 Siege Battery's time in France, *The Gambardier*, in which Thomas features as 'Thomas Tyler': 'Among the subalterns T. Tyler alone was reliable and useful...He carried on quietly and patiently...His serene and kindly presence and quiet dry humour did much to alleviate the squalid miseries of life [in France] for his companions.'[58] By January 1917 Thomas could no longer worry that he was one of those 'superfluous' men he had encountered in Turgenev, written about in *The Happy-Go-Lucky Morgans* and had once feared himself to be.

Edward's letters to Helen are for the most part filled with practical details – asking her to send his 'Jaeger waistcoat', detailed discussions of his attempts to find suitable baggage for France, the weather and the fact that she has sent too much 'underclothing' when he really needs more socks, a scarf and 'of course, the calico bags'.[59] He lists his duties: inspecting the cookhouse and latrines, lecturing to the battery. But his careful avoidance of anything emotional is undercut by his repeated 'goodbyes', sometimes in the middle of a letter, and an enigmatic request for her 'particular news', a possible reference to the pregnancy she longed for. He also gives detailed instructions about the children, being particularly concerned that Bronwen has taken to wearing, 'transparent stockings most unsuitable for a child of 14 who lives in the country and is not well off nor bait for a man who is well off'.[60] It is an example, he believes, of Helen's 'liking for prettiness go[ing] too far'. But (like his own father) he relents in his next letter.

By 23 January his 'latest news' is that their captain, Fenner, has reported sick and will almost certainly not be accompanying 244 Siege Battery to France. It is an uncertain time: 'We have no idea what will happen.'[61] By 24 January he is issued with a steel helmet, field dressings and iodine, which he supplements with Epsom salts, more soap and medicines sent by Helen. By 26 January a supply of motorbikes has arrived and a replacement for Fenner is imminent, namely Captain Franklin Lushington. The battery is now expecting to sail to France from Southampton on Monday 29 January.

Only during his last weekend in England does Thomas admit to feeling 'doleful'.[62] Though he blames 'a dirty east wind' and 'being lame' (from new boots troubling his ankles again) the real cause was almost certainly the thought of leaving the countryside he loved and his family. He had walked over the Downs by Cricklade Bottom and the Fonthills to the Ransomes' house at Hatch, near Tisbury, to see his youngest, Myfanwy. She was being looked after by Ivy Ransome, who insisted he stay the night. Before going to bed Myfanwy sat on his knee by the fire and told him that she had been singing some of the folk-songs he had taught her to Ivy's rather conventional mother. Her choice – 'Gor blimey O'Riley you are looking well' – amused him greatly. Riding back on a hired bicycle the next day, to save his blistered feet, he relished once again the beauty of the area, as he joined the Mere and Amesbury Road at Fonthill Bishop: 'hedgeless roads over long sloping downs with woods and sprinkled thorns, carved with old tracks which junipers line – an owl and many rabbits – a clear pale sky and but a faint sunset – a long twilight lasting till 6'.[63] If he needed a reminder of all he would be leaving the next day, it was this last ride back to camp in the gathering dusk.

On arrival back at camp, Thomas was told that the battery would be moving out at 6.30 a.m. the next day. Thorburn had left with the guns on the twenty-seventh after they had spent an evening discussing serious things – poetry, philosophical questions and the Bible. Now, on the twenty-eighth, dining with two more light-hearted fellow-officers, Horton and Smith, he was 'merry and hilarious', joining in with their 'imbecile jests', but he was fully aware of the dangers they faced, writing to Helen the same evening, 'I think we are for the Somme, right enough.' But it would be to Arras, where the next great battle of the war was planned, that Thomas was sent.

27

'No More Goodbyes Now'
(January–April 1917)[1]

> Cold, dirt, fatigue, uncertainty, and the accidental or amusing
> thing. If only one wasn't taught to think it was something else.
> But then this is the case everywhere, not only out here.
>   – Thomas to Walter de la Mare, 9 March 1917

Thomas's account of his two and a half months in France, in
the diary he had started on 1 January 1917, makes it seem
even more regrettable that he wrote no poetry there. Parts of it
read like embryonic Thomas poems, particularly his passages on
the birds he observes daily at the front – black-headed buntings,
thrushes, linnets, pigeons, magpies, hedge sparrows, rooks, kestrels,
chaffinches, pipits, owls, blackbirds and great tits, and the familiar
larks of war poetry – and some notes at the end of his diary, which
also read like germs of poems: 'The light of the new moon and
every star / And no more singing for the bird...' A separate jotting
inserted into it suggests that he may even have attempted verse at
one point, as he contemplated the dangers he faced, perhaps with
his poem 'Roads' in mind:

> Where any turn may lead to Heaven
> Or any corner may hide Hell
> Roads shining like river up hill after rain.

To begin with, however, Thomas's experiences at the end of January 1917, as he made his way to France with 244 Siege Battery, seemed more suited to the genius of two other war poets, both of whom were proceeding towards Arras during this same period, Siegfried Sassoon and Isaac Rosenberg. Rosenberg, for instance, has left a graphic account of the crossing all three took from Southampton to Le Havre in 'The Troop Ship':

> Grotesque and queerly huddled
> Contortionists to twist
> The sleepy soul to a sleep,
> We lie all sorts of ways
> But cannot sleep.
> The wet wind is so cold,
> And the lurching men so careless,
> That, should you drop to a doze,
> Wind's fumble or men's feet
> [Are] on your face.[2]

While Thomas would not have had to endure such discomfort on his ship, the *Mona Queen*, where three officers shared a cabin in relative comfort, once his battery reached its position in France he would suffer equally painful experiences.

Thomas's journey down to Southampton began at five o'clock on the bitterly cold morning of 29 January. As the 244th marched to Codford station in the dark with the men singing 'Pack up your troubles in your old kitbag', the song (though not to Thomas's musical taste) 'brought one tear' as he said in his last goodbye of all, to England.[3] With no food or tea to cheer either officers or men on the freezing journey to the port, when they arrived at 9.30 a.m. they had to wait in Southampton till dusk, when they sailed at 7 p.m. Though both the departure from England and arrival in France struck Thomas as 'beautiful and unforgettable', he found the journey as a whole tedious in the extreme.[4] Even after their arrival at Le Havre at 4 a.m. the next day, the 244th had another five-hour wait until they were allowed to march to the rest camp three miles away. Breakfast, when it finally materialized, was at 9.45 a.m.

Thomas resorts frequently to his favourite phrase for army life at this point, 'hanging about', which is what he felt he was doing for the next five days, his problems increased by the bad ankle and blisters he had acquired on his walk to see Myfanwy at the Ransomes. Still unable to read anything more demanding than a magazine, even less able to concentrate on serious writing of his own and not remotely interested in the endless card-games played around him, he spent most of his time censoring the men's correspondence and writing his own long letters to family and friends. 'The worst of this hanging about,' he told Eleanor, 'is that everybody gets on one's nerves, or my nerves.'[5] He would not be the first, or last, to compare such camps to 'a clearing house'.[6] Sassoon, who would set out for Arras a fortnight after Thomas, would describe his own transit camp at Rouen as a Military Sorting Office and find it a memorable target for his satire in 'Base Details':

> If I were fierce, and bald, and short of breath,
> I'd live with scarlet Majors at the Base
> And speed glum heroes up the line to death ...

Thomas's own account of life in *his* transit camp may lack the concentration and satiric punch of Sassoon's, but like most of his diary entries and letters written in France, it enables his readers in England (as Bottomley claimed) 'to see inconceivable things vividly' in a way which 'the usual photographs of the war correspondents' do not.[7] Thomas himself would dismiss the writing of one such journalist, William Beach Thomas of the *Daily Mail*, after reading his account of the ruins of Péronne: 'I am very glad it is not my job,' he wrote to his parents, 'and at the same time sure I could do it infinitely better... It is a pleasure not to have to write through one's hat.'[8]

Despite his claim that he was glad *not* to have to write about the war, however, it seems likely that Thomas was already contemplating a book on his experiences in France. This would help explain his return to diary-writing after a gap of 15 months. He also makes his intentions fairly clear when he asks Helen, three days after arriving at Le Havre: 'By the way, if you keep my letters, would you keep them in order, as they are so much fuller than my diary.'[9] With his parents he is more explicit: 'I wonder if you would mind keeping my letters, so that I might some day, if I wished, use them as a supplement to my diary.'[10] As it is, his diary and letters together paint a fascinating picture of conditions in France for a newly fledged officer and his unit in early 1917, their surroundings, their daily routine, their food, their discomforts and their unexpected pleasures.

There is, however, one notable omission from Thomas's account, that is, any attempt to give the political and military background to the Battle of Arras. In the case of his letters this is understandable, since it would have been regarded as sensitive information and censored accordingly. And in the case of his diary, which is quite frank in other areas, it may be that the soldiers knew very little of what was happening beyond their own small part in the grand scheme. Thomas's letter to Frost of 8 March suggests as much: 'You sound more hopeful than people are here. Not that they are despondent but that they just don't know what to think. They know that the newspapers are stupid and the Huns wise, and there practically is the end of their knowledge.'

Yet Arras was one of the great battles of the First World War and needs to be put into context for many modern readers. The year 1916 had ended in a sense of defeat for the Allies: the Somme offensive had not been the decisive victory many anticipated, Russian morale was at a low ebb, Romania had been overrun and, at sea, Jutland had been at best a negative encounter. Only the capture of Baghdad could really be counted as a success and that seemed to most English people too far away to be of much interest. One result of the growing dissatisfaction had been the change of political leadership in England, from Asquith to Lloyd George in December 1916, and a switch in military leadership in France where General Nivelle (who had successfully pushed back the Germans at Verdun, though not without attracting criticism for his costly counter-attacking strategy, and in the process coined the famous rallying cry '*Ils ne passeront pas*') replaced Marshal Joffre as Commander-in-Chief of the French Armies. While Lloyd George and his fellow politicians on the Allied side were rejecting German peace proposals in December as insincere, Joffre had been drawing up plans for one more great battle, in the belief that this would finally defeat the enemy.

Since Allied troops in France numbered about 3,900,000 men (one-third of them British) to the Germans' 2,500,000, Joffre had calculated that a concerted attack in spring 1917 should exhaust their reserves and bring the war to an end. When Nivelle took command in early 1917, while accepting Joffre's plan of a renewal of the Somme offensive on a widened front, in principle, he made several significant changes. He proposed to attack on both flanks of the Lens–Noyon–Rheims salient, with the French striking the greatest blow in Champagne after Allied attacks north and south of the Somme had claimed the Germans' main attention. His plan to avoid the old Somme battlefields but attack each side of them reduced the frontage of the British, who were ordered instead to take over the French front south of the Somme as far as Roye, in order to release more French troops for the main attack in Champagne. In spite of Haig's reservations, the battle was fixed for 1 April, an unfortunate date. It was an ingenious scheme, but even before it got under way (later than planned) on 9 April, the Germans had disrupted it, as Thomas would witness. Ludendorff, anticipating the Allies' move and anxious to avoid repeating the senseless butchery of the Somme, had already ordered a new, massively fortified line of defence to be built across the base of the Lens–Noyon–Rheims arc. This new line, completed early in 1917, would be known as the Hindenburg Line.

Had Thomas lived to write a book about his involvement in the Battle of Arras he would no doubt have offered his own interpretation of it. Despite this omission, there is a great deal to value in the account he has left us. It was not simply the bird-life he enjoyed; once out of Le Havre on 4 February, he found the countryside as a whole, including its human element, a familiar source of pleasure: 'We have passed between beautiful chalk hills and low country,' he wrote to Helen as his train started on its crawl up-country towards Arras, via Alaincourt and Amiens.[11] 'I must say I am enjoying this journey more than anything since I left home. It is a real journey…the wayside country and troops and Y.M.C.A. ladies and telegraph wires and poplars and now some big junction all snowy with black engines, and men carrying planks, and signals, and trees.' 'I don't think I really knew what travel was like till we left England,' he told Frost, offering the possibility that his unwritten book on France might have been his most interesting travel book of all.[12]

What also emerges from Thomas's account of his first real journey in France is an appreciation of the way the men coped with the discomfort of travelling. He was highly conscious of the fact that, while he shared a compartment with only one other officer and could lie down to rest, the men were packed in, 35 to a truck. He especially admired the way they used humour to deal with this and other difficulties, often with irreverent songs.

On this particular journey, which began with the usual long delays, they started with 'The nightingales are singing in the pale moonlight', crying 'All tickets' and imitating cattle as they were crowded into their cramped trucks (marked, in French, '40 men, 10 horses'). As they drew closer to the action their song of choice became 'We haven't seen the Kaiser for a hell of a time, / Hell of a time, / Hell of a time'. Though Thomas would grow tired of songs like 'Where does daddy go when he goes out', or 'Wait till I'm as old as father', he realized from the start how helpful such apparent 'nonsense' could be.[13] He even enjoyed their amusement when he nearly missed the train at one of their stops. He grew fond of the men generally, his servant in particular, whom he told Eleanor was a 'gem':

> He is a carpenter from Oxford named Taylor, rather slow but extraordinarily good-humoured, and thoughtful and ingenious. He washes and darns for me and pillages wood to keep our stove going and in between he keeps up a slow stream of nice rustic remarks. He won't lose anything if he can help it. He is the most devoted thing I have met since we lost our dog. He mutters 'They put upon good nature, don't they, Sir' but though I tell him not to listen to anyone but me he goes on being put upon without complaint.[14]

The journey also helped to harmonize the disparate group of six officers in charge of the 244th. Apart from his limited contact with the two 'boys' of 19 and 20, Rubin and Smith, he quickly learnt to appreciate one of the two regular soldiers among them, Captain Horton, who had come up from the ranks and by his mid-twenties had already been in the army for ten years. While regarding him as 'commonplace' and realizing that he could never have a 'serious' conversation with him, after a fortnight in France he was describing Horton to Frost as 'a rather fine specimen of the old English soldier, always bright and smart and capable, crude but goodhearted and frivolous and yet thorough in their work'.[15] He relished Horton's talk particularly, 'all…in sort of proverbs or cant sayings and bits of comic songs, coarse metaphors – practically all quotation'.[16] 'He and I get on excellently somehow', he told de la Mare, to his own evident surprise.[17]

The other regular soldier in their group, Captain (soon to be Major) Lushington, was also 14 years his junior. From his initial dismissal of him as 'a smooth…vain man', Thomas gradually learnt to respect, even like him. Lushington's younger brother had been killed in France only four months before he came to take command of the 244th and it could not have been easy for him. He also found it difficult at the beginning to give orders to someone so much older than himself, until he realized that Thomas did not appear to mind. According to Lushington the officers and men alike 'looked up to him [Thomas] as the kind of father of our happy family'.[18]

Thomas's opinion of the group was more qualified: 'We get on well enough but we six are rum company,' he wrote after two months with them.[19] One of the 'rummest' of all, yet ironically the one to whom he felt closest in many ways, was the only other officer over 30, John Thorburn. This 'Scotch philosopher' (a university lecturer in civilian life) he found 'an impossible unmilitary creature who looks far more dismal than he really can be'.[20] While appreciating the fact that there was one man he could talk to seriously, he thought him 'too gloomy, timid and apologetic and helpless to live with'.[21] On the one hand he welcomed the chance to discuss philosophy, poetry and the Bible, but Thorburn's 'screaming nightmares', his many neuroses and his inability to deal (as Thomas could) with the stream of 'dirty stories' favoured by Horton, Rubin and Smith were wearying.[22] He understood Thorburn's worries about not being able to laugh at the obscene jokes and his fear that his inefficiency might lose him his commission, but would be greatly relieved when he was posted elsewhere. Nevertheless this 'melancholy Scottish philosopher bred mostly in solitude under his mother's roof' had a salutary effect on Thomas, making him realize how 'dismal' he might himself have appeared at times and increasing his efforts to fit in with the people and situations around him, however uncongenial.[23] Thorburn in turn would tell Helen on the day Edward died of his 'great debt of gratitude' to him; he had been Thorburn's 'support' through work he found difficult and alien to his nature: 'I claim at least his friendship and…am terribly lonely out here without him.'[24]

Thomas himself noted the 'curious experience of getting on with quite incompatible people' and this ability to get on 'moderately well, or even more with all sorts of uncongenial people' (his own words to Bottomley) was one of a number of reasons Eleanor believed he was 'so excellent and so contented and so greatly liked' as a soldier:

Not that any aspect of war itself made him so, but that he was completely suited to the job required of him among men of all sorts for whom he was responsible: fitted for it by years spent in the open air on all roads in all weathers, of field-work and observation, of mixing naturally with uncomplicated people, of doing practical things in the elements he was at home in: knowing that he was doing all this well, and more than 'fairly pleased' that, without too much fear, he could enjoy in war-time France the sort of things he had enjoyed in peace-time England.[25]

Thomas would need all these qualities and more, even before the 244th arrived in the battle area. The journey there was exhausting, physically and mentally, their train taking 24 hours to cover the first hundred miles to Doullens, where they spent the first night. After much 'hanging about' there, Thomas was sent ahead to Mondicourt to choose billets for a second night, spent in bitterly cold lodgings in one of the highest spots in northern France. A third night in Bernaville, with a makeshift dinner of half-cold food, eaten mostly standing up, was followed by a march to their final destination – for the moment – Dainville, only two miles from Arras. Dinner that night was bully (corned beef), cheese and white wine.

Thomas endured all the discomforts of the journey without complaint, and seems even to have relished them at times. A streak of puritanism in his nature, verging on masochism, appears to have made physical suffering enjoyable or at least reassuring. Only when Horton's weekly parcels from Fortnum & Mason's arrive, or food sent by families and friends of other officers provide them with the occasional luxurious meal, did he complain, preferring the plain food served to the men. But there was no opportunity in France to try different diets and his improved appetite did not allow for faddishness. Similarly, Helen believed, he had 'little time for depression'.[26] Even his frequent illnesses and fears of illness disappear, a chill being the worst he complained of once the fighting is under way.

This preference for hard, plain living would serve Thomas well at the front. The journey over, he would spend the next week visiting Observation Posts and studying maps, work he much preferred to choosing billets for the men, supervising jobs and signing orders. He 'enjoyed' his first day out in the line, he told Eleanor, 'the exercise, the work with a map and field-glasses, the scene, the weather and the sense of being able to do a new job. Altogether I have never seen or done anything out of doors more exciting or interesting and not more pleasant.'[27] Walking to and from the Observation Posts in the 'fine clear weather' that mid-February, he thought it 'as good as any walking I ever did,' he told Hooton: 'The country is much like Salisbury Plain, chalky, with a few streams, and buildings of brick, chalky stone and red tiles.'[28] Even his first sight of a dead man 'lying like a monument covered with sacking' could not spoil his enjoyment.[29]

Manning an Observation Post appealed to Thomas not just because it made him feel both needed and responsible; it also gave him a legitimate opportunity to study the countryside – 'nice high hilly country' – more carefully.[30] When there was no firing to observe on 15 February, for example, he admitted to Helen that he 'turned [his] [field]glasses onto a kestrel and saw him pounce and come up with a mouse'.[31] Hardly the kind of observations he could include in his official report, they nevertheless added interest to his daily duties and helped to take his mind off the dangers he knew he ran 'sitting in a ruin within easy range of the Huns'.[32] With his keen sight there was little he missed, as the short-sighted Eleanor amusingly recalled. His efforts to teach her his countryman's knowledge had failed disastrously in England when he had pointed out a deer running across a road in Epping Forest:

> 'Where? Oh – I've missed it!' [Eleanor wrote] – but I knew that at most I should only have discerned some flicker of movement. And then the flicker cut across my sight. 'There goes another! I can see it now!'
> 'That one', said Edward, 'was a motor-car.'[33]

Thomas's dry sense of humour would serve him almost as well as his keen sight in France. An unusually dull day at one Observation Post, for instance, was enlivened for him by the sight of 'a mad captain', clearly of the game-hunting kind, 'with several men driving partridges over the open and whistling and crying "Mark over".'[34] Humour would also help him to endure three weeks at the Group 35 Heavy Artillery Headquarters in Arras as Orderly Officer. Instead of reacting strongly to what he viewed as being 'a glorified lackey or humble adjutant to an old Indian colonel perplexed in the extreme', he joked about it, repeating with relish the Colonel's comments on 'the old Hun', whose planes he considered 'confoundedly cheeky' for bringing down a number of British planes over Arras at the end of February.[35]

Thomas's secondment to Group Headquarters on 19 February had made him feel the least needed of the 244's subalterns, though he had probably been specially chosen for his map-reading skills, to help decipher the reconnaissance photographs taken from the air. 'Hang[ing] about' after a Heavy Artillery commander and trying to please him made him feel that his soul was 'less [his] own'.[36] He hated office work, disliked the lack of hard physical exercise, had no opportunity to speak the French that he had been practising at his battery and was convinced that his maths would grow stale. After his first week he was depressed by 'lots of food and too little exercise'.[37] Even Helen's news of Selwyn & Blount's proofs of his poems could not entirely cheer him up, though he was relieved to hear that they had been checked by Eleanor and John Freeman: 'My proofs sound as though they would be perfect.'[38] (They were not; the typesetting was careless and inconsistent and made Thomas's verse look like prose on occasions.) In his depression he had stopped reading a daily Shakespeare sonnet but vowed to begin reading again when his own poems arrived in book form. And, apart from his diary and letters home, he still 'couldn't think of writing'.[39] Experiences which inspired Sassoon, Rosenberg, Owen and countless other war poets to write their best work would fail to produce one complete poem from Thomas, whose genius flourished on less outwardly dramatic subject matter. When Helen told him that Frost had persuaded Henry Holt to publish an American edition of his *Poems* he seemed indifferent, sending no thanks for Frost's efforts, merely a brusque 'So you did find a publisher after all[40].' And he welcomed the acceptance of three of his poems by Harriet Monroe for *Poetry* (Chicago) as 'very good news' mainly because the magazine paid well: 'The money is the thing.'[41]

The nearer the battle came, the less his own work seemed to matter. He wanted now to be involved in action, not words, and what depressed him after two weeks at Headquarters were 'the long hours of waiting, nothing that ha[d] to be done and yet not free to do what [he] want[ed]'.[42] He missed his fellow officers at the 244th, one of the worst aspects of his job at HQ being the lack of people he liked much. 'I don't want friends,' he explained to Frost, 'I don't think I should like to have friends out here...But I want companions and I hardly expect to find them here.'[43] There were plenty of 'likeable people' – Colonel Witchall in his more charming and affable moments, Captain Angus, another subaltern Cassells and the Signalling Officer, Major Berrington – but he warmed to none of them.

One small consolation was that he could discuss poetry with Berrington, 'a hard clever pungent fellow', who was familiar with the verse publications the *New Age* and *Georgian Poetry*. Another advantage was the beauty of Arras, where it had survived heavy shelling, the great ruined Town Hall reminding him of Carreg Cennen in Wales. (Arras had just escaped being captured by the Germans in 1914.) The town itself brought to mind the elegance of Bath. He loved the white houses and shutters of the Place Victor Hugo and the numerous gardens, courtyards and open spaces with trees. He admired the beautiful eighteenth-century citadel with a church standing ruined in a great barrack square.

When, after two days at HQ, their billet was moved to a fine modern house at the corner of Rue de l'Abbé Halluin and Boulevard Vauban, he listed its luxurious features, its oak floors, panelling and decorated ceilings. At the same time he longed for the more primitive conditions of his cramped billets with the 244th, where he slept with the others, in his valise on the floor. The palatial house, intact apart from a shell hole on the first floor, was cold, draughty and unwelcoming. Ironically it also seemed less safe than his previous, far more exposed quarters. The daily reminders of how much Arras had already suffered and the heightened noise of the artillery within the confines of a city made him more conscious of danger than he had been. Frenetic air activity over Arras, during which he saw several English planes shot down in flames, increased his sense of danger. Though he fell asleep quickly at night, he was woken up regularly by relentless enemy shelling, which he began to fear for the first time, even to 'wonder if it is better to be on the window or outer side of the room or on the chimney or inner side, whether to be upstairs where you may fall or on the ground floor where you may be worse crushed'.[44]

While Thomas had been too busy to brood on such matters with the 244th, he was frequently bored at HQ, 'rather like a dog doing what it doesn't want to do – as [Hilaire] Belloc said of me years ago when I was going about with him on various errands of his before we could settle down to lunch together,' he told Helen.[45] He regarded his job as an interval or protracted railway waiting room and was merely looking for a good opportunity to let the Colonel know that he wanted to get back to his battery.

Meantime, he managed to persuade the Colonel to take him out to the Group's various batteries in the field. He had already shown himself useful in the office, reading and interpreting maps, writing letters, making inventories and arranging billets. Once out with the Colonel he was able to demonstrate his other skills. He also walked daily to see Horton, Thorburn, Rubin and Smith at the 244th, two miles out of Arras.

Being driven in the Colonel's car had its compensations, allowing him a panoramic view of the landscape: 'huge expanses of rolling high ploughed land and a few copses, all kinds of troops and Hun prisoners – a group of turbanned Indians standing by a barn door holding a poor sheep by a rope, a few dogs in the village and in one place hundreds of thousands of shells stacked up'.[46] He also saw more melancholy sights, the 'ruined churches, churchyard and railway' at Achicourt, with its 'sordid ruin of Estaminet...wet, mortar, litter, almanacs, bottles, broken glass, damp beds, dirty paper, knife, crucifix, statuettes, old chairs'.[47] Even more desolate was the sight of Faubourg Ronville, 'its whistling deserted ruined street, deserted roadways, pavements with single files of men. Cellars are dugouts, trenches behind and across road. Dead calf in stable. Rubble, rubbish, filth and old plush chair'.[48] Thomas's three weeks at HQ would also give him an insider's knowledge of the developing military situation denied to most soldiers on the ground. He had not only worked with air reconnaissance maps but on maps and plans that revealed the Artillery's role in proceedings. 'Subalterns are told nothing but I happen to know what is intended,' he could not resist telling Eleanor on 30 March.

Despite some undoubted advantages of his position at Headquarters, not least of which was his relative safety and the likelihood of promotion, Thomas remained fixed in his purpose, for the reasons he gave Bottomley: 'Observing is what I like best and I am very anxious to get back to a more physically active life than I lead here as a sort of Adjutant.'[49] As he put it more crudely in his diary, he was 'fed up with sitting on my arse doing nothing that anybody couldn't do better'.[50] While it had been a useful experience, he had no regrets when he was eventually allowed back to the front on 9 March.

When Thomas rejoined the 244 Siege Battery they had moved into a different battle position, an orchard within easy walking distance of Arras. Their new location attracted even more shells, probably aimed at the road which ran behind the orchard. Thomas, who had not experienced as much shelling as his fellow-officers at this point, was 'not very happy' with Lushington, Horton and Smith, who had the 'wind up'.[51] But the two regulars had been in the war from the start and had developed a healthy fear of enemy fire. Lushington himself observed that 'as the novelty and excitement wore off, and the horrors of experience impressed themselves on the mind, the fear of death and disablement became ever-present realities', stressing that this would affect the 'imaginative man' especially.[52] It would not be long before Thomas, too, would start to experience this fear. Like all the new sensations which crowded in on him in France, he would try to analyse what precisely it was and why, one of the many fascinations of his diary and letters from the front. To Bottomley, for instance, he would write on 23 March, after a prolonged period of shelling:

> Fear too, I have discovered – to that point where the worst moment is when you find that you have survived and that all your fear was useless. You screw yourself up for a second to bear anything and nothing comes – except a curious disappointment which I suppose is also relief. Sometimes at night I have been in this state a hundred times, but partly through inexperience, not knowing what might mean harm. Still, I shall never like the shell that flaps as it falls, or the one that suddenly bounces into hearing and in a second is bursting far off – no sooner does it open the gate than it is right in the door, or even the small one that complains and whimpers and is called a 'pipsqueak' or a 'whizzbang', and flies into that ghastly village all night long like flights of humming birds.

His agnosticism allowed him no comfort from religion. When Rubin tackled him about this, arguing after a particularly dangerous spell in No Man's Land that marvellous escapes were 'ordained', Thomas's sceptical response was that so, too, were 'the marvellous escapes of certain telegraph poles, houses' and so on.[53] The last words in his war diary would read 'I never understood quite what was meant by God.' He had already spelled out his attitude in 'February Afternoon', where 'God sits aloft ... / ... stone-deaf and stone-blind'.[54]

To begin with, at least in France, he seemed indifferent to his fate: 'If I come back it will be wounded or at the end of the war, I don't mind which,' he had written to Eleanor the day before returning to the dangers of the front.[55] Once back with his battery thoughts of the coming conflict, now only a month away, seemed more real. The 244th's Observation Posts, which had been moved to more exposed positions than those of three weeks earlier, were a constant reminder of the dangers involved. His first day back on duty, for instance, 11 March, was at Ronville, whose ruined streets, deserted roads, cellar dugouts and nearby trenches, all within sight of the German front line near Beaurains, together with the frequent shelling of his post, increased this awareness. The Germans' vantage-point of Telegraph Hill was only a few hundred yards west of his post and he knew that any incautious movement during his 24-hour stints there, even the glint of sun on his field-glasses, would provide their excellent snipers with an easy target. It might look innocent, home only to rabbits, but less than a fortnight after his return to the 244th he was leaving his diary at home, just 'in case'.[56]

Only by keeping his mind fixed on the job at hand could he cope with what was to come. Responding to Helen, who had asked for reassurances of his love, he explains:

> My dear, you must not ask me to say much more. I know that you must say much more because you feel much. But I, you see, must not feel anything. I am just as it were tunnelling underground and something sensible in my subconsciousness directs me not to think of the sun. At the end of the tunnel there is the sun. Honestly this is not the result of thinking; it is just an explanation of my state of mind which is really so entirely preoccupied with getting on through the tunnel that you might say I had forgotten there was a sun at either end, before or after this business. This will perhaps induce you to call me inhuman like the newspapers, just because for a time I have had my ears stopped – mind you I have not done it myself – to all but distant echoes of home and friends and England. If I could respond as you would like me to to your feelings I should be unable to go on with this job in ignorance whether it is to last weeks or months or years – I never even think whether it will be weeks or months or years. I don't even wonder if the drawers in the sitting room are kept locked![57]

The graphic central imagery of tunnelling in Edward's letter to Helen must come, consciously or not, from the many hours he had spent at the Ronville Observation Post. For Ronville was one of a number of starting points for an elaborate series of underground passages being developed beneath Arras, to enable the troops to arrive at the battlefield on 9 April secretly and in safety. The chalky soil of the region, which reminded Thomas of his own 'South Country', was easily excavated and engineers and miners, many from Bantam battalions drawn from the coal-pits of northern England, worked night and day to extend the existing vast network of caverns, underground quarries, galleries and sewage tunnels under Arras. The tunnels would eventually cover 12 miles and include tramways and a light railway, as well as footpaths, with their own electric lighting and hospital. By 9 April they would be big enough to conceal 24,000 men and the surprise element involved would help to account for the Allied success on the opening day of the Battle of Arras. Thomas might describe the streets of Ronville as 'deserted' but he would certainly have known from his time at Group Headquarters of the frantic activity going on beneath them.

Part of Thomas's own tunnelling process was, as he explained to Helen, to bury thoughts of home, though they proved impossible to avoid altogether. On 14 March, for instance, he was talking to two of the men about Gloucestershire and Wiltshire, which evidently reminded him of his last visit to Frost at Ledington and their unfortunate encounter with the gamekeeper. His attempt to climb a high, unstable chimney-stack the next day, under fire, may have been yet another attempt to prove that he was not the coward he had feared. But his failure to do so now mattered less, as he explained to Frost: 'It was just another experience like the gamekeeper – but it lies far less on my mind because the practical result of my failure was nil and I now see far more from the ground level than I could have seen then from 200ft up the factory chimney.'[58]

If Frost was right to claim that the gamekeeper incident was one reason Thomas needed to enlist, by March 1917 he had proved beyond doubt that he was no coward. During his last month he would spend almost half his time at the Observation Post, a particularly exhausting job physically and mentally, and 12 days on the battery guns firing at fixed lines as part of the Allies' assault barrage. His anxiety to do all that was required of him made even supervising the digging of new dugouts and shallow trenches for emergency use a tiring experience. By 2 April he had seen, he told Frost with some restraint, 'new things':

...and had mud and worse things to endure which do not become less terrible in anticipation but are less terrible once I am in the midst of them. Jagged gables at dawn when you are cold and tired out look a thousand times worse from their connection with a certain kind of enemy shell that has made them look like that, so that every time I see them I half think I hear the moan of the approaching and hovering shell and the black grisly flap that it seems to make as it bursts. I see and hear more than I did because changed conditions compel us to go up to the very front among the infantry to do our observation and we spend nights without shelter in the mud chiefly in waiting for morning and the arrival of the relief. It is a 24 hour job and takes more to recover from. But it is far as yet from being unendurable.

The mud had arrived with the rain, which had followed the snow, shortly after Thomas's return. One of the most feared aspects of life on the Western Front for men and General Staff alike, the mud turned the ground into a quagmire. And though it was at its worst in the trenches, it also had its effect on the Artillery who, as Thomas could testify from personal experience, had to 'stand up in mud, wet and cold all night':[59] 'You nearly pull your leg off, and often your boot off, at each step in the worst places – the stiff, soft clay sucks round the boot at each step.'[60]

Despite these and countless other discomforts, Thomas found 'many things to enjoy' in the second half of March.[61] His explanation for this was that being in France had made him 'surer of some primitive things' about himself and other people, and not simply due to being older:

In short, I am glad I came out and I think less about return than I thought I should – partly no doubt I inhibit the idea of return, I only think by flashes of the things at home that I used to enjoy and should again – I enjoy many of them out here when the sun shines and at early morning and late afternoon. I doubt if anybody here thinks less of home than I do and yet I doubt if anybody loves it more.[62]

It is evident from Thomas's letters and diary, however, that his thoughts were often of England as the battle drew nearer. (Even No Man's Land reminded him of Goodwood Racecourse.) On 24 March he told Merfyn that he was hoping 'to come back again', while at the same time appearing to prepare his son to take over as head of the family should he not return. Three days later he was writing more explicitly to Eleanor: 'I keep feeling that I should enjoy it more if I knew I would survive it. I can't help allowing it to trouble me, but it doesn't prey on me, and I have no real foreboding, only occasional trepidation and anxiety.'[63] Perhaps, like the narrator of 'Rain', he was lying awake at night 'Remembering again that I shall die'. So many of his feelings had been anticipated in verse during his months in England, but he allowed himself to say only so much in his letters to family and friends. He realized, he told Eleanor, that, while the coming fight would be 'worse than anything' he had known so far, it would be worse still for Eleanor, Helen and his mother.[64] It was a letter which meant more to Eleanor than any other from Edward, she said, because it was the only time he laid by his reserve and 'allowed me to know that he knew how much I loved him'.[65]

The pace of events increased for both Allied and German troops around Arras towards the end of March. Its most immediate effect on Thomas was the 244th's move on 26 March from the edge of Arras to the still more devastated village of Achicourt, or, rather, to a chalk pit halfway between Achicourt and Agny. (Thomas reported, with no apparent qualms, 'stealing a Decanville truck' to help lay out nightlines for their new position.[66]) Reminded by this new spot of the chalk pit near Lupton's house in Froxfield, Edward wrote appreciatively to Helen:

> It is almost a beautiful spot still and I am sitting warm in the sun on a heap of chalk with my back to the wall of the pit which is large and shallow. Fancy, an old chalk pit with moss and even a rabbit left in spite of the paths trodden almost all over it. It is beautiful and sunny and warm though cold in the shade. The chalk is dazzling.[67]

What Edward omitted from his description to Helen, deliberately no doubt, was the increased exposure and danger of this new position. Only a few hundred yards across the plain in front of the quarry lay a sunken road, running parallel to the enemy front, which had to be crossed on the way to the Observation Post. By the end of March this road was closely lined with guns and howitzers as far as the eye could see.

The 244th's move had been in response to one of the Germans' most brilliant strategic moves in the build-up to Arras, their retirement to the Hindenburg Line. Completed by 18 March, this had forced the Allies to revise their plans and, while new ones were being made, the troops in the line were ordered to move forward to conform with the enemy's retirement. In a further stroke of military cunning, German troops had been ordered to destroy the infrastructure of the country, causing Rosenberg (whose 40th Division was set to work to restore it) to write that 'as far as houses or signs of ordinary human living is concerned, we might as well be in the Sahara Desert'.[68] Thomas's own description of it to Helen when he first arrived in Beaurains, which formed the hinge on which the Germans had swung back, conveys the desolation even more graphically:

> I never thought it would be so bad. It is nothing but dunes of piled up brick and stone with here and there a jagged piece of wall, except that the little summerhouse place under the trees that I told Baba about is more or less perfect. The only place one could recognize was the churchyard. Scores of tombstones were quite undamaged. All the trees were splintered and snapped and dead until you got to the outskirts. The trench we observed from ran along inside a garden hedge with a cherry in it. No Man's Land below the village was simply churned up dead filthy ground with tangled rusty barbed wire over it.[69]

Preparations for the great offensive were 'ceaselessly pushed forward,' Lushington noted, reminding him of the period before the Battle of the Somme, which he had witnessed nine months earlier, 'with this difference, that now the number of guns seemed double as great, and the piles of ammunition that were dumped nightly on the battery positions, twice as many'.[70] Thomas, too, notes 'things close impending now'.[71] Whereas spring normally promised hope and renewal for him, it is now linked to more negative signs. His descriptions of birds, from the beginning of March, are frequently accompanied by references to the aeroplanes, bombs and bullets which share the sky with them, often dominating it. On 11 March, for instance, he records: 'Larks singing over No Man's Land – French mortars', on 14 March, 'blackbirds singing far off – a spatter of our machine guns – the spit of one enemy bullet'. As Rosenberg observed in 'Returning We Hear the Larks', at this point in the war 'Death could drop from the dark / As easily as song'.

Distracted briefly from his concentration on the immediate future by a review of *An Annual of New Poetry*, Thomas's reaction to it shows how important it was to him to be both poet and soldier. Responding to the

TLS reviewer's mixed praise of his 18 poems in the *Annual* – 'he is a real poet with the truth in him. At present…he has too little control over his eyes' – Thomas writes to Bottomley:

> It would be the one consolation in finishing up out here to provide such reviewers with a conundrum, except that I know they would invent an answer…Why do the idiots accuse me of using my eyes? Must I only use them with field-glasses and must I see only Huns in these beautiful hills eastwards and only hostile flashes in the night skies when I am at the Observation Post? [72]

There was little time for studying nature, however. As Thomas wrote in his letter of 4 April to John Freeman, who had sent him the *TLS* review together with some of his favourite York River tobacco, 'I only live now in the hours when I can smoke. Sometimes all through a wet cold night I do not live, I only smoke.' Things had been 'speeding up,' he told Freeman, and work and some exposure to weather and danger increased: 'I wonder what these days will bring forth.'

This 'speeding up' of events is reflected faithfully in Thomas's diary. On 2 April, a week before the date they all fear, he reports 'filling sandbags for dug out we are to have in battery for battle' and the next day, while noting filling sandbags again, he also records an equally important fact for himself, that he was reading one of Shakespeare's great tragedies, *Macbeth*, whose opening lines must have acquired new resonance for him:

> 1st Witch: When shall we three meet again
>   In thunder, lightning, or in rain?
>
> 2nd Witch: When the hurly-burly's done,
>   When the battle's lost and won.

Shakespeare's words no doubt help him to face the future, to put it into perspective and to say: 'Come what come may, / Time and the hour runs through the roughest day.' And any further worries about a failure of nerve on the day are perhaps calmed by Lady Macbeth's rousing response to her husband's fears: 'But screw your courage to the sticking-place, / And we'll not fail.'

After more than a week of rain, April had opened fine and sunny, but by the fourth it is 'showery cold muddy and slippery again'. By the evening Thomas, like the rest of the battery, is exhausted. But the full-scale bombardment is due to begin the next day and they are forced into further activity by the need to move to the dugout they are preparing for such an event. The next day, 5 April, begins just as miserably, with more rain and deafening artillery action from both sides, set to continue until the battle itself. But later in the day, with the arrival of sun and wind to dry the mud, Thomas's spirits lift again and he draws comfort from the sight of 'fine green feathers of yarrow' at the edge of the dugout. He is also cheered by reading another great Shakespeare tragedy, *Hamlet*, before bed, possibly those well-known lines which seem to suit his philosophical acceptance of his situation: 'There's a divinity that shapes our ends, / Rough-hew them how we will.'

On 6 April, when he drives with Horton to Avesnes and Fosseux, he witnesses continuous columns of infantry marching up to the line with their yellow gas-alert patches on their backs, and reports Horton's admiring remarks about the enemy's accurate shelling without comment: 'The Bosh [*sic*] is a damned good man, isn't he, a damned smart man, you must admit.'

With only two days to go, Thomas is up at the Observation Post on 7 April at 6 a.m. for a 'cold bright day of continuous shelling'. The infantry are now 'all over the place in [the] open', preparing the jokily named 'Prussian Way' with boards to enable the wounded to be carried away during battle.[73] Yet he still has time, during his relatively peaceful stint there, to note the larks, partridges, hedge sparrows and magpies, and to compare a huge explosion at Neuville-Vitasse to a birch tree or fountain. He is back with his battery by 7.30 p.m., 'in peace', until a continuous roar of artillery starts up again an hour later.

On 8 April, the last day of preparation before the battle – and also Easter Sunday – the General Staff organizes what Lushington calls 'a full dress rehearsal of the barrage for it; at the same time the Germans begin their own heavy bombardment of the 244th's neighbouring village, Achicourt, turning it into a holocaust of flame and death'.[74] The battery's guns, almost completely exposed in their quarry, are heavily shelled, a 5.9 plunging into the ground next to Thomas. By an extraordinary stroke of luck it fails to explode, although as Lushington (unlike the more reticent Thomas) relates, 'the wind of its passing knocked him down: that night in the mess somebody said, with unintended irony, "Thomas, you were evidently born to live through this war" and they all drank his health'.[75]

Twelve hours later Thomas was dead.

The Battle of Arras had opened at 7 a.m., with Thomas manning the 244th's Observation Post. Two minutes before zero hour, Lushington recalled in *The Gambardier*, he had looked at his watch: 'T[homas] should be at the O.P.... Why didn't [he] ring up? CRASH! The air was rent with a swelling thunder of sound, stunning, ear-splitting, deafening. The Battle of Arras had begun. A few minutes later a telephone message brought the sad news of T[homas]'s death.'[76] He had, in Lushington's words, been 'killed in the O.P. by a direct hit *through* the chest'.[77]

In case there could be any doubt attached to this account, written 13 years after the event, we have two contemporary reports of the death which leave little uncertainty as to the details. The first is from Thomas's fellow-officer Thorburn, who wrote to Helen the same day to inform her that her husband had been 'killed...by shell fire' that morning, with no mention of death by percussive force.[78] The second, more specific account followed the next day, 10 April, in Lushington's letter to Helen. He had waited until the body could be brought up from the Observation Post and buried the following day in 'a little military cemetery' a few hundred yards from the battery: 'With regard to his actual death...it should be of some comfort to you that he died at a moment of victory from *a direct hit* by a shell.'[79]

During his subsequent visit to a devastated Helen, Lushington may have unwittingly allowed her to devise a more bearable version of Edward's end than the facts strictly support by describing Thomas's miraculous survival of a shell-blast the day before his death, which she then transferred to his actual death. However it came about, a fragile Helen, on the edge of a breakdown that would last many years, wrote to tell Eleanor after Lushington's visit that he told her that as Edward stood by his dugout lighting his pipe all the Germans had retreated, but a last shell they sent over passed so close to him that the blast of air stopped his heart. 'He told me,' Helen writes,

> there was no wound and his beloved body was not injured. This was borne out by the fact that when the contents of his pockets were returned to me – a bundle of letters, a note-book and the Shakespeare

Sonnets I had given him, they were all strangely creased as though subject to some terrible pressure, most strange to see. There was no wound or disfigurement at all. He just died standing there in the early morning after the battle.[80]

In none of Lushington's written accounts does he give any grounds at all for such an interpretation. A blast from a shell knocked Thomas over, but on 8 April not the ninth, and in doing so, as the editor of Thomas's diary points out, may have been responsible for the curious creasing of its pages.[81] When asked by one of Thomas's earliest biographers, John Moore, for precise details, Lushington wrote on 29 February 1936 in words which leave no room for ambiguity:

> O.P. at that time was in rather an exposed piece of trench in the village of Beaurains in front of Arras. The next day, Easter Monday, was the date of the Battle of Arras. A few moments after Zero Hour (about 7 o'clock in the morning I think it was) I was rung up on the telephone from the O.P. A voice said that Thomas had been killed, *shot clean through the chest* by a pip-squeak (a 77mm shell) the very moment the battle began. A little later it began to snow.[82]

This letter has been buried for many years in the Berg Collection of the New York Public Library and Helen's version has persisted, lending a more dramatic twist to what was otherwise a fairly routine death in battle in the First World War.

But does the exact manner of Edward Thomas's death matter? Yes, it does. For the legendary version of his end places him in a realm of myth and threatens to obscure the real miracle of his life, his writing. The most authoritative poetry critic of his time, the innovator of new forms and approaches in a number of prose genres and among a handful of poets who helped reshape English verse in the early twentieth century, it is Thomas's achievements in life we should be remembering him for rather than the manner of his death.

Acknowledgements

My first thanks must go to the Edward Thomas Estate. The late Edward Cawston Thomas encouraged this project from the start and authorized access to unpublished and copyrighted material, which his successor, Mrs Rosemary Vellender, has allowed me freely to reproduce.

In writing this book I have been grateful for information about and insights into Thomas and his works to all his previous biographers, in particular to William Cooke and R. George Thomas, and to his many critics and editors, especially to Edna Longley for her *Annotated Collected Poems* (2008) and to Guy Cuthbertson and Lucy Newlyn for their selected edition of Thomas's *Prose Writings* (2011), still ongoing. Martin Gilbert was very supportive throughout with historical background. Sadly he died just before publication.

I am also indebted to present and past members of the Edward Thomas Fellowship for their help and encouragement: Richard Emeny, Anne Harvey, Colin Thornton, the late Alan Martin, Larry Skillman, Michael Howe, Robert Gomme, Frances Guthrie, Ian and Breeda Morton, the late Tim Wilton-Steer and his wife, Hilary, Paul Stephenson, Terry Lloyd, Richard Purver, John Monks, Judy Kendall, Joseph Turner, Christopher Martin, Mike Cope, and Alan Anderson. The Friends of the Dymock Poets have also given help and support at every stage: Roy and Pat Palmer, Linda Hart, Jeff Cooper, Ray Canham and Jonathan Lumby in particular.

Warmest thanks, too, are due to the following individuals, who have helped in a variety of ways: Michael Allan, Frances

Bradshaw, Michael Copp, Katie Gramich, Frances Hounsell, Pat and Stuart Laurence, Dave Massey, Wilhelm Meusburger, Robert Nye, Anne Sebba, Helen Smith, John Stape, Alison Thomas, Frances Twinn, Martha Vogeler, Joan Wheelton, Danny Wigley and Henry Woudhuysen.

I must thank, too, the following institutions, librarians and archivists throughout Britain and North America: Amherst College (Peter Nelson and staff at Special Collections), Battersea Public Library (Malcolm Holmes and Felix Lancashire at Wandsworth Heritage Service), Berg Collection, New York Public Library (Isaac Gewirtz, Stephen Crook and Anne Garner), Bodleian Library, Oxford (Colin Harris), British Library, Department of Manuscripts, Bryn Mawr College (Marianne Hansen at Special Collections), Dartmouth College, Massachusetts (Peter Carini and staff at Special Collections), Gloucester Archives (Mick Heath), Imperial War Museum (Tony Richards and Alan Wakefield), Lincoln College Library, Oxford (Andrew Mussell), Marquette University Library (Phil Runcorn), National Library of Wales (Martin Robson-Riley), Royal Artillery Museum, Woolwich (Paul Evans), Senate House Library, University of London (Richard Espley), State University of New York at Buffalo (Michael Basinski and James Maynard at the Lockwood Memorial Library), University of British Columbia Library, Norman Colbeck Collection (Katherine Kalsbeck), University of Durham (Richard Higgins at Special Collections), University of Gloucester's Dymock Poets' Archive (Lorna Scott), University of Rochester (Melinda Wallington at Rare Books and Special Collections) and the University of Texas at Austin (Molly Schwartzburg and all the staff at the Harry Ransom Center, who made my Fellowship there so fruitful and enjoyable). Thanks also to the trustees of the Wilfrid Gibson and Robert Frost literary estates.

I am grateful for the help of Tristram Woolf, Philip Woolf, Mike Cope and especially my husband, Cecil Woolf, in the preparation of this book for the press and the support, sympathy and forbearance of the other members of my family – Kate, Emma and Alice Woolf – during the writing of it. Finally, and not least, my warm thanks to Robin Baird-Smith, Jamie Birkett Mark Bostridge and Deborah Blake.

ABBREVIATIONS

Note: Throughout this book and in quotations from the works and letters of Edward Thomas, the word 'and' has been spelt out in full rather than being denoted by an ampersand.

MAIN CORRESPONDENTS

CB	Clifford Bax, HRC, UR
dlM	Walter de la Mare, Bodleian, *Poet to Poet*, Seren Books, 2012
DU	David ('Dad') Uzzell
ECH	Edna Clarke Hall
EF	Eleanor Farjeon, BPL
EG	Edward Garnett, HRC
ESP	Edward Sidney Pollock Haynes, HRC
FC	(Charles) Frank Cazenove DUL, Bodleian
GB	Gordon Bottomley, Cardiff
HGB	(Helton) Godwin Baynes
HH	Harry Hooton, UBC
HM	Harold Monro, Buffalo
HT	Helen Thomas, Cardiff, NLW
HWN	Henry Woodd Nevinson
IM	Ian MacAlister, BPL
JA/JH	Janet Hooton (née Aldis)
JAN	James Ashcroft Noble, Cardiff, NLW
JB	Jesse Berridge, *Letters of Edward Thomas to Jesse Berridge*, London, Enitharmon, 1983
JF	John Freeman, Berg
JG	James Guthrie
JT	Julian Thomas, Cardiff
JWH	John Wilton Haines, GA
LA	Lascelles Abercrombie

MT	Margaret Townsend, Bodleian
ND	Norman Douglas, Beinicke
RB	Rupert Brooke, Marquette
RF	Robert Frost, DC
RH	Ralph Hodgson, Beinicke
WHD	W. H. Davies, Beinicke
WHH	W. H. Hudson, Cardiff

ARCHIVES

Amherst	Amherst College, Massachussets
Beinicke	Beinicke Library, University of Yale
Berg	Berg Collection, New York Public Library
BL	British Library, London
Bodleian	Bodleian Library, Oxford
BPL	Battersea Public Library
Bryn Mawr	Bryn Mawr College
Buffalo	State University of New York at Buffalo
Cardiff	Edward Thomas Collection Cardiff University Library
DC	Dartmouth College, Hanover, New Hampshire
DUL	Durham University Library
GA	Gloucestershire Archives
HRC	Harry Ransom Center, University of Texas at Austin
IWM	Imperial War Museum Library
LCL	Lincoln College Library, Oxford
Marquette	Marquette University Library
NLS	National Library of Scotland
NLW	National Library of Wales, Aberystwyth
RAM	Royal Artillery Museum, Woolwich
SH	Senate House Library, University of London
UBC	University of British Columbia, Norman Colbeck Collection
UR	University of Rochester

ET'S WORKS
(Place of publication London, unless otherwise stated.)

ACS	*Algernon Charles Swinburne* (Martin Secker, 1912)
BCLAW	ed. *British Country Life in Autumn and Winter* (Hodder & Stoughton, 1907)
BCLSS	ed. *British Country Life in Spring and Summer* (Hodder & Stoughton, 1907)
BS	ed. *The Bible in Spain* by George Borrow (Dent, 1906)

BW	*Beautiful Wales* (A. & C. Black, 1905). Edition used OUP, 1983.
CC	*Cloud Castle* (Duckworth, 1922)
CET	*The Childhood of Edward Thomas* (Faber & Faber, 1938). Edition used Faber, 1983.
Cobbett	ed. *Rural Rides* by William Cobbett (Dent, 1912)
COE	*The Chessplayer and Other Essays* (Whittington Press, Andoversford, 1981)
Country	*The Country* (Batsford, 1913).
CS	*Celtic Stories* (Clarendon Press, Oxford, 1911)
ETY	*Essays of Today and Yesterday* (Harrap, 1926)
FB	*The Friend of the Blackbird* (Pear Tree Press, Flansham, 1938)
FIL	ed. *The Flowers I Love* (T. C. & E. C. Jack, 1916)
FIP	*Feminine Influence on the Poets* (Martin Secker, 1910)
FTB	*Four-and-Twenty Blackbirds* (Duckworth, 1915). Edition used the Cyder Press, Cheltenham, 2001
GB	*George Borrow* (Chapman & Hall, 1912)
HE	*The Heart of England* (Dent, 1906)
Herbert	ed. *The Temple and A Priest in the Temple* (Dent, 1908)
HGLM	*The Happy-Go-Lucky Morgans* (Duckworth, 1913)
HS	*Horae Solitariae* (Duckworth, 1902)
HV	ed. *The Hills and the Vale* by Richard Jefferies (Duckworth, 1909)
IOW	*The Isle of Wight* (Blackie & Son, 1911)
IPS	*In Pursuit of Spring* (Nelson & Sons, 1914)
IW	*The Icknield Way* (Constable, 1913)
JD	ed. *The Poems of John Dyer* (Fisher Unwin, 1903)
Keats	*Keats* (T. C. & E. C. Jack, 1916)
LDM	*The Life of the Duke of Marlborough* (Chapman & Hall, 1915)
LH	*Lafcadio Hearn* (Constable, 1912)
LNTBB	*A Language Not to be Betrayed* (Carcanet, Manchester, 1981)
LPE	*A Literary Pilgrim in England* (Methuen, 1917)
LS	*The Last Sheaf* (Jonathan Cape, 1938)
LT	*Light and Twilight* (Duckworth, 1911). Edition used Laurel Books, Holt, 2000
Marlowe	ed. *The Plays and Poems of Christopher Marlowe* (Dent, 1909)
MM	*Maurice Maeterlinck* (Methuen, 1911)
NT	*Norse Tales* (Constable, 1912)
Oxford	*Oxford* (A. & C. Black, 1903). Edition used Signal Books, Oxford, 2005
PBPS	ed. *The Pocket Book of Poems and Songs for the Open Air* (Grant Richards, 1907)
PGB	ed. *The Pocket George Borrow* (Chatto & Windus, 1912).
Prose	*The Prose of Edward Thomas* ed. Roland Gant (Falcon Press, 1948)
RA(1904)	*Rose Acre Papers* (Brown Langham, 1904)
RA(1910)	*Rose Acre Papers* (Duckworth, 1910)

RJ	*Richard Jefferies* (Hutchinson, 1909). Edition used Faber & Faber, 1978
RU	*Rest and Unrest* (Duckworth, 1910)
SC	*The South Country* (Dent, 1909). Edition used Little Toller Books, Stanbridge, 2009.
ST	*A Sportsman's Tale* (Tregara Press, Edinburgh, 1983)
Taylor	ed. *Words and Places* by Isaac Taylor (Dent, 1911)
TE	ed. *This England : An Anthology from her Writers* (OUP, Oxford, 1915)
TM	*The Tenth Muse* (Martin Secker, 1911)
WC	*Windsor Castle* (Blackie & Son, 1910)
WL	*The Woodland Life* (Blackwood, 1897)
WP	*Walter Pater* (Martin Secker, 1913)
ZGB	ed. *The Zincali* by George Borrow (Dent, 1914)

OTHER MAIN ABBREVIATIONS

(Place of publication London, unless otherwise stated)

ACP	*Annotated Collected Poems of Edward Thomas*, ed. Edna Longley
AIW/WWE	*As It Was* and *World Without End*, Helen Thomas
AM	*The Poetry of Edward Thomas*, Andrew Motion
B	*Bookman*
CP1978	*Collected Poems*, ed. R. George Thomas (Oxford: Clarendon, 1978)
DC	*Daily Chronicle*
Diary	ET's diary, 1900–12 (NLW) and 1915 (NLW)
ECHJ	Edna Clarke Hall Journal
ETFN	*Edward Thomas Fellowship Newsletter*
FNB	Field Notebooks, Berg
JK	Judy Kendall's edition of ET letters to dlM (*Poet to Poet*)
LFY	*The Last Four Years* (ET to EF letters) (Oxford: Oxford University Press, 1979)
LJB	*The Letters of Edward Thomas to Jesse Berridge* (Enitharmon, 1983)
LGB	*The Letters of Edward Thomas to Gordon Bottomley* (Oxford: Oxford University Press, 1968)
NN	'Notes on Nought' by ET, Lincoln College, LCL
PW	*Edward Thomas: Prose Writings* (Oxford: Oxford University Press, 2011), ed. Guy Cuthbertson and Lucy Newlyn
RGT	*Edward Thomas: A Portrait*, R. George Thomas (Oxford: Clarendon, 1985)
RW	Memories of ET collected by Rowland Watson
SL	*Edward Thomas: Selected Letters*, ed. R. G. Thomas (Oxford: Oxford University Press, 1995)
TLS	*Times Literary Supplement*
WD	War Diary (Transcribed in *CP1978*)

NOTES

(Place of publication London, unless otherwise stated)

INTRODUCTION

1   *New Bearings in English Poetry* (Pelican Books, 1972), p. 55.
2   *The Poetry of Edward Thomas* [*AM*] (Routledge & Kegan Paul, 1980), p. 11.
3   'Roads from France', *Saturday Guardian*, 28 June 2008.
4   *The Annotated Collected Poems* [*ACP*] (Bloodaxe Books, 2008), p. 11.
5   *ACP*, p. 22.
6   Ibid., pp. 36–7.
7   *AM*, p. 169.
8   Quoted by Richard Emeny in 'Edward Thomas Ninety Years On', *Journal of the Friends of the Dymock Poets*, no. 7, 2008, p. 57.
9   *ACP*, p. 48.
10 See Whiteman, *The Edward Thomas Country*, p. 18.
11 Field Notebook [FNB] 79, Berg Collection, New York Public Library.
12 *ACP*, p. 80.
13 *Listener*, vol. 70 (10 October 1963), p. 561.
14 *Selected Letters of Robert Frost*, ed. Thompson, p. 217.
15 *ACP*, p. 11.
16 ET to GB, 26 December 1907.
17 Christopher Somerville, *Greenwood Dark: A Traveller's Poems* (Haus Publishing, 2008), p. 91.
18 *ACP*, p. 105.
19 *The Icknield Way* [*IW*] (Constable, 1913), p. 280.
20 Coombes, *Edward Thomas*, p. 13.
21 *The Last Four Years*, ed. Anne Harvey (Stroud: Sutton Publishing, 1997), p. xv.
22 ET to GB, 7 March 1907.
23 Emeny, 'Edward Thomas Ninety Years On', pp. 50, 52.
24 Douglas, *Looking Back*, pp. 174, 175.
25 Faber paperback, 1978.
26 Letter of 8 May 1898, *Edward Thomas: Letters to Helen* (Manchester: Carcanet Press, 2000), pp. 126–8.

27 *Edward Thomas: Selected Poems* (Oxford: Oxford University Press, 1995), p. 31.

28 Ibid., p. 35.

29 *LJB*, p. 47.

30 ET to RF, 22 July 1915, DC.

31 Glyn Maxwell, 'Dead on a Side Track: On Frost's "War Thoughts at Home"', *Virginia Quarterly Review*, 1 October 2006.

32 Ibid.

33 Review of *North of Boston in Daily News* 22 July 1914.

CHAPTER 1 – Beginnings (1878–1880)

1   'Addenda to Autobiography', Berg.

2   [*Beautiful*] *Wales*, 1983, p. 16.

3   *SC*, p. 24.

4   Ibid, p. 25.

5   Now 14 Lansdowne Gardens, between South Lambeth and Wandsworth Roads, this runs north off an elegant circus of houses. Philip Henry and Mary Elizabeth Thomas had found rooms in one of the imposing four-storey, semi-detached villas in Upper Lansdowne Road after their marriage in Wales on 3 February 1877. Railway links to Lambeth in the mid-nineteenth century had encouraged the growth of this relatively recent suburb south of the Thames, where property and rents were still affordable, and which allowed Philip Thomas to commute daily to his new post as a clerk at the Board of Trade.

6   *SC*, pp. 23–24.

7   RF to ET, April 1915, DC.

8   *Collected Poems* (Faber & Faber, 1979), p. 8.

9   *PW*, vol. 1, p. 130.

10 Related to R. George Thomas by ET's second cousin, T. Treharne Thomas in 1966–7 (RGT, p. 10). ET wrote in his diary on 2 September 1907: 'Auntie scandalous about old Mr Townsend (grandfather of mother) and everyone else.'

11 Another relative, the First World War pilot Captain D. M. K. Marendaz, helps to explain the confusion over nationality, stating that the Marendaz family had been established in Switzerland since 1200, but were descended from the Marendaz du Douro of the town with the same name in Portugal. Edward Thomas's great-grandfather, David Emmanuel Marendaz, had met the Welshman Thomas Mansel Talbot of Margam Castle in Lausanne, during Talbot's Grand Tour of Europe and been invited to return with him to Wales some time between 1768 and 1772. Marendaz is reputed to have saved Talbot's life in a shipwreck on the journey and was granted the farm, Ty Draw, in thanks, on his marriage to Miss Ivans, a clergyman's daughter. Whatever the truth of this story, the foreign element clearly interested Thomas, who would contemplate taking 'Marendaz' as a pseudonym for his poems in 1915, before dismissing it as 'too un-English' for a country in the grip of war and patriotic fervour' (ET to EF, ?26 February 1915).

12 ET to HT, [1898] Cardiff.

13 LFY, p. 13.

14 *CET*, p. 18.

15 Ibid.

16 Ibid., p. 17.

17 Ibid., p. 48.

18 Rowland Watson's Introduction to the Memories of Edward Thomas he collected in the 1940s and 1950s. BPL [RW].

19 *CET*, p. 115.

20 ET to his father, 13 July [1892], Berg.

21 'How I Began', *PW*, vol. 1, p. 176.

22 RW, p. 5.

23 *CET*, p. 137.

24 Ibid., pp. 6–7.

25 Ibid., p. 83.

26 Ibid., p. 137.

27 Ibid., p. 104.

28 JAN to ET, 31 October 1895, Cardiff.

CHAPTER 2 – 'All Being, Doing and Suffering' (1880–1888)

1 ET to JF, 8 December, Berg. The chapter title also comes from an undated letter to Freeman.

2 *CET*, p. 13.

3 Ibid.

4 See FNB 68, *c.* November/December 1913–February 1914.

5 *CET*, p. 14.

6 I am grateful to Richard Purver for his research on ET's south London houses.

7 CET, pp. 23–4.

8 Ibid., p. 72.

9 Ibid., p. 88.

10 Ibid., p. 108.

11 Ibid.

12 Ibid., p. 73.

13 Ibid., p. 19.

14 Eckert, *Edward Thomas*, p. 23, n. 1.

15 RGT, p. 10.

16 *CET*, p. 57.

17 Ibid., p. 29.

18 Ibid., p. 28.

19 'How I Began', *Prose Writings*, vol. 1, p. 175.

20 *CET*, p. 33.

21 Ibid., p. 30.
22 Mark Holloway, *Norman Douglas: a Biography* (Secker & Warburg, 1976), p. 223.
23 'In Our Alley', *English Review*, November 1913, p. 540.
24 'Hampstead in August', *London Miniatures* (*The Lost Sheaf*), *Prose Writings*, vol. 2, p. 520.
25 *CET*, p. 40.
26 'Rain' (*Rose Acre Papers*), reprinted in *Essays of Today and Yesterday*, p. 42.
27 Ibid.
28 *PW*, vol. 2, p. 157.
29 'Old Man', *ACP*, p. 36.
30 *CET*, p. 60.
31 Ibid., p. 56.
32 Ibid., p. 43.
33 Ibid., p. 46.
34 ET to HH, 13 March 1898, UBC.
35 19 Cambria Place is now 171 Farringdon Road.
36 'How I Began', *PW*, vol. 1, p. 176.
37 R. G. Watts, 'Edward Thomas in Wiltshire', *Hatcher Review* (Salisbury), 1991, p. 36.
38 *CET*, p. 46.
39 Ibid., p. 47.
40 Ibid.
41 Ibid.
42 Ibid., p. 48.
43 FNB 9, *c.* 13 May 1907.
44 *CET*, p. 129.
45 'Notes on Naught'(NN), LCL.
46 *CET*, p. 132.
47 Ibid.
48 'Dad', Colbeck Collection, UBC.
49 Ibid.
50 'Dad' Uzzell would survive ET by more than two years, dying in December 1919, when he was interred in Swindon's Radnor Street Cemetery. See *ETFN*, no. 59, January 2008.

CHAPTER 3 – 'The Foolish Years' (1889–1893)

1   ET entry for 31 August 1899, 1899 notebook, Cardiff.
2   *CET*, p. 30.
3   Ibid., p. 64.
4   Ibid., p. 65.
5   Ibid., pp. 66–7.

6   Ibid., p. 71.
7   Ibid., pp. 34–5.
8   Ibid., p. 79.
9   Ibid., p. 83.
10   Ibid.
11   Entry for 31 August 1899, 1899 notebook, Cardiff.
12   *CET*, p. 77.
13   Ibid., p. 87.
14   Ibid., pp. 89–90.
15   Ibid., p. 99.
16   Ibid., p. 126.
17   Ibid., p. 136.
18   Ibid., p. 104.
19   Ibid., p. 105. This must have taken place in the 1880s, rather than the 1890s, since Davitt's last spell in prison was in 1883.
20   *SC*, p. 23.
21   *CET*, p. 103.
22   Ernest's memoirs of ET, RW.
23   Ibid.
24   'A Sportsman's Tale', ts, p. 1.
25   Ibid., p. 3.
26   *CET*, p. 117.
27   'A Sportsman's Tale', ts, p. 3.
28   Ibid.
29   Ibid., p. 4.
30   Arthur York Hardy sent his 'Memorial to Edward Thomas' to Guthrie from Pristina, Yugoslavia, on 3 February 1929, Eckert Collection, Bodleian.
31   *CET*, p. 134.
32   ET to H. H. Sturmer, 4 April 1900, Berg.
33   *BW*, p. 90.
34   Ibid.

CHAPTER 4 – St Paul's and Helen Noble: Alone Together (1894–1897)

1   *CET*, p. 146.
2   Ibid., p. 148.
3   *PW*, vol. 1, p. 321.
4   Report for July 1894, St Paul's School Archives.
5   Ibid.
6   Ibid. Robert F. Cholmeley (d. 1927) was headmaster of the Dame Alice Owen's Boys' School in Islington from 1909 to 1927.

7   *CET*, p. 142.

8   Ibid.

9   *CET*, p. 146.

10   Ibid., p. 144.

11   Ibid., p. 143.

12   RGT, pp. 20–1. The Keats sonnet is, of course, 'On First Looking into Chapman's Homer'.

13   See FNB 1, Berg.

14   FNB 1 entries for 12 February and 20 March 1895.

15   FNB 1, 18 March 1895.

16   Bentley, *Those Days*, p. 58.

17   *PW*, vol. 1, p. 307.

18   Ibid.

19   FNB 1, 4 February 1895.

20   *CET*, p. 144.

21   FNB 1, 13 and 21 March 1895.

22   Rev. Walter George Tarrant was minister of the Wandsworth Unitarian Church, East Hall, Wandsworth, from 1883 to 1921 and the author of seven books of prose and verse. Tarrant's name and some of his characteristics would contribute to the figures of Mr Torrance and Mr Stodham in Thomas's *The Happy-Go-Lucky Morgans*.

23   FNB 1, 14 January 1895.

24   Ibid., 25 January 1895.

25   Ibid., 4 and 27 January 1895. There are no surviving details of membership of the Selborne Society for 1895, but reviews of ET's *The Woodland Life* and *The Book of the Open Air* are included in *Nature Notes* for 1897 and 1907 respectively.

26   i.e. *The Pelican Papers* (1873), *Verses of a Prose Writer* (1887), *The Sonnet in England* (1893), *Impressions and Memories* (1895).

27   JAN to ET correspondence is housed at Cardiff and Aberystwyth.

28   No. 15 The Grove was later renamed 37 St Ann's Hill, but destroyed in July 1944 by a flying bomb. ETFN, no. 67, January 2012.

29   JAN to ET, 11 November 1895.

30   Ibid.

31   Ibid., 9 December 1895.

32   Ibid., 28 November 1895.

33   Ibid., 13 November 1895.

34   George Cotterell to JAN, 8 November 1895, in JAN/ET collection.

35   'Letter Three' of Conan Doyle's *The Stark Munro Letters* (1895). The extract Noble sent on 28 November 1895 has not survived but I have assumed he had this one, or something very similar, in mind.

36   A brief account of this walk is included in the diary section of *The Woodland Life*.

37   *AIW*, p. 18.

38   Ibid., p. 15.

39 *AIW*, p. 16.

40 HT to JA, 2 January 1896, RGT, p. 43.

41 ET's unpublished essay, 'The Winter Twilight' (Cardiff), may be based on this 7 February walk.

42 This move in December 1895 from 15 The Grove, may account for the loss of ET's replies to JAN's letters of October to December 1895.

43 ET to H. H. Sturmer, 4 May 1900, Berg.

44 The anemone is taken to symbolize unfading love, but its origin in Greek myth – that it sprang from Aphrodite's tears as she mourned the death of Adonis – implies, rather, the destruction of hope and all living things.

45 HT to JA, 27 July 1896.

46 *PW*, vol. 1, p. 178.

47 See *AIW*, pp. 33–4

48 RGT, p. 46.

49 HT to JA, in her January 1897 letter.

50 HT to EG, undated letter from High Beech, *c.* 1917–18, HRC.

51 ET to HT, 29 January 1898, Cardiff.

52 See ET to HH, 8 May 1898, UBC.

53 *SL*, p. 119.

54 Ibid.

55 HT to EG [undated], HRC.

56 See Sonnet 50, *Modern Love.*

57 HT to EG [undated], HRC.

58 i.e. Horst Roman who lived with his parents at the Hotel Metropole in London.

CHAPTER 5 – A Glimpse of Paradise (October 1897– September 1898)

1   ET to HH, 16 October 1897.

2   Ibid.

3   Ibid., 20 October 1897.

4   The *Speaker*, which ran from 1890 to 1907, was a weekly newspaper subtitled *A Review of Politics, Letters, Science and the Arts.*

5   ET to H. H. Sturmer, 4 April 1900, Berg.

6   'How I Began', *PW*, vol. 1, p. 177.

7   ET to HH, 13 November 1897.

8   Ibid., 24 November 1907.

9   Ibid.

10 Ibid.

11 *ACS*, p. 171.

12 ET to IM, 1 December 1897.

13 Ibid.

14 Ibid.

15 Ibid.

16 ET to HH, 13 December 1897.

17 IM's memories of ET, RW.

18 Ibid.

19 ET to IM, 1 December 1897.

20 ET to HH, 6 November 1897.

21 Ibid., 24 November 1897.

22 Ibid., 3 [April] 1898.

23 *Oxford*, pp. 171–2.

24 Moore, p. 38.

25 ET to IM, 8 March 1898.

26 Ibid.

27 ET to HT, 14 November 1897, Cardiff.

28 HT to HH, 27 January 1898.

29 Ibid., 8 May 1898.

30 Norman Brett-James's memories of ET, RW.

31 Ibid.

32 ET to DU, 22 May 98.

33 Ibid.

34 ET to DU, undated letter, *c.* 1898.

35 ET to IM, 12 September 1898.

36 RGT, p. 53.

37 ET to HH, 17 August 1898.

38 Ibid.

39 Ibid.

40 ET to GB, 19 September 1911.

41 ET to HH, early August 1898, Cardiff.

42 ET to GB, 19 September 1911.

43 Ibid.

44 ET to HH, early August 1898, Cardiff.

45 Ibid.

46 ET to IM, 12 September 1898.

47 RGT, p. 68.

48 ET to HT, 20 September 1898, NLW.

49 ET to HH, 19 October 1898.

CHAPTER 6 – Paradise Gained (1898–1899)

1   ET to HT, 14 October 1898, Cardiff.

2   ET to HH, 19 October 1898.

3   Gwen John's reminiscences, published in the *National Library of Wales Journal*, vol. 15 (Winter 1967). RGT gives this as Staircase 12, but the details do not tally with the present layout.

4   ET to HH, 19 October 1898.

5   RW.

6   See Michael Holroyd, *Lytton Strachey* (Penguin Books, 1971), pp. 129–30.

7   Ibid.

8   ET to HT, 9 June 1898, Cardiff.

9   Ibid.

10   Ibid.

11   Quoted in Alun John's unpublished thesis, 'The Life and Work of Edward Thomas', University College of South Wales and Monmouthshire, 1952–5, p. 16.

12   RW.

13   *Oxford*, p. 82.

14   ET to HH, 13 November 1898.

15   Ibid.

16   Ibid., 28 October 1898.

17   RF to Sidney Cox, 11 October 192[8], DC.

18   ET to HH, 26 December 1898.

19   NN, entry for '13-14.x.99', LCL.

20   ET to HH, 26 December 1898.

21   Six chapters of *Olivia Paterson* survive, at Berg.

22   *The Lawyer*, London, 1951, (Eyre and Spottiswoode, 1957), p. 168.

23   FNB 3, 6 October 1899.

24   Haynes, *Fritto Misto*, p. 19.

25   Ibid.

26   ET to HT, 22 February 1899, Cardiff.

27   Ibid.

28   Ibid., 28 August 1898, Cardiff.

29   Ibid.

30   ET to GB, 16 December 1902.

31   The *Academy and 'Literature'*, 8 February 1902. ET's first review had been in the *Daily Chronicle*, 25 November 1901.

32   *National Library of Wales Journal*, vol. 15 (Winter 1967).

33   His college exam was on 'Boissiers, "Ciceron et ses amis"'; the subject matter for the Lothian Essay Prize was 'Michel L'Hôpital, the famous politique under Catherine de Medici'.

34   RW.

35   ET to GB, 15 March 1910.

36   Clarendon Press, 1984–2000, p. 363.

37   *Oxford*, p. xxi.

38   ET to GB, 17 March 1904.

39 *Oxford*, p. 44.
40 Ibid., p. 84.
41 NN, Berg.
42 *AIW*, p. 52.
43 *Oxford*, p. 77.
44 Cooke, *Edward Thomas*, p. 31.
45 ET to RF, 19 May 1914.
46 *WP*, p. 220.
47 ET to HH, 13 November 1898 and ET to GB, 22 April 1907.
48 *WP*, p. 94.
49 *Oxford*, p. 77.
50 *AIW*, p. 80.
51 ET to HT, 22 February 1899, Cardiff.

CHAPTER 7 – Paradise Lost (1899–1900)

1   ET to HT, paraphrasing his father's accusations, *c.* 20 August 1899, Cardiff.
2   ET to HH, 16 May 1899.
3   *AIW*, p. 55.
4   ET to HT, 11 May 1900, Cardiff.
5   ET to ESPH, 8 January 1900, HRC.
6   ET to HT, 11 May 1899, Cardiff.
7   Ibid., 20 August 1899, Cardiff.
8   Ibid., 11 May 1899, Cardiff.
9   *Speaker*, 1 April 1899.
10 GB to C. C. Abbott, 7 December 1937, DUL.
11 ET to GB, 7 July 1906.
12 ET to ESPH, 8 January 1900, HRC.
13 *AIW*, p. 58.
14 ET to HT, 2 July 1899, Cardiff.
15 ET to ESPH, 12 August 99, HRC.
16 ET to HT, 20 August 1899, Cardiff.
17 31 August 1899 notebook, Cardiff.
18 ET to HT, 20 August 1899, Cardiff.
19 NN, 16 November 1899.
20 Ibid.
21 Ibid., 15 January 1900.
22 HT to ET, 26 November 1899, Cardiff.
23 NN, 16 February 1900.
24 ET to HT, 2 July 1899, Cardiff.
25 NN, 18 February 1900.
26 Haynes, *Personalia*, pp. 12–13.

27 FNB 42, 8 April 1910.
28 ET to H. B. Davies, 14 April 1900, Berg.
29 Ibid.
30 ET to JB, 30 September 1902, Cardiff.
31 *Oxford*, p. 136.
32 Ibid.
33 ET to H. B. Davies, 14 April 1900, Berg.
34 Ibid.
35 Ibid. Aesculapius is the Roman name for the son of Apollo, to whose temple pilgrims came for healing.
36 HT to ECH, from Forge House, Oxford, *c.* 1919, in the possession of Alison Thomas.
37 Ibid.
38 RGT, p. 82.
39 ET to HH, 8 May 1898.
40 ET to HT, 31 May 1900, Cardiff.
41 Ibid., 24 May 1900, Cardiff.
42 Ibid., 25 May 1900, Cardiff.
43 ET to GB, 24 July 1905.
44 RGT, p. 88.
45 *Helen and Edward Thomas: A Handful of Letters*, ed. R. George Thomas (Edinburgh: Tragara Press, 1985), p. 12.
46 ET to ESPH, 8 January 1900, HRC.
47 ET to HT, 10 May 1900, Cardiff.
48 Ibid., 25 May 1900, Cardiff.
49 Ibid.
50 ET to IM, 16 June 1900.
51 *WWE*, p. 80.
52 Related by GB in 'A Note on Edward Thomas', *Welsh Review*, vol. 4, no. 3 (September 1945).
53 See *LNTBB*, pp. v–vii.
54 RGT, 61.
55 Ibid., pp. 92–3.
56 Cooke, *Edward Thomas*, p. 30.
57 Moore, *The Life and Letters of Edward Thomas*, p. 42.
58 *Oxford*, p. 76.
59 Ibid., p. 78.
60 Ibid.

CHAPTER 8 – Grub Street (September 1900–September 1901)

1   ET had bills of at least £70 at Oxford, £50 of it for wine.
2   ET to ESPH, 12 August 1899, HRC.

3   ET to IM, 11 October 1900.

4   Ibid.

·   5   ET to Owen Edwards, 6 October 1900, *ETFN*, no. 57, January 2007.

6   ET to IM, 11 October 1900.

7   Ibid., 16 November 1900.

8   Nevinson, *Changes and Chances*, p. 195.

9   HH's note on an original letter from ET of 19 October 1901, Cardiff.

10 'A Poet's Wife', a review of Helen Thomas's *WWE*, in *Weekend Review*, 24 January 1931.

11 ET to GB, 17 February 1905.

12 HWN's 'Fame Too Late', a review of John Moore's *The Life and Letters of Edward Thomas*, in *Life and Letters Today*, March 1940, pp. 269–73.

13 Notes taken by A. D. Williams of conversations with ET, 1908–9, Bodleian.

14 ET to GB, [October] 1908.

15 Ibid., 20 November 1907; not published in *LJB*.

16 See Emeny, *Edward Thomas on the Georgians*, p. 7.

17 See ET to GB, 16 December 1902 and ET's review, *DC*, 8 January 1903.

18 Obituary of ET, *Westminster Gazette*, 28 April 1917.

19 *DC*, 23 November 1900.

20 See *Some Soldier Poets*, T. S. Moore, (London, 1919), pp. 77–85.

21 ET to GB, February 1905 and 22 March 1912.

22 ET to IM, 14 November 1900.

23 ET to GB, 30 June 1905.

24 *TLS*, 16 April 1917.

25 *Westminster Gazette*, 28 April 1917.

26 Introduction to *LGB*, p. 10.

27 ET to GB, 22 April 1907.

28 Milne, *The Memoirs of a Bookman*, p. 149.

29 ET to HM, 19 May 1911, Buffalo.

30 ET to IM, 16 November 1900.

31 Ibid.

32 ET to IM, 25 October 1900.

33 *HS*, p. 90.

34 Ibid., p. 93.

35 ET to IM, 25 October 1900.

36 ET to ECH, n.d., Berg.

37 Ibid.

38 ET to IM, 1 January 1901.

39 Ibid., 8 February 1901.   ·

40 ET to GB, 5 December 1913.

41 *HS*, p. 125.

42 ET to IM, 4 November 1900.

43 Diary, NLW.
44 Ibid., 19 January 1901.
45 Ibid., 23 February 1901.
46 Ibid., 25 February 1901.
47 Ibid., 8 March 1901.
48 Ibid., 11 March 1901.
49 ET to IM, 12 February 1901.
50 ET gives the address as '7 Blandfield Street [Road?], Nightingale Lane', which suggests that the entrance to his flat was at the side of Nightingale Parade in Blandfield Road.
51 ET to IM, 14 February 1901.
52 Ibid., 22 February 1901.
53 Ransome, *Autobiography*, p. 83.
54 Diary, 17 January 1901.
55 *The Letters of Edward Thomas to Jesse Berridge*, ed. A. Berridge (Enitharmon, 1983) [*LJB*], p. 85 in JB's 'Memoir' of ET.
56 ET to JB, 25 June 1901.
57 ET to RF, 15 April 1915.
58 JB's 'Memoir', *Letters*, p. 89.
59 ET to IM, 8 February–12 March 1901.
60 Ibid., 22 April 1901. ET gives opium up for several weeks after visiting Haynes.
61 Ibid., 4 July 1901.
62 *WWE*, p. 86.
63 *The Country* (Cheltenham: Cyder Press, 2000), p. 24.
64 ET to IM, 4 July 1901.
65 Ibid., 13 September 1901.
66 Diary, 8 August 1901.

CHAPTER 9 – Rose Acre Cottage (October 1901–July 1903)

1   *WWE*, p. 86.
2   Ibid., p. 87.
3   ET to GB, 16 December 1902.
4   FNB 42, *c*. April 1910.
5   Ibid.
6   ET to JB, 24 December 1901, *LJB*, p. 21.
7   ET to IM, 31 March 1902 and ET to DU, 21 December 1909.
8   ET to GB, 21 December 1909.
9   *ACP*, p. 69.
10 Ibid., pp. 79–80.
11 Ibid., p. 224.
12 ET to HH, 19 October 1901.
13 A. Duncan Williams, *Today*, May 1917.

14 These occur towards the end of NN.

15 ET to IM, 30 October 1901.

16 Ibid.

17 Ibid.

18 *WWE*, pp. 90–1.

19 ET to IM, 9 February 1902.

20 Ibid.

21 ET to HH, 11 March 1902.

22 Ibid., 14 March 1902.

23 HT to JH, 7 June 1902, UBC.

24 i.e. *Longman's Magazine, Cornhill, Good Words, Temple Magazine, Outlook, Spectator, Onlooker, Pall Mall Gazette, Pall Mall Magazine, Leisure Hours, Globe, Westminster Gazette* (ET to IM, 20 January 1902).

25 *HS*, p. 172.

26 Marsh, *Edward Thomas*, p. 18.

27 ET to JB, 3 May 1902, *LJB*, p. 27.

28 ET to IM, 8 June 1902.

29 ET to GB, 14 November 1908.

30 Moore, *The Life and Letters of Edward Thomas* p. 84.

31 *LJB*, p. 32.

32 Moore, pp. 78--9.

33 ET to IM, 8 June 1902.

34 'Some Letters of Edward Thomas', *Athenaeum*, 16 April 1920, p. 501.

35 ET to IM, 8 June 1902.

36 Ibid., 13 July 1902.

37 ET to IM, 10 October 1902.

38 ET to JB, 14 August 1902, *LJB*, p. 30.

39 *Welsh Review*, September 1945, p. 168.

40 'The Thankless Muse', *DC*, 5 December 1902.

41 *Sunday Times*, 5 May 1957.

42 *Welsh Review*, September 1945, p. 168.

43 Ibid., p. 170.

44 Ibid., p. 171.

45 'A Note on ET and "Eluned"', 16 December 1902.

46 ET to GB, 6 August 1904.

47 Ibid., 16 December 1902.

48 Ibid., 6 August 1904.

49 *Welsh Review*, p. 175.

50 'A Note on ET and "Eluned"', p. 15.

51 See *Welsh Review*, p. 171.

52 *LGB*, p. 8.

53 ET to GB, 31 October 1902.

54 *LJB*, 30 October 1902.
55 Ibid., 9 December 1906.
56 Unpublished memoir of his father, recorded by Merfyn Thomas, RW.
57 ET to IM, 2 May 1901.
58 *LFY*, p. 30.
59 Ibid., p. 20.
60 Ibid.
61 FNB 19.
62 Note of 29 March 1907, Berg.
63 ET to IM, 25 December 1902.
64 Ibid.

CHAPTER 10 – 'The Valley of the Shadow': Ivy Cottage, Bearsted Green (July 1903–May 1904)

1   HT to IM, 4 October 1903.
2   ET to IM, 30 June 1903.
3   Ibid.
4   Ibid.
5   *WWE*, p. 101.
6   ET to IM, 30 June 1903.
7   *WWE*, p. 103.
8   ET to GB, 17 April 1903.
9   ET to IM, 30 June 1903.
10 Moore, *The Life and Letters of Edward Thomas*, p. 101.
11 ET to IM, 16 March 1903.
12 See *Welsh Review*, September 1945, for a fuller account of the visit.
13 ET to IM, 4 October 1903.
14 Ibid., 30 June 1903.
15 Ibid., 6 October 1903.
16 HT to IM, 6 December 1903.
17 ET to IM, 5 September 1903.
18 Ibid.
19 Ibid.
20 Ibid.
21 Ibid., 23 September 1903.
22 Ibid.
23 Ibid., 17 November 1903.
24 Ibid., 7 December 1903.
25 Quoted by HT in her letter to IM of 6 December 1903.
26 HT to IM, 4 October 1903.
27 ET to IM, 1 November 1903.

28 HT to IM, 4 October 1903 and ET to GB, 2 February 1905.

29 Ibid.

30 ET to IM, 1 November 1903.

31 ET to GB, 14 April 1911.

32 Ibid., 22 March 1912.

33 ET to IM, 1 November 1903.

34 Ibid.

35 *ACP*, p.87.

36 *Hamlet* 3, 1, l. 85.

37 ET to IM, 1 November 1903.

38 ET to GB, 17 March 1904.

39 Cooke, p. 39.

40 Haynes, *Personalia*, p. 28.

41 JT to Eckert, 5 November 1939, Bodleian.

42 Diary, autumn 1903.

43 *WWE*, p. 101.

44 HT to IM, 8 October 1904.

45 ET to GB, 30 March 1908.

46 ET to RF, 19 May 1914.

47 ET to GB, 17 March 1904.

48 Ibid.

49 ET to IM, 7 December 1903, BPL.

50 ET to JB, 1 January 1904, *Letters*, p. 50.

51 Ransome, *Autobiography*, p. 82.

52 Ibid., p. 87.

53 ET to GB, 7 March 1904.

54 *The Week's Survey*, 24 December 1904.

55 ET to GB, 6 August 1904.

56 *The Souls of the Streets*, p. 37.

57 ET to GB, 28 September 1904.

58 Ibid., 24 April 1904.

59 FNB 5.

60 ET to GB, 6 August 1904.

61 Ibid., 24 April 1904.

62 Ibid., 12 May 1904.

CHAPTER 11 – Elses Farm (May 1904–October 1906)

1 ET to IM, 17 June 1904.

2 *WWE*, p. 105.

3 Ibid., p. 107.

4 *ACP*, p. 54.

5   Ibid., p. 95.
6   'Some Letters of Edward Thomas', *Athenaeum*, 16 April 1920.
7   Whistler, *Imagination of the Heart*, p. 196.
8   ET to GB, 7 February 1908.
9   Davies, *Later Days*, pp. 48–9.
10 ET to GB, 30 August 1904.
11 Ibid., 28 September 1904.
12 Ransome, *Autobiography*, p. 99.
13 Ibid., pp. 99–100,
14 See *Autobiography*, p. 99.
15 ET to GB, 4 September 1905.
16 Ibid., 24 August 1908: omitted by RGT from *LJB*.
17 *Autobiography*, p. 99.
18 ET to GB, 28 September 1904.
19 Ibid., 20 September 1904.
20 Ibid., 5 December 1904.
21 Ibid.
22 Ibid., 28 December 1904.
23 ET to IM, 31 October 1904.
24 Ibid., 11 November 1904.
25 ET to JB, 22 December 1904.
26 ET to IM, 11 November 1904.
27 ET to GB, 17 February 1905. ET's abandoned notes are at UBC.
28 *BW*, p. 10.
29 Ibid., p. 3.
30 Ibid., pp. 21–3.
31 Ibid., p. 125.
32 'A Note on Edward Thomas', *Welsh Review*, September 1945.
33 ET to GB, 27 February 1905.
34 Ibid., 3 May 1905.
35 ET to IM, 23 August 1905.
36 ET to GB, 3 May 1905.
37 *GB*, p. 322.
38 RGT, p. 121.
39 ET to GB, 19 September 1905.
40 ET already knew the Perris agency by 1901, when he had offered it *Olivia Paterson*.
41 I am indebted to Robert Gomme for his article, 'Edward Thomas and his Literary Agent', *ETFN*, no. 37, August 1997.
42 T. Burke, *City of Encounters* (Constable, 1932), p. 78.
43 Ibid.
44 Ibid., p. 85.
45 ET to FC, undated letter at HRC.

46 ET to JB, 16 April 1905.
47 ET to GB, 3 May 1905.
48 Ibid., 24 July 1905.
49 Ibid.
50 Ibid.
51 Ibid.
52 Ibid.
53 Ibid., 6 August 1905.
54 ET to JB, 8 August 1905.
55 ET to IM, 8 August 1905.
56 Ibid., 23 August 1905.
57 *BW*, p. 44.
58 Stonesifer, *W. H. Davies*, p. 68.
59 Preface to *The Autobiography of a Super-Tramp*, 1908.
60 NN, 11 October 1905.
61 GB to ET, 25 March 1910, Berg.
62 'A Poet at Last', *DC*, 21 October 1905.
63 ET to GB, 1 March 1906.
64 *W. H. Davies*, p. 84.
65 See FNB 8, August–December 1906.
66 WHD letters to ET are at Beinecke Library, Yale University.
67 *Later Days*, p. 138.

CHAPTER 12 – Berryfield Cottage: 'When First I Came Here I Had Hope' (December 1906–February 1907)

1   'When first', *APC*, p. 134.
2   ET to GB, 11 January 1906.
3   ET to Cazenove, 1906, DUL.
4   Review of 'An Annual of New Poetry', *Saturday Westminster Gazette*, 28 April 1917.
5   *HE*, p. 97.
6   ET to GB, 22 September 1907.
7   *HE*, p. 139.
8   Ibid., p. 21.
9   ET to GB, 26 April 1906.
10 *HE*, p. 17.
11 Ibid., p. 194.
12 ET to GB, 26 April 1906.
13 Undated letter from 'the Weald, Sevenoaks' from ET to HWN, asking if ET could dedicate *HE* to him. Collection of the late Tim Wilton-Steer.
14 *TLS*, 7 April 1910.

15 ET to GB, 27 September 1906.

16 Ibid., 11 November 1906.

17 Helen was probably mistaken about the house's construction. Malmstone is the main building material with brick reinforcements around the windows and doors. Malmstone is a calcareous sandstone, resembling chalk, and was formerly quarried in the Upper Greensand at the foot of the hangers.

18 ET to GB, 11 November 1906.

19 *WWE*, p. 114.

20 Ibid., pp. 114–15.

21 Ibid., p. 115.

22 ET to GB, 28 December 1914.

23 See Eckert, *Edward Thomas*, p. 89.

24 ET to WHH, 28 March 1907, Cardiff.

25 ET to GB, 26 February 1908.

26 Ibid.

27 See H. Thomas *Under Storm's Wing* (Manchester, Carcanet, 1998), pp. 236–8.

28 Hudson, *Letters from W. H. Hudson to Edward Garnett*, (Dent, 1925), pp. 134–5.

29 ET to EF, [postmarked 15/16 February 1915].

30 *IPS*, p. 245.

31 ET to GB, 14 May 1907.

32 Goldring, *South Lodge*, p. 50.

33 ET to GB, 22 April 1907.

34 dlM to Rowland Watson, 13 November 1950, Berg.

35 *Letters from W. H. Hudson to Edward Garnett*, p. 135.

36 RGT, p. 250.

37 FNB 46, [*c*. February] 1911.

38 dlM to Rowland Watson, 13 November 1950.

39 In the event ET settled for a quotation from Thomas Traherne.

40 FNB 36, 11 July 1909.

41 *LT*, 1911.

42 ET to GB, 14 December 1909.

43 *DC*, 14 August 1902.

44 ET to GB, 28 July 1906.

45 Ibid., 7 March 1907.

46 *DC*, 17 May 1904.

47 See *Poet to Poet: Edward Thomas's Letters to Walter de la Mare*, ed. Judy Kendall (Bridgend: Seren, 2012) [JK], p. 27.

48 ET to GB, 22 April 1907.

49 i.e. *DC*, 9 November 1906.

50 ET to RF, 28 June 1915.

51 The Square Club was founded by R. A. Scott James, Edward Garnett and Conal O'Riordan, to keep the memory of Henry Fielding alive. It had no rules, no officers

or elections, no minutes and it met once a month at various West End restaurants over its nearly 40 years of existence, including Paganini's in Baker Street, the Florence restaurant, Piccadilly, Simpson's in the Strand and the Wellington in Fleet Street. Its members included many of Thomas's friends – Nevinson, MacAlister, Hudson, Seccombe, Martin Freeman and, later, Muirhead Bone. Other literary figures were Yeats, Ford Madox Ford, Edgar Jepson, John Galsworthy, Percival Gibbon, Arthur Machen and John Drinkwater.

52 ET to GB, 31 October 1912, and ET to HT, 15 November 1912.
53 ET to RF, 28 June 1915.
54 Whistler, *Imagination of the Heart*, p. 113.
55 ET to GB, 7 July 1906.
56 *HE*, p. 226.
57 Ibid., pp. 226–7.
58 ET to GB, 7 July 1906.
59 Ibid., 11 November 1906.
60 Ibid., 9 December 1906.
61 Ibid.
62 ET to GB, 26 December 1906.
63 ET to GB, 3 March 1912.
64 See *DC*, 26 February 1906.
65 ET to GB, 16 February 1907.
66 Robin Guthrie to R. P. Eckert, MS Eng. Lett. C. 282, Bodleian.
67 ET to GB, 30 January 1915.
68 *Welsh Review*, August 1939, p. 28.
69 Ibid.
70 *LFY*, p. 27.
71 Robin Guthrie to R. P. Eckert, MS Eng. Lett. C. 282, Bodleian.
72 Ibid.
73 *LFY*, p. 27.
74 *Welsh Review*, August 1939, p. 24.

CHAPTER 13 – Hope and Loss of Hope (January 1907– December 1909)

1 ET to GB, 22 April 1907.
2 Ibid., 14 May 1907.
3 Ibid.
4 Ibid.
5 ET to GB, 27 March 1907.
6 Ibid.
7 ET to GB, 14 May 1907.

8   Ibid., 10 August 1907.

9   Ibid.

10 *WWE*, p. 126.

11 ET to GB, 22 September 1907.

12 Ibid.

13 ET to GB, 26 December 1907.

14 See article in *Barrier Miner* (Broken Hills, NSW, Australia) 11 March 1912, reprinted from *London Magazine*. Dr Savill had recently published *Clinical Lectures on Neurasthenia* (Henry Glaisher, 1906) when he first saw ET in 1907.

15 ET to GB, 15 January 1908.

16 Ibid., 7 February 1908. Evelyn Hope Webb was born on 30 November 1889, according to the London University Register of Students.

17 ET to GB, 7 February 1908.

18 FNB 29, 12 March 1909.

19 *ACP*, p. 113.

20 *WWE*, p. 123.

21 ET to dlM, 19 February 1908, JK, p. 47.

22 *ACP*, p. 280.

23 ET to dlM, 19 February 1908, JK, p. 47.

24 ET to GB, 26 February 1908.

25 FNB 15, *c.* 20 February 1908.

26 ET to GB, 15 January and 26 February 1908.

27 Diary, Monday, 2 March 1908.

28 ET to GB, 26 February 1908.

29 *WWE*, p. 125.

30 Eckert, *Edward Thomas* p. 104.

31 Moore, *The Life and Letters of Edward Thomas* p. 153.

32 Ibid.

33 RGT, p. 148.

34 Ibid., p. 146.

35 ET to dlM, 13 March 1908, JK, p. 47.

36 HT to JH, 15 March 1908, Cooke, *Edward Thomas*, pp. 35–6.

37 ET to GB, 30 March 1908.

38 Ibid., [n.d.] October 1908.

39 ET to JB, 14 November 1908, *LJB*, p. 59.

40 *Scrutiny*, vol. 6, no. 4 (March 1938), p. 436.

41 ET to GB, 7 February 1908.

42 *RJ*, p. 336.

43 ET to GB, 24 September 1908.

44 'A Memoir', *LJB*, p. 89.

45 ET to GB, August 1911.

46 Ibid., 'Christmas 1911'.

47 *CET*, p. 135.
48 ET to GB, 26 February 1908.
49 Ibid., 1 October 1908.
50 *SC* (2009), pp. 19–20, 26.
51 Ibid., p. 9.
52 Ibid., p. 7.
53 Ibid., p. 13.
54 Ibid.
55 *SC*, p. 29.
56 Ibid., p. 32.
57 Ibid., p. 83.
58 *WWE*, p. 129.
59 *ACP*, p. 22.
60 *SC*, p. 134.
61 ET to GB, 1 October 1908.
62 ET to Emily Bottomley, 15 September 1909, Cardiff.
63 GB to ET, 8 October 1909.
64 ET to GB, 14 December 1909, and GB to ET, 8 October 1909.
65 *SC*, p. 10.
66 ET to dlM, 26 October 1908, JK, p. 55.
67 Ibid., 6 January 1909, JK, p. 59.
68 ET to GB, 13 February 1909.
69 Ibid., 15 March 1909.
70 Introduction to *The Selected Poems of Edward Thomas* (Tregynon: Gregynog Press, 1927).
71 *TLS*, 10 March 1910, p. 82.
72 FNB 20, 19 February 1908.

CHAPTER 14 – 'Your Hurried and Harried Prose Man': Wick Green (December 1909–December 1910)

1 Rhys, *Letters from Limbo*, p. 139.
2 ET to GB, 3 January 1909.
3 Ibid.
4 Ibid., 13 February 1909.
5 Ibid., 26 August 1910.
6 Goldring, *South Lodge*, p. 35.
7 ET's 'The North-West Wind' appeared in *The Tramp* in March 1910, his 'Great Possessions' in April 1910 (reprinted in *The Last Sheaf* (1928)) and his 'Castle of Lostormellyn' in June 1910 (reprinted in *Light and Twilight* (1911)). ET had problems getting paid by Goldring and was angry with him. But he praised Goldring's work in

his review of *Georgian Poetry 1911–1912*, though Goldring did not appear in it, as 'invariably interesting, often brilliant' (Richard Emeny, *ET on the Georgians*, p. 23).

8   Goldring, *South Lodge*, p. 35.

9   ET reviewed Pound's *Personae* twice: in *DC*, 7 June 1909, and *English Review*, vol. 1, no. 3 (June 1909).

10 ET to HH, 16 September 1909.

11 Ibid.

12 ET to GB, 6 November 1908.

13 Ibid.

14 Diary, 16 December 1909: 'Helen unwell'.

15 ET to GB, 24 September 1908.

16 *WWE*, p. 131.

17 Ibid., p. 133.

18 FNB 41, 20 December 1909.

19 ET to GB, 22 December 1910.

20 Ibid., 'Friday' [Christmas 1911].

21 *NT*, 12.

22 *ACP*, p. 74.

23 Ibid., p. 75.

24 Ibid., p. 68.

25 ET to GB, 3 January 1910.

26 FNB 40, [c. 1910].

27 *PW*, vol. 2, p. 368.

28 Ibid., p. 388.

29 Ibid., pp. 381 and 383–4.

30 ET to GB, 14 December 1909.

31 Ibid., 25 November 1910.

32 Ibid., 14 December 1909.

33 Ibid., 22 April 1910.

34 GB to ET, 25 March 1910.

35 Ibid., 22 April 1910.

36 *FIP*, pp. 3, 16 & 145–50.

37 FNB 44, 16 August 1910.

38 *ACP*, p. 74.

39 ET to MT, 14 February 1915, Bodleian.

40 RH to Edward Marsh, 17 May 1945.

41 *DC*, 30 May 1907.

42 Diary, 2 March 1914, Bryn Mawr. Hodgson himself was a judge of bull terriers at Cruft's Dog Show.

43 Whistler, *Imagination of the Heart*, p. 172.

44 Ibid.

45 Ibid.

46 Helen Thomas, 'Mr Ralph Hodgson', *The Times*, 7 November 1962.

47 Ibid.

48 ET to HM, 19 May 1911.

49 ET's contributions to its eight numbers were: No. 1 (March 1913) 'Ella Wheeler Wilcox', pp. 33–42 and review of *Poems* by W. B. Yeats, pp. 53–6; No. 2 (June 1913) 'Thomas Hardy of Dorchester', pp. 180–4; No. 3 (September 1913) review of *Poems* by John Gould, pp. 363–5, review of *Poems* by John Alford, p. 366, review of *Eve and Other Poems* by Ralph Hodgson, pp. 370–1; No. 4 (December 1913) review of *Oxford Poetry 1910–1913* and *Cambridge Poets 1900–1913*, pp. 489–91; No. 5 (March 1914) 'Reviewing: an Unskilled Labour', pp. 37-41 and review of 'New Editions, Reprints & Anthologies', pp. 62–5; No. 6 (June 1914) review of 'Reprints & Anthologies', pp. 185–8; No. 7 (September 1914) review of 'Reprints & Anthologies', pp. 299–301; No. 8 (December 1914) 'War Poetry', pp. 341–5, review of 'Anthologies & Reprints', pp. 384–8.

50 *Morning Post*, 3 February 1910.

51 *DC*, 14 January 1913.

52 Hibberd, *Harold Monro*, pp. 96–7.

53 Hassall, *Rupert Brooke*, p. 239.

54 Marsh, *Edward Thomas* p. 105.

55 *DC*, 9 April 1912.

56 *Rupert Brooke*, p. 380.

57 RB to ET, [*c.* May 1913], Milwaukee University Library.

CHAPTER 15 – The Bax–Baynes Effect (1911–1912)

1   The National Insurance Act was passed in 1911, which included national social health insurance for primary care (not specialist or hospital care), initially for about one-third of the population – employed working-class wage earners but not their dependants.

2   A copy of the petition, signed by Hilaire Belloc, is at HRC.

3   *Welsh Review*, September 1945.

4   Douglas, p. 174.

5   Ibid., p. 175. The Horse Shoe was almost certainly the pub of that name in Tottenham Court Road, near to the British Museum Reading Room where Thomas and Douglas pursued their researches. The Dominion Theatre stands on the original site.

6   Ibid., p. 174.

7   Burke, *City of Encounters*, pp. 86–7.

8   EG to Douglas, 2 February 1912, Norman Douglas Collection, Vorarlberger Landesbibliothek, Bregenz.

9   *Looking Back*, p. 174.

10 Letter of 3 November 1912, Beinecke.

11 Douglas, *Looking Back*, p. 174.

12 Ibid.

13 *Welsh Review* (September 1945), p. 176.

14 Mark Holloway, *Norman Douglas: A Biography* (Secker & Warburg, 1976), pp. 174–5.

15 i.e. 'The Chessplayer' (October 1912), 'Green and Scarlet' (April 1913) together with a review of the Clarendon Press edition of Coleridge's *Poems*.

16 Podmore, who helped found the Fabian Society, was compelled to resign from a senior position in the Post Office because of alleged homosexual involvement. He committed suicide in August 1910, two months after Thomas's tea with his wife and Clifford Bax.

17 ET to GB, 31 October 1912.

18 ET to GB, 31 October 1913, and ET to CB [postmarked 19 September 1912, HRC].

19 The draft introduction to this is at the Berg.

20 See 'Twenty Chinese Poems', *Morning Post*, 16 May 1910.

21 Clifford Bax Papers, D254, Box 1, folder 10, Rare Books & Special Collections, University of Rochester.

22 Ibid.

23 Diary, 6 January 1911.

24 Ibid., 18 April 1911.

25 *Letters from W. H. Hudson to Edward Garnett* (London, 1925), p. 118.

26 ET to dlM, 19 November 1911.

27 Bax, *Inland Far*, p. 110.

28 Ibid.

29 *LFY*, p. 2.

30 Diary, 14 April 1912.

31 ET to GB, 18 April 1912.

32 Diary, 20 April 1912.

33 Hollis, *Now All Roads Lead to France*, p. 108.

34 HGB's private diary, quoted in Diana Baynes Jansen, *Jung's Apprentice* (Einsiedeln: Daimon Verlag, 2003), p. 137.

35 Ibid., p. 61.

36 *LFY*, p. 12.

37 ET to HT, 2 August 1912, NLW.

38 Ibid.

39 Moore, *The Life and Letters of Edward Thomas*, p. 181.

40 FNB 57, [n.d., but August 1912].

41 ET to HT, 6 August 1912, NLW.

42 Ibid.

43 ET to dlM, 31 October 1912.

44 ET to HT, 16 August 1912, NLW.

45 RGT, p. 223.

46 ET to GB, 22 May 1907.

47 ET to dlM, 11 January 1912.

48 Ibid., 3 January 1913.

49 ET to GB, 31 October 1912.

50 See Julian Thomas to Eckert, 2 May 1935, Eckert Collection, Bodleian.
51 FNB 38, [late 1909], Berg.
52 FNB 62, [May–June 1913].
53 Ibid.
54 ET to EG, 6 February 1913, HRC.
55 Hudson, *Letters from W. H. Hudson to Edward Garnett*, pp. 134–5.
56 *HGLM*, chap. V, *PW*, vol 1, p. 39.
57 *TLS* review by Charles Brodribb, 20 November 1913.
58 ET to EG, 25 November 1912.
59 ET to HT, 13 November 1912, HRC.
60 FNB 61, Berg.
61 ET to HT, 12 November 1912, NLW.
62 RGT, p. 203.

CHAPTER 16 – Pursued by the Other in Pursuit of Spring (January–September 1913)

1   ET to HM, 15 January 1913.
2   ET to dlM, [? January 1913], JK, p. 144.
3   *LFY*, pp. 4–5.
4   Ibid., p. 5.
5   *First and Second Love* (Michael Joseph, 1947; Oxford: Oxford University Press, 1959).
6   Annabel Farjeon, *Morning Has Broken* (Macrae, 1986), p. 124.
7   FNB 61.
8   *HGLM, PW*, vol. 1, p. 52.
9   *LFY*, p. 42.
10 Ibid., p. 12.
11 Ibid., p. 97. EF to Myfanwy Thomas, 24 February 1953, DC.
12 EF to Myfanwy Thomas, 24 February 1953, DC.
13 Ibid.
14 Ibid.
15 EF to Joseph Farjeon, *Morning Has Broken*, p. 122.
16 *LFY*, p. 7.
17 Ibid., p. 19.
18 See Whistler, *Imagination of the Heart*, pp. 214–16.
19 ET to GB, 20 July 1911.
20 *IW*, p. 91.
21 Ibid., p. 283.
22 Ibid., p. vii.
23 'Roads', *ACP*, p. 106.

24 FNB 18, *c.* 13 May 1908.

25 See W. H. Hudson, *A Traveller in Little Things* (1921).

26 *IW*, pp. vii and 106.

27 ET to GB, 16 September 1908.

28 ET to HT, 11 February 1913, NLW.

29 *IPS*, pp. 199–200.

30 'But these things also', *ACP*, p. 67.

31 *IPS*, p. 210.

32 Ibid.

33 *IPS*, pp. 219–20.

34 FNB 62, *c.* June 1913.

35 P. J. Kavanagh, *People and Places* (Manchester: Carcanet Press, 1988), p. 196.

36 Ibid., p. 197.

37 C. G. Jung, *Memories, Dreams, Reflections* (Fontana, 1983), p. 262.

38 FNB 62, *c.* June 1913.

39 *LS*, p. 52.

40 *Country*, p. ii.

41 ET to GB, 24 January 1906, and FNB 29, [February–March] 1909.

42 ET to IM, 31 November 1911.

43 ET's interview with A. D. Williams, Eckert Collection, Bodleian.

44 *ACP*, p. 40.

45 Ibid., p. 42.

46 Ibid.

47 HT to JH, 6 August 1913, *Time and Again*, p. 200.

48 *LFY*, p. 20.

49 Ibid.

50 FNB 62.

51 FNB 63.

52 Unfinished MS of *Ecstasy*, Berg.

CHAPTER 17 – 'The Only Brother I Ever Had'
(6 October 1913–March 1914)

1   ET to dlM, 6 October 1913, JK, p. 169.

2   *LFY*, p. 3

3   Ibid.

4   Ibid.

5   RF to Grace Walcott Hazard Conkling, 28 June 1921, DC.

6   'The Sun Used to Shine', *ACP*, p. 122.

7   ET to RF, 19 February 1914.

8   See note 31 below.

9   See *LFY*, p. 59, for ET's letter to EF of 26 January 1914. ET's review of dlM appeared in *DC* on 10 January 1914. One offshoot from this autobiographical exploration was an article 'How I Began', published in *T.P.'s Weekly*, 31 January 1914.

10   ET to JF, [December 1913], Berg.

11   Ibid.

12   Ibid.

13   Ibid., 11 December 1913 and [December 1913].

14   *ACP*, p. 16. RGT detects evidence of a similar impulse behind much of his uncommissioned writing from 1912 until mid-1914, e.g. *Rest and Unrest, Light and Twilight, The Happy-Go-Lucky Morgans, In Pursuit of Spring* and the final chapter of *Keats*. (RGT, p. 223).

15   *CET*, p. 14.

16   *ACP*, p. 53.

17   Ibid., pp. 136–7.

18   *LFY*, p. 221.

19   GB and his wife spent the winters of 1911–12 and 1912–13 at R. C. Trevelyan's house, The Shiffolds, Holmbury, approximately 20 miles from where ET was lodging near East Grinstead.

20   RF may have introduced the Imagist poet F. S. Flint to ET at this meeting at St George's restaurant. JF was certainly there, and ET expected W. H. Davies and RH to be present too.

21   ET to EF, 5 December 1913.

22   ET had accepted an invitation to a dinner at Pecorini's from HM for 11 November, attended by W. H. Davies, F. S. Flint, Ralph Hodgson, Victor Plarr, Maurice Hewlett, Alfred Storer, J. C. Squire, Robert Frost and Arundel del Re, but cancelled at the last minute.

23   Claud Lovat Fraser's diary entry for 6 January 1914, Bryn Mawr.

24   Ibid.

25   i.e. 67 Frith Street, a house visited by Charles and Mary Lamb, which had once been the Venetian Embassy.

26   Lovat Fraser's diary, Bryn Mawr.

27   Ibid.

28   ET to dlM, 23 January 1914, JK, p. 128.

29   ET to EF, 12 November 1913.

30   Ibid., 8 December 1913, BPL.

31   Leslie Lee Francis told me during an interview in June 2009 that she had heard her grandfather, Robert Frost, refer to Thomas's intention of leaving Helen in late 1913 and early 1914. She insisted that Frost had urged him not to and that it was on his advice that Thomas returned home: 'Robert viewed himself as a more mature person and he didn't want Thomas, or any of his friends, to divorce.' She was in close touch with her grandfather until his death in her thirty-second year. Frost's first biographer, Lawrance Thompson, who talked to Frost over many years, also remembered him saying that Thomas had been intending to leave his wife at this period.

32 RGT, p. 34.

33 See *LPE*, p. 1.

34 See ET to GB, 25 August 1914 and ET to EF, [postmarked 30 March 1914], BPL.

35 ET to EF, 22 February 1914, BPL.

36 *LFY*, p. viii.

37 RF to Sidney Cox, 11 October 1927, DC.

38 Ibid.

39 Ibid.

40 Ibid.

41 *LFY*, p. 79.

CHAPTER 18 – 'While We Two Walked Slowly Together': Thomas and Frost in Gloucestershire (April–July 1914)

1   ET to John Freeman, [end April], 1915.

2   RF to Sidney Cox, 18 May 1914, DC.

3   Elinor Frost to Leona White, *c.* 20 June 1914, *Selected Letters of RF*, p. 126.

4   The Gallows, as ET would have known it in 1914, no longer exists, save for steps leading up into the garden and one small section of the house, which collapsed *c.* 1933/6 after the thatched roof fell in. But the village in which The Gallows was situated, Ryton, is still there, with its narrow, winding roads, relatively unchanged except for the nearby M50 motorway.

5   Commissioned for the 7 November 1914 edn of the *Nation* and reprinted in *LS*.

6   'This England', *LNTBB*, p. 269.

7   See ET to EF, 21/22 April 1914.

8   Ibid.

9   Ibid.

10 'This England', *LNTBB*, pp. 269–70.

11 Ibid., p. 270.

12 Ibid.

13 *PN Review* 7, vol. 5, No. 3, April–June 1979.

14 *LNTBB*, p. 270.

15 RF to Sidney Cox, December 1914, DC.

16 Ibid.

17 Ibid.

18 Ibid.

19 Review of *North of Boston* in *Daily News and Leader*, 22 July 1914.

20 Preface to *Lyrical Ballads*.

21 *LFY*, p. 90.

22 Ibid.

23 Ibid., p. 91.

24 ET to GB, 29 May 1914.

25 *Frost: a Literary Life Reconsidered* (Amherst: University of Massachusetts Press, 1993), p. 75.

26 ET to RF, 19 May 1914.

27 RF to Grace Walcott Hazard Conkling, 28 June 1921, DC.

28 RF to Louis Untermeyer, DC.

29 Letter of 16 December 1925, Wesleyan University Library.

30 Ibid.

31 'The Frontiers of Prose', *Literature*, 23 September 1899.

32 See *DC*, 25 January 1906.

33 ET to RF, 19 May 1914.

34 Meyers, *Robert Frost*, p. 105.

35 Bonham's Catalogue (Oxford) for 2/3 December 1998: JWH's note inserted in his copy of *In Memoriam: ET Being Number Two of the Green Pastures Series*.

36 'This England', *LNTBB*, p. 270.

37 *ACP*, pp. 90–1.

38 See ibid., p. 245.

39 *The Queen's Vigil and Other Songs, DC*, 15 December 1902; *The Golden Helm & Other Verses, DC*, 6 November 1903; *The Web of Life, DC*, 18 April 1908; *Akra the Slave, DC*, 9 August 1911; *Fires*, Book I, *DC*, 9 March 1912; *Fires*, Books II and III, *DC*, 5 September 1912; *New Numbers*, Part 1, 21 March 1914; *Thoroughfares and Borderlands, Bookman*, November 1914. ET also reviewed WG's *The Nets of Love* (place and date unspecified) and *The Stanfolds* (place and date unspecified).

40 *DC*, 26 November 1903.

41 See Linda Hart, *Once They Lived in Gloucestershire*, p. 38.

42 *The Web of Life, DC*, 18 April 1908.

43 *DC*, 9 August 1911.

44 ET to HM, 3 January 1913.

45 ET to GB, 22 May 1914.

46 Ibid.

47 '4th August 1914 – Robert Frost', Helen Thomas, *PN Review*, vol. 5, no. 3.

48 Ibid.

49 ET to RF, [late May, early June] 1914.

50 ET to GB, 3 September 1914.

51 HT to RF, [*c.* March 1917], DC.

52 D. H. Lawrence to Edward Marsh, November 1913, Berg.

53 See ET's reviews of *New Numbers* in *New Weekly*, 21 March 1914, and *DC*, 29 April 1914.

54 ET to GB, 4 April 1914.

55 RF to Sidney Cox, [late 1914], DC.

56 ET to GB, 22 April 1914.

57 Ibid., 26 February 1908.

58 *RJ*, p.167.

59 Quoted in Emeny, *Edward Thomas on the Georgians*, p. 41.

60 *Bookman*, March 1914.

61 Ibid.

62 ET to GB, 21 September 1914.

63 Letter from a friend of GB's, Dixon Scott, to Alan Monkhouse, 3 October 1913, quoted by RGT in *LGB*, p. 184n.

64 Conversation with Jeff Cooper, February 2010.

65 'Memories of a Poet's Life', *Listener*, 15 November 1956.

66 Review of *Men and Huns*, B, July 1914; rev. of *Cromwell and Other Poems*, B, July 1914; revue of *Rebellion: a Play in 3 Acts*; revue of *New Numbers*, Part 1, *New Weekly*, 21 March [19]14; revue of *New Numbers, DC*, 29 April 1914.

67 *New Weekly*, 21 March 1914.

68 ET to JF, 8 March 1915.

69 ET to GB, 27 June 1914. *New Numbers*, Part III, was published in October 1914 but dated 'August 1914'.

70 *New Weekly*, 27 March 1914.

71 Hart, *Once They Lived in Gloucestershire*, p. 46.

72 ET to RF, 6 July 1914.

73 *ACP*, p. 137.

74 ET to EF, [20 June 1914].

75 This was a series of 24 drawings by Katherine Cameron with flower-poems of ET's choosing.

76 Elinor Frost to Leona Harvey [*c.* 20 June 1914], Thompson, *Selected Letters of Robert Frost*, p. 126.

77 'Robert Frost', *PN Review*, vol. 5, no. 3, p. 22.

78 Ibid.

79 RF to Sidney Cox, 11 October 1928, DC.

80 RF was at Steep for the weekend of 17 July 1914.

81 ET to EF, 17 July 1914.

82 ET to RF, 'Wednesday' [possibly 1 July 1914].

83 ET to HM, 2 July 1914.

CHAPTER 19 – The Sun Used to Shine (August–September 1914)

1 *WWE*, p. 158.

2 *LFY*, p. 80.

3 Ibid.

4 This was published in 1916 as *The Flowers I Love*.

5 *LFY*, p. 87.

6 'Robert Frost', *PN Review*, vol. 5, no. 3, p. 22.

7 *LFY*, p. 87.

8   Ibid.
9   ET to EF, 14 August 1914.
10 'Robert Frost', *PN Review*, vol. 5, no. 3, p. 22.
11 See *LFY*, p. 95. ET sent the words of both songs to EF, who had admired them when she heard them at a similar sing-song.
12 ET, 'The Combe', for instance, would appear in *The Bouquet* in April 1915.
13 ET to WHH, 20 November 1914, Cardiff.
14 HT, 'Robert Frost', loc. cit.
15 Ibid.
16 *LFY*, p. 88.
17 'Robert Frost', loc. cit.
18 ET to EF, 14 August 1914.
19 Ibid.
20 Ibid.
21 Ibid.
22 Ibid.
23 Ibid.
24 Ibid.
25 Last stanza of 'Fall In', published in *DC*, 31 August 1914, and reprinted next day in response to public enthusiasm. See Dominic Hibberd and John Onions, *Poetry of the Great War* (Macmillan, 1986), p. 190 for further details.
26 ET to JF, 14 August 1914.
27 At this stage ET was actively seeking war poems, reminding Eleanor on at least two occasions to save any for him.
28 ET to GB, 25 August 1914.
29 ET to HM, 14 September 1914.
30 Ibid., 19 September 1914.
31 'War Poetry', *LNTBB*, p. 132.
32 *ACP*, pp. 104-5.
33 Barker, *The Art of Edward Thomas*, p. 123.
34 Cooke, *Edward Thomas*, p. 215.
35 ET refers in 'War Poetry' to 'Harry & St Crispin', *LNTBB*, p. 133.
36 ET to JF, 14 August 1914.
37 ET to Cazenove, 17 August 1914, DUL.
38 Ibid., 19 August 1914.
39 Eckert, *Edward Thomas*, p. 146.
40 Ibid.
41 Ibid.
42 Unpub. notes by EF, some later rewritten and included in her Foreword to *You Come Too* (Bodley Head, 1964).
43 Ibid.
44 Ibid.

45 Ibid.
46 Ibid.
47 Ibid.
48 Ibid.
49 Interview with Frost's grand-daughter, Lesley Lee Francis, June 2009.
50 ET to EF, [postmarked 4 September 1914].
51 *LFY*, p. 91.
52 Ibid.
53 Ibid.
54 Ibid., p. 95.
55 EF to Maitland Radford, 29 August 1914, BL.
56 'This England', *LNTBB*, p. 271.
57 'Ickenham in September', from *London Miniatures, LS, PW*, vol. 2, p. 521.
58 *ACP*, p. 122.
59 *ACP*, p. 122.

CHAPTER 20 – The Road Taken (September–November 1914)

1   e.g. ET to GB, 21 September 1914 and ET to WHH, 20 November 1914.
2   ET to RF, 9 November 1914.
3   ET to GB, 3 September 1914.
4   This and all following quotations are from 'Tipperary', *English Review*, October 1914, unless otherwise indicated.
5   ET to JB, 3 September 1914, *LJB*, p. 74.
6   e.g. ET to EF, 4 September 1914 and ET to GB, 3 September 1914.
7   ET to EF, 13 September 1914.
8   ET to RF, 19 September 1914.
9   Mrs Gardner's house was Farm Corner, Tadworth, Surrey.
10 ET to RF, 19 September 1914.
11 ET to EF, 17 October 1914.
12 Ibid.
13 Ibid.
14 ET to EF, 17 October 1914; John Wilton Haines (1875–1960) had a wide circle of friends, including C. Day-Lewis, Herbert Howells, Walter de la Mare, Siegfried Sassoon and Vaughan Williams.
15 James Guthrie (ed.), *Green Pastures*, p. 13.
16 ET to EF, 17 October 1914.
17 ET to HT, [11 October?] 1914, *SL*, p. 97.
18 *Green Pastures*, p. 13.
19 Ibid.
20 ET to HT, 17 October 1914, *SL*, p. 98.
21 *ACP*, p. 101.

22 ET to RF, 31 October 1914.

23 ET to HM, n.d. [?9 or 10 November 1914?].

24 'Ralph Hodgson', *The Times*, 7 November 1962.

25 Harding, *Dreaming of Babylon*, pp. 114ff.

26 ET to HM, [undated letter].

27 ET to RH, 19 November 1914, Beinecke.

28 ET to HM [undated letter].

29 Hibberd, *Harold Monro*, p. 161.

30 ET to RF, 2 January 1916.

31 There are two versions of the poem and an annotated version of the prose piece at Buffalo.

32 ET to MT, 23 November 1914, Bodleian.

33 Ibid.

34 Letter from American film producer Elliott Baker to RGT, *ETFN* no. 63, January 2010.

35 Ibid.

36 ET to RF, 13 June 1915.

37 'The Signpost', *ACP*, p. 37.

38 Meyers, *Robert Frost*, p. 126.

39 *ACP*, p. 46.

40 RF to HM, December 1914, Thompson, *Selected Letters of Robert Frost*, p. 142.

41 Myfanwy Thomas to Linda Hart, 31 March 1997, in possession of the recipient.

42 Hollis, *Now All Roads Lead to France*, p. 176.

43 See *The Robert Frost Review*, no. 21, 2012 for Francis's review of Hollis.

44 GA.

45 Quoted by Jeff Cooper, 'The Frosts at Ryton', *Dymock Poems and Friends Newsletter* (2004), p. 62.

46 *ACP*, p. 46.

47 'Walking with Robert Frost', unpublished account by EF of RF's visit to her in May 1957.

CHAPTER 21 – 'The Only Begetter' (December 1914)

1 ET to GB, 19 December 1914.

2 *LNTBB*, p. 222; *English Review*, December 1914.

3 ET to HT, 11 October 1914, Cardiff.

4 ET to CB, 9 July 1912.

5 ET to HH, 19 May 1915.

6 Letter from Ezra Pound to T. S. Eliot, 24 February 1922,

7 ET to RF, 15 December 1914.

8 ET to GB, 26 February 1908.

9 *ACP*, p. 31.

10　'Ryton: Clothes on the line blowing violently in wind and crackle like a rising woodfire'. FNB 79.

11　'The White House', MS at Buffalo.

12　Marsh, *Edward Thomas*, p. 116.

13　ET to JF, 8 March 1915.

14　*W. H. Davies*, p. 116.

15　ET to RF, 15 December 1914.

16　ET to EF, 16 January 1915.

17　*ACP*, p. 16.

18　'November', *ACP*, p. 88.

19　*ACP*, p. 14.

20　ET to GB, 30 June 1915.

21　Ibid.

22　The most significant of the changes is the omission of some lines at Frost's suggestion, notably following line 11, where ET had originally written: 'Only cobblers (who keep away) / And a few odd men (who do not matter)', which he admitted had 'a touch nearing facetiousness in it'. He also omitted the phrase 'wing's light word' after Frost queries it. Both versions are contained in ET's notebook at Buffalo.

23　ET to EG, 13 March 1915, HRC. Shelley plays, in 'The Sensitive Plant', with the opposites of youth / decay, sadness / delight, reality / dreams.

24　*ACP*, p. 35.

25　Ibid., p. 148.

26　*IPS*, p. 178.

27　Whistler, *Imagination of the Heart*, pp. 213–16.

28　*IPS*, p. 197.

29　*ACP*, p. 35.

30　*WWE*, p. 156.

31　Edna Longley argues that 'March' was influenced by William Morris's 'The Message of the March Wind', *ACP*, p. 148.

32　*LPE*, p. 52.

33　ET review of Pound's *Personae*, *DC*, 7 June 1909.

34　'Old man' is the herb *Artemisia arbrotanum*, which has various uses in herbal medicine. It is often combined with the other herbs ET mentions, 'rosemary and lavender', to make scented sachets.

35　ET to GB, 21 May 1908.

36　Ibid., 6 April 1910.

37　FNB 79.

38　There is no evidence that Thomas had read *Chez Côte du Swann*, published in 1913. But it was reviewed in the *TLS* in 1914, so may have come to ET's notice.

39　*Listener*, 15 June 1978, review of ET's *RJ*.

40　Barker (ed.), *The Art of Edward Thomas*; essay by Robert Wells.

41　See pp. 2–3.

42 Coombes, p. 89, e.g. 'After Rain', 'The Source', 'Melancholy', 'Rain', 'Like the Touch of Rain', 'It Rains', 'What will they do?', 'The sorrow of true love'.

43 *LPE*, p. 48.

44 ET to GB, 9 August 1908.

45 Pub. in *RA* (1910), pp. 108 ff.

46 MS note in an undated folder at Berg labelled 'Subjects'.

47 *Cymbeline* III, iii, ll. 36–9.

48 FNB 79.

49 *ACP*, p. 38.

50 Since at least four early poems – 'Interval', 'The Other', 'Birds' Nests' and 'The Mountain Chapel' – are undated, they may also have been included in the batch he sent to HM.

51 ET to EF, undated letter.

52 Monro was said to be 'furious' at the Dymock Poets for publishing what he regarded as a competing publication to *Poetry and Drama*, *New Numbers*. Gibson had compounded his sins in Monro's eyes by marrying Monro's secretary, Geraldine Townsend, and taking her away from the Poetry Bookshop.

53 See Hibberd, *Harold Monro*, pp. 153–4, for the full picture.

54 ET to HM, 15 December 1914.

55 Ibid., n.d. but *c.* 21 December 1914.

56 Ibid.

57 Erica Royde Smith read from ET's poems on 29 December 1917 to an audience of 50.

58 Quoted in endnote to *Poetry Wales*, vol. 13, no. 14 (1978), p. 70.

59 Introduction to EF, *The Green Roads*, p. 15.

CHAPTER 22 – This England (January–February 1915)

1   ET to JF, 4 October 1914.

2   See ET to JB, 25 May 1915, *LJB*, p. 77, re having 'my name put down on possibly a very long list'.

3   ET to dlM, [mid-September] 1914, JK, p. 189.

4   ET to WHH, 26 November 1914.

5   ET to EF, 26 December 1914.

6   *LFY*, p. 154.

7   ET to IM, 19 January 1915.

8   ET to JF, 16 January 1915.

9   *ACP*, p. 49.

10 FNB 67, 5 December 1913.

11 *ACP*, p. 50.

12 FNB 54.

13 *ACP*, p. 50.

14 FNB 40, 7 December 1909.

15 *ACP*, p. 52.

16 *RJ*, pp. 208–9.

17 Ibid. Cf. FNB 58, for April 1913: 'hunt-scarlet'.

18 Cooke, p. 222.

19 See FNB 54.

20 FNB 75.

21 *ACP*, p. 51.

22 Harvey, *Adlestrop Revisited*, p. 57.

23 Margaret Drabble, *A Writer's Britain* (re 'Adlestrop').

24 *Adlestrop Revisited*, p. 21.

25 FNB 79.

26 *ACP*, p. 57.

27 Ibid., p. 52.

28 Ibid., p. 53. Is there a possible link in ET's mind between the 'lilies' here and the 'fleur-de-lys' of France?

29 Ibid., p. 66.

30 See p. 72 for Haynes's walks round Oxford with ET.

31 *ACP*, p. 72.

32 Ibid., p. 59.

33 ET to HT, 9 October 1914, Cardiff.

34 FNB 67, 11 December 1913.

35 FNB 40, 15 December [1909].

36 Diary.

37 ET to JF, 16 January 1915.

38 Ibid., 21 January 1915.

39 ET to IM, 19 January 1915.

40 Ibid.

41 Ibid.

42 ET to IM, 10 February 1915.

43 ET to EF, 24 January 1915.

44 *ACP*, p. 61.

45 ET to GB, 30 January 1915.

46 *This England*, quoted in *ACP*, p. 214.

47 ET to EF, 9 February 1915.

48 ET to GB, 30 January 1915.

49 Letter to the *TLS*, 19 April 1917.

50 *ACP*, p. 45. Whiteman in *The Edward Thomas Country* (p. 34), writes that the most likely model for this ancient farmhouse is Prior's Dean on Froxfield Plateau, north of Steep.

51 *ACP*, p. 94.

52 EF to William Blackwood, 1915, Blackwood Papers, NLS.

CHAPTER 23 – Marlborough and the Fields of Flanders
(March–July 1915)

1   ET to GB, 2 March 1915.
2   Ibid.
3   ET to GB, 30 January 1915.
4   Ibid.
5   *ACP*, p. 60.
6   FNB 80 and *ACP*, p. 63.
7   *ACP*, p. 128.
8   'The Owl', *ACP*, p. 65.
9   See pp. 352–3.
10 *ACP*, p. 80.
11 ET to GB, 6 and 17 May 1915.
12 Ibid., 17 May and 18 April 1915.
13 ET to RF, 22 April 1915.
14 Notes at DC on the MS (partial) of *Marlborough*.
15 *Marlborough*, pp. 95–6.
16 Ibid.
17 Ibid., p. 118.
18 Ibid., p. 11.
19 Ibid.
20 Ibid., p. 12.
21 ET to JB, 6 January 1915, *LJB*, p. 76. I am indebted to Edna Longley for part of what
    follows.
22 *Lob Lie-by-the-fire: or, The Luck of Lingborough and Other Tales* (1874).
23 EF to William Blackwood, 22 May 1915, and Blackwood to EF, 28 May 1915, NLS.
24 See 'From Hodge to Lob: Reconstructing the English Farm-labourer 1870–1914', Alan
    Hawkins, *Living and Learning* (Scolar Press, 1996), pp. 213–85.
25 *ACP*, p. 77.
26 ET to RF, 15 May 1915.
27 *ACP*, p. 90.
28 ET to RF, 9 Sept. 1916.
29 FNB 2, 18 June 1895.
30 *ACP*, p. 91.
31 ET to EG, 25 June 1915.
32 See *ACP*, p. 91.
33 ET to EF, / [n.d., but c. 25 June 1915] *LFY*, p. 148].
34 *LFY*, p. 148.
35 ET to RF, 13 June 1915.
36 RF to ET, 26 June 1915.
37 *ACP*, p. 96.

CHAPTER 24 – The Extreme Decision (July–November 1915)

1   'Tipperary', *English Review*, October 1914.
2   IM's memories of ET, RW.
3   ET to his parents, 9 July 1915, DC.
4   Eckert Collection, Bodleian.
5   ET to his parents, 9 July 1915.
6   ET to MT, 21 November 1915, Bodleian.
7   See 'Edward Thomas as War Poet', Barber, *The Art of Edward Thomas*, p. 126.
8   William Cooke corresponded with Wilfred Owen's brother, Harold, who wrote that 'Wilfred Owen never mentioned ET in conversation nor yet in any of his letters home.' Cooke, *Edward Thomas* p. 267.
9   ET to RF, [15] July 1915.
10 ET to his parents, 9 July 1915, DC.
11 ET to RF, 11 July 1915.
12 Ibid.
13 RF to ET, 31 July 1915.
14 RF to Lascelles Abercrombie, 21 September 1915.
15 See M. Thomas, *One of These Fine Days*, pp. 45–6.
16 *ACP*, p. 97.
17 Ibid.
18 RF to ET, 31 July 1915.
19 ET to EF, [postmarked 21 July 1915].
20 *ACP*, p. 98.
21 Ibid., p. 99.
22 *WWE*, pp. 160–1.
23 *LFY*, p. 152.
24 Ibid.
25 Ibid.
26 ET to GB, [15?] July 1915.
27 ET to EF, 21 July 1915.
28 *ACP*, p. 99.
29 Ibid., p. 109.
30 Ibid., p. 100.
31 ET to RF, 21 August 1915.
32 Ibid., 12 October 1915.
33 Ibid.
34 ET to EF, 5 September 1915.
35 ET to RF, 9 August 1915.
36 Ibid.
37 ET to RF, 21 August 1915.
38 ET to dlM, 31 August 1915, JK, p. 206.

39 ET to RF, 3 September 1915.
40 ET to MT, 21 November 1915, Bodleian.
41 ET to Elinor Frost, 27 November 1915, DC.
42 ET to dlM, [?16 October 1915], JK, p. 210.
43 ET to JWH, 28 September 1915, Eckert Collection, Bodleian.
44 Ibid.
45 ET to RF, [4 and 5 October 1915].
46 Ibid.
47 ET to dlM, October 1915 [in pencil], JK, p. 209.
48 *LFY*, p. 169.
49 *New Bearings*, p. 69.
50 *ACP*, p. 101.
51 HWN's review of Moore, *Today*, March 1940.
52 Haynes, *Personalia* (Selwyn & Blount, 1918).
53 *Welsh Review* (September 1945).
54 Moore, *The Life and Letters of Edward Thomas*, p. 228.
55 Nevinson, *Changes & Chances*, pp. 195–6.
56 *Poet and Painter. Being the Correspondence between Gordon Bottomley and Paul Nash 1910–1946* (London, 1955), p. 89.
57 *ACP*, p. 114.
58 ET to RF, 13 November 1915.
59 Ibid.
60 ET to JF, [15/16 October] Autumn 1915.
61 ET to RF, 6 November 1915.
62 Ibid.
63 Ibid.
64 Ibid.
65 Ibid.
66 Ibid.
67 Ibid., Wednesday [17 November 1915].
68 Ibid., 16 January 1916.
69 Ibid., Wednesday 24 November 1915.
70 ET to EF, [17/24 November 1915], *LFY*, p. 171.
71 *DC*, 2 May 1901.
72 ET to EF, Wednesday [24 November 1915].
73 *ACP*, p. 102.
74 ET to MT, 21 November 1915.
75 See *ACP*, p. 103.
76 Ibid., p. 104.
77 ET to RF, 6 December 1915.
78 ET to EF, [late November 1915].
79 ET to RF, 16 January 1916.

80 ET to GB, 20 December 1915.
81 All three men would survive the war and go on to have successful painting careers.
82 *ACP*, p. 114.
83 ET to EF, Wednesday [postmarked 29 June 1916].
84 *ACP*, p. 105.
85 Ibid. 'Rain' is quoted in full in the Introduction.
86 *ACP*, pp. 107–8.

CHAPTER 25 – 'A Heart that was Dark'
(November 1915–August 1916)

1   ET to RF, 5 March 1916.
2   *CP*, p. 105.
3   ET to HT, 24 April 1916, NLW.
4   ET to HT, [11 March 1916], NLW.
5   ECHJ, *c.* 1–19 January 1920.
6   Jad Adams, *Madder Music, Stronger Wine: The Life of Ernest Dowson, Poet and Decadent* (I. B. Tauris, 2002), p. 15.
7   ECHJ, 15–21 March 1919.
8   Ibid., 19 January–16 February 1920.
9   Ibid., 15–21 March 1919.
10 Ibid., 30 March–2 April 1919.
11 ET to GB, 20 December 1915.
12 HT to ECH, [December 1919], letter in possession of Prof. Alison Thomas.
13 ET to HT, 24 January 1916, *CP1978*, p. 409.
14 *ACP*, p. 112.
15 Ibid., p. 118.
16 Ibid., p. 121.
17 Ibid.
18 Ibid., p. 124.
19 ECHJ, 21 May 1919.
20 *ACP*, p. 106.
21 ET to RF, 2 January 1916.
22 ET to HT, 24 April 1916, NLW.
23 *ACP*, p. 111.
24 Ibid., p. 117.
25 ET to RF, 16 January 1916.
26 ET to EF, [postmarked 27 February 1916].
27 ET to Abercrombie, 2 March 1916, *SL*, pp. 119–20.
28 ET to RF, 16 March 1916.
29 ET to JWH, 14 April 1916, Eckert Collection, Bodleian.

30 ET to GB, 11 February 1916.

31 RW.

32 *Poet and Painter*, p. 89.

33 ET to RF, 21 May 1916.

34 Ibid.

35 Ibid.

36 *LFY*, p. 198.

37 ET to dlM, [?7 June 1916], JK, p. 222.

38 RGT, p. 268.

39 'A Note on Edward Thomas', *Welsh Review*, vol. 4, no. 3 (September 1945), p. 177.

40 ET to EF, 8 June 1915.

41 ET to GB, 30 July 1916.

42 Ibid.

43 ET to EF, 8 June 1915.

44 J. C. Squire, *Life and Letters* (Hodder & Stoughton, 1920), p. 35.

45 *ACP*, p. 119.

46 Cooke, *Edward Thomas* p. 199.

47 *ACP*, p. 120.

48 *DC*, 18 January 1907.

49 *ACP*, p. 120. The following quotation is from the same source.

50 ET to RF, 5 March [1916].

51 *ACP*, pp. 123-4.

52 Ibid., p. 123.

53 Ibid., p. 126.

54 EG's Introduction to ET's *Selected Poems* (Tregynon: Gregynog Press, 1927).

55 *ACP*, p. 128.

56 ET to EF, Wednesday [postmarked 29 June 1916].

57 ET to RF, 21 May [1916].

58 *WWE*, p. 165.

59 ET to RF, 28 July [1916].

60 Ibid.

61 *ACP*, p. 131.

62 *LFY*, p. 213.

63 ET to GB, 14 August 1916.

64 ET to EF, 15 August 1916.

CHAPTER 26 – The Long Goodbye (August 1916–January 1917)

1 *ACP*, p. 131. ET sent the '8 verses' of 'Gone, gone again' to EF in a letter dated 27 August 1916.

2 FNB 19, 11 June 1908.

3   *ACP*, p. 132.

4   Ibid., p. 133.

5   ET to RF, 9 September 1916.

6   Ibid.

7   Ibid.

8   *ACP*, p. 132.

9   The bulk of the Hospital building was demolished in the 1920s, when the institution was moved to the country, but the land was preserved as a public playground for children. The area in front of the original Hospital, lined with the 'cloisters' referred to by ET, may be 'the stony square sunlit' and 'that girl's clear eyes' may refer to one of the foundlings. Both squares contained mature plane trees by 1916.

10 *LJB*, p. 80.

11 ET to GB, 27 October 1916.

12 *ACP*, p. 133.

13 ET to GB, 2 October 1916.

14 ET to JF, 27 October 1916.

15 ET to RF, 9 September 1916.

16 *ACP*, p. 134.

17 *LFY*, p. 229 and ET to RF, 19 October 1916.

18 *WWE*, p. 170.

19 Ibid.

20 Ibid.

21 ET to GB, 27 October 1916.

22 *LFY*, p. 231.

23 *WWE*, p. 171.

24 ET to RF, 23 November 1916.

25 See *Welsh Review*, vol. IV, no. 3 (September 1945), pp. 177–8.

26 Marcia Allentuck, 'Isaac Rosenberg and Gordon Bottomley', *Harvard Library Bulletin*, vol. 23, no. 3 (July 1975), p. 264.

27 *Bookman* (September 1930), p. 324.

28 Ibid.

29 *ACP*, pp. 135–6.

30 *ETFN*, no. 54, August 2005, p. 10.

31 ET to EF, [postmarked 15 November 1916] 'Tuesday'.

32 ET to EF, 7 December 1916.

33 Ibid., 11 December 1916.

34 ET to HT, 10 December 1916, NLW.

35 ET to EF, 15 December 1916.

36 ET to RF, 24 November 1916.

37 *WWE*, p. 173.

38 ET to EF, 27 December 1916

39 Ibid.

40 *ACP*, p.138
41 *IPS*, p. 104
42 ET to EF, 27 December 1916.
43 *CP1978*, pp. 462–3.
44 Eleanor Farjeon, *First and Second Love* (Oxford: Oxford University Press, 1959), p. 50.
45 ET to HT, [postmarked January 1917], NLW.
46 Ibid., [postmarked 15 January 1917] Monday.
47 HT to JH, 29 January 1920.
48 ET to HT, [postmarked 12 January 1917], NLW
49 Quoted by Ingpen in a letter to RF, 17 April 1917, DC.
50 *ACP*, p. 139.
51 ET to RF, 31 December 1916.
52 'Edward Thomas, As I Knew Him', *Green Pastures*, p. 17.
53 Ibid.
54 Ibid., p. 18.
55 ET to HT, January 1917, NLW.
56 ET to EG, 19 January 1917.
57 ET to EF, [postmarked 19 January 1917].
58 Severn, *The Gambardier*, pp. 123–4.
59 ET to HT, [19 January 1917] NLW.
60 Ibid., [postmarked 15 January 1917] NLW.
61 Ibid., [postmarked 24 January 1917] NLW.
62 ET to EF, [postmarked 29 January 1917].
63 WD.

CHAPTER 27 – 'No More Goodbyes Now' (January–April 1917)

1   ET to EF, 31 January 1917.
2   Rosenberg crossed to France in June 1916. *Poems and Plays of Isaac Rosenberg* (Oxford: Oxford University Press, 2004), p. 127.
3   Diary, 29 January 1917.
4   ET to EF, 31 January 1917.
5   Ibid.
6   Ibid.
7   GB to ET, 28 March 1917.
8   ET to his parents, 22 March 1917, DC.
9   ET to HT, 2 February 1917, NLW.
10 ET to his parents, 13 February 1917, DC.
11 ET to HT, 5 February 1917, NLW.
12 ET to RF, 11 February 1917.
13 ET to dlM, 14 February 1917, JK, p. 22.

14 ET to EF, 13 February 1917.
15 ET to RF, 11 February 1917.
16 Ibid.
17 ET to dlM, 14 February 1917, JK, p. 227.
18 Franklin Lushington to HT, 10 April 1917, RGT, p. 294.
19 ET to RF, 11 February 1917.
20 Ibid.
21 Ibid.
22 Diary, 23 January 1917.
23 ET to Julian Thomas, 30 March 1917, DC.
24 Letter from Thorburn to HT, 9 April 1917, RGT, p. 294.
25 *LFY*, p. 248.
26 HT to RF, 2 March 1917.
27 ET to EF, 10 February 1917.
28 ET to HH, 16 February 1917.
29 ET to EF, 10 February 1917.
30 ET to HH, 16 February 1917.
31 ET to HT, 15 February 1917, NLW.
32 ET to EF, 10 February 1917.
33 *LFY*, p. 197.
34 Diary, 16 February 1917.
35 ET to EF, 1 March 1917.
36 ET to RF, 23 February 1917.
37 ET to HT, 27 February 1917, NLW.
38 ET to EF, 21 February 1917.
39 Ibid.
40 ET to RF, 8 March 1917.
41 Ibid.
42 Ibid., 6 March 1917.
43 Ibid.
44 Diary, 4 March 1917.
45 ET to HT, 27 February 1917, NLW.
46 ET to Merfyn Thomas, 20 February 1917, Cardiff.
47 Diary, 23 February 1917.
48 Ibid., 2 March 1917.
49 ET to GB, 26 February 1917.
50 Diary, 9 March 1917.
51 Ibid., 5 March 1917.
52 *The Gambardier*, pp. 57–8.
53 Diary, 23 March 1917.
54 *ACP*, p. 109.
55 ET to EF, 8 March 1917.

56 Diary, 20 March 1917.

57 ET to HT, 6 April 1917, NLW.

58 ET to RF, 2 April 1917.

59 ET to EF, 22 March 1917.

60 Ibid.

61 ET to RF, 2 April 1917.

62 Ibid.

63 ET to EF, 27 March 1917.

64 Ibid.

65 *LFY*, p. 259.

66 Diary, 27 March 1917.

67 ET to HT, 24 March 1917.

68 Isaac Rosenberg to GB, [postmarked 8 April 1917] IWM.

69 ET to HT, 24 March 1917, NLW.

70 *The Gambardier*, p. 127.

71 ET to RF, 2 April 1917.

72 *TLS*, 29 March 1917, p. 151 and ET to GB, 4 April 1917.

73 Diary, 7 April 1917.

74 *The Gambardier*, p. 128.

75 Ibid., p. 129.

76 Ibid.

77 Ibid. My italics.

78 RGT, p. 294.

79 Ibid. My italics.

80 *LFY*, p. 263.

81 WD.

82 Major Franklin Lushington to John Moore, 29 February 1936, Berg. My italics.

SELECT BIBLIOGRAPHY
(Place of publication London, unless otherwise stated)

Barker, J. (ed.), *The Art of Edward Thomas* (Bridgend: Poetry Wales Press, 1987)

Bax, C., *Inland Far* (Heinemann, 1925)

——. *Some I Knew Well* (Phoenix House, 1951)

Bentley, E. C., *Those Days* (Constable, 1940)

Bergonzi, B., *Heroes' Twilight* (Constable, 1965)

Bottomley, G., 'A Note on Edward Thomas', *Welsh Review*, Cardiff (September 1945)

Burke, T., *City of Encounters* (Constable, 1932)

Chambers, R., *The Last Englishman* (Faber & Faber, 2009)

Cooke, W., *Edward Thomas: A Critical Biography* (Faber & Faber, 1970)

Coombes, H., *Edward Thomas: A Critical Study* (Chatto & Windus, 1973)

Cooper, J. and Emeny, R. (eds), *A Bibliographical Checklist of the Works of Edward Thomas* (Blackburn: White Sheep Press, 2004)

Cuthbertson, G. and Newlyn, L. (eds), *Branch-Lines: Edward Thomas and Contemporary Poetry* (Enitharmon, 2007)

——. *Edward Thomas: Prose Writings*, vols 1 and 2 (Oxford: Oxford University Press, 2011)

Davies, W. H., *Later Days* (Jonathan Cape, 1925)

Douglas, N., *Looking Back: An Autobiographical Excursion* (Chatto & Windus, 1934)

Eckert, R. P., *Edward Thomas* (Dent, 1937)

Emeny, R., *Edward Thomas on the Georgians* (Cheltenham: Cyder Press, 2004)

Farjeon, E., *The Last Four Years* (Oxford: Oxford University Press, 1958) edition used OUP 1979 pbk.

Farndale, M., *History of the Royal Regiment of Artillery: Western Front, 1914–1918* (Royal Artillery Institution, 1987)

Francis, L.L., *An Adventure in Poetry: 1900–1918: Robert Frost* (New Brunswick: Transaction Publishing, 2004)

Fussell, P., *The Great War and Modern Memory* (Oxford: Oxford University Press, 1975)

Garnett, D., *The Golden Echo* (Chatto & Windus, 1953)

Garnett, E., 'Edward Thomas', *Athenaeum* (16 and 20 April 1920)

Gibbs, P., *Realities of War* (Hutchinson, 1919)

Gibson, A., *Postscript to Adventure* (Dent, 1930)

Gilbert, M., *First World War* (Weidenfeld & Nicolson, 1994)

Goldring, D., *South Lodge* (Constable, 1943)

Guthrie, J., 'Edward Thomas: Letters to W. H. Hudson', *London Mercury* (August 1920)

——. '*To the Memory of Edward Thomas*' (Flansham, 1937)

——. 'Edward Thomas', *Welsh Review* (August 1939)

Haines, J. W., *In Memoriam: Edward Thomas* (The Green Pasture Series, Morland Press, 1919)

——. 'Edward Thomas', *The Gloucester Journal* (16 February 1935)

Harding, J., *Dreaming of Babylon: The Life and Times of Ralph Hodgson* (Greenwich Exchange Publishing, 2008)

Hart, L. (ed.), *Once They Lived in Gloucestershire* (Cheltenham: Green Branch Press, 2000)

Harvey, A., *Adlestrop Revisited* (Stroud: Sutton Publishing, 1999)

Harvey, A. (ed.), *Elected Friends: Poems for and About Edward Thomas* (Enitharmon, 1991)

Hassall, C., *Edward Marsh: Patron of the Arts* (Longmans, 1959)

——. *Rupert Brooke: A Biography* (Faber & Faber, 1964)

Haynes, E. S. P., *Personalia* (Selwyn & Blount, 1918)

——. *Fritto Misto* (Cayme Press, 1924)

Hibberd, D., *Harold Monro* (Basingstoke: Palgrave, 2001)

——. *Wilfrid Owen: A New Biography* (Weidenfeld & Nicolson, 2002)

Hollis, M., *Now All Roads Lead to France: The Last Years of Edward Thomas* (Faber & Faber, 2011)

Hooker, J., *Poetry of Place* (Manchester: Carcanet Press, 1982)

Hudson, W. H., *Letters from W. H. Hudson to Edward Garnett* (Dent, 1925)

Jansen, D. B., *Jung's Apprentice* (Einsiedeln: Daimon Verlag, 2003)

Jeffery, D., *Dr. Harry Roberts – a Petersfield Philanthropist* (Petersfield, 1988)

Jepson, E., *Memories of an Edwardian and Neo-Georgian* (Martin Secker, 1938)

Johnson, T., *Edward Thomas on Thomas Hardy* (Cheltenham: Cyder Press, 2002)

Kendall, J., *Edward Thomas, Birdsong and Flight* (Cecil Woolf Publishers, 2014)

Kendall, J. (ed.), *Edward Thomas's Poets* (Manchester: Carcanet Press, 2007)

——. *Poet to Poet: Edward Thomas's Letters to Walter de la Mare* (Seren, 2012)

Kirkham, M., *The Imagination of Edward Thomas* (Cambridge: Cambridge University Press, 1986)

Longley, E., *Edward Thomas: The Annotated Collected Poems* (Bloodaxe Books, Tarset, 2008)

Lucas, E. V., *The Open Road* (Methuen, 1905)

MacFarlane, R., *The Old Ways* (Hamish Hamilton, 2012)

Marsh, J., *Edward Thomas: A Poet for His Country* (Paul Elek, 1978)

Mertins, L., *Life and Walks-Talking* (Oklahoma University Press, 1965)

Meyers, J., *Robert Frost* (Constable, 1996)

Milne, J., *The Memoirs of a Bookman* (John Murray, 1934)

Moore, J., *The Life and Letters of Edward Thomas* (Heinemann, 1939)

Motion, A. *The Poetry of Edward Thomas* (Hogarth Press, 1980)

Nevinson, H. W., *Changes and Chances* (Nisbet & Co., 1923)

Nicholson, J., *The Great Silence: 1918–1920: Living in the Shadow of the War* (John Murray, 2009)

Parini, J., *Robert Frost: A Life* (New York: Henry Holt, 1999)

Ransome, A., *Autobiography* (Jonathan Cape, 1975)

Rhys, E., *Letters from Limbo* (Dent, 1936)

Saunders, C., *Edward Thomas and the Great War* (Cecil Woolf Publishers, 2006)

Scannell, V., *Edward Thomas* (Longmans Green & Co., 1963)

Sebba, A., *Enid Bagnold* (Weidenfeld & Nicolson, 1986)

Severn, Mark, *The Gambardier* (Ernest Benn, 1930)

Silkin, J., *Out of Battle: The Poetry of the Great War* (Oxford: Oxford University Press, 1972)

Sims, G., *The Rare Book Game* (Philadelphia: Holmes Publishing, 1985)

Smith, S., *Edward Thomas* (Faber & Faber, 1986)

Spencer, M. (ed.), *Elected Friends: Robert Frost and Edward Thomas to One Another* (New York: Handsel Books, 2003)

Stonesifer, R. J., *W. H. Davies* (Jonathan Cape, 1963)

Thomas, A., *Portraits of Women: Gwen John and Her Forgotten Contemporaries* (Cambridge: Polity Press, 1994)

Thomas, H., *Under Storm's Wing* (Manchester: Carcanet Press, 1988)

Thomas, M., *One of These Fine Days: Memoirs* (Manchester: Carcanet Press, 1982)

Thomas, R. George, *Edward Thomas* (Cardiff: University of Wales Press, 1993)

Thomas, R. George, *Edward Thomas: A Portrait* (Oxford: Clarendon, 1985)

Thomas, R. George (ed.), *Letters from Edward Thomas to George Bottomley* (Oxford: Oxford University Press, 1968)

Thompson, L., *The Early Years: 1974–1915* (New York: Holt, Rinehart & Winston, 1966)

Thompson, L. (ed.), *Selected Letters of Robert Frost* (New York: Holt, Rinehart & Winston, 1964)

Untermeyer, L., *The Letters of Robert Frost to Louis Untermeyer* (Jonathan Cape, 1964)

Walsh, J. E., *Into My Own: The English Years of Robert Frost* (New York: Grove Weidenfeld, 1988)

Watts, K., *The Marlborough Downs* (Bradford on Avon: Ex Libris, 1993)

Webb, A., *Edward Thomas and World Literary Studies: Wales and Anglocentrism and English Literature* (Cardiff: University of Wales, 2013)

Whistler, T., *Imagination of the Heart: The Life of Walter de la Mare* (Duckworth, 1993)

Whiteman, W. M., *The Edward Thomas Country* (Southampton: Paul Cave Publications, 1978)

Wilson, J. M., *Isaac Rosenberg: The Making of a Great War Poet* (Weidenfeld & Nicolson, 2008)

———. *Siegfried Sassoon: Soldier, Poet, Lover, Friend* (Duckworth, 2013)

Wisniewski, J., *Edward Thomas: A Mirror of England* (Newcastle-upon-Tyne: Cambridge Scholars, 2009)

Wright, H. G., *Studies in Contemporary Literature* (Bangor: Jarvis & Foster, 1918)

INDEX

1. All works are listed under author name
2. The section, Edward Thomas: war, active service is indexed in chronological order

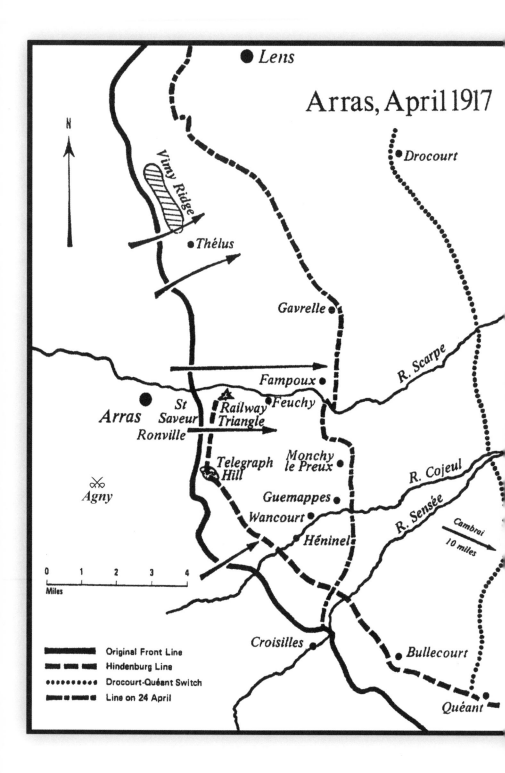